THE CROSSWORD COMPANION

THE CROSSWORD COMPANION

Being a work compiled expressly for the assistance and amusement of those who enjoy composing or solving crossword puzzles

by

M.R.W.∴.

NEW REVISED EDITION

BARRIE & JENKINS
COMMUNICA - EUROPA

6/4   493·732

© *Herbert Jenkins Ltd 1952, 1968, 1972, 1975*
First published by
Herbert Jenkins Ltd.
2 Clement's Inn,
London. WC2A 2EP

1952

ALL RIGHTS RESERVED

Reprinted 1962

Reprinted 1968

Reprinted 1972

Reprinted 1974

New, Revised Edition 1975

by Barrie & Jenkins Ltd.
24 Highbury Crescent, London N5 1RX

ISBN 0 257 65735 5

Printed in Great Britain by
A. Wheaton & Co., Exeter

INTRODUCTION

CROSSWORD puzzle enthusiasts will be quick to appreciate the
simplicity of this " Companion " which, ignoring meaning
and derivation, concerns itself only with the number of letters
any given word may contain. The general principle adopted
has been to take all the two-letter words in common usage
and group them together alphabetically under the one head,
then to do similarly with the three-letter words, the four-
letter words, the five-letter words and so on up to the twenty-
letter words. Thus all words of the same length have been
brought together in a form most likely to be of assistance to
the solver or compiler of crossword puzzles.

It may be objected that some of the groups—those of five,
six, and seven letters, in particular—comprise many hundreds
of words and that to search systematically through them
would involve a labour of some magnitude. In certain circum-
stances this may well be true, but the extent of the search will
be greatly reduced in cases where one or more letters of the
word are known, since these letters can be used as " keys."
The value of the key letters will depend both on the letters
themselves and on their position in the word. If the first letter
is known, the required word must obviously lie within the limits
of that letter in its appropriate group, and if both first and second
letters are available the search will be narrowed infinitely.

Often when only one letter is known, commonsense will
suggest the alternative letters which may precede it—or
follow it. In the word " scholar," for instance, if the letter
" c " were the only one known, a moment's thought would
reveal that the preceding letter must be one of " a," " e,"
" i," " o," " s," " u " and " y," and a rapid glance down the
list of seven letter words beginning with any of these letters
and having " c " as the second letter will quickly produce
the desired result.

Finally, where a single letter only is known—say, the fourth—
a very rapid inspection can be made by running the eye down

the fourth letter of the appropriate column, pausing for closer inspection only where the known letter occurs. Using again the word " scholar " as an example, " o " would be the known letter and, in glancing quickly down the list, only those words having " o " as the fourth letter would require a second thought.

A few minutes' practice will show how useful and rapid this book can be in producing the required word.

CONTENTS

CONTINENTS AND COUNTRIES
OF THE WORLD

*Where names of countries have been changed both new and former names
appear in the appropriate columns*

4 letters	5 letters	6 letters	7 letters
ASIA	BURMA	AFRICA	ALBANIA
BALI	CHILE	ANGOLA	ALGERIA
CHAD	CHINA	AZORES	AMERICA
CUBA	CONGO	ARABIA	ANDORRA
EIRE	CRETE	BELIZE	ANTIGUA
FIJI	EGYPT	BHUTAN	ARMENIA
GAZA	GABON	BORNEO	AUSTRIA
GUAM	GHANA	BRAZIL	BAHAMAS
IRAN	HAITI	BRUNEI	BAHRAIN
IRAQ	INDIA	CANADA	BELGIUM
JAVA	ITALY	CEYLON	BERMUDA
LAOS	JAPAN	CYPRUS	BOLIVIA
MALI	KENYA	EUROPE	BRITAIN
OMAN	KHMER	FRANCE	BURUNDI
PERU	KOREA	GAMBIA	CORSICA
SIAM	LIBYA	GREECE	CURACAO
TOGO	MACAO	GUIANA	DAHOMEY
USSR	MALAY	GUINEA	DENMARK
	MALTA	GUYANA	ECUADOR
	NEPAL	HAWAII	ENGLAND
	NIGER	ISRAEL	ERITREA
	PAPUA	JORDAN	ESTONIA
	QATOR	KUWAIT	FINLAND
	SABAH	LATVIA	FORMOSA
	SAMOA	MALAWI	GERMANY
	SPAIN	MEXICO	GRENADA
	SUDAN	MONACO	HOLLAND
	SYRIA	NORWAY	HUNGARY
	TIBET	PANAMA	ICELAND
	TIMOR	PERSIA	IRELAND
	TONGA	POLAND	JAMAICA
	WALES	RUSSIA	LAPLAND
	YEMEN	RWANDA	LEBANON
	ZAIRE	SOMALI	LESOTHO
		SERBIA	LIBERIA
		SWEDEN	MADEIRA
		TAI WAN	MAJORCA
		TOBAGO	MOROCCO
		TURKEY	NIGERIA
		UGANDA	REUNION
		ZAMBIA	RUMANIA
			ST. KITTS
			SARAWAK
			SENEGAL
			SOMALIA
			SUMATRA
			SURINAM
			TANGIER
			TUNISIA
			URUGUAY
			VIETNAM

9

CONTINENTS AND COUNTRIES OF THE WORLD—continued

8 letters

ANTILLES
BARBADOS
BOTSWANA
BULGARIA
CAMBODIA
COLOMBIA
CAMEROON
DOMINICA
ETHIOPIA
HONDURAS
HONG KONG
MALAGASY
MALAYSIA
MONGOLIA
PAKISTAN
PARAGUAY
PORTUGAL
RHODESIA
ST. HELENA
SALVADOR
SCOTLAND
SRI LANKA
TANZANIA
TASMANIA
THAILAND
TRINIDAD
ZANZIBAR

9 letters

ABYSSINIA
ARGENTINA
AUSTRALIA
CALEDONIA
COSTA RICA
GIBRALTAR
GOLD COAST
GREENLAND
GUATEMALA
INDO-CHINA
INDONESIA
LITHUANIA
MANCHURIA
MAURITIUS
NICARAGUA
NYASALAND
POLYNESIA
SAN MARINO
SINGAPORE
SWAZILAND
VENEZUELA

10 letters

ANTARCTICA
BANGLADESH
GUADELOUPE
IVORY COAST
LUXEMBOURG
MADAGASCAR
MAURITANIA
MONTENEGRO
MONTSERRAT
MOZAMBIQUE
NEW ZEALAND
PUERTO RICO
SEYCHELLES
SOMALILAND
SOUTH YEMEN
TANGANYIKA
UPPER VOLTA
WEST INDIES
YUGOSLAVIA

11 letters

AFGHANISTAN
AUSTRALASIA
COOK ISLANDS
NAURU ISLAND
NETHERLANDS
NEW HEBRIDES
PHILIPPINES
SAUDI ARABIA
SIERRA LEONE
SOUTH AFRICA
SWITZERLAND

12 letters

COCOS ISLANDS
FAROE ISLANDS
LIECHENSTEIN
UNITED STATES

13 letters

CAYMAN ISLANDS
CENTRAL AFRICA
CANARY ISLANDS
COMORO ISLANDS
NORFOLK ISLAND
TRUCIAL STATES
UNITED KINGDOM
VIRGIN ISLANDS

14 letters

CAROLINE ISLAND
CZECHOSLOVAKIA
GILBERT ISLANDS
LEEWARD ISLAND
MALDIVE ISLANDS
MARIANA ISLANDS
SOCIETY ISLANDS
SOLOMON ISLANDS

15 letters

BALEARIC ISLANDS
FALKLAND ISLANDS
MARSHALL ISLANDS
WINDWARD ISLANDS

16 letters

CAPE VERDE ISLANDS
VATICAN CITY STATE

17 letters

CONGOLESE REPUBLIC
SANTA CRUZ ISLANDS

18 letters

UNITED ARAB EMIRATES
UNITED ARAB REPUBLIC
SYRIAN ARAB REPUBLIC

COUNTIES OF THE UNITED KINGDOM

Both new and former names appear in the appropriate columns

4 letters

AVON
BUTE
DOWN
FIFE
KENT
ROSS

5 letters

ANGUS
CLWYD
DYFED
ESSEX
GWENT
MORAY
NAIRN
POWYS
SALOP

6 letters

ANTRIM
ARMAGH
DURHAM
LONDON
ORKNEY
SURREY
SUSSEX
TYRONE

7 letters

CUMBRIA
GWYNEDD
KINROSS
NORFOLK
PEEBLES
RENFREW
SELKIRK
SUFFOLK
WIGTOWN
ZETLAND

8 letters

ABERDEEN
AYRSHIRE
CHESHIRE
CORNWALL
CROMARTY
ROXBURGH
STIRLING

9 letters

BERKSHIRE
CAITHNESS
CLEVELAND
FERMANAGH
HAMPSHIRE
MIDDLESEX
WILTSHIRE
YORKSHIRE

10 letters

BANFFSHIRE
CUMBERLAND
DERBYSHIRE
DEVONSHIRE
FLINTSHIRE
WEST SUSSEX
MERSEYSIDE
HUMBERSIDE
EAST SUSSEX
KINCARDINE
LANCASHIRE
MIDLOTHIAN
PERTHSHIRE
SHROPSHIRE
SUTHERLAND

11 letters

ARGYLLSHIRE
CLACKMANNAN
DORSETSHIRE
EAST LOTHIAN
LANARKSHIRE
LONDONDERRY
OXFORDSHIRE
RADNORSHIRE
TYNE AND WEAR
WEST LOTHIAN
WESTMORLAND

12 letters

BEDFORDSHIRE
BERWICKSHIRE
DENBIGHSHIRE
LINCOLNSHIRE
MID GLAMORGAN
WEST MIDLANDS
RUTLANDSHIRE
WARWICKSHIRE

13 letters

CARDIGANSHIRE
DUMFRIESSHIRE
HEREFORDSHIRE
HERTFORDSHIRE
KIRKCUDBRIGHT
MONMOUTHSHIRE
PEMBROKESHIRE
SOMERSETSHIRE
STAFFORDSHIRE
WEST GLAMORGAN
WEST YORKSHIRE

14 letters

BRECKNOCKSHIRE
CAMBRIDGESHIRE
DUMBARTONSHIRE
GLAMORGANSHIRE
INVERNESS-SHIRE
LEICESTERSHIRE
MERIONETHSHIRE
NORTHUMBERLAND
NORTH YORKSHIRE
SOUTH GLAMORGAN
SOUTH YORKSHIRE
WORCESTERSHIRE

15 letters

BUCKINGHAMSHIRE
CAERNARVONSHIRE
CARMARTHENSHIRE
GLOUCESTERSHIRE
HUNTINGDONSHIRE
MONTGOMERYSHIRE
NOTTINGHAMSHIRE
ROSS AND CROMARTY

16 letters

NORTHAMPTONSHIRE

17 letters

GREATER MANCHESTER

20 letters

HEREFORD AND
WORCESTER

THE STATES OF THE UNITED STATES OF AMERICA

4 letters

IOWA
OHIO
UTAH

5 letters

IDAHO
MAINE
TEXAS

6 letters

ALASKA
KANSAS
NEVADA
OREGON

7 letters

ALABAMA
ARIZONA
FLORIDA
GEORGIA
INDIANA
MONTANA
NEW YORK
VERMONT
WYOMING

8 letters

ARKANSAS
COLORADO
COLUMBIA
DELAWARE
ILLINOIS
KENTUCKY
MARYLAND
MICHIGAN
MISSOURI
NEBRASKA
OKLAHOMA
VIRGINIA

9 letters

LOUISIANA
MINNESOTA
NEW JERSEY
NEW MEXICO
TENNESSEE
WISCONSIN

10 letters

CALIFORNIA
WASHINGTON

11 letters

CONNECTICUT
MISSISSIPPI
NORTH DAKOTA
RHODE ISLAND
SOUTH DAKOTA

12 letters

NEW HAMPSHIRE
PENNSYLVANIA
WEST VIRGINIA

13 letters

MASSACHUSETTS
NORTH CAROLINA
SOUTH CAROLINA

SOME FLOWERING PLANTS

3 letters
HOP
IVY
RUE
TEA
YAM

4 letters
ALOE
ARUM
BALM
COCO
COLE
FLAG
IRIS
LILY
MUSK
PINK
ROSE
SAGE
VINE

5 letters
AGAVE
ASPIC
ASTER
DAISY
LOTUS
LUPIN
OXLIP
PANSY
PEONY
PHLOX
POPPY
TANSY
TULIP
VIOLA
YUCCA

6 letters
AZALEA
BORAGE
CACTUS
CATNIP
CISTUS
CLOVER
COSMOS
CROCUS
DAHLIA
MADDER
MALLOW
MIMOSA
ORCHID
ROCKET
SESAME
SORREL
THRIFT
VIOLET
ZINNIA

7 letters
ACONITE
ANEMONE
BUGLOSS
BEGONIA
CAMPION
CATMINT
CLARKIA
COWSLIP
DAY LILY
DITTANY
DOG-ROSE
FUCHSIA
GENTIAN
JACINTH
JASMINE
JONQUIL
LOBELIA
MAY-LILY
OPUNTIA
PETUNIA
SEA-PINK
SYRINGA
SPIRAEA
VANILLA
VERBENA
VERVAIN

8 letters
AMARANTH
ANGELICA
ASPHODEL
AURICULA
BIGNONIA
BLUEBELL
CAMELLIA
CAMOMILE
CATCHFLY
CLEMATIS
DAFFODIL
DROPWORT
FOXGLOVE
GERANIUM
GIRASOLE
GLOXINIA
HAREBELL
HYACINTH
LARKSPUR
MARIGOLD
MUSK-ROSE
POND-LILY
PRIMROSE
SCABIOUS
SNOWDROP
STAPELIA
SWEETPEA
TOAD-FLAX
VALERIAN
VERONICA
WISTERIA

9 letters
AMARYLLIS
BUTTERCUP
CAMPANULA
CANDYTUFT
CARNATION
CELANDINE
CHINA-ROSE
CINERARIA
CLOVE-PINK
COLUMBINE
DANDELION
DIGITALIS
EDELWEISS
EGLANTINE
GLADIOLUS
GOLDEN-ROD
HELLEBORE
HOLLYHOCK
NELUMBIUM
PIMPERNEL
PYRETHRUM
SAXIFRAGE
SPEEDWELL
SPIKENARD
SUNFLOWER
WATER-LILY

10 letters
CHINA-ASTER
CORNFLOWER
CRANE'S BILL
DAMASK-ROSE
DELPHINIUM
FRITILLARY
GELDER ROSE
GRANADILLA
HEARTSEASE
HELIOTROPE
NASTURTIUM
ORANGE-LILY
POLYANTHUS
RANUNCULUS
SNAPDRAGON
SWEET-BRIAR
WALLFLOWER

11 letters
ANTIRRHINUM
CABBAGE-ROSE
CALCEOLARIA
CONVOLVULUS
EVERLASTING
FORGET-ME-NOT
GILLYFLOWER
GLOBE-FLOWER
HONEYSUCKLE
RAGGED ROBIN

12 letters
CORN MARIGOLD
LADY'S SLIPPER
PASQUE-FLOWER
SWEET WILLIAM
VIRGIN'S BOWER

13 letters
CHRYSANTHEMUM
MARSH MARIGOLD
ODONTOGLOSSUM
PASSION FLOWER
TRUMPET FLOWER

14 letters
CANTERBURY BELL

15 letters
MICHAELMAS DAISY

SOME SHRUBS AND TREES

3 letters	4 letters	5 letters	6 letters	7 letters
ASH	ALOE	ABELE	ACACIA	AMBATCH
		ALDER	ALMOND	APRICOT
BEN	BASS	ALMUG	ANANAS	ARBUTUS
BAY		APPLE	AZALEA	
BOX	COLA	ARECA		BEBEERU
	CORK	ASPEN		BLUE-GUM
ELM	CRAB		BANANA	BOX-WOOD
		BEECH	BANYAN	BUCK-EYE
FIG	GALE	BIRCH	BEOBAB	
FIR	GEAN			CAJUPUT
		CAROB	CARAPA	CASSAVA
NUT	LIME	CEDAR	CASHEW	CHAMPAC
		CLOVE	CHERRY	COWTREE
OAK	PALM	COCOA	CITRON	CYPRESS
	PEAR	CYCAD	COFFEE	
SAL	PINE		CORNEL	DOG-WOOD
	PLUM	EBONY		DURMAST
YEW	ROSE	ELDER	DAMSON	
			DAPHNE	FAN-PALM
	SORB	GUAVA	DEODAR	
			DURIAN	GUM-TREE
	TEAK	HAZEL		
		HENNA	GOMUTI	HICKORY
	UPAS	HOLLY		HOLM-OAK
			JAROOL	
		LARCH	JARRAH	JUNIPER
		LEMON	JUJUBE	
		LIANA		LIVE-OAK
			LAUREL	
		MANGO	LINDEN	MAMMOTH
		MAPLE		
		MYRRH	MALLEE	OIL-PALM
			MEDLAR	
		OLIVE	MYRTLE	RED-PINE
		OSIER		RED-WOOD
			NUTMEG	
		PEACH		SEQUOIA
		PLANE	ORANGE	SYRINGA
				SPINDLE
		SUMAC	PLATAN	
			POPLAR	TAMARIX
		THORN		
			QUINCE	WYCH-ELM
		YUCCA		
			RATTAN	
			SALLOW	
			SPRUCE	
			STORAX	
			SUMACH	
			WALNUT	
			WATTLE	
			WILLOW	

THE CROSSWORD COMPANION

SOME SHRUBS AND TREES—continued

8 letters	9 letters	10 letters	11 letters
AILANTUS	AZEDARACH	ALMOND-TREE	CABBAGE-PALM
			CAJUPUT-TREE
BAYBERRY	BEAR-BERRY	BIRD-CHERRY	CAMEL'S-THORN
BEAM-TREE	BLUEBERRY	BLACK-THORN	CAMPHOR-TREE
BERBERIS	BUCKTHORN	BOTTLE-TREE	COTTONEASTER
BERGAMOT	BUSSU-PALM	BRUSH-WOOD	COTTON-PLANT
BUDDLEIA	BUTTER-NUT	BUTTER-TREE	
		BUTTON-BUSH	GUELDER-ROSE
CARNAUBA	CASUARINA	BUTTON-WOOD	
CHESTNUT	CHERIMOYA		LAURUSTINUS
CINCHONA	CHINKAPIN	COTTON-TREE	
CINNAMON	CRAB-APPLE	COWRIE-PINE	PALMYRA-PALM
CLEMATIS	CRANBERRY		POMEGRANATE
COCCULUS	CROWBERRY	DRAGON-TREE	PRICKLY-PEAR
CRAB-TREE			
	GELSEMIUM	EUCALYPTUS	SERVICE-TREE
DATE-PALM			SHITTAH-TREE
DATE-TREE	HYDRANGEA	FIDDLE-WOOD	SPINDLE-TREE
DATE PLUM			
DIVI-DIVI	LANCE-WOOD	GOOSE-BERRY	VARNISH-TREE
		GREEN-HEART	
EUCALYPT	PERSIMMON		12 letters
	PISTACHIO	HACKMATACK	
GUAIACUM	PITCH-PINE		CALABASH-TREE
	PLANE-TREE	JAPATI-PALM	CHRIST'S-THORN
HAWTHORN			
HEMP-PALM	SAGE-BRUSH	QUERCITRON	MONKEY-PUZZLE
HORN-BEAM	SAPODILLA		
	SATIN-WOOD	SANDAL-WOOD	PLANTAIN-TREE
IRON-BARK	SCREW-PILE	SUGAR-MAPLE	
	SILVER-FIR		RHODODENDRON
JACK-TREE	SNOW-BERRY	TALLOW-TREE	
	STONE-PINE		SPURGE-LAUREL
LABURNUM		WHITE-THORN	
	TULIP-TREE	WITCH-HAZEL	WELLINGTONIA
MAGNOLIA			WHORTLE-BERRY
MAHOGANY	WAX-MYRTLE		
MESQUITE	WHITEBEAM		13 letters
MULBERRY	WHITE-WOOD		
MUSK-PEAR	WYCH-HAZEL		BUTCHER'S-BROOM
MUSK-PLUM			
			HORSE-CHESTNUT
OLEANDER			
			TRAVELLER'S-JOY
PINASTER			
PLANTAIN			14 letters
ROSE-WOOD			BREADFRUIT-TREE
SAGO-PALM			STRAWBERRY-TREE
SCRUB-OAK			
SHADDOCK			TRAVELLER'S-TREE
SWEET-BAY			
SYCAMINE			TURPENTINE-TREE
SYCAMORE			
			15 letters
TREE-FERN			
			TREMBLING-POPLAR
VIBURNUM			
WISTERIA			
WITCH-ELM			

15

MAMMALS

2 letters	3 letters	4 letters	5 letters	
OX	APE	BEAR	ADDAX	TABBY
	ASS	BOAR	ARNEE	TAPIR
		BUCK		TIGER
	BAT	BULL	BISON	
			BITCH	VIXEN
	CAT	CALF	BRUIN	
	COB	CAVY	BUNNY	WHALE
	COW	COLT		WHELP
	CUB		CAMEL	
	CUR	DEER	CIVET	ZEBRA
			COATI	ZIBET
	DAM	FAWN	CONEY	ZORIL
	DOE	FOAL	CUDDY	
	DOG			
		GAUR	DAMAN	
	ELK	GOAT	DHOLE	
	EMU		DINGO	
	EWE	HACK		
		HARE	ELAND	
	FOX	HART		
		HIND	FILLY	
	GNU		FITCH	
		IBEX		
	HOG		GAYAL	
		LAMB	GENET	
	KID	LION	GORAL	
		LOVO	GRICE	
	NAG	LYNX		
			HINNY	
	PIG	MARE	HORSE	
	PUG	MACE	HOUND	
		MINK	HYENA	
	RAT	MOLE	HYRAX	
	RAM	MULE		
		MUSK	LEMUR	
	TOD		LLAMA	
	TUP	NEAT	LORIS	
	YAK	ORYX	MANIS	
			MOOSE	
		PACA	MOUSE	
		PONY		
		PUMA	OTTER	
			OUNCE	
		SEAL		
		STAG	PANDA	
			PUNCH	
		TIKE	PUPPY	
		URUS	SABLE	
			SAIGA	
		VOLE	SASIN	
			SHEEP	
		WOLF	SHREW	
		WORM	SKUNK	
			SLOTH	
		ZEBU	STEER	
			STOAT	
			SWINE	

THE CROSSWORD COMPANION

MAMMALS—continued

6 letters

AGOUTI
ALPACA
ARGALI
ASWAIL
AYE-AYE

BABOON
BADGER
BANDOG
BEAGLE
BEAVER

CASTOR
CATTLE
CHACMA
CHETAH
COCKER
CONGAR
COYOTE
COYPOU
CUSCUS

DESMAN
DONKEY

ERMINE

FARROW
FERRET
FOX-BAT

GALAGO
GIBBON
GOPHER

HACKEE

JACKAL
JAGUAR
JENNET
JERBOA

KITTEN
KOODOO

MARMOT
MARTEN
MARINO
MATACO
MUSK-OX

NILGAU

OCELOT
ONAGER

PALLAH
POODLE
PUG-DOG
PYGARG

QUAGGA

RABBIT
RACOON
RHESUS

SERVAL
SETTER

TARPAN
TENREE
TOM-CAT
TUSKER

URCHIN

VICUNA

WAIRUS
WALRUS
WAPITI
WEASEL
WETHER
WOMBAT

7 letters

ANT-BEAR
AUROCHS

BIGHORN
BLESBOK
BROCKET
BUFFALO
BULL-DOG
BULLOCK
BUSH-CAT

CARACAL
CARIBOO
CHAMOIS
CHEETAH
CHIKARA

DOLPHIN

EANLING
ECHIDNA
ECHINUS

FIN-BACK
FITCHET
FOUMART

GAZELLE
GEMSBOK
GIRAFFE
GLUTTON
GORILLA
GUANACO

HAMSTER
HARRIER

JACKASS

LEMMING
LEOPARD
LEVERET
LIONESS
LURCHER

MAMMOTH
MANATEE
MOUFLON
MUSK-RAT

NARWHAL

OPOSSUM

PANTHER
POLE-CAT

RACCOON
RED-DEER
ROE-BUCK
ROE-DEER
RORQUAL

SAPAJOU
SEA-BEAR
SEA-CALF
SEA-LION
SIAMANG
SPANIEL

TERRIER
TIGRESS

URODELE

VOENGRA

WALLABY
WART-HOG
WILD-ASS
WILD-CAT
WISTITI
WOLF-DOG

8 letters

AARDVARK
ANT-EATER
ANTELOPE

BULL-CALF

CACHELOT
CAPTBARA
CAPUCHIN
CARCAJOU
CARIACOU
CAVE-BEAR
CHIPMUNK
CIVET-CAT
COACH-DOG

DEMI-WOLF
DUCK-BILL
DUCK-MOLE

EARTH-HOG
ELEPHANT

FOX-HOUND

GALLOWAY

HEDGEHOG

KANGAROO
KINKAJOU
KIWI-KIWI

MACROPOD
MANDRILL
MARMOSET
MUSK-DEER

OUISTITI

PANGOLIN
PLATYPUS
PORPOISE

REINDEER
RIVER-HOG

SQUIRREL
STALLION
STEENBOK
TABBY-CAT
TIGER-CAT

WANDEROO
WATER-RAT
WILD-BOAR

MAMMALS—continued

9 letters

ARMADILLO

BABYRUSSA
BANDICOOT
BINTURONG
BUCK-HOUND

CANPAGNOL
CATAMOUNT

DACHSHUND
DEER-HOUND
DEER-MOUSE
DROMEDARY
DZIGGETAI

EARTH-WOLF

GREYHOUND
GROUND-HOG
GUINEA-PIG

ICHNEUMON

PADEMELON
PHALANGER
PIPISTREL
PORCUPINE

RAZOR-BACK
RETRIEVER

SHORT-HORN
SHREW-MOLE
SILVER-FOX
SPRING-BOK

WATER-MOLE
WATER-VOLE
WOLVERINE
WOODCHUCK

10 letters

BLOOD-HOUND
BOTTLE-NOSE

CAMELOPARD
CHIMPANZEE
CHINCHILLA

FIELD-MOUSE
FREE-MARTIN

PANTHERESS
PRAIRIE-DOG

RHINOCEROS
ROCK-RABBIT

SEA-LEOPARD
SEA-UNICORN
SPERM-WHALE

VAMPIRE-BAT

11 letters

BULL-TERRIER

FLYING LEMUR

GLOBIGERINA

HORNED-HORSE

MOUNTAIN-CAT

ORANG-OUTANG

SEA-ELEPHANT
SLEUTH-HOUND

12 letters

FLITTER-MOUSE

HARVEST-MOUSE
HIPPOPOTAMUS

SPIDER-MONKEY

OURANG-OUTANG

WATER-SPANIEL

14 letters

FLYING-SQUIRREL

GROUND-SQUIRREL

FISH AND AQUATIC ANIMALS

3 letters	4 letters	5 letters	6 letters
COD	BASS	BLEAK	ANGLER
DAB	CARP	BORER	BARBEL
EEL	CHAR	BREAM	BLENNY
HAG	CHUB	BRILL	BONITO
RAY	CLAM		BARBOT
	CRAB	DORSE	
			CAPLIN
	DACE	FLUKE	CHEVIN
	DORY		COCKLE
		GAPER	CONGER
	GOBY		CUTTLE
		LOACH	
	HAKE	LEECH	DOCTOR
			DUGONG
	KELT	MATTY	
		MUREX	GURAMI
	LING		GRILSE
	LUCE	PERCH	GURNET
		PRAWN	
	PARR		KELTIE
	PIKE	ROACH	
			LIMPET
	RUDD	SHARK	
		SIREN	MEDUSA
	SCAD	SKATE	MILTER
	SHAD	SMELT	MINNOW
	SOLE	SMOLT	MUD-EEL
		SNAIL	MULLET
	TOPE	SPRAT	(red and grey)
		SQUID	MUSSEL
		TENCH	NEREID
		TORSK	
		TROUT	OYSTER
		TUNNY	
			PHOLAS
		WHELK	PLAICE
			POLLAN
			REMORA
			SALMON
			SEACAT
			SEADOG
			SEA-EEL
			SEA-FOX
			SHANNY
			SHRIMP
			SUCKER
			TARPON
			TAUTOG
			TEREDO
			TURBOT
			WEEVER
			WRASSE

FISH AND AQUATIC ANIMALS—continued

7 letters	8 letters	9 letters	10 letters
ALEWIFE	ARGONAUT	ANGEL-FISH	ACORN-SHELL
ANCHOVY			ARCHER-FISH
	BAND-FISH	BARRACUDA	
CATFISH		BLACK-FISH	BOTTLE-FISH
COD FISH	CALAMARY	BRANDLING	
CODLING	CHIMAERA	BULL-TROUT	CANDLE-FISH
	COAL-FISH		CUTTLE-FISH
DOG FISH	CRAYFISH	CERATODUS	
DOLPHIN			FLYING-FISH
	DEAL-FISH	DEVIL-FISH	
EEL-POUT		DIMYARIAN	HAMMER-FISH
	EAR-SHELL		HERMIT-CRAB
GARFISH		FISH-LOUSE	HORSE-LEECH
GRAMPUS	FILE-FISH		
GUDGEON	FLOUNDER	GLOBE-FISH	PARROT-FISH
	FOX-SHARK		PERIWINKLE
HADDOCK		HOUND-FISH	PURPLE-FISH
HALIBUT	GOLD-FISH		
HERRING	GRAYLING	LAMP-SHELL	RIBBON-FISH
			RIBBON-WORM
LAMPERN	JOHN DORY	OSTRACIAN	
LAMPREY			SAND-HOPPER
LOBSTER	KING-CRAB	PILOT-FISH	SILVER-FISH
MUDFISH	LANCELET	SEA-NEEDLE	
MURAENA	LUMP-FISH	SEA-NETTLE	
		SEA-SQUIRT	
OCTOPOD	MACKEREL	SEA-URCHIN	
OCTOPUS	MALARMAT	SURMULLET	
	MENHADEN	SWORD-FISH	
PIDDOCK	MONKFISH		
POLLACK		TIFFEN BAT	
	OCTOPEDE	TRUNK-FISH	
ROTIFER			
	PENNY-DOG	WHITE-BAIT	
SAND-EEL	PICKEREL		
SARDINE	PILCHARD		
SAW-FISH	PIPE-FISH		
SCALLOP	PHYSALIA		
SCULPIN			
SEA-COW	RHIZOPOD		
SEA-HARE			
SEA-PIKE	SEA-ACORN		
SEA-SLUG	SEA-DEVIL		
SEA-WOLF	SEA-LEMON		
SUNFISH	SEA-LOUSE		
	SEA-SNIPE		
TORPEDO	STARFISH		
TREPANG	STING-RAY		
	STURGEON		
WHITING			
	TOAD-FISH		
	WOLF-FISH		
	ZOOPHYTE		

FISH AND AQUATIC ANIMALS—continued

11 letters

BELLOWS-FISH
BRINE-SHRIMP

CALLING-CRAB

FLYING-SQUID

HIPPO-CAMPUS
HOLOTHURIAN

PAPER-SAILOR
PEARL-MUSSEL
PEARL-OYSTER

SALMON-TROUT
SEA-CUCUMBER
SEA-HEDGEHOG
SERPENT-FISH
STICKLEBACK
SUCKING-FISH

TRUMPET-FISH

WHEEL-ANIMAL

12 letters

SEA-PORCUPINE

13 letters

HORSE-MACKEREL
PAPER-NAUTILUS

AMPHIBIANS AND REPTILES

3 letters

ASP

BOA

EFT

4 letters

FROG

NEWT

PAMA

TOAD

5 letters

ABOMA
ADDER
ASPIC

COBRA

GECKO

SKINK
SNAKE

VIPER

6 letters

CAYMAN

DRAGON

IGUANA

LIZARD

PYTHON

TRITON
TURTLE

7 letters

AXOLOTL

PADDOCK

SERPENT

TADPOLE

URODELA

8 letters

ANACONDA

BASILISK
BULL-FROG

TORTOISE
TERRAPIN
TREE-FROG

9 letters

ALLIGATOR

BLIND-WORM

CHAMELEON
CROCODILE

PUFF-ADDER

10 letters

FER-DE-LANCE

GLASS-SNAKE

SALAMANDER

WATER-SNAKE

11 letters

RATTLE-SNAKE

13 letters

ICHTHYOSAURUS

14 letters

BOA-CONSTRICTOR

COBRA-DE-CAPELLO

SNAPPING-TURTLE

INSECTS AND INVERTEBRATES

3 letters	4 letters	5 letters	6 letters	7 letters
ANT	CLEG	APHIS	BEETLE	ANT-LION
	FLEA	BRIZE	BOTFLY	ANNELID
BEE				
BUG	GNAT	DRONE	CHAFER	BEAN-FLY
	GRIG		CHIGOE	BEE-MOTH
DOR	GRUB	EMMET	CHINCH	BLOW-FLY
			CICADA	BOAT-FLY
FLY	LICE	FLUKE		
			DAYFLY	CESTOID
NIT	MITE	LARVA		CRICKET
	MOTH	LOUSE	EARWIG	
			ELATOR	EPIZOON
	SLUG	MIDGE		
			GADFLY	FIREFLY
	TICK	SNAIL		FROG-FLY
			HORNET	
	WASP			GALL-FLY
	WORM		JIGGER	
				HIVE-BEE
			LOCUST	
				KATYDID
			MAGGOT	
			MANTIS	LOBWORM
			MAYBUG	LUGWORM
			MAYFLY	
				MAWWORM
			SAW-FLY	MOLLUSC
			SCARAB	
			SPIDER	SAND-FLY
			THRIPS	TERMITE
			TSETSE	
				WOOD-ANT
			WEEVIL	

INSECTS AND INVERTEBRATES—continued

8 letters

BOOK-WORM

CASE-WORM
CRANE-FLY

EPHEMERA

FLATWORM
FLESH-FLY

GALL-GNAT
GLOW-WORM

HAIR-WORM
HONEY-BEE
HORSE-FLY
HOUSE-FLY

ITCH-MITE

LADY-BIRD

MILLIPED
MOSQUITO
MYRIAPOD

SCORPION
SHIP-WORM

TAPE-WORM

WATER-BUG
WHEAT-FLY
WHIRLWIG
WIRE-WORM

9 letters

BOOK-LOUSE
BREEZE-FLY
BUMBLE-BEE
BUTTER-FLY

CANKER-FLY
CENTIPEDE
CHEESE-FLY
CHRYSALIS
CLAVICORN
COCHINEAL
COCKROACH
COFFEE-BUG
COLEOPTER

DRAGON-FLY

EARTH-WORM

HUMBLE-BEE

TARANTULA
TURNIP-FLY

WATER-FLEA
WOOD-LOUSE

10 letters

ARTHROPODS

BIRD-SPIDER
BLISTER-FLY
BLUE-BOTTLE

CADDICE-FLY
CANKER-WORM
COCKCHAFER
CORN-BEETLE

DEATH'S-HEAD
DEATH-WATCH

FROG-HOPPER

HARVEST-BUG
HESSIAN-FLY

LEAF-INSECT

PALMER-WORM
PHYLLOXERA

RIBBON-WORM

SHEEP-LOUSE
STAG-BEETLE

WHEAT-MIDGE

11 letters

BLACK BEETLE
BLOOD-SUCKER

CABBAGE-MOTH
CATERPILLAR
CLOTHES-MOTH

GRASSHOPPER

SCOLOPENDRA
STICK-INSECT

TIGER-BEETLE

12 letters

BOOK-SCORPION
BUZZARD-CLOCK

SPRING-BEETLE

WALKING-STICK
WATER-BOATMAN

13 letters

BLISTER-BEETLE

CARPENTER'S-BEE

DADDY-LONG-LEGS

PRAYING-MANTIS

15 letters

SERRICORN-BEETLE

16 letters

CABBAGE-BUTTERFLY

23

BIRDS

3 letters	4 letters	5 letters	6 letters	
AUK	CHAT	AGAMI	ARGALA	SCOTER
DAW	COOT		AVOCET	SEA-EEL
	COCK	BOOBY		SEA-MEW
EMU	CROW		BANTAM	SHRIKE
		CAPON	BARBET	SISKIN
FOP	DODO	CRAKE	BULBUL	
	DOVE	CRANE		THRUSH
	DUCK		CANARY	TOMTIT
HEN	DUPE	DIVER	CHOUGH	TOUCAN
		DRAKE	CONDOR	TROGON
JAY	ERNE		CORBIE	TURKEY
	EYAS	EAGLE	CUCKOO	
MEW		EGRET	CULVER	WIGEON
	FOWL	EIDER	CURLEW	
MOA			CUSHAT	
(running	GULL	FINCH	CYGNET	
bird)				
	HAWK	GLEDE	DARTER	
OWL	HERN	GOOSE	DIPPER	
		GEESE	DUNLIN	
PIE	IBIS	GREBE		
			FALCON	
ROC	KAKA	HARPY		
	KITE	HERON	GANDER	
TIT	KIWI	HOBBY	GANNET	
	KNOT		GARROT	
		MACAW	GODWIT	
	LARK	MAVIS	GROUSE	
	LOON	MERLE		
	LORY		HAMMER	
		NODDY	HOOPER	
	MINA		HOOPOE	
		OUZEL	HOWLET	
	RAIL	OWLET		
	RHEA		JACANA	
	ROOK	PIPIT		
	RUFF		LANNER	
	RUNT	QUAIL	LINNET	
	SHAG	RAVEN	MAGPIE	
	SKUA	REEVE	MARTIN	
	SMEW	ROBIN	MERLIN	
	SWAN			
		SAKER	ORIOLE	
	TEAL	SCAUP	OSPREY	
	TERN	SNIPE		
		SQUAB	PARROT	
	WREN	STORK	PEEWIT	
		SWIFT	PETREL	
			PIGEON	
		WADER	PLOVER	
			POUTER	
			PUFFIN	
			PULLET	
			RACAMA	

BIRDS—continued

7 letters

BARN OWL
BITTERN
BLUECAP
BUNTING
BUSTARD
BUZZARD

CATBIRD
CHICKEN
COLIBRI
COURSER
CREEPER

DOR-HAWK

EGG-BIRD

FANTAIL
FERN-OWL

GADWALL
GOBBLER
GORCOCK
GOR-CROW
GOSHAWK
GOSLING
GRACKLE
GRAYLEG
GRAY-OWL
GRIFFIN

HAGGARD
HARRIER

JACKDAW

KESTREL
KINGLET

LAPWING

MALLARD
MANAKIN
MARTLET
MOORHEN

ORTOLAN
OSTRICH

PARTLET
PEACOCK
PEAFOWL
PELICAN
PENGUIN
PINTAIL
POCHARD
PUTTOCK

REDPOLL
REDWING
RUDDOCK

SEA-DUCK
SKYLARK
SPARROW
SUN-BIRD
SWALLOW

TANAGER
TIERCEL
TITLARK
TITLING
TUMBLER

VULTURE

WAGTAIL
WARBLER
WAXWING
WIDGEON
WRYNECK

8 letters

ADJUTANT
AMADAVAT

BARNACLE
BEE-EATER
BLACKCAP
BLUEBIRD
BOBOLINK

CARDINAL
COCKATOO
COCKEREL
CURASSOW

DABCHICK
DIDAPPER
DOTTEREL
DUCKLING

EAGLE-OWL

FLAMINGO

GAMECOCK

HAWFINCH
HERNSHAW

KIWI-KIWI

LANDRAIL
LOVEBIRD
LYRE-BIRD

MEGAPODE
MOOR-COCK
MOOR-FOWL
MUSK-DUCK

NIGHTJAR
NUTHATCH

PHEASANT
POPINJAY

REDSHANK
REDSTART
RICE-BIRD
RING-DOVE

SAGE-COCK
SEA-EAGLE
SHELDUCK
SKUA-GULL
STARLING

THROSTLE
TITMOUSE
TRAGOPAN

WATERHEN
WHEATEAR
WHIMBREL
WHINCHAT
WOODCOCK
WOODLARK

THE CROSSWORD COMPANION

BIRDS—continued

9 letters

ALBATROSS

BALD-EAGLE
BEAN-GOOSE
BECCAFICO
BEEF-EATER
BLACKBIRD
BLACKCOCK
BLACK GAME
BOTTLE-TIT
BOWERBIRD
BRAMBLING
BULLFINCH

CAMPANERO
CASSOWARY
CHAFFINCH
CORMORANT
CORNCRAKE
CROSSBILL

FIELDFARE

GALLINULE
GER FALCON
GIER-EAGLE
GOLDCREST
GOLDENEYE
GOLDFINCH
GOOSANDER
GUILLEMOT

HEATH-COCK
HERON-SHAW

NIGHT-HAWK

PARRAKEET
PARTRIDGE
PASSERINE
PEREGRINE
PHALAROPE
PINE-FINCH
PTARMIGAN

RAZORBILL
REDBREAST
RINGOUZEL

SALANGANE
SANDPIPER
SEA-PARROT
SHELDRAKE
SNAKE-BIRD
SNOW-FLECK
SPOONBILL
STILT-BIRD
STOCKDOVE
STONECHAT

TRUMPETER
TURNSTONE

WATER-FOWL
WATERRAIL
WILD GOOSE
WINDHOVER

10 letters

ABERDEVINE

BRENT-GOOSE
BURROW-DUCK
BUSH-SHRIVE
BUTTER-BIRD

CANVAS BACK
COW-BUNTING

DEMOISELLE
DIDUNCULUS

FALLOW-CHAT
FLYCATCHER

GOATSUCKER
GREENFINCH
GREENSHANK
GUINEAFOWL

HARPY-EAGLE
HENHARRIER

KINGFISHER

NIGHT-HERON
NUTCRACKER

SAGE-GROUSE
SANDERLING
SAND-GROUSE
SANDMARTIN
SCREECH-OWL
SEA-SWALLOW
SHEARWATER
SOLAN-GOOSE
SONGTHRUSH
SUMMER-DUCK

TAILOR-BIRD
TROPIC-BIRD
TURTLE-DOVE

WATER-OUSEL
WEAVER-BIRD
WILLOW-WREN
WOOD-GROUSE
WOODPECKER
WOOD-PIGEON

11 letters

BARN-SWALLOW
BRUSH-TURKEY
BUTCHER-BIRD

COCHIN CHINA

FALLOW-FINCH
FRIGATE-BIRD

HUMMING-BIRD

KING-VULTURE

LAMMERGEIER

MOCKING-BIRD

NIGHTINGALE

REED-BUNTING
REED-SPARROW

SCISSOR-BILL
SNOW-BUNTING
SNOW ORTOLAN
SONG-SPARROW
SPARROW-HAWK
STILT-PLOVER

WHITETHROAT
WOODWARBLER

BIRDS—continued

12 letters

ADJUTANT-BIRD

BURROWING-OWL

CAPERCAILZIE
CARDINAL-BIRD

FALCON-GENTIL

HEDGE-SPARROW
HEDGE-WARBLER

MARSH-HARRIER
MISSEL-THRUSH

SEDGE-WARBLER
SERPENT-EATER
STONE-CHATTER
STUBBLE-GOOSE

WATTLE-TURKEY
WHIP-POOR-WILL

YELLOW HAMMER

13 letters

SECRETARY BIRD

{ TURKEY-BUZZARD
{ TURKEY-VULTURE

WILLOW-WARBLER

YELLOW-BUNTING

14 letters

BIRD-OF-PARADISE

SOME MYTHOLOGICAL NAMES

2 letters

EA
RA

3 letters

ANU
HAP
NOX
NUT
PAN
SET
SOL
TIW
TYR

4 letters

AJAX
APIS
ATON
BAST
EROS
HAPI
HERA
ISIS
JUNO
LEDA
LOKI

4 letters (cont)

LUNA
MAAT
MARS
ODIN
PTAH
SIVA
THOR
ZEUS

5 letters

AMMON
ASHUR
ATLAS
CERES
COMUS
CUPID
DAGON
DIANA
DURGA
ENLIL
FLORA
FRIGU
HORUS
HYMEN
INDRA
JANUS
JASON

5 letters (cont)

MAZDA
MIDAS
PLUTO
THOTH
VENUS
WODEN
WOTAN

6 letters

ADONIS
ANUBIS
APOLLO
ATHENA
AURORA
BAALIM
HATHOR
HERMES
ISHTAR
MARDUK
MEDUSA
MILCOM
MOLOCH
OSIRIS
PSYCHE
SATURN
SOMNUS
VISHNU
VULCAN

7 letters

ARIADNE
BACCHUS
BELLONA
JUPITER
MERCURY
MINERVA
MITHRAS
PERSEUS
PROTEUS
SERAPIS
ULYSSES

8 letters

HERCULES
NEPHTHYS

9 letters

APHRODITE
ASHTAROTH
MANICHAEUS
PYGMALION

CHEMICAL ELEMENTS, METALS, ALLOYS AND MANUFACTURED SUBSTANCES

2 letters	3 letters	4 letters	5 letters
MU	TIN	ALUM	ARGON
		COKE	BORAX
		GOLD	BORON
			BRASS
		IRON	ETHER
		LEAD	GLASS
		LIME	INVAR
		MOND	LYSOL
		(metal)	MUNTZ
		SODA	NITON
		ZINC	NITRE
			NYLON
			OZONE
			RADON
			SALOL
			STEEL
			WOOTZ
			XENON

CHEMICAL ELEMENTS, METALS, ALLOYS AND
MANUFACTURED SUBSTANCES—continued

6 letters

ALKALI
AMATOL

BARIUM
BARYTA
BRONZE

CARBON
CASEIN
CERIUM
COBALT
COPPER
CRESOL

ERBIUM

HELIUM

INDIUM
IODINE
IONIUM

NICKEL

OSMIUM
OXYGEN

PEWTER
PHENOL
POTASH

RADIUM

SILVER
SODIUM
SOLDER
STARCH

TANNIN

7 letters

ALCOHOL
ALUMINA
AMALGAM
AMMONAL
AMMONIA
ANILINE
ARSENIC
ASPIRIN

BENZENE
BISMUTH
BROMIDE
BROMINE

CADMIUM
CALCIUM
CALOMEL
CAMPHOR
COCAINE
CODEINE
CYANIDE

EBONITE

FERMIUM

GALLIUM
GELATIN
GLUCOSE

HAFNIUM
HOLMIUM

IRIDIUM

KRYPTON

LITHIUM

MENTHOL
MERCURY

NIOBIUM

PERSPEX

QUININE

RED-LEAD
RHENIUM
RHODIUM

SILICON
SODA-ASH
SULPHUR

THORIUM
TOLUESE

URANIUM

VERONAL
VITRIOL

YTTRIUM

8 letters

ACTINIUM
ANTIMONY
ASTATINE
ATROPINE

BAKELITE

CAFFEINE
CHARCOAL
CHLORINE
CHROMIUM
CINCHONA

DIDYMIUM

EUROPIUM

FLUORINE
FORMALIN
FRANCIUM

GLUCINUM
GRAPHITE
GUNMETAL

HYDROGEN

IODOFORM

LITHARGE
LUTECIUM

MANGANIN
MASURIUM
MORPHINE

NICHROME
NICOTINE
NITROGEN

PLATINUM
PLUMBAGO
POLONIUM

RUBIDIUM

SAMARIUM
SCANDIUM
SELERIUM

TANTALUM
THALLIUM
TITANIUM
TUNGSTEN

9 letters

ACETYLENE
ALUMINIUM

BERYLLIUM
BLACKLEAD

CELLULOSE
COLUMBIUM

DEUTERIUM
DIGITALIN
DURALUMIN

GERMANIUM
GUNCOTTON
GUNPOWDER

LANTHANUM

MAGNESIUM
MANGANESE

NEPTUNIUM

PALLADIUM
PLUTONIUM
POTASSIUM

QUICKLIME

STRONTIUM

VERDIGRIS
VULCANITE

WHITE-LEAD

YTTERBIUM

ZIRCONIUM

29

CHEMICAL ELEMENTS, METALS, ALLOYS AND MANUFACTURED SUBSTANCES—continued

10 letters

CAOUTCHOUC
CHLOROFORM
CONSTANTIN

DYSPROSIUM

GADOLINIUM

MOLYBDENUM

PHOSPHORUS
PROMETHIUM

11 letters

CARBORUNDUM

EINSTEINIUM

GLAUBER-SALT

IPECACUANHA

PARALDEHYDE

QUICK-SILVER

12 letters

PRAESODYMIUM

13 letters

PROTO-ACTINIUM

14 letters

BRITANNIA-METAL

PHOSPHOR-BRONZE

MINERAL ORES

4 letters	5 letters	6 letters	7 letters	8 letters
ALUM	AGATE	ALBITE	APATITE	ASBESTOS
	AMBER	AUGITE	ASPHALT	
CALX	ARGON		AZURITE	BLUE-JOHN
CAUK		CERITE		BORACITE
CLAY	BERYL		BARYTES	BRONZITE
COAL	BORAX	GALENA	BAUXITE	BROOKITE
		GARNET	BITUMEN	
GRIT	CHALK	GYPSUM	BORNITE	CALAMINE
	CHERT			CALCSPAR
LIAS		IOLITE	CALCITE	CHLORITE
	EMERY		CALICHE	CHROMITE
MAWL		JARGON		CINNABAR
MICA	FLINT	JASPER	DIAMOND	CORUNDUM
				CRYOLITE
ONYX	NITRE	KAOLIN	EMERALD	
OPAL			EPIDOTE	DIOPTASE
	PITCH	MARBLE		DOLOMITE
RUBY			FELSPAR	
	SILEX	POTASH		FLUORITE
SPAR		PYRITE	GRANITE	
				GRAPHITE
TALC		QUARTZ	KAINITE	
TUFA				HYACINTH
		SCHORL	LIQUITE	
WADD		SILICA		IDOCRASE
			OLIVINE	ILMENITE
		THORIA		
			PYRITES	LIMONITE
		ZIRCON		
			REALGAR	MAGNESIA
				MASSICOT
			SULPHUR	MELANITE
				MONAZITE
			TRIPOLI	
				ORPIMENT
			WOLFRAM	
			WURGITE	PYROXENE
			ZEOLITE	ROCK-SALT
				ROCK-SOAP
				ROCKWOOD
				SAPPHIRE
				SIDERITE
				STEATITE
				STIBNITE
				TINSTONE
				ZIRCONIA

MINERAL ORES—continued

9 letters

ALABASTER
AMIANTHUS
ANGLESITE
ANHYDRITE
ARAGONITE
ARGENTITE

BYSSOLITE

CASHOLONG
CAT-SILVER
COLUMBITE

EARTH-FLAX

FLUORSPAR

GREENSAND

IRON-STONE

LIMESTONE
LODESTONE

MAGNESITE
MAGNETITE
MALACHITE
MARCASITE
MISPICKEL

OZOCERITE

PETROLEUM

SALT PETRE
SCAPOLITE
STREAM-TIN

TRIDYMITE
TURQUOISE

10 letters

ACTINOLITE
ANTHRACITE
AQUAMARINE

CARNALLITE
CHALCEDONY
CHALYBEATE

HORNBLENDE

INFUSORIAL
(EARTH)

KIESELGUHR

MEERSCHAUM

PYROLUSITE

SERPENTINE
SPHALERITE

TOURMALINE

11 letters

CASSITERITE
CHRYSOPRASE
CHALCEDONYX

ICELAND-SPAR

LAPIS-LAZULI

PITCH BLENDE

ROCK-CRYSTAL

12 letters

AEROSIDERATE

CHALCOPYRITE

FULLER'S-EARTH

MOUNTAIN-CORK

MOUNTAIN-FLAX

SILVER-GLANCE
STRONTIANITE

14 letters

BRITANNIA-METAL

TWO-LETTER WORDS

AH!	GO	MA	SI
AM		ME	SO
AN		MI	
AS		MY	
AT			
AX	HA!		
AY	HE		TO
	HI!		
	HO!	NO	
BE			UP
BO			US
BY	IF	OD	
	I'M	OF	
	IN	OH!	
	IS	ON	
	IT	OR	WE
DI		OX	WO!
DO			
	JO		
		PA	YE
EH!		PO	
EM			
	LA		
	LO!		
		RE	
FA			
FY!			

33

THREE-LETTER WORDS

A							
ABB	BIB	DAN	FAG	HAG	JOB	MET	OWN
ABY	BID	DAP	FAR	HAH!	JOE	MEW	
ACE	BIG	DAW	FAT	HAM	JOG	MID	**P**
ACT	BIN	DAY	FAY	HAP	JOT	MIX	
ADD	BIS	DEE	FED	HAS	JOY	MOA	PAD
ADO	BIT	DEN	FEE	HAT	JUG	MOB	PAH
ADZ	BOA	DEW	FEN	HAW	JUT	MOO	PAL
AFT	BOB	DEY	FEU	HAY		MOP	PAN
AGA	BOG	DID	FEW	HEM		MOW	PAP
AGE	BOO	DIE	FEY	HEN	**K**	MUD	PAR
AGO	BOT	DIG	FEZ	HER		MUG	PAS
AHA!	BOW	DIM	FIB	HEW	KAW	MUM	PAT
AID	BOX	DIN	FID	HEY!	KAY		PAW
AIL	BOY	DIP	FIE	HID	KEG		PAX
AIM	BUD	DOE	FIG	HIE	KEN	**N**	PAY
AIR	BUG	DOG	FIN	HIM	KEX		PEA
AIT	BUM	DON	FIR	HIN	KEY	NAB	PED
ALB	BUN	DOR	FIT	HIP	KID	NAG	PEE
ALE	BUR	DOT	FIX	HIS	KIN	NAP	PEG
ALL	BUS	DRY	FLU	HIT	KIP	NAY	PEN
ALP	BUT	DUB	FLY	HOB	KIT	NEB	PEP
ALT	BUY	DUD	FOB	HOD	KYE	NEE	PER
AND	BYE	DUE	FOE	HOE		NET	PET
ANT		DUG	FOG	HOG		NEW	PEW
ANY		DUN	FOH	HOP	**L**	NIB	PIE
APE	**C**	DUO	FOP	HOT		NIL	PIG
APT		DUX	FOR	HOW	LAC	NIP	PIN
ARC	CAB	DYE	FOY	HOY	LAD	NIT	PIP
ARE	CAD		FOX	HUB	LAG	NOD	PIT
ARK	CAM		FRO	HUE	LAP	NOG	PIX
ARM	CAN	**E**	FRY	HUG	LAW	NOR	PLY
ART	CAP		FUN	HUH!	LAX	NOT	POD
ASH	CAR	EAR	FUR	HUM	LAY	NOW	POH
ASK	CAT	EAT		HUN	LEA	NUN	POP
ASP	CAW	EAU		HUT	LED	NUT	POT
ASS	CAY	EBB	**G**		LEE	NUX	POX
ATE	CIT	EEL			LEG		PRY
AUK	COB	E'EN	GAB	**I**	LEO		PUB
AVE	COD	E'ER	GAD		LET	**O**	PUG
AWE	COG	EFT	GAG	ICE	LID		PUN
AWL	COL	EGG	GAM	ICY	LIE	OAF	PUP
AWN	CON	EGO	GAP	ILK	LIP	OAK	PUR
AXE	COO	EKE	GAR	ILL	LIT	OAR	PUS
AYE	COR	ELD	GAS	IMP	LOB	OAT	PUT
	COT	ELF	GAT	INK	LOG	OBI	PYX
	COW	ELK	GAY	INN	LOO	ODD	
	COX	ELL	GEM	IOU	LOP	ODE	
B	COY	ELM	GET	IRE	LOT	O'ER	**Q**
	COZ	EMU	GIG	IRK	LOW	OFF	
BAA	CRY	END	GIN	IVY	LUG	OFT	QUA
BAD	CUB	ENS	GNU		LYE	OHM	
BAG	CUD	EON	GOB			OHO!	
BAH!	CUE	ERA	GOD	**J**		OIL	**R**
BAN	CUP	ERE	GOT		**M**	OKE	
BAR	CUR	ERG	GUM	JAB		OLD	RAG
BAT	CUT	ERN	GUN	JAG	MAC	ONE	RAM
BAY		ERR	GUT	JAH	MAD	OPE	RAN
BED		EVE	GUY	JAM	MAM	ORB	RAP
BEE	**D**	EWE	GYM	JAR	MAN	ORE	RAT
BEG		EYE	GYP	JAW	MAP	ORT	RAW
BEN	DAB			JAY	MAR	OUR	RAY
BET	DAD			JET	MAT	OUT	RED
BEY	DAG	**F**	**H**	JEW	MAW	OVA	REP
	DAK			JIB	MAY	OWE	RET
	DAM	FAD	HAD	JIG	MEN	OWL	

34

RIB	SAD	SOD	TAP	TOP		WED	
RID	SAG	SOG	TAR	TOR	**V**	WEE	**Y**
RIG	SAL	SOL	TAW	TOT		WEN	
RIM	SAP	SON	TAX	TOW	VAN	WET	YAK
RIP	SAT	SOP	TAY	TOY	VAT	WEY	YAM
ROB	SAW	SOT	TEA	TRY	VEX	WHO	YAP
ROC	SAY	SOU	TED	TUB	VIA	WHY	YAW
ROD	SEA	SOW	TEE	TUG	VIE	WIG	YEA
ROE	SEE	SOY	TEN	TUM	VIM	WIN	YEN
ROI	SET	SPA	THE	TUN	VIS	WIT	YES
ROT	SEW	SPY	THO'	TUP	VOW	WOE	YET
ROW	SEX	STY	THY	TUT!		WON	YEW
RUB	SHE	SUB	TIC	TWO		WOO	YON
RUE	SHY	SUE	TIE		**W**	WOP	YOU
RUG	SIC	SUM	TIN			WOT	
RUM	SIN	SUN	TIP	**U**	WAD	WRY	
RUN	SIP	SUP	'TIS		WAG		**Z**
RUT	SIR		TIT	UGH!	WAN		
RYE	SIT		T.N.T.	URN	WAP	**X**	ZAX
	SIX	**T**	TOD	USE	WAR		ZOO
	SKI		TOE	UNA	WAS	—	
S	SKY	TAB	TOM		WAX		
	SLY	TAG	TON		WAY		
SAC	SOB	TAN	TOO		WEB		

FOUR-LETTER WORDS

A

ABBA
ABBE
ABED
ABET
ABIB
ABLE
ABLY
ABUT
ACES
ACHE
ACID
ACME
ACNE
ACRE
ADAM
ADAR
ADIT
ADRY
ADZE
AEON
AERO
AERY
AFAR
AFFY
AGED
AGES
AGIO
AGOG
AGUE
AHOY
AIDE
AIRY
AJAR
AKEE
AKIN
ALAR
ALAS
ALEE
ALFA
ALLY
ALMA
ALMS
ALOE
ALOW
ALPS
ALSO
ALTO
ALUM
AMAH
AMBO
AMEN
AMID
AMIR
AMOK
AMYL
ANAL
ANEW
ANNA
ANON
ANTE
ANTI
ANUS

APEX
APSE
AQUA
ARAB
ARCH
AREA
ARIA
ARID
ARIL
ARMS
ARMY
ARNI
ARUM
ASCI
ASHY
ASIA
ASPS
ATOM
ATOP
AUNT
AURA
AUTO
AVER
AVID
AVIS
AVON
AVOW
AWAY
AWED
AWRY
AXES
AXIL
AXIS
AXLE
AYAH
AYES
AZYM

B

BAAL
BABE
BABU
BABY
BACH
BACK
BADE
BAGS
BAIL
BAIT
BAKE
BALD
BALE
BALK
BALL
BALM
BAND
BANE
BANG
BANK
BANT
BARB
BARD
BARE

BARK
BARM
BARN
BASE
BASH
BASK
BASS
BAST
BATE
BATH
BAWD
BAWL
BEAD
BEAK
BEAM
BEAN
BEAR
BEAT
BEAU
BECK
BEEF
BEEN
BEER
BEET
BELL
BELT
BEMA
BEND
BENT
BERE
BERG
BERM
BEST
BEVY
BIAS
BICE
BIDE
BIER
BIFF
BIGG
BIKE
BILE
BILK
BILL
BIND
BINE
BING
BIRD
BISE
BISK
BITE
BITT
BLAB
BLAE
BLED
BLEW
BLOB
BLOT
BLOW
BLUE
BLUR
BOAR
BOAT
BODE
BODY

BOER
BOGY
BOIL
BOLD
BOLE
BOLL
BOLT
BOMB
BOND
BONE
BONY
BOOB
BOOK
BOOM
BOON
BOOR
BOOT
BORE
BORN
BORT
BOSH
BOSK
BOSS
BOTH
BOTT
BOUT
BOWL
BOZO
BRAD
BRAE
BRAG
BRAN
BRAT
BRAY
BRED
BREW
BRIG
BRIM
BRIO
BROW
BUBO
BUCK
BUFF
BUHL
BULB
BULK
BULL
BUMP
BUND
BUNG
BUNK
BUNT
BUOY
BURG
BURL
BURN
BURR
BURY
BUSH
BUSK
BUSS
BUST
BUSY
BUTT
BUZZ

BYRE

C

CADE
CADI
CAFE
CAGE
CAIN
CAKE
CALF
CALK
CALL
CALM
CALP
CALX
CAME
CAMP
CANE
CANT
CAN'T
CAPE
CARD
CARE
CARK
CARL
CARP
CART
CASE
CASH
CASK
CAST
CATE
CAUK
CAUL
CAVE
CAVY
CEDE
CEIL
CELL
CELT
CENT
CERE
CESS
CHAM
CHAP
CHAR
CHAT
CHAW
CHAY
CHEF
CHEW
CHIC
CHID
CHIN
CHIP
CHIT
CHOP
CHOW
CHUB
CHUM
CIEL
CIST
CITE

CITY
CIVE
CLAD
CLAM
CLAN
CLAP
CLAW
CLAY
CLEF
CLEG
CLEM
CLEW
CLIP
CLOD
CLOG
CLOT
CLOY
CLUB
CLUE
COAL
COAT
COAX
COCA
COCK
COCO
CODE
COIF
COIL
COIN
COIR
COKE
COLA
COLD
COLE
COLT
COMA
COMB
COME
CONE
CONK
CONY
COOK
COON
COOP
COOT
COPE
COPT
COPY
CORD
CORE
CORF
CORK
CORM
CORN
COSE
COST
COSY
COTE
COUP
COVE
COWS
COZY
CRAB
CRAG
CRAM

CRAN
CRAW
CREW
CRIB
CROP
CROW
CRUM
CRUT
CRUX
CUBE
CUES
CUFF
CULL
CULM
CULT
CURB
CURD
CURE
CURE
CURL
CURT
CUSP
CUSS
CUTE
CYMA
CYME
CYST
CZAR

D

DACE
DADO
DAFF
DAFT
DAGO
DAIS
DALE
DAME
DAMN
DAMP
DANE
DANK
DARE
DARK
DARN
DART
DASH
DATA
DATE
DAUB
DAUK
DAVY
DAWK
DAWN
DAZE
DEAD
DEAF
DEAL
DEAN
DEAR
DEBT
DECK

DEE

DEED
DEEM
DEEP
DEER
DEFT.
DEFY
DELF
DELL
DELT
DEME
DEMI
DEMY
DENE
DENT
DENY
DERM
DESK
DEVA
DEWY
DHAK
DHAL
DHOW
DIAL
DIBS
DICE
DICK
DIDO
DIED
DIEM
DIES'
DIET
DIKE
DILL
DIME
DINE
DING
DINT
DIRE
DIRK
DIRT
DISC
DISH
DISK
DISS
DIVA
DIVE
DIXY
DOAB
DOCK
DODO
DOER
DOES
DOFF
DOGE
DOIT
DOLE
DOLL
DOLT
DOME
DONE
DON'T
DOOL
DOOM
DOOR
DOPE
DORA
DORP
DORR
DORY
DOSE

DOSS
DOST
DOTE
DOTH
DOUR
DOUT
DOVE
DOWL
DOWN
DOXY
DOZE
DOZY
DRAB
DRAG
DRAM
DRAT
DRAW
DRAY
DREG
DREW
DRIP
DROP
DRUB
DRUG
DRUM
DUAL
DUAN
DUCK
DUCT
DUDE
DUEL
DUET
DUKE
DULL
DULY
DUMB
DUMP
DUNE
DUNG
DUPE
DUSK
DUST
DUTY
DYAD
DYER
DYKE
DYNE

E

EACH
EARL
EARN
EARS
EASE
EAST
EASY
EBON
ECHO
EDDA
EDDY
EDEN
EDGE
EDGY
EDIT
EELS
EFTS
EGAD!
EGGS

EGIS
EIRE
ELAN
ELMO
ELMY
ELSE
ELUL
EMEU
EMIR
EMIT
ENDS
ENEW
ENID
ENOW
ENVY
EPHA
EPIC
EPOS
ERGO
ERIN
ERNE
EROS
ERSE
ERST
ESPY
ETCH
ETNA
ETUI
EVEN
EVER
EVIL
EWER
EWES
EXAM
EXIT
EXON
EYAS
EYED
EYES
EYOT
EYRE
EYRY

F

FACE
FACT
FADE
FAIL
FAIN
FAIR
FAKE
FALL
FAMA
FAME
FANE
FANG
FARE
FARL
FARM
FARO
FASH
FAST
FATE
FAUN
FAUX
FAWN
FAYS
FEAR

FEAT
FEED
FEEL
FEES
FEET
FELL
FELT
FEND
FENT
FEOD
FERN
FETE
FEUD
FIAT
FIBS
FICO
FIEF
FIFE
FIGS
FILE
FILL
FILM
FIND
FINE
FINN
FIRE
FIRM
FISC
FISH
FISK
FIST
FITS
FIVE
FIZZ
FLAG
FLAK
FLAM
FLAN
FLAP
FLAT
FLAW
FLAX
FLAY
FLEA
FLED
FLEE
FLEW
FLEX
FLIP
FLIT
FLOE
FLOG
FLOP
FLOW
FLUE
FLUX
FOAL
FOAM
FOCI
FOES
FOGY
FOIL
FOIN
FOLD
FOLK
FOND
FONT
FOOD
FOOL
FOOT

FORD
FORE
FORK
FORM
FORT
FOSS
FOUL
FOUR
FOWL
FOXY
FRAY
FREE
FRET
FRIT
FROG
FROM
FUEL
FULL
FUME
FUMY
FUND
FUNK
FURL
FURY
FUSE
FUSS
FUZE
FUZZ
FYRD

G

GABY
GAEL
GAFF
GAGE
GAIL
GAIN
GAIT
GALA
GALE
GALL
GAME
GAMP
GAMY
GANG
GOAL
GAPE
GARB
GASH
GASP
GATE
GAUD
GAUL
GAUR
GAVE
GAWD
GAWK
GAZE
GEAN
GEAR
GEAT
GELD
GENS
GENT
GERM
GEST
GHÂT

GHEE
GIBE
GIFT
GILD
GILL
GILT
GIMP
GINN
GIRD
GIRL
GIRT
GIST
GIVE
GLAD
GLEE
GLEN
GLIB
GLOW
GLUE
GLUM
GLUT
GNAT
GNAW
GNOO
GOAD
GOAL
GOAT
GOBY
GO-BY
GOER
GOLD
GOLF
GONE
GONG
GOOD
GORE
GORY
GOSH!
GOTH
GOUR
GOUT
GOWK
GOWN
GRAB
GRAM
GRAY
GREW
GREY
GRID
GRIG
GRIM
GRIN
GRIP
GRIT
GROG
GROT
GROW
GRUB
GRUM
GULF
GULL
GULP
GURU
GUSH
GUST
GUTS
GYAL
GYBE
GYRE
GYRI

GYVE

H

HACK
HADE
HADJ
HAFT
HA'HA
HAIL
HAIR
HAKE
HALE
HALF
HALL
HALM
HALO
HALT
HAME
HAND
HANG
HANK
HARD
HARE
HARK
HARM
HARP
HART
HASH
HASP
HATE
HATH
HAUL
HAUM
HAVE
HAWK
HAZE
HAZY
HEAD
HEAL
HEAP
HEAR
HEAT
HEED
HEEL
HEFT
HEIR
HELD
HELL
HELM
HELP
HEMP
HERB
HERD
HERE
HERN
HERO
HERR
HERS
HEST
HEWN
HIDE
HIGH
HILL
HILT
HIND
HINT
HIRE
HISS

HIST
HIVE
HOAR
HOAX
HOCK
HOLD
HOLE
HOLM
HOLP
HOLT
HOLY
HOME
HONE
HOOD
HOOF
HOOK
HOOP
HOOT
HOPE
HOPS
HORN
HOSE
HOST
HOUR
HOVE
HOWL
HUED
HUFF
HUGE
HULK
HULL
HUMP
HUNG
HUNK
HUNT
HURL
HURT
HUSH
HUSK
HYMN

I

IAMB
IBEX
IBIS
ICED
ICON
IDEA
IDEM
IDES
IDLE
IDLY
IDOL
IDYL
IKON
ILEX
IMAM
IMAN
IMPI
INCA
INCH
INKY
INLY
INTO
IONA
IOTA
IRAN
IRIS

IRON
ISIS
ISLE
ITCH
ITEM

J

JACK
JADE
JAIL
JAMB
JAPE
JARL
JAWS
JAZZ
JEAN
JEER
JEHU
JERK
JESS
JEST
JIBE
JILT
JINN
JOBS
JOIN
JOKE
JOLE
JOLL
JOLT
JOSS
JOVE
JOWL
JUBE
JUDY
JULY
JUMP
JUNE
JUNK
JUNO
JURY
JUST
JUTE

K

KADI
KAIL
KAKA
KALE
KALI
KATE
KAVA
KEEK
KEEL
KEEN
KEEP
KELP
KELT
KENT
KEPT
KERB
KERF
KERN
KEYS
KHAN
KIBE

KICK
KILL
KILN
KILT
KIND
KINE
KING
KINK
KINO
KIRK
KISS
KITE
KITH
KIWI
KNAG
KNAP
KNAR
KNEE
KNEW
KNIT
KNOB
KNOP
KNOT
KNOW
KNUB
KOHL
KOLA
KRIS

L

LACE
LACK
LACY
LADE
LADY
LAIC
LAID
LAIN
LAIR
LAKE
LAKH
LAKY
LAMA
LAMB
LAME
LAMP
LAND
LANE
LANK
LARD
LARK
LASH
LASS
LAST
LATE
LATH
LAUD
LAVA
LAVE
LAWN
LAZY
LEAD
LEAF
LEAK
LEAL
LEAN
LEAP
LEEK

LEER
LEES
LEFT
LEND
LENO
LENS
LENT
LESS
LEST
LEVY
LEWD
LIAR
LIAS
LICE
LICH
LICK
LIDO
LIED
LIEF
LIEN
LIER
LIES
LIEU
LIFE
LIFT
LIKE
LILT
LILY
LIMB
LIME
LIMN
LIMP
LIMY
LINE
LING
LINK
LINN
LINO
LINT
LIPS
LION
LIRA
LIRE
LISP
LIST
LITH
LIVE
LOAD
LOAF
LOAM
LOAN
LOTH
LOBE
LOCH
LOCK
LOCI
LODE
LOFT
LOIN
LOLL
LONE
LONG
LOOK
LOOM
LOON
LOOP
LOOT
LOPE
LOPS
LORD

LORE
LORN
LORY
LOSE
LOSS
LOST
LOTE
LOTH
LOTO
LOUD
LOUT
LOTS
LOVE
LUCE
LUCK
LUFF
LULL
LUMP
LUNA
LUNE
LUNG
LURE
LURK
LUSH
LUST
LUTE
LYNX
LYRE

M

MA'AM
MACE
MADE
MAGE
MAGI
MAID
MAIL
MAIM
MAIN
MAKE
MALE
MALL
MALM
MALT
MAMA
MANE
MANX
MANY
MARE
MARK
MARL
MARS
MART
MASH
MASK
MASS
MAST
MATE
MATE
MATH
MATT
MAUD
MAUL
MAZE
MAZY
MEAD
MEAL
MEAN

MEAT
MEED
MEEK
MEET
MELT
MEND
MENU
MERE
MERK
MESH
MESS
METE
MEWL
MEWS
MICA
MICE
MIEN
MIFF
MILD
MILE
MILK
MILL
MILT
MIME
MINA
MIND
MINE
MINK
MINT
MINX
MINY
MIRE
MIRY
MISS
MIST
MITE
MITT
MITY
MOAN
MOAT
MOCK
MODE
MOIL
MOLD
MOLE
MOLY
MONK
MOOD
MOON
MOOR
MOOT
MOPE
MORE
MORN
MOSS
MOST
MOTE
MOTH
MOUE
MOVE
MOYA
MUCH
MUCK
MUFF
MULE
MULL
MUMM
MUMP
MURK
MUSE

MUSK
MUST
MUTE
MYTH

N

NAIF
NAIL
NAME
NAPE
NARD
NAVE
NAVY
NEAP
NEAR
NEAT
NECK
NEED
NE'ER
NEON
NERO
NESS
NEST
NETT
NEWS
NEWT
NEXT
NICE
NICK
NIGH
NINE
NISI
NODE
NOEL
NOME
NONE
NONE
NOOK
NOON
NORE
NORM
NOSE
NOTE
NOUN
NOUS
NUDE
NULL
NUMB
NUTS

O

OAKS
OAKY
OARS
OARY
OAST
OATH
OATS
OBEY
OBIT
OBOE
ODDS
ODIC
ODOR
OGEE
OGLE
OGRE

OGPU, OILY, OLIO, OLLA, OMEN, OMIT, ONCE, ONER, ONLY, ONUS, ONYX, OOID, OOZE, OOZY, OPAL, OPEN, OPUS, ORAL, ORBY, ORGY, ORTS, ORYX, OTTO, OUCH, OUST, OVAL, OVEN, OVER, OVUM, OWED, OWNS, OXEN, OYER, OYES!, OYEZ!

P

PACA, PACE, PACK, PACO, PACT, PAGE, PAID, PAIL, PAIN, PAIR, PALE, PALI, PALL, PALM, PALP, PALT, PALY, PANE, PANG, PAPA, PARA, PARD, PARE, PARK, PARR, PART, PASS, PAST, PATE, PATH, PAUL, PAVE, PAWL, PAWN, PEAK, PEAL, PEAR, PEAT, PECK, PEEL, PEEN, PEEP, PEER, PEKE, PELF, PELL, PELT, PEND, PENT, PEON, PERI, PERK, PERT, PESO, PEST, PHEW!, PHIZ, PICA, PICE, PICK, PIED, PIER, PIKE, PILE, PILL, PIMP, PINE, PING, PINK, PINT, PINY, PIPE, PIPY, PISÉ, PISH!, PISS, PITH, PITY, PIXY, PLAN, PLAT, PLAY, PLEA, PLIM, PLOD, PLOP, PLOT, PLOW, PLUG, PLUM, PLUS, POCK, POEM, POET, POKE, POLE, POLL, POLO, POME, POMP, POND, PONY, POOH!, POOL, POOP, POOR, POPE, PORE, PORK, PORT, PORY, POSE, POST, POSY, POUR, POUT, PRAM, PRAY, PREY, PRIG, PRIM, PROA, PROD, PROP, PROW, PUCE, PUCK, PUFF, PUKE, PULE, PULL, PULP, PUMA, PUMP, PUNK, PUNT, PUNY, PUPA, PURE, PURL, PURR, PUSH, PUSS, PUTT, PYRE

Q

QUAD, QUAG, QUAY, QUID, QUIP, QUIT, QUIZ

R

RACE, RACK, RACY, RAFF, RAFT, RAGE, RAHU, RAID, RAIL, RAIN, RAKE, RÂLE, RAMP, RAND, RANG, RANK, RANT, RAPE, RAPT, RARE, RASE, RASH, RASP, RATE, RATH, RAVE, RAZE, READ, REAL, REAM, REAP, REAR, RECK, REED, REEF, REEK, REEL, REIN, RELY, REND, RENO, RENT, REPP, REST, RHEA, RICE, RICH, RICK, RIDE, RIFE, RIFT, RILL, RIME, RIMY, RIND, RING, RINK, RIOT, RIPE, RIPT, RISE, RISK, RITE, RIVE, ROAD, ROAM, ROAN, ROAR, ROBE, ROCK, RODE, ROIL, ROLE, ROLL, ROME, ROMP, ROOD, ROOF, ROOK, ROOM, ROOT, ROPE, ROPY, ROSE, ROSY, ROTA, ROTE, ROUE, ROUP, ROUT, ROVE, RUBY, RUCK, RUDD, RUDE, RUFF, RUGA, RUIN, RULE, RUMP, RUNE, RUNG, RUNT, RUSE, RUSH, RUSK, RUSS, RUST, RUTH, RYOT

S

SACK, SAFE, SAGA, SAGE, SAGO, SAID, SAIL, SAKE, SALE, SALT, SAME, SAMP, SAND, SANE, SANK, SANS, SARD, SARK, SASH, SATE, SAVE, SCAB, SCAD, SCAN, SCAR, SCAT, SCOT, SCOW, SCUD, SCUM, SCUT, SCYE, SEAL, SEAM, SEAR, SEAT, SECT, SEED, SEEK, SEEL, SEEM, SEEN, SEEP, SEER, SEIN, SELF, SELL, SEMI, SEND, SEPT, SERB, SERE, SERF, SETA, SHAD, SHAG, SHAH, SHAM, SHAW, SHEA, SHED, SHEW, SHIN, SHIP, SHOD, SHOE, SHOG, SHOP, SHOT, SHOW, SHUN, SHUT, SICE, SICK, SIDE, SIFT, SIGH, SIGN, SIKH, SILK, SILL, SILO, SILT, SINE, SING, SINK, SIRE, SIST, SITE, SIZE, SIZY, SKEW, SKID, SKIM, SKIN, SKIP, SKIT, SKUA, SKYE, SLAB, SLAG, SLAM, SLAP, SLAT, SLAV, SLAY, SLED, SLEW, SLEY, SLID, SLIM, SLIP, SLIP, SLOE, SLOP, SLOT, SLOW, SLUB, SLUE, SLUG, SLUM, SLUR, SLUT, SMEE, SMEW, SMIT, SMUG, SMUT, SNAG, SNAP, SNIP, SNOB, SNOT, SNOW, SNUB, SNUG, SOAK, SOAP, SOAR, SOCK, SODA, SOFA, SOFT, SOHO, SOIL, SOLD, SOLE, SOLI, SOLO, SOMA, SOME, SONG, SOON, SOOT, SOPH, SORB, SORE, SORN, SORT, SO-SO, SOUL, SOUK, SOUR, SOYA, SPAN, SPAR, SPAT, SPAY, SPEC, SPED, SPEW, SPIN, SPIR, SPIT, SPOT, SPRY

SPUD	TALL	TINT	TUSH	VERB	WAXY	WOMB
SPUE	TAME	TINY	TUSK	VERT	WEAK	WON'T
SPUN	TAMP	TIRE	'TWAS	VERY	WEAL	WONT
SPUR	TANG	TIRO	TWIG	VEST	WEAN	WOOD
STAB	TANK	TOAD	TWIN	VETO	WEAR	WOOF
STAG	TAPE	TO-DO	TWIT	VIAL	WEED	WOOL
STAR	TARE	TOED	TYPE	VICE	WEEK	WORD
STAY	TARN	TOFT	TYRE	VIDE	WEEN	WORE
STEM	TARO	TOGA	TYRO	VIEW	WEEP	WORK
STEP	TART	TOIL	TZAR	VILE	WEFT	WORM
STET	TASK	TOLD		VILL	WEIR	WORN
STEW	TASS	TOLL		VINE	WELD	WORT
STIR	TA-TA	TOLU	**U**	VINY	WELL	WOVE
STOA	TAUT	TOMB		VIOL	WELT	WRAP
STOP	TAXI	TOME	UGLY	VISE	WEND	WREN
STOW	TEAK	TONE	ULAN	VISE	WENT	WRIT
STUB	TEAL	TONG	ULNA	VIVA	WEPT	WYCH
STUD	TEAM	TONY	UMBO	VLEI	WERE	
STUN	TEAR	TOOK	UNDO	VLEY	WERT	
STYE	TEAT	TOOL	UNIT	VOCE	WEST	**Y**
SUCH	TEEM	TOOT	UNTO	VOID	WHAT	
SUCK	TEEN	TOPE	UPAS	VOLE	WHEN	YARD
SUDS	TEIL	TORE	UPON	VOLT	WHET	YARE
SUER	TELL	TORN	URDU	VOTE	WHEW!	YARN
SUET	TEMS	TORT	UREA		WHEY	YAWL
SUEZ	TEND	TORI	URGE		WHIG	YAWN
SUIT	TENE	TORY	URIC	**W**	WHIM	YAWS
SULK	TENT	TOSS	URIM		WHIN	YEAN
SUMP	TERM	TOUR	URSA	WADD	WHIP	YEAR
SUNG	TERN	TOUT	URUS	WADE	WHIR	YELK
SUNK	TEST	TOWN	USED	WADI	WHIT	YELL
SUNN	TEXT	TRAM	USER	WADY	WHIZ	YELP
SURD	THAN	TRAP	UTAH	WAFT	WHOA!	YOKE
SURE	THAT	TRAY	UVEA	WAGE	WHOP	YOLK
SURF	THAW	TREE		WAIF	WHOM	YORE
SWAB	THEE	TREK		WAIL	WICK	YOUR
SWAG	THEM	TRET	**V**	WAIN	WIDE	YOWL
SWAM	THEN	TRIG		WAIT	WIFE	YO-YO
SWAN	THEW	TRIM	VAIL	WAKE	WILD	YULE
SWAP	THEY	TRIO	VAIN	WALE	WILE	Y-WIS
SWAY	THIN	TRIP	IVAN	WALK	WILL	
SWIG	THIS	TROD	VAIR	WALL	WILT	
SWIM	THOU	TROT	VALE	WAND	WILY	**Z**
SWOP	THRO'	TROW	VAMP	WANE	WIND	
SWUM	THUD	TROY	VANE	WANT	WINE	ZANY
	THUG	TRUE	VARY	WARD	WING	ZEAL
	THUS	TSAR	VASE	WARE	WINK	ZEBU
T	TIED	TUBA	VAST	WARM	WINY	ZEND
	TICK	TUBE	VEAL	WARN	WIPE	ZERO
TACH	TIDE	TUCK	VEDA	WARP	WIRE	ZEST
TACK	TIDY	TUFA	VEER	WART	WIRY	ZEUS
TACT	TIER	TUFF	VEGA	WARY	WISE	ZINC
TAEL	TIFF	TUFT	VEIL	WASH	WISH	ZION
TA'EN	TIKE	TUNA	VEIN	WASP	WISP	ZOEA
TAIL	TILE	TUNE	VELD	WAST	WITH	ZONE
TAKE	TILL	TURF	VELA	WATT	WIVE	ZOON
TALC	TILT	TURK	VENA	WAUL	WOAD	ZULU
TALE	TIME	TURN	VEND	WAVE	WOLD	
TALK	TINE	TUSH!	VENT	WAVY	WOLF	

FIVE-LETTER WORDS

A

ABACA
ABACK
ABAOI
ABAFT
ABASE
ABASH
ABATE
ABBEY
ABBOT
ABEAM
ÁBELE
ABHOR
ABIDE
ABIES
ABODE
ABORT
ABOUT
ABOVE
ABUSE
ABYSM
ABYSS
ACERB
ACHED
ACHOR
ACORN
ACRED
ACRID
ACTED
ACTON
ACTOR
ACUTE
ADAGE
ADAYS
ADDAX
ADDED
ADDER
ADDLE
ADEPT
ADIEU
ADMIT
ADMIX
ADOBE
ADOPT
ADORE
ADORN
ADOWN
ADSUM
ADULT
ADUST
AEGIS
AERIE
AESOP
AFFIX
AFOOT
AFIRE
AFRIT
AFTER
AGAIN
AGAMI
AGAPE
AGATE

AGAVE
AGENT
AGILE
AGIST
AGLET
AGNEL
AGNUS
AGONY
AGORA
AGREE
AGRIN
AGUED
AHEAD
AHEAP
AIDER
AIRED
AISLE
AITCH
ALACK!
ALARM
ALATE
ALBUM
ALDER
ALERT
ALGAL
ALGID
ALGUM
ALIAS
ALIBI
ALIEN
ALIGN
ALIKE
ALIVE
ALLAH
ALLAY
ALLEY
ALLOT
ALLOW
ALLOY
ALMUG
ALOES
ALOFT
ALONE
ALONG
ALOOF
ALOUD
ALPHA
ALTAR
ALTER
ALULA
ALWAY
AMAIN
AMASS
AMATE
AMAZE
AMBER
AMBIT
AMBLE
AMEBA
AMBRY
AMEER
AMEND
AMENT
AMICE
AMIDE

AMISS
AMITY
AMMON
AMONG
AMORT
AMOUR
AMPLE
AMPLY
AMUCK
AMUSE
ANCLE
ANDES
ANEAR
ANELE
ANENT
ANGEL
ANGER
ANGLE
ANGLO
ANGRY
ANILE
ANIME
ANISE
ANKER
ANKLE
ANNEX
ANNOY
ANNUL
ANODE
ANTIC
ANTRE
ANURA
ANVIL
AORTA
APACE
APART
APEAK
APERY
APHIS
APING
APISH
APPAL
APPLE
APPLY
APPUI
APRIL
APRON
APSIS
APTLY
ARACK
ARBOR
AREAS
ARECA
ARENA
ARGIL
ARGOL
ARGON
ARGOT
ARGUE
ARGUS
ARIAN
ARIEL
ARIES
ARISE
ARMED

ARMOR
ARNEE
AROMA
AROSE
ARRAN
ARRAS
ARRAY
ARRIS
ARROW
ARSIS
ARSON
ARYAN
ASCUS
ASHEN
ASHES
ASIAN
ASIDE
ASKED
ASKER
ASKEW
ASPEN
ASPIC
ASSAY
ASSES
ASSET
ASTER
ASTIR
ASTRA
ATAXY
ATILT
ATLAS
ATOLL
ATONE
ATONY
ATRIP
ATTAR
ATTIC
AUDIT
AUGER
AUGHT
AUGUR
AULIC
AURAL
AURIC
AVAIL
AVAST
AVENS
AVERT
AVION
AVOID
AWAIT
AWAKE
AWARD
AWARE
AWASH
AWFUL
AWNED
AWNER
AXIAL
AXILE
AXIOM
AXLED
AZOTE
AZURE

B

BABEL
BABOO
BACON
BADGE
BADLY
BAGGY
BAIRN
BAIZE
BAKED
BAKER
BALAS
BALER
BALMY
BANAL
BANCO
BANDY
BANJO
BANKS
BANNS
BARBS
BARED
BARGE
BARIC
BARKY
BARMY
BARON
BASAL
BASED
BASEL
BASES
BASIC
BASIL
BASIN
BASIS
BASON
BASSE
BASSO
BASTA
BASTE
BATCH
BATED
BATHE
BATON
BATTA
BATTY
BAULK
BAVIN
BAWDY
BAYED
BAZAR
BEACH
BEADS
BEADY
BE-ALL
BEAMY
BEARD
BEAST
BEAUS
BEAUX
BEDAD!
BEDEL

BEDEW
BEDIM
BEECH
BEEFY
BEERY
BEFAL
BEFIT
BEFOG
BEGAN
BEGET
BEGIN
BEGUM
BEGUN
BEIGE
BEING
BELAY
BELCH
BELIE
BELLE
BELLY
BELOW
BENCH
BENNE
BERME
BERRY
BERTH
BERYL
BESET
BESOM
BESOT
BETEL
BETON
BETLE
BEVEL
BEZEL
BHANG
BIBLE
BIDET
BIFID
BIGHT
BIGLY
BIGOT
BIJOU
BILBO
BILGE
BINGE
BIPED
BIRCH
BIRTH
BISON
BITCH
BITER
BLACK
BLADE
BLAIN
BLAME
BLAND
BLANK
BLARE
BLASE
BLAST
BLAZE
BLEAK
BLEAR
BLEAT

BLEED	BOWEL	BULKY	CARGO	CHINK	COACT
BLEND	BOWER	BULLA	CARIB	CHIRK	COALY
BLESS	BOWIE	BULLY	CARLE	CHIRM	COAST
BLEST	BOXEN	BULSE	CAROB	CHIRP	COATI
BLIND	BOXER	BUNCH	CAROL	CHIVE	COBLE
BLINK	BOYAR	BUNNY	CAROM	CHODE	COBRA
BLISS	BRACE	BURGH	CARRY	CHOIR	COCOA
BLITE	BRACH	BURIN	CARSE	CHOKE	CODEX
BLITZ	BRACT	BURKE	CARTE	CHOKY	COIGN
BLOAT	BRAID	BURLY	CARUS	CHORD	COLIC
BLOBS	BRAIL	BURNT	CARVE	CHOSE	COLLY
BLOCK	BRAIN	BURRY	CASTE	CHUCK	COLON
BLOKE	BRAKE	BURSA	CATCH	CHUFF	COLOR
BLOND	BRAKY	BURSE	CATER	CHUMP	COLZA
BLOOD	BRAND	BURST	CATES	CHUNK	COMER
BLOOM	BRANK	BUSES	CATTY	CHURL	COMET
BLOWN	BRANT	BUSBY	CAULK	CHURN	COMIC
BLOWS	BRASH	BUSHY	CAUSE	CHUSE	COMMA
BLOWY	BRASS	BUSSU	CAVIL	CHUTE	CONCH
BLUES	BRAVE	BUTTE	CAVIN	CHYLE	CONEY
BLUFF	BRAVO	BUTTY	CEASE	CHYME	CONGE
BLUNT	BRAWL	BUXOM	CEDAR	CIBOL	CONIC
BLURS	BRAWN	BUYER	CELTS	CIDER	COOEE
BLURT	BRAXY	BY-END	CENSE	CIGAR	COOIE
BLUSH	BRAZE	BY-LAW	CENTO	CILIA	COOMB
BOARD	BREAD	BYSSI	CEORL	CINCH	CO-OPT
BOAST	BREAK	BY-WAY	CHACO	CIPPI	COPAL
BODLE	BREAM		CHAFE	CIRRI	COPED
BOGEY	BREED		CHAFF	CIVET	COPRA
BOGGY	BRENT	**C**	CHAIN	CIVIC	COPSE
BOGIE	BREVE		CHAIR	CIVIL	COPSY
BOGLE	BRIAR	CAABA	CHALK	CLACK	CORAL
BOGUS	BRIBE	CABAL	CHAMP	CLAIM	CORKY
BOHEA	BRICK	CABAS	CHANK	CLAMP	CORNY
BOIAR	BRIDE	CABBY	CHANT	CLANG	CORPS
BOLAR	BRIEF	CABER	CHAOS	CLANK	CORSE
BOLAS	BRIER	CABIN	CHAPE	CLARY	CORVE
BOLUS	BRILL	CABLE	CHAPT	CLASH	COSEN
BONED	BRINE	CABOB	CHARD	CLASP	COSEY
BONNE	BRING	CACAO	CHARE	CLASS	COUCH
BONNY	BRINK	CACHE	CHARM	CLAVE	COUGH
BONUS	BRINY	CACTI	CHARR	CLEAN	COULD
BONCE	BRISE	CADDY	CHART	CLEAR	COUNT
BOOBY	BRISK	CADET	CHARY	CLEAT	COUPE
BOOKS	BRIZE	CADGE	CHASE	CLEEK	COURT
BOOSE	BROAD	CADRE	CHASM	CLEFT	COVED
BOOSY	BROCK	CAECA	CHAYA	CLEPE	COVER
BOOTH	BROIL	CAIRN	CHEAP	CLERK	COVET
BOOTS	BROKE	CAIRO	CHEAT	CLICK	COVEY
BOOTY	BROME	CALID	CHECK	CLIFF	COVIN
BOOZE	BROOD	CALIF	CHEEK	CLIMB	COWER
BOOZY	BROOK	CALVE	CHEEP	CLIME	COWRY
BORAX	BROOM	CALYX	CHEER	CLING	COYLY
BORED	BROSE	CAMEL	CHELA	CLINK	COYPU
BORER	BROTH	CAMEO	CHERT	CLOAK	COZEN
BORIC	BROWN	CANAL	CHESS	CLOCK	CRACK
BORNE	BRUIN	CANDY	CHEST	CLOFF	CRAFT
BORON	BRUIT	CANNY	CHIAN	CLOKE	CRAKE
BOSKY	BRUNT	CANOE	CHICA	CLOMB	CRAMP
BOSOM	BRUSH	CANON	CHICH	CLOSE	CRANE
BOSSY	BRUTE	CANTO	CHICK	CLOTH	CRANK
BOTCH	BUDGE	CANTY	CHICO	CLOUD	CRAPE
BOTHY	BUFFO	CAPER	CHIDE	CLOUT	CRASH
BOUGH	BUFFY	CAPON	CHIEF	CLOVE	CRASS
BOUND	BUGGY	CAPOT	CHILD	CLOWN	CRATE
BOURG	BUGLE	CARAP	CHILL	CLUBS	CRAVE
BOURN	BUILD	CARAT	CHIMB	CLUCK	CRAWL
BOUSE	BUILT	CARED	CHIME	CLUMP	CRAZE
BOUTS	BULGE	CARET	CHINA	CLUNG	CRAZY
BOWED	BULGY	CAREX	CHINE	COACH	CREAK

CREAM		DIRTY	DRYAD	EMBAY	EXTRA
CREDO	**D**	DITCH	DRYER	EMBED	EXUDE
CREED		DITTO	DRYLY	EMBER	EXULT
CREEK	DADDY	DITTY	DUCAL	EMEND	EYRIE
CREEL	DAILY	DIVAN	DUCAT	EMERY	
CREEP	DAIRY	DIVER	DUCHY	EMMET	
CREPE	DAISY	DIXIE	DULLY	EMPTY	**F**
CREPT	DALLY	DIZEN	DULSE	ENACT	
CRESS	DAMAN	DIZZY	DUMMY	ENDER	FABLE
CREST	DAMAR	DOCKS	DUMPY	ENDOW	FACED
CRICK	DANCE	DODGE	DUNCE	ENDUE	FACER
CRIED	DANDY	DOGAL	DUPER	ENEMA	FACET
CRIER	DARIC	DOGGO	DUPLE	ENEMY	FADDY
CRIME	DARKY	DOGMA	DURRA	ENJOY	FADGE
CRIMP	DATUM	DOILY	DURST	ENNUI	FAERY
CRISP	DAUBY	DOING	DUSKY	ENROL	FAGOT
CROAK	DAUNT	DONNA	DUSTY	ENTIA	FAINT
CROCK	DAVIT	DONOR	DUTCH	ENSKY	FAIRY
CROFT	DAZED	DOOLY	DWALE	ENSUE	FAITH
CRONE	DEARY	DORIC	DWARF	ENTER	FAKIR
CRONY	DEATH	DORSE	DWELL	ENTRY	FALSE
CROOK	DEBAR	DOTAL	DYING	ENURE	FAMED
CROON	DEBIT	DOTER		ENVOY	FANCY
CRORE	DEBUT	DOTTY		EOLIC	FARAD
CROSS	DECAD	DOUBT	**E**	EPACT	FARCE
CROUP	DECAY	DOUGH		EPHAH	FARCY
CROWD	DECOY	DOUSE	EAGER	EPHOD	FATAL
CROWN	DECRY	DOWDY	EAGLE	EPHOR	FATED
CRUDE	DEDAL	DOWEL	EAGRE	EPOCH	FATLY
CRUEL	DEFER	DOWER	EARED	EPODE	FATTY
CRUET	DEIFY	DOWLE	EARLY	EPSOM	FAUGH
CRUMB	DEIGN	DOWNY	EARTH	EQUAL	FAULT
CRUMP	DEISM	DOWRY	EASEL	EQUIP	FAUNA
CRUSE	DEIST	DOWSE	EATER	ERASE	FAVOR
CRUSH	DEITY	DOZEN	EAVES	ERATO	FAVUS
CRUST	DELAY	DOZER	EBLIS	ERECT	FEAST
CRWTH	DELFT	DRAFF	EBONY	ERGOT	FEAZE
CRYER	DELTA	DRAFT	ECLAT	ERICA	FECAL
CRYPT	DELVE	DRAIN	EDEMA	ERODE	FECES
CUBEB	DEMED	DRAKE	EDGED	EROSE	FEIGN
CUBIC	DEMIT	DRAMA	EDICT	ERRED	FEINT
CUBIT	DEMON	DRANK	EDIFY	ERROR	FELLY
CUDDY	DEMOS	DRAPE	EDILE	ERUCT	FELON
CUISH	DEMUR	DRAVE	EDUCE	ERUPT	FEMUR
CULCH	DENSE	DRAWL	EDUCT	ESKAR	FENCE
CULLY	DEPOT	DRAWN	EERIE	ESKER	FENNY
CUMIN	DEPTH	DREAD	EGEST	ESSAY	FEOFF
CUPEL	DERBY	DREAM	EGGER	ESTOP	FERAE
CUPID	DERMA	DREAR	EGRET	ETERN	FERAL
CURDY	DETER	DREGS	EIDER	ETHER	FERNY
CURER	DEUCE	DRESS	EIGHT	ETHIC	FERRY
CURIA	DEVIL	DREST	EIKON	ETHOS	FESSE
CURIO	DHOLE	DRIER	EJECT	ETHYL	FETAL
CURLY	DIANA	DRIFT	ELAND	ETWEE	FETCH
CURRY	DAIRY	DRILL	ELATE	EUCRE	FETED
CURSE	DICED	DRILY	ELBOW	EVADE	FETID
CURST	DICER	DRINK	ELDER	EVENS	FETOR
CURVE	DICKY	DRIVE	ELECT	EVENT	FETUS
CUTCH	DICTA	DROIT	ELEGY	EVERY	FEVER
CUTIS	DIDST	DROLL	ELEMI	EVICT	FEWER
CYCAD	DIGHT	DRONE	ELFIN	EVOKE	FIBRE
CYCLE	DIGIT	DROOP	ELIDE	EXACT	FICHU
CYDER	DIKYN	DROPS	ELITE	EXALT	FIELD
CYMAR	DILDO	DROSS	ELMEN	EXCEL	FIEND
CYNIC	DILLY	DROVE	ELOGE	EXEAT	FIERY
CZECH	DIMLY	DROWN	ELOGY	EXERT	FIFER
	DINER	DRUID	ELOPE	EXILE	FIFTH
	DINGO	DRUNK	ELUDE	EXIST	FIFTY
	DINGY	DRUPE	ELVAN	EXPEL	FIGHT
	DIRGE	DRUSE	ELVES	EXTOL	FILCH

FILER	FORAY	GAMMA	GODLY	GUISE	HILAR
FILLY	FORCE	GAMUT	GOING	GULAR	HILLY
FILMY	FORDO	GAPER	GOODS	GULCH	HILUM
FILTH	FORGE	GARTH	GOODY	GULES	HINDU
FINAL	FORGO	GASSY	GOOSE	GULLY	HINGE
FINCH	FORKY	GATED	GORGE	GUMMY	HINNY
FINER	FORME	GAUDY	GORSE	GUNNY	HIRED
FINIS	FORTE	GAUGE	GORSY	GUSTO	HIRER
FINNY	FORTH	GAULT	GOUDA	GUSTY	HITCH
FIORD	FORTY	GAUNT	GOUGE	GUTTA	HIVES
FIRER	FORUM	GAUZE	GOURD	GYPSY	HOARD
FIRRY	FOSSA	GAUZY	GOUTY	GYRAL	HOARY
FIRST	FOSSE	GAWKY	GOWAN	GYRUS	HOBBY
FIRTH	FOUND	GAYAL	GRAAL		HOCUS
FISHY	FOUNT	GAYLY	GRACE		HODGE
FISTY	FRAIL	GAZEL	GRADE	**H**	HOIST
FITCH	FRAME	GAZER	GRAFF		HOLLA!
FITLY	FRANC	GECKO	GRAFT	HABIT	HOLLO!
FIVES	FRANK	GEESE	GRAIL	HADES	HOLLY
FIXED	FRANK	GELID	GRAIN	HAILY	HOMER
FJORD	FRAUD	GEMMA	GRAIP	HAIRY	HONEY
FLAIL	FREAK	GEMMY	GRAND	HAKIM	HONOR
FLAKE	FREED	GENET	GRANT	HALLO!	HOOFS
FLAKY	FREER	GENIE	GRAPE	HALMA	HOOKY
FLAME	FRESH	GENII	GRAPY	HALOS	HOPPY
FLAMY	FRIAR	GENRE	GRASP	HALVE	HORAL
FLANK	FRIED	GENUS	GRASS	HANCH	HORDE
FLARE	FRILL	GET-UP	GRATE	HANDY	HORNY
FLASH	FRISK	GHAUT	GRAVE	HAPLY	HORSE
FLASK	FRITH	GHOST	GRAVY	HAPPY	HORSY
FLAWY	FRIZZ	GHOUL	GRAZE	HARDS	HORUS
FLAXY	FROCK	GIANT	GREAT	HARDY	HOTEL
FLEAM	FROND	GIBER	GREBE	HAREM	HOTLY
FLECK	FRONT	GIBUS	GREED	HARPY	HOUGH
FLEER	FRORE	GIDDY	GREEK	HARRY	HOUND
FLEET	FROST	GIGOT	GREEN	HARSH	HOURI
FLESH	FROTH	GIPSY	GREET	HARUM	HOUSE
FLICK	FROWN	GIRTH	GRICE	HASTE	HOVEL
FLIER	FRUIT	GIVEN	GRIDE	HASTY	HOVER
FLIES	FRUMP	GIVER	GRIEF	HATCH	HOWEL
FLING	FRUSH	GLADE	GRILL	HATER	HUFFY
FLINT	FUDGE!	GLADY	GRIME	HATTI	HULKY
FLIRT	FUGAL	GLAIR	GRIMY	HAUGH	HULLO!
FLOAT	FUGUE	GLAND	GRIND	HAULM	HULLY
FLOCK	FULLY	GLARE	GRIPE	HAUNT	HUMAN
FLOOD	FUMID	GLASS	GRIST	HAVEN	HUMID
FLOOR	FUNGI	GLAVE	GROAN	HAWSE	HUMOR
FLORA	FUNNY	GLAZE	GROAT	HAZEL	HUMPH!
FLOSS	FUROR	GLEAM	GROIN	HEADY	HUMPY
FLOUR	FURRY	GLEAN	GROOM	HEALD	HUMUS
FLOUT	FURZE	GLEBE	GROPE	HEARD	HUNCH
FLOWN	FURZY	GLEBY	GROSS	HEART	HUNKS
FLUFF	FUSEE	GLEDE	GROUP	HEATH	HURLY
FLUID	FUSEL	GLEED	GROUT	HEAVE	HURRA!
FLUKE	FUSIL	GLEET	GROVE	HEAVY	HURRY
FLUME	FUSSY	GLIDE	GROWL	HEDGE	HURST
FLUNG	FUSTY	GLINT	GROWN	HEIGH!	HUSKY
FLUOR	FUZEE	GLOAT	GRUEL	HELIX	HUSSY
FLUSH	FUZZY	GLOBE	GRUFF	HELLO!	HUTCH
FLUTE		GLOOM	GRUME	HELOT	HUZZA!
FLUTY		GLORY	GRUNT	HELVE	HYADS
FLYER	**G**	GLOSS	GUANO	HEMAL	HYDRA
FOAMY		GLOVE	GUARD	HENCE	HYDRO
FOCAL	GABEL	GLOZE	GUAVA	HENNA	HYENA
FOCUS	GABLE	GLUEY	GUESS	HERBY	HYMEN
FOGEY	GAILY	GLUME	GUEST	HERON	HYOID
FOGGY	GALEA	GNARL	GUIDE	HERSE	HYRAX
FOIST	GALOP	GNARR	GUILD	HEWER	HYSON
FOLIO	GAMEY	GNASH	GUILE	HIDER	
FOLLY	GAMIN	GNOME	GUILT	HIGHT	

I

IAMBI
ICHOR
ICTUS
IDEAL
IDIOM
IDIOT
IDLER
IDOLA
ILEUM
ILIAC
ILIUM
IMAGE
IMAGO
IMAUM
IMBED
IMBUE
IMPEL
IMPLY
INANE
INAPT
INCOG
INCUR
INCUS
INDEX
INDIA
INDUE
INEPT
INERT
INFER
INFIX
INGOT
INKLE
INLAY
INLET
INNER
INSET
INTER
INURE
INURN
IODIC
IONIC
IRADE
IRATE
IRISH
IRONS
IRONY
ISLAM
ISLET
ISSUE
TCHY
IVIED
IVORY
IXTLE

J

JABOT
JAGGY
JALAP
JAPAN
JASEY
JAUNT
JAWED
JELLY
JEMMY
JENNY
JERID
JERKY
JESUS
JETTY
JEWEL
JEWRY
JIFFY
JIGOT
JINGO
JINKS
JOINT
JOIST
JOKER
JOLLY
JORUM
JOUST
JUDAS
JUDGE
JUICE
JUICY
JULEP
JUMPY
JUNTA
JUNTO
JUROR
JUTTY

K

KAABA
KAFIR
KALIF
KAROB
KAURI
KAYAK
KEDGE
KEEVE
KELPY
KERNE
KETCH
KEYED
KHAKI
KIOSK
KNACK
KNARL
KNAVE
KNEAD
KNEED
KNEEL
KNELL
KNELT
KNIFE
KNOCK
KNOLL
KNOUT
KNOWN
KNUBS
KNURL
KODAK
KORAN
KRAAL
KUDOS

L

LABEL
LABIA
LABOR
LADEN
LADLE
LAGER
LAIRD
LAITY
LAMED
LANCE
LANDE
LANKY
LAPEL
LAPSE
LARCH
LARDY
LARGE
LARGO
LARUM
LARVA
LASSO
LATCH
LATER
LATEX
LATHE
LATHY
LATIN
LAUGH
LAURA
LAVER
LAWNY
LAXLY
LAYER
LAZAR
LEACH
LEADY
LEAFY
LEAKY
LEARN
LEASE
LEASH
LEAST
LEAVE
LEAVY
LEDGE
LEDGY
LEECH
LEGAL
LEGGY
LEMAN
LEMMA
LEMON
LEMUR
LENTO
LEPER
LEPTA
LETCH
LETHE
LEVEE
LEVEL
LEVER
LEVIN
LEWIS
LIANA
LIBEL
LIBER
LIBRA
LICIT
LIEGE
LIEVE
LIGAN
LIGHT
LIKEN
LILAC
LIMBO
LIMIT
LINEN
LINER
LINGO
LINKS
LISLE
LISSE
LISTS
LITHE
LITRE
LIVED
LIVER
LIVES
LIVID
LIVRE
LLAMA
LOACH
LOAMY
LOATH
LOBAR
LOBBY
LOBED
LOCAL
LOCUS
LODGE
LOFTY
LOGAN
LOGIC
LOGOS
LOOBY
LOOFA
LOOSE
LORIS
LORRY
LOSER
LOTAS
LOTTO
LOTUS
LOUSE
LOUSY
LOVER
LOWED
LOWER
LOWLY
LOYAL
LUCID
LUCKY
LUCRE
LUMPY
LUNAR
LUNCH
LUNGE
LUPUS
LURCH
LURID
LUSTY
LYING
LYMPH
LYNCH
LYRIC

M

MACAW
MACER
MACLE
MADAM
MADIA
MADLY
MADRE
MAGIC
MAGMA
MAHDI
MAIZE
MAJOR
MAKER
MALAR
MALAY
MALIC
MAMMA
MANED
MANES
MANGE
MANGO
MANGY
MANIA
MANIS
MANLY
MANNA
MANOR
MANSE
MANUS
MAORI
MAPLE
MARCH
MARGE
MARLY
MARRY
MARSH
MASON
MASSY
MATCH
MATER
MATIN
MATTE
MATTY
MAUND
MAUVE
MAVIS
MAXIM
MAYOR
MAZER
MEALY
MEANS
MEANT
MEASE
MECCA
MEDAL
MEDIA
MEDOC
MÊLÉE
MELON
MERCY
MERGE
MERIT
MERLE
MERRY
MESHY
MESNE
METAL
METER
METRE
MEZZO
MIAUL
MIDGE
MIDST
MIGHT
MILAN
MILCH
MILKY
MIMIC
MINCE
MINER
MINIM
MINOR
MINUS
MIRTH
MISDO
MISER
MISTY
MITER
MITRE
MIXED
MIXEN
MIXER
MIZEN
MODAL
MODEL
MODUS
MOGUL
MOHUR
MOIRE
MOIST
MOLAR
MONAD
MONDE
MONEY
MONTE
MONTH
MOODY
MOONY
MOOSE
MOPER
MORAL
MOREL
MORSE
MOSSY
MOTET
MOTHY
MOTIF
MOTOR
MOTTO
MOULD
MOULT
MOUND
MOUNT
MOURN
MOUSE
MOUTH
MOVER
MOWER
MUCKY
MUCUS
MUDDY
MUFTI
MUGGY
MULCH
MULCT
MULSH
MUMMY
MUMMU
MUNCH
MUNGO
MURAL
MUREX
MURKY
MURRY

MUSER
MUSES
MUSIC
MUSKY
MUSTY
MUZZY
MYOPE
MYOPS
MYRRH

N

NABOB
NACRE
NADIR
NAIAD
NAIVE
NAKED
NAMER
NANDU
NAPPY
NASAL
NASTY
NATAL
NATCH
NATTY
NAVAL
NAVEL
NAVEW
NAVVY
NAWAB
NEEDS
NEEDY
NEESE
NEGRO
NEGUS
NEIGH
NERVE
NERVY
NETTY
NEVER
NEWEL
NEWLY
NEXUS
NICHE
NIDOR
NIDUS
NIECE
NIGHT
NINNY
NINON
NINTH
NIOBE
NISAN
NITRE
NITRY
NIVAL
NIZAM
NOBBY
NOBLE
NOBLY
NODAL
NODDY
NOILS
NOISE
NOISY
NOMAD
NONCE

NONES
NOOSE
NORSE
NORTH
NOSED
NOTCH
NOTED
NOVEL
NOWAY
NOYAU
NUDGE
NURSE
NUTTY
NYLON
NYMPH

O

OAKEN
OAKUM
OARED
OASIS
OASES
OATEN
OATHS
OBEAH
OBESE
OCCUR
OCEAN
OCHER
OCHRE
OCHRY
OCREA
ODDLY
ODEON
ODEUM
ODIUM
ODOUR
OFFAL
OFFER
OFTEN
OGHAM
OGLER
OILED
OILER
OLDEN
OLEIC
OLIVE
OMBRE
OMEGA
ONION
ONSET
OOZED
OPERA
OPINE
OPIUM
OPTIC
ORACH
ORANG
ORATE
ORBED
ORBIT
ORDER
OREAD
ORGAN
ORIEL
ORION
ORLOP
ORMER

ORNIS
ORPIN
ORRIS
OSCAN
OSIER
OTARY
OTHER
OTTER
OUGHT
OUNCE
OUSEL
OUTDO
OUTER
OUTGO
OUTRE
OUZEL
OVARY
OVATE
OVERT
OVINE
OVOID
OVOLO
OVULE
OWING
OWLET
OWNER
OX-EYE
OXIDE
OXLIP
OZONE

P

PACED
PACER
PACHA
PADDY
PADRE
PAEAN
PAGAN
PAINS
PAINT
PALEA
PALMY
PALPI
PALSY
PANDA
PANED
PANEL
PANIC
PANSY
PAPAL
PAPAW
PAPER
PAPPY
PARCH
PARED
PARER
PARRY
PARSE
PARTY
PASHA
PASSE
PASTE
PASTY
PATCH
PATED
PATEN
PATHS

PATIN
PATTY
PAUSE
PAVER
PAVID
PAWED
PAYEE
PAYER
PEACE
PEACH
PEAKY
PEARL
PEASE
PEATY
PECAN
PEDAL
PEKOE
PENAL
PENCE
PENIS
PENNY
PEONY
PERCH
PERDU
PERIL
PERKY
PERRY
PETAL
PETIT
PETTO
PETTY
PEWIT
PHARO
PHASE
PHIAL
PHLOX
PHONE
PHOTO
PHYLA
PIANO
PICRA
PICUL
PIECE
PIEND
PIETY
PIGMY
PIKED
PILAU
PILAW
PILCH
PILES
PILOT
PINCH
PINEY
PINNA
PIOUS
PIPED
PIPER
PIPIT .
PIQUE
PITCH
PITHY
PIVOT
PIXIE
PLACE
PLACK
PLAID
PLAIN
PLAIT
PLANE

PLANK
PLANT
PLASH
PLATE
PLEAD
PLICA
PLUCK
PLUMB
PLUME
PLUMP
PLUMY
PLUSH
PLUTO
PLYER
POACH
POCKY
PODGY
POESY
POINT
POISE
POKER
POLAR
POLKA
POLYP
POPPY
PORCH
PORER
PORES
PORGY
PORTE
POSER
POSIT
POSSE
POUCH
POULT
POUND
POWER
PRANK
PRASE
PRATE
PRAWN
PREEN
PRESS
PRICE
PRICK
PRIDE
PRIER
PRIMA
PRIME
PRINK
PRINT
PRIOR
PRISE
PRISM
PRIVY
PRIZE
PROBE
PROEM
PRONE
PRONG
PROOF
PROSE
PROSY
PROUD
PROVE
PROWL
PROXY
PRUDE
PRUNE
PSALM

PSHAW
PSOAS
PSORA
PUBES
PUBIC
PUDGY
PUFFY
PUKKA
PULPY
PULSE
PUNCH
PUNIC
PUNKA
PUPAE
PUPAL
PUPIL
PUPPY
PURGE
PURSE
PURSY
PUSSY
PUTID
PUTTY
PYGMY
PYLON

Q

QUACK
QUAFF
QUAIL
QUAKE
QUAKY
QUALM
QUART
QUASH
QUASI
QUEAN
QUEEN
QUEER
QUELL
QUERN
QUERY
QUEST
QUEUE
QUICK
QUIET
QUILL
QUILT
QUINT
QUIRE
QUIRK
QUITE
QUITS
QUOIN
QUOIT
QUOTA
QUOTE
QUOTH

R

RABBI
RABID
RACED
RACER
RADAR
RADII

		S			
RADIO	RETCH		SCOLD	SHARK	SIREN
RADIX	REVEL		SCOOP	SHARP	SIRUP
RAGED	REVET	SABER	SCOPE	SHAVE	SISAL
RAINY	RHEUM	SABLE	SCORE	SHAWL	SITES
RAISE	RHOMB	SABOT	SCORN	SHAWM	SIVAN
RAJAH	RHUMB	SABRE	SCOTS	SHEAF	SIXTH
RAKED	RHYME	SACRE	SCOTT	SHEAL	SIXTY
RAKER	RIANT	SADLY	SCOUR	SHEAR	SIZAR
RALLY	RIDER	SAHIB	SCOUT	SHEEN	SIZED
RAMEE	RIDGE	SAIGA	SCOWL	SHEEP	SIZER
RAMIE	RIDGY	SAINT	SCRAG	SHEER	SIZES
RANCH	RIFLE	SAJOU	SCRAM	SHEET	SKAIN
RANGE	RIGHT	SAKER	SCRAP	SHEIK	SKALD
RAPHE	RIGID	SAKIA	SCREW	SHELF	SKATE
RAPID	RIGOR	SALAD	SCRIP	SHELL	SKEAN
RASPY	RILED	SALEP	SCRUB	SHERD	SKEIN
RATCH	RINSE	SALES	SCRUM	SHEWN	SKIFF
RATED	RIPEN	SALIC	SCUDO	SHIAH	SKILL
RATEL	RISEN	SALIX	SCUDI	SHIFT	SKINK
RATER	RISER	SALLY	SCULK	SHILY	SKIRT
RATHE	RISKY	SALMI	SCULL	SHINE	SKULK
RATIO	RIVAL	SALON	SCURF	SHINY	SKULL
RATTY	RIVEL	SALOP	SCUTE	SHIPS	SKUNK
RAVEL	RIVER	SALSE	SEALS	SHIRE	SKIES
RAVEN	RIVET	SALTS	SEAMY	SHIRK	SKYEY
RAVED	ROACH	SALTY	SEDAN	SHIRT	SLABS
RAVER	ROAST	SALVE	SEDGE	SHIVE	SLACK
RAVIN	ROBIN	SALVO	SEDGY	SHOAL	SLAIN
RAWLY	ROBOT	SAMBO	SEEDY	SHOCK	SLAKE
RAYED	ROCKY	SANDY	SEEMS	SHOES	SLANG
RAYON	RODEO	SAPAN	SEINE	SHOON	SLANT
RAZOR	ROGER	SAPID	SEIZE	SHOER	SLASH
REACH	ROGUE	SAPOR	SEMEN	SHONE	SLATE
REACT	ROMAN	SAPPY	SENNA	SHOOK	SLATY
READY	ROMEO	SASIN	SEÑOR	SHOOT	SLAVE
REALM	RONDO	SATIN	SENSE	SHORE	SLEEK
REAST	ROOKY	SATYR	SEPAL	SHORL	SLEEP
REAVE	ROOMY	SAUCE	SEPIA	SHORN	SLEET
REBEC	ROOST	SAUCY	SEPIC	SHORT	SLICE
REBEL	ROOTY	SAVED	SEPOY	SHOUT	SLIDE
REBUS	ROPER	SAVER	SEPTA	SHOVE	SLILY
REBUT	RORIC	SAVIN	SERAI	SHOWN	SLIME
RECTO	ROSIN	SAVOR	SERGE	SHOWY	SLIMY
RECUR	ROTOR	SAVOY	SERIF	SHRED	SLING
REDAN	ROUGE	SAWER	SERUM	SHREW	SLINK
REDLY	ROUGH	SAXON	SERVE	SHRUB	SLIPS
REEDY	ROUND	SAYER	SETAE	SHRUG	SLOID
REEFY	ROUSE	SCALA	SETON	SHUCK	SLOOP
REEKY	ROUST	SCALD	SET-TO	SHUNT	SLOPE
REEVE	ROUTE	SCALE	SEVEN	SHYLY	SLOPS
REFER	ROVER	SCALL	SEVER	SIBYL	SLOPY
REFIT	ROWAN	SCALP	SEWER	SIDED	SLOTH
REFIX	ROWDY	SCALY	SEXES	SIDER	SLOTS
REGAL	ROWEL	SCAMP	SHACK	SIDES	SLOYD
REIGN	ROWER	SCANT	SHADE	SIDLE	SLUMP
REINS	ROYAL	SCAPA	SHADY	SIEGE	SLUNG
RELAX	RUBLE	SCAPE	SHAFT	SIEVE	SLUNK
RELAY	RUCHE	SCAPI	SHAKE	SIGHT	SLUSH
RELET	RUDDY	SCARE	SHAKO	SILEX	SLYLY
RELIC	RUGAE	SCARP	SHAKY	SILKY	SMACK
RELIT	RULER	SCART	SHALE	SILLY	SMALL
REMIT	RUMBA	SCATT	SHALL	SILTY	SMALT
RENAL	RUMEN	SCAUP	SHALM	SILVA	SMART
RENEW	RUMMY	SCAUP	SHALT	SIMAR	SMASH
RENTE	RUNIC	SCAUR	SHAME	SINCE	SMEAR
REPAY	RUPEE	SCENA	SHANK	SINEW	SMELL
REPEL	RURAL	SCENE	SHAN'T	SINGE	SMELT
REPLY	RUSHY	SCENT	SHAPE	SINKS	SMILE
RESET	RUSTY	SCION	SHARD	SINUS	SMIRK
RESIN	RUTTY	SCOFF	SHARE	SIOUX	SMITE

SMITH	SPEAK	STARK	SUGAR	TAKEN	THIEF
SMOCK	SPEAR	STARS	SUINT	TAKER	THIGH
SMOKE	SPECK	START	SUITE	TAKES	THILL
SMOKY	SPECS	STATE	SULCI	TALES	THINE
SMOLT	SPEED	STAVE	SULKS	TALLY	THING
SMOTE	SPELL	STAYS	SULKY	TALON	THINK
SNACK	SPELT	STEAD	SULLY	TALUS	THIRD
SNAIL	SPEND	STEAK	SUMAC	TAMED	THOLE
SNAKE	SPENT	STEAL	SUNNY	TAMER	THONG
SNAKY	SPERM	STEAM	SUPER	TAMIL	THORN
SNARE	SPICE	STEED	SURAH	TAMIS	THORP
SNARL	SPICK	STEEL	SURAL	TAMMY	THOSE
SNARY	SPICY	STEEP	SURFY	TANGO	THOWL
SNEAK	SPIES	STEER	SURGE	TANKS	THREE
SNEER	SPIKE	STELA	SURGY	TANSY	THREW
SNICK	SPIKY	STELE	SURLY	TAPER	THRID
SNIFF	SPILE	STEPS	SWAIN	TAPIR	THROB
SNIPE	SPILL	STERN	SWAMP	TAPIS	THROE
SNOOD	SPILT	STICH	SWANG	TARDY	THROW
SNOOP	SPINE	STICK	SWARD	TARES	THRUM
SNORE	SPINY	STIES	SWARE	TARGE	THUMB
SNORT	SPIRE	STIFF	SWARM	TARRY	THUMP
SNOUT	SPIRT	STILE	SWART	TARSI	THYME
SNOWY	SPIRY	STILL	SWASH	TASKS	THYMY
SNUFF	SPITE	STILT	SWATH	TASSE	TIARA
SOAKY	SPLAY	STING	SWEAR	TASTE	TIBIA
SOAPY	SPLIT	STINK	SWEAT	TASTY	TICKS
SOBER	SPODE	STINT	SWEDE	TAUNT	TIDAL
SOCKS	SPOIL	STIPE	SWEEP	TAWER	TIERS
SOCLE	SPOKE	STOAT	SWEET	TAWNY	TIGER
SODDY	SPOOK	STOCK	SWELL	TAXED	TIGHT
SOFAS	SPOOL	STOIC	SWEPT	TAXER	TILED
SOFTA	SPOON	STOKE	SWIFT	TAZZA	TILER
SOKEN	SPOOR	STOLE	SWILL	TEACH	TILES
SOLAN	SPORE	STOMA	SWINE	TEARS	TILTH
SOLAR	SPORT	STONE	SWING	TEASE	TIMED
SOLES	SPOTS	STONY	SWINK	TECHY	TIMES
SOL-FA	SPOUT	STOOD	SWIPE	TEENS	TIMID
SOLID	SPRAT	STOOK	SWIRL	TEETH	TINCT
SOLON	SPRAY	STOOL	SWISH	TEIND	TINED
SOLOS	SPREE	STOOP	SWISS	TELIC	TINGE
SOLUS	SPRIG	STORE	SWOLN	TEMPO	TINNY
SOLVE	SPRIT	STORK	SWOON	TEMPT	TIPSY
SONGS	SPUME	STORM	SWOOP	TEMSE	TIRES
SOOTH	SPUMY	STORY	SWORD	TENCH	TIROS
SOOTY	SPUNK	STOUP	SWORE	TENDS	TISAN
SOPPY	SPURN	STOUT	SWORN	TENET	TISRI
SORRY	SPURT	STOVE	SWUNG	TENON	TITAN
SORTS	SPUTA	STRAP	SYLPH	TENOR	TITHE
SORUS	SQUAB	STRAW	SYLVA	TENSE	TIZRI
SOUGH	SQUAD	STRAY	SYNOD	TENTH	TOADY
SOULS	SQUAT	STREW	SYRUP	TEPID	TOAST
SOUND	SQUAW	STRIA	SYTHE	TERCE	TO-DAY
SOUSE	SQUIB	STRIP		TERMS	TODDY
SOUTH	SQUID	STROP		TERRA	TOFFY
SOWAR	STACK	STROW	**T**	TERSE	TOILS
SOWER	STADE	STRUM		TESTY	TOISE
SPACE	STAFF	STRUT	TABBY	THANE	TOKAY
SPADE	STAGE	STUCK	TABES	THANK	TOKEN
SPAIN	STAGY	STUBS	TABID	THAWS	TOLLS
SPAIT	STAID	STUDY	TABLE	THECA	TOMAN
SPAKE	STAIN	STUFF	TABOO	THEFT	TONAL
SPANK	STAIR	STUMP	TABOR	THEGN	TONED
SPARE	STAKE	STUNG	TACHE	THEIR	TONGA
SPARK	STALE	STUNK	TACKS	THEME	TONGS
SPASM	STALK	STUNT	TACIT	THERE	TONIC
SPATE	STALL	STUPE	TAFIA	THERM	TONKA
SPATS	STAMP	STYLE	TAILS	THESE	TOOLS
SPAWL	STAND	SUAVE	TAINT	THEWS	TOOTH
SPAWN	STARE	SUETY		THICK	

TOPAZ	TRYST	UNMEW	VIRUS	WENCH	WORST
TOPER	TUBBY	UNPIN	VISIT	WHACK	WORTH
TOPIC	TUBER	UNSAY	VISOR	WHALE	WOULD
TOPSY	TUDOR	UNSET	VISTA	WHARF	WOUND
TOQUE	TUFTS	UNSEX	VITAL	WHEAL	WRACK
TORCH	TUFTY	UNTIE	VITTA	WHEAT	WRAPT
TORSK	TULIP	UNTIL	VIVID	WHEEL	WRATH
TORSO	TULLE	UNWED	VIXEN	WHELK	WREAK
TORUS	TUMID	UPPER	VIZOR	WHELM	WRECK
TOTAL	TUMOR	UPSET	VOCAL	WHELP	WREST
TOTEM	TUNED	URBAN	VODKA	WHERE	WRING
TOUCH	TUNER	URGES	VOGUE	WHICH	WRIST
TOUGH	TUNIC	URINE	VOICE	WHIFF	WRITE
TOUSE	TUNNY	USAGE	VOMER	WHILE	WRONG
TOWED	TURFS	USHER	VOMIT	WHIMS	WROTE
TOWEL	TURFY	USUAL	VOTER	WHINE	WROTH
TOWER	TURNS	USURP	VOUCH	WHIRL	WRUNG
TOXIC	TURPS	USURY	VOWEL	WHISK	WRYLY
TOXIN	TURVY	UTTER	VULVA	WHIST	
TOYER	TUSKS	UVULA	VYING	WHITE	
TRACE	TUSKY			WHIZZ	**X**
TRACK	TUTOR			WHOLE	
TRACT	TWAIN	**V**	**W**	WHOOP	XEBEC
TRADE	TWANG			WHORE	XYLEM
TRAIL	TWANK	VAGUE	WACKE	WHORL	
TRAIN	TWEAK	VALET	WADDY	WHORT	
TRAIT	TWEED	VALID	WADER	WHOSE	**Y**
TRAMP	TWICE	VALUE	WAFER	WHOSO	
TRAPE	TWILL	VALVE	WAFTS	WIDEN	YACCA
TRAPS	TWINE	VAPID	WAGER	WIDOW	YACHT
TRASH	TWINS	VAPOR	WAGES	WIDTH	YAGER
TRASS	TWIRL	VARIX	WAGON	WIELD	YAHOO
TRAVE	TWIST	VATIC	WAILS	WIGAN	YEARN
TRAWL	'TWIXT	VAULT	WAIST	WIGHT	YEARS
TREAD	TYPIC	VAUNT	WAITS	WILES	YEAST
TREAT	TYROS	VEDIC	WAIVE	WILLY	YEATS
TREND		VEINY	WAKED	WINCE	YIELD
TRESS		VELAR	WAKEN	WINCH	YODEL
TREWS	**U**	VELDT	WAKER	WINDY	YODLE
TRIAD		VELUM	WAKES	WINGS	YOGIN
TRIAL	UDDER	VENAL	WALTZ	WINZE	YOGIS
TRIAS	UHLAN	VENOM	WANLY	WIPED	YOICK
TRIBE	UKASE	VENUE	WARES	WIPER	YOKEL
TRICE	ULCER	VENUS	WARMS	WIRED	YOUNG
TRICK	ULNAR	VERGE	WARNS	WISER	YOURS
TRIED	ULTRA	VERSE	WARPS	WISPY	YOUTH
TRIER	UMBEL	VERSO	WARTY	WITAN	YUCCA
TRILL	UMBER	VERST	WASHY	WITCH	
TRINE	UMBRA	VERTU	WASTE	WITHE	
TRIPE	UNAPT	VERVE	WATCH	WITHY	**Z**
TRITE	UNBAR	VESTA	WATER	WITTY	
TROLL	UNBID	VETCH	WAVED	WIVES	ZAMBO
TROMP	UNCAP	VEXED	WAVER	WIZEN	ZAMIA
TROOP	UNCLE	VEXER	WAVES	WOFUL	ZEBEC
TROPE	UNCUT	VIAND	WAXED	WOMAN	ZEBRA
TROTH	UNDER	VICAR	WAXEN	WOMEN	ZIBET
TROUT	UNDUE	VIEWS	WEALD	WOODS	ZINCO
TRUCE	UNFIT	VIEWY	WEARY	WOODY	ZINKY
TRUCK	UNFIX	VIGIL	WEAVE	WOOER	ZONAL
TRULL	UNHAT	VIGOR	WEBBY	WOOTZ	ZONED
TRULY	UNIFY	VILLA	WEDGE	WORDY	ZOOID
TRUMP	UNION	VILLI	WEEDY	WORKS	ZORIL
TRUNK	UNITE	VIOLA	WEEDS	WORLD	ZYMIC
TRUGG	UNITS	VIPER	WEIGH	WORMY	
TRUST	UNITY	VIRGO	WEIRD	WORRY	
TRUTH	UNMAN	VIRTU	WELSH	WORSE	

SIX-LETTER WORDS

A

ABACUS
ABASER
ABATED
ABATER
ABATIS
ABBACY
ABBESS
ABBEYS
ABDUCE
ABDUCT
ABJECT
ABJURE
ABLAZE
ABLOOM
ABOARD
ABROAD
ABOUND
ABRADE
ABROAD
ABRUPT
ABSENT
ABSORB
ABSURD
ABUSER
ACACIA
ACAJOU
ACARUS
ACCEDE
ACCENT
ACCEPT
ACCESS
ACCORD
ACCOST
ACCRUE
ACCUSE
ACETIC
ACHEAN
ACHENE
ACHING
ACQUIT
ACROSS
ACTING
ACTION
ACTIVE
ACTUAL-
ACUMEN
ADAGIO
ADAMIC
ADDICT
ADDUCE
ADHERE
ADIEUS
ADIEUX
ADIPIC
ADJOIN
ADJURE
ADJUST
ADMIRE
ADNATE
ADNOUN
ADONIS
ADORER

ADRIFT
ADROIT
ADVENE
ADVENT
ADVERB
ADVERT
ADVICE
ADVISE
ADYTUM
AEDILE
AERATE
AERIAL
AERIFY
AEROSE
AFFAIR
AFFECT
AFFEER
AFFIRM
AFFLUX
AFFORD
AFFRAY
AFFUSE
AFGHAN
AFIELD
AFLAME
AFLOAT
AFRAID
AFRESH
AFREET
AGAMIC
AGARIC
AGENCY
AGENDA
AGHAST
AGNAIL
AGNATE
AGOING
AGOUTA
AGOUTI
AGUISH
AIGLET
AIGRET
AIR-BED
AIR-GAS
AIR-GUN
AIRILY
AIRING
AIR-SAC
AIR-WAY
AISLED
AKIMBO
ALALIA
ALARUM
ALBATA
ALBEDO
ALBEIT
ALBINO
ALBITE
ALBUGO
ALCAIC
ALCOVE
ALDERN
ALDINE
ALEGAR
ALGINE

ALGOUS
ALIGHT
ALIPED
ALKALI
ALLEGE
ALLIED
ALLIES
ALLUDE
ALLURE
ALMOND
ALMOST
ALPACA
ALPINE
ALUMNI
ALVEUS
ALVINE
ALWAYS
AMADOU
AMAZON
AMBLER
AMBLES
AMBUSH
AMENDE
AMENDS
AMENTA
AMERCE
AMIDST
AMNION
AMOEBA
AMORCE
AMORET
AMOUNT
AMPERE
AMULET
AMUSER
AMYLIC
ANANAS
ANARCH
ANCHOR
ANDEAN
ANEMIA
ANERGY
ANGINA
ANGLED
ANGLER
ANGORA
ANIGHT
ANIMAL
ANIMUS
ANKLED
ANKLET
ANNALS
ANNEAL
ANNUAL
ANOINT
ANSWER
ANTHEM
ANTHER
ANTIAR
ANTLER
ANTLIA
ANYHOW
ANYWAY
AORIST
AORTAL

AORTIC
APACHE
APATHY
APEPSY
APERCU
APEXES
APIARY
APICAL
APICES
APIECE
APLOMB
APNOEA
APODAL
APOGEE
APPALL
APPEAL
APPEAR
APPEND
APPOINT
APTOTE
ARABIC
ARABLE
ARBOUR
ARCADE
ARCHED
ARCHER
ARCHIL
ARCHLY
ARCHON
ARCTIC
ARDENT
ARDOUR
AREOLA
ARGALA
ARGALI
ARGENT
ARGIVE
ARGOSY
ARGUER
ARGUTE
ARIGHT
ARMADA
ARMFUL
ARMLET
ARMOUR
ARMPIT
ARNICA
AROUND
AROUSE
AROINT!
AROYNT!
ARRACK
ARRANT
ARREAR
ARRECT
ARREST
ARRIDE
ARRIVE
ARROBA
ARROWY
ARTERY
ARTFUL
ARTIST
ASCEND
ASCENT

ASHAME
ASHLAR
ASHLER
ASHORE
ASKANT
ASLANT
ASLEEP
ASLOPE
ASPECT
ASPICK
ASPIRE
ASSAIL
ASSENT
ASSERT
ASSESS
ASSETS
ASSIGN
ASSIST
ASSIZE
ASSOIL
ASSORT
ASSUME
ASSURE
ASTERN
ASTHMA
ASTONY
ASTRAL
ASTRAY
ASTRUT
ASTUTE
ASWARM
ASYLUM
ATAXIA
ATOMIC
ATONED
ATONIC
ATRIAL
ATRIUM
ATTACH
ATTACK
ATTAIN
ATTEND
ATTEST
ATTIRE
ATTORN
ATTUNE
AUBADE
AUBURN
AUGEAN
AUGITE
AUGURY
AUGUST
AURATE
AURIGA
AURIST
AURORA
AUTHOR
AUTUMN
AVANTI
AVATAR
AVAUNT
AVENGE
AVENUE
AVERSE
AVIARY

AVOCET
AVOSET
AVOUCH
AVOWAL
AVOWER
AWAKEN
AWAKES
AWEARY
AWEIGH
AWHILE
AWNING
AXILLA
AYE-AYE
AZALEA
AZOTIC

B

BABBLE
BABISH
BABOON
BABIES
BACKER
BADGER
BAFFLE
BAGMAN
BAGNIO
BAG-WIG
BAILIE
BAKERY
BAKING
BALATA
BALDLY
BALEEN
BALKAN
BALLAD
BALLET
BALLOT
BALSAM
BAMBOO
BANANA
BANDED
BANDIT
BANDOG
BANGLE
BANIAN
BANISH
BANKER
BANNER
BANTAM
BANTER
BANYAN
BAOBAB
BARBED
BARBEL
BARBER
BARBET
BARDIC
BAREGE
BARELY
BARGEE
BARIUM
BARLEY
BARONY
BARQUE
BARREL
BARREN
BARROW
BARTER

BARYTA
BASALT
BASELY
BASHAW
BASKET
BASNET
BASQUE
BASSET
BATEAU
BATHER
BATHOS
BATIST
BATLET
BATMAN
BATOON
BATTEN
BATTER
BATTLE
BATTUE
BAUBLE
BAWBLE
BAWDRY
BAYARD
BAY-RUM
BAZAAR
BEACON
BEADED
BEADLE
BEAGLE
BEAKED
BEAKER
BEARER
BEATER
BEAUTY
BEAVER
BECALM
BECAME
BECKON
BECOME
BEDAUB
BEDECK
BEDELL
BEDLAM
BEDRID
BEDROP
BEECHY
BEETLE
BEEVES
BEFALL
BEFELL
BEFOOL
BEFORE
BEFOUL
BEGGAR
BEGIRD
BEGONE
BEHALF
BEHAVE
BEHEAD
BEHEST
BEHIND
BEHOLD
BEHOOF
BEHOVE
BEIRAM
BELACE
BELATE
BELAUD
BELDAM
BELFRY

BELIAL
BELIEF
BELIKE
BELLED
BELLOW
BELONG
BELTED
BELUGA
BEMIRE
BEMOAN
BENIGN
BENUMB
BERATE
BERBER
BEREFT
BERLIN
BESEEM
BESIDE
BESMUT
BESPOT
BESTIR
BESTOW
BESTUD
BETAKE
BETIDE
BETONY
BETOOK
BETRAY
BETTER
BETTOR
BEWAIL
BEWARE
BEWEEP
BEWRAY
BEYOND
BEZANT
BEZOAR
BIASED
BIASES
BIAXAL
BIBBER
BICEPS
BICKER
BICORN
BIDDER
BIDERY
BIFFIN
BIFOLD
BIFORM
BIGAMY
BIGGIN
BIJOUX
BILLED
BILLET
BILLON
BILLOW
BIMANA
BINARY
BINATE
BINDER
BIOTIC
BIREME
BISECT
BISHOP
BISQUE
BISSON
BISTRE
BITING
BITTER
BLADED

BLAMER
BLANCH
BLAZER
BLAZON
BLEACH
BLENCH
BLENDE
BLENNY
BLIGHT
BLITHE
BLONDE
BLOODY
BLOOMY
BLOTCH
BLOUSE
BLOWER
BLOWZE
BLOWZY
BLUFFY
BLUISH
BOBBIN
BOB-WIG
BODICE
BODIED
BODILY
BODKIN
BOGGLE
BOILER
BOLARY
BOLDLY
BOLERO
BOLIDE
BOLTER
BON-BON
BONDED
BONDER
BONITO
BON-MOT
BONNET
BON-TON
BOOTED
BOOTES
BORAGE
BORATE
BORDER
BOREAL
BORROW
BOTANY
BOTCHY
BOT-FLY
BOTHER
BOTHIE
BOTTLE
BOTTOM
BOUGHT
BOUGIE
BOUNCE
BOUNTY
BOURNE
BOURSE
BOVINE
BOWERY
BOWLER
BOWMAN
BOWMEN
BOW-SAW
BOWYER
BOXING
BOYISH
BRAINS

BRAISE
BRAIZE
BRANCH
BRANDY
BRANKS
BRANNY
BRASSY
BRAVOS
BRAWNY
BRAYER
BRAZEN
BRAZIL
BREACH
BREAST
BREATH
BREECH
BREEKS
BREEZE
BREEZY
BRETON
BREVET
BREWER
BRIARY
BRIBER
BRIBES
BRICKY
BRIDAL
BRIDGE
BRIDLE
BRIERY
BRIGHT
BRIONY
BRITON
BROACH
BROGUE
BROKEN
BROKER
BROMIC
BRONZE
BROOCH
BROODY
BROOMY
BROWSE
BRUISE
BRUMAL
BRUSHY
BRUTAL
BRYONY
BUBBLE
BUBBLY
BUBOES
BUCCAL
BUCKER
BUCKLE
BUCKRA
BUDDLE
BUDGET
BUDLET
BUFFER
BUFFET
BUGLER
BULBED
BULBEL
BULBIL
BULIMY
BULLET
BUMPER
BUNCHY
BUNDLE
BUNGLE

BUNION	CALKIN	CASERN	CHANCE	CITRON
BUNKER	CALLER	CASHEW	CHANGE	CIVICS
BUNKUM	CALLET	CASING	CHAPEL	CIVISM
BUNYON	CALLOW	CASINO	CHAPPY	CLAMMY
BURBOT	CALLUS	CASKET	CHARGE	CLAMOR
BURDEN	CALMER	CASQUE	CHARRY	CLAQUE
BUREAU	CALMLY	CASSIA	CHASER	CLARET
BURGEE	CALMUC	CASTER	CHASTE	CLAUSE
BURGLE	CALQUE	CASTLE	CHATTY	CLAWED
BURGOO	CALXES	CASTOR	CHEERY	CLAYEY
BURIAL	CAMBER	CASUAL	CHEESE	CLEANS
BURIED	CAMERA	CATSUP	CHEESY	CLEAVE
BURLAP	CAMLET	CATENA	CHELAE	CLENCH
BURNER	CANAAN	CATGUT	CHEMIC	CLERGY
BURNET	CANARD	CATHAY	CHEQUE	CLERIC
BURROW	CANARY	CATKIN	CHERRY	CLEVER
BURSAR	CANCAN	CAT-LAP	CHERTY	CLICHE
BURTON	CANCEL	CATNIP	CHERUB	CLIENT
BUSHEL	CANCER	CATTLE	CHETAH	CLIFFY
BUSILY	CANDID	CAUCUS	CHEVIN	CLIMAX
BUSKIN	CANDLE	CAUDAL	CHIGOE	CLINCH
BUSSED	CANDOR	CAUDEX	CHIGRE	CLINGY
BUSTLE	CANINE	CAUDLE	CHILDE	CLINIC
BUTLER	CANING	CAUGHT	CHILLI	CLIQUE
BUTTER	CANKER	CAUKER	CHILLY	CLOACA
BUTTON	CANNON	CAULIS	CHINCH	CLODDY
BUZZER	CANNOT	CAUSAL	CHINED	CLOGGY
BY-BLOW	CANNIE	CAUSER	CHINKY	CLONIC
BY-GONE	CANOPY	CAUSEY	CHINTZ	CLOSER
BY-LANE	CANTAB	CAUTEL	CHIPPY	CLOSET
BY-NAME	CANTER	CAVASS	CHISEL	CLOTHE
BY-PATH	CANTHI	CAVEAT	CHITIN	CLOTTY
BY-PLAY	CANTLE	CAVERN	CHITON	CLOUDY
BY-ROAD	CANTOS	CAVIAR	CHOICE	CLOUGH
BYSSUS	CANTON	CAVITY	CHOLER	CLOVEN
BY-VIEW	CANTOR	CAWASS	CHOOSE	CLOVER
BY-WORD	CANUTE	CAYMAN	CHOPIN	CLUMPY
	CANVAS	CEDARA	CHOPPY	CLUMSY
	CANYON	CEDRAN	CHORAL	CLUTCH
	CAPFUL	CELERY	CHOREA	COAITA
	CAPIAS	CELLAR	CHOREE	COARSE
C	CAPLIN	CELLED	CHORIC	COATEE
	CAPOTE	CELTIC	CHORUS	COAXER
CABALA	CAPPED	CEMENT	CHOSEN	CO-AXAL
CABMAN	CAPRIC	CENSER	CHOUGH	COBALT
CACHET	CAPTOR	CENSOR	CHOUSE	COBBLE
CACHOU	CARACK	CENSUS	CHOWRY	COBURG
CACKLE	CARAFE	CENTAL	CHRISM	COBWEB
CACOON	CARBON	CENTER	CHRIST	COCCYX
CACTUS	CARBOY	CENTOS	CHROME	COCKED
CADDIE	CARDER	CENTRE	CHROMO	COCKER
CADDIS	CAREEN	CERATE	CHUBBY	COCKET
CADENT	CAREER	CEREAL	CHUFFY	COCKLE
CADGER	CARESS	CEREUS	CHURCH	COCOON
CAECAL	CARIES	CERIPH	CICADA	CODDED
CAECUM	CARINA	CERISE	CICOLA	CODDLE
CAESAR	CARMAN	CERITE	CICELY	CODIFY
CAFFRE	CARMEN	CERIUM	CICUTA	CODLIN
CAIMAN	CARNAL	CEROON	CIERGE	COERCE
CAIQUE	CARPAL	CERTES	CINDER	COEVAL
CAIRUS	CARPEL	CERUSE	CINQUE	COFFEE
CAJOLE	CARPET	CESTUS	CIPHER	COFFER
CALASH	CARPUS	CESURA	CIPPUS	COFFIN
CALCAR	CARROT	CHABUK	CIRCLE	COGENT
CALCES	CARTEL	CHACMA	CIRCUS	COGNAC
CALCIC	CARTER	CHAFER	CIRQUE	COHEIR
CALEFY	CARTON	CHAFFY	CIRRUS	COHERE
CALVES	CARVEL	CHAISE	CISTUS	COHORT
CALICE	CARVER	CHALET	CITHER	COIFED
CALICO	CASEIN	CHALKY	CITRIC	COILED
CALIPH				
CALKER				

COINER	CORTEX	CROAKY	CYCLIC	DEBILE
COLDLY	CORVEE	CROCUS	CYCLOP	DEBLAI
COLLAR	CORYMB	CROPPY	CYGNET	DEBRIS
COLLET	CORYZA	CROSSE	CYMBAL	DEBTOR
COLLIE	COSHER	CROTCH	CYMOSE	DECADE
COLLOP	COSILY	CROTON	CYMOUS	DECAMP
COLONY	CO-SINE	CROUCH	CYMRIC	DECANT
COLOUR	COSMIC	CRUISE	CYPHER	DECEIT
COLTER	COSMOS	CRUIVE	CYPRUS	DECENT
COLUMN	COSSET	CRUMBY	CYSTIC	DECERN
COLURE	COSTAL	CRUMMY		DECIDE
COMBAT	COSTER	CRUNCH		DECKER
COMBED	COSTLY	CRURAL	**D**	DECOCT
COMBER	COTTAR	CRUSET		DECREE
COMEDO	COTTER	CRUSTS	DABBER	DEDUCE
COMEDY	COTTON	CRUSTY	DABBLE	DEDUCT
COMELY	COTYLE	CRUTCH	DACAPO	DEEPEN
COMFIT	COUGAR	CRYING	DACOIT	DEEPLY
COMFRY	COULEE	CUBAGE	DACTYL	DEFACE
COMING	COUNTS	CUBOID	DAEDAL	DEFAME
COMITY	COUNTY	CUCKOO	DAEMON	DEFEAT
COMMIT	COUPLE	CUDDLE	DAGGER	DEFECT
COMMIX	COUPON	CUDGEL	DAGGLE	DEFEND
COMMON	COURSE	CUISSE	DAGOBA	DEFIER
COMPEL	COUSIN	CULDEE	DAHLIA	DEFILE
COMPLY	COVERT	CULLER	DAIMIO	DEFINE
CONCUR	COVING	CULLET	DAINTY	DEFORM
CONDOR	COWARD	CULLIS	DAKOIT	DEFRAY
CONFAB	COW-BOY	CULMEN	DAMAGE	DEFTLY
CONFER	COWLED	CULTCH	DAMASK	DEFYER
CONGEE	COW-POX	CULTER	DAMMAR	DEGREE
CONGER	COYOTE	CULTUS	DAMNED	DEHORT
CONGOU	COYPOU	CULVER	DAMPEN	DEIFIC
CONICS	COZILY	CUMBER	DAMPER	DEJECT
CONOID	CRADLE	CUMMIN	DAMSEL	DELATE
CONSUL	CRAFTY	CUMULI	DAMSON	DELETE
CONVEX	CRAGGY	CUNEAL	DANCER	DELIAN
CONVEY	CRAMBO	CUPFUL	DANDLE	DELUDE
CONVOY	CRANCH	CUPOLA	DANGER	DELUGE
COOLER	CRANKY	CUPRIC	DANGLE	DELVER
COOLIE	CRANNY	CUPULA	DANISH	DEMAIN
COOLLY	CRASIS	CUPULE	DAPPER	DEMAND
COOPER	CRATER	CURACY	DAPPLE	DEMEAN
COPECK	CRAVAT	CURARE	DARING	DEMENT
COPIER	CRAVEN	CURARI	DARKEN	DEMISE
COPING	CRAVER	CURATE	DARKLE	DEMURE
COPPER	CRAYON	CURDLE	DARKLY	DENARY
COPTIC	CRAZED	CURFEW	DARNEL	DENGUE
COPULA	CREAKY	CURIOS	DARNER	DENIAL
COPYER	CREAMY	CURLED	DARTER	DENIER
COQUET	CREASE	CURLER	DARTRE	DENOTE
CORBEL	CREASY	CURLEW	DARWIN	DENTAL
CORBIE	CREATE	CURSED	DASHER	DENTIL
CORCLE	CRECHE	CURSER	DATIVE	DENUDE
CORDED	CREDIT	CURTAL	DAUBER	DEODAR
CORDON	CREEKY	CURTLY	DAWDLE	DEPART
CORIUM	CREEPY	CURTSY	DAY-BED	DEPEND
CORKED	CREESE	CURULE	DAYFLY	DEPICT
CORNEA	CREMOR	CURVED	DAZZLE	DEPLOY
CORNED	CREOLE	CURVET	DEACON	DEPONE
CORNEL	CRESSY	CUSCUS	DEADEN	DEPORT
CORNER	CRESTA	CUSHAT	DEADLY	DEPOSE
CORNET	CRETIN	CUSTOM	DEAFEN	DEPUTE
CORONA	CREWEL	CUSTOS	DEAFLY	DEPUTY
CORPSE	CRINAL	CUTLER	DEALER	DERIDE
CORPUS	CRINGE	CUTLET	DEARLY	DERIVE
CORRAL	CRISES	CUT-OFF	DEARTH	DERMAL
CORRIE	CRISIS	CUTTER	DEBARK	DERMIC
CORSET	CRISPY	CUTTLE	DEBASE	DERMIS
CORTES	CRITIC	CYANIC	DEBATE	DERVIS

DESCRY	DIVERS	DUFFEL	ELICIT	EPODIC
DESERT	DIVERT	DUGONG	ELIJAH	EPONYM
DESIGN	DIVEST	DULCET	ELISHA	EPOPEE
DESIRE	DIVIDE	DUMBLY	ELIXIR	EQUATE
DESIST	DIVINE	DUNDER	ELOHIM	EQUERY
DESMAN	DIVING	DUNLIN	ELTCHI	EQUINE
DESPOT	DJERID	DUNNER	ELVISH	EQUITY
DETACH	DOCILE	DUPERY	ELYTRA	ERASER
DETAIL	DOCKET	DUPLEX	EMBALM	ERBIUM
DETAIN	DOCTOR	DURBAR	EMBANK	EREBUS
DETECT	DODDER	DURESS	EMBARK	ERENOW
DETENT	DODGER	DURIAN	EMBLEM	ERINGO
DETEST	DOGATE	DURION	EMBODY	ERMINE
DETOUR	DOG-DAY	DURING	EMBOSS	EROTIC
DEUCED	DOGGED	DUSTER	EMBRUE	ERRAND
DEVEST	DOGGER	DYNAMO	EMBRYO	ERRANT
DEVICE	DOINGS	DYNAST	EMERGE	ERRATA
DEVISE	DOLENT	DYSURY	EMETIC	ERYNGO
DEVOID	DOLLAR		ÉMEUTE	ESCAPE
DEVOIR	DOLMAN		ÉMIGRÉ	ESCARP
DEVOTE	DOLMEN	**E**	EMPALE	ESCHAR
DEVOUR	DOLOUR		EMPERY	ESCHEW
DEVOUT	DOMAIN	EAGLET	EMPIRE	ESCORT
DEWLAP	DOMINO	EARING	EMPLOY	ESCUDO
DEXTER	DONATE	EARNER	ENABLE	ESKIMO
DHURRA	DONJON	EARTHY	ENAMEL	ESPIAL
DIADEM	DONKEY	EAR-WAX	ENCAGE	ESPIED
DIAPER	DOOMED	EARWIG	ENCAMP	ESPIER
DIATOM	DORIAN	EASILY	ENCAVE	ESPRIT
DIBBER	DORMER	EASTER	ENCORE	ESSENE
DIBBLE	DORSAL	EATAGE	ENCYST	ESTATE
DICAST	DOSAGE	EATING	ENDEAR	ESTEEM
DICING	DOSSIL	ECARTÉ	ENDING	ESTHER
DICKER	DOTAGE	ECHOES	ENDIVE	ESTRAY
DICKEY	DOTARD	ECLAIR	ENDURE	ETCHER
DICTUM	DOTING	ECTYPE	ENERGY	ETHICS
DIDDLE	DOUBLE	ECZEMA	ENFOLD	ETHNIC
DIETER	DOUBLY	EDDISH	ENGAGE	ETYMIC
DIFFER	DOUCHE	EDENIC	ENGINE	ETYMON
DIGEST	DOUGHY	EDGING	ENGIRD	ETYPIC
DIGGER	DOWLAS	EDIBLE	ENGORE	EUCHRE
DILATE	DRACHM	EDITOR	ENGULF	EUCLID
DILUTE	DRAFFY	EFFACE	ENIGMA	EULOGY
DIMITY	DRAGON	EFFECT	ENJOIN	EUNUCH
DIMPLE	DRAPER	EFFETE	ENLACE	EUREKA
DIMPLY	DRAWEE	EFFIGY	ENLIST	EUTAXY
DINGEY	DRAWER	EFFLUX	ENNUYÉ	EVENLY
DINGHY	DREAMT	EFFORT	ENOUGH	EVICTS
DINGLE	DREAMY	EFFUSE	ENRAGE	EVINCE
DINNER	DREARY	EFREET	ENRICH	EVOLVE
DIODON	DREDGE	EGENCE	ENROBE	EXARCH
DIPLEX	DREGGY	EGESTA	ENROLE	EXCAMB
DIPLOE	DRENCH	EGG-CUP	ENSIGN	EXCEED
DIPNOI	DRESSY	EGGLER	ENSILE	EXCEPT
DIPPER	DRIFTY	EGGERY	ENSURE	EXCESS
DIRECT	DRIVEL	EGG-NOG	ENTAIL	EXCISE
DISARM	DRIVER	EGOISM	ENTICE	EXCITE
DISBAR	DROPSY	EGOIST	ENTIRE	EXCUSE
DISBUD	DROSKY	EGRESS	ENTITY	EXEMPT
DISCAL	DROSSY	EIGHTH	ENTOMB	EXHALE
DISCUS	DROUTH	EIGHTY	ENTRAP	EXHORT
DISHES	DROVER	EITHER	ENTREE	EXHUME
DISMAL	DROWSE	ELAPSE	ENVIER	EXODUS
DISMAY	DROWSY	ELATED	ENWRAP	EXOGEN
DISOWN	DRUDGE	ELATER	EOCENE	EXOTIC
DISPEL	DRY-ROT	ELDEST	EOLIAN	EXPAND
DISTAL	DUCKER	ELECTS	EOZOIC	EXPECT
DISTIL	DUELLO	ELENCH	EPARCH	EXPEND
DISUSE	DUENNA	ELEVEN	EPAULE	EXPERT
DITONE	DUETTO	ELFISH	EPIZOA	EXPIRE

EXPIRY
EXPORT
EXPOSE
EXPUGN
EXTANT
EXTASY
EXTEND
EXTENT
EXTERN
EXTORT
EXTRAS
EX-VOTO
EYELET
EYELID

F

FABIAN
FABLED
FABRIC
FACADE
FACETE
FACIAL
FACILE
FACING
FACTOR
FACULA
FADING
FAECAL
FAECES
FAG-END
FAGGOT
FAILLE
FAIRLY
FAKEER
FALCON
FALLOW
FALTER
FAMILY
FAMINE
FAMISH
FAMOUS
FANGED
FANNER
FANTOM
FARDEL
FARINA
FARMER
FAR-OFF
FARROW
FASCES
FASCIA
FASTEN
FASTER
FASTLY
FATHER
FATHOM
FATTEN
FAUCES
FAUCET
FAULTY
FAUNAL
FAVOSE
FAVOUR
FAWNER
FEALTY
FECULA
FECUND
FEEBLE

FEEBLY
FEEDER
FEELER
FELLAH
FELLER
FELLOE
FELLOW
FELONY
FEMALE
FENCED
FENCER
FENDER
FENIAN
FENNEC
FENNEL
FEODAL
FERIAL
FERINE
FERITY
FERRET
FERRIC
FERULE
FERVID
FERVOR
FESCUE
FESTAL
FESTER
FETICH
FETISH
FETTER
FETTLE
FEUDAL
FIACRE
FIANCÉ
FIASCO
FIBBER
FIBRIL
FIBRIN
FIBULA
FICKLE
FIDDLE
FIDGET
FIERCE
FIGURE
FILIAL
FILING
FILLER
FILLET
FILLIP
FILOSE
FILTER
FILTHY
FINALE
FINDER
FINELY
FINERY
FINGER
FINIAL
FINING
FINISH
FINITE
FINNED
FINNER
FIN-RAY
FIORIN
FIRING
FIRKIN
FIRMAN
FIRMLY

FISCAL
FISHES
FISHER
FISTIC
FITFUL
FITTER
FIXITY
FIZGIG
FIZZLE
FLABBY
FLAGGY
FLAGON
FLAMEN
FLANGE
FLASHY
FLATLY
FLAUNT
FLAVOR
FLAXEN
FLAYER
FLÉCHE
FLEDGE
FLEECE
FLEECY
FLENSE
FLESHY
FLEXOR
FLIGHT
FLIMSY
FLINCH
FLINTY
FLITCH
FLOCKY
FLOPPY
FLORAL
FLORET
FLORID
FLORIN
FLOSSY
FLOURY
FLOWER
FLUENT
FLUFFY
FLUNKY
FLURRY
FLUTED
FLYING
FODDER
FOEMAN
FOEMEN
FOETAL
FOETUS
FOGEYS
FOGIES
FOIBLE
FOILER
FOISON
FOLDER
FOLIAR
FOLLOW
FOMENT
FONDLE
FONDLY
FONTAL
FOOTED
FORAGE
FORBID
FORCAT
FORCED
FORCER

FOREGO
FOREST
FORGER
FORGET
FORGOT
FORKED
FORMAL
FORMER
FORMIC
FORTED
FOSSAE
FOSSIL
FOSTER
FOTHER
FOUGHT
FOULLY
FOURTH
FOWLER
FOX-BAT
FRACAS
FRAISE
FRAMER
FREELY
FREEZE
FRENCH
FRENZY
FRESCO
FRETTY
FRIDAY
FRIEND
FRIEZE
FRIGHT
FRIGID
FRINGE
FRINGY
FRISKY
FRIZZY
FROLIC
FROSTY
FROTHY
FROUZY
FROWZY
FROZEN
FRUGAL
FRUITY
FRUSTA
FRYING
FUCOID
FUDDLE
FULCRA
FULFIL
FULGID
FULLER
FULMAR
FUMBLE
FUNGAL
FUNGUS
FUNNEL
FURFUR
FURORE
FURRED
FURROW
FURIES
FURTHER
FUSION
FUSTED
FUSTET
FUSTIC
FUTILE
FUTURE

FYLFOT

G

GABBLE
GABIES
GABION
GABLES
GABLET
GADDER
GADFLY
GADOID
GAELIC
GAFFER
GAGGLE
GAIETY
GAINER
GAINLY
'GAINST
GAITED
GAITER
GALAXY
GALENA
GALIOT
GALLEY
GALLIC
GALLON
GALLOP
GALORE
GALOSH
GAMBIR
GAMBIT
GAMBLE
GAMBOL
GAMING
GAMMER
GAMMON
GANDER
GANGER
GANGUE
GANNET
GANOID
GAOLER
GARBLE
GARDEN
GARGLE
GARISH
GARLIC
GARNER
GARNET
GARRET
GARROT
GARTER
GASCON
GASIFY
GAS-JET
GASKET
GAS-TAR
GATHER
GAUCHO
GAUGER
GAYETY
GAMBIT
GEMINI
GEMMAE
GENDER
GENERA
GENEVA
GENIAL

GENIUS	GORGON	GYPSUM	HECKLE	HOOKER
GENTES	GOSPEL	GYRATE	HECTIC	HOOPER
GENTLE	GOSSIP	GYROSE	HECTOR	HOOPOE
GENTLY	GOTHIC		HEDDLE	HOOPOO
GENTRY	GOTTEN		HEDGER	HOOVES
GEORGE	GOVERN	**H**	HEGIRA	HOPPER
GERMAN	GRAINY		HEIFER	HOPPLE
GERMEN	GRAITH	HACKEE	HEIGHT	HORARY
GERUND	GRAKLE	HACKLE	HEJIRA	HORNED
GESTIC	GRAMME	HADJEE	HELMED	HORNER
GETTER	GRANGE	HAEMAL	HELMET	HORNET
GEW-GAW	GRASSY	HAGBUT	HELPER	HORRID
GEYSER	GRATER	HAGGED	HEMPEN	HORROR
GHETTO	GRATIS	HAGGIS	HEPTAD	HORSEY
GIBBER	GRAVEL	HAGGLE	HERALD	HOSIER
GIBBET	GRAVER	HAIRED	HERBAL	HOSTEL
GIBBON	GRAVES	HALVES	HEREAT	HOT-BED
GIB-CAT	GRAVID	HALLOH!	HEREBY	HOUDAH
GIBLET	GRAYLY	HALLOO!	HEREIN	HOURLY
GIFTED	GRAZER	HALLOW	HEREOF	HOUSES
GIGGLE	GREASE	HALLUX	HEREON	HOUSEL
GIGLET	GREASY	HALTER	HERESY	HOWDAH
GIGLOT	GREAVE	HALVES	HERETO	HOWLER
GILDER	GREEDY	HAMATE	HERIOT	HOWLET
GILLIE	GREENY	HAMITE	HERMIT	HOYDEN
GIMLET	GRIEVE	HAMLET	HERNIA	HUBBUB
GINGER	GRILLE	HAMMER	HEROES	HUCKLE
GIRDER	GRILSE	HAMOSE	HEROIC	HUDDLE
GIRDLE	GRIMLY	HAMOUS	HERPES	HUGELY
GLACIS	GRIPPE	HAMPER	HERMAN	HUMANE
GLADLY	GRISLY	HANDED	HEYDAY	HUMBLE
GLAIVE	GRITTY	HANDLE	HIATUS	HUMBLY
GLANCE	GROATS	HANGER	HIBRID	HUMBUG
GLASSY	GROCER	HANKER	HICCUP	HUMERI
GLAZER	GROGGY	HANSOM	HICKUP	HUMMER
GLEAMY	GROOVE	HAPPEN	HIDDEN	HUMOUR
GLIBLY	GROPED	HARASS	HIDING	HUMOUS
GLOOMY	GROTTO	HARBOR	HIEMAL	HUMPED
GLORIA	GROUND	HARDEN	HIGGLE	HUNGER
GLOSSY	GROUSE	HARDLY	HIGHER	HUNGRY
GLOVED	GROVEL	HARKEN	HIGHLY	HUNTER
GLOVER	GROWER	HARLOT	HILTED	HURDLE
GLOWED	GROWTH	HARPER	HINDER	HURLER
GLUMLY	GROYNE	HARROW	HINDOO	HURRAH
GLUTEN	GRUDGE	HASTEN	HIPPED	HURTLE
GNARLY	GRUMPY	HATRED	HISPID	HUSKED
GNAWER	GUEBER	HATTED	HITHER	HUSSAR
GNEISS	GUEBRE	HATTER	HITTER	HUSSIF
GNOMIC	GUFFAW	HAULER	HOARSE	HUSTLE
GNOMON	GUGGLE	HAUNCH	HOBBLE	HYADES
GNOSIS	GUIDON	HAVANA	HOBNOB	HYAENA
GOBBET	GUILTY	HAVING	HOCKEY	HYBRID
GOBBLE	GUINEA	HAVOCK	HODMAN	HYEMAL
GOBLET	GUISER	HAWHAW	HOIDEN	HYETAL
GOBLIN	GUITAR	HAWKER	HOLDER	HYMNAL
GOBIES	GULDEN	HAWSER	HOLILY	HYMNIC
GO-CART	GULLET	HAZARD	HOLLOA!	HYPHEN
GODSON	GUM-LAC	HEADED	HOLLOW	HYSSOP
GODWIT	GUNNEL	HEADER	HOLPEN	
GOFFER	GUNNER	HEALER	HOMAGE	
GOGGLE	GUN-WAD	HEALTH	HOMELY	**I**
GOITER	GURGLE	HEARER	HOMILY	
GOITRE	GURNET	HEARSE	HOMING	IAMBIC
GOLDEN	GUSHER	HEARTH	HOMINY	IAMBUS
GOLFER	GUSSET	HEARTY	HONEST	IATRIC
GOLOSH	GUTTAE	HEATER	HONOUR	IBISES
GOMUTI	GUTTER	HEATHY	HOODED	ICE-SAW
GOODLY	GUTTLE	HEAVEN	HOOFED	ICICLE
GOPHER	GUZZLE	HEAVER	HOOKAH	IDIOCY
GORGET	GYMNIC	HEBREW	HOOKED	IDOLON

IGNITE	INKING	JARGON	KECKSY	LANCET
IGNORE	INKSAC	JAROOL	KEELED	LANDAU
IGUANA	INLAID	JARRAH	KEENLY	LANDED
ILLUDE	INLAND	JASPER	KEEPER	LANKLY
ILLUME	INMATE	JAUNTY	KELPIE	LANNER
IMBIBE	INMOST	JEERER	KELSON	LAPDOG
IMBODY	INNATE	JEJUNE	KELTIC	LAPPER
IMBRUE	INNING	JENNET	KENNEL	LAPPET
IMMESH	INROAD	JERBOA	KERMES	LAPSED
IMMUNE	INRUSH	JEREED	KERNEL	LARDER
IMMURE	INSANE	JERKED	KERSEY	LARIAT
IMPACT	INSECT	JERKIN	KETTLE	LARVAE
IMPAIR	INSERT	JERSEY	KIBBLE	LARVAL
IMPALE	INSIDE	JESSED	KIBLAH	LARYNX
IMPARK	INSIST	JESTER	KICKER	LASCAR
IMPART	INSPAN	JESUIT	KIDNAP	LASHER
IMPAWN	INSTEP	JETSAM	KIDNEY	LASTLY
IMPEDE	INSTIL	JETSON	KILLER	LATEEN
IMPEND	INSULT	JEWELS	KILTED	LATELY
IMPISH	INSURE	JEWESS	KIMONO	LATENT
IMPLEX	INTACT	JEWISH	KINCOB	LATHEN
IMPORT	INTAKE	JIGGER	KINDLE	LATHER
IMPOSE	INTEND	JINGAL	KINDLY	LATISH
IMPOST	INTENT	JINGLE	KINGLY	LATTEN
IMPUGN	INTERN	JINNEE	KIPPER	LATTER
IMPURE	INTONE	JOBBER	KIRTLE	LAUNCH
IMPUTE	INTUIT	JOCKEY	KISMET	LAUREL
INARCH	INVADE	JOCOSE	KIT-CAT	LAVISH
INBORN	INVENT	JOCUND	KITTEN	LAWFUL
INBRED	INVERT	JOGGER	KNAGGY	LAWYER
INCAGE	INVEST	JOGGLE	KNIVES	LAXITY
INCASE	INVITE	JOINER	KNIGHT	LAYMAN
INCEST	INVOKE	JOSEPH	KNOBBY	LAZILY
INCISE	INWALL	JOSTLE	KNOTTY	LAZULI
INCITE	INWARD	JOTTER	KNOWER	LEADED
INCOME	INWORN	JOVIAL	KOBOLD	LEADEN
INCUBI	INWRAP	JOYFUL	KOODOO	LEADER
INCULT	IODIDE	JOYOUS	KOSMOS	LEAFED
INCUSE	IODINE	JUBATE	KRAKEN	LEAGUE
INDEED	IODISM	JUDAIC	KRONER	LEANLY
INDENT	IODIZE	JUGATE	KUMISS	LEAN-TO
INDIAN	IOLITE	JUGGLE	KÜMMEL	LEAPER
INDICT	IONIAN	JUJUBE		LEASED
INDIGO	IREFUL	JULIAN		LEAVED
INDITE	IRIDAL	JUMBLE	**L**	LEAVEN
INDIUM	IRISES	JUMPER		LEAVES
INDOOR	IRISED	JUNGLE	LAAGER	LECHER
INDUCE	IRITIS	JUNGLY	LABIAL	LEDGER
INDUCT	IRONER	JUNIOR	LABIUM	LEEWAY
INFAMY	ISABEL	JUNKER	LABOUR	LEGACY
INFANT	ISLAND	JUNKET	LABRET	LEGATE
INFECT	ISOBAR	JURIST	LABRUM	LEGATO
INFELT	ISOPOD	JURIES	LACHES	LEGEND
INFEST	ISSUED	JUSTLE	LACING	LEGGED
INFIRM	ITALIC	JUSTLY	LACKER	LEGION
INFLOW	ITSELF		LACKEY	LEGIST
INFLUX			LACMUS	LEGUME
INFOLD		**K**	LACTIC	LENDER
INFORM	**J**		LACUNA	LENGTH
INFULA		KAFFIR	LADDER	LENITY
INFUSE	JABBER	KAFTAN	LADING	LENSES
INGEST	JACANA	KAISER	LADIES	LENTEN
INHALE	JACKAL	KALIUM	LAGOON	LENTIL
INHERE	JAGGER	KALMUK	LAMBIE	LINTER
INHERE	JADISH	KAMALA	LAMELY	L'ENVOI
INHUME	JAGGED	KAOLIN	LAMENT	L'ENVOY
INJECT	JAGUAR	KARROO	LAMINA	LESION
INJURE	JAILER	KAVASS	LAMMAS	LESSEE
INJURY	JAILOR	KAWASS	LANATE	LESSEN
INK-BAG	JANGLE	KEBLAH	LANCER	LESSER

LESSON	LOCKET	MAGNUM	MATRON	MIDWAY
LESSOR	LOCK-UP	MAGPIE	MATTED	MIGHTY
LETHAL	LOCULI	MAGYAR	MATTER	MIKADO
LETTER	LOCUST	MAHOUT	MATURE	MILDEN
LEVANT	LODGER	MAIDEN	MAUGRE	MILDEW
LEVIER	LOGGAT	MAIGRE	MAY-BUG	MILDLY
LEVITE	LOG-HUT	MAINLY	MAY-DAY	MILKER
LEVIES	LOGGIA	MAKE-UP	MAY-DEW	MILLED
LEVITY	LOGGIE	MAKING	MAY-FLY	MILLER
LEWDLY	LOITER	MALADY	MAYHAP	MILLET
LIABLE	LOMENT	MALAGA	MAYHEM	MILTER
LIBYAN	LONELY	MALICE	MAYING	MIMOSA
LICHEN	LOOKER	MALIGN	MAZARD	MINDED
LICTOR	LOOSEN	MALLEE	MAZILY	MINDER
LIDDED	LOPPER	MALLET	MEADOW	MINGLE
LIFTER	LORATE	MALLOW	MEAGRE	MINIFY
LIGHTS	LORCHA	MALTHA	MEANLY	MINIMA
LIGNUM	LORDLY	MAMMAE	MEASLY	MINING
LIGULA	LORICA	MAMMAL	MEATUS	MINION
LIGULE	LORRIE	MAMMEE	MEDDLE	MINISH
LIGURE	LOSING	MAMMON	MEDIAL	MINIUM
LIKELY	LOTION	MANAGE	MEDIAN	MINNOW
LIKING	LOUDLY	MANANA	MEDICA	MINTER
LILIES	LOUNGE	MANCHU	MEDICI	MINUET
LIMBED	LOUVRE	MANEGE	MEDIUM	MINUTE
LIMBER	LOVELY	MANFUL	MEDLAR	MIRAGE
LIMNER	LOVING	MANGER	MEDLEY	MIRROR
LIMOUS	LOWERY	MANGLE	MEDUSA	MISERY
LIMPET	LOWEST	MANIAC	MEEKLY	MISFIT
LIMPID	LOWING	MANILA	MEETLY	MISHAP
LINDEN	LUBBER	MANIOC	MEGILP	MISLAY
LINEAL	LUCENT	MANITO	MEGOHM	MISSAL
LINEAR	LUCERN	MANNER	MEGRIM	MISSEE
LINGAM	LUGGER	MANTEL	MELLAY	MISTER
LINGER	LUMBAR	MANTIS	MELLEY	MISUSE
LINHAY	LUMBER	MANTLE	MELLOW	MITRAL
LINING	LUMPER	MANTUA	MELODY	MITRED
LINNET	LUNACY	MANUAL	MELTER	MITTEN
LINTEL	LUNATE	MANURE	MEMBER	MIZZEN
LIONEL	LUNGED	MAORIS	MEMOIR	MIZZLE
LIONET	LUNULA	MARAUD	MEMORY	MOB-CAP
LIPLET	LUNULE	MARBLE	MENACE	MOBILE
LIPPED	LUPINE	MARBLY	MENAGE	MOB-LAW
LIQUID	LURDAN	MARCID	MENDER	MOCKER
LIQUOR	LURKER	MARGIN	MENHIR	MODERN
LISPER	LUSTRA	MARINE	MENIAL	MODEST
LISSOM	LUSTRE	MARISH	MENSES	MODIFY
LISTEN	LUTINE	MARKED	MENTAL	MODISH
LITANY	LUTIST	MARKEE	MENTOR	MODULE
LITHIA	LUXATE	MARKER	MERCER	MOHAIR
LITHIC	LUXURY	MARKET	MERELY	MOIETY
LITMUS	LYCEUM	MARMOT	MERINO	MOLDER
LITTER	LYDIAN	MAROON	MERLIN	MOLEST
LITTLE	LYRATE	MARQUE	MERLON	MOLLAH
LIVELY	LYRIST	MARROW	MERMAN	MOLOCH
LIVERY		MARSHY	MESIAL	MOLTEN
LIVING		MARTEN	METAGE	MOMENT
LIZARD	**M**	MARTIN	METEOR	MONDAY
LLANOS		MARTYR	METHOD	MONEYS
LLOYD'S	MACRON	MARVEL	METHYL	MONGER
LOADED	MACULA	MASCLE	METOPE	MONGOL
LOADER	MADCAP	MASCOT	METRIC	MONIED
LOAFER	MADDEN	MASHER	METTLE	MONISM
LOATHE	MADDER	MASKED	MIASMA	MONIST
LOAVES	MADMAN	MASKER	MICKLE	MONKEY
LOBATE	MAENAD	MASQUE	MID-AIR	MONODY
LOBULE	MAGGOT	MASTED	MID-DAY	MOORVA
LOCALE	MAGIAN	MASTER	MIDDEN	MOPISH
LOCATE	MAGILP	MASTIC	MIDDLE	MOPSEY
LOCKER	MAGNET	MATRIX	MID-LEG	MORALE

MORASS		NOTARY	OMENED	OVERDO
MORBID	**N**	NOTICE	ONAGER	OVISAC
MOREEN		NOTIFY	ONRUSH	OWLERY
MORGUE	NAEVUS	NOTION	ONWARD	OWLISH
MORION	NAILER	NOUGAT	OOIDAL	OXALIC
MORMON	NAMELY	NOUGHT	OOLITE	OX-EYED
MOROSE	NANKIN	NOUNAL	OOLOGY	OX-GALL
MORRIS	NAPERY	NOVICE	OOM!AK	OXGANG
MORROW	NAPKIN	NOWAYS	OPAQUE	OXYGEN
MORSEL	NARIAL	NOWISE	OPENED	OXYMEL
MORTAL	NARROW	NOZZLE	OPENER	OYSTER
MORTAR	NARWAL	NUANCE	OPENLY	
MORULA	NASEBY	NUBILE	OPHITE	
MOSAIC	NASUTE	NUCHAL	OPIATE	**P**
MOSLEM	NATANT	NUCLEI	OPPOSE	
MOSQUE	NATION	NUDELY	OPPUGN	PACIFY
MOSTLY	NATIVE	NUDGED	OPTICS	PACKER
MOTETT	NATRON	NUDITY	OPTION	PACKET
MOTHER	NATURE	NUGGET	ORACHE	PADDER
MOTILE	NAUGHT	NULLAH	ORACLE	PADDLE
MOTION	NAUSEA	NUMBER	ORALLY	PAGODA
MOTIVE	NEAPED	NUNCIO	ORANGE	PAIGLE
MOTLEY	NEARLY	NURSED	ORATOR	PALACE
MOTORY	NEATLY	NUTANT	ORCHID	PALATE
MOTTLE	NEBULA	NUTMEG	ORCHIS	PALEAE
MOTTOS	NECKED	NUTRIA	ORDAIN	PALELY
MOULDY	NECTAR	NUZZLE	ORDEAL	PALING
MOUSER	NEEDED	NYLGAU	ORDERS	PALISH
MOUTHS	NEEDLE		ORDURE	PALLAH
MOVING	NEEDLY		OREGON	PALLET
MOWING	NEPHEW	**O**	ORGASM	PALLID
MUCOSE	NEREID		ORGEAT	PALLIA
MUCOUS	NERVED	OAFISH	ORGIES	PALLOR
MUDDLE	NESTLE	OBELUS	ORIENT	PALMAR
MUFFIN	NETHER	OBEYER	ORIGIN	PALMED
MUFFLE	NETTED	OBJECT	ORIOLE	PALMER
MUFTEE	NETTLE	OBLATE	ORISON	PALPUS
MULISH	NEURAL	OBLIGE	ORMOLU	PALTER
MULLEN	NEUTER	OBLONG	ORNATE	PALTRY
MULLET	NEWARK	OBOIST	OROIDE	PAMPAS
MUMBLE	NEWISH	OBOLUS	ORPHAN	PAMPER
MUMMER	NIBBLE	OBSESS	ORPHIC	PANARY
MUMPER	NICELY	OBTAIN	ORRERY	PANDER
MURDER	NICENE	OBTEST	OSIERY	PANDIT
MURMUR	NICETY	OBTUSE	OSMIUM	PANTRY
MURREY	NICHED	OCCULT	OSMOSE	PAPACY
MUSCAT	NICKEL	OCCUPY	OSPRAY	PAPERY
MUSCLE	NIDIFY	OCELLI	OSPREY	PAPIST
MUSEUM	NIELLO	OCELOT	OSSEIN	PAPPUS
MUSING	NIGGER	OCHREA	OSSIFY	PAPULA
MUSKET	NILGAU	OCTANT	OSTLER	PAPYRI
MUSK-OX	NIMBLE	OCTAVE	OSWALD	PARADE
MUSLIM	NIMBLY	OCTAVO	OTALGY	PARAPH
MUSLIN	NIMBUS	OCTROI	OTIOSE	PARCEL
MUSSEL	NINETY	OCULAR	OTITIS	PARDON
MUSTER	NIPPER	ODDITY	OUSTER	PARENT
MUTELY	NIPPLE	ODIOUS	OUTBID	PARGET
MUTINY	NITRIC	OEDEMA	OUTCRY	PARIAH
MUTTER	NOBODY	OFF-DAY	OUTFIT	PARIAN
MUTTON	NODDLE	OFFEND	OUTING	PARING
MUTUAL	NODOSE	OFFICE	OUTLAW	PARISH
MUZZLE	NODULE	OFFING	OUTLAY	PARITY
MYOPIA	NOETIC	OFFSET	OUTLET	PARLEY
MYOSIS	NOGGIN	OGHAM	OUTPUT	PARLOR
MYOTIC	NOMADE	OIDIUM	OUTRUN	PARODY
MYRIAD	NONAGE	OILERY	OUTSET	PAROLE
MYRTLE	NON-EGO	OIL-GAS	OUTSIT	PARROT
MYSELF	NOODLE	OLDISH	OUTVIE	PARSEE
MYSTIC	NORMAL	OMASUM	OUTWIT	PARSON
MYTHIC	NORMAN	OMELET	OVALLY	PARTLY

PARVIS
PASSEE
PASSER
PASSIM
PASTEL
PASTIL
PASTOR
PASTRY
PATCHY
PATENT
PATERA
PATHOS
PATINA
PATOIS
PATROL
PATRON
PATTEN
PATTER
PAUNCH
PAUPER
PAVING
PAVIOR
PAVISE
PAWNER
PAX-WAX
PAY-DAY
PAYNIM
PEACHY
PEAKED
PEA-NUT
PEARLY
PEBBLE
PEBBLY
PECKER
PECTEN
PECTIC
PEDANT
PEDATE
PEDDLE
PEDLAR
PEDLER
PEELER
PEEPER
PEEWIT
PEGGED
PEG-TOP
PELAGE
PELLET
PELTRY
PELVIC
PELVIS
PENCIL
PENMAN
PENMEN
PENNER
PENNON
PENULT
PENURY
PEOPLE
PEPLUS
PEPPER
PEPSIN
PEPTIC
PERDUE
PERIOD
PERISH
PERMIT
PERRON
PERSON
PERTLY

PERUKE
PERUSE
PESETA
PESTER
PESTLE
PETARD
PETITE
PETREL
PETROL
PEWTER
PHAROS
PHASES
PHASIS
PHLEGM
PHLOEM
PHOLAS
PHONIC
PHRASE
PHYLUM
PHYSIC
PIANOS
PIAZZA
PICKED
PICKER
PICKET
PICKLE
PICNIC
PICRIC
PIDDLE
PIECER
PIERCE
PIGEON
PIGGIN
PIG-NUT
PIG-STY
PILEUS
PILFER
PILING
PILLAR
PILLAU
PILLAW
PILLOW
PILULE
PIMPLE
PIMPLY
PINEAL
PINERY
PINION
PINKED
PINNAE
PINTLE
PIPING
PIPKIN
PIPPIN
PIQUET
PIRACY
PIRATE
PISCES
PISGAH
PISTIL
PISTOL
PISTON
PITCHY
PITIER
PITMAN
PIT-SAW
PITTED
PLACER
PLACID
PLAGUE

PLAICE
PLAINT
PLANET
PLAQUE
PLASHY
PLASMA
PLATAN
PLATEN
PLATER
PLAYER
PLEACH
PLEASE
PLEDGE
PLEIAD
PLENTY
PLENUM
PLEURA
PLEXUS
PLIANT
PLIERS
PLIGHT
PLINTH
PLOUGH
PLOVER
PLUCKY
PLUMED
PLUMPY
PLUNGE
PLURAL
POACHY
POCKET
PODDED
PODIUM
POETIC
POETRY
POISER
POISON
POLICE
POLICY
POLISH
POLITE
POLITY
POLLAN
POLLED
POLLEN
POLLEX
POLONY
POLYPE
POLYPI
POMACE
POMADE
POMMEL
PONCHO
PONDER
PONGEE
PONIES
POODLE
POONAC
POORLY
POPERY
POPGUN
POLISH
POPLAR
POPLIN
POPPET
PORGIE
PORISM
PORKER
POROUS
PORTAL

PORTER
PORTLY
POSSET
POSTAL
POSTER
POT-ALE
POTASH
POTATO
POT-BOY
POTEEN
POTENT
POTHER
POTION
POTTER
POTTLE
POUNCE
POUTER
POWDER
PRAISE
PRANCE
PRATER
PRAXIS
PRAYER
PREACH
PRECIS
PREFER
PREFIX
PREPAY
PRESTO
PRETOR
PRETTY
PRICED
PRIEST
PRIMAL
PRIMER
PRIMLY
PRIMUS
PRINCE
PRIORY
PRISON
PRIVET
PROFIT
PROLEG
PROLIX
PROMPT
PROPEL
PROPER
PROSER
PROVEN
PROVER
PRUNER
PRYING
PSEUDO
PSYCHE
PUBLIC
PUCKER
PUDDLE
PUDDLY
PUFFER
PUFFIN
PUG-DOG
PUISNE
PULING
PULKHA
PULLET
PULLEY
PULPIT
PUMICE
PUMMEL
PUMPER

PUNCHY
PUNDIT
PUNISH
PUNKAH
PUNTER
PUPPET
PURELY
PURFLE
PURGER
PURIFY
PURISM
PURIST
PURITY
PURPLE
PURSER
PURSUE
PURVEY
PUTLOG
PUTRID
PUTTER
PUZZLE
PYGARG
PYTHON

Q

QUAGGA
QUAGGY
QUAINT
QUAKER
QUARRY
QUARTE
QUARTO
QUARTZ
QUAVER
QUEASY
QUENCH
QUINCE
QUINOA
QUINSY
QUIRKY
QUITCH
QUIVER
QUORUM
QUOTER
QUOTHA!

R

RABBET
RABBIS
RABBIN
RABBIT
RABBLE
RABIES
RACEME
RACHIS
RACIAL
RACILY
RACING
RACKER
RACKET
RACOON
RADDLE
RADIAL
RADISH
RADIUM
RADIUS

RAFFIA
RAFFLE
RAFTER
RAGGED
RAGMAN
RAGOUT
RAIDER
RAILER
RAISER
RAISIN
RAKING
RAKISH
RAMBLE
RAMIFY
RAMMER
RAMOSE
RAMOUS
RAMROD
RAMSON
RANCHE
RANCHO
RANCID
RANDOM
RANGER
RANKLE
RANKLY
RANSOM
RANTER
RAPIDS
RAPIER
RAPINE
RAPPEE
RAPPER
RAREFY
RARELY
RARITY
RASCAL
RASHER
RASHLY
RASPER
RASURE
RATHER
RATIFY
RATING
RATION
RATIOS
RATITE
RATLIN
RAT-PIT
RATTAN
RATTEN
RATTER
RATTLE
RAVAGE
RAVINE
RAVING
RAVISH
RAWISH
RAZZIA
READER
REALLY
REALTY
REAPER
REALOFI
REAVER
REBATE
REBECK
REBUFF
REBUKE
RECALL

RECANT
RECAST
RECEDE
RECENT
RECESS
RECIPE
RECITE
RECKON
RECOIL
RECORD
RECOUP
RECTOR
RECTUM
REDACT
REDCAR
REDDEN
REDDLE
REDEEM
RED-HOT
REDOUT
REDRAW
REDUCE
RE-ECHO
REECHY
REEDED
REEFER
REFILL
REFINE
REFLEX
REFLUX
REFOLD
REFORM
RE-FORM
REFUGE
REFUND
REFUSE
REFUTE
REGAIN
REGALE
REGARD
REGENT
REGIME
REGINA
REGION
REGIUS
REGLET
REGNAL
REGRET
REHASH
REHEAR
REJECT
REJOIN
RELATE
RELENT
RELICT
RELIEF
RELIER
RELISH
RELIVE
RELUME
REMAIN
REMAKE
REMAND
REMANT
RE-MARK
REMEDY
REMIND
REMISS
REMORA
REMOTE

REMOVE
RENAME
RENARD
RENDER
RENNET
RENOWN
RENTAL
RENTER
REOPEN
REPAID
REPAIR
REPAND
REPASS
REPAST
REPEAL
REPEAT
REPENT
REPINE
REPORT
REPOSE
REPUTE
RESCUE
RESEAT
RESECT
RESENT
RESHIP
RESIDE
RESIGN
RESILE
RESINY
RESIST
RESORB
RESORT
RESULT
RESUME
RETAIL
RETAIN
RETAKE
RETARD
RETINA
RETIRE
RETORT
RETURN
RETUSE
REVAMP
REVEAL
REVELS
REVERE
REVERT
REVIEW
REVILE
REVISE
REVIVE
REVOKE
REVOLT
REWARD
REXINE
RHESUS
RHEUMY
RHINAL
RHYMER
RHYTHM
RIALTO
RIALTY
RIBALD
RIBAND
RIBBED
RIBBON
RICHES
RICHLY

RIDDLE
RIDING
RIFELY
RIFLER
RIGGER
RIGOUR
RILLET
RIMPLE
RINGED
RINGER
RINSER
RIOTER
RIPELY
RIPPLE
RIPRAP
RISING
RISKER
RITUAL
RIVAGE
RIVERY
ROAMER
ROARER
ROBBER
ROBUST
ROCHET
ROCKER
ROCKET
ROCOCO
RODENT
ROLLER
ROMAIC
ROMISH
RONDEL
RONION
RONYON
ROOFER
ROOTED
ROPERY
ROPILY
ROSARY
ROSERY
ROSINY
ROSTER
ROSTRA
ROTARY
ROTATE
ROTTEN
ROTUND
ROUBLE
RUBBER
RUBBLE
RUBIED
RUBIES
RUBIGO
RUBINE
RUBRIC
RUDDER
RUDDLE
RUDDOC
RUDELY
RUEFUL
RUFFLE
RUFOUS
RUGATE
RUGGED
RUGOSE
RUGOUS
RUINER
RULING
RUMBLE

RUMMER
RUMOUR
RUMFLE
RUMPUS
RUNLET
RUNNEL
RUNNER
RUNNET
RUNRIG
RUSHES
RUSKIN
RUSSET
RUSTIC
RUSTLE

S

SACHEM
SACHET
SACKER
SACQUE
SACRAL
SACRED
SACRUM
SADDEN
SADDLE
SAFELY
SAFETY
SAGELY
SAGGER
SAILER
SAILOR
SAKIEH
SALAAM
SALAMI
SALARY
SALIFY
SALINA
SALINE
SALIVA
SALLOW
SALMIS
SALMON
SALOON
SALOOP
SALTER
SALTLY
SALUTE
SALVER
SALVOR
SAMARA
SAMIAN
SAMITE
SAMLET
SAMPAN
SAMPLE
SANDAL
SANDIX
SANDYX
SANIES
SANITY
SANIAK
SANTON
SAPPER
SARONG
SASINE
SATEEN
SATINY
SATIRE

SATRAP	SEARED	SEXUAL	SIMILE	SMOOTH
SATURN	SEASON	SHABBY	SIMMER	SMUDGE
SAUCER	SEA-WAY	SHADOW	SIMONY	SMUGLY
SAVAGE	SECANT	SHAGGY	SIMOOM	SMUTCH
SAVANT	SECEDE	SHAGGY	SIMOUS	SMUTTY
SAVINE	SECERN	SHAKEN	SIMPER	SNAGGY
SAVING	SECOND	SHAKER	SIMPLE	SNARER
SAVORY	SECRET	SHALLI	SIMPLY	SNATCH
SAVOUR	SECTOR	SHAMMY	SINAIC	SNEAKY
SAW-FLY	SECUND	SHAMOY	SINEWY	SNEEZE
SAW-PIT	SECURE	SHANNY	SINFUL	SNIVEL
SAWYER	SEDATE	SHANTY	SINGER	SNOBBY
SAYING	SEDUCE	SHAPER	SINGLE	SNOOZE
SCABBY	SEEDED	SHARER	SINGLY	SNORER
SCALED	SEEING	SHAVER	SINKER	SNOUTY
SCALER	SEEKER	SHEAFY	SINNER	SNUFFY
SCANTY	SEEMER	SHEARS	SINTER	SNUGLY
SCAPUS	SEEMLY	SHEATH	SIPHON	SOAKED
SCARAB	SEE-SAW	SHEAVE	SIPPET	SOAKER
SCARCE	SEETHE	SHEENY	SIRDAR	SOCAGE
SCARFS	SEGGAR	SHEERS	SIRIUS	SOCIAL
SCARRY	SEINER	SHEKEL	SIRRAH	SOCKET
SCATHE	SEIZER	SHELFY	SISKIN	SODDEN
SCENIC	SEIZIN	SHELLY	SISTER	SODIUM
SCHEIK	SEJANT	SHELVE	SITTER	SODOMY
SCHEME	SELDOM	SHELVY	SIZING	SOEVER
SCHISM	SELECT	SHERRY	SKATER	SOFFIT
SCHIST	SELLER	SHEWED	SKERRY	SOFTEN
SCHOOL	SELVES	SHIELD	SKETCH	SOFTLY
SCONCE	SEMITE	SHIFTY	SKEWER	SOIREE
SCORCH	SEMOLA	SHINER	SKINNY	SOLACE
SCORER	SENARY	SHINTY	SKIVER	SOLDER
SCORIA	SENATE	SHIVER	SKURRY	SOLELY
SCOTCH	SENDAL	SHOALY	SLABBY	SOLEMN
SCOTER	SENDER	SHODDY	SLAGGY	SOLEUS
SCOTIA	SENECA	SHOPPY	SLANGY	SOLVER
SCRAPE	SENEGA	SHORED	SLATED	SOMBRE
SCRAWL	SENILE	SHOULD	SLATER	SOMITE
SCREAK	SENIOR	SHOVEL	SLAVER	SONANT
SCREAM	SENNIT	SHOWER	SLAVIC	SONATA
SCREED	SEÑORA	SHREWD	SLAYER	SONNET
SCREEN	SENTRY	SHRIEK	SLEAVE	SOOTHE
SCREES	SEPTET	SHRIFT	SLEAZY	SOPHIE
SCRIBE	SEPTIC	SHRIKE	SLEDGE	SORDID
SCRIMP	SEPTUM	SHRILL	SLEEKY	SORELY
SCRIPT	SEQUAL	SHRIMP	SLEEPY	SORREL
SCROLL	SEQUIN	SHRINE	SLEETY	SORROW
SCUMMY	SERAPH	SHRINK	SLEEVE	SORTER
SCURFY	SERENE	SHRIVE	SLEEZY	SORTIE
SCURRY	SERIAL	SHROUD	SLEIGH	SOULED
SCURVY	SERIES	SICKEN	SLICER	SOURCE
SCUTCH	SERIPH	SICKLE	SLIDER	SOURLY
SCUTUM	SERMON	SICKLY	SLIGHT	SOVRAN
SCYTHE	SEROON	SIDING	SLIVER	SOWANS
SEA-CAT	SEROUS	SIENNA	SLOGAN	SOWENS
SEA-COW	SERVAL	SIERRA	SLOPPY	SPADIX
SEA-DOG	SERVER	SIESTA	SLOUCH	SPARRY
SEA-EAR	SESAME	SIFTER	SLOUGH	SPARSE
SEA-EEL	SESTET	SIGNAL	SLOVEN	SPARTA
SEA-EGG	SET-OFF	SIGNER	SLOWLY	SPATHE
SEA-FIR	SETOSE	SIGNET	SLUDGE	SPAVIN
SEA-FOX	SETTEE	SIGNOR	SLUDGY	SPECIE
SEA-GOD	SETTER	SILAGE	SLUICE	SPEECH
SEALER	SETTLE	SILENT	SLUICY	SPEEDY
SEAMAN	SEVERE	SILICA	SLUSHY	SPENCE
SEAMER	SEVERN	SILKEN	SMILER	SPHERE
SEA-MEW	SEVRES	SILURE	SMIRCH	SPHERY
SEANCE	SEWAGE	SILVAN	SMITER	SPHINX
SEARCE	SEWING	SILVER	SMITHY	SPIDER
SEARCH	SEXTON	SIMIAN	SMOKER	SPIGOT
		SIMION		

SPILTH	STEAMY	STYMIE		TEATED
SPINAL	STEELY	SUABLE	**T**	TEA-URN
SPINED	STEEPY	SUBDUE		TEDDER
SPINEL	STEEVE	SUBLET	TABARD	TEDIUM
SPINET	STELAE	SUBMIT	TABLET	TEEMER
SPINNY	STENCH	SUBORN	TABOUR	TEETHE
SPIRAL	STEPPE	SUBTLE	TABRET	TELLER
SPIRED	STEREO	SUBTLY	TABULA	TELSON
SPIRIT	STICKY	SUBURB	TACKLE	TEMPER
SPLASH	STIFLE	SUBWAY	TACTIC	TEMPLE
SPLEEN	STIGMA	SUCCOR	TAENIA	TENANT
SPLICE	STILLY	SUCKER	TAG-RAG	TENDER
SPLINT	STINGO	SUCKLE	TAILED	TENDON
SPOKEN	STINGY	SUDDEN	TAILOR	TENNIS
SPONGE	STIPES	SUFFER	TAKING	TENREC
SPONGY	STITCH	SUFFIX	TALCKY	TENSOR
SPOONY	STITHY	SUGARY	TALENT	TENTED
SPORAN	STIVER	SUITOR	TALION	TENTER
SPOTTY	STODGE	SULCUS	TALKER	TENURE
SPOUSE	STODGY	SULLEN	TALLOW	TEPEFY
SPRAIN	STOCKS	SULTAN	TALMUD	TERAPH
SPRANG	STOKER	SULTRY	TAMELY	TERCEL
SPRAWL	STOLEN	SUMACH	TAMINE	TEREDO
SPREAD	STOLID	SUMMER	TAMINY	TERETE
SPRING	STOLON	SUMMIT	TAMPER	TERGAL
SPRINT	STONER	SUMMON	TAM-TAM	TERMLY
SPRITE	STONES	SUN-BOW	TAN-BED	TERROR
SPROUT	STOOGE	SUNDAY	TANDEM	TESTER
SPRUCE	STORAX	SUNDER	TANGLE	TETCHY
SPRUNG	STORER	SUN-DEW	TANGLY	TETHER
SPUNGE	STOREY	SUNDRY	TANIST	TETRAD
SPURGE	STORMY	SUNKEN	TANNER	TETTER
SPUTUM	STRAIN	SUNLIT	TANNIC	TEUTON
SQUALL	STRAIT	SUNSET	TANNIN	THALER
SQUAMA	STRAKE	SUPERB	TAN-PIT	THANKS
SQUARE	STRAND	SUPINE	TANREC	THATCH
SQUASH	STRASS	SUPPER	TAN-VAT	THEBES
SQUAWK	STRATA	SUPPLE	TAPPET	THECAL
SQUEAK	STRATH	SUPPLY	TARGET	THEINE
SQUEAL	STRAWY	SURELY	TARGUM	THEISM
SQUILL	STREAK	SURETY	TARIFF	THEIST
SQUINT	STREAM	SURTAX	TARPAN	THENCE
SQUIRE	STREET	SURVEY	TARPON	THEORY
SQUIRM	STRESS	SUTILE	TARPUM	THESES
SQUIRT	STRIAE	SUTLER	TARSAL	THESIS
STABLE	STRICT	SUTTEE	TARSIA	THETIS
STABLY	STRIDE	SUTURE	TARSUS	THEWED
STACTE	STRIFE	SWAMPY	TARTAN	THIEVE
STAFFS	STRIKE	SWARDY	TARTAR	THINLY
STAGER	STRING	SWARTH	TARTER	THIRST
STAGEY	STRIPE	SWATHE	TARTLY	THIRTY
TSAITH	STRIVE	SWEATY	TASKER	THISBE
STALKY	STROKE	SWEEPY	TASSEL	THORAX
STAMEN	STROLL	SWERVE	TASTER	THORNY
STANCH	STRONG	SWINGE	TATTER	THORPE
STANZA	STROVE	SWIPES	TATTLE	THOUGH
STAPES	STRUCK	SWITCH	TATTOO	THOWEL
STAPLE	STRUMA	SWIVEL	TAURUS	THRALL
STARCH	STRUNG	SYLVAN	TAUTOG	THRASH
STARED	STUBBY	SYMBOL	TAVERN	THREAD
STARER	STUCCO	SYNDIC	TAWDRY	THREAT
STARRY	STUDIO	SYNTAX	TAWERY	THRENE
STARVE	STUFFY	SYPHON	T CLOTH	THRESH
STATED	STUMPY	SYRIAC	TEA-CUP	THRICE
STATIC	STUPID	SYRIAN	TEA-POT	THRIFT
STATUE	STUPOR	SYRINX	TEAPOY	THRILL
STATUS	STURDY	SYRUPY	TEARER	THRIPS
STAVES	STYLAR	SYSTEM	TEASEL	THRIVE
STAYER	STYLET	SYZYGY	TEASER	THROAT
STEADY	STYLUS		TEA-SET	THRONE

THRONG	TONSOR	TRUANT	UNCIAL	UNTOLD
THROVE	TOOTER	TRUDGE	UNCOIL	UNTROD
THROWN	TOOTHY	TRUISM	UNCORD	UNTRUE
THRUSH	TOPPER	TRUMPS	UNCORK	UNTUNE
THRUST	TOPPLE	TRUSTY	UNCURL	UNUSED
THWACK	TORIES	TRYING	UNDINE	UNVEIL
THWART	TORPID	TSETSE	UNDOER	UNWARY
THYMOL	TORPOR	TUBFUL	UNDONE	UNWELL
THYMUS	TORQUE	TUBING	UNDULY	UNWEPT
THYRSE	TORRID	TUBULE	UNEASY	UNWIND
THYRSI	TOSSER	TUCKER	UNEVEN	UNWISE
TIBIAL	TOSS-UP	TUCKET	UNFAIR	UNWORN
TICKET	TOTHER	TUFTED	UNFELT	UNWRAP
TICKLE	TOTTER	TUGGER	UNFOLD	UNYOKE
TIDBIT	TOUCAN	TULWAR	UNFREE	UPBEAR
TIDILY	TOUCHY	TUMBLE	UNFURL	UPBIND
TIERCE	TOUPEE	TUMEFY	UNGIRD	UPCAST
TIE-ROD	TOUPET	TUMOUR	UNGLUE	UPCOIL
TIE-WIG	TOUSLE	TUMULT	UNGUAL	UPCURL
TIFFIN	TOUTER	TUNDRA	UNHAND	UPHILL
TIGHTS	TOWAGE	TUNING	UNHOLY	UPHOLD
TILERY	TOWARD	TUNNEL	UNHOOD	UPKEEP
TILING	TOWERY	TURBAN	UNHOOK	UPLAND
TILLER	TOYMAN	TURBID	UNHUNG	UPLIFT
TILTER	TRACER	TURBOT	UNHURT	UP-LINE
TIMBER	TRACES	TUREEN	UNHUSK	UPMOST
TIMBRE	TRADER	TURFEN	UNIPED	UPPISH
TIMELY	TRAGIC	TURGID	UNIQUE	UPREAR
TIMIST	TRANCE	TURKEY	UNISON	UPRISE
TIMOUS	TRAPAN	TURNER	UNITED	UPROAR
TINDER	TRAPES	TURNIP	UNITER	UPROOT
TINGES	TRASHY	TURRET	UNJUST	UPRUSH
TINGLE	TRAVEL	TURTLE	UNKIND	UPSHOT
TINKER	TRAVIS	TURVES	UNKNIT	UPSIDE
TINKLE	TREATY	TUSCAN	UNLACE	UPSOAR
TINMAN	TREBLE	TUSKED	UNLADE	UPWARD
TINNER	TREBLY	TUSKER	UNLESS	URANIC
TINSEL	TREMOR	TUSSLE	UNLIKE	URANUS
TIP-CAT	TRENCH	TUYERE	UNLINK	URBANE
TIPPET	TREPAN	TWELVE	UNLOAD	URCHIN
TIPPLE	TRESSY	TWENTY	UNLOCK	UREMIA
TIPTOE	TRIBAL	TWIGGY	UNMAKE	URETER
TIPTOP	TRICKY	TWINGE	UNMASK	URGENT
TIRADE	TRIFID	TWITCH	UNMEET	URINAL
TIRING	TRIFLE	TWO-PLY	UNMIXT	URSINE
TISSUE	TRIGON	TYMPAN	UNMOOR	USABLE
TITBIT	TRIGYN	TYPHUS	UNPACK	USANCE
TITHER	TRIMLY	TYPIFY	UNPAID	USEFUL
TITLED	TRINAL	TYPIST	UNREAD	USURER
TITTER	TRIPLE	TYRANT	UNREAL	UTERUS
TITTLE	TRIPLY	TYRIAN	UNREST	UTMOST
TMESIS	TRIPOD		UNRIPE	UTOPIA
TOCSIN	TRIPOS		UNROBE	UVULAR
TODDLE	TRITON	**U**	UNROLL	
TOFFEE	TRIUNE		UNROOF	
TOGGLE	TRIUNE	UBIETY	UNROOT	**V**
TOILER	TRIVET	UGLILY	UNRULY	
TOILET	TRIUNE	ULLAGE	UNSAFE	VACANT
TOLLER	TROCAR	ULSTER	UNSAID	VACATE
TOMATO	TROCHE	ULTIMO	UNSEAL	VACUUM
TOMAUN	TROGON	UMBLES	UNSEAT	VAGARY
TOMBAC	TROJAN	UMLAUT	UNSEEN	VAGINA
TOMBAK	TROLLY	UMPIRE	UNSENT	VAINLY
TOMBOY	TROOPS	UNABLE	UNSHED	VALISE
TOM-CAT	TROPHI	UNBEND	UNSHIP	VALLAR
TOMTIT	TROPHY	UNBIAS	UNSHOD	VALLEY
TOMTOM	TROPIC	UNBIND	UNSOLD	VALOUR
TONGUE	TROUGH	UNBOLT	UNSTOP	VALUER
TONITE	TROUPE	UNBORN	UNSUNG	VALVED
TONSIL	TROWEL	UNCASE	UNTIDY	VAMPER

VANDAL	VIRAGO	WAR-CRY	WICKER	WRESTS
VANISH	VIRGIN	WARDEN	WICKET	WRETCH
VANITY	VIRILE	WARDER	WIDELY	WRIGHT
VAPOUR	VIROSE	WARILY	WIELDY	WRITER
VARIED	VIRTUE	WARMER	WIFELY	WRITHE
VARLET	VISAGE	WARMLY	WIGEON	WRONGS
VASSAL	VISCID	WARMTH	WIGGED	WYVERN
VASTLY	VISCUM	WARNER	WIGWAM	
VATFUL	VISIER	WARPED	WILDER	
VAWARD	VISION	WARPER	WILDLY	**X**
VEINED	VISUAL	WARREN	WILFUL	
VELLUM	VITALS	WASHER	WILILY	XYLOID
VELVET	VITRIC	WASTER	WILLOW	XYSTUS
VENDEE	VITTAE	WATERY	WIMBLE	
VENDER	VIVACE	WATTLE	WIMPLE	
VENDOR	VIVIFY	WAX-END	WINCER	**Y**
VENDUE	VIZIER	WAYLAY	WINCEY	
VENEER	VOICED	WEAKEN	WINDER	YANKEE
VENERY	VOIDER	WEAKLY	WINDOW	YARROW
VENIAL	VOLANT	WEALTH	WIND-UP	YCLEPT
VENOSE	VOLLEY	WEAPON	WINGED	YEARLY
VENOUS	VOLUME	WEARER	WINKER	YEASTY
VENTER	VOLUTE	WEASEL	WINKLE	YELLOW
VERBAL	VOODOO	WEAVER	WINNER	YEOMAN
VERGER	VORTEX	WEAZEN	WINNOW	YEOMEN
VERIFY	VOTARY	WEBBED	WINSEY	YESTER
VERILY	VOTIVE	WEB-EYE	WINTER	YIELDS
VERITY	VOYAGE	WEDDED	WINTRY	YOICKS!
VERMIN	VULCAN	WEEDER	WISDOM	YONDER
VERNAL	VULGAR	WEEKLY	WISELY	YTTRIA
VERSED		WEEPER	WISHER	
VERSUS		WEEVER	WITHAL	
VERTEX	**W**	WEEVIL	WITHER	**Z**
VESPER		WEIGHT	WITHIN	
VESSEL	WABBLE	WELDER	WITTED	ZAFFRE
VESTAL	WADDLE	WELKIN	WIVERN	ZANDER
VESTED	WADMAL	WELTER	WIZARD	ZAREBA
VESTRY	WAFFLE	WETHER	WOBBLE	ZEALOT
VETCHY	WAFTER	WHALER	WOEFUL	ZEBECK
VIABLE	WAGGLE	WHARFS	WOLVES	ZECHIN
VIBRIO	WAGGON	WHEEZE	WOMBAT	ZENANA
VICTIM	WAITER	WHEEZY	WONDER	ZENITH
VICTOR	WAINER	WHENCE	WONTED	ZEPHYR
VICUNA	WALKER	WHERRY	WOODED	ZEREBA
VIELLE	WALLER	WHEYEY	WOODEN	ZEUGMA
VIEWER	WALLET	WHILOM	WOOING	ZIGZAG
VIGOUR	WALLOW	WHILST	WOOLLY	ZINCKY
VIKING	WALNUT	WHIMSY	WORKER	ZIRCON
VILELY	WALRUS	WHINER	WORMED	ZITHER
VILIFY	WAMPUM	WHINNY	WORRIT	ZODIAC
VINERY	WANDER	WHISKY	WORSEN	ZONARY
VINOUS	WANION	WHITEN	WORSER	ZONATE
VINOSE	WANTER	WHITES	WORTHY	ZONULE
VIOLAS	WANTON	WHOLLY	WRAITH	ZOUAVE
VIOLET	WAPITI	WHOOPS!	WREATH	ZOUNDS!
VIOLIN	WARBLE	WICKED	WRENCH	ZYGOMA

SEVEN-LETTER WORDS

A

AARONIC
ABALONE
ABANDON
ABATTIS
ABAXIAL
ABDOMEN
ABETTER
ABIDING
ABIETIC
ABIGAIL
ABILITY
ABLUENT
ABOLISH
ABREAST
ABRIDGE
ABROACH
ABSCESS
ABSCIND
ABSCOND
ABSENCE
ABSOLVE
ABSTAIN
ABUSIVE
ABYSMAL
ABYSSAL
ACADEMY
ACANTHA
ACCLAIM
ACCOMPT
ACCOUNT
ACCURSE
ACCUSED
ACCUSER
ACEROUS
ACETATE
ACETIFY
ACETOUS
ACHAEAN
ACHIEVE
ACICULA
ACIDIFY
ACIDITY
ACOLYTE
ACONITE
ACORNED
ACQUIRE
ACREAGE
ACROBAT
ACROGEN
ACTABLE
ACTINIA
ACTINIC
ACTRESS
ACTUARY
ACTUATE
ACUTELY
ADAGIAL
ADAMANT
ADAMITE
ADAPTER
ADDABLE
ADDIBLE

ADDRESS
ADDUCER
ADENOID
ADHERER
ADHIBIT
ADIPOSE
ADJOURN
ADJUDGE
ADJUNCT
ADJURER
ADMIRAL
ADMIRER
ADOPTER
ADULATE
ADVANCE
ADVERSE
ADVISED
ADVISER
AEOLIAN
AERATOR
AFFABLE
AFFABLY
AFFIXAL
AFFLICT
AFFRONT
AFRICAN
AGAINST
AGATINE
AGATIZE
AGGRESS
AGILELY
AGILITY
AGITATE
AGNOMEN
AGONIST
AGONIZE
AGRAFFE
AGROUND
AIDLESS
AILMENT
AIMLESS
AIR-BATH
AIR-CELL
AIRLESS
AIR-PUMP
AJUTAGE
ALAMODE
ALBUMEN
ALCALDE
ALCAZAR
ALCHEMY
ALCOHOL
ALCORAN
ALE-COST
ALEMBIC
ALE-WIFE
ALFALFA
ALGEBRA
ALIFORM
ALIMENT
ALIMONY
ALIQUOT
ALKANET
ALKORAN
ALLEGRO

ALL-HAIL
ALLOWER
ALMANAC
ALMONER
ALMONRY
ALMS-MAN
ALOETIC
ALREADY
ALUMINA
ALUMNUS
AMALGAM
AMATEUR
AMATIVE
AMATORY
AMAZING
AMBATCH
AMBIENT
AMENDER
AMENITY
AMENTIA
AMIABLE
AMIABLY
AMIANTH
AMMONIA
AMNESIA
AMNESTY
AMORINO
AMOROUS
AMPHORA
AMPLIFY
AMPULLA
AMUSING
AMUSIVE
AMYLENE
AMYLOID
ANAEMIA
ANAEMIC
ANAGOGE
ANAGRAM
ANALECT
ANALOGY
ANALYSE
ANALYST
ANALYZE
ANAPEST
ANARCHY
ANATOMY
ANBERRY
ANCHOVY
ANCIENT
ANDANTE
ANDIRON
ANEMONE
ANEROID
ANGELIC
ANGELUS
ANGEVIN
ANGLIFY
ANGLING
ANGRILY
ANGUISH
ANGULAR
ANILINE
ANIMATE
ANIMISM

ANIMIST
ANISEED
ANNATES
ANNATTO
ANNELID
ANNOTTO
ANNUENT
ANNUITY
ANNULAR
ANNULET
ANNULUS
ANODYNE
ANOMALY
ANOREXY
ANOSMIA
ANOTHER
ANTACID
ANT-BEAR
ANTENNA
ANT-HILL
ANTHINE
ANTHRAX
ANTIQUE
ANT-LION
ANTONYM
ANUROUS
ANXIETY
ANXIOUS
ANYBODY
ANYWISE
APANAGE
APATITE
APEPSIA
APHASIA
APHEMIA
APHESIS
APHETIC
APHONIA
APHTHAE
APISHLY
APOCOPE
APOLOGY
APOSTLE
APPAREL
APPEASE
APPLAUD
APPOINT
APPRISE
APPROVE
APPULSE
APRICOT
APRIORI
APROPOS
APSIDAL
APTERYX
APTNESS
AQUATIC
AQUEOUS
ARABIAN
ARACHIS
ARAMAIC
ARAMEAN
ARANEID
ARBITER
ARBLAST

ARBUTUS
ARCADED
ARCANUM
ARCHAIC
ARCHERY
ARCHIVE
ARCHWAY
ARCUATE
ARDENCY
ARDUOUS
AREOLAR
ARGYRIA
ARIETTA
ARIDITY
ARMHOLE
ARMIGER
ARMILLA
ARMORIC
ARMOURY
ARNOTTO
ARRAIGN
ARRANGE
ARRIVAL
ARSENAL
ARSENIC
ARTISAN
ARTISTE
ARTLESS
ARUSPEX
ASCETIC
ASCITES
ASCRIBE
ASEXUAL
ASHAMED
ASIATIC
ASININE
ASKANCE
ASPERSE
ASPHALT
ASPIRER
ASQUINT
ASSAGAI
ASSAULT
ASSAYER
ASSEGAI
ASSIZER'
ASSUAGE
ASSUMER
ASSURED
ASSURER
ASTATIC
ASTERIA
ASTOUND
ASTRICT
ASTRIDE
ASUNDER
ATAVISM
ATELIER
ATHEISM
ATHEIST
ATHEOUS
ATHIRST
ATHLETE
ATHWART
ATOMISM

ATOMIST	BANDAGE	BEES-WAX	BISTORT	BOREDOM
ATOMIZE	BANDANA	BEGGARY	BITTERN	BOROUGH
ATROPAL	BANDBOX	BEGHARD	BITTERS	BOSCAGE
ATROPHY	BANDEAU	BEGONIA	BITUMEN	BOSKAGE
ATROPIN	BANDLET	BEGUILE	BIVALVE	BOTANIC
ATTACHE	BANDORE	BEGUINE	BIVOUAC	BOTARGO
ATTAINT	BANDROL	BELGIAN	BIZARRE	BOTCHER
ATTEMPT	BANDSAW	BELIEVE	BLABBER	BOTTINE
ATTRACT	BANEFUL	BELLIED	BLACKEN	BOUDOIR
AUCTION	BANKING	BELLITE	BLACKLY	BOUILLI
AUDIBLE	BANQUET	BELL-MAN	BLADDER	BOULDER
AUDIBLY	BANSHEE	BELLOWS	BLANKET	BOUNCER
AUDITOR	BAPTISM	BELOVED	BLANKLY	BOUNDED
AUGITIC	BAPTIST	BELTANE	BLARNEY	BOUNDEN
AUGMENT	BAPTIZE	BELTING	BLASTER	BOUQUET
AUGURAL	BARBULE	BEMUSED	BLATANT	BOURDON
AURATED	BARGAIN	BENCHER	BLEAKLY	BOW-HAND
AURELIA	BARILLA	BENEATH	BLEATER	BOWLINE
AUREOLA	BAR-IRON	BENEFIT	BLEMISH	BOWLING
AURICLE	BARK-BED	BENIGHT	BLES-BOK	BOWSHOT
AUROCHS	BARMAID	BENISON	BLESSED	BOX-TREE
AURORAL	BARN-OWL	BENZENE	BLEWITS	BOXWOOD
AUSPICE	BARONET	BENZOIN	BLINDED	BOYCOTT
AUSTERE	BAROQUE	BEQUEST	BLINDER	BOYHOOD
AUSTRAL	BARRACK	BEREAVE	BLINDLY	BRABBLE
AUTO-CAR	BARRAGE	BERRIED	BLINKER	BRACING
AVARICE	BARRIER	BESEECH	BLISTER	BRACKEN
AVENGER	BAR-SHOT	BESHREW	BLOATED	BRACKET
AVERAGE	BARWOOD	BESIEGE	BLOATER	BRAD-AWL
AVERTER	BARYTES	BESMEAR	BLOSSOM	BRAGGET
AVIATOR	BARYTIC	BESPEAK	BLOTCHY	BRAHMAN
AVIDITY	BASCULE	BESTEAD	BLOTTER	BRAIDED
AVOIDER	BASHFUL	BESTIAL	BLOUSED	BRAINED
AWARDER	BASILAR	BESTREW	BLOW-FLY	BRAMBLE
AWFULLY	BASSOON	BETHINK	BLOWZED	BRAMBLY
AWKWARD	BASTARD	BETIMES	BLUBBER	BRANCHY
AXIALLY	BASTION	BETOKEN	BLUCHER	BRANDED
AXILLAR	BATTERY	BETROTH	BLUE-CAP	BRANDER
AXOLOTL	BATTISH	BETWEEN	BLUE-GUM	BRANGLE
AZIMUTH	BAYONET	BETWIXT	BLUEING	BRAN-NEW
AZOTISE	BAY-SALT	BEWITCH	BLUNDER	BRASIER
AZURITE	BAY-WOOD	BEZETTA	BLUNTLY	BRATTLE
AZYGOUS	BEACHED	BEZIQUE	BLUSTER	BRAVADO
	BEAMING	BIBASIC	BOARDED	BRAVELY
	BEARDED	BICYCLE	BOARDER	BRAVERY
B	BEARING	BIDDING	BOARISH	BRAVURA
	BEARISH	BIFILAR	BOASTER	BRAWLER
BAALISM	BEASTLY	BIGGISH	BOAT-FLY	BRAZIER
BAALITE	BEATIFY	BIG-HORN	BOATMAN	BREADTH
BABBLER	BEATING	BIGNESS	BOBSTAY	BREAKER
BABYISH	BEAUISH	BIGOTED	BOB-TAIL	BREAK-UP
BABYISM	BEBEERU	BIGOTRY	BODEFUL	BREATHE
BACCATE	BECAUSE	BILIARY	BOGGLER	BRECCIA
BACCHIC	BECHARM	BILIOUS	BOILING	BREEDER
BACKING	BECLOUD	BILLION	BOLETUS	BREVIER
BADDISH	BEDDING	BILL-MAN	BOLLARD	BREVITY
BADNESS	BEDEGAR	BILLOWY	BOLSTER	BREWAGE
BAFFLER	BEDEVIL	BINACLE	BOMBARD	BREWERY
BAGASSE	BEDIGHT	BINDERY	BOMBAST	BREWING
BAGGAGE	BEDIZEN	BINDING	BONANZA	BRIBERY
BAGGING	BEDOUIN	BINOCLE	BONDAGE	BRICOLE
BAGPIPE	BED-POST	BIOGENY	BONDMAN	BRIDOON
BAIRILY	BED-TICK	BIOTAXY	BONE-ASH	BRIEFLY
BALANCE	BEECHEN	BIPLANE	BONFIRE	BRIGADE
BALANUS	BEEF-TEA	BIPOLAR	BOOKISH	BRIGAND
BALCONY	BEE-HIVE	BIRCHEN	BOOKLET	BRIMFUL
BALEFUL	BEE-LINE	BIRETTA	BOOKMAN	BRIMMER
BALLADE	BEE-MOTH	BISCUIT	BOORISH	BRINDED
BALLAST	BEESTIE	BISMUTH	BORACIC	BRINDLE
BALLOON				BRINGER

BRINISH
BRISKET
BRISKLY
BRISTLE
BRISTLY
BRITISH
BRITTLE
BROADEN
BROADLY
BROCADE
BROCAGE
BROCARD
BROCKET
BROIDER
BROILER
BROKAGE
BROKING
BROMATE
BROMIDE
BROMINE
BRONZED
BROTHEL
BROTHER
BROUGHT
BROWNIE
BRUISER
BRUSQUE
BRUTIFY
BRUTISH
BRYOZOA
BUCK-EYE
BUCKISH
BUCKLER
BUCKRAM
BUCOLIC
BUDDING
BUFFALO
BUFFOON
BUGBEAR
BUGLOSS
BUILDER
BULBOUS
BULIMIA
BULLACE
BULLATE
BULL-DOG
BULLION
BULLOCK
BULRUSH
BULWARK
BUM-BOAT
BUMPKIN
BUNGLER
BUNTING
BUOYAGE
BUOYANT
BURDOCK
BURGAGE
BURGEON
BURGESS
BURGHAL
BURGHER
BURGLAR
BURMESE
BURNING
BURNISH
BURROCK
BURSARY
BURTHEN
BUSH-CAT

BUSHMAN
BUSTARD
BUSTLER
BUTCHER
BUTMENT
BUTTERY
BUTTOCK
BUTYRIC
BUXOMLY
BUZZARD
BY-GONES
BYSSINE

C

CABARET
CABBAGE
CABBALA
CABINED
CABINET
CABOOSE
CACHEXY
CACIQUE
CACKLER
CACOLET
CADDICE
CADENCE
CADENZA
CADMEAN
CADMIUM
CAESIUM
CAESURA
CAISSON
CAITIFF
CAJOLER
CAJUPUT
CALAMUS
CALCIFY
CALCINE
CALCITE
CALCIUM
CALDRON
CALENDS
CALIBRE
CALIPEE
CALIVER
CALL-BOY
CALLING
CALLOUS
CALMUCK
CALOMEL
CALORIC
CALOTTE
CALOYER
CALTROP
CALUMBA
CALUMET
CALUMNY
CALVARY
CALYCLE
CAMAIEU
CAMBIST
CAMBIUM
CAMBRIC
CAMELRY
CAMPHOR
CAMPION
CAMWOOD
CANAKIN

CANDENT
CANDIED
CANDOUR
CANELLA
CANNERY
CANNULA
CANONRY
CANTATA
CANTEEN
CANTHUS
CANTING
CANTLET
CANVASS
CANZONE
CAPABLE
CAP-A-PIE
CAPERER
CAPITAL
CAPITOL
CAPRICE
CAPRINE
CAPSIZE
CAPSTAN
CAPSULE
CAPTAIN
CAPTION
CAPTIVE
CAPTURE
CARACAL
CARAMEL
CARAVAN
CARAVEL
CARAWAY
CARBIDE
CARBINE
CARCASS
CARDIAC
CARDOON
CAREFUL
CARIBOO
CARIOLE
CARIOUS
CARLINE
CARLIST
CARLOCK
CARMINE
CARNAGE
CARNIFY
CAROCHE
CAROLUS
CAROTID
CAROUSE
CARPING
CARRACK
CARRIER
CARRION
CARROTY
CARTAGE
CARTOON
CART-WAY
CARVING
CASCADE
CASEOUS
CASHIER
CASSADA
CASSAVA
CASSOCK
CASTING
CASTLED
CAST-OFF

CASUIST
CATALAN
CATARRH
CATAWBA
CATBIRD
CATCALL
CATCHER
CATCHUP
CATECHU
CATERAN
CATERER
CAT-FISH
CAT-HEAD
CATHODE
CATHOOD
CATLING
CATMINT
CAT'S-EYE
CAT'S-PAW
CAUDATE
CAULINE
CAUSTIC
CAUTERY
CAUTION
CAVALRY
CAVESON
CAVIARE
CAYENNE
CAZIQUE
CEDILLA
CEDRATE
CEILING
CELADON
CELLULE
CENSURE
CENTAGE
CENTAUR
CENTIME
CENTNER
CENTRAL
CENTRIC
CENTURY
CERAMIC
CEREOUS
CERTAIN
CERTIFY
CERUMEN
CERVINE
CESSION
CESTOID
CETACEA
CHABLIS
CHABOUK
CHAFFER
CHAGRIN
CHALDEE
CHALICE
CHAMADE
CHAMBER
CHAMFER
CHAMOIS
CHAMPAC
CHANCEL
CHANCRE
CHANGER
CHANNEL
CHANTER
CHANTRY
CHAOTIC
CHAPLET

CHAPMAN
CHAPPED
CHAPTER
CHARADE
CHARGER
CHARILY
CHARIOT
CHARITY
CHARMED
CHARMER
CHARNEL
CHARPIE
CHARPOY
CHARQUI
CHARTER
CHASMED
CHASSIS
CHASTEN
CHATEAU
CHATTEL
CHATTER
CHEAPEN
CHEAPLY
CHEATER
CHECKER
CHEDDAR
CHEERER
CHEERLY
CHEETAH
CHEMISE
CHEMIST
CHEQUER
CHERISH
CHEROOT
CHERVIL
CHESNUT
CHESSEL
CHESTED
CHEVIOT
CHEVRON
CHIASMA
CHICANE
CHICKEN
CHICORY
CHIEFLY
CHIGNON
CHIKARA
CHILIAD
CHIMERE
CHIMNEY
CHINESE
CHINNED
CHIPPER
CHIRPER
CHIRRUP
CHISLEU
CHLAMYS
CHLORAL
CHLORIC
CHOLERA
CHOOSER
CHOPINE
CHOPPER
CHORION
CHORIST
CHOROID
CHRISOM
CHROMIC
CHRONIC
CHUCKLE

CHUTNEY	COAL-BED	COMPLOT	CONVERT	COWHERD
CHYLIFY	COAL-GAS	COMPORT	CONVICT	COWHIDE
CHYLOUS	COAL-PIT	COMPOSE	CONVOKE	COW-ITCH
CHYMIFY	COAL-TAR	COMPOST	COOKERY	COWSLIP
CHYMOUS	COAMING	COMPUTE	COOLISH	COW-TREE
CILIARY	COASTER	COMRADE	COOPERY	COXCOMB
CIMBRIC	COATING	CONACRE	COPAIBA	COYNESS
CIMETER	CO-AXIAL	CONCAVE	COPYIST	COZENER
CINDERY	GOBBLER	CONCEAL	COPIOUS	CRABBED
CIPOLIN	COCAINE	CONCEDE	COPPERY	CRAB-OIL
CIRCEAN	COCHLEA	CONCEIT	COPPICE	CRACKED
CIRCLED	COCKADE	CONCEPT	CORACLE	CRACKER
CIRCLER	COCKNEY	CONCERN	CORCULE	CRACKLE
CIRCLET	COCK-PIT	CONCERT	CORDAGE	CRAGGED
CIRCUIT	COCO-NUT	CONCISE	CORDATE	CRAMMER
CIRROSE	COCTION	CONCOCT	CORDIAL	CRAMPED
CISSOID	CODICIL	CONCORD	CORDITE	CRAMPON
CISTERN	CODILLA	CONCUSS	CORK-LEG	CRANAGE
CITABLE	CODLING	CONDEMN	CORNICE	CRANIAL
CITADEL	COEHORN	CONDIGN	CORNISH	CRANIUM
CITHARA	COELIAC	CONDOLE	COROLLA	CRANKLE
CITHERN	COEQUAL	CONDONE	CORONAL	CRANNOG
CITIZEN	COEXIST	CONDUCE	CORONER	CRAUNCH
CITRINE	COGENCY	CONDUCT	CORONET	CRAVING
CIVILLY	COGNATE	CONDUIT	CORRECT	CRAWLER
CLACHAN	COGNIZE	CONDYLE	CORRODE	CRAZILY
CLACKER	COHABIT	CONFECT	CORRUPT	CREATIN
CLAMANT	COHIBIT	CONFESS	CORSAGE	CREATOR
CLAMBER	COINAGE	CONFEST	CORSAIR	CREDENT
CLAMOUR	COITION	CONFIDE	CORSNED	CREEPER
CLAP-NET	COJUROR	CONFINE	CORTEGE	CREMATE
CLAPPER	COLDISH	CONFIRM	CORVINE	CREMONA
CLARION	COLIBRI	CONFLUX	COSAQUE	CRENATE
CLARITY	COLICKY	CONFORM	COSMISM	CRESSET
CLASPER	COLLATE	CONFUSE	COSSACK	CRESTED
CLASSIC	COLLECT	CONFUTE	COSTARD	CREVICE
CLATTER	COLLEGE	CONGEAL	COSTATE	CRIBBLE
CLAVATE	COLLIDE	CONGEST	COSTIVE	CRICKET
CLAVIER	COLLIER	CONICAL	COSTREL	CRICOID
CLAY-PIT	COLLOID	CONIFER	COSTUME	CRIMPER
CLEANER	COLLUDE	CONJOIN	COTERIE	CRIMPLE
CLEANLY	COLONEL	CONJURE	COTHURN	CRIMSON
CLEANSE	COLOURY	CONJURY	COTIDAL	CRINGER
CLEARER	COLTISH	CONNATE	COTTAGE	CRINGLE
CLEARLY	COLUMBA	CONNECT	COTTIER	CRINITE
CLEAVER	COMBINE	CONNING	COTTONY	CRINKLE
CLEMENT	COMBING	CONNIVE	COUCHEE	CRINOID
CLERISY	COMFORT	CONNOTE	COUCHER	CRIPPLE
CLERKLY	COMFREY	CONQUER	COUGHER	CRISPER
CLICKER	COMICAL	CONSENT	COULOMB	CRISPIN
CLIMATE	COMIQUE	CONSIGN	COULTER	CRISPLY
CLIMBER	COMITIA	CONSOLE	COUNCIL	CRIZZEL
CLINGER	COMMAND	CONSOLS	COUNSEL	CROAKER
CLINKER	COMMEND	CONSORT	COUNTER	CROCHET
CLIPPER	COMMENT	CONSULT	COUNTRY	CROCKET
CLIVERS	COMMODE	CONSUME	COUPLER	CROFTER
CLOACAL	COMMOVE	CONTACT	COUPLET	CROOKED
CLOSELY	COMMUNE	CONTAIN	COUPURE	CROPPER
CLOSING	COMMUTE	CONTEMN	COURAGE	CROQUET
CLOSURE	COMPACT	CONTEND	COURIER	CROSIER
CLOTHES	COMPACT	CONTEND	COURSER	CROSSED
CLOUDER	COMPANY	CONTENT	COURTER	CROSSLY
CLOVERY	COMPARE	CONTEST	COUNTLY	CROWBAR
CLOVERY	COMPART	CONTEXT	COUVADE	CROWDED
CLOYING	COMPASS	CONTORT	COVERER	CROWNED
CLUB-LAW	COMPEER	CONTOUR	COVETER	CROZIER
CLUSTER	COMPEND	CONTROL	COW-BANE	CRUCIAL
CLUTTER	COMPETE	CONTUSE	COW-CALF	CRUCIFY
CLYSTER	COMPILE	CONVENE	COWHAGE	CRUDELY
COAGENT	COMPLEX	CONVENT	COW-HEEL	CRUDITY

CRUELLY	CZARINA	DEFACER	DEVELOP	DISCOUS
CRUELTY		DEFAMER	DEVIATE	DISCUSS
CRUISER		DEFAULT	DEVILRY	DISDAIN
CRUISIE	**D**	DEFENCE	DEVIOUS	DISEASE
CRUMBLE		DEFIANT	DEVISEE	DISGUST
CRUMBLY	DABBLER	DEFICIT	DEVISER	DISHING
CRUMPET	DACOITY	DEFILER	DEVISOR	DISJOIN
CRUMPLE	DAISIED	DEFINED	DEVOLVE	DISLIKE
CRUPPER	DAKOITY	DEFINER	DEVOTED	DISLINK
CRUSADE	DALLIER	DEFLECT	DEVOTEE	DISMASK
CRUSADO	DAMNIFY	DEFORCE	DEW-CLAW	DISMAST
CRUSHER	DAMNING	DEFRAUD	DEWDROP	DISMISS
CRYPTAL	DAMPISH	DEFUNCT	DEWFALL	DISOBEY
CRYPTIC	DANDIFY	DEGRADE	DEXTRAL	DISPARK
CRYSTAL	DANGLER	DEHISCE	DIABASE	DISPART
CTENOID	DAPPLED	DEICIDE	DIAGRAM	DISPLAY
CUBHOOD	DARKISH	DEICTIC	DIALECT	DISPONE
CUBICAL	DARLING	DEIFORM	DIALIST	DISPORT
CUBICLE	DASHING	DEISTIC	DIALYSE	DISPOSE
CUBITAL	DASH-POT	DELAINE	DIAMOND	DISPUTE
CUCKOLD	DASTARD	DELAYER	DIAPASM	DISROBE
CUDBEAR	DASYURE	DELIGHT	DIARCHY	DISROOT
CUDWEED	DAUNTER	DELIVER	DIARIAN	DISRUPT
CUIRASS	DAUPHIN	DELPHIC	DIARIST	DISSECT
CUISINE	DAWDLER	DELTAIC	DIBBLER	DISSENT
CULLION	DAWNING	DELTOID	DICE-BOX	DISTAFF
CULPRIT	DAY-BOOK	DELUDER	DICKENS	DISTAIN
CULTURE	DAY-LILY	DEMERIT	DICTATE	DISTANT
CULVERT	DAYLONG	DEMESNE	DICTION	DISTEND
CUMFREY	DAYSMAN	DEMI-GOD	DIETARY	DISTICH
CUMSHAW	DAY-STAR	DEMIREP	DIETIST	DISTORT
CUMULUS	DAYTIME	DEMONIC	DIFFORM	DISTURB
CUNEATE	DAYWORK	DEMOTIC	DIFFUSE	DISYOKE
CUNNING	DAZZLER	DENIZEN	DIGAMMA	DITCHER
CUPPING	DEAD-EYE	DENSELY	DIGGING	DITTANY
CUPROUS	DEAD-PAY	DENSITY	DIGITAL	DIURNAL
CUPRITE	DEAD-SET	DENTATE	DIGNIFY	DIVERGE
CURABLE	DEALING	DENTINE	DIGNITY	DIVERSE
CURACAO	DEANERY	DENTIST	DIGRAPH	DIVIDER
CURATOR	DEATHLY	DEODAND	DIGRESS	DIVINER
CURIOUS	DEBACLE	DEPLETE	DILATER	DIVISOR
CURLING	DEBASED	DEPLORE	DILATOR	DIVORCE
CURRANT	DEBASER	DEPLUME	DILEMMA	DIVULGE
CURRENT	DEBATER	DEPOSER	DILUENT	DIZZILY
CURRIER	DEBAUCH	DEPOSIT	DIMETER	DJEREED
CURRISH	DEBOUCH	DEPRAVE	DIMMISH	DOCKAGE
CURSING	DECADAL	DEPRESS	DIMNESS	DOESKIN
CURSIVE	DECAGON	DEPRIVE	DIMPLED	DOG-CART
CURSORY	DECAGYN	DERANGE	DIMYARY	DOGFISH
CURSTLY	DECANAL	DERIDER	DINETTE	DOGGISH
CURTAIL	DECAPOD	DERIVER	DIOCESE	DOG-HOLE
CURTAIN	DECEASE	DERMOID	DIORAMA	DOG-ROSE
CURVITY	DECEIVE	DERRICK	DIORITE	DOG'S-EAR
CUSHION	DECENCY	DERVISH	DIOXIDE	DOG-SICK
CUSTARD	DECIDED	DESCANT	DIPLOMA	DOGSKIN
CUSTODY	DECIDER	DESCEND	DIPLOPY	DOG-STAR
CUT-AWAY	DECIDUA	DESCENT	DIPOLAR	DOG-TROT
CUTICLE	DECIMAL	DESERVE	DIPTYCH	DOGWOOD
CUTLASS	DECLAIM	DESIRER	DIREFUL	DOLABRA
CUTLERY	DECLARE	DESPAIR	DIRT-BED	DOLEFUL
CUTTING	DECLINE	DESPISE	DIRTILY	DOLPHIN
CYANEAN	DECORUM	DESPOIL	DIRT-PYE	DOLTISH
CYANIDE	DECREER	DESPOND	DISABLE	DOMICAL
CYCLIST	DECREET	DESSERT	DISAVOW	DOMINIE
CYCLOID	DECRIAL	DESTINE	DISBAND	DONNISH
CYCLONE	DECRIER	DESTINY	DISCAGE	DOORWAY
CYCLOPS	DECUMAN	DESTROY	DISCARD	DOR-HAWK
CYNICAL	DECUPLE	DETERGE	DISCERN	DORMANT
CYPRESS	DEEDFUL	DETRACT	DISCOID	DOUBLET
CYPRIAN	DEEP-SEA	DETRUDE	DISCORD	DOUBTER

DOUCEUR
DOUGHTY
DOVE-COT
DOVELET
DOWAGER
DOWERED
DRACHMA
DRAGGLE
DRAG-NET
DRAGOON
DRAINER
DRAPERY
DRASTIC
DRAUGHT
DRAWING
DRAYAGE
DRAYMAN
DREAMER
DREDGER
DRESSER
DRIBBLE
DRIBLET
DRIFTER
DRINKER
DRIZZLE
DRIZZLY
DROMOND
DRONISH
DROPLET
DROPPER
DROUGHT
DROUTHY
DRUGGET
DRUIDIC
DRUMMER
DRUNKEN
DRYNESS
DRY-SHOD
DUALISM
DUALIST
DUALITY
DUBIETY
DUBIOUS
DUCALLY
DUCHESS
DUCTILE
DUDGEON
DUKEDOM
DULCIFY
DULLARD
DULLISH
DULNESS
DUMPISH
DUNCERY
DUNGEON
DUNNAGE
DUNNISH
DUPABLE
DURABLE
DURABLY
DURAMEN
DURANCE
DURMAST
DUSKILY
DUSKISH
DUST-MAN
DUTEOUS
DUTIFUL
DUUMVIR
DWELLER

DWINDLE
DYE-WOOD
DYE-WORK
DYINGLY
DYNAMIC
DYNASTY
DYSLOGY
DYSURIA
DYSURIC

E

EAGERLY
EANLING
EAR-ACHE
EAR-DROP
EAR-DRUM
EAR-HOLE
EARLDOM
EARLESS
EAR-MARK
EARNEST
EARNING
EAR-PICK
EAR-RING
EAR-SHOT
EARTHEN
EARTHLY
EASEFUL
EASTERN
EASTING
EATABLE
EBB-TIDE
EBONITE
EBONIZE
EBRIETY
ECBATIC
ECBOLIC
ECDYSIS
ECHELON
ECHIDNA
ECHINUS
ECLIPSE
ECLOGUE
ECONOMY
ECSTASY
ECTOPIA
ECTOZOA
ECTYPAL
EDACITY
EDICTAL
EDIFICE
EDITION
EDUCATE
EEL-BUCK
EEL-POUT
EFFABLE
EFFENDI
EFFULGE
EGG-BIRD
EGG-FLIP
EGOTISM
EGOTIST
EGOTIZE
EJECTOR
ELASTIC
ELATION
ELDERLY
ELECTOR

ELECTRO
ELEGANT
ELEGIAC
ELEGIST
ELEGIZE
ELEMENT
ELEVATE
ELF-BOLT
ELF-LAND
ELF-LOCK
ELISION
ELIXATE
ELLAGIC
ELLIPSE
ELOGIUM
ELOHIST
ELUSION
ELUSIVE
ELUSORY
ELYSIAN
ELYSIUM
ELYTRON
ELYTRUM
ELZEVIR
EMANANT
EMANATE
EMBARGO
EMBASSY
EMBLAZE
EMBOSOM
EMBOWEL
EMBOWER
EMBRACE
EMBROIL
EMBROWN
EMBRYOS
EMERALD
EMERODS
EMINENT
EMOTION
EMPEROR
EMPIRIC
EMPOWER
EMPRESS
EMPRISE
EMPTIER
EMPYEMA
EMULATE
EMULOUS
ENACTOR
ENAMOUR
ENCENIA
ENCHAIN
ENCHANT
ENCHASE
ENCLASP
ENCLAVE
ENCLOSE
ENCRUST
ENDEMIC
ENDLESS
ENDLONG
ENDOGEN
ENDORSE
ENDOWER
ENDWISE
ENERGIC
ENFEOFF
ENFORCE
ENGAGED

ENGLISH
ENGORGE
ENGRAFT
ENGRAIL
ENGRAIN
ENGRAVE
ENGROSS
ENHANCE
ENJOYER
ENLARGE
ENLIVEN
ENNOBLE
ENOUNCE
ENQUIRE
ENSLAVE
ENSNARE
ENTASIS
ENTENTE
ENTERIC
ENTHRAL
ENTICER
ENTITLE
ENTOMIC
ENTONIC
ENTRAIL
ENTRAIN
ENTRANT
ENTREAT
ENTRUST
ENTWINE
ENTWIST
ENVELOP
ENVIOUS
ENVENOM
ENVIRON
EPACRIS
EPARCHY
EPAULET
EPERGNE
EPICARP
EPICENE
EPICURE
EPIDERM
EPIDOTE
EPIGENE
EPIGRAM
EPISODE
EPISTLE
EPITAPH
EPITHET
EPITOME
EPIZOAN
EPIZOON
EPOCHAL
EQUABLE
EQUABLY
EQUALLY
EQUATOR
EQUERRY
EQUINOX
ERASION
ERASURE
ERECTER
ERECTOR
ERECTLY
ERELONG
EREMITE
ERGOTED
ERISTIC
ERMINED

ERODENT
EROSION
EROSIVE
ERRATIC
ERRATUM
ERRHINE
ERUDITE
ESCAPER
ESCHEAT
ESCUAGE
ESPARTO
ESPOUSE
ESQUIRE
ESSAYER
ESSENCE
ESTHETE
ESTIVAL
ESTRADE
ESTREAT
ESTUARY
ETAGERE
ETCHING
ETERNAL
ETESIAN
ETHICAL
ETHMOID
EUGENIC
EULOGIC
EUPEPSY
EUPHONY
EUPNOEA
EVANGEL
EVANISH
EVASION
EVASIVE
EVENING
EVICTOR
EVIDENT
EVOLVER
EXACTER
EXACTOR
EXALTER
EXAMINE
EXAMPLE
EXCERPT
EXCITER
EXCLAIM
EXCLAVE
EXCLUDE
EXCRETA
EXCRETE
EXCUSER
EXECUTE
EXEGETE
EXERGUE
EXHAUST
EXHIBIT
EXIGENT
EXOGAMY
EXPANSE
EXPENSE
EXPIATE
EXPLAIN
EXPLODE
EXPLOIT
EXPLORE
EXPOSED
EXPOSER
EXPOUND
EXPRESS

EXPUNGE
EXSCIND
EXTATIC
EXTINCT
EXTRACT
EXTREME
EXTRUDE
EXUVIAE
EXUVIAL
EYEBALL
EYEBROW
EYELASH
EYELESS
EYESHOT
EYESORE

F

FABLIAU
FACETTE
FACTION
FACTORY
FACULAR
FACULTY
FADDIST
FADDISH
FADEDLY
FAECULA
FAGOTTO
FAIENCE
FAILING
FAILURE
FAINTLY
FAIRILY
FAIRING
FAIRISH
FALCATE
FALLACY
FALSELY
FALSIFY
FALSISM
FALSITY
FAMULUS
FANATIC
FANCIED
FANCIER
FANCIES
FANFARE
FAN-PALM
FANTAIL
FANTASM
FARADIC
FARCEUR
FARCING
FARDAGE
FARMING
FARMOST
FARNESS
FARRAGO
FARRIER
FARTHER
FASCINE
FASHION
FAST-DAY
FATALLY
FATEFUL
FATIGUE
FATLING
FATNESS

FATUITY
FATUOUS
FAUNIST
FAUX-PAS
FEARFUL
FEASTER
FEATHER
FEATURE
FEBRILE
FEDERAL
FEEDING
FEELING
FEIGNED
FEIGNER
FELSITE
FELSPAR
FELTING
FELUCCA
FENCING
FEODARY
FEOFFEE
FEOFFER
FEOFFOR
FERMENT
FERNERY
FERN-OWL
FERRUGO
FERRULE
FERTILE
FERVENT
FERVOUR
FESTIVE
FESTOON
FETLOCK
FEUDARY
FEWNESS
FIANCÉE
FIASCOS
FIBSTER
FIBRINE
FIBROID
FIBROUS
FICTILE
FICTION
FICTIVE
FIDGETY
FIELDER
FIERILY
FIFTEEN
FIFTHLY
FIGHTER
FIGMENT
FIGURAL
FIGURED
FILBERT
FILCHER
FILEMOT
FILIATE
FILIBEG
FILICAL
FILINGS
FILLING
FINABLE
FINALLY
FINANCE
FINBACK
FINDING
FINESSE
FINICAL
FINIKIN

FINLESS
FINNISH
FIREARM
FIRE-BOX
FIRE-DOG
FIREFLY
FIREMAN
FIRE-NEW
FIRE-PAN
FIRE-POT
FIRSTLY
FISHERY
FISH-FAG
FISHING
FISSILE
FISSION
FISSURE
FISTULA
FITCHET
FITCHEW
FITNESS
FITTING
FIXABLE
FIXEDLY
FIXTURE
FLACCID
FLAMING
FLANEUR
FLANKER
FLANNEL
FLAPPER
FLARING
FLATTEN
FLATTER
FLAUNTY
FLAVOUR
FLEECED
FLEECER
FLEERER
FLEETLY
FLEMING
FLEMISH
FLESHED
FLESHER
FLESHLY
FLEURET
FLEXILE
FLEXION
FLEXURE
FLICKER
FLIGHTY
FLIPPER
FLITTER
FLOATER
FLOGGER
FLOORER
FLORIST
FLOTSAM
FLOUNCE
FLOUTER
FLOWAGE
FLOWERY
FLOWING
FLUENCY
FLUNKEY
FLUORIC
FLUSTER
FLUTINA
FLUTING
FLUTIST

FLUTTER
FLUVIAL
FLUXION
FOGGAGE
FOGYISM
FOGGILY
FOLIAGE
FOLIATE
FOLIOLE
FOOLERY
FOOLISH
FOOTING
FOOTMAN
FOOTPAD
FOOTWAY
FOPLING
FOPPERY
FOPPISH
FORAGER
FORAMEN
FORAYER
FORBADE
FORBEAR
FORBORE
FORCEPS
FORCING
FOREARM
FOREIGN
FORELEG
FOREMAN
FORERUN
FORESEE
FORETOP
FOREVER
FORFEIT
FORFEND
FORGAVE
FORGERY
FORGING
FORGIVE
FORGOER
FORLORN
FORMULA
FORSAKE
FORTIFY
FORTLET
FORTUNE
FORWARD
FOSSICK
FOULARD
FOUMART
FOUNDER
FOUNDRY
FOURGON
FOVEATE
FRAGILE
FRAILTY
FRAMING
FRANKLY
FRANTIC
FRAUGHT
FRECKLE
FRECKLY
FREEDOM
FREEMAN
FREIGHT
FRESHEN
FRESHET
FRESHLY
FRETFUL

FRETTED
FRIABLE
FRIBBLE
FRIEZED
FRIGATE
FRINGED
FRISIAN
FRISKET
FRITTER
FRIZZLE
FRIZZLY
FROCKED
FROGGED
FRONTAL
FRONTED
FROUNCE
FROWARD
FRUSTUM
FUCHSIA
FUDDLER
FUGUIST
FULCRUM
FULGENT
FULLING
FULMINE
FULNESS
FULSOME
FULVOUS
FUMBLER
FUMETTE
FUNERAL
FUNGOID
FUNGOUS
FUNICLE
FUNNILY
FURBISH
FURCATE
FURCULA
FURIOSO
FURIOUS
FURLONG
FURMITY
FURNACE
FURNISH
FURRIER
FURRING
FURROWY
FURTHER
FURTIVE
FUSCOUS
FUSIBLE
FUSSILY
FUSTIAN

G

GABBLER
GABELLE
GADWELL
GAINFUL
GAINING
GAINSAY
GAIRISH
GALANGA
GALEATE
GALENIC
GALILEE
GALIPOT
GALLANT

GALLEON	GIBBOSE	GOUACHE	GUANACO	HATCHER
GALLERY	GIBBOUS	GOURMET	GUARDED	HATCHET
GALLING	GIDDILY	GOUTILY	GUDGEON	HATEFUL
GALLIOT	GIGGLER	GRABBER	GUERDON	HAUBERK
GALLIUM	GILDING	GRACILE	GUESSER	HAUGHTY
GALLOON	GIMBALS	GRACKLE	GUILDER	HAULAGE
GALLOWS	GIMBLET	GRADATE	GUILDRY	HAUNTED
GALUMPH	GINGHAM	GRADUAL	GUIPURE	HAUNTER
GAMBIER	GINSENG	GRAFTER	GUMMING	HAUTBOY
GAMBLER	GIPSIES	GRAINED	GUMMOUS	HAUTEUR
GAMBOGE	GIRAFFE	GRAMARY	GUNNERY	HAWKING
GAMBREL	GIRLISH	GRAMMAR	GUNSHOT	HAZELLY
GANGWAY	GITTERN	GRAMPUS	GUNWALE	HEADILY
GANTLET	GIZZARD	GRANARY	GURNARD	HEADING
GARBAGE	GLACIAL	GRANDAM	GUSHING	HEADWAY
GARBLER	GLACIER	GRANDEE	GUTTATE	HEALING
GARBOIL	GLADDEN	GRANDLY	GUTTLER	HEALTHY
GARDANT	GLAMOUR	GRANGER	GUZZLER	HEARING
GARFISH	GLARING	GRANITE	GYMNAST	HEARKEN
GARGOIL	GLAZIER	GRANTEE		HEARSAY
GARLAND	GLEANER	GRANTER		HEARTED
GARMENT	GLEBOUS	GRANTOR	**H**	HEARTEN
GARNISH	GLEEFUL	GRANULE		HEATHEN
GAROTTE	GLEEMAN	GRAPERY	HABITAT	HEATHER
GARROTS	GLIMMER	GRAPHIC	HABITED	HEATING
GASEITY	GLIMPSE	GRAPNEL	HABITUÉ	HEAVILY
GASEOUS	GLISTEN	GRAPPLE	HACHURE	HEBRAIC
GASTRIC	GLISTER	GRASPER	HACKBUT	HECKLER
GATEWAY	GLITTER	GRATIFY	HACKING	HECTARE
GAUDILY	GLOBATE	GRATING	HACKLER	HEDGING
GAUFFER	GLOBOSE	GRAVELY	HACKNEY	HEDONIC
GAULISH	GLOBOUS	GRAVITY	HADDOCK	HEEDFUL
GAUNTLY	GLOBULE	GRAYISH	HAGGARD	HEINOUS
GAVOTTE	GLORIFY	GRAZIER	HAGGISH	HEIRDOM
GAYNESS	GLOSSER	GRAZING	HAGGLER	HEIRESS
GAZELLE	GLOSSIC	GREATLY	HALBERD	HELICAL
GAZETTE	GLOTTAL	GREAVES	HALCYON	HELICES
GEARING	GLOTTIC	GRECIAN	HALIBUT	HELLISH
GEHENNA	GLOTTIS	GREENLY	HALIDOM	HELOTRY
GELATIN	GLOWING	GREENTH	HALYARD	HELPFUL
GELDING	GLUCINA	GRENADE	HAMITIC	HEMLOCK
GELIDLY	GLUCOSE	GRIDDLE	HAMMOCK	HENBANE
GEMMATE	GLUTEAL	GRIFFIN	HAMSTER	HENNERY
GEMMULE	GLUTTON	GRIFFON	HANAPER	HENOTIC
GENERAL	GLYPHIC	GRIMACE	HANDFUL	HEPATIC
GENERIC	GLYPTIC	GRIMILY	HANDILY	HERBAGE
GENESIS	GNARLED	GRINDER	HANDSEL	HERBOSE
GENETTE	GNATHIC	GRIPING	HANGING	HERETIC
GENETIC	GNOSTIC	GRIPPER	HANGMAN	HERNIAL
GENEVAN	GOATISH	GRISKIN	HAPLESS	HEROINE
GENIPAP	GOBBLER	GRISLED	HAPPILY	HEROISM
GENITAL	GODDESS	GRISTLE	HARBOUR	HEROIZE
GENITOR	GODHEAD	GRISTLY	HARDILY	HERONRY
GENTEEL	GODLESS	GRIZZLE	HARDISH	HERRING
GENTIAN	GODLIKE	GRIZZLY	HARELIP	HERSELF
GENTILE	GODLILY	GROCERY	HARICOT	HESSIAN
GENUINE	GODSEND	GROGRAM	HARMFUL	HETAERA
GENUSES	GODSHIP	GROGRAN	HARMONY	HETAIRA
GEODESY	GODWARD	GROINED	HARNESS	HEXAGON
GEOGENY	GOITRED	GROOVED	HARPIST	HEXAPLA
GEOGONY	GOLFING	GROSSLY	HARPOON	HEXAPOD
GEOLOGY	GONDOLA	GROTTOS	HARRIER	HICKORY
GERMANE	GOOSERY	GRUBBER	HARVEST	HIDEOUS
GESTURE	GORDIAN	GRUDGER	HASHISH	HIGGLER
GHASTLY	GORILLA	GRUFFLY	HASSOCK	HIGHWAY
GHERKIN	GORMAND	GRUMBLE	HASTATE	HILDING
GHOSTLY	GOSHAWK	GRUMOUS	HASTILY	HILLOCK
GIANTLY	GOSLING	GRUNTER	HATABLE	HILLTOP
GIANTRY	GOSSIPY	GRUYÉRE	HATCHEL	HIMSELF

73

HIPPISH	ICEFOOT	INDUSIA	IRIDIAN	KEELSON
HIRCINE	ICHNITE	INDWELL	IRIDIUM	KEEPING
HIRSUTE	ICINESS	INEPTLY	IRKSOME	KERAMIC
HISTORY	IDEALLY	INERTIA	ISCHIUM	KESTREL
HOARDER	IDENTIC	INERTLY	ISOLATE	KETCHUP
HOBNAIL	IDIOTCY	INEXACT	ISONOMY	KHALIFF
HOGGISH	IDIOTIC	INFANCY	ISTHMUS	KHANATE
HOLDING	IDOLIZE	INFANTA	ITALIAN	KHEDIVE
HOLIBUT	IDYLLIC	INFANTE	ITERATE	KILLING
HOLIDAY	IGNEOUS	INFEOFF		KINDRED
HOLLAND	IGNOBLE	INFIDEL		KINETIC
HOLSTER	IGNOBLY	INFLAME	**J**	KINGDOM
HOMERIC	ILLAPSE	INFLATE		KINGLET
HOMONYM	ILLEGAL	INFLECT	JACINTH	KINLESS
HONESTY	ILLICIT	INFLICT	JACKASS	KINSMAN
HOPEFUL	ILLNESS	INFULAE	JACKDAW	KINSMEN
HOPLITE	IMAGERY	INGESTA	JACOBIN	KIRTLED
HORIZON	IMAGINE	INGOING	JACOBUS	KITCHEN
HORNLET	IMBIBER	INGRAFT	JACONET	KNACKER
HORRENT	IMBOSOM	INGRAIL	JAGGERY	KNAGGED
HOSANNA	IMBOWEL	INGRAIN	JAGHIRE	KNARRED
HOSEMAN	IMBOWER	INGRATE	JANITOR	KNARLED
HOSIERY	IMBROWN	INGRESS	JANUARY	KNAVERY
HOSPICE	IMITANT	INHABIT	JARGOON	KNAVISH
HOSTAGE	IMITATE	INHALER	JASMINE	KNEELER
HOSTESS	IMMENSE	INHERIT	JASPERY	KNITTER
HOSTILE	IMMERGE	INHIBIT	JAVELIN	KNOBBED
HOSTLER	IMMERSE	INHUMAN	JEALOUS	KNOCKER
HOTNESS	IMMORAL	INITIAL	JEHOVAH	KNOTTED
HOTSPUR	IMPANEL	INJURER	JEJUNUM	KNOWING
HOUSING	IMPASTE	INKHORN	JELLIES	KNUCKLE
HOWBEIT	IMPASTO	INKLING	JEMADAR	KOUMISS
HOWEVER	IMPEACH	INLAYER	JEMIDAR	KREUZER
HOWLING	IMPEARL	INNERVE	JEOPARD	KURSAAL
HUELESS	IMPERIL	INQUEST	JETTIES	KYANIZE
HUFFISH	IMPETUS	INQUIRE	JEWELRY	
HULKING	IMPIETY	INQUIRY	JOBBERY	
HUMANLY	IMPINGE	INSHORE	JOCULAR	**L**
HUMDRUM	IMPIOUS	INSIGHT	JOINERY	
HUMERAL	IMPLANT	INSIPID	JOINING	LABIATE
HUMERUS	IMPLEAD	INSNARE	JOINTED	LACONIC
HUMIDLY	IMPLORE	INSPECT	JOINTLY	LACQUER
HUMMOCK	IMPOUND	INSPIRE	JOLLILY	LACTEAL
HUMORAL	IMPRESS	INSTALL	JOLLITY	LACTINE
HUNDRED	IMPRINT	INSTANT	JONQUIL	LACTOSE
HUNTING	IMPROVE	INSTATE	JOTTING	LACUNAE
HURRIED	IMPULSE	INSTEAD	JOURNAL	LACUNAR
HURTFUL	IMPUTER	INSULAR	JOURNEY	LADANUM
HUSBAND	INANITY	INSURER	JOUSTER	LAGGARD
HUSKILY	INBOARD	INTEGER	JOYLESS	LAICIZE
HUSSITE	INBREAK	INTENSE	JUBILEE	LAKELET
HUSWIFE	INBREED	INTERIM	JUDAISM	LAMBENT
HYALINE	INCENSE	INTITLE	JUDAIZE	LAMBKIN
HYALITE	INCISOR	INTRANT	JUDASES	LAMELLA
HYALOID	INCIVIL	INTROIT	JUGATED	LAMINAE
HYDATID	INCLINE	INTRUDE	JUGGLER	LAMINAR
HYDRANT	INCLOSE	INTRUST	JUGULAR	LAMPION
HYDRATE	INCLUDE	INTWINE	JUNIPER	LAMPOON
HYDRIDE	INCOMER	INTWIST	JUPITER	LAMPREY
HYDROUS	INCRUST	INVADER	JURYMAN	LANDING
HYGEIAN	INCUBUS	INVALID	JUSSIVE	LANGUID
HYGIENE	INCURVE	INVEIGH	JUSTICE	LANGUOR
HYMNODY	INDEXES	INVERSE	JUSTIFY	LANIARY
	INDEXER	INVITER		LANTERN
	INDICES	INVOICE		LANYARD
	INDITER	INVOLVE	**K**	LAPELLE
	INDOORS	INWARDS		LAPILLI
I	INDORSE	INWEAVE	KAINITE	LAPWING
	INDUCER	IRANIAN	KALMUCK	LARCENY
IAMBIZE	INDULGE	IRICISM	KATYDID	LARGELY
IBERIAN				
ICEBERG				

LARGESS	LIGHTER	LUMPING	MANNISH	MERCIES
LASHING	LIGHTLY	LUMPISH	MANNITE	MERCURY
LASTING	LIGNIFY	LUNATED	MANSION	MERMAID
LATCHET	LIGNINE	LUNATIC	MANTLET	MERRILY
LATENCY	LIGNITE	LUNETTE	MANUMIT	MERSION
LATERAL	LIMITED	LUNULAR	MARABOU	MESEEMS
LATHING	LIMITER	LUNULET	MARINER	MESSAGE
LATRINE	LIMOSIS	LUPULIN	MARITAL	MESSIAH
LATTICE	LINEAGE	LURCHER	MARLINE	MESTIZO
LAUGHER	LINEATE	LURDANE	MARPLOT	METAYER
LAUNDRY	LINGUAL	LUSTFUL	MARQUEE	METTLED
LAWLESS	LINGULA	LUSTILY	MARQUIS	MIASMAL
LAWSUIT	LINNEAN	LUSTRAL	MARRIED	MICROBE
LAXNESS	LINSEED	LUSTRUM	MARROWY	MICROHM
LAZARET	LIONESS	LYCOPOD	MARSALA	MIDLAND
LEADING	LIONISM	LYINGLY	MARSHAL	MIDLENT
LEAFAGE	LIONIZE	LYRATED	MARTIAL	MIDMOST
LEAFLET	LIQUATE	LYRICAL	MARTLET	MIDNOON
LEAGUED	LIQUEFY		MASONIC	MIDRIFF
LEAGUER	LIQUEUR		MASONRY	MIDSHIP
LEAKAGE	LISSOME	**M**	MASSAGE	MIDWIFE
LEARNED	LITERAL		MASSIVE	MIGRANT
LEARNER	LITHIUM	MACHETE	MASTERY	MIGRATE
LEASING	LITHOID	MACHINE	MASTICH	MILEAGE
LEATHER	LITOTES	MACULAE	MASTIFF	MILFOIL
LECHERY	LITUATE	MADDING	MASTOID	MILIARY
LECTERN	LITURGY	MADEIRA	MATADOR	MILITIA
LECTION	LIVERED	MADNESS	MATINÉE	MILKMAN
LECTURE	LOADING	MADONNA	MATRASS	MILKSOP
LEEWARD	LOATHER	MAESTRO	MATTERY	MILLING
LEGALLY	LOATHLY	MAGENTA	MATTING	MILLION
LEGATEE	LOBATED	MAGGOTY	MATTOCK	MILREIS
LEGGING	LOBELET	MAGICAL	MAUDLIN	MIMETIC
LEGHORN	LOBELIA	MAGNATE	MAUNDER	MIMICRY
LEGIBLE	LOBIPED	MAGNIFY	MAWKISH	MINARET
LEGIBLY	LOBSTER	MAHATMA	MAWWORM	MINCING
LEGITIM	LOBULAR	MAJESTY	MAXILLA	MINDFUL
LEGLESS	LOBWORM	MALAISE	MAXIMAL	MINERAL
LEISTER	LOCALLY	MALARIA	MAXIMUM	MINIATE
LEISURE	LOCKAGE	MALAYAN	MAYORAL	MINIKIN
LEMMING	LODGING	MALEFIC	MAZURKA	MINIMUM
LENGTHY	LOFTILY	MALISON	MAZZARD	MINIVER
LENIENT	LOGICAL	MALLARD	MEADOWY	MINSTER
LENTOID	LOGWOOD	MALLEUS	MEALIES	MINTAGE
LENTIGO	LOLLARD	MALMSEY	MEANDER	MINUEND
LEONINE	LOMBARD	MALTESE	MEANING	MIOCENE
LEOPARD	LONGING	MALTING	MEASLED	MIRACLE
LEPROSE	LONGISH	MALTMAN	MEASLES	MIRIFIC
LEPROSY	LOOSELY	MAMELON	MEASURE	MISCALL
LEPROUS	LOPPING	MAMMARY	MECHLIN	MISDATE
LETHEAN	LORGNON	MAMMOTH	MECONIC	MISDEED
LETTUCE	LOTTERY	MANACLE	MEDALET	MISDEEM
LEUCOMA	LOUNGER	MANAGER	MEDDLER	MISDOER
LEVATOR	LOUTISH	MANAKIN	MEDIATE	MISERLY
LEVELLY	LOVABLE	MANATEE	MEDICAL	MISGIVE
LEVERET	LOWLAND	MANCHET	MEDIUMS	MISLEAD
LEVITIC	LOWNESS	MANCHOO	MEDULLA	MISLIKE
LEXICAL	LOYALLY	MANDATE	MEDUSAE	MISNAME
LEXICON	LOYALTY	MANDREL	MEETING	MISRULE
LIAISON	LOZENGE	MANDRIL	MEIOSIS	MISSILE
LIASSIC	LUCARNE	MANGLER	MÉLANGE	MISSING
LIBERAL	LUCENCY	MANHOLE	MELANIC	MISSION
LIBERTY	LUCERNE	MANIHOC	MELILOT	MISSIVE
LIBRARY	LUCIDLY	MANIHOT	MELODIC	MISTAKE
LIBRATE	LUCIFER	MANIKIN	MELTING	MISTILY
LICENCE	LUCKILY	MANILLA	MEMENTO	MISTIME
LICENSE	LUGGAGE	MANIPLE	MENISCI	MIXABLE
LICITLY	LUGWORM	MANITOU	MENTHOL	MIXEDLY
LIDLESS	LULLABY	MANKIND	MENTION	MIXTURE
LIGHTEN	LUMBAGO	MANLIKE	MERCERY	MOANFUL

MOBBISH	MULLION	NEPTUNE	OBLIGOR	ORATION
MOCKERY	MULTURE	NERVOUS	OBLIQUE	ORATORY
MODALLY	MUMBLER	NERVURE	OBLOQUY	ORBITAL
MODESTY	MUMMERY	NETTING	OBOVATE	ORCHARD
MODICUM	MUMMIFY	NEUTRAL	OBSCENE	ORDERER
MODISTE	MUMPISH	NEWNESS	OBSCURE	ORDERLY
MODULAR	MUNCHER	NEWSMAN	OBSERVE	ORDINAL
MODULUS	MUNDANE	NIBBLER	OBTRUDE	ORGANIC
MOIDORE	MURAENA	NIBLICK	OBVERSE	ORGANON
MOISTEN	MURICES	NICTATE	OBVIATE	ORGANUM
MOLLIFY	MURIATE	NIGGARD	OBVIOUS	ORIFICE
MOLLUSC	MURKILY	NIGHTLY	OCARINA	ORLEANS
MOLLUSK	MURRAIN	NILOTIC	OCCIPUT	OROGENY
MOMENTA	MURTHER	NINTHLY	OCCLUDE	OROLOGY
MONADIC	MUSCLED	NIOBIUM	OCEANIC	OROTUND
MONARCH	MUSCOID	NIPPERS	OCELLUS	ORPHEAN
MONEYED	MUSICAL	NITRATE	OCREATE	ORTOLAN
MONEYER	MUSROLE	NITRIFY	OCTAGON	OSCULUM
MONGREL	MUSTANG	NITROUS	OCTAVOS	OSIERED
MONITOR	MUSTARD	NIVEOUS	OCTOBER	OSMANLI
MONKEYS	MUSTILY	NOCTURN	OCTOPOD	OSMOTIC
MONKISH	MUTABLE	NODATED	OCTOPUS	OSSEINE
MONOCLE	MUTABLY	NODDING	OCTUPLE	OSSELET
MONODIC	MYALGIA	NODULAR	OCULATE	OSSEOUS
MONOGYN	MYCELIA	NOISILY	OCULIST	OSSICLE
MONSOON	MYELOID	NOISOME	ODALISK	OSSIFIC
MONSTER	MYLODON	NOMADIC	ODDMENT	OSSUARY
MONTERO	MYOLOGY	NOMARCH	ODDNESS	OSTIOLE
MONTHLY	MYOTOMY	NOMINAL	ODOROUS	OSTITIS
MOONISH	MYRRHIC	NOMINEE	OESTRUS	OSTRICH
MOORAGE	MYSTERY	NONAGON	OFFENCE	OTALGIA
MOORING	MYSTIFY	NONPLUS	OFFENSE	OTARIES
MOORISH		NONSUIT	OFFERER	OTOCYST
MORAINE		NOOLOGY	OFFICER	OTOLITE
MORALLY	**N**	NOONDAY	OGREISH	OTOLITH
MORASSY		NOONING	OLDNESS	OTOLOGY
MORCEAU	NAILERY	NOSEGAY	OLITORY	OTTOMAN
MORDANT	NAIVELY	NOSTRIL	OLIVINE	OURSELF
MORISCO	NAIVETE	NOSTRUM	OLYMPIC	OUTCAST
MORNING	NAKEDLY	NOTABLE	OMENTUM	OUTCOME
MOROCCO	NAMABLE	NOTABLY	OMENTAL	OUTCROP
MORPHIA	NANKEEN	NOTHING	OMINOUS	OUTDARE
MORRICE	NAPHTHA	NOURISH	OMNIBUS	OUTDOOR
MORTICE	NAPLESS	NOVELTY	ONENESS	OUTFACE
MORTIFY	NARDINE	NOWHERE	ONERARY	OUTFALL
MORTISE	NARRATE	NOXIOUS	ONEROUS	OUTFLOW
MOSELLE	NARTHEX	NUCLEUS	ONESELF	OUTGROW
MOTHERY	NARWHAL	NULLIFY	ONGOING	OUTLAST
MOTTLED	NASALLY	NULLITY	ONICOLO	OUTLIER
MOTTOES	NASCENT	NUMBLES	ONWARDS	OUTLINE
MOUFLON	NASTILY	NUMERAL	OOLITIC	OUTLIVE
MOULDER	NATTILY	NUMMARY	OOTHECA	OUTLOOK
MOUNTED	NATURAL	NUNNERY	OPACITY	OUTMOST
MOURNER	NAUGHTY	NUNNISH	OPACOUS	OUTPOST
MOUSING	NAVVIES	NUPTIAL	OPALINE	OUTPOUR
MOUTHED	NEBULAE	NURSERY	OPALIZE	OUTRAGE
MOUTHER	NEBULAR	NURTURE	OPENING	OUTRIDE
MOVABLE	NECKLET		OPERANT	OUTROOT
MOVABLY	NECTARY		OPERATE	OUTRUSH
MOWBURN	NEEDFUL	**O**	OPEROSE	OUTSAIL
MUCIFIC	NEEDILY		OPINION	OUTSIDE
MUDDILY	NEGLECT	OAKLING	OPOSSUM	OUTSPAN
MUEZZIN	NEGRESS	OARSMAN	OPPIDAN	OUTSTAY
MUEDDIN	NEGROES	OBCONIC	OPPOSED	OUTSTEP
MUFFLED	NEGROID	OBELISK	OPPOSER	OUTTALK
MUFFLER	NEITHER	OBELIZE	OPPRESS	OUTVOTE
MUGGISH	NELUMBO	OBESITY	OPTICAL	OUTWALK
MUGWORT	NEMESIS	OBLIGED	OPULENT	OUTWARD
MULATTO	NEMORAL	OBLIGEE	OPUNTIA	OUTWEAR
MULLEIN	NEOLOGY	OBLIGER	OPUSCLE	OUTWORK

OVARIAN	PANTHER	PEDDLER	PHAETON	PISTOLE
OVARIAL	PANTILE	PEDICEL	PHALANX	PITCHER
OVATION	PANTLER	PEDLARY	PHALLIC	PITEOUS
OVERACT	PAPALLY	PEDLERY	PHALLUS	PITFALL
OVERAWE	PAPILLA	PEERAGE	PHANTOM	PITHILY
OVERBID	PAPULAE	PEERESS	PHARYNX	PITIFUL
OVERDUE	PAPULAR	PEEVISH	PHILTER	PIVOTAL
OVEREAT	PAPYRUS	PELAGIC	PHILTRE	PIVOTED
OVERJOY	PARABLE	PELECAN	PHLOEUM	PLACARD
OVERLAP	PARADOX	PELICAN	PHOEBUS	PLACATE
OVERLAY	PARAGON	PELISSE	PHOENIX	PLACKET
OVERLIE	PARAPET	PELORIA	PHONICS	PLACOID
OVERPAY	PARASOL	PELORIC	PHRENIC	PLAGUER
OVERRUN	PARBOIL	PELTATE	PHYSICS	PLAIDED
OVERSEA	PAREIRA	PENALLY	PHYTOID	PLAINLY
OVERSEE	PARESIS	PENALTY	PIANINO	PLAITED
OVERSET	PARETIC	PENANCE	PIANIST	PLAITER
OVERTAX	PARLOUR	PENATES	PIASTER	PLANISH
OVERTLY	PARODIC	PENDANT	PIASTRE	PLANNER
OVERTOP	PARONYM	PENDENT	PIBROCH	PLANTAR
OVIDUCT	PAROTID	PENDING	PICADOR	PLANTER
OVIFORM	PARQUET	PENFOLD	PICCOLO	PLASMIC
OVOIDAL	PARSLEY	PENGUIN	PICEOUS	PLASTER
OXIDATE	PARSNIP	PENNANT	PICKAXE	PLASTIC
OXIDIZE	PARTAKE	PENNIES	PICKING	PLATANE
OXONIAN	PARTIAL	PENSILE	PICOTEE	PLATEAU
OXYTONE	PARTING	PENSION	PICQUET	PLATINA
OZONIZE	PARTLET	PENSIVE	PICTURE	PLATING
	PARTNER	PENTILE	PIDDOCK	PLATOON
	PARTOOK	PEONAGE	PIEBALD	PLATTER
P	PARTIES	PEONISM	PIERAGE	PLAUDIT
	PARVENU	PEPPERY	PIERCER	PLAYFUL
PABULAR	PARVISE	PEPSINE	PIETISM	PLEADER
PABULUM	PASCHAL	PEPTICS	PIETIST	PLEASER
PACABLE	PASQUIL	PERCHER	PIGGERY	PLEDGEE
PACIFIC	PASQUIN	PERCUSS	PIGGISH	PLEDGER
PACKAGE	PASSAGE	PERDURE	PIGMENT	PLEDGET
PACKING	PASSANT	PERFECT	PIKEMAN	PLEIADS
PACTION	PASSING	PERFIDY	PILEATE	PLENARY
PADDING	PASSION	PERFORM	PILGRIM	PLENISH
PADDLER	PASSIVE	PERFUME	PILLAGE	PLEURAE
PADDOCK	PASTERN	PERHAPS	PILLION	PLEURAL
PADELLA	PASTIME	PERIAPT	PILLORY	PLIABLE
PADLOCK	PASTURE	PERIGEE	PILLOWY	PLIABLY
PAGEANT	PATCHER	PERIWIG	PILULAR	PLIANCY
PAILFUL	PATELLA	PERJURE	PIMENTO	PLICATE
PAINFUL	PATERAE	PERJURY	PIMENTA	PLODDER
PAINTER	PATHWAY	PERMIAN	PIMPLED	PLOTTER
PAKTONG	PATIENT	PERMUTE	PINCASE	PLUCKER
PALADIN	PATRIAL	PERPEND	PINCERS	PLUGGER
PALATAL	PATRIOT	PERPLEX	PINCHER	PLUMAGE
PALAVER	PATRIST	PERSIAN	PINETUM	PLUMBER
PALETOT	PATTERN	PERSIST	PINFOLD	PLUMBIC
PALETTE	PATTIES	PERTAIN	PINHOLE	PLUMERY
PALFREY	PAUCITY	PERTURB	PINNACE	PLUMMET
PALLIAL	PAULINE	PERTUSE	PINNATE	PLUMOSE
PALLIUM	PAUNCHY	PERUSAL	PINNERS	PLUMOUS
PALMARY	PAVIOUR	PERUSER	PINNULA	PLUMPER
PALMATE	PAYABLE	PERVADE	PINNULE	PLUMPLY
PALUDAL	PAYMENT	PERVERT	PINTAIL	PLUMULE
PAMPEAN	PEACOCK	PESSARY	PIONEER	PLUNDER
PANACEA	PEARLED	PETALED	PIOUSLY	PLUNGER
PANBEAR	PEABULL	PETHYP	PIQUANT	PLURIAL
PANDECT	PEBBLED	PETRINE	PIRAGUA	POACHER
PANDORE	PECCANT	PETROUS	PIRATIC	POCHARD
PANICLE	PECCARY	PETTILY	PIROGUE	PODAGRA
PANNIER	PECCAVI	PETTISH	PISCINA	POETESS
PANOPLY	PECKISH	PETUNIA	PISCINE	POETICS
PANSIES	PECTOSE	PEWTERY	PISMIRE	POETIZE
				POINTED

POINTER	PRELECT	PROTEIN		RATTEEN
POITREL	PRELUDE	PROTEND	**Q**	RAUCOUS
POLACCA	PREMIER	PROTEST		RAVAGER
POLEMIC	PREMISE	PROUDLY	QUADRAT	RAVELIN
POLENTA	PREMISS	PROVERB	QUESTER	RAWNESS
POLITIC	PREMIUM	PROVIDE	QUAFFER	RAYLESS
POLLACK	PREPAID	PROVISO	QUALIFY	REACHER
POLLARD	PREPARE	PROVOKE	QUALITY	READILY
POLLUTE	PREPUCE	PROVOST	QUANTUM	READING
POLYGON	PRESAGE	PROWESS	QUARREL	READMIT
POLYGYN	PRESENT	PROWLER	QUARTAN	REAGENT
POLYPUS	PRESIDE	PROXIMO	QUARTER	REALGAR
POLYZOA	PRESUME	PRUDENT	QUARTET	REALISM
POMATUM	PRETEND	PRUDERY	QUARTZY	REALIST
POMPION	PRETENT	PRUDISH	QUASSIA	REALITY
POMPOUS	PRETEXT	PRURIGO	QUAYAGE	REALIZE
PONIARD	PREVAIL	PSALTER	QUEENLY	REANNEX
PONTAGE	PREVENT	PSYCHIC	QUEERLY	REARGUE
PONTIFF	PREVISE	PTARMIC	QUELLER	REBOUND
PONTOON	PRICKER	PUBERTY	QUERIST	REBUILD
POPEDOM	PRICKET	PUBLISH	QUERIES	REBUKER
POPPIED	PRICKLE	PUCKERY	QUESTOR	RECEIPT
POPULAR	PRICKLY	PUDDING	QUIBBLE	RECEIVE
PORCINE	PRIDIAN	PUDDLER	QUICKEN	RECENCY
PORIFER	PRIMACY	PUDENCY	QUICKLY	RECENSE
PORRIGO	PRIMAGE	PUDENDA	QUIETEN	RECITAL
PORTAGE	PRIMARY	PUERILE	QUIETLY	RECITER
PORTEND	PRIMATE	PUFFERY	QUIETUS	RECLAIM
PORTENT	PRIMELY	PULLEYS	QUILLED	RECLINE
PORTICO	PRIMING	PULSATE	QUINARY	RECLUSE
PORTION	PRINTER	PUMPION	QUININE	RECOUNT
PORTRAY	PRITHEE	PUMPKIN	QUINTAL	RECOVER
POSSESS	PRIVACY	PUNCHER	QUINTAN	RECRUIT
POSTAGE	PRIVATE	PUNGENT	QUINTET	RECTIFY
POSTBOY	PRIVILY	PUNNING	QUONDÀM	RECTORY
POSTERN	PRIVITY	PUNSTER		RECURVE
POSTFIX	PROBANG	PUPPIES		REDCOAT
POSTMAN	PROBATE	PURGING	**R**	REDDISH
POSTURE	PROBITY	PURITAN		REDNESS
POTABLE	PROBLEM	PURLIEU	RABIDLY	REDOUBT
POTASSA	PROCEED	PURLOIN	RACCOON	REDOUND
POTENCY	PROCESS	PURPLES	RADIANT	REDPOLL
POTTAGE	PROCTOR	PURPORT	RADIATE	REDRAFT
POTTERY	PROCURE	PURPOSE	RADICAL	REDRESS
POUCHED	PRODIGY	PURPURA	RADICLE	REDSKIN
POULTRY	PRODUCE	PURSUER	RAFFISH	REDTAIL
POUNCED	PRODUCT	PURSUIT	RAGWORT	REDUCER
POUNDER	PROFANE	PURVIEW	RAILING	REDWING
POVERTY	PROFESS	PUSHING	RAILWAY	REDWOOD
POWDERY	PROFFER	PUSTULE	RAIMENT	REFEREE
PRAETOR	PROFILE	PUTREFY	RAINBOW	REFINED
PRAIRIE	PROFUSE	PUTTOCK	RAMADAN	REFINER
PRAISER	PROGENY	PUZZLER	RAMBLER	REFLECT
PRANCER	PROJECT	PYAEMIA	RAMMISH	REFORGE
PRATING	PROLATE	PYAEMIC	RAMPAGE	REFOUND
PRATTLE	PROLONG	PYGMEAN	RAMPANT	REFRACT
PRAVITY	PROMISE	PYGMIES	RAMPART	REFRAIN
PRAYING	PROMOTE	PYLORUS	RAMPION	REFRESH
PREBEND	PRONELY	PYLORIC	RAMSONS	REFUGEE
PRECEDE	PRONGED	PYRAMID	RANCOUR	REFUSAL
PRECEPT	PRONOUN	PYRETIC	RANSACK	REFUSER
PRECISE	PROPHET	PYREXIA	RAPIDLY	REFUTER
PREDATE	PROPOSE	PYRITES	RAPTURE	REGALER
PREDIAL	PROSAIC	PYRITIC	RAREBIT	REGALIA
PREDICT	PROSODY	PYRRHIC	RASORES	REGALLY
PREDOOM	PROSPER	PYTHIAN	RATABLE	REGATTA
PREFACE	PROTEAN		RATABLY	REGENCY
PREFECT	PROTECT		RATAFIA	REGIMEN
PRELACY	PROTÉGÉ		RATCHET	REGNANT
PRELATE	PROTEID		RATLINE	REGORGE

REGRANT	RESTORE	ROMPISH	SAILING	SCARFED
REGRATE	RETIARY	RONDEAU	SAINTED	SCARIFY
REGREET	RETINAL	ROOFING	SAINTLY	SCARLET
REGRESS	RETINUE	ROOKERY	SALABLE	SCARPED
REGULAR	RETIRAL	ROOMFUL	SALICIN	SCATTER
REGULUS	RETIRED	ROOMILY	SALIENT	SCENERY
REINTER	RETOUCH	ROOSTER	SALIQUE	SCEPTER
REISSUE	RETRACE	ROOTLET	SALLIES	SCEPTIC
REJOICE	RETRACT	RORQUAL	SALMIAC	SCEPTRE
REJUDGE	RETREAT	ROSEATE	SALSIFY	SCHEMER
RELAPSE	REUNION	ROSEOLA	SALTANT	SCHERZO
RELATED	REUNITE	ROSETTE	SALTERN	SCHNAPS
RELATER	REVELRY	ROSOLIO	SALTIER	SCHOLAR
RELATOR	REVENGE	ROSTRAL	SALTIRE	SCHOLIA
RELEASE	REVENUE	ROSTRUM	SALTISH	SCHORLY
RELIANT	REVERER	ROTATOR	SALUTER	SCIATIC
RELIEVE	REVERIE	ROTIFER	SALVAGE	SCIENCE
RELIEVO	REVERSE	ROTUNDA	SAMOVAR	SCISSEL
RELIGHT	REVILER	ROUGHEN	SAMPLER	SCISSIL
REMARRY	REVISAL	ROUGHLY	SANABLE	SCOFFER
REMNANT	REVISER	ROULADE	SANCTUM	SCOLDER
REMODEL	REVISIT	ROULEAU	SANCTUS	SCOLLOP
REMORSE	REVIVAL	ROUNDEL	SANICLE	SCOOPER
REMOULD	REVIVER	ROUNDER	SANIOUS	SCORIAE
REMOUNT	REVOLVE	ROUNDLY	SAPAJOU	SCORIFY
REMOVAL	REWRITE	ROUSING	SAPIENT	SCORNER
REMOVED	REYNARD	ROUTINE	SAPLESS	SCORPIO
REMOVER	RHENISH	ROWLOCK	SAPLING	SCOURER
RENEWAL	RHIZOID	ROYALLY	SAPPHIC	SCOURGE
RENEWER	RHIZOMA	ROYALTY	SARACEN	SCRAGGY
RENTIER	RHIZOME	RUBASSE	SARCASM	SCRAPER
RENUENT	RHODIUM	RUBBING	SARCODE	SCRAPPY
REPAINT	RHOMBIC	RUBBISH	SARCOID	SCRATCH
REPINER	RHOMBUS	RUBELLA	SARCOMA	SCREECH
REPLACE	RHUBARB	RUBEOLA	SARCOUS	SCREWER
REPLANT	RIBBING	RUBIFIC	SARDINE	SCRIBAL
REPLETE	RICKETS	RUCKING	SARDIUS	SCROTAL
REPLEVY	RICKETY	RUDDILY	SATANIC	SCROTUM
REPLICA	RIGGING	RUDDOCK	SATCHEL	SCRUBBY
REPLIER	RIGHTER	RUFFIAN	SATIATE	SCRUNCH
REPOSAL	RIGHTLY	RUFFLED	SATIETY	SCRUPLE
REPOSER	RIGIDLY	RUFFLER	SATINET	SCUDDER
REPOSIT	RILIEVO	RUINATE	SATIRIC	SCUFFLE
REPRESS	RINGENT	RUINOUS	SATISFY	SCULLER
REPRINT	RINGLET	RULABLE	SATRAPY	SCULPIN
REPROOF	RIOTOUS	RUMMAGE	SATYRIC	SCUMBLE
REPROVE	RIPOSTE	RUNAWAY	SAUCILY	SCUMMER
REPTANT	RISIBLE	RUNDLET	SAUNTER	SCUPPER
REPTILE	RISIBLY	RUNNING	SAURIAN	SCUTAGE
REPULSE	RISSOLE	RUPTURE	SAUROID	SCUTATE
REQUEST	RIVALRY	RURALLY	SAUSAGE	SCUTTLE
REQUIEM	RIVETED	RUSSIAN	SAVABLE	SCYTHED
REQUIRE	RIVETER	RUSTILY	SAVANNA	SEALING
REQUITE	RIVULET	RUTHFUL	SAVELOY	SEAWARD
REREDOS	ROADWAY	RUTTISH	SAVIOUR	SEBACIC
RESCIND	ROARING		SAVOURY	SECEDER
RESCUER	ROASTER		SAWDUST	SECLUDE
RESEIZE	ROBBERY	**S**	SCABBED	SECRECY
RESERVE	ROCKERY		SCABIES	SECRETE
RESIDUE	ROEBUCK	SABAOTH	SCABRID	SECTARY
RESOLVE	ROGUERY	SABBATH	SCALDIC	SECTILE
RESOUND	ROGUISH	SACCULE	SCALENE	SECTION
RESPELL	ROISTER	SACKAGE	SCALLED	SEDULAR
RESPIRE	ROLLICK	SACKBUT	SCALLOP	SECURER
RESPITE	ROLLING	SACKING	SCALPEL	SEDILIA
RESPOND	ROLLOCK	SACRING	SCAMPER	SEDUCER
RESTFUL	ROMANCE	SACRIST	SCANDAL	SEEDILY
RESTIFF	ROMANIC	SADDLER	SCANTLY	SEEMING
RESTIVE	ROMMANY	SADNESS	SCAPULA	SEGMENT
	ROMAUNT	SAFFRON	SCARVES	

SEISMAL	SHERIFF	SIXFOLD	SOAKAGE	SPHERIC
SEISMIC	SHIFTER	SIXTEEN	SOAKING	SPICATE
SEIZURE	SKIMMER	SIXTHLY	SOBERLY	SPICERY
SEJEANT	SHINESS	SIZABLE	SOCCAGE	SPICILY
SELENIC	SHINGLE	SKEPTIC	SOCIETY	SPICULA
SELFISH	SHINGLY	SKETCHY	SOFTISH	SPICULE
SELVAGE	SHINING	SKILFUL	SOJOURN	SPILLER
SEMINAL	SHIPPER	SKILLED	SOLDIER	SPINACH
SEMITIC	SHIPPON	SKILLET	SOLICIT	SPINAGE
SENATOR	SHIPPER	SKIMMER	SOLIDLY	SPINDLE
SENATUS	SHIRKER	SKINFUL	SOLIPED	SPINNER
SENSORY	SHIVERY	SKINNER	SOLOIST	SPINNEY
SENSUAL	SHOOTER	SKIPPER	SOLUBLE	SPINOSE
SEQUELA	SHOPMAN	SKIRRET	SOLVENT	SPINOUS
SEQUENT	SHORTEN	SKULKER	SOMATIC	SPIRAEA
SEQUOIA	SHORTLY	SKULPIN	SOMEHOW	SPIRANT
SERAPHS	SHOTTEN	SKYLARK	SONANCE	SPITTER
SERFDOM	SHOUTER	SKYWARD	SONLESS	SPITTLE
SERIATE	SHOWERY	SLABBER	SONSHIP	SPLASHY
SERIOUS	SHOWILY	SLACKEN	SOOTHER	SPLEENY
SERPENT	SHOWING	SLACKLY	SOPHISM	SPLENIC
SERPIGO	SHOWMAN	SLANDER	SOPHIST	SPLOTCH
SERRATE	SHREDDY	SLANGEY	SOPRANI	SPOILER
SERRIED	SHRILLY	SLANTLY	SOPRANO	SPONDEE
SERVANT	SHRIVEL	SLASHED	SORCERY	SPONGER
SERVICE	SHRUBBY	SLATING	SORGHUM	SPONSOR
SERVILE	SHUDDER	SLAVERY	SORORAL	SPOONEY
SESSILE	SHUFFLE	SLAVISH	SOROSIS	SPORRAN
SESSION	SHUTTER	SLEEKLY	SORRILY	SPORULE
SETTING	SHUTTLE	SLEEPER	SOTTISI!	SPOTTED
SETTLED	SHYNESS	SLEEVED	SOUFFLE	SPOUSAL
SETTLER	SIAMANG	SLEIGHT	SOUNDLY	SPOUTER
SEVENTH	SIAMESE	SLENDER	SOURISH	SPRAYEY
SEVENTY	SICCATE	SLIDING	SOUTANE	SPRIGGY
SEVERAL	SICCITY	SLINESS	SPACIAL	SPRIGHT
SEXTAIN	SICKISH	SLINGER	SPANGLE	SPRINGE
SEXTANT	SIGHTED	SLIPPER	SPANGLY	SPRINGY
SHACKLE	SIGHTLY	SLITTER	SPANIEL	SPURNER
SHADILY	SIGMOID	SLOBBER	SPANISH	SPURRED
SHADING	SIGNIFY	SLOUGHY	SPANKER	SPURNER
SHADOOF	SIGNIOR	SLUBBER	SPANNER	SPURNEY
SHADOWY	SIGNORA	SLUMBER	SPARELY	SPUTTER
SHAFTED	SILENCE	SLYNESS	SPARING	SQUABBY
SHALLOP	SILICIC	SMARTEN	SPARKLE	SQUALID
SHALLOT	SILICLE	SMARTLY	SPARRER	SQUALLY
SHALLOW	SILICON	SMASHER	SPARROW	SQUALOR
SHAMBLE	SILIQUA	SMATTER	SPARTAN	SQUAMAE
SHAMMER	SILIQUE	SMELLER	SPASTIC	SQUASHY
SHAMPOO	SILLERY	SMELTER	SPATHAL	SQUEEZE
SHANDRY	SILLILY	SMILING	SPATHED	SQUELCH
SHANKED	SILURUS	SMITTEN	SPATHIC	SQUINCH
SHAPELY	SILVERN	SMOKILY	SPATIAL	STABBER
SHARDED	SILVERY	SMOKING	SPATTER	STABLER
SHARPEN	SILIMAR	SMOLDER	SPATTLE	STADDLE
SHARPER	SIMIOUS	SMOTHER	SPATULA	STADIUM
SHARPLY	SIMITAR	SMUGGLE	SPAWNER	STAGGER
SHASTER	SINCERE	SNAFFLE	SPEAKER	STAGING
SHASTRA	SINEWED	SNAKISH	SPECIAL	STAIDLY
SHATTER	SINKING	SNAPPER	SPECIES	STAINER
SHAVING	SINLESS	SNARLER	SPECIFY	STALKED
SHEAVES	SINOPLE	SNEERER	SPECKLE	STALKER
SHEARER	SINUATE	SNIGGER	SPECTER	STAMINA
SHEATHY	SINUOUS	SNIPPER	SPECTRE	STAMMER
SHEBEEN	SIRENIA	SNIPPET	SPECTRA	STAMPER
SHEDDER	SIRLOIN	SNORTER	SPECULA	STANDER
SHELLAC	SIRNAME	SNOUTED	SPELLER	STANIEL
SHELLED	SIROCCO	SNOWISH	SPELTER	STANNIC
SHELTER	SISTRUM	SNUFFER	SPENCER	STANZAS
SHELVES	SITTING	SNUFFLE	SPENDER	STAPLER
SHERBET	SITUATE	SNUGGLE	SPHERAL	STARCHY

STARING
STARKLY
STARLIT
STARRED
STARTER
STARTLE
STATELY
STATICS
STATION
STATIST
STATUED
STATURE
STATUTE
STAUNCH
STEALER
STEALTH
STEAMER
STEARIC
STEARIN
STEEPEN
STEEPER
STEEPLE
STEEPLY
STEERER
STELLAR
STENCIL
STEPPER
STEPSON
STERILE
STERLET
STERNAL
STERNED
STERNLY
STERNUM
STEWARD
STHENIC
STIBIAL
STICHIC
STICKER
STICKLE
STIFFEN
STIFFLY
STIGMAS
STILLER
STILTED
STILTON
STIMULI
STINTER
STIPEND
STIPPLE
STIPULE
STIRRER
STIRRUP
STOICAL
STOMACH
STOMATA
STONILY
STOPPER
STOPPLE
STORAGE
STORIED
STORIES
STOUTLY
STOWAGE
STRANGE
STRATUM
STRATUS
STRAYER
STREAKY
STREAMY

STRETCH
STRIATE
STRIGIL
STRIKER
STRINGY
STRIPED
STRIVER
STROKER
STROPHE
STRUMAE
STUBBED
STUBBLE
STUBBLY
STUDDED
STUDENT
STUDIED
STUDIER
STUDIES
STUFFER
STUMBLE
STUMPER
STUNNER
STUNTED
STUPEFY
STUTTER
STYGIAN
STYLISH
STYLIST
STYLITE
STYLOID
STYPTIC
SUASION
SUASIVE
SUAVELY
SUAVITY
SUBACID
SUBDEAN
SUBDUAL
SUBDUCE
SUBDUCT
SUBDUED
SUBDUER
SUBERIC
SUBJECT
SUBJOIN
SUBLIME
SUBSIDE
SUBSIDY
SUBSIST
SUBSOIL
SUBSUME
SUBTEND
SUBTILE
SUBVENE
SUBVERT
SUCCEED
SUCCESS
SUCCORY
SUCCOUR
SUCCUMB
SUCKING
SUCROSE
SUCTION
SUFFICE
SUFFUSE
SUGGEST
SUICIDE
SULCATE
SULKILY
SULLENS

SULPHUR
SULTANA
SUMLESS
SUMMARY
SUMMONS
SUMPTER
SUNBEAM
SUNDOWN
SUNFISH
SUNLESS
SUNRISE
SUNWARD
SUPPORT
SUPPOSE
SUPREME
SURBASE
SURCOAT
SURFACE
SURFEIT
SURGEON
SURGERY
SURLILY
SURLOIN
SURMISE
SURNAME
SURPASS
SURPLUS
SURTOUT
SURVIVE
SUSPECT
SUSPEND
SUSTAIN
SUTLING
SUTURAL
SUTURED
SWABBER
SWADDLE
SWAGGER
SWALLOW
SWARTHY
SWEARER
SWEATER
SWEDISH
SWEEPER
SWEETEN
SWEETLY
SWELTER
SWELTRY
SWIFTLY
SWILLER
SWIMMER
SWINDLE
SWINGLE
SWINISH
SWITZER
SWOLLEN
SYCOSIS
SYENITE
SYLPHID
SYNCOPE
SYNODAL
SYNODIC
SYNONYM
SYNOVIA
SYRINGA
SYRINGE
SYSTOLE

T

TABARET
TABBIES
TABETIC
TABINET
TABLEAU
TABORER
TABORET
TABULAE
TABULAR
TACITLY
TACTICS
TACTILE
TACTION
TACTUAL
TADPOLE
TAFFETA
TAFFETY
TALCOSE
TALCOUS
TALIPED
TALIPES
TALIPOT
TALKING
TALLAGE
TALLIER
TALLOWY
TALLIES
TAMABLE
TAMBOUR
TAMPION
TANAGER
TANGENT
TANGHIN
TANKARD
TANLING
TANNAGE
TANNERY
TANNING
TANTIVY
TANTRUM
TAPIOCA
TAPPING
TAPSTER
TARDILY
TARNISH
TARTISH
TASTILY
TATTING
TATTLER
TAUNTER
TAURINE
TAXABLE
TAXICAB
TEACHER
TEARFUL
TEASING
TECHILY
TECHNIC
TEDIOUS
TEEMING
TEGULAR
TELLING
TEMPERA
TEMPEST
TEMPLAR
TEMPLET
TEMPTER

TENABLE
TENANCY
TENDRIL
TENFOLD
TENIOID
TENSELY
TENSILE
TENSION
TENSITY
TENTHLY
TENUITY
TENUOUS
TERBIUM
TERMINI
TERMITE
TERNARY
TERNATE
TERRACE
TERRENE
TERRIER
TERRIFY
TERSELY
TERTIAN
TESSERA
TESTACY
TESTATE
TESTIFY
TESTILY
TETANIC
TETANUS
TEXTILE
TEXTUAL
TEXTURE
THALAMI
THALLUS
THANAGE
THEATER
THEATRE
THEORBO
THEOREM
THEREAT
THEREBY
THEREIN
THEREOF
THEREON
THERETO
THERMAE
THERMAL
THERMIC
THEURGY
THICKEN
THICKET
THICKLY
THIEVES
THILLER
THIMBLE
THINKER
THIRDLY
THIRSTY
THISTLE
THISTLY
THITHER
THROMBI
THOUGHT
THREADY
THRIFTY
THRIVER
THROATY
THROUGH
THROWER

THRUMMY	TORTIVE	TRINGLE	TWIBILL	UNIFORM
THUGGEE	TORTURE	TRINITY	TWIDDLE	UNITARY
THUMBED	TORYISM	TRINKET	TWINING	UNITIVE
THUMMIN	TOTALLY	TRIOLET	TWINKLE	UNITIES
THUMPER	TOTEMIC	TRIPANG	TWINNED	UNKEMPT
THUNDER	TOTTERY	TRIPERY	TWISTER	UNKNOWN
THYROID	TOUCHER	TRIPLET	TWITTER	UNLATCH
THYRSUS	TOUGHEN	TRIPOLI	TYMPANA	UNLEARN
THYSELF	TOUGHLY	TRIPPER	TYPHOID	UNLEASH
TIARAED	TOURIST	TRIREME	TYPHOON	UNLOOSE
TICKING	TOURNEY	TRISECT	TYPHOUS	UNLUCKY
TICKLER	TOWARDS	TRISMUS	TYPICAL	UNMANLY
TIDINGS	TOWERED	TRITELY	TYRANNY	UNMIXED
TIERCEL	TOXICAL	TRIUMPH	TZARINA	UNMOVED
TIFFANY	TOYSHOP	TRIVIAL		UNNAMED
TIGHTEN	TRACERY	TROCHAR		UNNERVE
TIGHTLY	TRACHEA	TROCHEE	**U**	UNNOTED
TIGRESS	TRACING	TRODDEN		UNOWNED
TIGRINE	TRACKER	TROLLER	ULCERED	UNPAVED
TIGRISH	TRADING	TROLLEY	ULULATE	UNQUIET
TILLAGE	TRADUCE	TROLLOP	UMBILIC	UNRAVEL
TIMBREL	TRAFFIC	TROOPER	UMBRAGE	UNREADY
TIMEOUS	TRAGEDY	TROPIST	UNACTED	UNSCREW
TIMIDLY	TRAILER	TROTTER	UNAIDED	UNSHORN
TINDERY	TRAINED	TROUBLE	UNARMED	UNSIZED
TINNING	TRAINER	TROUNCE	UNASKED	UNSLING
TINTING	TRAIPSE	TRUANCY	UNAWARE	UNSOUND
TINWARE	TRAITOR	TRUCKER	UNBEGOT	UNSPENT
TIPPLER	TRAMMEL	TRUCKLE	UNBLEST	UNSWEPT
TIPSILY	TRAMPER	TRUFFLE	UNBOSOM	UNSWORN
TITANIC	TRAMPLE	TRUMPET	UNBOUND	UNTAMED
TITHING	TRAMWAY	TRUNDLE	UNBRACE	UNTAXED
TITLARK	TRANSIT	TRUNKED	UNBURNT	UNTEACH
TITLING	TRANSOM	TRUSSED	UNCANNY	UNTRIED
TITMICE	TRAPEZE	TRUSTEE	UNCARED	UNTRULY
TITRATE	TRAPPER	TRUSTER	UNCHAIN	UNTRUTH
TITULAR	TRAVAIL	TRIABLE	UNCIVIL	UNTWINE
TOADIES	TRAWLER	TRYABLE	UNCLASP	UNTWIST
TOASTER	TREACLE	TUBBING	UNCLEAN	UNUSUAL
TOBACCO	TREADER	TUBBISH	UNCLOAK	UNWEAVE
TOBOGAN	TREADLE	TUBULAR	UNCLOSE	UNWOOED
TODDLER	TREASON	TUESDAY	UNCOUTH	UNWRUNG
TOGATED	TREATER	TUITION	UNCOVER	UPBRAID
TOILFUL	TREDDLE	TUMBLER	UNCROWN	UPBREAK
TOLLAGE	TREFOIL	TUMBREL	UNCTION	UPHEAVE
TOMBOLA	TRELLIS	TUMBRIL	UNDATED	UPRAISE
TOMFOOL	TREMBLE	TUMIDLY	UNDERDO	UPRIGHT
TOMPION	TREMOLO	TUMULAR	UNDERGO	UPROUSE
TONGUED	TRENAIL	TUMULUS	UNDOING	UPSTART
TONNAGE	TRENTAL	TUNABLE	UNDRESS	UPTHROW
TONSILE	TREPANG	TUNABLY	UNDYING	UPWARDS
TONSURE	TRESSED	TUNEFUL	UNEARTH	URAEMIA
TONTINE	TRESSEL	TUNNAGE	UNEQUAL	URANIUM
TOOLING	TRESTLE	TUNNIES	UNFITLY	URETHRA
TOOTHED	TRIABLE	TURBINE	UNFROCK	URGENCY
TOPIARY	TRIADIC	TURGENT	UNGLOVE	URINARY
TOPICAL	TRIBUNE	TURKISH	UNGODLY	URINATE
TOPLESS	TRIBUTE	TURKOIS	UNGUENT	URODELA
TOPMAST	TRICKER	TURMOIL	UNHANDY	URODELE
TOPMOST	TRICKLE	TURNERY	UNHAPPY	USELESS
TOPPING	TRICKSY	TURNING	UNHARDY	USUALLY
TORMENT	TRIDENT	TURNKEY	UNHEARD	USURPER
TORMINA	TRIFLER	TURNSOL	UNHINGE	UTENSIL
TORNADO	TRIFORM	TUSSOCK	UNHITCH	UTERINE
TORPEDO	TRIGAMY	TUTELAR	UNHOPED	UTILITY
TORPIFY	TRIGGER	TWADDLE	UNHORSE	UTILIZE
TORREFY	TRIGRAM	TWADDLY	UNHOUSE	UTOPIAN
TORRENT	TRILITH	TWANGLE	UNIAXIAL	UTRICLE
TORSION	TRILOGY	TWATTLE	UNICORN	UTTERER
TORTILE	TRIMMER	TWELFTH	UNIDEAL	UTTERLY

UXORIAL

V

VACANCY
VACCINE
VACUITY
VACUOLE
VACUOUS
VACUUMS
VAGINAE
VAGINAL
VAGRANT
VAGUELY
VALANCE
VALENCE
VALENCY
VALIANT
VALIDLY
VALLARY
VALLEYS
VALONIA
VALVATE
VALVULE
VAMPIRE
VANILLA
VANTAGE
VAPIDLY
VAPOURY
VARIANT
VARIETY
VARIOLA
VARIOUS
VARICES
VARNISH
VASCULA
VATICAN
VAULTED
VAULTER
VAUNTER
VAVASOR
VEDETTE
VEERING
VEGETAL
VEHICLE
VEINING
VEINLET
VELARIA
VELVETY
VENDACE
VENISON
VENTAGE
VENTRAL
VENTURE
VERANDA
VERBENA
VERBOSE
VERDANT
VERDICT
VERDURE
VERMEIL
VERNIER
VERNINE
VERSIFY
VERSION
VERTIGO
VERVAIN
VESICAL
VESICLE

VESTIGE
VESTURE
VETERAN
VEXILLA
VIADUCT
VIBRANT
VIBRATE
VIBRIOS
VICEROY
VICIOUS
VICTORY
VICTUAL
VICUGNA
VIDETTE
VIDIMUS
VIDUITY
VILLAGE
VILLAIN
VILLEIN
VILLOUS
VILLOSE
VINCULA
VINEGAR
VINTAGE
VINTNER
VIOLATE
VIOLENT
VIOLIST
VIRELAY
VIRGATE
VIRTUAL
VISAGED
VISCERA
VISCOUS
VISIBLE
VISIBLY
VISITER
VISITOR
VISORED
VITALLY
VITIATE
VITRIFY
VITRIOL
VIVARIA
VIVIDLY
VIVIFIC
VIXENLY
VOCABLE
VOCALIC
VOCALLY
VOLAPUK
VOLCANO
VOLLEYS
VOLTAIC
VOLUBLE
VOLUBLY
VOLUMED
VOLUTED
VOUCHER
VOYAGER
VULGATE
VULPINE
VULTURE
VULTURE

W

WADDING
WADDLER
WADDLES

WADMOLL
WAFTAGE
WAGERER
WAGGERY
WAGGISH
WAGONER
WAGTAIL
WAILING
WAKEFUL
WAKENER
WALKING
WALLABY
WALLING
WALLOON
WALTZER
WANNESS
WANNISH
WARBLER
WARFARE
WARLIKE
WARNING
WARRANT
WARRING
WARRIOR
WASHING
WASPISH
WASSAIL
WASTAGE
WASTING
WATCHER
WATERED
WATTLED
WAVELET
WAVERER
WAYSIDE
WAYWARD
WAYWORN
WEALDEN
WEALTHY
WEARILY
WEARING
WEASAND
WEAZAND
WEATHER
WEAVING
WEBBING
WEDDING
WEDLOCK
WEEPING
WEEVILY
WEIGHER
WEIGHTY
WELCOME
WELFARE
WENCHER
WERGILD
WERWOLF
WESTERN
WESTING
WETNESS
WETTISH
WHALING
WHARVES
WHEATEN
WHEEDLE
WHEELED
WHEELER
WHENE'ER
WHEREAS
WHEREAT

WHEREBY
WHEREIN
WHEREOF
WHEREON
WHERETO
WHERE'ER
WHETHER
WHETTER
WHIFFLE
WHIMPER
WHIMSEY
WHIPPER
WHIRLER
WHISKER
WHISKEY
WHISPER
WHISTLE
WHITHER
WHITING
WHITISH
WHITLOW
WHITSUN
WHITTLE
WHOEVER
WHOPPER
WHORISH
WHORLED
WIDGEON
WIDOWER
WIELDER
WIGGERY
WIGGING
WIGLESS
WILDING
WILDISH
WILEFUL
WILLING
WILLOWY
WINDAGE
WINDING
WINDROW
WINGLET
WINNING
WINSOME
WINTERY
WISHFUL
WISTFUL
WISTITI
WITHERS
WITHOUT
WITHIES
WITLESS
WITLING
WITNESS
WITTILY
WIZENED
WOFULLY
WOLFISH
WOLFKIN
WOLFRAM
WOMANLY
WOODMAN
WORDIER
WORDILY
WORDING
WORKING
WORKMAN
WORLDLY
WORRIER

WORSHIP
WORSTED
WOUNDER
WOURALI
WRANGLE
WRAPPER
WREATHE
WREATHY
WRECKER
WRESTER
WRESTLE
WRIGGLE
WRINGER
WRINKLE
WRINKLY
WRITING
WRITTEN
WRONGER
WRONGLY
WROUGHT
WRYNECK
WRYNESS

X

XANTHIC
XANTHIN
XERASIA
XEROTES
XIPHOID

Y

YACHTER
YCLEPED
YELLING
YIELDER
YOUNGLY
YOUNKER
YTTRIUM

Z

ZANYISM
ZEALOUS
ZEBRINE
ZEDOARY
ZEOLITE
ZETETIC
ZINCODE
ZINCOID
ZINCOUS
ZITHERN
ZONULAR
ZONULET
ZOOGAMY
ZOOGONY
ZOOGENY
ZOOLITE
ZOOLOGY
ZOONOMY
ZOOTOMY
ZYMOGEN
ZYMOSIS
ZYMOTIC
ZYMURGY

EIGHT-LETTER WORDS

A

AARDVARK
AARDWOLF
ABATTOIR
ABBATIAL
ABDICANT
ABDICATE
ABDUCENT
ABDUCTOR
ABERRANT
ABETMENT
ABEYANCE
ABHORRER
ABJECTLY
ABLATION
ABLATIVE
ABLEPSIA
ABLUTION
ABNEGATE
ABOMASUS
ABORTION
ABORTIVE
ABRADANT
ABRASION
ABROGATE
ABRUPTLY
ABSCISSA
ABSENTEE
ABSENTLY
ABSINTHE
ABSOLUTE
ABSOLVER
ABSONANT
ABSTERGE
ABSTRACT
ABSTRUSE
ABSURDLY
ABUNDANT
ABUTMENT
ACADEMIC
ACANTHUS
ACARIDAN
ACARPOUS
ACAULOUS
ACAULINE
ACCADIAN
ACCENTOR
ACCEPTER
ACCIDENT
ACCOLADE
ACCOUTRE
ACCREDIT
ACCRESCE
ACCURACY
ACCURATE
ACCURSED
ACCUSTOM
ACENTRIC
ACERBITY
ACERVATE
ACESCENT
ACHIEVER
ACICULAR

ACIDIFIC
ACIERAGE
ACONITIC
ACONITIN
ACORN-CUP
ACOSMISM
ACOUSTIC
ACQUAINT
ACQUIRER
ACREABLE
ACRIDITY
ACRIMONY
ACRITUDE
ACROLITH
ACROMION
ACROSTIC
ACROTISM
ACTINISM
ACTIVELY
ACTIVITY
ACTUALLY
ACULEATE
ADAMITIC
ADDENDUM
ADDITION
ADDITIVE
ADDUCENT
ADDUCTOR
ADENITIS
ADEQUACY
ADEQUATE
ADHERENT
ADHESION
ADHESIVE
ADIANTUM
ADJACENT
ADJUSTER
ADJUTANT
ADMONISH
ADOPTION
ADOPTIVE
ADORABLE
ADORABLY
ADROITLY
ADSCRIPT
ADULATOR
ADULTERY
ADUNCOUS
ADVANCER
ADVISORY
ADVOCACY
ADVOCATE
ADVOWSON
AERATION
AERIALLY
AERIFORM
AEROCYST
AEROLITE
AEROLOGY
AERONAUT
AEROSTAT
AESTHETE
AESTIVAL
AFFECTED
AFFERENT

AFFIANCE
AFFINITY
AFFIRMER
AFFLATUS
AFFLUENT
AFFOREST
AFFRIGHT
AFFUSION
AGAR-AGAR
AGASTRIC
AGGRIEVE
AGIOTAGE
AGITATED
AGITATOR
AGNOSTIC
AGNUS DEI
AGRAPHIA
AGRARIAN
AGRESTIC
AGRIMONY
AGRONOMY
AGUE-CAKE
AIGUILLE
AILANTUS
AIR-BORNE
AIR-BRAKE
AIR-BUILT
AIR-DRAIN
AIRINESS
AIR-PLANT
AIR-SHAFT
AIR-TIGHT
ALACRITY
ALARM-GUN
ALARMING
ALARMIST
ALBACORE
ALBINISM
ALBURNUM
ALCHEMIC
ALDEHYDE
ALDERMAN
ALEATORY
ALE-BERRY
ALE-HOUSE
ALGERIAN
ALGIDITY
ALGUAZIL
ALIENAGE
ALIENATE
ALIENISM
ALIENIST
ALKALIFY
ALKALIZE
ALKALINE
ALKALOID
ALKARSIN
ALLEGORY
ALL-FOURS
ALLIANCE
ALLOCATE
ALLODIAL
ALLODIUM
ALLOPATH
ALLOYAGE

ALLSPICE
ALLURING
ALLUSION
ALLUSIVE
ALLUVIAL
ALLUVION
ALLUVIUM
ALMIGHTY
ALMS-DEED
ALOPECIA
ALPHABET
ALPINERY
ALQUIFOU
ALSATIAN
ALTARAGE
ALTERANT
ALTHOUGH
ALTITUDE
ALTRUISM
ALUMINUM
ALUM-ROOT
ALVEOLAR
ALVEOLUS
AMADAVAT
AMARANTH
AMAZEDLY
AMBITION
AMBLOTIC
AMBLYGON
AMBROSIA
AMBULANT
AMENABLE
AMENABLY
AMERICAN
AMETHYST
AMICABLE
AMICABLY
AMMONIAC
AMMONITE
AMMONIUM
AMOEBEAN
AMORETTI
AMORTIZE
AMPHIBIA
AMPHIPOD
AMPHORAL
AMPUTATE
ANABASIS
ANACONDA
ANAGLYPH
ANALOGUE
ANALYSIS
ANALYTIC
ANARCHIC
ANASARCA
ANATHEMA
ANCESTOR
ANCESTRY
ANCHORET
ANECDOTE
ANEURISM
ANGELICA
ANGLICAN
ANIMATED
ANISETTE

ANK EIGHT-LETTER WORDS BEA

ANKYLOSE
ANNALIST
ANNOTATE
ANNOUNCE
ANNUALLY
ANNULATA
ANNULATE
ANNULOSE
ANOINTER
ANSERINE
ANSWERER
ANTALGIC
ANT-EATER
ANTECEDE
ANTEDATE
ANTELOPE
ANTEPAST
ANTERIOR
ANTEROOM
ANTIDOTE
ANTILOGY
ANTIMASK
ANTIMONY
ANTIPHON
ANTIPODE
ANTIPOPE
ANTITYPE
ANTLERED
ANYTHING
ANYWHERE
AORISTIC
APERIENT
APERTURE
APHELION
APHORISM
APIARIST
APODOSIS
APOLOGUE
APOPLEXY
APOSTASY
APOSTATE
APOSTEME
APOTHEGM
APPANAGE
APPARENT
APPENDIX
APPETENT
APPETITE
APPETIZE
APPLAUSE
APPLE-PIE
APPOSITE
APPRAISE
APPROACH
APPROVAL
APPROVER
APTEROUS
APTITUDE
APYRETIC
AQUARIUM
AQUARIUS
AQUEDUCT
AQUIFORM
AQUILINE
ARBALIST
ARBORIST
ARBOURED
ARCADIAN
ARCHAEAN

ARCHAISM
ARCHDUKE
ARCHNESS
ARCHWISE
ARCTURUS
ARDENTLY
ARGENTAL
ARGONAUT
ARGUABLE
ARGUMENT
ARHIZOUS
ARIANISM
ARMAMENT
ARMATURE
ARMENIAN
ARMINIAN
ARMORIAL
ARMOURER
ARMY-LIST
ARMY-WORM
AROMATIC
ARPEGGIO
ARQUEBUS
ARRANGER
ARRESTER
ARROGANT
ARROGATE
ARTERIAL
ARTESIAN
ARTFULLY
ARTIFICE
ARTISTIC
ARUSPICY
ASBESTOS
ASCIDIAN
ASCIDIUM
ASPERITY
ASPHODEL
ASPHYXIA
ASPIRANT
ASPIRATE
ASPIRING
ASPOROUS
ASSAILER
ASSASSIN
ASSAYING
ASSEMBLE
ASSEMBLY
ASSENTER
ASSERTOR
ASSESSOR
ASSIGNEE
ASSIGNER
ASSONANT
ASSORTED
ASSUAGER
ASSUMING
ASSYRIAN
ASTERISK
ASTERISM
ASTEROID
ASTHENIA
ASTONISH
ASTRAGAL
ASTUCITY
ASTUTELY
ATHELING
ATHENIAN
ATHEROMA

ATHLETIC
ATLANTES
ATLANTIC
ATMOLOGY
ATOMIZER
ATONABLE
ATROCITY
ATTACKER
ATTEMPER
ATTENDER
ATTESTER
ATTICISM
ATTITUDE
ATTORNEY
AUCIPIAL
AUDACITY
AUDIENCE
AUDITORY
AUGURIAL
AUGUSTAN
AUGUSTLY
AURICULA
AURIFORM
AUSTRIAN
AUTOCRAT
AUTO-DE-FE
AUTO-DA-FE
AUTONOMY
AUTOPSIA
AUTOTYPE
AUTUMNAL
AVE-MARIA
AVERMENT
AVERSION
AVIATION
AVIFAUNA
AVOUCHER
AVOWABLE
AVOWEDLY
AVULSION
AWEATHER

B

BABYHOOD
BACCARAT
BACCHANT
BACHELOR
BACILLAR
BACILLUS
BACKBITE
BACKBONE
BACK-DOOR
BACKHAND
BACKMOST
BACKSIDE
BACK-STAY
BACKWARD
BACONIAN
BACULITE
BADIGEON
BAGGAGE
BAILABLE
BAILMENT
BAKSHISH
BALANCER
BALD-ERNE
BALDNESS
BALDRICK

BALE-FIRE
BALL-COCK
BALLISTA
BALSAMIC
BALUSTER
BANDELET
BAND-FISH
BANISHER
BANISTER
BANK-NOTE
BANKRUPT
BANNERED
BANNERET
BANTERER
BANTLING
BANXRING
BAPTIZER
BARBACAN
BARBARIC
BARBECUE
BARBERRY
BARBETTE
BARBICAN
BARDLING
BAREFOOT
BARENESS
BARGEMAN
BARITONE
BARNACLE
BARN-YARD
BARONAGE
BARONESS
BARONIAL
BAROUCHE
BARRATOR
BARRATRY
BARRETOR
BARTERER
BARTIZAN
BARYTONE
BASALTIC
BASANITE
BASCINET
BASE-BALL
BASE-BORN
BASELESS
BASE-LINE
BASEMENT
BASENESS
BASICITY
BASILICA
BASILISK
BASS-CLEF
BASSINET
BASS-VIOL
BASTARDY
BATAVIAN
BAT-HORSE
BAYADERE
BAYBERRY
BDELLIUM
BEACONED
BEAD-ROLL
BEADS-MAN
BEAM-ENDS
BEAMLESS
BEAM-TREE
BEAN-KING
BEARABLE
BEARABLY

85

BEARSKIN
BEARWARD
BEATIFIC
BEAUTIFY
BEAVERED
BECHAMEL
BECHANCE
BECOMING
BEDABBLE
BEDESMAN
BEDRENCH
BEDSTEAD
BEDSTRAW
BEEF-WOOD
BEES'-WING
BEETLING
BEET-ROOT
BEFRIEND
BEGETTER
BEGGARLY
BEGINNER
BEGRUDGE
BEGUILER
BEHEMOTH
BEHOLDEN
BEHOLDER
BELABOUR
BELIEVER
BELITTLE
BELL-PULL
BELL-ROPE
BELLYFUL
BELLY-GOD
BEMOANER
BENDABLE
BENEDICK
BENEFICE
BENGALEE
BENIGNLY
BENJAMIN
BEPRAISE
BEQUEATH
BERGAMOT
BERGMEHL
BERTHAGE
BESIEGER
BESLAVER
BESOTTED
BESPREAD
BESPRENT
BESTIARY
BESTOWAL
BESTOWER
BESTRIDE
BETEL-NUT
BETRAYAL
BETRAYER
BEVERAGE
BEWAILER
BEWILDER
BEZONIAN
BIBLICAL
BIBULOUS
BICONVEX
BICUSPID
BIDDABLE
BIDENTAL
BIENNIAL
BIGAMIST
BIGNONIA

BILANDER
BILBERRY
BILL-HOOK
BILLY-BOY
BILOBATE
BIMANOUS
BIMENSAL
BIND-WEED
BINNACLE
BINOMIAL
BIOLOGIC
BIOMETRY
BIOPLASM
BIPAROUS
BIRAMOUS
BIRD-BOLT
BIRD-CALL
BIRD-LIME
BIRD'S-EYE
BIRTHDAY
BISERIAL
BISEXUAL
BISTOURY
BITHEISM
BITING-IN
BITINGLY
BITNOBEN
BITTACLE
BITTERLY
BIWEEKLY
BLACK-CAP
BLACKING
BLACKISH
BLACK-LEG
BLACK-TIN
BLACK-WAD
BLADDERY
BLAMABLE
BLAMABLY
BLAMEFUL
BLANDISH
BLASTULA
BLAZONER
BLAZONRY
BLEACHER
BLEEDING
BLENHEIM
BLESSING
BLINDAGE
BLINDING
BLINKARD
BLISSFUL
BLISTERY
BLITHELY
BLIZZARD
BLOCKADE
BLOCKISH
BLOCK-TIN
BLOODILY
BLOOMERY
BLOOMING
BLOSSOMY
BLOW-HOLE
BLOWPIPE
BLUDGEON
BLUEBELL
BLUE-BIRD
BLUE-BOOK
BLUENESS
BLUE-PILL

BLUNTISH
BLUSHING
BOARDING
BOASTFUL
BOAT-BILL
BOAT-HOOK
BOBBINET
BOBOLINK
BOCK-BEER
BODEMENT
BODILESS
BOG-EARTH
BOGGLING
BOHEMIAN
BOLDNESS
BOLT-HEAD
BOLT-ROPE
BOMBAZET
BONA FIDE
BONDMAID
BONE-DUST
BONE-LACE
BONE-MILL
BONIFACE
BONNETED
BOOBYISH
BOOK-DEBT
BOOK-OATH
BOOK-POST
BOOK-WORM
BOOKWORM
BOOT-HOOK
BOOT-HOSE
BOOT-JACK
BOOT-LACE
BOOTLESS
BOOT-RACK
BOOT-TREE
BOOT-LAST
BORACHIO
BORACITE
BORDERER
BORECOLE
BORROWER
BOSTANGI
BOTANIST
BOTANIZE
BOTCHERY
BOTHERER
BOTRYOID
BOTTOMED
BOTTOMRY
BOUNCING
BOUNDARY
BOURGEON
BOW-DRILL
BOWSPRIT
BOYISHLY
BRACELET
BRACHIAL
BRACKISH
BRADYPOD
BRAGGART
BRAIDING
BRAINISH
BRAKEMAN
BRAKE-VAN
BRANCHED
BRANDIED
BRANDISH

BRAND-NEW
BRATTICE
BRAWLING
BRAZENLY
BREAD-NUT
BREAKAGE
BREASTED
BREATHER
BREECHED
BREECHES
BREEDING
BRETHREN
BRETTICE
BREVIARY
BREVIATE
BREVIPED
BREWSTER
BRIBABLE
BRICKBAT
BRICK-TEA
BRIGHTEN
BRIGHTLY
BRIMLESS
BRIMMING
BRINDLED
BRINE-PAN
BRINE-PIT
BRISTLED
BRITZSKA
BROACHER
BROCADED
BROCATEL
BROCCOLI
BROCHURE
BROIDERY
BROKENLY
BROMELIA
BRONCHIA
BRONCHUS
BRONZITE
BROOKLET
BROUGHAM
BROWBEAT
BROWNING
BROWNISH
BRUNETTE
BRUTALLY
BRYOLOGY
BUCK-SHOT
BUCKSKIN
BUDDHISM
BUDDHIST
BUFONITE
BUILDING
BUKSHISH
BULK-HEAD
BULL-CALF
BULLETIN
BULL-FROG
BULL-HEAD
BULL'S-EYE
BULRUSHY
BUNCOMBE
BUNGALOW
BUNG-HOLE
BUNGLING
BUNTLINE
BUOYANCY
BURGAMOT
BURGANET

BURGEOIS
BURGLARY
BURGRAVE
BURGUNDY
BURLETTA
BURNABLE
BURNOOSE
BURNT-EAR
BURROWER
BUSINESS
BUSKINED
BUSY-BODY
BUTCHERY
BUTTRESS
BY-CORNER
BY-STREET

C

CA3ALLER
CABIN-BOY
CABRIOLE
CACHALOT
CACHUCHA
CACODYLE
CACOLOGY
CADASTRE
CADUCEAN
CADUCEUS
CADUCOUS
CAESURAL
CAFFEINE
CAGELING
CAIMACAM
CAJOLERY
CALABASH
CALAMARY
CALAMINE
CALAMINT
CALAMITE
CALAMITY
CALCINER
CALC-SPAR
CALC-TUFF
CALCULAR
CALCULUS
CALENDAR
CALENDER
CALF-LOVE
CALIFATE
CALIPASH
CALIPERS
CALISAYA
CALL-BIRD
CALL-NOTE
CALMNESS
CALOTYPE
CALYCINE
CALYCOID
CALYPTRA
CAMBRIAN
CAMELEON
CAMELLINE
CAMELLIA
CAMISADE
CAMISOLE
CAMOMILE
CAMPAIGN
CAMPHINE

CANADIAN
CANAILLE
CANALIZE
CANASTER
CANCELLI
CANCROID
CANDIDLY
CANE-MILL
CANISTER
CANNIBAL
CANNIKIN
CANOEIST
CANONESS
CANONIST
CANONIZE
CANOPIED
CANOROUS
CANTICLE
CANTONAL
CANZONET
CAPACITY
CAPELINE
CAPITATE
CAPRIOLE
CAPSICUM
CAPSIZAL
CAPSULAR
CAPTIOUS
CAPUCHIN
CAPYBARA
CARABINE
CARACARA
CARACOLE
CARAPACE
CARAP-OIL
CARBOLIC
CARBONIC
CARBURET
CARCAJOU
CARCANET
CARDAMOM
CARD-CASE
CARDIGAN
CARDINAL
CARDITIS
CARELESS
CARE-WORN
CARIACOU
CARIATID
CARILLON
CARINATE
CARNALLY
CARNAUBA
CARNEOUS
CARNIVAL
CAROLINE
CAROUSAL
CAROUSEL
CAROUSER
CARRIAGE
CARRIOLE
CARROCHE
CARTLOAD
CARTROOT
CARUCATE
CARUNCLE
CARYATID
CASCABEL
CASEMATE
CASEMENT

CASE-SHOT
CASE-WORM
CASH-BOOK
CASHMERE
CASTANET
CASTAWAY
CAST-IRON
CASTLING
CASTRATE
CASUALLY
CASUALTY
CATACOMB
CATAPULT
CATARACT
CATCHFLY
CATCHING
CATEGORY
CATENARY
CATERESS
CATHEDRA
CATHETER
CATONIAN
CAT'S-TAIL
CAUDICLE
CAULDRON
CAULICLE
CAUSABLE
CAUSALLY
CAUSEWAY
CAUTIOUS
CAVALIER
CAVATINA
CAVE-BEAR
CAVERNED
CAVICORN
CAVILLER
CELERITY
CELIBACY
CELIBATE
CELLARER
CELLARET
CELLULAR
CEMETERY
CENOBITE
CENOTAPH
CENTUARY
CENTOIST
CENTUPLE
CEPHALIC
CERASTES
CERATOSE
CERBERUS
CEREBRAL
CEREBRIN
CEREBRUM
CEREMONY
CERULEAN
CERULEIN
CERUSITE
CERVICAL
CESAREAN
CESSPOOL
CETACEAN
CETALITY
CHAIRMAN
CHALDAIC
CHALDRON
CHAMFRON
CHAMPION
CHANCERY

CHANDLER
CHANTAGE
CHAP-BOOK
CHAPERON
CHAPITER
CHAPLAIN
CHAPTREL
CHARCOAL
CHARLOCK
CHARMING
CHARTISM
CHARTIST
CHASE-GUN
CHASSEUR
CHASTELY
CHASTISE
CHASTITY
CHASUBLE
CHAUFFER
CHEATERY
CHEATING
CHEERFUL
CHEERILY
CHEERING
CHEMICAL
CHENILLE
CHERUBIC
CHESS-MAN
CHESTNUT
CHETVERT
CHICANER
CHICK-PEA
CHIEFDOM
CHIEFERY
CHIEFESS
CHILDBED
CHILDING
CHILDISH
CHILDREN
CHILIASM
CHILLING
CHIMAERA
CHINA-INK
CHINAMAN
CHINLESS
CHIPMUNK
CHIPPING
CHIRAGRA
CHIT-CHAT
CHIVALRY
CHLOASMA
CHLORIDE
CHLORINE
CHLORITE
CHOICELY
CHOLERIC
CHOPPING
CHORAGUS
CHORALLY
CHOULTRY
CHOW-CHOW
CHRISMAL
CHRISTEN
CHROMATE
CHROMIUM
CHROMITE
CHUFFILY
CHURLISH
CHYLURIA
CHYMICAL

CIBORIUM
CICATRIX
CICERONE
CIDERKIN
CI-DEVANT
CILIATED
CIMOLITE
CINCHONA
CINCTURE
CINERARY
CINNABAR
CINNAMON
CIRCULAR
CIRRIPED
CISELURE
CISTELLA
CITATION
CITATORY
CIVET-CAT
CIVILIAN
CIVILIST
CIVILITY
CIVILIZE
CLAIMANT
CLAMANCY
CLANGOUR
CLANNISH
CLANSHIP
CLANSMAN
CLAP-SILL
CLAPTRAP
CLAQUEUR
CLARENCE
CLASSIFY
CLAVECIN
CLAVICLE
CLAWBACK
CLAY-COLD
CLAY-MARL
CLAY-MILL
CLAYMORE
CLEANSER
CLEARING
CLEAVAGE
CLEAVERS
CLEMATIS
CLEMENCY
CLENCHER
CLERICAL
CLEVERLY
CLEW-LINE
CLIENTAL
CLIMATIC
CLIMBING
CLINCHER
CLINICAL
CLIPPING
CLIQUISH
CLIQUISM
CLOAK-BAG
CLODDISH
CLODPOLL
CLOISTER
CLOTHIER
CLOTHING
CLOUDILY
CLOUDLET
CLOVERED
CLOWNISH
CLUBBIST

CLUB-FOOT
CLUB-MOSS
CLUB-ROOM
CLUMSILY
CLYPEATE
COACH-BOX
COACH-DOG
COACHMAN
COACTIVE
COAGENCY
COAGULUM
COALESCE
COAL-FISH
COAL-MINE
COAL-WORK
COARSELY
COASTING
COBALTIC
CO-BISHOP
COBWEBBY
COCCULUS
COCKADED
COCKATOO
COCK-BOAT
COCK-CROW
COCKEREL
COCK-LOFT
COCKSURE
COCKTAIL
CODIFIER
COERCION
COERCIVE
COEXTEND
COFFERED
COGENTLY
COGITATE
COGNOMEN
COG-WHEEL
COHERENT
COHESION
COHESIVE
COHOBATE
COIFFURE
COINCIDE
CO-INHERE
COLANDER
COLDNESS
COLE-SEED
COLEWORT
COLICKED
COLLAPSE
COLLARET
COLLATOR
COLLIERY
COLLOQUY
COLONIAL
COLONIST
COLONIZE
COLOPHON
COLOSSAL
COLOSSUS
COLOURED
COLUMNAR
COLUMNED
COMATOSE
COMBINED
COMBINER
COMEDIAN
COMETARY
COMITIAL

COMMENCE
COMMERCE
COMMONER
COMMONLY
COMMUNAL
COMPILER
COMPLAIN
COMPLECT
COMPLETE
COMPLICE
COMPLIER
COMPLINE
COMPOSED
COMPOSER
COMPOUND
COMPRESS
COMPRISE
COMPUTER
CONCEDER
CONCEIVE
CONCERTO
CONCHOID
CONCLAVE
CONCLUDE
CONCRETE
CONDENSE
CONFEREE
CONFERVA
CONFLATE
CONFLICT
CONFOUND
CONFRERE
CONFRONT
CONFUSED
CONGENER
CONGLOBE
CONGRESS
CONGREVE
CONICITY
CONIFORM
CONJOINT
CONJUGAL
CONJUNCT
CONJURER
CONNIVER
CONQUEST
CONSERVE
CONSIDER
CONSOLER
CONSPIRE
CONSTANT
CONSTRUE
CONSULAR
CONSUMER
CONSUMPT
CONTANGO
CONTEMPT
CONTINUE
CONTRACT
CONTRARY
CONTRAST
CONTRITE
CONTRIVE
CONVENER
CONVERGE
CONVERSE
CONVEYAL
CONVEYER
CONVINCE

CONVOLVE
CONVULSE
CONY-WOOL
COOLNESS
COPPERAS
COPULATE
COPY-BOOK
COPYHOLD
COQUETRY
COQUETTE
CORACOID
CORAL-RAG
CORBEILE
CORDOVAN
CORDUROY
CORDWAIN
COREGENT
CORELESS
CORMOGEN
CORNEOUS
CORNERED
CORNETCY
CORN-FLAG
CORN-LAWS
CORN-MILL
CORN-PIPE
CORN-ROSE
CORN-RENT
CORNUTED
CORONACH
CORONARY
CORONOID
CORPORAL
CORRIDOR
CORRIVAL
CORSELET
CORTICAL
CORUNDUM
CORVETTE
CORYBANT
CORYPHEE
CO-SECANT
COSENAGE
COSMETIC
COST-FREE
COSTLESS
COSTMARY
COSTUMED
CO-SURETY
CO-TENANT
COTQUEAN
COTTAGER
COTYLOID
COUCHANT
COULISSE
COUNTESS
COUPLING
COURSING
COURT-DAY
COURTESY
COURTIER
COUSINLY
COVENANT
COVERING
COVERLET
COVERLID
COVERTLY
COVETOUS
COVINOUS
COWARDLY

COW-BERRY	CUCUMBER	DANSEUSE	DEFERENT
COWORKER	CUCURBIT	DARINGLY	DEFERRER
COXSWAIN	CUL-DE-SAC	DARKLING	DEFIANCE
COZENAGE	CULINARY	DARKNESS	DEFILADE
CRAB-WOOD	CULPABLE	DARKSOME	DEFINITE
CRAB-TREE	CULPABLY	DASTARDY	DEFLOWER
CRACKNEL	CULTRATE	DATELESS	DEFLUENT
CRAFTILY	CULTURAL	DATE-PALM	DEFORMED
CRAGSMEN	CULTURED	DATE-TREE	DEFORMER
CRANE-FLY	CULVERIN	DATE-PLUM	DEFRAYAL
CRANKILY	CUMBRIAN	DATURINE	DEFRAYER
CRANNIED	CUMBROUS	DAUGHTER	DEFTNESS
CRAWFISH	CUMULATE	DAVY-LAMP	DEGRADED
CRAYFISH	CUPBOARD	DAYBREAK	DEJECTED
CREAMERY	CUPIDITY	DAY-DREAM	DEJEUNER
CREASOTE	CUPREOUS	DAYLIGHT	DELATION
CREATION	CURASSOU	DAZZLING	DELEGATE
CREATIVE	CURATIVE	DEAD-BEAT	DELETION
CREATURE	CURATRIX	DEAD-BORN	DELICACY
CREDENCE	CURBABLE	DEAD-FALL	DELICATE
CREDIBLE	CURB-ROOF	DEADHEAD	DELIRIUM
CREDIBLY	CURCULIO	DEAD-HEAT	DELIVERY
CREDITOR	CURELESS	DEAD-LOCK	DELPHIAN
CREMATOR	CURRENCY	DEAD-MEAT	DELUSION
CRENELLE	CURRICLE	DEADNESS	DELUSIVE
CREOSOTE	CURSEDLY	DEAD-WORK	DELUSORY
CRESCENT	CURSORES	DEAF-MUTE	DEMANDER
CRETONNE	CURTAL-AX	DEAFNESS	DEMENTED
CREUTZER	CURTNESS	DEAL-FISH	DEMENTIA
CREVASSE	CUSHIONY	DEANSHIP	DEMIJOHN
CRIBBAGE	CUSPIDOR	DEARNESS	DEMI-LUNE
CRIBRATE	CUSTOMER	DEATH-BED	DEMIURGE
CRIMEFUL	CUTPURSE	DEATHFUL	DEMI-VOLT
CRIMINAL	CUTWATER	DEBASING	DEMI-WOLF
CRIMPING	CYANOGEN	DEBILITY	DEMOCRAT
CRISPATE	CYANOSIS	DEBONAIR	DEMOLISH
CRISTATE	CYCLAMEN	DEBUTANT	DEMONIAC
CRITICAL	CYCLONIC	DECADENT	DEMONIST
CRITIQUE	CYCLOPIC	DECAGRAM	DEMONIZE
CROAKING	CYCLOPES	DECANTER	DEMURELY
CROCKERY	CYLINDER	DECEASED	DEMURRER
CROMLECH	CYNANCHE	DECEIVER	DENARIUS
CROMORNE	CYNICISM	DECEMBER	DENDRITE
CROP-FULL	CYNOSURE	DECEMVIR	DENDROID
CROP-SICK	CYRENAIC	DECENTLY	DENIABLE
CROSSBOW	CYRILLIC	DECIMATE	DENOUNCE
CROSSCUT	CYSTITIS	DECIPHER	DENTICLE
CROSS-EYE	CZAREVNA	DECISION	DEPARTED
CROSSING		DECISIVE	DEPENDER
CROSSLET		DECK-LOAD	DEPILATE
CROSSWAY	**D**	DECK-HAND	DEPLORER
CROTCHED		DECLARED	DEPONENT
CROTCHET	DABCHICK	DECLARER	DEPRAVED
CROUPIER	DACRYOMA	DECLINAL	DEPRAVER
CROW-FOOT	DACTYLIC	DECOLOUR	DEPRIVER
CROWNING	DAFFODIL	DECORATE	DEPURATE
CROWNLET	DAHABIEH	DECOROUS	DERANGED
CROWN-SAW	DAINTILY	DECREASE	DERELICT
CRUCIBLE	DAIRYING	DECREPIT	DERISION
CRUCIFER	DIARYMAN	DECRETAL	DERISIVE
CRUCIFIX	DALESMAN	DECURION	DERMATIC
CRUMPLED	DALMATIC	DEDICATE	DEROGATE
CRUSADER	DAY-SPRING	DEEPLESS	DESCRIED
CRUSHING	DAMNABLE	DEEP-LAID	DESCRIER
CRUSTILY	DAMNABLY	DEEPNESS	DESERTER
CRUTCHED	DAMPNESS	DEER-HAIR	DESERVER
CRYOLITE	DANDRUFF	DEFECATE	DESIGNER
CUBATURE	DANDYISH	DEFENDEE	DESIROUS
CUBIFORM	DANDYISM	DEFENDER	DESOLATE

DESPATCH
DESPISER
DESPOTIC
DETACHED
DETAILED
DETAILER
DETAINER
DETECTOR
DETESTER
DETHRONE
DETONATE
DETONIZE
DETRITAL
DETRITUS
DEUCEDLY
DEVILISH
DEVONIAN
DEVOTION
DEVOUTLY
DEW-BERRY
DEWINESS
DEW-POINT
DEXTRINE
DEXTROSE
DIABETES
DIABETIC
DIABOLIC
DIACONAL
DIADELPH
DIADEMED
DIAGLYPH
DIAGNOSE
DIAGONAL
DIALLAGE
DIALLING
DIALOGUE
DIALYSER
DIALYSIS
DIAMETER
DIAPASON
DIASTASE
DIASTEMA
DIASTOLE
DIATOMIC
DIATONIC
DIATRIBE
DICHROIC
DICLINIC
DICTATOR
DIDACTIC
DIDAPPER
DIDYMIUM
DIDYMOUS
DIERESIS
DIETETIC
DIFFRACT
DIFFUSER
DIGESTER
DIGGABLE
DIGITATE
DIGYNIAN
DIGYNOUS
DIHEDRAL
DIHEDRON
DILATION
DILATIVE
DILATORY
DILIGENT
DILUTION
DILUVIAL

DILUVIAN
DILUVION
DILUVIUM
DIMEROUS
DIMINISH
DINGDONG
DINORNIS
DINOSAUR
DIOCESAN
DIOECIAN
DIOPSIDE
DIOPTASE
DIOPTRIC
DIORAMIC
DIPLOMAT
DIPLOPIA
DIPTERAL
DIRECTLY
DIRECTOR
DISABUSE
DISAGREE
DISANNEX
DISANNUL
DISARRAY
DISASTER
DISBURSE
DISCIPLE
DISCLAIM
DISCLOSE
DISCOUNT
DISCOVER
DISCREET
DISCRETE
DISCROWN
DISEASED
DISENDOW
DISGORGE
DISGRACE
DISGUISE
DISHEVEL
DISHORSE
DISINTER
DISJOINT
DISJUNCT
DISLODGE
DISLOYAL
DISMALLY
DISMOUNT
DISORDER
DISPATCH
DISPEACE
DISSEVER
DISSOLVE
DISSUADE
DISTALLY
DISTANCE
DISTASTE
DISTINCT
DISTRACT
DISTRAIN
DISTRAIT
DISTRESS
DISTRICT
DISTRUST
DISUNION
DISUNITE
DISUSAGE
DITHEISM
DITHEIST
DIURETIC

DIVIDEND
DIVI-DIVI
DIVIDUAL
DIVINELY
DIVINITY
DIVISION
DIVISIVE
DIVORCEE
DIVORCER
DOCILITY
DOCIMASY
DOCKYARD
DOCTORAL
DOCTRINE
DOCUMENT
DODDERED
DOG-CHEAP
DOG-EARED
DOGGEDLY
DOGGEREL
DOG-GRASS
DOG-LATIN
DOGMATIC
DOG'S-BANE
DOG-SLEEP
DOG-TOOTH
DOG-WATCH
DOLDRUMS
DOLERITE
DOLOMITE
DOLOROUS
DOMAINAL
DOMESTIC
DOMICILE
DOMINANT
DOMINATE
DOMINEER
DOMINION
DOMINOES
DONATION
DONATIVE
DOOMSDAY
DOOMSMAN
DOOR-NAIL
DOOR-POST
DOOR-STEP
DORMANCY
DORMOUSE
DOTATION
DOTINGLY
DOTTEREL
DOUBLING
DOUBLOON
DOUBTFUL
DOUGH-NUT
DOVETAIL
DOWNCAST
DOWN-COME
DOWNFALL
DOWNHILL
DOWN-LINE
DOWNPOUR
DOWNWARD
DOXOLOGY
DRACONIC
DRAGOMAN
DRAGONET
DRAINAGE
DRAMATIC
DRAM-SHOP

DRAUGHTY
DRAWABLE
DRAWBACK
DRAW-WELL
DREADFUL
DREAMILY
DREARILY
DRESSING
DRIFT-NET
DRILLING
DRIPPING
DROLLERY
DROPPING
DROPSIED
DROPWORT
DROUGHTY
DROWSILY
DRUBBING
DRUDGERY
DRUGGIST
DRUIDISM
DRUMHEAD
DRUNKARD
DRY-NURSE
DRY-POINT
DUBITATE
DUCATOON
DUCK-BILL
DUCKLING
DUCK-MOLE
DUCK-WEED
DUELLING
DUELLIST
DULCIMER
DULLNESS
DUMB-BELL
DUMBNESS
DUMPLING
DUNG-FORK
DUNGHILL
DUODENUM
DUOLOGUE
DURATION
DUST-BALL
DUST-CART
DUTIABLE
DWARFISH
DWELLING
DYE-HOUSE
DYE-STUFF
DYNAMICS
DYNAMITE
DYNASTIC
DYSPNOEA

E

EAGLE-OWL
EAR-SHELL
EARTH-HOG
EARTH-PIG
EARTH-NUT
EASEMENT
EASINESS
EASTERLY
EASTWARD
EAU DE VIE
EBURNEAN
EBURNINE

ECAUDATE	EMACIATE	ENSAMPLE	ERRORIST
ECHINATE	EMBALMER	ENSCONCE	ERUCTATE
ECHINITE	EMBATTLE	ENSEMBLE	ERUPTION
ECHINOLD	EMBEZZLE	ENSHRINE	ERUPTIVE
ECLECTIC	EMBITTER	ENSIFORM	ERYTHEMA
ECLIPTIC	EMBLAZON	ENSILAGE	ESCALADE
ECONOMIC	EMBOLDEN	ENSLAVER	ESCALLOP
ECOSTATE	EMBOLISM	ENTAILER	ESCAPADE
ECRASEUR	EMBRASOR	ENTANGLE	ESCHALOT
ECSTATIC	EMERGENT	ENTELLUS	ESCULENT
ECUMENIC	EMERITUS	ENTHRALL	ESOTERIC
EDACIOUS	EMERSION	ENTHRONE	ESPALIER
EDENTATA	EMIGRANT	ENTICING	ESPECIAL
EDENTATE	EMIGRATE	ENTIRELY	ESPOUSAL
EDGE-BONE	EMINENCE	ENTIRETY	ESPOUSER
EDGELESS	EMISSARY	ENTOMOID	ESSAYIST
EDGE-TOOL	EMISSION	ENTOZOAL	ESQUIMAU
EDGEWAYS	EMISSIVE	ENTOZOIC	ESTHETIC
EDGEWISE	EMISSORY	ENTOZOON	ESTIMATE
EDIFYING	EMPANNEL	ENTR'ACTE	ESTOPPEL
EDITRESS	EMPHASIS	ENTRANCE	ESTOVERS
EDUCABLE	EMPHATIC	ENTREATY	ESTRANGE
EDUCATOR	EMPLOYEE	ENTRENCH	ESURIENT
EDUCIBLE	EMPLOYER	ENTREPOT	ETERNITY
EEL-SPEAR	EMPOISON	ENTRESOL	ETERNIZE
EERINESS	EMPORIUM	ENURESIS	ETHELING
EFFECTER	EMPURPLE	ENVELOPE	ETHEREAL
EFFECTOR	EMPYREAL	ENVIABLE	ETHERIFY
EFFERENT	EMPYREAN	ENVIABLY	ETHERISM
EFFICACY	EMULATOR	ENVIRONS	ETHERIZE
EFFLUENT	EMULGENT	ENVISAGE	ETHICIST
EFFUSION	EMULSIFY	ENZOOTIC	ETHIOPIC
EFFUSIVE	EMULSION	EOLIPILE	ETHNICAL
EGESTION	EMULSIVE	EPHEMERA	ETHOLOGY
EGG-APPLE	ENACTIVE	EPHESIAN	ETHYLENE
EGG-GLASS	ENALLAGE	EPICALYX	ETIOLATE
EGG-PLANT	ENCEINTE	EPICYCLE	ETIOLOGY
EGG-SHELL	ENCHORIC	EPIDEMIC	ETRUSCAN
EGG-SLICE	ENCIRCLE	EPIGEOUS	ETYPICAL
EGG-SPOON	ENCLITIC	EPIGRAPH	EUCALYPT
EGOISTIC	ENCOMIUM	EPILEPSY	EUGENICS
EGRESSOR	ENCRINAL	EPILOGIC	EULOGIST
EGYPTIAN	ENCRINIC	EPILOGUE	EULOGIUM
EIGHT-DAY	ENCROACH	EPINASTY	EULOGIZE
EIGHTEEN	ENCUMBER	EPIPHANY	EUPEPSIA
EIGHTHLY	ENCYCLIC	EPIPHYTE	EUPEPTIC
EJECTION	ENDAMAGE	EPIPLOIC	EUPHONIC
ELAPSION	ENDANGER	EPIPLOON	EUPHRASY
ELATEDLY	ENDERMIC	EPISODIC	EUPHUISM
EL DORADO	ENDOCARP	EPISPERM	EUPHUIST
ELECTION	ENDOGAMY	EPISTLER	EURASIAN
ELECTIVE	ENDORSER	EPONYMIC	EUROPEAN
ELECTRIC	ENDURING	EPULOTIC	EVACUANT
ELECTRON	ENERGIZE	EPYORNIS	EVACUATE
ELEGANCE	ENERVATE	EQUALITY	EVADABLE
ELEGANCY	ENFEEBLE	EQUALIZE	EVADIBLE
ELEGIAST	ENFILADE	EQUATION	EVALUATE
ELENCHUS	ENFOREST	EQUIPAGE	EVANESCE
ELEPHANT	ENGENDER	EQUITANT	EVENNESS
ELEVATOR	ENGINEER	EQUIVOKE	EVENTFUL
ELEVENTH	ENGORGED	ERASTIAN	EVENTIDE
ELF-ARROW	ENGRAVER	ERECTILE	EVENTUAL
ELIGIBLE	ENHANCER	ERECTION	EVERSION
ELIGIBLY	ENKINDLE	ERECTIVE	EVERSIVE
ELLIPSIS	ENLARGED	EREMICAL	EVERYDAY
ELLIPTIC	ENLARGER	EREMITIC	EVERYONE
ELONGATE	ENNEAGON	ERETHISM	EVICTION
ELOQUENT	ENORMITY	ERGOTINE	EVIDENCE
ELUDIBLE	ENORMOUS	ERGOTISM	EVILDOER
ELVISHLY	ENROLLER	EROTETIC	EVILNESS
		ERRANTRY	

EVULSION
EXACTING
EXACTION
EXAMINEE
EXAMINER
EXCAVATE
EXCHANGE
EXCISION
EXCITANT
EXCITING
EXCURSUS
EXECRATE
EXECUTOR
EXEGESIS
EXEGETIC
EXEMPLAR
EXEQUIAL
EXEQUIES
EXERCISE
EXERTION
EXHALANT
EXHALENT
EXHORTER
EXIGENCE
EXIGENCY
EXIGIBLE
EXIGUOUS
EXIGUITY
EXISTENT
EXORABLE
EXORCISE
EXORCISM
EXORCIST
EXORCIZE
EXORDIAL
EXORDIUM
EXOSMOSE
EXOTERIC
EXPECTER
EXPEDITE
EXPELLER
EXPERTLY
EXPIABLE
EXPIATOR
EXPLICIT
EXPLORER
EXPONENT
EXPORTER
EXPOSURE
EXSERTED
EXTENDER
EXTENSOR
EXTERIOR
EXTERNAL
EXTOLLER
EXTRADOS
EXTRORSE
EXULTANT
EXUVIATE
EYE-GLASS
EYE-PIECE
EYESIGHT
EYE-TOOTH
EYE-WATER

F

FABULIST
FABULOUS

FACE-ACHE
FACETIAE
FACIALLY
FACILITY
FACTIOUS
FACTOTUM
FADELESS
FADINGLY
FAIRNESS
FAITHFUL
FALCATED
FALCHION
FALCONER
FALCONET
FALCONRY
FALLIBLE
FALLIBLY
FALL-TRAP
FALSETTO
FAMELESS
FAMILIAR
FAMOUSLY
FANCIFUL
FANDANGO
FANFARON
FAN-LIGHT
FANTASIA
FARCICAL
FARCY-BUD
FAREWELL
FARMABLE
FARMYARD
FARRIERY
FARTHEST
FARTHING
FASCIATE
FASCICLE
FASHIOUS
FASTENER
FASTNESS
FATALISM
FATALIST
FATALITY
FATHERLY
FATTENER
FAULTILY
FAUTEUIL
FAVONIAN
FAVOURED
FAVOURER
FEARLESS
FEASIBLE
FEASIBLY
FEATHERY
FEATURED
FEBRUARY
FECULENT
FEDERATE
FEED-PIPE
FEED-PUMP
FELDSPAR
FELICITY
FELLNESS
FELO-DE-SE
FELSTONE
FEME-SOLE
FENCIBLE
FERACITY
FERETORY
FERINGEE

FERN-SEED
FEROCITY
FERREOUS
FERRETER
FERRIAGE
FERRYMAN
FERVENCY
FERVIDLY
FESTALLY
FESTIVAL
FETATION
FETICIDE
FEUDALLY
FEVERFEW
FEVERISH
FIBRILLA
FIBROSIS
FIDELITY
FIDUCIAL
FIELD-DAY
FIELD-GUN
FIENDISH
FIERCELY
FIFTIETH
FIGHTING
FIGULINE
FIGURANT
FIGURATE
FIGURINE
FIGURING
FILAMENT
FILATORY
FILATURE
FILE-FISH
FILIALLY
FILICIDE
FILICOID
FILIFORM
FILIGREE
FILLIBEG
FILTHILY
FILTRATE
FINALITY
FINEDRAW
FINENESS
FINESPUN
FINGERED
FINISHER
FINITELY
FINITUDE
FIREBALL
FIRE-CLAY
FIRE-DAMP
FIRELOCK
FIRE-PLUG
FIRE-SHIP
FIRESIDE
FIREWOOD
FIRMNESS
FISH-HOOK
FISHWIFE
FISTULAR
FITFULLY
FIVEFOLD
FIXATION
FIXATIVE
FLABBILY
FLABELLA
FLAGELLA
FLAGGING
FLAGRANT

FLAMBEAU
FLAMINGO
FLASHILY
FLATTING
FLATLONG
FLATNESS
FLATTERY
FLATTING
FLATWISE
FLAUNTER
FLAUTIST
FLAWLESS
FLEABITE
FLECTION
FLEETING
FLESHPOT
FLEXIBLE
FLEXIBLY
FLEXUOSE
FLEXUOUS
FLIMSILY
FLIPPANT
FLOATAGE
FLOATING
FLOCCOSE
FLOGGING
FLOODING
FLOORING
FLORALLY
FLORIDLY
FLOSCULE
FLOTILLA
FLOUNDER
FLOURISH
FLOWERED
FLOWERET
FLUENTLY
FLUIDITY
FLUMMERY
FLUORITE
FLUXIBLE
FOCALIZE
FOGEYISM
FOLIATED
FOLLICLE
FOLLOWER
FOMENTER
FONDLING
FONDNESS
FONTANEL
FOODLESS
FOOLSCAP
FOOTBALL
FOOTFALL
FOOTGEAR
FOOTHOLD
FOOTMARK
FOOTPATH
FOOTSTEP
FORAMINA
FORBORNE
FORCEDLY
FORCEFUL
FORCIBLE
FORCIBLY
FORCLOSE
FORDABLE
FOREBODE
FORECAST
FOREDATE

FOREDOOM	FRIBBLER	GALVANIC	GLAUCOMA
FOREFEND	FRICTION	GAMENESS	GLAUCOUS
FOREGOER	FRIENDLY	GAMESOME	GLEESOME
FOREGONE	FRIGHTEN	GAMESTER	GLIBNESS
FOREHAND	FRIGIDLY	GANGLIAC	GLISSADE
FOREHEAD	FRILLING	GANGLION	GLOAMING
FOREKNOW	FRIPPERY	GANGRENE	GLOBATED
FORELAND	FRISKILY	GANISTER	GLOBULAR
FORELOCK	FRONTAGE	GANTLOPE	GLOBULET
FOREMAST	FRONTIER	GARDENER	GLOBULIN
FOREMOST	FRONTLET	GARDENIA	GLOOMILY
FORENOON	FROSTILY	GARGOYLE	GLORIOLE
FORENSIC	FROSTING	GARISHLY	GLORIOUS
FOREPART	FROTHILY	GARLICKY	GLOSSARY
FOREPEAK	FRUCTIFY	GAROTTER	GLOSSILY
FORESAID	FRUCTOSE	GARRISON	GLOWWORM
FORESAIL	FRUGALLY	GARROTTE	GLOXINIA
FORESHEW	FRUITAGE	GASALIER	GLUCINUM
FORESHOW	FRUITERY	GASELIER	GLUMNESS
FORESIDE	FRUITFUL	GASOGENE	GLUTTONY
FORESKIN	FRUITION	GASTRULA	GLYPTICS
FORESTAL	FRUMENTY	GATHERER	GNATLING
FORESTER	FRUMPISH	GAUNTLET	GNOMICAL
FORESTRY	FRUSTULE	GAZOGENE	GNOMONIC
FORETELL	FRUSTUMS	GELATINE	GOATHERD
FOREWARN	FUGACITY	GELIDITY	GODCHILD
FOREWARD	FUGITIVE	GEMINATE	GODWARDS
FORMALIN	FUGLEMAN	GEMINOUS	GOITERED
FORMALLY	FULCRATE	GEMMEOUS	GOITROUS
FORMERLY	FULCRUMS	GENDARME	GOLGOTHA
FORMLESS	FULGENCY	GENERANT	GONFALON
FORMULAE	FULLNESS	GENERATE	GONFANON
FORSAKER	FULMINIC	GENEROUS	GONIDIUM
FORSOOTH	FUMAROLE	GENEVESE	GOODNESS
FORSWEAR	FUMELESS	GENIALLY	GORGEOUS
FORTIETH	FUMIGATE	GENITALS	GOSSAMER
FORTRESS	FUMITORY	GENITIVE	GOSSIPRY
FORTUITY	FUNCTION	GENIUSES	GOURMAND
FORWARDS	FUNDABLE	GEODESIC	GOUTWORT
FOSTERER	FUNEREAL	GEODETIC	GOUTWEED
FOULNESS	FUNGUSES	GEOGNOSY	GOVERNOR
FOUNDERY	FURBELOW	GEOLATRY	GOWNSMAN
FOUNTAIN	FURCATED	GEOMANCY	GRAAFIAN
FOURFOLD	FURLOUGH	GEOMETER	GRACEFUL
FOURTEEN	FURMENTY	GEOMETRY	GRACIOUS
FOURTHLY	FURRIERY	GEOPONIC	GRADIENT
FOXGLOVE	FURTHEST	GEORGIAN	GRADUATE
FRACTION	FUSAROLE	GERANIUM	GRAFFITI
FRACTURE	FUSIFORM	GERMANIC	GRAFFITO
FRAGMENT	FUSILEER	GERMINAL	GRAINING
FRAGRANT	FUTILELY	GESTURAL	GRALLOCK
FRAMPOLD	FUTILITY	GIANTESS	GRANDEUR
FRANKISH	FUTURITY	GIBINGLY	GRANDSON
FRANKLIN		GIGANTIC	GRANITIC
FRAUDFUL		GIGGLING	GRANULAR
FREAKISH	**G**	GIMCRACK	GRAPHITE
FRECKLED		GINGERLY	GRASPING
FREEBORN	GABIONED	GIRASOLE	GRATEFUL
FREEDMAN	GADABOUT	GIRLHOOD	GRATUITY
FREEHAND	GADHELIC	GLABROUS	GRAVAMEN
FREEHOLD	GAINLESS	GLACIATE	GRAVELLY
FREENESS	GALACTIC	GLADIATE	GRAYLING
FREEZING	GALANGAL	GLADIOLI	GRAYNESS
FRONTIER	GALANTINE	GLADNESS	GREELALY
FRENZIED	GALEATED	GLADSOME	GREEDILY
FREQUENT	GALLIARD	GLANDERS	GREENERY
FRESCOES	GALLICAN	GLANDULE	GREENING
FRESCOED	GALLIPOT	GLAREOUS	GREENISH
FRESHMAN	GALLOPER	GLASSFUL	GREETING
FRETWORK	GALLOWAY	GLASSILY	GREWSOME

GRIDIRON
GRIEVOUS
GRILLADE
GRIMNESS
GRINDING
GRISETTE
GRIZZLED
GROINING
GROSBEAK
GROSCHEN
GROTTOES
GROUPING
GROWLING
GRUDGING
GRUESOME
GRUMBLER
GRUMPILY
GRUMPISH
GRUNTING
GUAIACUM
GUARDIAN
GUERNSEY
GUERILLA
GUICOWAR
GUIDABLE
GUIDANCE
GUILEFUL
GUILTILY
GULLIBLE
GUMPTION
GUNSMITH
GURGOYLE
GUTTURAL
GYMNASIA
GYMNOGEN
GYMNOTUS
GYNANDER
GYNARCHY
GYPSEOUS
GYRATION
GYRATORY
GYROIDAL
GYROSTAT

H

HABITANT
HABITUAL
HABITUDE
HACIENDA
HAEMATIC
HAEMATIN
HAIRLESS
HALENESS
HALLIARD
HAMIFORM
HANDBILL
HANDBOOK
HANDCUFF
HANDGRIP
HANDICAP
HANDLINE
HANDMAID
HANDRAIL
HANDSOME
HANGNAIL
HARANGUE
HARDENED
HARDNESS

HARDSHIP
HARDWARE
HAREBELL
HARLOTRY
HARMLESS
HARMONIC
HARRIDAN
HARUSPEX
HASTENER
HATCHWAY
HAUTBOIS
HAVANNAH
HAVILDAR
HAWTHORN
HAYMAKER
HAZINESS
HEADACHE
HEADACHY
HEADLAND
HEADLESS
HEADLONG
HEADMOST
HEADSHIP
HEADSMAN
HEALABLE
HEARTILY
HEAVENLY
HEBETATE
HEBETUDE
HEBRAISM
HEBRAIST
HEBRAIZE
HECATOMB
HEDGEHOG
HEDGEROW
HEDONISM
HEDONIST
HEEDLESS
HEELBALL
HEGELIAN
HEGEMONY
HEIGHTEN
HEIRLOOM
HEIRSHIP
HELIACAL
HELICOID
HELLENIC
HELMETED
HELMSMAN
HELOTISM
HELPLESS
HELPMATE
HELVETIC
HEMATINE
HEMATITE
HEMIPTER
HENCHMAN
HENEQUEN
HEPATITE
HEPATIZE
HEPTAGON
HERALDIC
HERALDRY
HERBARIA
HERDSMAN
HEREDITY
HEREUNTO
HEREUPON
HEREWITH
HERITAGE

HERMETIC
HERNSHAW
HEROSHIP
HERPETIC
HESITANT
HESITATE
HETARISM
HIATUSES
HIBERNAL
HICCOUGH
HIDDENLY
HIERARCH
HIERATIC
HIGHLAND
HIGHNESS
HIGHROAD
HILARITY
HINDERER
HINDMOST
HINDUISM
HIRELING
HISTORIC
HITHERTO
HOARDING
HOARSELY
HOGSHEAD
HOLDFAST
HOLINESS
HOLLANDS
HOLLOWLY
HOMEBORN
HOMEFELT
HOMELESS
HOMESPUN
HOMEWARD
HOMICIDE
HOMILIST
HOMILIES
HOMODONT
HOMOLOGY
HOMONYMY
HOMOPTER
HOMOTYPE
HONESTLY
HONORARY
HONOURER
HOODWINK
HOPELESS
HORATIAN
HORNBEAM
HORNBILL
HORNPIPE
HORNWORK
HOROLOGE
HOROLOGY
HORRIBLE
HORRIBLY
HORRIDLY
HORRIFIC
HORSEMAN
HOSEPIPE
HOSPITAL
HOSTELRY
HOTCHPOT
HOWITZER
HUCKSTER
HUGENESS
HUGUENOT
HUMANELY
HUMANISM

HUMANIST
HUMANITY
HUMANIZE
HUMBLING
HUMIDITY
HUMILITY
HUMORIST
HUMOROUS
HUMPBACK
HUNGERER
HUNGRILY
HUNTRESS
HUNTSMAN
HURTLESS
HUSTINGS
HYACINTH
HYDROGEN
HYDROMEL
HYDROPIC
HYDROZOA
HYGIENIC
HYMENEAL
HYMENEAN
HYMENIUM
HYPNOSIS
HYPNOTIC
HYSTERIA
HYSTERIC

I

IAMBUSES
IATRICAL
ICHOROUS
IDEALESS
IDEALISM
IDEALIST
IDEALITY
IDEALIZE
IDEATION
IDENTIFY
IDENTITY
IDEOGRAM
IDEOLOGY
IDIOTISM
IDLENESS
IDOCRASE
IDOLATER
IDOLATRY
IDOLIZER
IGNITION
IGNOMINY
IGNORANT
ILLATION
ILLATIVE
ILLUMINE
ILLUSION
ILLUSIVE
ILLUSORY
IMBECILE
IMBITTER
IMBLAZON
IMBOLDEN
IMBORDER
IMBUTION
IMITABLE
IMITANCY
IMITATOR
IMMANATE

IMMANENT	INFERNAL	INTRORSE	JOKINGLY
IMMANUEL	INFILTER	INTRUDER	JOLTHEAD
IMMATURE	INFINITE	INUNDATE	JOVIALLY
IMMINENT	INFINITY	INVASION	JOYFULLY
IMMINGLE	INFIRMLY	INVASIVE	JOYOUSLY
IMMOBILE	INFLATED	INVEIGLE	JUBILANT
IMMODEST	INFLATUS	INVENTOR	JUBILATE
IMMOLATE	INFLEXED	INVERTED	JUDAICAL
IMMORTAL	INFLUENT	INVESTOR	JUDGMENT
IMMUNITY	INFORMAL	INVITING	JUDICIAL
IMPANATE	INFORMER	INVOCATE	JUGGLERY
IMPARITY	INFRINGE	INVOLUTE	JULIENNE
IMPERIAL	INFUSION	INWARDLY	JUNCTION
IMPETIGO	INFUSIVE	IODOFORM	JUNCTURE
IMPLICIT	INFUSORY	IREFULLY	JURASSIC
IMPOISON	INGUINAL	IRISATED	JURISTIC
IMPOLICY	INHALANT	IRISCOPE	JUSTNESS
IMPOLITE	INHALENT	IRISHISM	JUVENILE
IMPORTER	INHERENT	IRIDITIS	
IMPOSING	INHESION	IRONBARK	
IMPOSTOR	INIMICAL	IRONICAL	**K**
IMPOTENT	INIQUITY	IRONSIDE	
IMPRIMIS	INITIATE	IRONWARE	KAKEMONO
IMPRISON	INJECTOR	IRRIGATE	KAKODYLE
IMPROPER	INKINESS	IRRISION	KALENDER
IMPROVER	INKSTAND	IRRITANT	KANGAROO
IMPUDENT	INLANDER	IRRITATE	KEELHAUL
IMPUGNER	INLAYING	ISABELLA	KEENNESS
IMPUNITY	INNATELY	ISAGOGIC	KEEPSAKE
IMPURELY	INNOCENT	ISCHURIA	KERCHIEF
IMPURITY	INNOVATE	ISLAMISH	KERNELLY
IMPURPLE	INNUENDO	ISLAMITE	KEROSENE
INACTION	INQUIRER	ISLANDER	KEYSTONE
INACTIVE	INSANELY	ISOCHEIM	KICKSHAW
INASMUCH	INSANITY	ISOCRYME	KILOGRAM
INCEPTOR	INSCRIBE	ISOGONIC	KILOWATT
INCHOATE	INSECURE	ISOLATED	KINDLING
INCIDENT	INSERTED	ISOMERIC	KINDNESS
INCISION	INSIGNIA	ISOTHERM	KINETICS
INCISIVE	INSOLATE	ISSUABLE	KINGLIKE
INCISORY	INSOLENT	ITERANCE	KINGLING
INCISURE	INSOMNIA		KINGSHIP
INCLINED	INSOMUCH		KINKAJOU
INCOMING	INSPIRED	**J**	KINSFOLK
INCREASE	INSPIRER		KNAPSACK
INCUBATE	INSPIRIT	JACKETED	KNICKERS
INDAGATE	INSTANCE	JACOBEAN	KNIGHTLY
INDEBTED	INSTINCT	JACOBITE	KNITTING
INDECENT	INSTRUCT	JAILBIRD	KNOTLESS
INDENTED	INSULATE	JALOUSIE	KNOWABLE
INDEVOUT	INTAGLIO	JANIZARY	KREASOTE
INDIAMAN	INTEGRAL	JAPANNER	KREOSOTE
INDICANT	INTENDED	JAPHETIC	KREUTZER
INDICATE	INTENTLY	JAUNDICE	KRYOLITE
INDIGENE	INTERACT	JAUNTILY	
INDIGENT	INTEREST	JEALOUSY	
INDIRECT	INTERIOR	JEHOVIST	**L**
INDOCILE	INTERMIT	JEJUNELY	
INDOLENT	INTERMIX	JEOPARDY	LABIALLY
INDURATE	INTERNAL	JEREMIAD	LABOURED
INDUSIUM	INTERVAL	JEROBOAM	LABOURER
INDUSIAL	INTHRALL	JESUITIC	LABURNUM
INDUSTRY	INTIMACY	JESUITRY	LACERATE
INELITION	INTIMATE	JETTISON	LACONISM
INEQUITY	INTONATE	JEWELLER	LACROSSE
INEXPERT	INTRADOR	JEWISHLY	LACRYMAL
INFAMOUS	INTRENCH	JOCOSELY	LACUNOUS
INFANTRY	INTREPID	JOCOSITY	LADYHOOD
INFECUND	INTRIGUE	JOCUNDLY	LADYLIKE
INFERIOR	INTROMIT	JOINTURE	LADYSHIP

LAICALLY
LAMASERY
LAMBLIKE
LAMBLING
LAMBSKIN
LAMELLAE
LAMELLAR
LAMENESS
LAMINARY
LAMINATE
LANCELET
LANDFALL
LANDLADY
LANDLESS
LANDLORD
LANDMARK
LANDSLIP
LANDSMAN
LANDSMEN
LANDWARD
LANDWEHR
LANGSYNE
LANGUAGE
LANGUISH
LANKNESS
LANNERET
LANOLINE
LANTHORN
LAPELLED
LAPIDARY
LAPIDATE
LAPIDIFY
LAPPETED
LAPSABLE
LARBOARD
LARCENER
LARKSPUR
LARYNGES
LARYNXES
LATENESS
LATENTLY
LATINISM
LATINIST
LATINITY
LATINIZE
LATITUDE
LATTERLY
LAUDABLE
LAUDABLY
LAUDANUM
LAUGHTER
LAUREATE
LAVATORY
LAVENDER
LAVISHLY
LAWFULLY
LAWGIVER
LAXATIVE
LAZINESS
LEADLESS
LEAFLESS
LEANNESS
LEARNING
LEATHERN
LEATHERY
LEAVINGS
LECTURER
LEGALISM
LEGALITY
LEGALIZE

LEGATINE
LEGATION
LEISURED
LEMONADE
LENGTHEN
LENIENCE
LENIENCY
LENITIVE
LEPORINE
LETHARGY
LETTERED
LEUCOSIS
LEVANTER
LEVELLER
LEVERAGE
LEVIABLE
LEVIGATE
LEVIRATE
LEVITATE
LEWDNESS
LEWISSON
LIBATION
LIBATORY
LIBELLER
LIBERATE
LIBRETTO
LICENSEE
LICENSER
LICHENED
LICHENIC
LICORICE
LIEGEMAN
LIENTERY
LIFELESS
LIFELIKE
LIFELONG
LIFETIME
LIGAMENT
LIGATION
LIGATURE
LIGNEOUS
LIGNITIC
LIGULATE
LIKEABLE
LIKENESS
LIKEWISE
LIMITARY
LIMONITE
LINCTURE
LINEALLY
LINEARLY
LINEATED
LINGERER
LINGUIST
LINIMENT
LINNAEAN
LINOLEUM
LINSTOCK
LIPOGRAM
LIQUIDLY
LISTENER
LISTLESS
LITERARY
LITERATE
LITERATO
LITERATI
LITHARGE
LITIGANT
LITIGATE
LITTORAL

LITURGIC
LIVELILY
LIVELONG
LIVERIED
LIVIDITY
LIXIVIAL
LIXIVIUM
LOADSTAR
LOANABLE
LOATHFUL
LOATHING
LOCALISM
LOCALITY
LOCALIZE
LOCATION
LOCATIVE
LOCUTION
LODESTAR
LODGMENT
LOGICIAN
LOGISTIC
LOGOGRAM
LOGOTYPE
LOITERER
LOLLARDY
LOLLIPOP
LOMENTUM
LONESOME
LONGEVAL
LONGHAND
LONGSOME
LONGWAYS
LONGWISE
LOOPHOLE
LORDLING
LORDSHIP
LORICATE
LORIKEET
LOTHARIO
LOUDNESS
LOVELESS
LOVINGLY
LOWERING
LOYALIST
LUBBERLY
LUCERNAL
LUCIDITY
LUCKLESS
LUCULENT
LUKEWARM
LUMBERER
LUMINARY
LUMINOUS
LUMPFISH
LUNATION
LUNCHEON
LUNGWORT
LUNULATE
LUPULINE
LUSCIOUS
LUSTRATE
LUSTRING
LUSTROUS
LUSTRUMS
LUTANIST
LUTENIST
LUTHERAN
LUXATION
LYCOPODE
LYMPHOID

M

MACARONI
MACAROON
MACERATE
MACKEREL
MACROPOD
MACRURAL
MACULATE
MADRIGAL
MAESTOSO
MAGAZINE
MAGDALEN
MAGICIAN
MAGNESIA
MAGNETIC
MAGNIFIC
MAGNOLIA
MAHARANI
MAHOGANY
MAIDENLY
MAIEUTIC
MAINLAND
MAINTAIN
MAJESTIC
MAJOLICA
MAJORATE
MAJORITY
MALAPERT
MALARIAL
MALARIAN
MALIGNLY
MALINGER
MALODOUR
MALSTICK
MALTSTER
MALTREAT
MALTWORM
MAMMALIA
MAMMIFER
MAMMILLA
MANCIPLE
MANDAMUS
MANDARIN
MANDIBLE
MANDOLIN
MANDRAKE
MANDRILL
MANELESS
MANEQUIN
MANFULLY
MANGANIC
MANGONEL
MANGROVE
MANIACAL
MANICHEE
MANICURE
MANIFEST
MANIFOLD
MANIFORM
MANNERED
MANNERLY
MANORIAL
MANSUETE
MANTELET
MANTILLA
MANUALLY
MANURIAL
MARABOUT

MARABOUT	MELASSES	MINUSCLE	MONOLITH
MARASMUS	MELIBEAN	MINUTELY	MONOPOLY
MARAUDER	MELINITE	MINUTIAE	MONOTONE
MARAVEDI	MELODEON	MIRINESS	MONOTONY
MARBLING	MELODICS	MIRTHFUL	MONSIEUR
MARGINAL	MELODIST	MISAPPLY	MONTICLE
MARGINED	MELODIZE	MISCARRY	MONUMENT
MARGRAVE	MEMBERED	MISCHIEF	MOONBEAM
MARIGOLD	MEMBRANE	MISCIBLE	MOONLESS
MARINADE	MEMORIAL	MISCOUNT	MOONSHEE
MARITIME	MEMORIZE	MISDOUBT	MOORLAND
MARJORAM	MENHADEN	MISGUIDE	MOOTABLE
MARKEDLY	MENINGES	MISJUDGE	MORALIST
MARKSMAN	MENISCUS	MISNOMER	MORALITY
MARMOSET	MENOLOGY	MISOGAMY	MORALIZE
MARONITE	MENSTRUA	MISOGYMY	MORAVIAN
MARQUESS	MENTAGRA	MISPLACE	MORBIDLY
MARQUISE	MENTALLY	MISPRINT	MORBIFIC
MARRIAGE	MEPHITIC	MISPRISE	MORCEAUX
MARRYING	MEPHITIS	MISPRIZE	MOREOVER
MARTAGON	MERCHANT	MISQUOTE	MORESQUE
MARTINET	MERCIFUL	MISSHAPE	MORIBUND
MASCOTTE	MERCURIC	MISSPEAK	MOROSELY
MASSACRE	MERIDIAN	MISSPELL	MORPHINE
MASSEUSE	MEROSOME	MISSPEND	MORTALLY
MASSETER	MESMERIC	MISSPENT	MORTGAGE
MASSICOT	MESOZOIC	MISSTATE	MORTMAIN
MASTERLY	MESQUITE	MISTAKEN	MORTUARY
MASTICOT	MESSMATE	MISTITLE	MOSAICAL
MASTITIS	MESSUAGE	MISTRESS	MOSQUITO
MASTLESS	MESTIZOS	MISTRUST	MOTHERLY
MASTODON	METALLED	MITIGANT	MOTILITY
MATELESS	METALLIC	MITIGATE	MOTIVITY
MATERIAL	METAMERE	MITTIMUS	MOTORIAL
MATERNAL	METAPHOR	MNEMONIC	MOUFFLON
MATRICES	METEORIC	MOBILITY	MOULDING
MATRONAL	METEWAND	MOBILIZE	MOUNTAIN
MATRONLY	METEYARD	MOCCASIN	MOUNTING
MATTRESS	METHINKS	MODALITY	MOURNFUL
MATURELY	METHODIC	MODELLER	MOURNING
MATURITY	METHYLIC	MODERATE	MOUTHFUL
MAXILLAE	METONYMY	MODESTLY	MOVELESS
MAXILLAR	METRICAL	MODIFIER	MOVEMENT
MAXIMIST	MEZEREON	MODISHLY	MOVINGLY
MAXIMIZE	MIASMATA	MODULATE	MUCHNESS
MAYORESS	MICROBIC	MOISTURE	MUCIFORM
MAZARINE	MICROZOA	MOLASSES	MUCILAGE
MAZINESS	MIDDLING	MOLECULE	MUCOSITY
MAZOURKA	MIDNIGHT	MOLESKIN	MULBERRY
MEAGRELY	MIGHTILY	MOLOSSUS	MULETEER
MEANNESS	MILDNESS	MOLYBDIC	MULISHLY
MEANTIME	MILESIAN	MOMENTLY	MULTIFID
MEASURED	MILITANT	MOMENTUM	MULTIPED
MECHANIC	MILITARY	MONACHAL	MULTIPLE
MEDALLIC	MILITATE	MONANDER	MULTIPLY
MEDALIST	MILKMAID	MONANDRY	MUMBLING
MEDDLING	MILLEPED	MONARCHY	MUNGOOSE
MEDIATOR	MILLIPED	MONASTIC	MUNIMENT
MEDICATE	MILLIARD	MONETARY	MUNITION
MEDICINE	MILLINER	MONETIZE	MURDERER
MEDIEVAL	MIMICKER	MONGOOSE	MURIATIC
MEDIOCRE	MINATORY	MONISTIC	MURICATE
MEDITATE	MINIMIZE	MONITION	MURIFORM
MEDULLAR	MINIMIZE	MONITORY	MURITURER
MEEKNESS	MINIMUMS	MONITRIX	MURRHINE
MEETNESS	MINISTER	MONOCARP	MUSCADEL
MEGAPODE	MINISTRY	MONOCRAT	MUSCATEL
MEIOCENE	MINORITE	MONODIST	MUSCULAR
MELANISM	MINORITY	MONOGAMY	MUSHROOM
MELANITE	MINSTREL	MONOGRAM	MUSICIAN

MUSINGLY
MUSLINET
MUSQUASH
MUSQUITO
MUSTACHE
MUTATION
MUTCHKIN
MUTENESS
MUTILATE
MUTINEER
MUTINOUS
MUTTERER
MUTUALLY
MYCELIUM
MYCOLOGY
MYELITIS
MYRIAPOD
MYRMIDON
MYSTICAL
MYTHICAL

N

NACREOUS
NAINSOOK
NAMEABLE
NAMELESS
NAMESAKE
NAPIFORM
NAPOLEON
NARCOSIS
NARCOTIC
NARGHILE
NARGILEH
NARRATOR
NARROWLY
NASALIZE
NASCENCY
NASICORN
NASIFORM
NATATION
NATATORY
NATIONAL
NATIVELY
NATIVITY
NAUMACHY
NAUSEATE
NAUSEOUS
NAUTICAL
NAUTILUS
NAVIGATE
NAZAREAN
NAZARENE
NAZARITE
NEARCTIC
NEARNESS
NEATHERD
NEATNESS
NEBULOSE
NEBULOUS
NECKLACE
NECROSIS
NECROSED
NECTARED
NEEDFIRE
NEEDLESS
NEGATION
NEGATIVE
NEIGHBOR

NEMATODE
NEMATOID
NEOLOGIC
NEOPHYTE
NEOTERIC
NEPENTHE
NEPHRITE
NEPOTISM
NEPOTIST
NESTLING
NEURITIS
NEUROSIS
NEUROTIC
NICENESS
NICKELIC
NICKNAME
NICOTIAN
NICOTINE
NIHILISM
NIHILIST
NIHILITY
NINEPINS
NINETEEN
NITROGEN
NOACHIAN
NOBILITY
NOBLEMAN
NOBLESSE
NOCTURNE
NODOSITY
NOETICAL
NOMADISH
NOMARCHY
NOMINATE
NOMOLOGY
NONESUCH
NONSENSE
NOONTIDE
NORMALLY
NORSEMAN
NORTHERN
NOSELESS
NOSOLOGY
NOTARIAL
NOTATION
NOTCHING
NOTELESS
NOTIONAL
NOVELIST
NOVEMBER
NOVERCAL
NOWADAYS
NUCIFORM
NUCLEATE
NUCLEOLI
NUDENESS
NUGATORY
NUISANCE
NUMBERER
NUMBNESS
NUMERARY
NUMERATE
NUMEROUS
NUMMULAR
NUMSKULL
NUPTIALS
NURSLING
NUTATION
NUTRIENT
NYMPHEAN

O

OBDURACY
OBDURATE
OBEDIENT
OBITUARY
OBJECTOR
OBLATION
OBLIGANT
OBLIGATE
OBLIGATO
OBLIGING
OBLIVION
OBSCURER
OBSERVER
OBSIDIAN
OBSOLETE
OBSTACLE
OBSTRUCT
OBTAINER
OBTRUDER
OBTURATE
OBTUSELY
OBVOLUTE
OCCASION
OCCIDENT
OCCULTLY
OCCUPANT
OCCUPIER
OCCELATE
OCHREOUS
OCTOPEDE
OCTOROON
OCULARLY
OCULATED
ODIOUSLY
ODOMETER
ODONTOID
OENOLOGY
OFFENDER
OFFERING
OFFICIAL
OFFSHOOT
OFTTIMES
OILINESS
OINTMENT
OLEANDER
OLIBANUM
OLIGARCH
OLYMPIAD
OLYMPIAN
OMISSION
OMISSIVE
OMNIFORM
OMOHYOID
OMOPLATE
OMPHALIC
ONCOMING
ONCOTOMY
ONLOOKER
ONTOGENY
ONTOLOGY
OOLOGIST
OPAQUELY
OPENNESS
OPERATIC
OPERATOR
OPERETTA
OPHIDIAN

OPOPANAX
OPPONENT
OPPOSITE
OPTATIVE
OPTICIAN
OPTIMISM
OPTIMIST
OPTIMIZE
OPTIONAL
OPULENCE
OPUSCULE
ORACULAR
ORAGIOUS
ORANGERY
ORATORIC
ORBITARY
ORCADIAN
ORCHELLA
ORDAINER
ORDINAND
ORDINANT
ORDINARY
ORDINATE
ORDNANCE
ORDUROUS
ORGANISM
ORGANIST
ORGANIZE
ORICHALC
ORIENTAL
ORIGINAL
ORNAMENT
ORNATELY
ORNITHIC
ORPIMENT
ORTHODOX
ORTHOEPY
ORTHOGON
OSCITANT
OSCULANT
OSCULATE
OSMANLIS
OSNABURG
OTIOSITY
OTOSCOPE
OUISTITI
OUTARGUE
OUTBRAVE
OUTBREAK
OUTBURST
OUTDOORS
OUTFLANK
OUTGOING
OUTLAWRY
OUTLYING
OUTMARCH
OUTRANCE
OUTREACH
OUTRIDER
OUTRIGHT
OUTSHINE
OUTSIDER
OUTSKIRT
OUTSPEAK
OUTSTARE
OUTSTRIP
OUTSWEAR
OUTVALUE
OUTWARDS
OUTWATCH

OUTWEIGH	PALATINE	PARTIZAN	PERIGEAN
OVERALLS	PALENESS	PASHALIC	PERILOUS
OVERARCH	PALESTRA	PASSABLE	PERINEUM
OVERBEAR	PALINODE	PASSABLY	PERINEAL
OVERBOLD	PALISADE	PASSERES	PERIODIC
OVERBRIM	PALLIATE	PASSIBLE	PERIPLUS
OVERCAST	PALLMALL	PASSOVER	PERJURER
OVERCOAT	PALMATED	PASSPORT	PERMEATE
OVERCOME	PALMETTE	PASTILLE	PERONEAL
OVERDATE	PALMETTO	PASTORAL	PERORATE
OVERDOSE	PALMIPED	PATAGIUM	PEROXIDE
OVERDRAW	PALMITIC	PATCHERY	PERRUQUE
OVERFLOW	PALPABLE	PATENTEE	PERSIMON
OVERGROW	PALPABLY	PATERNAL	PERSONAL
OVERHAND	PALSTAFF	PATHETIC	PERSPIRE
OVERHANG	PALSTAVE	PATHLESS	PERSUADE
OVERHAUL	PALTERER	PATIENCE	PERTNESS
OVERHEAD	PALUDINE	PATULOUS	PERTUSED
OVERHEAR	PALUDISM	PAULDRON	PERUVIAN
OVERHEAT	PALUDOSE	PAVEMENT	PERVERSE
OVERHUNG	PAMPERER	PAVILION	PERVIOUS
OVERLAND	PAMPHLET	PAVONINE	PESTERER
OVERLEAP	PANCREAS	PAWNSHOP	PETALINE
OVERLIVE	PANDANUS	PEACEFUL	PETALOID
OVERLOAD	PANDEMIC	PEARLASH	PETIOLAR
OVERLOOK	PANGOLIN	PEASECOD	PETIOLED
OVERLORD	PANICLED	PECCABLE	PETITION
OVERMUCH	PANNIKIN	PECCANCY	PETITORY
OVERNICE	PANORAMA	PECTINAL	PETRIFIC
OVERPASS	PANTHEON	PECTORAL	PETRONEL
OVERPLUS	PAPALIST	PECULATE	PETROSAL
OVERRATE	PAPALIZE	PECULIAR	PETTIFOG
OVERRIDE	PAPILLAE	PEDAGOGY	PETULANT
OVERRIPE	PAPISTIC	PEDANTIC	PEWTERER
OVERRULE	PAPISTRY	PEDANTRY	PHALANGE
OVERSEAS	PAPULOSE	PEDESTAL	PHANTASM
OVERSEER	PAPULOUS	PEDICURE	PHANTASY
OVERSHOE	PARABOLA	PEDIGREE	PHARISEE
OVERSMAN	PARADIGM	PEDIMANE	PHARMACY
OVERSTAY	PARADISE	PEDIMENT	PHEASANT
OVERSTEP	PARAFFIN	PEDUNCLE	PHENOGAM
OVERTAKE	PARAGOGE	PEERLESS	PHILABEG
OVERTASK	PARAGRAM	PELAGIAN	PHILIBEG
OVERTIME	PARAKEET	PELASGIC	PHILOMEL
OVERTONE	PARALLAX	PELERINE	PHOLADES
OVERTURE	PARALLEL	PELLAGRA	PHONETIC
OVERTURN	PARALYSE	PELLICLE	PHORMINX
OVERWEEN	PARALYZE	PELLUCID	PHORMIUM
OVERWIND	PARAMERE	PELTATED	PHTHISIC
OVERWISE	PARAMOUR	PEMMICAN	PHTHISIS
OVERWORK	PARASANG	PENCHANT	PHYLARCH
OVERWORN	PARASITE	PENDENCY	PHYLETIC
OXIDIZER	PARCENER	PENDULUM	PHYLLOID
OXYMORON	PARDONER	PENITENT	PHYSALIA
	PARENTAL	PENKNIFE	PHYSICAL
	PARERGON	PENOLOGY	PHYSIQUE
P	PARHELIC	PENSTOCK	PIACULAR
	PARHELIA	PENTACLE	PIANETTE
PACIFIER	PARIETAL	PENTAGON	PIASSAVA
PACKFONG	PARISIAN	PENTAGYN	PICAROON
PADISHAH	PARLANCE	*PENUMBRA	PICIFORM
PADUASOY	PARMESAN	PEPERINE	PICKEREL
PAGANISH	PARODIST	PEPERINO	PICKLOCK
PAGANISM	PAROXYSM	PERCEIVE	PIERCING
PAGANIZE		PERFORCE	PIGEONRY
PAGINATE	PARTAKER	PERFUMER	PILASTER
PAINLESS	PARTERRE	PERIAGUA	PILCHARD
PAINTING	PARTHIAN	PERIANTH	PILEATED
PAIRWISE	PARTIBLE	PERICARP	PILEWORT
PALATIAL	PARTISAN	PERIDERM	PILFERER

PILIFORM
PILLAGER
PILLARED
PILLOWED
PILLWORM
PILOTAGE
PINAFORE
PINASTER
PINDARIC
PINNACLE
PINNATED
PINNIPED
PINWHEEL
PIQUANCY
PISCATOR
PISIFORM
PISOLITE
PITHLESS
PITIABLE
PITIABLY
PITILESS
PITTANCE
PITYROID
PLACABLE
PLACEMAN
PLACENTA
PLACIDLY
PLAGIARY
PLAGUILY
PLANCHET
PLANGENT
PLANLESS
PLANTAIN
PLANTLET
PLASTERY
PLASTRON
PLATEAUS
PLATEAUX
PLATFORM
PLATINUM
PLATONIC
PLATTING
PLATYPUS
PLAUSIVE
PLAYBILL
PLAYGOER
PLAYMATE
PLEADING
PLEASANT
PLEASING
PLEASURE
PLEBEIAN
PLECTRUM
PLEIADES
PLEONASM
PLETHORA
PLEURISY
PLIANTLY
PLICATED
PLIGHTER
PLIOCENE
PLODDING
PLOUGHER
PLUCKILY
PLUMBAGO
PLUMBEAN
PLUMBERY
PLUMBING
PLUMBERY
PLUMELET

PLUMIPED
PLURALLY
PLUTONIC
PLUVIOUS
PODAGRAL
PODAGRIC
PODALGIA
POETICAL
POIGNANT
POISONER
POLARITY
POLARIZE
POLEMICS
POLICIES
POLISHED
POLISHER
POLITELY
POLITICS
POLLUTER
POLTROON
POLYGAMY
POLYGLOT
POLYGRAM
POLYGYNY
POLYPARY
POLYPITE
POLYPODY
POLYPOUS
POLYZOON
POMANDER
POMOLOGY
POORNESS
POPINJAY
POPISHLY
POPULACE
POPULATE
POPULOUS
PORIFORM
PORISTIC
POROSITY
POROUSLY
PORPHYRY
PORPOISE
PORRIDGE
PORT-WINE
PORTABLE
PORT-FIRE
PORT-HOLE
PORTICOS
PORTRAIT
PORTRESS
POSITION
POSITIVE
POSSIBLY
POST-CARD
POST-DATE
POST-HORN
POST-MARK
POST-OBIT
POST-PAID
POSTPONE
POST-TOWN
POSTURER
POTASSIC
POTATION
POTATOES
POTATORY
POTENTLY
POT-HOUSE
POTSHERD

POULTICE
POUNDAGE
POWDERED
POWERFUL
PRACTICE
PRACTISE
PRANDIAL
PRANKISH
PRATTLER
PREACHER
PREAMBLE
PRECINCT
PRECIOUS
PRECLUDE
PRE-EXIST
PREGNANT
PREJUDGE
PRELATIC
PREMOLAR
PREMORSE
PRENTICE
PREPARER
PREPENSE
PRESCIND
PRESENCE
PRESERVE
PRESSING
PRESSMAN
PRESSURE
PRESTIGE
PRETENCE
PRETENSE
PRETERIT
PRETTILY
PREVIOUS
PRICKING
PRIDEFUL
PRIE-DIEU
PRIESTLY
PRIGGISH
PRIMEVAL
PRIMNESS
PRIMROSE
PRINCELY
PRINCESS
PRINTING
PRIORATE
PRIORESS
PRIORITY
PRIORIES
PRISMOID
PRISONER
PRISTINE
PROBABLE
PROBABLY
PROCEEDS
PROCLAIM
PROCUROR
PRODIGAL
PRODUCER
PROEMIAL
PROFANER
PROFOUND
PROGRESS
PROHIBIT
PROLAPSE
PROLIFIC
PROLOGUE
PROMISER
PROMOTER

PROMPTER
PROMPTLY
PROPENSE
PROPERLY
PROPERTY
PROPHECY
PROPHESY
PROPLASM
PROPOLIS
PROPOSAL
PROPOSER
PROPOUND
PROPYLON
PROROGUE
PROSODIC
PROSPECT
PROSTATE
PROSTYLE
PROTASIS
PROTOCOL
PROTOZOA
PROTRACT
PROTRUDE
PROVABLE
PROVABLY
PROVIDED
PROVIDER
PROVINCE
PROXIMAL
PRUDENCE
PRUNELLA
PRURIENT
PRUSSIAN
PSALMIST
PSALMODY
PSALTERY
PSYCHIST
PTEROPOD
PTOMAINE
PTYALISM
PUBLICAN
PUBLICLY
PUDDLING
PUFF-BALL
PUGILISM
PUGILIST
PUISSANT
PULINGLY
PULMONIC
PUMPROOM
PUNCHEON
PUNCTATE
PUNCTUAL
PUNCTURE
PUNGENCY
PUNINESS
PUNISHER
PUNITIVE
PUNITORY
PUPARIAL
PUPILAGE
PUPILARY
PUPPYISH
PUPPYISM
PURBLIND
PURCHASE
PURENESS
PURIFIER
PURPLISH
PURSEFUL

PURSENET
PURSLANE
PURSUANT
PURULENT
PURVEYOR
PUSTULAR
PUTATIVE
PYOGENIC
PYRIFORM
PYROLOGY
PYROXENE
PYTHONIC
PYXIDIUM

Q

QUADRANT
QUADRATE
QUADRIGA
QUADROON
QUAESTOR
QUAGMIRE
QUAINTLY
QUALMISH
QUANDARY
QUANTITY
QUARRIER
QUARTERN
QUATRAIN
QUEASILY
QUEERISH
QUENCHER
QUESTION
QUIBBLER
QUICKSET
QUIDDITY
QUIDNUNC
QUIETISM
QUIETIST
QUIETUDE
QUILLING
QUILTING
QUINCUNX
QUIRKISH
QUITRENT
QUIVERED
QUIXOTIC
QUOTABLE
QUOTIENT

R

RABBINIC
RACEMOSE
RACHITIC
RACHITIS
RACINESS
RACK-RENT
RADIALLY
RADIANCE
RADICATE
RAGGEDLY
RAG-STONE
RAILLERY
RAILROAD
RAINBAND
RAINFALL

RAINLESS
RAISABLE
RAISONNE
RAKEHELL
RAKISHLY
RAMBLING
RAMPANCY
RANCHERO
RANCIDLY
RANKNESS
RANSOMER
RAPACITY
RAPE-CAKE
RAPIDITY
RAPTORES
RAPTURED
RARENESS
RASCALLY
RASHNESS
RASORIAL
RATIONAL
RATSBANE
RAVENOUS
RAVINGLY
RAVISHER
RE-ABSORB
REACTION
REACTIVE
READABLE
READABLY
READJUST
REAFFIRM
REALISER
REALNESS
REAPPEAR
REARMOST
REARWARD
REASONER
REASSERT
REASSIGN
REASSUME
REASSURE
REATTACH
REBUTTAL
REBUTTER
RECANTER
RECEIVER
RECENTLY
RECESSED
RECKLESS
RECKONER
RECOMMIT
RECONVEY
RECORDER
RECOURSE
RECOVERY
RECREANT
RECREATE
RECUSANT
REDACTOR
REDARGUE
REDEEMER
REDOUBLE
REDSHANK
REDSTART
REED-BAND
REED-MACE
REED-PIPE
RE-ENGAGE

RE-ENLIST
RE-EXPORT
RE-FASTEN
REFERRER
REFINERY
REFLEXED
REFLEXLY
REFLUENT
REFOREST
REFORMED
REFORMER
REFUNDER
REGALITY
REGARDER
REGATHER
REGICIDE
REGIMENT
REGIONAL
REGISTER
REGISTRY
REGRATER
REGROWTH
REGULATE
REHEARSE
REIMPORT
REIMPOSE
REINLESS
REINSERT
REINSURE
REINVEST
REJECTER
REJOICER
REKINDLE
RELATIVE
RELEASER
RELEGATE
RELEVANT
RELIABLE
RELIABLY
RELIANCE
RELIEVER
RELIGION
RELISTEN
REMANENT
REMARKER
REMARQUE
REMEDIAL
REMEMBER
REMINDER
REMISSLY
REMITTAL
REMITTEE
REMITTER
REMOTELY
RENDERER
RENDIBLE
RENEGADE
RENIFORM
RENNETED
RENOUNCE
RENOVATE
RENOWNED
REOCCUPY
REOMETER
REORDAIN
REPAIRER
REPARTEE
REPEALER
REPEATER

REPELLER
REPENTER
REPEOPLE
REPERUSE
REPETEND
REPLEVIN
REPORTER
REPOUSSE
REPRIEVE
REPRISAL
REPROACH
REPROVAL
REPROVER
REPTILIA
REPUBLIC
REQUITAL
REQUITER
REREWARD
RESCRIPT
RESEARCH
RESEMBLE
RESENTER
RESERVED
RESERVER
RESETTER
RESIDENT
RESIDUAL
RESIDUUM
RESIGNED
RESIGNER
RESINOUS
RESISTER
RESOLUTE
RESOLVED
RESOLVER
RESONANT
RESORTER
RESOURCE
RESPONSE
RESTLESS
RESTORER
RESTRAIN
RESTRICT
RESUPINE
RETAILER
RETAINER
RETARDER
RETICENT
RETICULE
RETIFORM
RETIRING
RETRENCH
RETRIEVE
RETROACT
RETRORSE
RETURNER
REVEALER
REVEILLE
REVELLER
REVENGER
REVEREND
REVERENT
REVIEWAL
REVIEWER
REVISION
REVIVIFY
REVOLTER
REVOLUTE
REVOLVER

REWARDER	ROTATORY	SAMAROID	SCHEMING
RHAPSODE	ROTIFORM	SAMENESS	SCHEMIST
RHAPSODY	ROTTENLY	SAMPHIRE	SCHIEDAM
RHEOSTAT	ROULETTE	SANATIVE	SCHNAPPS
RHEOTOME	ROWDYISM	SANATORY	SCHOLIUM
RHETORIC	ROYALISM	SANCTIFY	SCHOONER
RHIZANTH	ROYALIST	SANCTION	SCIATICA
RHIZOGEN	RUBICUND	SANCTITY	SCILICET
RHIZOPOD	RUBIDIUM	SAND-BANK	SCIMITAR
RHOMBOID	RUBRICAL	SAND-BATH	SCIOLISM
RHONCHUS	RUDENESS	SAND-FLEA	SCIOLIST
RHYTHMIC	RUDIMENT	SAND-HILL	SCIOLOUS
RIBALDRY	RUEFULLY	SANDIVER	SCIOPTIC
RICHNESS	RUFFLING	SAND-MOLE	SCIRRHUS
RICOCHET	RUGGEDLY	SANDWICH	SCISSION
RIDDANCE	RUGOSITY	SANENESS	SCISSORS
RIDICULE	RUINABLE	SANGAREE	SCIURINE
RIFENESS	RULELESS	SANGUINE	SCLEROMA
RIFFRAFF	RUMINANT	SANITARY	SCOLDING
RIFLEMAN	RUMINATE	SANSKRIT	SCOOP-NET
RIGADOON	RUMMAGER	SAP-GREEN	SCORNFUL
RIGHTFUL	RUM-SHRUB	SAPIDITY	SCORPION
RIGIDITY	RUNAGATE	SAPIENCE	SCOT-FREE
RIGOROUS	RUNOLOGY	SAPONIFY	SCOTSMAN
RING-BOLT	RURALISM	SAPPHIRE	SCOTTICE
RING-BONE	RURALISE	SARABAND	SCOTTISH
RING-DOVE	RUTABAGA	SARCENET	SCOURGER
RINGWORM	RUTHLESS	SARDONIC	SCOWLING
RIPARIAL	RYE-GRASS	SARDONYX	SCRABBLE
RIPENESS		SARGASSO	SCRAGGED
RITUALLY		SARMENTA	SCRAMBLE
RIVERINE	**S**	SARSENET	SCRANNEL
RIVETING		SATIABLE	SCRAPING
ROAD-BOOK	SABBATIC	SATIRIST	SCRAWLER
ROADSTER	SABULOUS	SATIRIZE	SCREAMER
ROBORANT	SACCULAR	SATURATE	SCREECHY
ROBURITE	SACREDLY	SATURDAY	SCREW-KEY
ROCK-CORK	SACRISTY	SAUCE-BOX	SCRIBBLE
ROCK-ROSE	SADDLERY	SAUCE-PAN	SCROFULA
ROCK-RUBY	SADDUCEE	SAVAGELY	SCROLLED
ROCK-SALT	SAFENESS	SAVAGERY	SCRUBBER
ROCK-SOAP	SAGACITY	SAVAGISM	SCRUB-OAK
ROCK-WOOD	SAGAMORE	SAVANNAH	SCRUPLER
ROCK-WORK	SAGE-COCK	SAVINGLY	SCRUTINY
RODENTIA	SAGENESS	SAVOYARD	SCUFFLER
ROLL-CALL	SAILLESS	SAW-FRAME	SCULLERY
ROLY-POLY	SAIL-LOFT	SAXATILE	SCULLION
ROMANCER	SAINFOIN	SAXONISM	SCULPTOR
ROMANISM	SALAD-OIL	SAXONIST	SCURRILE
ROMANIST	SALARIED	SCABBARD	SCURVILY
ROMANIZE	SALARIES	SCABIOUS	SCUTCHER
ROMANTIC	SALEABLE	SCABROUS	SCUTELLA
ROOD-BEAM	SALEABLY	SCAFFOLD	SCYTHIAN
ROOD-LOFT	SALESMAN	SCALABLE	SEA-ACORN
ROOFLESS	SALICINE	SCALLION	SEA-BOARD
ROOF-TREE	SALIENCE	SCAMMONY	SEA-COAST
ROOT-CROP	SALIVANT	SCAMPISH	SEA-DEVIL
ROOTEDLY	SALIVARY	SCANDENT	SEA-EAGLE
ROPE-WALK	SALIVATE	SCANSION	SEAFARER
ROPINESS	SALMONET	SCANTILY	SEAFIGHT
ROSARIAN	SALT-BUSH	SCAPHOID	SEA-GOING
ROSEMARY	SALT-JUNK	SCAPULAR	SEA-GRASS
ROSE-PINK	SALTLESS	SCARCELY	SEA-GREEN
ROSEWOOD	SALT-LICK	SCARCITY	SEA-HORSE
ROSINESS	SALT-MINE	SCATHING	SEA-LEMON
ROSOGLIO	SALTNESS	SCENARIO	SEA-LEVEL
ROSTELLA	SALT-WORK	SCENICAL	SEA-LOUSE
ROSTRATE	SALTWORT	SCENTFUL	SEAL-SKIN
ROTATION	SALUTARY	SCEPTRAD	SEAMLESS
ROTATIVE	SALVABLE	SCHEDULE	SEA-ONION

SEARCHER
SEA-ROVER
SEA-SCAPE
SEA-SHORE
SEA-SNAKE
SEASONAL
SEASONER
SEA-WRACK
SECLUDED
SECONDER
SECONDLY
SECRETLY
SECTORAL
SECURELY
SECURITY
SEDATELY
SEDATIVE
SEDERUNT
SEDIMENT
SEDITION
SEDULITY
SEDULOUS
SEED-CAKE
SEED-CORN
SEEDLING
SEEDSMAN
SEERSHIP
SEIGNIOR
SEIGNORY
SEIZABLE
SELECTOR
SELENITE
SELENIUM
SELF-HELP
SELF-LOVE
SELF-MADE
SELF-SAME
SELF-WILL
SELVEDGE
SEMESTER
SEMI-DOME
SEMI-MUTE
SEMINARY
SEMITONE
SEMOLINA
SENILITY
SENORITA
SENSIBLE
SENSIBLY
SENSIFIC
SENSUOUS
SENTENCE
SENTIENT
SENTINEL
SENTRIES
SEPALINE
SEPALOID
SEPALOUS
SEPARATE
SEPTETTE
SEPTICLE
SEQUENCE
SERAGLIO
SERAPHIM
SERAPHIC
SERENADE
SERENELY
SERENITY
SERGEANT

SERIALLY
SERIATIM
SERJEANT
SEROSITY
SERRATED
SERVITOR
SESAMOID
SESS-POOL
SESTERCE
SESTETTE
SETIFORM
SETTLING
SEVERELY
SEVERITY
SEWERAGE
SEXANGLE
SEXTUPLE
SEXUALLY
SHABBILY
SHABRACK
SHADDOCK
SHAFTING
SHAGREEN
SHALLOON
SHAMANIC
SHAMBLES
SHAMEFUL
SHAMROCK
SHANTIES
SHAPABLE
SHARP-CUT
SHARP-SET
SHATTERY
SHEALING
SHEARING
SHEATHED
SHEEP-DOG
SHEEPISH
SHEEP-RUN
SHEETING
SHEILING
SHELVING
SHEMITIC
SHEPHERD
SHILLING
SHIN-BONE
SHINGLED
SHINGLES
SHIPMATE
SHIPMENT
SHIPPING
SHIP-WORM
SHIP-YARD
SHIRTING
SHOCKING
SHOE-HORN
SHOELESS
SHOOTING
SHORTAGE
SHORT-RIB
SHOT-BELT
SHOULDER
SHOW-ROOM
SHRAPNEL
SHREWDLY
SHREWISH
SHRIMPER
SHRUNKEN
SHUFFLER
SIBILANT

SIBILATE
SICK-LIST
SICKNESS
SICK-ROOM
SIDE-ARMS
SIDE-DISH
SIDELONG
SIDEREAL
SIDERITE
SIDESMAN
SIDE-WALK
SIDEWAYS
SIDE-WIND
SIDEWISE
SIGMATIC
SIGNABLE
SIGNALLY
SIGNETED
SIGN-POST
SILENTLY
SILICATE
SILICIFY
SILICULA
SILICULE
SILICIUM
SILIQUAE
SILK-MILL
SILK-WORM
SILLABUB
SILURIAN
SILVERLY
SIMONIAC
SIMPERER
SIMPLIFY
SIMULATE
SINAITIC
SINAPISM
SINCIPUT
SINECURE
SINFULLY
SING-SONG
SINGULAR
SINISTER
SINOLOGY
SIPHONAL
SIPHONIC
SIRENIAN
SISTERLY
SITOLOGY
SITUATED
SITZ-BATH
SIXPENCE
SIXPENNY
SIXTIETH
SIZEABLE
SKEAN-DHU
SKELETAL
SKELETON
SKERRIES
SKETCHER
SKEW-BALD
SKILLESS
SKIN-DEEP
SKINLESS
SKIN-WOOL
SKIP-JACK
SKIPPING
SKIRMISH
SKIRRHUS

SKITTISH
SKITTLES
SKUA-GULL
SKULLESS
SKY-LIGHT
SLAP-DASH
SLASHING
SLATTERN
SLAVERER
SLAVONIC
SLEEPILY
SLEEPING
SLIGHTLY
SLIME-PIT
SLIMNESS
SLIP-DOCK
SLIPPERY
SLIP-SHOD
SLIPSLOP
SLOBBERY
SLOP-SHOP
SLOTHFUL
SLOVENLY
SLOWNESS
SLOW-WORM
SLUGGARD
SLUGGISH
SLUTTERY
SLUTTISH
SMACKING
SMALLAGE
SMELLING
SMELTERY
SMITHERY
SMOKE-BOX
SMOOTHEN
SMOOTHLY
SMOTHERY
SMOULDER
SMUGGLER
SMUGNESS
SMUT-BALL
SMUTTILY
SNAPPISH
SNAP-SHOT
SNARLING
SNATCHER
SNEAKING
SNEEZING
SNIVELLY
SNOBBERY
SNOBBISH
SNOBBISM
SNOW-BALL
SNOW-BIRD
SNOW-BOOT
SNOW-DROP
SNOW-LINE
SNOW-SHOE
SNOW-SLIP
SNUB-NOSE
SNUFF-BOX
SNUFFLER
SNUGGERY
SNUGNESS
SOBRIETY
SOCIABLE
SOCIABLY
SOCIALLY
SOCINIAN

SOCRATIC	SPECIMEN	STAGNANT	STRAIGHT
SODOMITE	SPECIOUS	STAGNATE	STRAINED
SOFTENER	SPECKLED	STAIR-ROD	STRAINER
SOFTNESS	SPECTRAL	STAKE-NET	STRAITEN
SOIL-PIPE	SPECTRUM	STALKING	STRAITLY
SOLATIUM	SPECULAR	STALLAGE	STRANGER
SOLDERER	SPECULUM	STALLION	STRANGLE
SOLDIERY	SPEEDILY	STALWART	STRAPPER
SOLECISM	SPELAEAN	STAMENED	STRATEGY
SOLECIST	SPELLING	STAMINAL	STRATIFY
SOLECIZE	SPERM-OIL	STAMP-ACT	STREAMER
SOLEMNLY	SPHAGNUM	STAMPEDE	STRENGTH
SOLENESS	SPHENOID	STAMPING	STRIATED
SOLIDIFY	SPHERICS	STANCHER	STRICKEN
SOLIDITY	SPHEROID	STANCHLY	STRICKLE
SOLITARY	SPHERULE	STANDARD	STRICTLY
SOLITUDE	SPHYGMIC	STANDING	STRIDENT
SOLSTICE	SPICULAR	STANDISH	STRIKING
SOLUTION	SPIKELET	STANHOPE	STRINGED
SOLVABLE	SPIKE-OIL	STANNARY	STRINGER
SOLVENCY	SPINELLE	STANZAIC	STRIPPER
SOMATIST	SPINIFEX	STAPELLA	STROBILE
SOMBRELY	SPINSTER	STARCHED	STRONGLY
SOMBRERO	SPIRICLE	STARCHER	STRONTIA
SOMBROUS	SPIRALLY	STARFISH	STROPHIC
SOMEBODY	SPIRILLA	STARLESS	STRUGGLE
SOMERSET	SPIRITED	STARLIKE	STRUMOSE
SOME-SUCH	SPITEFUL	STARLING	STRUMOUS
SOMETIME	SPITFIRE	STATEDLY	STRUMPET
SOMEWHAT	SPITTOON	STATICAL	STRUTTER
SOMNIFIC	SPLENDID	STATUARY	STUBBLED
SONG-BIRD	SPLENDOR	STEADILY	STUBBORN
SONGLESS	SPLINTER	STEALING	STUD-BOOK
SONGSTER	SPLITTER	STEALTHY	STUDIOUS
SON-IN-LAW	SPLOTCHY	STEAM-TUG	STUFFING
SONORITY	SPLUTTER	STEARINE	STULTIFY
SONOROUS	SPOLIATE	STEATITE	STUMBLER
SOOTHING	SPONDAIC	STEDFAST	STUNNING
SOPRANOS	SPONSION	STEELING	STUPIDLY
SORCERER	SPONTOON	STEENBOK	STUPRATE
SORDIDLY	SPOOKISH	STEEPLED	STURDILY
SORENESS	SPOONFUL	STEERAGE	STURGEON
SORTABLE	SPORADIC	STELLARY	SUBACRID
SORTMENT	SPORIDIA	STELLATE	SUBACUTE
SOUCHONG	SPORTFUL	STEM-LEAF	SUBCLASS
SOULLESS	SPORTING	STEMLESS	SUBEROSE
SOUNDING	SPORTIVE	STERLING	SUBEROUS
SOURNESS	SPOTLESS	STIBNITE	SUB-GENUS
SOUTHERN	SPRIGGED	STICKLER	SUB-LEASE
SOUTHING	SPRINGER	STILETTO	SUBLUNAR
SOUVENIR	SPRINKLE	STIMULUS	SUBMERGE
SOW-BREAD	SPRUCELY	STINGILY	SUBMERSE
SPACIOUS	SPURGALL	STINGING	SUBORDER
SPADEFUL	SPUR-GEAR	STING-RAY	SUBORNER
SPALPEEN	SPURIOUS	STINK-POT	SUBOVATE
SPANDREL	SQUABBLE	STIPULAR	SUBPOENA
SPANGLED	SQUADRON	STIRLESS	SUB-POLAR
SPANIARD	SQUAMATE	STIRRING	SUBSERVE
SPANKING	SQUAMOUS	STOCKADE	SUBTLETY
SPAN-ROOF	SQUANDER	STOCK-POT	SUB-TONIC
SPARABLE	SQUARELY	STOICISM	SUBTRACT
SPAR-DECK	SQUATTER	STOMATIC	SUBULATE
SPARERIB	SQUEAKER	STOOPING	SUBURBAN
SPARKISH	SQUEEZER	STOP-COCK	SUCCINCT
SPARSELY	SQUIRREL	STOPPAGE	SUCCINIC
SPATHOSE	STABLE-BOY	STOPPING	SUCHWISE
SPAVINED	STABLE-MAN	STORMFUL	SUCKLING
SPEAKING	STABLING	STOWAWAY	SUDATORY
SPEARMAN	STABLISH	STRADDLE	SUDDENLY
SPECIFIC	STACCATO	STRAGGLE	SUFFERER

SUFFRAGE		TECHNICS	THINKING
SUICIDAL	**T**	TECTONIC	THINNESS
SUITABLE		TEETHING	THINNISH
SUITABLY	TABBINET	TEETOTAL	THIRSTER
SULCATED	TABBY-CAT	TEE-TOTUM	THIRTEEN
SULLENLY	TABLEAUX	TEGUMENT	THOLE-PIN
SULPHATE	TABOURET	TELEGRAM	THORACIC
SULPHOID	TABULATE	TELLABLE	THORINUM
SULPHITE	TACITURN	TELL-TALE	THOROUGH
SULPHURY	TACKLING	TELLURAL	THOUSAND
SULTANIC	TACKSMAN	TELLURIC	THRALDOM
SUMMONER	TACTICAL	TEMERITY	THRASHER
SUN-BURNT	TACTLESS	TEMPERED	THREATEN
SUNLIGHT	TAENIOID	TEMPORAL	THRENODY
SUN-SHADE	TAFFERAL	TEMPTING	THRIVING
SUNSHINE	TAFFEREL	TEMULENT	THROMBUS
SUNSHINY	TAILLESS	TENACITY	THROSTIC
SUPERADD	TAIL-RACE	TENANTRY	THROTTLE
SUPERBLY	TAKINGLY	TENDANCE	THRUMMER
SUPERIOR	TALISMAN	TENDENCY	THUMPING
SUPINELY	TALLIAGE	TENDERLY	THUNDERY
SUPPLANT	TALLNESS	TENEMENT	THURIBLE
SUPPLIER	TALLOWER	TENESMIC	THURIFER
SUPPOSER	TALLYMAN	TENESMUS	THURSDAY
SUPPRESS	TALMUDIC	TENON-SAW	THWARTER
SURCEASE	TAMEABLE	TENT-WINE	THWARTLY
SURGICAL	TAMANDUA	TENTACLE	TICKLING
SURMISER	TARAMACK	TERMINAL	TICKLISH
SURMOUNT	TAMARIND	TERMINUS	TIDE-GATE
SURPLICE	TAMARISK	TERMLESS	TIDELESS
SURROUND	TAMELESS	TERRAPIN	TIDE-MILL
SURVEYOR	TAMENESS	TERRIBLE	TIDE-WAVE
SURVIVAL	TAMPERER	TERRIBLY	TIDINESS
SURVIVOR	TAN-BALLS	TERRIFIC	TIGERISH
SUSPENSE	TANGENCY	TERTIARY	TILLABLE
SUTTLING	TANGIBLE	TESSERAE	TIMBERED
SUZERAIN	TANGIBLY	TESTATOR	TIME-BALL
SWANNERY	TANISTRY	TESTICLE	TIME-BILL
SWANSKIN	TANNABLE	TETANOID	TIME-FUSE
SWASHING	TANTALUM	TETRAGON	TIMELESS
SWEEPING	TAPE-LINE	TETRAPOD	TIME-WORN
SWEET-BAY	TAPESTRY	TETRARCH	TIMIDITY
SWEETING	TAPE-WORM	TEUTONIC	TIMOROUS
SWEETISH	TAP-HOUSE	TEXT-BOOK	TINCTURE
SWEET-PEA	TARA-FERN	TEXT-HAND	TINKLING
SWEET-SOP	TARBOOSH	THALAMUS	TINPLATE
SWELLING	TARGETED	THALLINE	TINSMITH
SWIMMING	TARLATAN	THALLIUM	TINTLESS
SWINDLER	TARTARIC	THANEDOM	TIP-STAFF
SWORD-ARM	TARTNESS	THANKFUL	TIRESOME
SYBARITE	TARTRATE	THATCHER	TITANIAN
SYCAMINE	TASK-WORK	THEARCHY	TITANIUM
SYCAMORE	TASTABLE	THEATRIC	TITHABLE
SYLLABIC	TASTEFUL	THEISTIC	TITHE-PIG
SYLLABLE	TATTERED	THEMATIC	TITMOUSE
SYLLABUS	TATTLING	THEOCRAT	TITULARY
SYMBOLIC	TATTOOER	THEODICY	TOAD-FISH
SYMMETRY	TAUNTING	THEOGONY	TOAD-FLAX
SYMPATHY	TAVERNER	THEOLOGY	TOAD-SPIT
SYMPHONY	TAWDRILY	THEORIST	TOADYISM
SYMPOSIA	TAXATION	THEORIZE	TO-AND-FRO
SYNOPSIS	TAXOLOGY	THEORIES	TOBOGGAN
~~SYNTONIN~~	~~TEA-PARTY~~	~~THERAPY~~	~~TOILETTE~~
SYPHILIS	TEA-CHEST	THESPIAN	TOILSOME
SYSTEMIC	TEACHING	THEURGIC	TOIL-WORN
SYSTOLIC	TEAMSTER	THICKISH	TOLBOOTH
SYZYGIES	TEAR-DROP	THICKSET	TOLERANT
	TEARLESS	THIEVERY	TOLERATE
	TEASELER	THIEVISH	TOLLABLE

TOLL-GATE
TOLL-MAN
TOMAHAWK
TOMATOES
TOMBLESS
TOMENTUM
TOM-NODDY
TOMORROW
TONALITY
TONELESS
TONICITY
TONSILAR
TONSURED
TOOTHFUL
TOP-BOOTS
TOP-DRESS
TOP-HEAVY
TOPONOMY
TOREADOR
TOREUTIC
TORTIOUS
TORTOISE
TORTUOSE
TORTUOUS
TORTURER
TOTALITY
TOTEMISM
TOTTERER
TOUCHILY
TOUCHING
TOUGHISH
TOURNURE
TOWARDLY
TOWERING
TOWN-HALL
TOWNSHIP
TOWNSMAN
TOWN-TALK
TOWNWARD
TOXICANT
TRACHEAL
TRACHYTE
TRACKAGE
TRACTATE
TRACTION
TRACTIVE
TRADUCER
TRAGICAL
TRAGOPAN
TRAIL-NET
TRAINING
TRAIN-OIL
TRAMPLER
TRAM-ROAD
TRANQUIL
TRANSACT
TRANSEPT
TRANSFER
TRANSFIX
TRANSHIP
TRANSMIT
TRANSUDE
TRAP-BALL
TRAP-DOOR
TRAPEZIA
TRAPPEAN
TRAPPING
TRAPPIST
TRAP-TUFA
TRASHILY

TRAVELED
TRAVELER
TRAVERSE
TRAVESTY
TRAWLING
TRAWL-NET
TREASURE
TREASURY
TREATING
TREATISE
TREELESS
TREENAIL
TREMBLER
TRENCHER
TREPHINE
TRESPASS
TRIANDER
TRIANGLE
TRIARCHY
TRIASSIC
TRIBRACH
TRIBUNAL
TRICHINA
TRICHOMA
TRICHORD
TRICKERY
TRICKING
TRICKISH
TRICYCLE
TRIFLING
TRIGLYPH
TRIGONAL
TRIGRAPH
TRILLION
TRIMETER
TRIMMING
TRIMNESS
TRIPPING
TRIPTOTE
TRIPTYCH
TRIUMVIR
TRIVALVE
TROCHAIC
TROCHOEA
TROCHOID
TROLLING
TROMBONE
TROOPIAL
TROPHIED
TROPHIES
TROPICAL
TROUBLER
TROUSERS
TROUTLET
TROUVERE
TRUCKAGE
TRUCKLER
TRUEBLUE
TRUEBORN
TRUEBRED
TRUELOVE
TRUENESS
TRUFFLED
TRUMPERY
TRUNCATE
TRUNNION
TRUSSING
TRUSTFUL
TRUSTILY
TRUTHFUL

TUBERCLE
TUBEROSE
TUBEROUS
TUBEWELL
TUBIFORN
TUBULOSE
TUBULOUS
TUMBLING
TUMIDITY
TUNELESS
TUNGSTEN
TUNGSTIC
TUNICATE
TURANIAN
TURBANED
TURGIDLY
TURMERIC
TURN-COAT
TURN-COCK
TRUNPIKE
TURNSOLE
TURNSPIT
TURRETED
TUTELAGE
TUTELARY
TUTORAGE
TUTORESS
TUTORIAL
TWADDLER
TWEAZERS
TWILIGHT
TWIN-BORN
TWINLING
TWITCHER
TWO-EDGED
TWO-FACED
TWOPENCE
TWOPENNY
TYMPAMIC
TYMPANUM
TYPIFIER
TYPOLOGY
TYRANNIC
TYROLESE

U

UBIQUITY
UDOMETER
UGLINESS
ULCERATE
ULCEROUS
ULTERIOR
ULTIMATE
ULTRAISM
ULTRAIST
UMBONATE
UMBRELLA
UMPIRAGE
UNABATED
UNALLIED
UNATONED
UNAVOWED
UNAWARES
UNBELIEF
UNBIASED
UNBIDDEN
UNBOLTED
UNBOUGHT

UNBROKEN
UNBUCKLE
UNBURDEN
UNBURIED
UNBURNED
UNBUTTON
UNCALLED
UNCANDID
UNCHASED
UNCHURCH
UNCIFORM
UNCINATE
UNCLOTHE
UNCOMELY
UNCOMMON
UNCOUPLE
UNCTUOUS
UNDECKED
UNDERBID
UNDERBUY
UNDERLAY
UNDERLIE
UNDERPIN
UNDULATE
UNEARNED
UNEASILY
UNENDING
UNENVIED
UNERRING
UNEVENLY
UNFADING
UNFAIRLY
UNFASTEN
UNFETTER
UNFILIAL
UNFORGOT
UNFORMED
UNFUNDED
UNGAINLY
UNGENTLE
UNGENTLY
UNGLAZED
UNGULATE
UNHANGED
UNHARMED
UNHEEDED
UNHOLILY
UNIAXIAL
UNIFILAR
UNIONISM
UNIONIST
UNIPOLAR
UNIQUELY
UNITEDLY
UNIVALVE
UNIVERSE
UNIVOCAL
UNJUSTLY
UNKENNEL
UNKINDLY
UNLAWFUL
UNLIKELY
UNLIMBER
UNLOVELY
UNMEETLY
UNMUFFLE
UNMUZZLE
UNPATHED
UNPEOPLE
UNPITIED

UNPOETIC
UNPOLITE
UNPROVED
UNREASON
UNREPAID
UNRIDDLE
UNSADDLE
UNSAFELY
UNSEALED
UNSEEMLY
UNSETTLE
UNSHAKEN
UNSHAPEN
UNSHROUD
UNSIFTED
UNSLAKED
UNSOCIAL
UNSOILED
UNSOUGHT
UNSOURED
UNSPOKEN
UNSTABLE
UNSTEADY
UNSTRING
UNSTRUNG
UNSUITED
UNSWATHE
UNTASTED
UNTHREAD
UNTHRIFT
UNTIDILY
UNTIMELY
UNTINGED
UNTIRING
UNTITLED
UNTOWARD
UNVALUED
UNVARIED
UNVERSED
UNVOICED
UNWARILY
UNWARPED
UNWASHED
UNWASHEN
UNWIELDY
UNWISDOM
UNWISELY
UNWISHED
UNWANTED
UNWORTHY
UPGROWTH
UPHEAVAL
UPHOLDER
UPLANDER
UPRISING
UPSPRING
UP-STROKE
URBANITY
URETHRAL
URGENTLY
UROSCOPY
URSULINE
URTICATE
USEFULLY
USUFRUCT
USURIOUS
UXORIOUS

V

VACATION
VAGABOND
VAGINATE
VAGRANCY
VAINNESS
VALERIAN
VALIDATE
VALIDITY
VALOROUS
VALUABLE
VALUATOR
VALVULAR
VANADIUM
VANDALIC
VANGUARD
VANQUISH
VAPORIZE
VAPOROSE
VAPOROUS
VAPOURER
VARIABLE
VARIABLY
VARIANCE
VARICOSE
VARIETAL
VARIFORM
VARIOLAR
VARIORUM
VARLETRY
VASCULAR
VASCULUM
VASELINE
VASIFORM
VASSALRY
VASTNESS
VAULTING
VEGETATE
VEHEMENT
VEILLESS
VEINLESS
VELARIUM
VELLEITY
VELOCITY
VENALITY
VENATION
VENDETTA
VENDIBLE
VENDIBLY
VENERATE
VENEREAL
VENETIAN
VENGEFUL
VENIALLY
VENOMOUS
VENOSITY
VENTURER
VERACITY
VERANDAH
VERATRIN
VERBALLY
VERBATIM
VERBIAGE
VERDANCY
VERDERER
VERDITER
VERDURED
VERIFIER

VERJUICE
VERONICA
VERSICLE
VERTEXES
VERTICES
VERTICLE
VERTICAL
VESICANT
VESICATE
VESPIARY
VESTMENT
VESTURED
VESUVIAN
VEXATION
VEXILLAR
VEXILLUM
VIATICUM
VIBRATOR
VICARAGE
VICARIAL
VICENARY
VICINAGE
VICINITY
VICTORIA
VICTRESS
VIENNESE
VIEWLESS
VIGILANT
VIGNERON
VIGNETTE
VIGOROUS
VILENESS
VILIFIER
VILIPEND
VILLAGER
VILLAINY
VINCIBLE
VINCULUM
VINE-CLAD
VINEYARD
VINOSITY
VINTAGER
VINTNERY
VIOLABLE
VIOLATOR
VIOLENCE
VIPERINE
VIPERISH
VIPEROUS
VIRGINAL
VIRIDITY
VIRILITY
VIRTUOSO
VIRTUOUS
VIRULENT
VISCERAL
VISCOUNT
VISIGOTH
VISIONAL
VISITANT
VISITING
VITALISM
VITALIST
VITALITY
VITALIZE
VITELLUS
VITIATOR
VITREOUS
VITULINE
VIVACITY

VIVARIUM
VIVA VOCE
VIXENISH
VOCALIST
VOCALITY
VOCALIZE
VOCATION
VOCATIVE
VOICEFUL
VOIDABLE
VOIDANCE
VOIDNESS
VOLATILE
VOLCANIC
VOLITION
VOLITIVE
VOLTAISM
VOMITING
VOMITORY
VORACITY
VORTICES
VORTICLE
VOTARESS
VOTARIST
VOTARIES
VOTIVELY
VOUSSOIR
VOWELISM
VOWELLED
VOYAGEUR
VOLCANIC
VULGARLY

W

WAGONAGE
WAINSCOT
WAITRESS
WALL-EYED
WALLOWER
WALL-TREE
WANDERER
WANDEROO
WANTONLY
WAR-DANCE
WARDENRY
WARDROBE
WARD-ROOM
WARDSHIP
WAR-HORSE
WARINESS
WARMNESS
WAR-PAINT
WARRANTY
WARRENER
WAR-WHOOP
WASHABLE
WASTEFUL
WATCH-DOG
WATCHFUL
WATCHMAN

WATER-GAS
WATER-HEN
WATERING
WATERMAN
WATER-POT
WATER-POX
WATER-RAM

WATER-RAT
WATTLING
WAVELESS
WAVE-WORN
WAX-CLOTH
WAXED-END
WAXINESS
WAX-LIGHT
WAYFARER
WEAKLING
WEAKNESS
WEANLING
WEAPONED
WEARABLE
WEEKLIES
WEEVILED
WELCOMER
WELDABLE
WELLADAY
WELL-BORN
WELL-BRED
WELL-KNIT
WELL-READ
WELL-ROOM
WELL-TO-DO
WELL-WORN
WEREWOLF
WESLEYAN
WESTERLY
WESTMOST
WESTWARD
WET-NURSE
WHARFAGE
WHATEVER
WHEATEAR
WHEAT-EEL
WHEAT-FLY
WHEEDLER
WHEELMAN
WHENEVER
WHEREVER
WHERRIES
WHEY-FACE
WHIFFLER
WHIGGERY
WHIGGISH
WHIMBREL
WHIMSIES

WHIN-CHAT
WHIP-CORD
WHIP-HAND
WHIP-LASH
WHIPPING
WHIPSTER
WHIRLWIG
WHIRRING
WHISTLER
WHITEBOY
WHITE-LEG
WHITENER
WHOREDOM
WHORESON
WICKEDLY
WICKERED
WIDENESS
WIFEHOOD
WIFELIKE
WIG-BLOCK
WILD-BOAR
WILDFIRE
WILD-FOWL
WILDNESS
WILD-WOOD
WILFULLY
WILINESS
WINDFALL
WINDGALL
WINDLASS
WINDLESS
WIND-MILL
WINDOWED
WINDPIPE
WINDROSE
WIND-SAIL
WINDWARD
WING-CASE
WINGLESS
WINNOWER
WINTERLY
WIRE-DRAW
WIRE-ROPE
WIRE-WORM
WIRE-WOVE
WIRINESS
WISEACRE
WISENESS

WISH-BONE
WISTERIA
WITCH-ELM
WITCHERY
WITCHING
WITHDRAW
WITHHOLD
WOEFULLY
WOLF-FISH
WOMANISH
WONDERER
WONDROUS
WOODBINE
WOOD-COAL
WOODCOCK
WOODENLY
WOODLAND
WOOD-LARK
WOODRUFF
WOOD-WORK
WOOINGLY
WOOL-DYED
WOOL-MILL
WOOLPACK
WOOLSACK
WOOLWARD
WORD-BOOK
WORKABLE
WORKADAY
WORKSHOP
WORM-CAST
WORMLING
WORMWOOD
WORRYING
WORTHILY
WRANGLER
WRAPPAGE
WRAPPING
WRATHFUL
WRECKAGE
WRESTLER
WRETCHED
WRIGGLER
WRINKLED
WRISTLET
WRONGFUL
WRONGOUS

X

XANTHOMA
XANTHOUS
XENOGAMY
XYLOCARP

Y

YACHTING
YATAGHAN
YEANLING
YEAR-BOOK
YEARLING
YEARNING
YEOMANLY
YEOMANRY
YIELDING
YOKE-MATE
YOUNGISH
YOURSELF
YOUTHFUL
YULE-TIDE

Z

ZAMINDAR
ZEALOTRY
ZEMINDAR
ZENITHAL
ZEOLITIC
ZIGZAGGY
ZODIACAL
ZOETROPE
ZOOLATRY
ZOOPHILE
ZOOPHILY
ZOOPHYTE
ZOOSPERM
ZOOSPORE
ZOOTOMIC
ZYMOLOGY

NINE-LETTER WORDS

A

ABANDONED
ABANDONER
ABASHMENT
ABATEMENT
ABBOTSHIP
ABDOMINAL
ABDUCTION
ABERRANCE
ABHORRENT
ABHORRING
ABIDINGLY
ABJECTION
ABNEGATOR
ABOLISHER
ABOLITION
ABOMINATE
ABORIGINE
ABRAHAMIC
ABSCONDER
ABSINTHIC
ABSORBENT
ABSTAINER
ABSTINENT
ABSURDITY
ABUNDANCE
ABUSIVELY
ACALEPHAE
ACCENTUAL
ACCESSARY
ACCESSION
ACCESSORY
ACCIDENCE
ACCIPITER
ACCLIMATE
ACCLIVITY
ACCLIVOUS
ACCOMPANY
ACCORDANT
ACCORDING
ACCORDION
ACCRETION
ACCRETIVE
ACCUMBENT
ACCUSABLE
ACESCENCE
ACETIFIER
ACETYLENE
ACIDIFIER
ACIDULATE
ACIDULENT
ACIDULOUS
ACINIFORM
ACOUSTICS
ACQUIESCE
ACQUITTAL
ACROMATIC
ACROPOLIS
ACROSPIRE
ACTUALIST
ACTUALITY
ACUMINATE
ACUTENESS

ADAPTABLE
ADDICTION
ADDRESSED
ADDRESSEE
ADDRESSER
ADDUCIBLE
ADDUCTION
ADENOTOMY
ADHERENCE
ADIPOCERE
ADJACENCE
ADJECTIVE
ADJOINING
ADJUTANCY
ADMEASURE
ADMINICLE
ADMIRABLE
ADMIRABLY
ADMIRALTY
ADMISSION
ADMIXTION
ADMIXTURE
ADMONITOR
ADOPTABLE
ADORATION
ADORINGLY
ADORNMENT
ADULATION
ADULTERER
ADULTNESS
ADUMBRANT
ADUMBRATE
ADVANTAGE
ADVENTUAL
ADVENTURE
ADVERBIAL
ADVERSARY
ADVERSELY
ADVERTENT
ADVERTISE
ADVISABLE
ADVISABLY
ADVISEDLY
ADVOCATOR
AEGOPHONY
AEPYORNIS
AEROMETER
AEROMETRY
AEROPHYTE
AEROPLANE
AESTHETIC
AETIOLOGY
AFFECTING
AFFECTION
AFFIANCED
AFFIDAVIT
AFFILIATE
AFFIRMANT
AFFLATION
AFOREHAND
AFORESAID
AFORETIME
AFTER-CROP
AFTER-DAMP
AFTER-GLOW

AFTER-LIFE
AFTERMATH
AFTERMOST
AFTERNOON
AFTERWARD
AGGRAVATE
AGGREGATE
AGGRESSOR
AGITATION
AGONISTIC
AGONIZING
AGREEABLE
AGREEABLY
AGREEMENT
AIMLESSLY
AIR-ENGINE
AIR-JACKET
AITCHBONE
AITIOLOGY
ALABASTER
ALACK-A-DAY
ALARM-BELL
ALBATROSS
ALBESCENT
ALBUGINEA
ALBURNOUS
ALCHEMIST
ALCOHOLIC
ALE-CONNER
ALERTNESS
ALGEBRAIC
ALIENABLE
ALIENATOR
ALIGNMENT
ALIMENTAL
ALIZARINE
ALLANTOIS
ALLAYMENT
ALLEGORIC
ALLELUIAH
ALLEVIATE
ALL-HALLOW
ALLIGATOR
ALLOGRAPH
ALLOPATHY
ALLOTMENT
ALLOTROPY
ALLOWABLE
ALLOWABLY
ALLOWANCE
ALMA MATER
ALMANDINE
ALMOND-OIL
ALMS-GIVER
ALMS-HOUSE
ALOES-WOOD
ALONGSIDE
ALBEULORA
ALTAR-TOMB
ALTERABLE
ALTERCATE
ALTERNATE
ALTISCOPE
ALUMINIUM
ALUMINOUS

AMARYLLIS
AMASSMENT
AMAUROSIS
AMAUROTIC
AMAZEMENT
AMAZINGLY
AMAZONIAN
AMBERGRIS
AMBIGUITY
AMBIGUOUS
AMBITIOUS
AMBLYOPIA
AMBROSIAL
AMBULACRA
AMBULANCE
AMBUSCADE
AMENDABLE
AMENDMENT
AMIANTHUS
AMIDSHIPS
AMOROUSLY
AMORPHOUS
AMPERSAND
AMPHIBIAN
AMPHIBOLE
AMPHIGORY
AMPHIOXUS
AMPLENESS
AMPLIFIER
AMPLITUDE
AMUSEMENT
AMUSINGLY
AMUSIVELY
ANALECTIC
ANALGESIA
ANALOGIST
ANALOGIZE
ANALOGOUS
ANALYTICS
ANANDROUS
ANAPESTIC
ANAPLASTY
ANARCHIST
ANASTATIC
ANATOMISM
ANATOMIST
ANATOMIZE
ANATROPAL
ANCESTRAL
ANCHORAGE
ANCHORITE
ANCHYLOSE
ANCIENTLY
ANCILLARY
ANECDOTAL
ANGLE-IRON
ANGLICISM
ANGLICIZE
ANGULARLY
ANGULATED
ANHYBRITE
ANHYDROUS
ANIMALISM
ANIMALITY
ANIMALIZE

ANIMATING
ANIMATION
ANIMISTIC
ANIMOSITY
ANKYLOSIS
ANNOTATOR
ANNOUNCER
ANNOYANCE
ANNUITANT
ANNULARLY
ANNULMENT
ANOMALOUS
ANONYMITY
ANONYMOUS
ANTALKALI
ANTARCTIC
ANTE-CHOIR
ANTELUCAN
ANTEMETIC
ANTENATAL
ANTHELION
ANTHEMION
ANTHEROID
ANTHODIUM
ANTHOLOGY
ANTHOZOON
ANTHROPIC
ANTICHLOR
ANTIDOTAL
ANTIPAPAL
ANTIPATHY
ANTIPHONY
ANTIPODAL
ANTIPODES
ANTIPYRIN
ANTIQUARY
ANTIQUITY
ANTI-TRADE
ANXIOUSLY
APARTMENT
APATHETIC
APERITIVE
APETALOUS
APHERESIS
APHYLLOUS
APISHNESS
APLANATIC
APOCOPATE
APOCRYPHA
APOLOGIST
APOLOGIZE
APOPHYSIS
APOSTOLIC
APOTHECIA
APPALLING
APPARATUS
APPARITOR
APPELLANT
APPELLATE
APPENDAGE
APPENDANT
APPERTAIN
APPETENCE
APPETIZER
APPLE-JOHN
APPLIANCE
APPLICANT
APPOINTED
APPORTION
APPRAISER

APPREHEND
APPROBATE
ARABESQUE
ARACHNIDA
ARACHNOID
ARAUCARIA
ARBITRAGE
ARBITRARY
ARBITRATE
ARBOREOUS
ARBORETUM
ARCHANGEL
ARCHDUCAL
ARCHDUCHY
ARCHETYPE
ARCHITECT
ARCHIVIST
ARCHSTONE
ARCTOGEAL
ARCUATION
ARDUOUSLY
AREOMETER
AREOPAGUS
ARGENTINE
ARMADILLO
ARMILLARY
ARMISTICE
ARMY-CORPS
AROMATIZE
ARRAIGNER
ARRHIZOUS
ARRISWISE
ARROGANCE
ARROWROOT
ARSENICAL
ARSENIOUS
ARTHRITIC
ARTHRITIS
ARTICHOKE
ARTICULAR
ARTIFICER
ARTILLERY
ARTLESSLY
ASAFETIDA
ASBESTINE
ASCENDANT
ASCENSION
ASCERTAIN
ASPARAGUS
ASPERMOUS
ASPERSION
ASPERSIVE
ASPHALTIC
ASPHALTUM
ASPLENIUM
ASSAILANT
ASSERTION
ASSERTIVE
ASSIDUITY
ASSIDUOUS
ASSISTANT
ASSOCIATE
ASSONANCE
ASSUASIVE
ASSURABLE
ASSURANCE
ASSUREDLY
ASTHMATIC
ASTRADDLE
ASTRAKHAN

ASTROLABE
ASTROLOGY
ASTRONOMY
ASTUCIOUS
ASYMMETRY
ASYMPTOTE
ASYNDETIC
ASYNDETON
ATHANASIA
ATHEISTIC
ATHENAEUM
ATHLETICS
ATMOLYSIS
ATMOMETER
ATONEMENT
ATROCIOUS
ATTAINDER
ATTENDANT
ATTENTION
ATTENTIVE
ATTENUANT
ATTENUATE
ATTOLLENT
ATTRACTER
ATTRIBUTE
ATTRITION
AUDACIOUS
AUDIPHONE
AUGMENTER
AUGURSHIP
AURICULAR
AURISCOPE
AUSTERELY
AUSTERITY
AUTHENTIC
AUTHORESS
AUTHORIAL
AUTHORITY
AUTHORIZE
AUTOCRACY
AUTOGRAPH
AUTOMATIC
AUTOMATON
AUXILIARY
AVAILABLE
AVALANCHE
AVOCATION
AVOIDABLE
AVOIDANCE
AVUNCULAR
AWAKENING
AWE-STRUCK
AWFULNESS
AWKWARDLY
AXIOMATIC
AZEDARACH
AZIMUTHAL

B

BABIRUSSA
BACCHANAL
BACCHANTE
BACCIFORM
BACKBITER
BACKBOARD
BACKSHISH
BACKSLIDE
BACKSTAIR

BACKSWORD
BACKWOODS
BACTERIUM
BADMINTON
BAGATELLE
BAILIWICK
BAKEHOUSE
BALCONIED
BALDACHIN
BALD-EAGLE
BALD-FACED
BALEFULLY
BALLADIST
BALLISTIC
BALLOT-BOX
BAMBOOZLE
BANDEROLE
BANDICOOT
BANDOLEER
BANDOLINE
BANEFULLY
BANK-AGENT
BANK-STOCK
BANQUETER
BANQUETTE
BAPTISMAL
BARBARIAN
BARBARISM
BARBARITY
BARBARIZE
BARBAROUS
BAREFACED
BARGAINER
BARNACLES
BAROGRAPH
BAROMETER
BARONETCY
BAROSCOPE
BARRELLED
BARRICADE
BARRISTER
BASHFULLY
BASILICON
BAS-RELIEF
BASTINADO
BASTIONED
BATH-BRICK
BATH-CHAIR
BATRACHIA
BATTALION
BATTLE-AXE
BAWDINESS
BAY-WINDOW
BEACONAGE
BEAN-FEAST
BEAN-GOOSE
BEAR-BERRY
BEARDLESS
BEATITUDE
BEAU-IDEAL
BEAUMONDE
BEAUTEOUS
BEAUTIFUL
BERBERINE
BECCAFICO
BEDLAMITE
BEDRAGGLE
BEDRIDDEN
BEECH-MAST
BEEF-EATER

BEER-HOUSE
BEER-MONEY
BEESTINGS
BEFITTING
BEGINNING
BEHAVIOUR
BELEAGUER
BELEMNITE
BELIEVING
BELL-GLASS
BELLICOSE
BELL-METAL
BELL-PUNCH
BELL-TOWER
BELLY-BAND
BELONGING
BELVEDERE
BENCH-MARK
BENEFICED
BENIGNANT
BENIGNITY
BERGAMASK
BERSERKER
BERYLLINE
BESEECHER
BESEEMING
BESETTING
BESPANGLE
BESPATTER
BESPECKLE
BESTIALLY
BETROTHAL
BEVEL-GEAR
BEWITCHER
BIANGULAR
BIBACIOUS
BIBLICIST
BICAMERAL
BICIPITAL
BICONCAVE
BICYCLIST
BIESTINGS
BIFARIOUS
BIFOLIATE
BIFURCATE
BIGOTEDLY
BILABIATE
BILATERAL
BILINGUAL
BILITERAL
BILLIARDS
BILOCULAR
BIMONTHLY
BINDINGLY
BINERVATE
BINOCULAR
BINOMINAL
BINTURONG
BIOGRAPHY
BIOLOGIST
BIPARTITE
BIPENNATE
■IR■II WIII■
■I■■ ■■■ I II
BIRD'S-FOOT
BIRD'S-NEST
BIRTH-MARK
BIRTH-ROOT
BISECTION
BISEGMENT

BISHOPRIC
BISMUTHAL
BISULCATE
BITTERISH
BLACK-BALL
BLACK-BAND
BLACKBIRD
BLACKCOCK
BLACK-FISH
BLACK-GAME
BLACK-IRON
BLACK-JACK
BLACK-LEAD
BLACK-LIST
BLACK-MAIL
BLACKNESS
BLADDERED
BLADE-BONE
BLAEBERRY
BLAMELESS
BLANDNESS
BLANKNESS
BLASPHEME
BLASPHEMY
BLAST-PIPE
BLEACHERY
BLEAKNESS
BLEAR-EYED
BLESSEDLY
BLINDFOLD
BLINDNESS
BLIND-WORM
BLOCKADER
BLOCKHEAD
BLOND-LACE
BLONDNESS
BLOOD-HEAT
BLOODLESS
BLOODSHED
BLOOD-SHOT
BLOSSOMED
BLUE-GRASS
BLUE-STONE
BLUFFNESS
BLUNDERER
BLUNTNESS
BLUSTERER
BOATSWAIN
BODY-GUARD
BOG-BUTTER
BOLD-FACED
BOLTSPRIT
BOMBARDON
BOMBASTIC
BOMBAZINE
BOMB-KETCH
BOMB-PROOF
BOMB-SHELL
BOND-SLAVE
BONE-BLACK
BONE-BROWN
BONE-EARTH
■ ■II WWWII I
■ ■ ■ IIIIII II
BOOK-LOUSE
BOOK-MAKER
BOOK-PLATE
BOOK-STALL
BOOMERANG
BOORISHLY

BOOT-MAKER
BOTTLE-TIT
BOULEVARD
BOUNDLESS
BOUNTEOUS
BOUNTIFUL
BOURGEOIS
BOWER-BIRD
BOW-LEGGED
BOW-STRING
BOW-WINDOW
BOXING-DAY
BOX-KEEPER
BOYCOTTER
BRACHYURA
BRACTEATE
BRAHMANIC
BRAINLESS
BRAIN-SICK
BRAMBLING
BRANCHIAE
BRANCHIAL
BRANCHLET
BRAND-IRON
BRANDLING
BRASS-BAND
BRAVENESS
BRAZIL-NUT
BREAD-CORN
BREAKABLE
BREAK-DOWN
BREAKFAST
BREAK-NECK
BREAST-PIN
BREATHING
BREECHING
BREEZE-FLY
BRESSOMER
BRIAR-ROOT
BRIC-A-BRAC
BRICK-CLAY
BRICK-KILN
BRICKWORK
BRIDE-CAKE
BRIDESMAN
BRIDEWELL
BRIEFLESS
BRIEFNESS
BRIER-ROOT
BRIGADIER
BRILLIANT
BRIMSTONE
BRIQUETTE
BRISKNESS
BRITANNIC
BROAD-BRIM
BROADCAST
BROADNESS
BROADSIDE
BROIDERER
BROKERAGE
BRONCHIAL
■■■● ●I I ●●■II
■■.▼ ▼II.■.▼.■
BROTHERLY
BROWNNESS
BRUSHWOOD
BRUSQUELY
BRUTALITY
BRUTALIZE

BRUTISHLY
BUCCANEER
BUCENTAUR
BUCKETFUL
BUCK-HOUND
BUCKSHISH
BUCKTHORN
BUCK-TOOTH
BUCKWHEAT
BUFF-STICK
BUFF-WHEEL
BUGLE-HORN
BUHRSTONE
BULGARIAN
BULKINESS
BULL-FIGHT
BULL-TROUT
BUMBAILIF
BUMBLE-BEE
BUMBLEDOM
BUMPTIOUS
BUOYANTLY
BURLESQUE
BURLINESS
BURNISHER
BURSIFORM
BUSHINESS
BUSH-METAL
BUSSU-PALM
BUTTER-BUR
BUTTERCUP
BUTTERFLY
BUTTERINE
BUTTER-NUT
BY-PRODUCT
BYSSOLITE
BY-STANDER
BYZANTINE

C

CABALLINE
CABBALISM
CABBALIST
CABLEGRAM
CABRIOLET
CACHAEMIA
CACHOLONG
CACODEMON
CACOETHES
CACOPHONY
CADASTRAL
CADAVERIE
CADETSHIP
CAESAREAN
CAESARISM
CAINOZOIC
CAIRNGORM
CALAMANCO
CALCANEUM
CALCEDONY
■■■.●●■■■II
I.■.I▼L.▼II■
CALCULOUS
CALENDRER
CALENTURE
CALIBERED
CALIBRATE
CALIPHATE

CALLIPERS
CALLOSITY
CALLOUSLY
CALMATIVE
CALORIFIC
CALVINISM
CALVINIST
CALVITIES
CAMARILLA
CAMBISTRY
CAMERATED
CAMPAGNOL
CAMPANERO
CAMPANILE
CAMPANULA
CAMPHORIC
CAMP-STOOL
CANAANITE
CANCEROUS
CANDIDATE
CANDLE-NUT
CANDLEMAS
CANDYTUFT
CANE-BRAKE
CANE-CHAIR
CANESCENT
CANE-SUGAR
CANKER-FLY
CANKEROUS
CANNELURE
CANNONADE
CANNONEER
CANONICAL
CANTICLES
CANVASSER
CAPACIOUS
CAPARISON
CAPILLARY
CAPILLOSE
CAPITALLY
CAPITULAR
CAPITULUM
CAPONIERE
CAPRICCIO
CAPRICORN
CAPRIFORM
CAPSICINE
CAPSULATE
CAPTAINCY
CAPTIVATE
CAPTIVITY
CARAMBOLA
CARAMBOLE
CARBONADO
CARBONATE
CARBONIZE
CARBUNCLE
CARCINOMA
CARDBOARD
CAREENAGE
CAREFULLY
CARE-TAKER
CARMELITE
CARNALIST
CARNALITY
CARNALIZE
CARNATION
CARNELIAN
CARNIVORA
CARNIVORE

CARPENTER
CARPENTRY
CARPET-BAG
CARPETING
CARPET-ROD
CARPINGLY
CARPOLOGY
CARRAGEEN
CARRONADE
CARRON-OIL
CARROUSEL
CARTESIAN
CART-HORSE
CARTILAGE
CARTRIDGE
CARTULARY
CASE-KNIFE
CASEMATED
CASHEW-NUT
CASSAREEP
CASSATION
CASSEROLE
CASSIMERE
CASSOCKED
CASSONADE
CASSOWARY
CASTALIAN
CASTELIAN
CASTIGATE
CASTILIAN
CASTOR-OIL
CAST-STEEL
CASUALISM
CASUALIST
CASUARINA
CASUISTIC
CASUISTRY
CATACLYSM
CATALEPSY
CATALOGUE
CATAMARAN
CATAMENIA
CATAMOUNT
CATAPLASM
CATARRHAL
CATCHMENT
CATCH-POLL
CATCH-WORD
CATECHISM
CATECHIST
CATECHIZE
CATERWAUL
CATHARIST
CATHARTIC
CATHEDRAL
CATOPTRIC
CAT-SILVER
CATTLE-PEN
CAUCASIAN
CAUSALITY
CAUSATION
CAUSATIVE
CAUSELESS
CAUTELOUS
CAUTERIZE
CAUTIONER
CAVALCADE
CAVERNOUS
CEASELESS
CEBADILLA

CELANDINE
CELEBRANT
CELEBRATE
CELEBRITY
CELESTIAL
CELESTINE
CELLARAGE
CELLARMAN
CELLULOID
CELLULOSE
CELTICISM
CENOBITIC
CENSORIAL
CENTENARY
CENTERING
CENTIPEDE
CENTRALLY
CENTRE-BIT
CENTURIAL
CENTURION
CEPHALATE
CEPHALOID
CERACEOUS
CERATITIS
CERATODUS
CERAUNITE
CERBEREAN
CERCARIAN
CERECLOTH
CEROGRAPH
CERTAINLY
CERTAINTY
CERTIFIER
CERTITUDE
CESPITOSE
CESSATION
CETACEOUS
CEVADILLA
CHAFFERER
CHAFFINCH
CHAIN-GANG
CHAIN-PIER
CHAIN-PUMP
CHAIN-SHOT
CHALLENGE
CHALYBITE
CHAMBERED
CHAMBERER
CHAMELEON
CHAMOMILE
CHAMPAGNE
CHAMPAIGN
CHANCEFUL
CHANDLERY
CHANGEFUL
CHARACTER
CHARINESS
CHARIOTED
CHARIVARI
CHARLATAN
CHARTERED
CHARTERER
CHAR-WOMAN
CHASTENER
CHASTISER
CHATOYANT
CHATTERER
CHAUFFEUR
CHAW-BACON
CHEAP-JACK

CHEAPNESS
CHEATABLE
CHECKMATE
CHEEK-BONE
CHEERLESS
CHEESE-FLY
CHELONIAN
CHEMISTRY
CHEMITYPE
CHEQUERED
CHERIMOYA
CHERISHER
CHERRY-PIT
CHEVALIER
CHEVELURE
CHEVRONED
CHIBOUQUE
CHICKLING
CHICKWEED
CHIDINGLY
CHIEFTAIN
CHILBLAIN
CHILDHOOD
CHILDLESS
CHILDLIKE
CHILIARCH
CHILLNESS
CHINAWARE
CHINA-CLAY
CHINA-ROOT
CHINA-ROSE
CHINA-SHOP
CHINCAPIN
CHINCHONA
CHINCOUGH
CHINKAPIN
CHIROLOGY
CHISELLED
CHIVALRIC
CHLOROSIS
CHLOROTIC
CHOCK-FULL
CHOCOLATE
CHOKE-BORE
CHOKE-DAMP
CHOKE-FULL
CHOLAEMIA
CHOLERAIC
CHONDRIFY
CHOP-HOUSE
CHORISTER
CHRISTIAN
CHRISTMAS
CHROMATIC
CHRONICLE
CHRYSALID
CHRYSALIS
CHTHONIAN
CHUBB LOCK
CHUB-FACED
CHURCHING
CHURCHISM
CHURCHMAN
CICATRIZE
CIGARETTE
CILIOFORM
CIMMERIAN
CINCHONIC
CINCHONIN
CINCTURED

CINERARIA
CINEREOUS
CINGALESE
CIRCINATE
CIRCULATE
CIRRHOSIS
CISALPINE
CIVILIZED
CIVILIZER
CLACK-DISH
CLAIMABLE
CLAMOROUS
CLAMOURER
CLAPBOARD
CLARET-CUP
CLARET-JUG
CLARIFIER
CLARIONET
CLASSABLE
CLASSICAL
CLASS-MATE
CLAUSTRAL
CLAUSALAR
CLAVICORN
CLAY-SLATE
CLAY-STONE
CLEANNESS
CLEARANCE
CLEARNESS
CLEAVABLE
CLEMENTLY
CLEPSYDRA
CLERGYMAN
CLERICISM
CLERKSHIP
CLEVERISH
CLIENTAGE
CLIENTELE
CLIMATIZE
CLIMBABLE
CLOAK-ROOM
CLOCK-WORK
CLOG-DANCE
CLOISTRAL
CLOSENESS
CLOSE-TIME
CLOTH-HALL
CLOTH-YARD
CLOUDLESS
CLOVE-PINK
CLUBBABLE
CLUB-HOUSE
COACH-HIRE
COADJUTOR
COADUNATE
COAGULANT
COAGULATE
COAL-BLACK
COAL-BRASS
COAL-FIELD
COALITION
COAL-PLANT
COAST-LINE
COASTWISE
COAXINGLY
COCCOLITE
COCCOLITH
COCCYGEAL
COCHINEAL
COCHLEATE

COCK-A-HOOP
COCK-FIGHT
COCKLE-HAT
COCKNEYFY
COCKROACH
COCK'S-COMB
COCKSWAIN
COCOONERY
COEMPTION
COENOBITE
COENOSARE
COEQUALLY
COERCIBLE
COETERNAL
COFFEE-BUG
COFFEE-POT
COFFER-DAM
COFOUNDER
COGITABLE
COGNATION
COGNITION
COGNITIVE
COGNIZANT
COHEIRESS
COHERENCE
COLCHICUM
COLCOTHAR
COLD-BLAST
COLD-CREAM
COLEOPTER
COLLATION
COLLATIVE
COLLEAGUE
COLLECTOR
COLLEGIAL
COLLEGIAN
COLLIGATE
COLLIMATE
COLLINEAR
COLLISION
COLLOCATE
COLLODION
COLLOIDAL
COLLUSION
COLLUSIVE
COLLYRIUM
COLOCYNTH
COLONELCY
COLONIZER
COLONNADE
COLOPHONY
COLORIFIC
COLOSSEUM
COLOSTRUM
COLOURING
COLOURIST
COLOURMAN
COLTISHLY
COLT'S-FOOT
COLUBRINE
COLUMBARY
COLUMBINE
COLUMBIUM
COLUMBITE
COLUMELLA
COMBATANT
COMBATIVE
COMICALLY
COMMANDER
COMMENDAM

COMMENDER
COMMENSAL
COMMENTER
COMMINGLE
COMMINUTE
COMMITTAL
COMMITTEE
COMMITTER
COMMODITY
COMMODORE
COMMONAGE
COMMOTION
COMMUNION
COMMUNISM
COMMUNIST
COMMUNITY
COMPACTLY
COMPANION
COMPELLER
COMPETENT
COMPLAINT
COMPLEXLY
COMPLEXUS
COMPLIANT
COMPONENT
COMPOSITE
COMPOSURE
COMRADERY
CONCAVELY
CONCAVITY
CONCEALER
CONCEITED
CONCENTRE
CONCERNED
CONCERTED
CONCILIAR
CONCISELY
CONCISION
CONCOCTER
CONCORDAT
CONCOURSE
CONCREATE
CONCUBINE
CONDEMNER
CONDENSER
CONDIMENT
CONDITION
CONDUCIVE
CONDUCTOR
CONFERRER
CONFESSED
CONFESSOR
CONFIDANT
CONFIDENT
CONFIDING
CONFIGURE
CONFIRMED
CONFIRMEE
CONFIRMER
CONFLUENT
CONFORMER
CONFUCIAN
CONFUSION
CONFUTING
CONGERIES
CONGESTED
CONGRUENT
CONGRUITY
CONGRUOUS
CONICALLY

CONJUGATE
CONNATURE
CONNECTOR
CONNEXION
CONNUBIAL
CONQUEROR
CONSCIOUS
CONSCRIPT
CONSENSUS
CONSERVER
CONSIGNEE
CONSIGNER
CONSONANT
CONSPIRER
CONSTABLE
CONSTANCY
CONSTRAIN
CONSTRICT
CONSTRUCT
CONSULATE
CONSULTER
CONSUMING
CONTAGION
CONTAGIUM
CONTAINER
CONTEMNER
CONTENDER
CONTENTED
CONTICENT
CONTINENT
CONTINUAL
CONTINUED
CONTINUER
CONTORTED
CONTRALTO
CONTRIVER
CONTUMACY
CONTUMELY
CONTUSION
CONUNDRUM
CONVERTER
CONVEXITY
CONVIVIAL
CONVOCATE
CONVOLUTE
COOPERAGE
CO-OPERANT
CO-OPERATE
COPARTNER
COPE-STONE
COPIOUSLY
COPPERING
COPPERISH
COPROLITE
COPROLOGY
COPSE-WOOD
COPYRIGHT
CORALLINE
CORALLITE
CORALLOID
CORAL-REEF
CORAL-TREE
CORAL-WORT
CORBEILLE
CORDELIER
CORDIALLY
CORDIFORM
CORIANDER
CORKSCREW
CORMORANT

CORN-CRAKE
CORNELIAN
CORNETIST
CORN-FLOUR
CORNOPEAN
CORN-POPPY
COROLLARY
COROLLINE
CORONETED
COROZO-NUT
CORPORATE
CORPOREAL
CORPOSANT
CORPULENT
CORPUSCLE
CORRECTLY
CORRECTOR
CORRELATE
CORRODENT
CORROSION
CORROSIVE
CORRUGATE
CORRUPTED
CORRUPTER
CORRUPTLY
CORTICATE
CORTICOSE
CORUSCANT
CORUSCATE
CORYMBOSE
COSMOGONY
COSMOLOGY
COSMORAMA
COSTIVELY
COSTUMIER
CO-TANGENT
COTHURNUS
COTILLION
CO-TRUSTEE
COTTONADE
COTTON-GIN
COTYLEDON
COUMARINE
COUNTABLE
COUNTLESS
COUNTSHIP
COURTEOUS
COURTESAN
COURTHAND
COURTLING
COURT-ROLL
COURTSHIP
COURT-YARD
COVERTURE
COVERT-WAY
COVETABLE
COWARDICE
COWFEEDER
COXCOMBRY
CRAB-APPLE
CRABBEDLY
CRAB-STICK
CRACKLING
CRAFTLESS
CRAFTSMAN
CRAMP-IRON
CRANBERRY
CRANKNESS
CRAPULENT
CRAPULOUS

CRASSNESS
CRAVATTED
CRAVINGLY
CRAZINESS
CREAM-CAKE
CREAM-LAID
CREAM-WOVE
CREATABLE
CREATRESS
CREDENDUM
CREDULITY
CREDULOUS
CREEPHOLE
CREMATION
CREMATORY
CRENATION
CRENATURE
CRENELATE
CREPITANT
CREPITATE
CRESCENDO
CRESTLESS
CRETINISM
CRICKETER
CRIMELESS
CRIMINATE
CRIMINOUS
CRINOLINE
CRISPNESS
CRITERION
CRITICISM
CRITICIZE
CROCODILE
CROOKEDLY
CROP-EARED
CROSIERED
CROSSBILL
CROSS-BRED
CROSS-FIRE
CROSS-HEAD
CROSSNESS
CROSS-ROAD
CROSSWISE
CROTCHETY
CROW-BERRY
CROWNLESS
CROWN-WORK
CROW-QUILL
CROW'S-BILL
CROW'S-FEET
CROW'S-FOOT
CROW'S-NEST
CRUCIFIER
CRUCIFORM
CRUDENESS
CRUSH-ROOM
CRUSTACEA
CRYPTOGAM
CRYPTONYM
CUBICALLY
CUBICULAR
CUCKOLDLY
CUCKOLDOM
CUCKOLDRY
CUCULLATE
CULULAWAN
CULLENDER
CULMINATE
CULPATORY

CULTIVATE
CUMBRANCE
CUNEIFORM
CUNNINGLY
CUP-BEARER
CURB-STONE
CURDINESS
CURIOSITY
CURIOUSLY
CURLINESS
CURRENTLY
CURRY-COMB
CURSORIAL
CURSORILY
CURSTNESS
CURTAILER
CURVATURE
CUSHIONED
CUSPIDATE
CUSTODIAL
CUSTODIAN
CUSTODIER
CUSTOMARY
CUTANEOUS
CUT-THROAT
CUTTINGLY
CYCLOIDAL
CYCLOPEAN
CYLINDRIC
CYMBALIST
CYMOPHANE
CYNEGITIC
CYNICALLY
CYSTIFORM
CYSTOTOMY
CYTHEREAN
CYTOBLAST

D

DACHSHUND
DAIRY-FARM
DAIRY-MAID
DALLIANCE
DAMASCENE
DAMASKEEN
DAMNATION
DAMNATORY
DAMPISHLY
DANDELION
DANDIPRAT
DANGEROUS
DAPPLE-BAY
DARE-DEVIL
DARWINIAN
DARWINISM
DASH-BOARD
DASH-WHEEL
DASTARDLY
DASYMETER
DATE-SUGAR
DAUNTLESS
DAY-LABOUR
DAY-SCHOOL
DAYSPRING
DEACONESS
DEAD-DRUNK
DEAD-HOUSE
DEAD-LIGHT

DEAD-MARCH
DEAFENING
DEATH-BELL
DEATH-BLOW
DEATH-FIRE
DEATHLESS
DEATHLIKE
DEATH-RATE
DEATH'S-MAN
DEBARMENT
DEBATABLE
DEBAUCHED
DEBAUCHEE
DEBAUCHER
DEBENTURE
DEBUTANTE
DECACHORD
DECADENCE
DECAGONAL
DECALCIFY
DECALITRE
DECALOGUE
DECAMETRE
DECAPODAL
DECASTYLE
DECEITFUL
DECEPTION
DECEPTIVE
DECIDABLE
DECIDEDLY
DECIDUATE
DECIDUOUS
DECILITRE
DECILLION
DECIMALLY
DECIMATOR
DECIMETRE
DECK-CARGO
DECLAIMER
DECLINATE
DECLINOUS
DECLINING
DECLIVITY
DECLIVOUS
DECOCTION
DECOLLATE
DECOMPLEX
DECOMPOSE
DECORATED
DECORATOR
DECOY-DUCK
DECREMENT
DECRETIST
DECRETIVE
DECRETORY
DECUMBENT
DECURRENT
DECUSSATE
DEDICATEE
DEDICATOR
DEDUCIBLE
DEDUCTION
DEDUCTIVE
DEER-HOUND
DEER-MOUSE
DEFALCATE
DEFAULTER
DEFECTION
DEFECTIVE
DEFENDANT

DEFENSIVE
DEFENSORY
DEFERENCE
DEFERMENT
DEFIANTLY
DEFICIENT
DEFINABLE
DEFINABLY
DEFLECTED
DEFLECTOR
DEFLORATE
DEFLUXION
DEFOLIATE
DEFORMITY
DEFRAUDER
DEGRADING
DEHISCENT
DEINORNIS
DEIPAROUS
DEJECTION
DELICIOUS
DELIGHTED
DELINEATE
DELIQUIUM
DELIRIANT
DELIRIOUS
DELIVERER
DELUDABLE
DEMAGOGIC
DEMAGOGUE
DEMANDANT
DEMEANOUR
DEMI-DEVIL
DEMI-LANCE
DEMI-MONDE
DEMISABLE
DEMISSION
DEMIURGIC
DEMOCRACY
DEMULCENT
DEMURRAGE
DENDRITIC
DENOTABLE
DENOUNCER
DENSENESS
DENTATELY
DENTIFORM
DENTISTRY
DENTITION
DENYINGLY
DEODORANT
DEODORIZE
DEOXIDATE
DEOXIDIZE
DEPARTURE
DEPASTURE
DEPENDANT
DEPENDENT
DEPICTURE
DEPLETION
DEPLETIVE
DEPLETORY
DEPLORABLE
DEPOSITOR
DEPRAVITY
DEPRECATE
DEPREDATE
DEPRESSED
DEPRESSOR
DEPURATOR

DERIVABLE
DERIVABLY
DERMATOID
DERRINGER
DESCANTER
DESCENDER
DESCRIBER
DESECRATE
DESERTION
DESERVING
DESSICANT
DESSICATE
DESIGNATE
DESIGNING
DESIRABLE
DESIRABLY
DESMOLOGY
DESOLATER
DESOLATOR
DESPAIRER
DESPERADO
DESPERATE
DESPOILER
DESPONDER
DESPOTISM
DESTINATE
DESTINIST
DESTITUTE
DESTROYER
DESUETUDE
DESULTORY
DETECTION
DETECTIVE
DETENTION
DETERGENT
DETERMENT
DETERMINE
DETERRENT
DETERSION
DETERSIVE
DETHRONER
DETONATOR
DETRACTER
DETRACTOR
DETRIMENT
DETRITION
DETRUSION
DEVASTATE
DEVELOPER
DEVIATION
DEVIL-FISH
DEVILMENT
DEVIL'S-BIT
DEVILSHIP
DEVIOUSLY
DEVISABLE
DEVITRIFY
DEVONPORT
DEVOTEDLY
DEWLAPPED
DEXTERITY
DEXTEROUS
DEXTRORSE
DIABLERIE
DIABOLISM
DIABROSIS
DIACHYLON
DIACHYLUM
DIACONATE
DIACRITIC

DIATRINIC
DIAERESIS
DIAGNOSIS
DIALECTAL
DIALECTIC
DIALOGISM
DIALOGIST
DIALOGIZE
DIAL-PLATE
DIAMETRIC
DIAMETRAL
DIAMONDED
DIANDROUS
DIANOETIC
DIAPHRAGM
DIARRHOEA
DIASTOLIC
DIATHESIS
DIATHETIC
DIATOMITE
DICASTERY
DICHOGAMY
DICHOTOMY
DICHROISM
DICKY-BIRD
DECLINOUS
DICOELOUS
DICTATION
DICTATURE
DICTATORY
DICTATRIX
DIDACTICS
DIDACTILE
DIDELPHIA
DIDELPHIC
DIE-SINKER
DIETARIAN
DIETETICS
DIETETIST
DIFFERENT
DIFFICULT
DIFFIDENT
DIFFLUENT
DIFFUSION
DIFFUSIVE
DIGENESIS
DIGESTION
DIGESTIVE
DIGITALIN
DIGITALIS
DIGITATED
DIGNIFIED
DIGNITARY
DILATABLE
DILIGENCE
DIMENSION
DIMIDIATE
DIMISSORY
DIMYARIAN
DINGINESS
DINOCERAS
DINOTHERE
DIOECIOUS
DIONYSIAC
DIONYSIAN
DIOPTRICS
DIPHTHONG
DIPHYCERC
DIPLOMACY
DIPTEROUS

DIRECTION
DIRECTIVE
DIRECTORY
DIRECTRIX
DIREFULLY
DIRIGIBLE
DIRTINESS
DISAFFECT
DISAFFIRM
DISAPPEAR
DISAVOUCH
DISAVOWAL
DISAVOWER
DISBELIEF
DISBURDEN
DISBURSER
DISCERNER
DISCHARGE
DISCHURCH
DISCOIDAL
DISCOLOUR
DISCOMFIT
DISCOMMON
DISCOURSE
DISCOVERY
DISCREDIT
DISCUSSER
DISEMBARK
DISEMBODY
DISENABLE
DISENGAGE
DISENROLL
DISENTAIL
DISENTOMB
DISESTEEM
DISFAVOUR
DISFIGURE
DISFOREST
DISGORGER
DISGRACER
DISGUISER
DISH-CLOTH
DISH-CLOUT
DISHONEST
DISHONOUR
DISINFECT
DISINHUME
DISLOCATE
DISMANTLE
DISMEMBER
DISMISSAL
DISNATURE
DISOBLIGE
DISPARAGE
DISPARATE
DISPARITY
DISPAUPER
DISPELLER
DISPENSER
DISPEOPLE
DISPERSAL
DISPERSER
DISPLAYER
DISPLEASE
DISPONDEE
DISPOSURE
DISPRAISE
DISPROVAL
DISPUTANT
DISREGARD

DISRELISH
DISREPAIR
DISREPUTE
DISSECTOR
DISSEIZOR
DISSEMBLE
DISSENTER
DISSIDENT
DISSIPATE
DISSOLUTE
DISSOLVER
DISSONANT
DISTANTLY
DISTILLER
DISTEMPER
DISTORTED
DISTRAINT
DISTURBER
DITHYRAMB
DIURNALLY
DIVERGENT
DIVERSELY
DIVERSIFY
DIVERSION
DIVERSITY
DIVERTING
DIVIDABLE
DIVISIBLE
DIVISIBLY
DIVORCIVE
DIVULSION
DIVULSIVE
DIZZINESS
DOCTORATE
DOCTORESS
DOCTRINAL
DODECAGON
DOGMATICS
DOGMATISM
DOGMATIST
DOGMATIZE
DOLEFULLY
DOMINATOR
DOMINICAL
DOMINICAN
DOOR-PLATE
DORMITIVE
DORMITORY
DOUBTABLE
DOUBTLESS
DOUGHTILY
DOWERLESS
DOWNINESS
DOWNRIGHT
DOWNTHROW
DOWN-TRAIN
DOWNWARDS
DRAFTSMAN
DRAGONISH
DRAGON-FLY
DRAINABLE
DRAIN-TILE
DRAIN-TRAP
DRAMATIST
DRAMATIZE
DRAPERIED
DRAVIDIAN
DRAY-HORSE
DREADLESS
DREAMLAND

DREAMLESS
DRESS-COAT
DRIFTLESS
DRIFT-WEED
DRIFT-WOOD
DRINKABLE
DRIVELLER
DROMEDARY
DROP-PRESS
DROP-SCENE
DROPSICAL
DRUIDICAL
DRUM-MAJOR
DRUM-STICK
DRYSALTER
DUALISTIC
DUBIOUSLY
DUCTILELY
DUCTILITY
DULCAMARA
DUMBFOUND
DUODECIMO
DUODENARY
DUPLICATE
DUPLICITY
DURA-MATER
DUSKINESS
DUST-BRAND
DUTEOUSLY
DUTIFULLY
DYER'S-WEED
DYNAMICAL
DYNAMITER
DYSCRASIA
DYSENTERY
DYSPEPSIA
DYSPEPTIC
DZIGGETAI

E

EAGERNESS
EAGLE-EYED
EAGLE-WOOD
EALDORMAN
EAR-COCKLE
EARLINESS
EARNESTLY
EARTH-BORN
EARTH-FLAX
EARTHLING
EARTHWARD
EARTH-WOLF
EARTHWORK
EARTHWORM
EASY-CHAIR
EAVESDROP
EBULLIENT
ECCENTRIC
ECHINATED
ECLAMPSIA
ECONOMICS
ECONOMIST
ECONOMIZE
ECSTASIED
ECTOBLAST
ECTOPLASM
EDELWEISS
EDIBILITY

EDIFICIAL
EDITORIAL
EDUCATION
EDUCATIVE
EEL-BASKET
EFFECTIVE
EFFECTUAL
EFFICIENT
EFFLUENCE
EFFLUVIAL
EFFLUVIUM
EFFLUXION
EFFODIENT
EFFULGENT
EGLANTINE
EGOTHEISM
EGOTISTIC
EGREGIOUS
EGRESSION
EIDER-DUCK
EIDER-DOWN
EIDOGRAPH
EIGHTFOLD
EIGHTIETH
EIRENICON
EJACULATE
EJECTMENT
ELABORATE
ELATERIUM
ELBOW-ROOM
ELDERSHIP
ELDER-WINE
ELECTORAL
ELECTRIFY
ELECTUARY
ELEGANTLY
ELEMENTAL
ELEVATION
ELEVATORY
ELIMINATE
ELLIPSOID
ELMO'S-FIRE
ELOCUTION
ELOHISTIC
ELOPEMENT
ELOQUENCE
ELSEWHERE
ELUCIDATE
ELUTRIATE
EMACIATED
EMANATION
EMBARRASS
EMBATTLED
EMBAY-MENT
EMBELLISH
EMBER-DAYS
EMBER-TIDE
EMBER-WEEK
EMBEZZLER
EMBLEMENT
EMBRACEOR
EMBRACERY
EMBRASURE
EMBROCATE
EMBROIDER
EMBRYONAL
EMBRYONIC
EMBRYOTIC
EMENDATOR
EMERGENCE

EMERGENCY
EMINENTLY
EMMENSITE
EMOLLIENT
EMOLUMENT
EMOTIONAL
EMPHASIZE
EMPHYSEMA
EMPIRICAL
EMPTINESS
EMPYREUMA
EMULATION
EMULATIVE
EMULATORY
EMULOUSLY
EMUNCTORY
ENACTMENT
ENAMELIST
ENCAUSTIC
ENCHANTED
ENCHANTER
ENCHORIAL
ENCLOSURE
ENCOMIAST
ENCOMPASS
ENCOUNTER
ENCOURAGE
ENCRIMSON
ENCRINATE
ENDEARING
ENDEAVOUR
ENDECAGON
ENDEICTIC
ENDEMICAL
ENDLESSLY
ENDOLYMPH
ENDOMORPH
ENDOPLASM
ENDOPLAST
ENDOMOSE
ENDOSPERM
ENDOSTEUM
ENDOSTOME
ENDOWMENT
ENDURABLE
ENDURABLY
ENDURANCE
ENERGETIC
ENERGICAL
ENFEEBLER
ENGINEMAN
ENGISCOPE
ENGLISHRY
ENGRAILED
ENGRAINER
ENGRAVING
ENGROSSER
ENGYSCOPE
ENHYDROUS
ENIGMATIC
ENJOYABLE
ENJOYMENT
ENLIGHTEN
ENLIVENER
ENNEANDER
ENRAPTURE
ENROLMENT
ENTELECHY
ENTERALGY
ENTERITIS

ENTERTAIN
ENTHYMEME
ENTOMICAL
ENTOPHYTE
ENTREATER
ENTREMETS
ENTROCHAL
ENTROPIUM
ENUCLEATE
ENUMERATE
ENUNCIATE
ENVIOUSLY
ENVOYSHIP
EPAULETTE
EPHEMERAL
EPHEMERIS
EPHEMERON
EPICLINAL
EPICUREAN
EPICURISM
EPIDERMAL
EPIDERMIC
EPIDERMIS
EPIDICTIC
EPIGAEOUS
EPIGENOUS
EPIGRAPHY
EPIGYNOUS
EPILEPTIC
EPILOGIZE
EPIPHRAGM
EPIPHYSIS
EPIPHYTIC
EPIPHYTAL
EPISCOPAL
EPISODIAL
EPISTOLIC
EPITAPHIC
EPITOMIST
EPITOMIZE
EPIZOOTIC
EPONYMOUS
EPSOM-SALT
EQUALNESS
EQUIPMENT
EQUIPOISE
EQUISETUM
EQUITABLE
EQUITABLY
EQUIVALVE
EQUIVOCAL
EQUIVOQUE
ERADICATE
ERASEMENT
ERECTNESS
EREMITISM
ERIOMETER
ERISTICAL
ERRONEOUS
ERSTWHILE
ERUDITELY
ERUDITION
ERUGINOUS
ERYTHRITE
ESCAPABLE
ESCHEATOR
ESCLANDRE
ESOTERISM
ESPIONAGE
ESPLANADE

ESSENTIAL
ESTAFETTE
ESTAMINET
ESTIMABLE
ESTIMABLY
ESTUARIAN
ESTUARINE
ESURIENCE
ESURIENCY
ET CAETERA
ETERNALLY
ETHICALLY
ETHIOPIAN
ETHMOIDAL
ETHNICISM
ETHNOLOGY
ETIQUETTE
ETYMOLOGY
EUCHARIST
EUCHOLOGY
EULOGICAL
EUPHEMISM
EUPHEMIZE
EUPHONIUM
EUPHORBIA
EVAGINATE
EVANGELIC
EVAPORATE
EVASIVELY
EVENTUATE
EVERGREEN
EVERYBODY
EVIDENTLY
EVOCATION
EVOLUTION
EVOLUTIVE
EXACTNESS
EXAMINANT
EXAMINING
EXANTHEMA
EXARCHATE
EXCAVATOR
EXCEEDING
EXCELLENT
EXCENTRIC
EXCEPTING
EXCEPTION
EXCESSIVE
EXCHANGER
EXCHEQUER
EXCIPIENT
EXCISABLE
EXCISEMAN
EXCITABLE
EXCLAIMER
EXCLUSION
EXCLUSIVE
EXCORIATE
EXCREMENT
EXCRETION
EXCRETIVE
EXCRETORY
EXCULPATE
EXCURRENT
EXCURSION
EXCURSIVE
EXCUSABLE
EXCUSABLY
EXECRABLE
EXECRABLY

EXECUTANT
EXECUTION
EXECUTIVE
EXECUTORY
EXECUTRIX
EXEGETIST
EXEGETICS
EXEMPLARY
EXEMPLIFY
EXEMPTION
EXEQUATUR
EXERCISER
EXFOLIATE
EXHALABLE
EXHAUSTED
EXHIBITER
EXHIBITOR
EXISTENCE
EXOGAMOUS
EXOGENOUS
EXONERATE
EXORCISER
EXOSMOSIS
EXOSMOTIC
EXPANSILE
EXPANSION
EXPANSIVE
EXPECTANT
EXPEDIENT
EXPENSIVE
EXPIATION
EXPIATORY
EXPIRABLE
EXPISCATE
EXPLAINER
EXPLETIVE
EXPLETORY
EXPLICATE
EXPLOITER
EXPLOSION
EXPLOSIVE
EXPOSITOR
EXPOUNDER
EXPRESSLY
EXPULSION
EXPULSIVE
EXPURGATE
EXQUISITE
EXSERTILE
EXSICCATE
EXSICCANT
EXTEMPORE
EXTENSILE
EXTENSION
EXTENSITY
EXTENSIVE
EXTENUATE
EXTERNALS
EXTIRPATE
EXTORTION
EXTRACTOR
EXTRADITE
EXTREMELY
EXTREMIST
EXTREMITY
EXTRICATE
EXTRINSIC
EXTRORSAL
EXTRUSION
EXUBERANT

EXUDATION
EYE-BRIGHT

F

FABACEOUS
FABRICATE
FACETIOUS
FACSIMILE
FACTITIVE
FACTORAGE
FACTORIAL
FAGOT-VOTE
FAINTNESS
FAIRY-LAND
FAITH-CURE
FAITHLESS
FALCATION
FALCONINE
FALDSTOOL
FALLOPIAN
FALSEHOOD
FALSENESS
FALSIFIER
FALTERING
FANATICAL
FANCILESS
FANCY-BALL
FANCY-FAIR
FANCY-FREE
FANCY-WORK
FANTASTIC
FARMHOUSE
FARMSTEAD
FAR-SOUGHT
FASCIATED
FASCICLED
FASCICULE
FASCINATE
FASHIONER
FASTENING
FATEFULLY
FATTINESS
FAULTLESS
FAVEOLATE
FAVOURITE
FEARFULLY
FEATHERED
FEBRICULA
FEBRIFUGE
FECULENCE
FECUNDATE
FECUNDITY
FEELINGLY
FEIGNEDLY
FELLOW-MAN
FELONIOUS
FEMME-SOLE
FENESTRAL
FENIANISM
FENUGREEK
FEODALITY
FERACIOUS
FEROCIOUS
FERROTYPE
FERRY-BOAT
FERTILELY
FERTILITY
FERTILIZE

FERVENTLY
FERVIDITY
FESTINATE
FESTIVELY
FESTIVITY
FETICIDAL
FOETICIDE
FETIDNESS
FETICHISM
FETISHISM
FETLOCKED
FEUDALISM
FEUDALIST
FEUDALITY
FEUDALIZE
FEUDATORY
FEU-DE-JOIE
FIBRIFORM
FIBRINOUS
FICTIONAL
FIDDLE-BOW
FIDUCIARY
FIELD-BOOK
FIELDFARE
FIELD-WORK
FIERINESS
FIFE-MAJOR
FIFTEENTH
FIGURABLE
FIGURANTE
FILACEOUS
FILIATION
FILIGREED
FILLETING
FILLISTER
FILMINESS
FILOPLUME
FIMBRIATE
FINANCIAL
FINANCIER
FINEDRAWN
FINGERING
FINICALLY
FINICKING
FIRE-ALARM
FIRE-BRAND
FIRE-BRICK
FIRE-EATER
FIRE-GUARD
FIRE-IRONS
FIREPLACE
FIRE-PROOF
FIRMAMENT
FIRST-BORN
FIRST-HAND
FIRSTLING
FIRST-RATE
FISHERMAN
FISHINESS
FISH-JOINT
FISH-LOUSE
FISH-PLATE
FISH-SLICE
FISH-SPEAR
FISHWOMAN
FISTULOSE
FISTULOUS
FITTINGLY
FIXEDNESS

FLABELLUM
FLACCIDLY
FLAGELLUM
FLAGEOLET
FLAGRANCY
FLAKINESS
FLAP-EARED
FLATTERER
FLATULENT
FLAUNTING
FLAVOROUS
FLAVOURED
FLAYFLINT
FLECKLESS
FLEETNESS
FLESH-HOOK
FLESHINGS
FLESHLESS
FLESH-MEAT
FLIGHTILY
FLINT-LOCK
FLIPPANCY
FLOOD-GATE
FLOOD-MARK
FLOOD-TIDE
FLOREATED
FLORIDITY
FLOSCULAR
FLOSS-SILK
FLOTATION
FLOWERING
FLOWER-POT
FLUCTUANT
FLUCTUATE
FLUOR-SPAR
FLUXIONAL
FLYBITTEN
FLY-FISHER
FLYING-FOX
FOGGINESS
FOG-SIGNAL
FOLIATION
FOLLOWING
FOOLHARDY
FOOLISHLY
FOOT-BOARD
FOOT-CLOTH
FOOT-POUND
FOOTPRINT
FOOT-STALK
FOOTSTOOL
FOPPISHLY
FORASMUCH
FORBEARER
FROBIDDEN
FORCELESS
FORCEMEAT
FORECLOSE
FOREFRONT
FOREGOING
FOREIGNER
FOREJUDGE
FORENAMED
FORESTALL
FORESTINE
FORETASTE
FORETOKEN
FORETOOTH
FOREWOMAN
FORFEITER

FORGATHER
FORGETFUL
FORGIVING
FORGOTTEN
FORLORNLY
FORMALISM
FORMALIST
FORMALITY
FORMATION
FORMATIVE
FORMICARY
FORMULARY
FORMULATE
FORMULIZE
FORNICATE
FORTHWITH
FORTIFIER
FORTITUDE
FORTNIGHT
FORTUNATE
FOSSILIZE
FOSTERSON
FOUNDLING
FOUNDRESS
FOUNDRIES
FOURPENCE
FOURSCORE
FOVEOLATE
FOXHUNTER
FRACTIONS
FRAGRANCE
FRAGRANCY
FRANCHISE
FRANCOLIN
FRANGIBLE
FRANKNESS
FRATERNAL
FRAUDLESS
FREEMASON
FREESTONE
FREEZIBLE
FREIGHTER
FRENCHMAN
FREQUENCY
FRESHNESS
FRETFULLY
FRICASSEE
FRICATIVE
FRIGHTFUL
FRIGIDITY
FRIVOLITY
FRIVOLOUS
FRONTLESS
FROSTBITE
FROSTWORK
FROWARDLY
FRUGALITY
FRUITERER
FRUITLESS
FRUTICOSE
FRUTICOUS
FUGACIOUS
FULGURITE
FULGUROUS
FULMINATE
FULSOMELY
FUNDAMENT
FUNGIFORM
FUNGOLOGY
FUNICULAR

FUNNELLED
FURBISHER
FURCATION
FURFUROUS
FURIOUSLY
FURNISHED
FURNISHER
FURNITURE
FURTHERER
FURTIVELY
FUSILLADE
FUSSINESS
FUSTIGATE
FUSTINESS

G

GABARDINE
GABIONAGE
GAINSAYER
GALANTINE
GALENICAL
GALINGALE
GALLANTLY
GALLANTRY
GALLERIES
GALLICISM
GALLINULE
GALLIVANT
GALLOONED
GALLOPADE
GALLOWSES
GALVANISM
GALVANIST
GALVANIZE
GAMBADOES
GANGLIONS
GANNISTER
GARDENING
GARGARISM
GARMENTED
GARNISHER
GARNITURE
GARRETEER
GARROTTER
GARRULITY
GARRULOUS
GASCONADE
GASHOLDER
GASOMETER
GASOMETRY
GASPINGLY
GASTROPOD
GASTRALGY
GASTRITIS
GATHERING
GAUCHERIE
GAUDEAMUS
GAUDINESS
GAUGEABLE
GAVELKIND
GAZETTEER
GELSEMIUM
GEMMATION
GENEALOGY
GENERABLE
GENERALLY
GENERATOR
GENERICAL

GENETICAL
GENIALITY
GENITIVAL
GENTEELLY
GENTILITY
GENTLEMAN
GENTLEMEN
GENUFLECT
GENUINELY
GEODESIST
GEOGRAPHY
GEOLOGIST
GEOLOGIAN
GEOMANCER
GEOMANTIC
GEOMETRIC
GEOPONICS
GERFALCON
GERMANDER
GERMANIUM
GERMICIDE
GERMINANT
GERMINATE
GERUNDIAL
GERUNDIVE
GIANTSHIP
GIBBERISH
GIBBOSITY
GIBBOUSLY
GIDDINESS
GINGLYMUS
GIPSOLOGY
GIRANDOLE
GLADIATOR
GLANDERED
GLANDULAR
GLASSWORT
GLAUCOSIS
GLOBOSITY
GLOBULOSE
GLOMERATE
GLOWINGLY
GLUEYNESS
GLUTINATE
GLUTINOUS
GLYCERINE
GLYPTODON
GNATHONIC
GNOMONICS
GNOMONIST
GODFATHER
GODLESSLY
GODLINESS
GODMOTHER
GOFFERING
GOLDFINCH
GOLDSMITH
GONOPHORE
GOOSANDER
GORGONEAN
GORGONIZE
GOSPELLER
GOSSIPING
GOSSIPPED
GOTHICISM
GOUTINESS
GOVERNESS
GRACELESS
GRACILITY
GRADATION

GRADATORY
GRADUALLY
GRADUATOR
GRAMINEAL
GRAMMATIC
GRANDIOSE
GRANDNESS
GRANDSIRE
GRANITOID
GRANTABLE
GRANULATE
GRANULITE
GRANULOUS
GRANULOSE
GRASPABLE
GRATIFIER
GRATITUDE
GRATULATE
GRAUWACKE
GRAVELESS
GRAVENESS
GRAVITATE
GRAYHOUND
GRAYWACKE
GREATCOAT
GREATNESS
GREENBACK
GREENHORN
GREENNESS
GREGORIAN
GRENADIER
GRENADINE
GREYHOUND
GRIEVANCE
GRIMALKIN
GRIMINESS
GRIPINGLY
GRISAILLE
GROCERIES
GROOMSMAN
GROPINGLY
GROSSBEAK
GROSSNESS
GROTESQUE
GROUNDSEL
GROVELLER
GRUFFNESS
GUARANTEE
GUARANTOR
GUARDABLE
GUARDEDLY
GUARDSMAN
GUERRILLA
GUIDELESS
GUILDHALL
GUILELESS
GUILLEMOT
GUILTLESS
GUMMINESS
GUNPOWDER
GUSHINGLY
GUSTATORY
GUTTIFORM
GYMNADIUM
GYMNASTIC
GYNOECIUM
GYNOPHORE
GYRFALCON
GYROSCOPE

H

HABERGEON
HABITABLE
HABITUATE
HACKBERRY
HACKNEYED
HAEMATOID
HAGGARDLY
HAGIOLOGY
HAILSTONE
HAIRINESS
HALFPENNY
HALFPENCE
HALLOWMAS
HALOPHYTE
HALOSCOPE
HAMADRYAD
HAMMERMAN
HAMSTRING
HANDINESS
HANDIWORK
HANDSPIKE
HARANGUER
HARBOURER
HARDIHOOD
HARDINESS
HARLEQUIN
HARMFULLY
HARMONICA
HARMONICS
HARMONIST
HARMONIUM
HARMONIZE
HARMOTOME
HARNESSER
HARPOONER
HARSHNESS
HARVESTER
HASTINESS
HATCHMENT
HATEFULLY
HAUGHTILY
HAVERSACK
HAYMAKING
HAZARDOUS
HEADINESS
HEALTHFUL
HEALTHILY
HEARTACHE
HEARTBURN
HEARTFELT
HEARTLESS
HEARTSOME
HEATHENRY
HEAVINESS
HEBRAICAL
HEBRIDIAN
HEEDFULLY
HEGEMONIC
HEINOUSLY
HELICLINE
HELIOTYPE
HELLEBORE
HELLENISM
HELLENIST
HELLENIZE
HELLISHLY
HEMATOSIS

HEMICYCLE
HEMIPLEGY
HEMISTICH
HENDIADYS
HEPATICAL
HEPTAGLOT
HEPTARCHY
HERBALIST
HERBARIUM
HERBIVORE
HERCULEAN
HEREABOUT
HEREAFTER
HERETICAL
HERITABLE
HERITABLY
HERMITAGE
HERMITARY
HERONSHAW
HESITANCY
HESITATOR
HESPERIAN
HETAIRISM
HETERODOX
HETERONYM
HETEROPOD
HEURISTIC
HEXACHORD
HEXAGONAL
HEXAMETER
HEXASTYLE
HEXATEUCH
HIBERNATE
HIBERNIAN
HIDEOUSLY
HIEMATION
HIERARCHY
HIEROGRAM
HIEROLOGY
HILARIOUS
HILLINESS
HINDRANCE
HINDOOISM
HIPPIATRY
HIPPOCRAS
HIRUNDINE
HISPIDITY
HISTOGENY
HISTOLOGY
HISTORIAN
HOARHOUND
HOARINESS
HOBGOBLIN
HOBNAILED
HODIERNAL
HODOMETER
HOIDENISH
HOLLYHOCK
HOLOCAUST
HOLOGRAPH
HOMESTEAD
HOMEWARDS
HOMICIDAL
HOMILETIC
HOMOGRAPH
HOMOLOGUE
HOMOPHONE
HOMUNCULE
HONORABIC
HONORABLE

HOPEFULLY
HOREHOUND
HOROLOGER
HOROMETRY
HOROSCOPE
HOROSCOPY
HORSEBACK
HORSEWHIP
HORTATION
HORTATIVE
HORTATORY
HOSTILELY
HOSTILITY
HOTTENTOT
HOUNDFISH
HOUSEHOLD
HOUSELESS
HOUSEMAID
HOUSEROOM
HOUSEWIFE
HOWSOEVER
HUCKABACK
HUFFINESS
HUMANNESS
HUMECTATE
HUMILIATE
HUMOURIST
HUNCHBACK
HUNDREDTH
HUNGARIAN
HURRICANE
HURRIEDLY
HURTFULLY
HUSBANDLY
HUSBANDRY
HUSKINESS
HYBRIDISM
HYBRIDITY
HYBRIDIZE
HYDRANGEA
HYDRAULIC
HYDROLOGY
HYDROPULT
HYDROSOMA
HYDROZOON
HYETOLOGY
HYGIENISM
HYLOZOISM
HYMNOLOGY
HYPALLAGE
HYPERBOLA
HYPERBOLE
HYPETHRAL
HYPNOTISM
HYPNOTIZE
HYPOCAUST
HYPOCRISY
HYPOCRITE
HYPOGAEON
HYPONASTY
HYPOSTYLE
HYSTERICS

I

ICELANDER
ICELANDIC
ICHNEUMON
ICHNOLITE

ICHNOLOGY
ICHTHYOID
ICONOLOGY
IDEALIZER
IDENTICAL
IDEOGRAPH
IDIOGRAPH
IDIOMATIC
IDIOPATHY
IDIOTICAL
IGNITABLE
IGNORAMUS
IGNORANCE
IGUANODON
ILLEGALLY
ILLEGIBLE
ILLEGIBLY
ILLIBERAL
ILLICITLY
ILLOGICAL
IMAGINARY
IMBRICATE
IMBROGLIO
IMBUEMENT
IMITATION
IMITATIVE
IMMANENCE
IMMANENCY
IMMEDIACY
IMMEDIATE
IMMENSELY
IMMENSITY
IMMERSION
IMMIGRANT
IMMIGRATE
IMMINENCE
IMMODESTY
IMMOLATOR
IMMORALLY
IMMOVABLE
IMMOVABLY
IMMUTABLE
IMMUTABLY
IMPARTIAL
IMPASSION
IMPASSIVE
IMPATIENT
IMPEACHER
IMPEDANCE
IMPELLENT
IMPENDENT
IMPERFECT
IMPERIOUS
IMPETRATE
IMPETUOUS
IMPINGENT
IMPIOUSLY
IMPLEADER
IMPLEMENT
IMPLICATE
IMPLIEDLY
IMPOLITIC
IMPORTANT
IMPORTUNE
IMPOSABLE
IMPOSTURE
IMPOTENCE
IMPOTENCY
IMPOUNDER
IMPRECATE

IMPROBITY
IMPROMPTU
IMPROVING
IMPROVISE
IMPRUDENT
IMPUDENCE
IMPULSION
IMPULSIVE
IMPUTABLE
INABILITY
INAMORATO
INAMORATA
INANIMATE
INANITION
INAUDIBLE
INAUGURAL
INBREATHE
INCAPABLE
INCARNATE
INCAUTION
INCENTIVE
INCEPTION
INCEPTIVE
INCESSANT
INCIDENCE
INCIPIENT
INCLEMENT
INCLOSURE
INCLUSIVE
INCOGNITO
INCOGNITA
INCOMMODE
INCORRECT
INCORRUPT
INCREMATE
INCREMENT
INCUBATOR
INCUBUSES
INCULCATE
INCULPATE
INCUMBENT
INCURABLY
INCURVATE
INDECORUM
INDELIBLE
INDELIBLY
INDEMNIFY
INDEMNITY
INDENTURE
INDEXICAL
INDICATOR
INDICTION
INDIGENCE
INDIGNANT
INDIGNITY
INDISPOSE
INDOLENCE
INDUCIBLE
INDUCTILE
INDUCTION
INDUCTIVE
INDUEMENT
INDULGENT
INDWELLER
INEBRIANT
INEBRIATE
INEBRIETY
INEBRIOUS
INEFFABLE
INEFFABLY

INELASTIC
INELEGANT
INEQUABLE
INERTNESS
INFANTILE
INFANTINE
INFATUATE
INFECTION
INFECTIVE
INFERABLE
INFERENCE
INFERTILE
INFIRMARY
INFIRMITY
INFLATION
INFLEXION
INFLUENCE
INFLUENZA
INFLUXION
INFORMANT
INFURIATE
INFUSIBLE
INFUSORIA
INGENIOUS
INGENUITY
INGENUOUS
INGLUVIES
INHABITER
INHERENCE
INHERENCY
INHERITOR
INHUMANLY
INJECTION
INJURIOUS
INJUSTICE
INNERMOST
INNERVATE
INNKEEPER
INNOCENCE
INNOCENCY
INNOCUOUS
INNOVATOR
INNUENDOS
INOCULATE
INODOROUS
INORGANIC
INQUILINE
INQUIRING
INQUIRIES
INSATIATE
INSENSATE
INSERTION
INSIDIOUS
INSINCERE
INSINUATE
INSOLENCE
INSOLUBLE
INSOLVENT
INSPECTOR
INSTANTLY
INSTIGATE
INSTITUTE
INSULARLY
INSULATOR
INSULTING
INSURABLE
INSURANCE
INSURGENT
INTEGRANT
INTEGRATE

INTEGRITY
INTELLECT
INTENDANT
INTENSELY
INTENSIFY
INTENSION
INTENSITY
INTENSIVE
INTENTION
INTERMENT
INTERCEDE
INTERCEPT
INTERDICT
INTERFACE
INTERFERE
INTERFUSE
INTERJECT
INTERLACE
INTERLARD
INTERLINE
INTERLOCK
INTERLOPE
INTERLUDE
INTERMENT
INTERNODE
INTERPOSE
INTERPRET
INTERRUPT
INTERSECT
INTERVENE
INTERVIEW
INTESTACY
INTESTATE
INTESTINE
INTORTION
INTRICACY
INTRICATE
INTRIGUER
INTRINSIC
INTRODUCE
INTROVERT
INTRUSION
INTRUSIVE
INTUITION
INTUITIVE
INTUMESCE
INUREMENT
INUTILITY
INVECTIVE
INVENTION
INVENTIVE
INVENTORY
INVERSELY
INVERSION
INVIDIOUS
INVIOLATE
INVISIBLE
INVISIBLY
INVOLUTED
INWREATHE
INWROUGHT
IRASCIBLE
IRKSOMELY
IRONSMITH
IRRADIANT
IRRADIATE
IRREGULAR
IRRIGUOUS
IRRITABLE

IRRITABLY
IRRUPTION
IRRUPTIVE
ISINGLASS
ISOCLINAL
ISOCLINIC
ISOLATION
ISOMERISM
ISOMETRIC
ISOSCELES
ISRAELITE
ISSUELESS
ITCHINESS
ITERATIVE
ITERATION
ITINERANT
ITINERARY
ITINERATE

J

JABORANDI
JACOBINIC
JACOBITIC
JANSENIST
JANSENISM
JEALOUSLY
JEERINGLY
JENNETING
JEREMIADE
JERFALCON
JESSAMINE
JESUITISM
JETTINESS
JEWELLERY
JOCUNDITY
JOCULARLY
JOLLINESS
JOURNEYER
JOVIALITY
JOYLESSLY
JUDGESHIP
JUDICIARY
JUDICIOUS
JUICELESS
JUICINESS
JUNIORITY
JURIDICAL
JUSTIFIER
JUXTAPOSE

K

KAINOZOIC
KENTLEDGE
KERATITIS
KERNELLED
KIDNAPPER
KILOMETRE
KILLINGLY
KINDLINGS
KINGCRAFT
KINSWOMAN
KITCHENER
KITTENISH
KITTIWAKE
KNAVISHLY
KNIGHTAGE

KNOWINGLY
KNOWLEDGE
KRUMMHORN

L

LABIALIZE
LABORIOUS
LABOURING
LABYRINTH
LACERABLE
LACERATED
LACERTINE
LACHRYMAL
LACINIATE
LACONICAL
LACTATION
LACTIFUGE
LACUNARIA
LACUSTRAL
LAEVIGATE
LAMINATED
LARGENESS
LARGHETTO
LARVIFORM
LARYNGEAL
LARYNGEAN
LASSITUDE
LASTINGLY
LATERALLY
LAUDATORY
LAUGHABLE
LAUGHABLY
LAUNDRESS
LAURELLED
LAWGIVING
LAWLESSLY
LAZARETTO
LEAFINESS
LEAKINESS
LEARNEDLY
LEASEHOLD
LECHEROUS
LEGENDARY
LEGIONARY
LEGISLATE
LEISURELY
LENGTHILY
LENIENTLY
LENTIFORM
LEPROUSLY
LEPROSITY
LETHARGIC
LETTERING
LEVANTINE
LEVELLING
LEVELNESS
LEVIATHAN
LEVIGABLE
LEVITICAL
LEXICALLY
LIBATIONS
LIBELLOUS
LIBERALLY
LIBERATOR
LIBRARIAN
LIBRATION
LIBRATORY
LICHENOUS

LICKERISH
LIENTERIC
LIGATURED
LIGHTNESS
LIGHTNING
LIGHTSOME
LIGNIFORM
LIGULATED
LIMACEOUS
LIMESTONE
LIMITABLE
LIMITEDLY
LIMITLESS
LIMPIDITY
LIMPINGLY
LINEAMENT
LINEOLATE
LINGERING
LINGULATE
LIPPITUDE
LIQUATION
LIQUEFIER
LIQUIDATE
LIQUIDITY
LIQUORICE
LISTERISM
LITERALLY
LITHENESS
LITHESOME
LITHOIDAL
LITHOLOGY
LITHOTOMY
LITHOTYPY
LITIGABLE
LITIGATOR
LITURGIES
LITURGIST
LIVERWORT
LIVERYMAN
LIVIDNESS
LIXIVIATE
LIXIVIOUS
LODESTONE
LOATHSOME
LOCKSMITH
LOCOMOTOR
LOFTINESS
LOGARITHM
LOGICALLY
LOGOMACHY
LOGOMANIA
LONGEVITY
LONGEVOUS
LONGICORN
LONGINGLY
LONGITUDE
LOOPHOLED
LOOSENESS
LOQUACITY
LORGNETTE
LORICATED
PATRIARCH
LOWERMOST
LOWLANDER
LOWLINESS
LUBRICATE
LUBRICITY
LUCIDNESS
LUCIFUGAL

LUCKINESS
LUCRATIVE
LUBRICATE
LUBRICITY
LUCIDNESS
LUCUBRATE
LUDICROUS
LUMPISHLY
LUNULATED
LUSTFULLY
LUSTINESS
LUXURIANT
LUXURIATE
LUXURIOUS
LYMPHATIC

M

MACARONIS
MACARONIC
MACHINATE
MACHINERY
MACHINIST
MACINTOSH
MACROCOSM
MACRUROUS
MADREPORE
MAGDALENE
MAGICALLY
MAGNALIUM
MAGNESIAN
MAGNESIUM
MAGNETISM
MAGNETIZE
MAGNIFIER
MAGNITUDE
MAHARAJAH
MAHARANEE
MAHOMEDAN
MAHOMETAN
MAJORSHIP
MAJUSCULE
MALACHITE
MALADROIT
MALARIOUS
MALICIOUS
MALIGNANT
MALIGNITY
MALLEABLE
MALLEOLUS
MAMMALIAN
MAMMALOGY
MAMMONISM
MAMMONIST
MAMMONITE
MANDATARY
MANDATORY
MANDOLINE
MANDUCATE
MANGANESE
MANGANITE
MANICHEAN
MANIFESTO
MANIPULAR
MANLINESS
MANNERISM
MANNERIST
MANOEUVRE
MANOMETER

MARCASITE
MARCHPANE
MARGARINE
MARKETING
MARMALADE
MARMOREAL
MARQUETRY
MARSUPIAL
MARSUPIUM
MARTIALLY
MARTINMAS
MARTYRDOM
MARTYRIZE
MASCULINE
MASSAGIST
MASSINESS
MASSIVELY
MASTERFUL
MASTICATE
MATCHABLE
MATCHLESS
MATCHLOCK
MATERNITY
MATRICIDE
MATRIMONY
MATRONAGE
MATRONIZE
MATUTINAL
MAUNDERER
MAUSOLEAN
MAUSOLEUM
MAWKISHLY
MAXILLARY
MAYONAISE
MAYORALTY
MEALINESS
MEANINGLY
MEANWHILE
MEATINESS
MECHANICS
MECHANISM
MECHANIST
MECHANIZE
MEDALLION
MEDALLIST
MEDIAEVAL
MEDIATELY
MEDIATIVE
MEDIATIZE
MEDICABLE
MEDICALLY
MEDICINAL
MEDULLARY
MEGAFARAD
MELANOSIS
MELAPHYRE
MELIBOEAN
MELIORATE
MELODIOUS
MELODRAMA
MELODRAME
MELTINGLY
MEMOIRIST
MEMORABLE
MEMORANDA
MEMORIZER
MENAGERIE
MENDACITY
MENDICANT
MENDICITY

MENISCOID
MENSTRUAL
MENSTRUUM
MENTATION
MERCENARY
MERCILESS
MERCURIAL
MERCUROUS
MERGANSER
MERRIMENT
MESENTERY
MESMERISM
MESMERIST
MESMERIZE
MESSENGER
MESSIANIC
MESSIEURS
METALLINE
METALLIST
METALLIZE
METALLOID
METEORITE
METHEGLIN
METHODISM
METHODIST
METHODIZE
METHOUGHT
METHYSTIC
METONYMIC
METROLOGY
METRONOME
MEZZANINE
MEZZOTINT
MIASMATIC
MICACEOUS
MICROBIAL
MICROBIAN
MICROCOSM
MICROCYTE
MICROLOGY
MICROPYLE
MICROTOME
MICROZOON
MICROZYME
MICTURATE
MIDDLEMAN
MIDSUMMER
MIDWIFERY
MIDWINTER
MIGRATION
MIGRATORY
MILESTONE
MILITANCY
MILKINESS
MILLIPORE
MILLINERY
MILLIONTH
MILLSTONE
MIMETICAL
MINDFULLY
MINEINGLY
MINIATURE
MINORSHIP
MIRIFICAL
MIRTHLESS
MISBEHAVE
MISBELIEF
MISCHANCE
MISCREANT
MISDEMEAN

MISDIRECT
MISEMPLOY
MISERABLE
MISERABLY
MISGIVING
MISGOVERN
MISINFORM
MISMANAGE
MISREPORT
MISSELTOE
MISSHAPEN
MISTINESS
MISTLETOE
MITRIFORM
MNEMONICS
MOBOCRACY
MOCKINGLY
MODELLING
MODERATOR
MODERNISM
MODERNIST
MODERNIZE
MODILLION
MODULATOR
MOISTNESS
MOLECULAR
MOLLIFIER
MOMENTARY
MOMENTOUS
MONACHISM
MONADICAL
MONADELPH
MONARCHAL
MONARCHIC
MONASTERY
MONATOMIC
MONEYLESS
MONGOLIAN
MONITRESS
MONKEYISM
MONOCHORD
MONODRAMA
MONOGRAPH
MONOLOGUE
MONOMANIA
MONOPLANE
MONOPTOTE
MONOSPERM
MONSIGNOR
MONSTROUS
MONTICULE
MOODINESS
MOONLIGHT
MOONSHINE
MOONSHINY
MOONSTONE
MORALIZER
MORBIDITY
MORDACITY
MORMONISM
MORMONITE
MORMONIST
MORTALITY
MORTGAGEE
MORTGAGER
MOSAICIST
MOSSINESS
MOULDABLE
MOUSTACHE
MUCRONATE

MUDDINESS
MUFFETTEE
MULTIFOIL
MULLIONED
MULTIFORM
MULTIPLEX
MULTITUDE
MUMPISHLY
MUNDANELY
MUNICIPAL
MURDERESS
MURDEROUS
MURICATED
MURMURING
MUSCADINE
MUSCOLOGY
MUSCOVADO
MUSCOVITE
MUSICALLY
MUSKETTER
MUSKETOON
MUSKETRY
MUSSULMAN
MUSTINESS
MUTILATOR
MUTTERING
MYOGRAPHY
MYONICITY
MYRIORAMA
MYROBALAN
MYSTERIES
MYSTICISM
MYTHOLOGY

N

NAILERESS
NAKEDNESS
NAPPINESS
NARCISSUS
NARCOTISM
NARCOTIZE
NARRATION
NARRATIVE
NASEBERRY
NASTINESS
NATROLITE
NATTINESS
NATURALLY
NAUGHTILY
NAUTILOID
NAVIGABLE
NAVIGABLY
NAVIGATOR
NECESSARY
NECESSITY
NECKCLOTH
NECROLOGY
NECTAREAL
NECTAREAN
NECTARINE
NECTAROUS
NEEDFULLY
NEEDINESS
NEFARIOUS
NEGLIGENT
NEGOCIATE
NEGOTIATE
NEIGHBOUR

NEOLITHIC
NEOLOGIAN
NEOLOGISM
NEOLOGIST
NEOLOGIZE
NEOTERISM
NEOTERIZE
NEPENTHES
NEPHALISM
NEPHALIST
NEPHELOID
NEPHRITIC
NEPHRITIS
NEPTUNIAN
NERVATION
NERVELESS
NERVOUSLY
NESCIENCE
NESTORIAN
NEURALGIA
NEURALGIC
NEURILITY
NEUROLOGY
NEUROPTER
NEUROTOMY
NEUTRALLY
NEVERMORE
NEWSPAPER
NEWTONIAN
NICTATION
NICTITATE
NIGGARDLY
NIGHTFALL
NIGHTLESS
NIGHTMARE
NIGHTWARD
NIGRITUDE
NINETIETH
NOBLENESS
NOCTURNAL
NOISELESS
NOISINESS
NOISOMELY
NOMINALLY
NOMINATOR
NONENTITY
NONPAREIL
NORMALIZE
NORTHERLY
NORTHWARD
NORWEGIAN
NOSTALGIA
NOTOCHORD
NOTORIETY
NOTORIOUS
NOURISHER
NOVELTIES
NOVENNIAL
NOVITIATE
NOWHITHER
NOXIOUSLY
NULLIFIER
NULLIPIER
NUMERABLE
NUMERALLY
NUMERATOR
NUMERICAL
NUMMULARY
NUMMULITE
NUNNERIES

NUTRIMENT
NUTRITION
NUTRITIVE
NYSTAGMUS

O

OASTHOUSE
OBBLIGATO
OBCONICAL
OBCORDATE
OBEDIENCE
OBEISANCE
OBESENESS
OBFUSCATE
OBJECTIFY
OBJECTION
OBJECTIVE
OBJURGATE
OBLIQUELY
OBLIQUITY
OBLIVIOUS
OBNOXIOUS
OSBCENELY
OBSCENITY
OBSCURANT
OBSCURELY
OBSCURITY
OBSECRATE
OBSEQUIES
OBSERVANT
OBSERVING
OBSESSION
OBSTETRIC
OBSTINACY
OBSTINATE
OBSTRUENT
OBTRUSION
OBTRUSIVE
OBTURATOR
OBVIOUSLY
OBVOLUTED
OCCIPITAL
OCCLUSION
OCCULTISM
OCCUPANCY
OCELLATED
OCTAGONAL
OCTASTYLE
OCTENNIAL
OCTOPUSES
OCULIFORM
ODALISQUE
ODDFELLOW
ODONTALGY
ODOROUSLY
ODOURLESS
OENANTHIC
OFFENSIVE
OFFERTORY
OFFICIATE
OFFICIAL
OFFICIOUS
OFFSPRING
OLECRANON
OLEOGRAPH
OLFACTORY
OLIGARCHY
OMINOUSLY

OMISSIBLE
ONEROUSLY
ONSLAUGHT
OPERATION
OPERATIVE
OPERCULAR
OPERCULUM
OPEROSELY
OPEROSITY
OPHIOLOGY
OPINIONED
OPODELDOC
OPPORTUNE
OPPOSABLE
OPPRESSOR
OPPUGNANT
OPTICALLY
OPTIMATES
OPTIMETER
OPTOMETER
OPULENTLY
ORANGEADE
ORANGEMAN
ORANGEISM
ORBICULAR
ORCHESTRA
ORDERLESS
ORDINANCE
ORGANICAL
ORGANIZED
ORGANIZER
ORGANZINE
ORGIASTIC
ORIENTATE
ORIFLAMME
ORIGINATE
OROGRAPHY
ORPHANAGE
ORTHODOXY
ORTHOEPIC
ORTHOGAMY
ORTHOPTER
OSCILLATE
OSCITANCY
OSSIFRAGE
OSTENSIVE
OSTEOLOGY
OSTEOTOMY
OSTIOLATE
OSTRACEAN
OSTRACION
OSTRACISM
OSTRACIZE
OSTROGOTH
OTHERNESS
OTHERWISE
OTOLOGIST
OTORRHOEA
OUBLIETTE
OURSELVES
OUTERMOST
OUTFITTER
OUTNUMBER
OUTRIGGER
OUTSPOKEN
OUTSPREAD
OUTWARDLY
OVERBOARD
OVERBUILD

OVERCLOUD
OVERCROWD
OVERDRESS
OVERDRIVE
OVERGORGE
OVERISSUE
OVERMATCH
OVERNIGHT
OVERPOWER
OVERREACH
OVERSHOOT
OVERSIGHT
OVERSLEEP
OVERSTATE
OVERSTOCK
OVERTHROW
OVERTRADE
OVERVALUE
OVERWEIGH
OVERWHELM
OVIFEROUS
OVIGEROUS
OVIPAROUS
OVULATION
OWNERSHIP
OXIDATION
OXYGENATE
OXYGENIZE
OXYGENOUS
OZOCERITE
OZOKERITE

P

PACHYDERM
PACKSHEET
PADEMELON
PAEDAGOGY
PAGEANTRY
PAILLASSE
PAINFULLY
PALAESTRA
PALANKEEN
PALATABLE
PALATABLY
PALEOLOGY
PALESTRAL
PALESTRIC
PALFREYED
PALLADIUM
PALMARIAN
PALMATELY
PALMISTER
PALMISTRY
PALPATION
PALPEBRAL
PALPIFORM
PALPITATE
PALSGRAVE
PALUSTRAL
PANDERESS
PANDERISM
PANDURATE
PANEGYRIC
PANELLING
PANOPLIED
PANTALETS
PANTALOON
PANTHEISM

PANTHEIST
PANTOMIME
PAPILLARY
PAPILLATE
PAPILLOSE
PARABASIS
PARABOLIC
PARACHUTE
PARACLETE
PARAGRAPH
PARALYSIS
PARALYTIC
PARAMATTA
PARAMOUNT
PARANYMPH
PARAPETED
PARAPODIA
PARATAXIS
PARBUCKLE
PARCHMENT
PAREGORIC
PARENESIS
PARENETIC
PARENTAGE
PARGETING
PARHELION
PAROCHIAL
PARODICAL
PAROTITIS
PARQUETRY
PARRAKEET
PARRICIDE
PARSEEISM
PARSIMONY
PARSONAGE
PARTIALLY
PARTITION
PARTITIVE
PARTRIDGE
PASSENGER
PASSERINE
PASSIONAL
PASSIVELY
PASSIVITY
PASTICCIO
PASTORATE
PASTURAGE
PATCHOULI
PATCHOULY
PATCHWORK
PATERNITY
PATHOLOGY
PATIENTLY
PATRIARCH
PATRICIAN
PATRIMONY
PATRIOTIC
PATRISTIC
PATRONAGE
PATRONESS
PATRONIZE
PAUPERISM
PAUPERIZE
PAYMASTER
PEACEABLE
PEACEABLY
PEASANTRY
PECCANTLY
PECCARIES
PECTINATE

PECULATOR
PECUNIARY
PEDAGOGIC
PEDAGOGUE
PEDICULAR
PEDOMETER
PEEVISHLY
PERIASTIC
PELASGIAN
PELLITORY
PENCILLED
PENDENTLY
PENDULATE
PENDULOUS
PENETRANT
PENETRATE
PENINSULA
PENITENCE
PENNILESS
PENNONCEL
PENSIONER
PENSIVELY
PENTAGLOT
PENTAGRAM
PENTANDER
PENTARCHY
PENTECOST
PENTHOUSE
PENULTIMA
PENURIOUS
PERCEIVER
PERCHANCE
PERCOLATE
PERDITION
PERENNIAL
PERFECTER
PERFECTLY
PERFERVID
PERFORATE
PERFORMER
PERFUMERY
PERIMETER
PERIPETIA
PERIPHERY
PERISPERM
PERISPORE
PERISTOME
PERISTYLE
PERMANENT
PERMEABLE
PERMEABLY
PERMITTEE
PERMITTER
PERPETUAL
PERSECUTE
PERSIMMON
PERSONAGE
PERSONATE
PERSONIFY
PERSONNEL
PERSUADER
PERTINENT
PERTURBER
PERTUSION
PERVASIVE
PERVERTER
PESSIMISM
PESSIMIST
PESSIMIZE
PESTILENT

PETARDIER
PETECHIAE
PETECHIAL
PETIOLARY
PETIOLATE
PETROLOGY
PETROLEUM
PETTICOAT
PETTINESS
PETTISHLY
PETTITOES
PETULANCE
PETULANCY
PHAENOGAM
PHALANGER
PHALANGES
PHALANXES
PHALAROPE
PHARISAIC
PHAROLOGY
PHENICIAN
PHILATELY
PHILIPPIC
PHILOGYNY
PHILOLOGY
PHILOMATH
PHILOMELA
PHLEBITIS
PHOCACEAN
PHONATION
PHONETICS
PHONOGRAM
PHONOLOGY
PHONOTYPE
PHONOTYPY
PHOSPHATE
PHOSPHIDE
PHOTOLOGY
PHOTOTYPE
PHOTOTYPY
PHRENETIC
PHRENITIS
PHYCOLOGY
PHYLLOPOD
PHYSICIAN
PHYSICISM
PHYSICIST
PHYTOGENY
PHYTOTOMY
PICANINNY
PICKABACK
PICKTHANK
PICTORIAL
PEACEMEAL
PIETISTIC
PIGMENTAL
PIKESTAFF
PILLORIED
PIMPERNEL
PINCHBECK
PINNATELY
PIPISTREL
PIQUANTLY
PIRATICAL
PIROUETTE
PISCIFORM
PISOLITIC
PISTACHIO
PITCHFORK
PITCHPIPE

PITEOUSLY
PITHECOID
PITHINESS
PITIFULLY
PITUITARY
PITUITOUS
PITYINGLY
PIZZICATO
PLACELESS
PLACENTAL
PLACIDITY
PLAINNESS
PLAINTIFF
PLAINTIVE
PLANETARY
PLANETOID
PLANTLESS
PLAQUETTE
PLASMATIC
PLASTERER
PLATINIZE
PLATINOID
PLATINOUS
PLATITUDE
PLATONISM
PLATONIST
PLAUSIBLE
PLAUSIBLY
PLAYFULLY
PLAYHOUSE
PLAYTHING
PLEASANCE
PLENARILY
PLENITUDE
PLENTEOUS
PLENTIFUL
PLEURITIS
PLEURITIC
PLICATION
PLICATURE
PLOUGHBOY
PLOUGHMAN
PLUMBEOUS
PLUMELESS
PLUMPNESS
PLUNDERER
PLURALISM
PLURALIST
PLURALITY
PLURALIZE
PLUTOCRAT
PLUTONIAN
PLUTONIST
PNEUMATIC
PNEUMONIA
PNEUMONIC
POCKETFUL
POENOLOGY
POETASTER
POETICULE
POIGNANCY
POINTEDLY
POINTSMAN
POISONOUS
POLARIZER
POLEMICAL
POLICEMAN
POLITICAL
POLITICLY

POLLARCHY
POLLENIZE
POLLINATE
POLLUTION
POLONAISE
POLYANDRY
POLYARCHY
POLYGONAL
POLYGRAPH
POLYPHONY
POLYPIDOM
POLYSCOPE
POLYSTYLE
POLYZONAL
POMACEOUS
POMPHOLYX
POMPOSITY
POMPOUSLY
PONDEROUS
PONTONIER
POORHOUSE
POPLITEAL
POPULARLY
PORBEAGLE
PORCELAIN
PORCUPINE
PORTERAGE
PORTICOES
PORTICOED
PORTIONER
PORTRAYER
POSSESSOR
POSTILION
POSTULANT
POSTULATE
POSTURIST
POTASSIUM
POTENTATE
POTENTIAL
POTENTITE
POULTERER
POUSSETTE
POWERLESS
PRACTICAL
PRACTISED
PRACTISER
PRAGMATIC
PRAYERFUL
PREACHIFY
PREACHING
PREBENDAL
PRECEDENT
PRECENTOR
PRECEPTOR
PRECIPICE
PRECISELY
PRECISION
PRECOCITY
PRECURSOR
PREDATORY
PREDICANT
PREDICATE
PREDICTOR
PREFATORY
PREFERRER
PREFIGURE
PREFIXION
PREGNABLE
PREGNANCY
PREJUDICE

PRELATIST
PRELATURE
PRELECTOR
PRELUSIVE
PREMATURE
PREMONISH
PREOCCUPY
PREORDAIN
PREPOTENT
PREPUTIAL
PRESBYTER
PRESCIENT
PRESCRIBE
PRESCRIPT
PRESENTEE
PRESENTLY
PRESERVER
PRESIDENT
PRESUMING
PRETENDED
PRETENDER
PRETERITE
PRETERMIT
PRETTYISH
PREVALENT
PREVENTER
PREVISION
PRICELESS
PRIESTESS
PRIMARILY
PRIMATIAL
PRIMITIVE
PRINCEDOM
PRINCIPAL
PRINCIPIA
PRINCIPLE
PRIORSHIP
PRISMATIC
PRIVATEER
PRIVATELY
PRIVATION
PRIVATIVE
PRIVILEGE
PROBATION
PROBATIVE
PROBATORY
PROBOSCIS
PROCEDURE
PROCLITIC
PROCOELUS
PROCONSUL
PROCREANT
PROCREATE
PROCURACY
PRODIGIES
PROFANELY
PROFANITY
PROFESSED
PROFESSOR
PROFFERER
PROFILIST
PROFUSELY
PROGNOSIS
PROGNOSIS
PROGRAMME
PROJECTOR
PROLEPSIS
PROLEPTIC
PROLETARY
PROLIXITY

PROLUSION
PROMENADE
PROMINENT
PROMISING
PROMOTION
PROMOTIVE
PRONATION
PRONENESS
PRONOUNCE
PROOEMIUM
PROPAGATE
PROPELLER
PROPHETIC
PROROGATE
PROSCRIBE
PROSECTOR
PROSECUTE
PROSELYTE
PROSINESS
PROSODIAL
PROSODIAN
PROSODIST
PROSTRATE
PROTECTOR
PROTESTER
PROTHORAX
PROTOTYPE
PROTOZOAL
PROTOZOON
PROUDNESS
PROVENCAL
PROVENDER
PROVIDENT
PROVISION
PROVISORY
PROVOKING
PROXIMATE
PROXIMITY
PRUDENTLY
PRUDISHLY
PRURIENCE
PRURIENCY
PSALMODIC
PSEUDONYM
PSORIASIS
PSYCHICAL
PSYCHOSIS
PTARMIGAN
PTERYGOID
PTOLEMAIC
PUBESCENT
PUBLICIST
PUBLICITY
PUBLISHER
PUERILELY
PUERILITY
PUERPERAL
PUFFINESS
PUGNACITY
PUISSANCE
PULMONARY
PULPINESS
PULSATILE
PULSATION
PULSATIVE
PULSATORY
PULSELESS
PULVERIZE
PULVEROUS

PULVINATE
PUMICEOUS
PUNCTILIO
PUNCTUATE
PUNGENTLY
PURCHASER
PURGATION
PURGATIVE
PURGATORY
PURITANIC
PURLOINER
PURPOSELY
PURPOSIVE
PURPUREAL
PURSINESS
PURSUANCE
PURULENCE
PURULENCY
PUSHINGLY
PUSTULATE
PUSTULOUS
PUTRIDITY
PUZZOLANA
PYRAMIDAL
PYRAMIDIC
PYRETHRUM
PYRITICAL
PYROGENIC
PYROLATER
PYROMETER
PYROXYLIC
PYRRHONIC
PYTHONESS
PYTHONISM
PYTHONIST

Q

QUADRATIC
QUADRIFID
QUADRILLE
QUADRUPED
QUADRUPLE
QUAKERESS
QUAKERISH
QUAKERISM
QUALIFIED
QUALITIES
QUARRYMAN
QUARTERLY
QUARTETTE
QUARTZITE
QUARTZOSE
QUEENHOOD
QUEERNESS
QUERULOUS
QUICKENER
QUICKLIME
QUICKNESS
QUICKSAND
QUIESCENT
QUIETNESS
QUINTETTE
QUINTUPLE
QUITCLAIM
QUITTANCE
QUIXOTISM
QUIZZICAL
QUODLIBET

QUOTATION
QUOTIDIAN

R

RABIDNESS
RACKAROCK
RADIANTLY
RADIATELY
RADIATION
RADICALLY
RAILINGLY
RAININESS
RAJAHSHIP
RAMPANTLY
RANCHERIA
RANCIDITY
RANCOROUS
RANTIPOLE
RAPACIOUS
RAPIDNESS
RAPTORIAL
RAPTUROUS
RAREESHOW
RASCALDOM
RASCALISM
RASCALITY
RASPBERRY
RATIONALE
RAVISHING
REACHABLE
REACHLESS
READDRESS
READINESS
READJOURN
REALISTIC
REALITIES
REANIMATE
REAPPOINT
REARRANGE
REASONING
REATTEMPT
REBAPTISM
REBAPTIZE
REBELLION
REBUILDER
REBUKEFUL
RECAPTURE
RECEIPTOR
RECEIVING
RECENSION
RECEPTION
RECEPTIVE
RECESSION
RECESSIVE
RECHAUFFE
RECHERCHE
RECIPIENT
RECKONING
RECLINATE
RECLUSELY
RECLUSIVE
RECOGNISE
RECOLLECT
RECOMMEND
RECONCILE
RECONDITE
RECONDUCT
RECONQUER

RECOVERER
RECREANCY
RECREMENT
RECRUITER
RECTANGLE
RECTIFIER
RECTITUDE
RECTORIAL
RECTORATE
RECUMBENT
RECURRING
RECURVATE
RECUSANCY
RECUSANCE
REDACTION
REDBREAST
REDDITION
REDELIVER
REDOLENCE
REDOLENCY
REDOUBTED
REDUCIBLE
REDUCTION
REDUNDANT
REFECTION
REFECTORY
REFERABLE
REFERENCE
REFERMENT
REFINEDLY
REFITMENT
REFLECTOR
REFLEXION
REFLEXIVE
REFORMING
REFORTIFY
REFRACTOR
REFRESHER
REFULGENT
REFURBISH
REFURNISH
REFUSABLE
REFUTABLE
REGARDANT
REGARDFUL
REGARDING
REGENESIS
REGICIDAL
REGIMINAL
REGISTRAR
REGRETFUL
REGULARLY
REGULATOR
REHEARSAL
REHEARSER
REIMBURSE
REIMPLANT
REIMPRINT
REINFORCE
REINSPECT
REINSPIRE
REINSTALL
REINSURER
REITERATE
REJECTION
REJOICING
REJOINDER
RELEVANCE
RELEVANCY
RELIEVING

RELIGIOUS
RELIQUARY
REMAINDER
REMIGRATE
REMINDFUL
REMISSION
REMISSIVE
REMISSORY
REMITTENT
REMOVABLE
RENASCENT
RENDITION
RENEWABLE
RENITENCE
RENITENCY
RENOUNCER
RENOVATOR
REPARABLE
REPARABLY
REPAYABLE
REPAYMENT
REPEATING
REPELLENT
REPENTANT
REPERCUSS
REPERTORY
REPERUSAL
REPLENISH
REPLETION
REPLETORY
REPLICANT
REPORTING
REPOSEFUL
REPOSSESS
REPREHEND
REPRESENT
REPRESSER
REPRIMAND
REPROBATE
REPRODUCE
REPTATORY
REPTILIAN
REPUBLISH
REPUDIATE
REPUGNANT
REPULSION
REPULSIVE
REPUTABLE
REPUTEDLY
REQUISITE
RESCUABLE
RESECTION
RESENTFUL
RESERVOIR
RESIDENCE
RESIDENCY
RESIDUARY
RESILIENT
RESISTANT
RESISTENT
RESOLVENT
RESONANCY
RESONATOR
RESPECTER
RESTFULLY
RESTIFORM
RESTIVELY
RESTRAINT
RESULTANT
RESUMABLE

RESURGENT
RETAINING
RETALIATE
RETENTION
RETENTIVE
RETICENCE
RETICULUM
RETINITIS
RETIREDLY
RETRACTOR
RETRIEVAL
RETRIEVER
RETROCEDE
RETROUSSE
REVERENCE
REVERSELY
REVERSION
REVERSIVE
REVETMENT
REVIVABLE
REVOCABLE
REVOLTING
REVULSION
REVULSIVE
RHACHITIS
RHAPSODIC
RHEOMETER
RHEUMATIC
RHINOLITH
RHIZODONT
RHYMELESS
RHYTHMICS
RIBBONISM
RIBBONMAN
RIDDLINGS
RIGHTNESS
RIGIDNESS
RIGMAROLE
RINGLETED
RIOTOUSLY
RITUALISM
RITUALIST
RIVALSHIP
ROADSTEAD
ROCAMBOLE
ROCKINESS
ROGUISHLY
ROISTERER
ROKAMBOLE
ROMANCIST
ROMANIZER
ROMPISHLY
ROOMINESS
ROSACEOUS
ROSTELLUM
ROSTRATED
ROTUNDITY
ROUGHNESS
ROUNDELAY
ROUNDHEAD
ROUNDNESS
RUBESCENT
RUDDINESS
RUFFIANLY
RUINATION
RUINOUSLY
RUMINATOR
RUNCINATE
RUNECRAFT
RUSTICATE

RUSTICITY
RUSTINESS
RUTHENIUM

S

SABADILLA
SABRETASH
SACCHARIC
SACCHARIN
SACCIFORM
SACKCLOTH
SACRAMENT
SACRIFICE
SACRILEGE
SACRISTAN
SADDUCEAN
SAFEGUARD
SAFFLOWER
SAGACIOUS
SAGITTATE
SAILBORNE
SAINTFOIN
SAINTHOOD
SAINTSHIP
SALACIOUS
SALANGANE
SALERATUS
SALICYLIC
SALIENTLY
SALIMETER
SALMONOID
SALTATION
SALTATORY
SALTPETRE
SALUBRITY
SALVATION
SAMARITAN
SANCTUARY
SANDALLED
SANDARACH
SANDINESS
SANDPIPER
SANDSTONE
SANJAKATE
SAPIDNESS
SAPIENTLY
SAPODILLA
SAPPINESS
SARCASTIC
SARCOCARP
SARGASSUM
SARMENTUM
SARTORIAL
SARTORIUS
SASSAFRAS
SASSENACH
SATANICAL
SATELLITE
SATIATION
SATURABLE
SATURNIAN
SATURNINE
SAUCINESS
SAUNTERER
SAVOURILY
SAXIFRAGE
SAXOPHONE
SCAGLIOLA

SCALINESS
SCALLOPED
SCANSORES
SCANTNESS
SCANTLING
SCAPEMENT
SCAPIFORM
SCAPOLITE
SCAPULARY
SCARECROW
SCARIFIER
SCARPINES
SCATHEFUL
SCATTERED
SCATTERER
SCAVENGER
SCENTLESS
SCEPTICAL
SCHEMATIC
SCHEMEFUL
SCHISTOSE
SCHISTOUS
SCHOLARLY
SCHOLIAST
SCHOLIUMS
SCHOOLING
SCHOOLMAN
SCHORLOUS
SCIATICAL
SCIENTIAL
SCIENTIST
SCINTILLA
SCIOMACHY
SCIOMANCY
SCIOPTRIC
SCIRRHOID
SCIRRHOUS
SCISSIBLE
SCLEROSIS
SCLEROTIC
SCORBUTIC
SCORCHING
SCORPIOID
SCOTCHMAN
SCOUNDREL
SCRAGGILY
SCRAMBLER
SCRATCHER
SCREAMING
SCRIBBLER
SCRIMMAGE
SCRIPTORY
SCRIPTURE
SCRIVENER
SCRUTOIRE
SCULPTURE
SCUMBLING
SCUMMINGS
SCUTCHEON
SCUTELLUM
SCUTIFORM
SCYTHEMAN
SEAFARING
SEABOARD
SEASONING
SEBACEOUS
SECERNENT
SECESSION
SECLUSION
SECLUSIVE

SECONDARY
SECRETARY
SECRETION
SECRETIVE
SECRETORY
SECTARIAN
SECTIONAL
SECTORIAL
SECULARLY
SECUNDINE
SECURABLE
SEDENTARY
SEDITIOUS
SEDUCIBLE
SEDUCTION
SEDUCTIVE
SEEDINESS
SEEMINGLY
SEGMENTAL
SEGREGATE
SEIGNIORY
SELACHIAN
SELECTION
SELECTIVE
SELENIOUS
SELFISHLY
SELVEDGED
SEMAPHORE
SEMBLANCE
SEMIBREVE
SEMICOLON
SEMIOLOGY
SEMITONIC
SENESCENT
SENESCHAL
SENIORITY
SENSATION
SENSELESS
SENSITIVE
SENSITIZE
SENSORIAL
SENSORIUM
SENSUALLY
SENTENCER
SENTIMENT
SEPARABLE
SEPARABLY
SEPARATOR
SEPTEMBER
SEPTENARY
SEPULCHRE
SEPULTURE
SEQUESTER
SERASKIER
SERENADER
SERGEANCY
SERGEANTY
SERIALITY
SERICEOUS
SERIOUSLY
SERMONIZE
SERRATION
SERRATURE
SERVIETTE
SERVILELY
SERVILITY
SERVITUDE
SESSIONAL
SETACEOUS

SEVENFOLD
SEVENTEEN
SEVENTHLY
SEVERABLE
SEVERALLY
SEVERALTY
SEVERANCE
SEXENNIAL
SEXUALITY
SEXUALIZE
SFORZANDO
SHADINESS
SHAKINESS
SHALLOWLY
SHAMANISM
SHAMBLING
SHAMELESS
SHAPEABLE
SHAPELESS
SHARPNESS
SHAVELING
SHEARLING
SHEATHING
SHEBEENER
SHEEPFOLD
SHEEPHOOK
SHELDRAKE
SHIFTLESS
SHILLELAH
SHINGLING
SHIPBOARD
SHIPWRECK
SHOEBLACK
SHOEMAKER
SHORELESS
SHORTHAND
SHORTNESS
SHOVELFUL
SHOVELLER
SHOWINESS
SHRINKAGE
SHRUBBERY
SHUFFLING
SIBILANCE
SIBILANCY
SIBYLLINE
SICCATION
SICCATIVE
SICKENING
SICKLEMAN
SIDEBOARD
SIGHINGLY
SIGHTLESS
SIGMOIDAL
SIGNALIZE
SIGNATORY
SIGNATURE
SIGNITARY
SIGNORINA
SILICEOUS
SILIQUOSE
SILKINESS
SILLINESS
SILVERING
SILVERIZE
SIMILARLY
SIMPERING
SIMPLETON
SIMULATOR
SINCERELY

SINCERITY
SINEWLESS
SINISTRAL
SINLESSLY
SINOLOGUE
SINUATION
SINUOSITY
SINUOUSLY
SIPHONAGE
SIPHUNCLE
SITUATION
SIXTEENMO
SIXTEENTH
SIZARSHIP
SKETCHILY
SKILFULLY
SKINFLINT
SLACKNESS
SLAKENESS
SLANDERER
SLANTWISE
SLATINESS
SLAUGHTER
SLAVONIAN
SLAVISHLY
SLEEKNESS
SLEEPLESS
SLENDERLY
SLIMINESS
SLIPPERED
SLOUCHING
SLUMBERER
SLUMBROUS
SMALLNESS
SMARTNESS
SMATTERER
SMILINGLY
SMOKELESS
SMOKINESS
SMUGGLING
SNIVELLER
SOBERNESS
SOBRIQUET
SOCIALISM
SOCIALIST
SOCIALITY
SOCIALIZE
SOCIETIES
SOCIOLOGY
SOFTENING
SOJOURNER
SOLDERING
SOLDIERLY
SOLEMNESS
SOLEMNITY
SOLEMNIZE
SOLFATARA
SOLFEGGIO
SOLICITOR
SOLIDNESS
SOLILOQUY
SOLITAIRE
SOMETHING
SOMETIMES
SOMEWHERE
SOMNOLENT
SONNETEER
SONNETIZE
SONOMETER
SOOTINESS

SOPHISTER
SOPHISTIC
SOPHISTRY
SOPHOMORE
SOPORIFIC
SOPRANIST
SORCERESS
SORRINESS
SORROWFUL
SORTILEGE
SOTTISHLY
SOUBRETTE
SOUNDABLE
SOUNDINGS
SOUNDLESS
SOUNDNESS
SOUTHERLY
SOUTHMOST
SOUTHWARD
SOVEREIGN
SPARENESS
SPARINGLY
SPARKLING
SPARTERIE
SPASMODIC
SPATIALLY
SPATULATE
SPEAKABLE
SPEARMINT
SPECIALLY
SPECIALTY
SPECTACLE
SPECTATOR
SPECULATE
SPECULUMS
SPEECHIFY
SPEEDWELL
SPERMATIC
SPHACELUS
SPHERICAL
SPHINCTER
SPICINESS
SPICULATE
SPIKENARD
SPILLIKIN
SPINDRIFT
SPININESS
SPINNAKER
SPINNERET
SPINOSITY
SPIRILLUM
SPIRITUAL
SPLEENFUL
SPLEENISH
SPLENDENT
SPLENDOUR
SPLENETIC
SPLENITIS
SPLINTERY
SPOKESMAN
SPOLIATOR
SPONGIOLE
SPORANGIA
SPORIDIUM
SPOROCYST
SPORTSMAN
SPOUTLESS
SPRIGHTLY
SPRINGING
SPRINGLET

SPRINKLER
SPUMINESS
SPUTTERER
SQUALIDLY
SQUARROSE
SQUEAMISH
STABILITY
STAGNANCY
STAIDNESS
STAINLESS
STAIRCASE
STALACTIC
STALENESS
STALKLESS
STALWORTH
STAMINATE
STAMMERER
STANCHION
STARBOARD
STARCHILY
STARINGLY
STARLIGHT
STARTLING
STATEMENT
STATESMAN
STATIONAL
STATIONER
STATISTIC
STATUETTE
STATUTORY
STAYMAKER
STEADFAST
STEELYARD
STEEPNESS
STEERSMAN
STELLATED
STELLULAR
STEPCHILD
STERILITY
STERILIZE
STERNMOST
STERNNESS
STEVEDORE
STEWARTRY
STIFFENER
STIFFNESS
STIGMATIC
STILLNESS
STIMULANT
STIMULATE
STINTLESS
STIPITATE
STIPULATE
STITCHING
STOCKDOVE
STOICALLY
STOLIDITY
STOMACHAL
STOMACHER
STOMACHIC
STONINESS
STOUTNESS
STRAGGLER
STRANGELY
STRANGLES
STRANGURY
STRAPPING
STRATAGEM
STRATEGIC
STREAMLET

STRENUOUS
STRETCHER
STRIATION
STRICTURE
STRINGENT
STRIPLING
STROBILUS
STRONTIUM
STRUCTURE
STRUGGLER
STRYCHNIA
STUDIEDLY
STUPEFIER
STUPIDITY
STUTTERER
STYLISHLY
STYLISTIC
STYLOBATE
SUABILITY
SUASIVELY
SUBAERIAL
SUBALPINE
SUBALTERN
SUBARCTIC
SUBCOSTAL
SUBDEACON
SUBDIVIDE
SUBDUABLE
SUBEREOUS
SUBFAMILY
SUBGENERA
SUBJACENT
SUBJUGATE
SUBLESSEE
SUBLIMATE
SUBLIMELY
SUBLIMITY
SUBLUNARY
SUBMARINE
SUBMERSED
SUBREGION
SUBSCRIBE
SUBSCRIPT
SUBSIDIZE
SUBSIDIES
SUBSTANCE
SUBSULTUS
SUBTENANT
SUBTILELY
SUBTILIZE
SUBTORRID
SUBVERTER
SUCCEEDER
SUCCESSOR
SUCCOURER
SUCCULENT
SUCCURSAL
SUCTORIAL
SUDORIFIC
SUFFERING
SUFFIXION
SUFFOCATE
SUGGESTER
SULCATION
SULKINESS
SULPHURET
SULPHURIC
SULTANESS

SULTANATE
SUMMARILY
SUMMARIST
SUMMARIZE
SUMMARIES
SUMMATION
SUMMERSET
SUMMONSES
SUMPTUARY
SUMPTUOUS
SUNFLOWER
SUNNINESS
SUNRISING
SUNSTROKE
SUPERABLE
SUPERFINE
SUPERHEAT
SUPERPOSE
SUPERSEDE
SUPERVENE
SUPERVISE
SUPPLIANT
SUPPORTER
SUPPURATE
SUPREMACY
SUPREMELY
SURCHARGE
SURCINGLE
SURGEONCY
SURLINESS
SURMISING
SURMULLET
SURPLICED
SURPRISAL
SURPRISED
SURRENDER
SURROGATE
SURVEYING
SUSPENDER
SUSPENSOR
SUSPICION
SUSTAINER
SWAGGERER
SWALLOWER
SWANSDOWN
SWARTHILY
SWEEPINGS
SWEETENER
SWEETMEAT
SWEETNESS
SWIFTNESS
SWIMMERET
SWINDLING
SWINEHERD
SWINGEING
SWINISHLY
SWORDSMAN
SYBARITIC
SYCOPHANT
SYLLABIFY
SYLLOGISM
SYLLOGIZE
SYMBIOTIC
SYMBOLISM
SYMBOLIST
SYMBOLIZE
SYMBOLOGY
SYMPHONIC
SYMPHYSIS

SYMPOSIAC
SYMPOSIUM
SYNAGOGUE
SYNCHRONY
SYNCLINAL
SYNCOPATE
SYNCOPIZE
SYNDICATE
SYNERESIS
SYNIZESIS
SYNODICAL
SYNONYMIC
SYNTACTIC
SYNTHESIS
SYNTHETIC
SYPHILIZE
SYSTEMIZE

T

TABASHEER
TABULARLY
TACAMAHAC
TACTICIAN
TAILORESS
TAILORING
TAINTLESS
TALEGALLA
TALKATIVE
TALMUDIST
TANTALIZE
TARANTISM
TARANTULA
TARAXACUM
TARBOUCHE
TARDINESS
TARENTULA
TARGETEER
TARGETIER
TARNISHER
TARPAULIN
TARTAREAN
TARTARIZE
TARTAROUS
TASIMETER
TASMANIAN
TASSELLED
TASTELESS
TATTOOING
TAURIFORM
TAUTOLOGY
TAWNINESS
TAXIDERMY
TAXONOMIC
TEACHABLE
TECHINESS
TECHNICAL
TECTONICS
TEDIOUSLY
TEGULATED
TELEGRAPH
TELEMETER
TELEMETRY
TETEOLOGY
TELEPATHY
TELEPHONE
TELEPHONY
TELESCOPE
TELESCOPY

TELLURIAN
TEMPERATE
TEMPERING
TEMPORARY
TEMPORIZE
TEMPTABLE
TEMPTRESS
TEMULENCE
TENACIOUS
TENDINOUS
TENEBROUS
TENSENESS
TENSILITY
TENTACLED
TENTATIVE
TEPIDNESS
TEREBINTH
TERMAGANT
TERMINATE
TERMITARY
TERRITORY
TERRORISM
TERRORIST
TERRORIZE
TERSENESS
TESSELLAR
TESTACEAN
TESTAMENT
TESTATRIX
TESTIFIER
TESTIMONY
TESTINESS
TETRALOGY
TETRARCHY
TEXTORIAL
TEXTUALLY
THALLOGEN
THANATOID
THANEHOOD
THANESHIP
THANKLESS
THATCHING
THEANDRIC
THEMATIST
THEOCRACY
THEOCRASY
THEOGONIC
THEOLOGIC
THEOMACHY
THEOMANCY
THEOPHANY
THEOREMIC
THEORETIC
THEORIZER
THEOSOPHY
THEREAWAY
THEREFORE
THEREFROM
THEREINTO
THEREUPON
THEREWITH
THERMALLY
THEURGIST
THICKNESS
THINKABLE
THIRSTILY
THIRTIETH
THRASHING
THRESHING

THREEFOLD	TRANSFORM	TRUCELESS	UNDERNBRED
THRENETIC	TRANSFUSE	TRUCULENT	UNDERGRID
THRESHOLD	TRANSIENT	TRUEPENNY	UNDERHAND
THRIFTILY	TRANSLATE	TRUMPETER	UNDERHUNG
THRILLING	TRANSMUTE	TRUNCATED	UNDERLINE
THROBLESS	TRANSPIRE	TRUNCHEON	UNDERLING
THROTTLER	TRANSPORT	TRUSTLESS	UNDERMINE
THROWSTER	TRANSPOSE	TRUTHLESS	UNDERMOST
THUMBLESS	TRAPEZIUM	TUBERCLED	UNDERPLOT
THUNDERER	TRAPEZOID	TUBICOLAR	UNDERPROP
THYLACINE	TRAPPINGS	TUBULATED	UNDERRATE
TIERCELET	TRAUMATIC	TUFACEOUS	UNDERSELL
TIGHTNESS	TRAVELLED	TUMIDNESS	UNDERSHOT
TIMBERING	TRAVELLER	TUNEFULLY	UNDERSIGN
TIMIDNESS	TRAVERSER	TUNICATED	UNDERTAKE
TIPSINESS	TRAVERTIN	TURBIDITY	UNDERWEAR
TIREDNESS	TREACHERY	TURBINATE	UNDERWOOD
TITILLATE	TREADMILL	TURBULENT	UNDESIRED
TITRATION	TREASURER	TURFINESS	UNDILUTED
TITTLEBAT	TREATMENT	TURGIDITY	UNDIVIDED
TITULARLY	TREMATODE	TURNSTILE	UNDOUBTED
TOLERABLE	TREMATOID	TURNSTONE	UNDREAMED
TOLERABLY	TREMBLING	TURPITUDE	UNDRESSED
TOLERANCE	TREMULOUS	TURQUOISE	UNDULATED
TOLERATOR	TRENCHANT	TUSSILAGO	UNDUTIFUL
TOLLBOOTH	TRIATOMIC	TUTORSHIP	UNEARTHLY
TOMENTOSE	TRIBALISM	TWENTIETH	UNEATABLE
TOMENTOUS	TRIBESMAN	TWINKLING	UNENDOWED
TONGUELET	TRIBUNATE	TYPICALLY	UNENGAGED
TONSILLAR	TRIBUTORY	TYRANNIZE	UNENGLISH
TONSORIAL	TRICKSOME	TYRANNOUS	UNEQUABLE
TOOTHACHE	TRICKSTER		UNEQUALLY
TOOTHLESS	TRICLINIC		UNEXPIRED
TOOTHPICK	TRICOLOUR	**U**	UNEXPOSED
TOOTHSOME	TRICUSPID		UNFEELING
TOPIARIAN	TRIENNIAL	ULIGINOUS	UNFEIGNED
TOPICALLY	TRIFACIAL	ULTIMATUM	UNFITNESS
TORMENTER	TRIFLORAL	UMBELLATE	UNFITTING
TORMENTIL	TRIFORIUM	UMBILICAL	UNFLEDGED
TORMENTOR	TRIGAMIST	UMBILICUS	UNFOUNDED
TORNADOES	TRIGONOUS	UMBONATED	UNGALLANT
TORPEDOES	TRIGYNIAN	UNABASHED	UNGENTEEL
TORPIDITY	TRIGYNOUS	UNADORNED	UNGUARDED
TORQUATED	TRIHERDAL	UNADVISED	UNGUIFORM
TORRIDITY	TRIHEDRON	UNALLOYED	UNHANDILY
TORSIONAL	TRILINEAR	UNAMIABLE	UNHAPPILY
TORTILITY	TRILITHON	UNANIMITY	UNHARNESS
TOTALNESS	TRILITHIC	UNANIMOUS	UNHEALTHY
TOUCHABLE	TRILOBATE	UNASSURED	UNHEEDFUL
TOUCHWOOD	TRILOBITE	UNAVENGED	UNHEEDING
TOUGHNESS	TRILOGIES	UNBENDING	UNHOPEFUL
TOURMALIN	TRIMEROUS	UNBIASSED	UNIFACIAL
TOWELLING	TRIMESTER	UNBLESSED	UNIFORMLY
TOWNSFOLK	TRINERVED	UNBOUNDED	UNIGENOUS
TOWNWARDS	TRINKETER	UNBRIDLED	UNINJURED
TRABECULA	TRINKETRY	UNBURTHEN	UNIPAROUS
TRACEABLE	TRINOMIAL	UNCEASING	UNISERIAL
TRACEABLY	TRISERIAL	UNCERTAIN	UNISEXUAL
TRACHEARY	TRITENESS	UNCIVILLY	UNISONANT
TRACHYTIC	TRITHEISM	UNCLEANLY	UNISONOUS
TRACKLESS	TRITURATE	UNCLOUDED	UNITARIAN
TRACTABLE	TRIUMPHAL	UNCONCERN	UNIVALENT
TRACTABLY	TRIUMPHER	UNCORRUPT	UNIVALVED
TRADESMAN	TRIVIALLY	UNCOURTLY	UNIVERSAL
TRADITION	TROCHLEAR	UNCOUTHLY	UNJOINTED
TRADITIVE	TROPOLOGY	UNCROSSED	UNKNOWING
TRAGEDIAN	TROUBLOUS	UNCROWNED	UNLEARNED
TRAINABLE	TROUSERED	UNDAUNTED	UNLIMITED
TRAITRESS	TROUSSEAU	UNDECEIVE	UNLUCKILY
TRANSCEND	TROUTLING	UNDEFINED	

UNMATCHED
UNMEANING
UNMERITED
UNMINDFUL
UNMIXEDLY
UNMORTISE
UNMUSICAL
UNNATURAL
UNNOTICED
UNOPPOSED
UNPITYING
UNPLUMBED
UNPOPULAR
UNQUIETLY
UNREALITY
UNREFINED
UNRELATED
UNRESTING
UNRUFFLED
UNSAVOURY
UNSCATHED
UNSELFISH
UNSETTLED
UNSHACKLE
UNSHAPELY
UNSHEATHE
UNSIGHTLY
UNSKILFUL
UNSKILLED
UNSOUNDLY
UNSPARING
UNSPOTTED
UNSTAINED
UNSTAMPED
UNSTINTED
UNSTUDIED
UNSUBDUED
UNSULLIED
UNTAINTED
UNTAMABLE
UNTENABLE
UNTHANKED
UNTHOUGHT
UNTHRIFTY
UNTIMEOUS
UNTOUCHED
UNTRACKED
UNTRAINED
UNTRODDEN
UNTUNABLE
UNTUTORED
UNUSUALLY
UNVARYING
UNVISITED
UNWARLIKE
UNWATCHED
UNWATERED
UNWEARIED
UNWEIGHED
UNWELCOME
UNWILLING
UNWINKING
UNWITTINGLY
UNWOMANLY
UNWORLDLY
UNWOUNDED
UNWREATHE
UNWRITTEN
UNWROUGHT
UPHOLSTER

UPPERMOST
UPRIGHTLY
URCEOLATE
URTICARIA
USELESSLY
USHERSHIP
UTILITIES
UTRICULAR
UTTERABLE
UTTERANCE
UTTERMOST

V

VACANCIES
VACCINATE
VACILLATE
VAGINATED
VAGUENESS
VAINGLORY
VALENTINE
VALIANTLY
VALUATION
VALUELESS
VAMPIRISM
VANDALISM
VAPIDNESS
VAPORABLE
VAPORIFIC
VAPOURISH
VARIATION
VARICELLA
VARIEGATE
VARIETIES
VARIOLOUS
VARIOLOID
VARIOUSLY
VARNISHER
VASCULOSE
VASOMOTOR
VASSALAGE
VEERINGLY
VEGETABLE
VEHEMENCE
VEHEMENCY
VEHICULAR
VELLICATE
VELVETEEN
VELVETING
VENEERING
VENERABLE
VENERABLY
VENERATOR
VENGEANCE
VENIALITY
VENTILATE
VENTRICLE
VENTUROUS
VERACIOUS
VERATRINE
VERBALISM
VERBALIST
VERBALIZE
VERBOSELY
VERBOSITY
VERDANTLY
VERDIGRIS
VERIDICAL
VERITABLE

VERITABLY
VERMICIDE
VERMIFORM
VERMIFUGE
VERMINATE
VERMINOUS
VERNATION
VERRUCOSE
VERRUCOUS
VERSATILE
VERSIFIER
VERTEBRAE
VERTEBRAL
VESICULAR
VESTIBULE
VESTIGIAL
VETCHLING
VEXATIOUS
VEXILLARY
VIABILITY
VIBRACULA
VIBRATILE
VIBRATION
VIBRATORY
VIBRISSAE
VICARIATE
VICARIOUS
VICARSHIP
VICENNIAL
VICIOUSLY
VICTIMIZE
VICTORESS
VICTORINE
VICTORIES
VIDELICET
VIGESIMAL
VIGILANCE
VILLIFORM
VILLOSITY
VINACEOUS
VINDICATE
VIOLATION
VIOLENTLY
VIOLINIST
VIRESCENT
VIRGILIAN
VIRGINITY
VIRTUALLY
VIRTUOSOS
VIRULENCE
VISCERATE
VISCIDITY
VISCOUNTY
VISIONARY
VISUALITY
VITELLINE
VITIATION
VITRIFIED
VITRIFORM
VITRIOLIC
VITRUVIAN
VIVACIOUS
VIVISECTS
VIZIERATE
VIZIERIAL
VOCALNESS
VOICELESS
VOLCANISM
VOLCANIST
VOLCANOES

VOLUMETER
VOLUNTARY
VOLUNTEER
VOODOOISM
VORACIOUS
VORTICOSE
VOUCHSAFE
VULCANISM
VULCANIAN
VULCANITE
VULCANIZE
VULGARIAN
VULGARISM
VULGARITY
VULGARIZE
VULNERARY
VULPICIDE
VULPINITE
VULTURINE
VULTURISH
VULTUROUS

W

WAGGISHLY
WAGONETTE
WAILINGLY
WAISTBAND
WAISTCOAT
WAKEFULLY
WALDENSES
WALLABIES
WANDERING
WAPENSHAW
WAPENTAKE
WAREHOUSE
WARNINGLY
WARRANTER
WARRANTOR
WASHINESS
WASPISHLY
WASSAILER
WASTENESS
WATCHWORD
WATERFALL
WATERLESS
WATERSHED
WAYFARING
WAYWARDLY
WEALTHILY
WEARINESS
WEARISOME
WEATHERED
WEATHERLY
WEDNESDAY
WEEPINGLY
WEIGHABLE
WEEVILLED
WEIGHTILY
WEIRDNESS
WESTERING
WESTWARDLY
WHALEBONE
WHEEDLING
WHEREFORE
WHEREINTO
WHERENESS
WHEREUNTO
WHEREUPON

WHEREWITH
WHERRYMAN
WHETSTONE
WHICHEVER
WHIMPERER
WHIMSICAL
WHININGLY
WHINSTONE
WHIRLIGIG
WHIRLPOOL
WHIRLWIND
WHISKERED
WHISPERER
WHITENESS
WHITEWASH
WHOLENESS
WHOLESALE
WHOLESOME
WHOSOEVER
WIDOWHOOD
WIELDABLE
WILLINGLY
WINDINESS

WINDINGLY
WINNINGLY
WINGFULLY
WISTFULLY
WITHERING
WITHSTAND
WITLESSLY
WITNESSER
WITTICISM
WITTINESS
WITTINGLY
WOEBEGONE
WOFULNESS
WOLFISHLY
WOLVERENE
WOMANHOOD
WOMANKIND
WOMANLIKE
WONDERFUL
WOODCRAFT
WOODINESS
WORDINESS
WORKHOUSE

WORKMANLY
WORKWOMAN
WORLDLING
WORRIMENT
WORSHIPER
WORTHLESS
WOUNDABLE
WRISTBAND
WRONGNESS
WRYNECKED

X

XERODERMA
XYLOGRAPH
XYLOPHONE

Y

YACHTSMAN
YANKEEISM

YELLOWISH
YESTERDAY
YESTEREVE
YOUNGLING
YOUNGNESS
YOUNGSTER
YTTERBIUM

Z

ZEALOUSLY
ZEMINDARY
ZEUGLODON
ZEUGMATIC
ZIRCONIUM
ZOOGRAPHY
ZOOLOGIST
ZOOPHYTIC
ZOOTOMIST
ZUMBOORUK
ZYGOMATIC
ZYMOMETER

TEN-LETTER WORDS

A

ABBREVIATE
ABDICATION
ABDOMINOUS
ABERDEVINE
ABERRATION
ABHORRENCE
ABIOGENIST
ABJECTNESS
ABJURATION
ABJURATORY
ABLE-BODIED
ABNEGATION
ABNORMALLY
ABOMINABLE
ABOMINABLY
ABORIGINAL
ABORIGINES
ABORTIVELY
ABOVE-BOARD
ABRIDGMENT
ABROGATION
ABROGATIVE
ABRUPTNESS
ABSCISSION
ABSENTMENT
ABSINTHIAN
ABSOLUTELY
ABSOLUTION
ABSOLUTISM
ABSOLUTORY
ABSORBABLE
ABSORBEDLY
ABSORPTION
ABSORPTIVE
ABSTEMIOUS
ABSTENTION
ABSTERGENT
ABSTERSION
ABSTINENCE
ABSTRACTED
ABSTRACTLY
ABSTRUSELY
ABSURDNESS
ABUNDANTLY
ABYSSINIAN
ACADEMICAL
ACCELERATE
ACCENTUATE
ACCEPTABLE
ACCEPTABLY
ACCEPTANCE
ACCEPTANCY
ACCESSIBLE
ACCESSIBLY
ACCIPITRAL
ACCOMPLICE
ACCOMPLISH
ACCORDANCE
ACCOUCHEUR
ACCOUNTANT
ACCRESCENT

ACCUBATION
ACCUMBENCY
ACCUMULATE
ACCURATELY
ACCUSATION
ACCUSATIVE
ACCUSATORY
ACCUSTOMED
ACEPHALOUS
ACETABULUM
ACETARIOUS
ACETIMETER
ACETOPATHY
ACHIEVANCE
ACHROMATIC
ACIDIMETER
ACINACEOUS
ACORN-SHELL
ACOTYLEDON
ACQUAINTED
ACQUIRABLE
ACROAMATIC
ACROGENOUS
ACRONYCHAL
ACROTERIUM
ACTINOLITE
ACTINOZOON
ACTIONABLE
ACTIVENESS
ADAMANTINE
ADAM'S-APPLE
ADAPTATION
ADDER-STONE
ADDER'S-WORT
ADDITIONAL
ADEQUATELY
ADHERENTLY
ADHESIVELY
ADHIBITION
ADIACTINIC
ADJACENTLY
ADJECTIVAL
ADJUDGMENT
ADJUDICATE
ADJUNCTION
ADJUNCTIVE
ADJURATION
ADJURATORY
ADJUSTABLE
ADJUSTMENT
ADMEASURER
ADMINISTER
ADMIRATION
ADMIRINGLY
ADMISSIBLE
ADMITTABLE
ADMITTANCE
ADMITTATOR
ADMITTEDLY
ADMONISHER
ADMONITION
ADMONITIVE
ADMONITORY
ADOLESCENT
ADROITNESS

ADULTERANT
ADULTERATE
ADULTERESS
ADULTERINE
ADULTEROUS
ADVENTURER
ADVERTENCE
ADVERTISER
AERIFEROUS
AEROLOGIST
AERONAUTIC
AEROSTATIC
AERUGINOUS
AESTHETICS
AFFABILITY
AFFECTEDLY
AFFILIABLE
AFFIRMABLE
AFFLICTING
AFFLICTION
AFFLICTIVE
AFFRONTING
AFORENAMED
AFRICANDER
AFTER-BIRTH
AFTER-GRASS
AFTER-IMAGE
AFTER-PAINS
AFTER-PIECE
AFTER-STATE
AFTER-TASTE
AFTERWARDS
AGALLOCHUM
AGGRANDIZE
AGGRESSION
AGGRESSIVE
AGRYPNOTIC
AIDE-DE-CAMP
AIR-BLADDER
AIR-CUSHION
ALARMINGLY
ALBESCENCE
ALBUMINOID
ALBUMINOUS
ALCOHOLISM
ALCOHOLIZE
ALDERMANCY
ALDERMANIC
ALDERMANLY
ALEXANDERS
ALGEBRAIST
ALIENATION
ALIMENTARY
ALINEATION
ALLEGATION
ALLEGIANCE
ALLEGORIST
ALLEGORIZE
ALLEGRETTO
ALLEVIATOR
ALLIACEOUS
ALLIGATION
ALLITERATE
ALLOCATION
ALLOCUTION

ALLOPATHIC	ANGLO-IRISH	APPROACHER
ALLUREMENT	ANGLOMANIA	APPROVABLE
ALLURINGLY	ANGLO-SAXON	AQUAMARINE
ALLUSIVELY	ANGORA-WOOL	AQUIFEROUS
ALMOND-CAKE	ANGULARITY	ARACHNIDAN
ALMOND-TREE	ANHUNGERED	ARBITRATOR
ALMS-GIVING	ANIMADVERT	ARBOR-VITAE
ALONGSHORE	ANIMALCULE	ARCHBISHOP
ALPENSTOCK	ANISOMERIC	ARCHDEACON
ALPHABETIC	ANNEXATION	ARCHER-FISH
ALTAR-BREAD	ANNIHILATE	ARCHETYPAL
ALTAR-CLOTH	ANNOTATION	ARCHITRAVE
ALTAR-PIECE	ANNUNCIATE	AREFACTION
ALTAZIMUTH	ANOINTMENT	ARENACEOUS
ALTERATION	ANSWERABLE	AREOLATION
ALTERATIVE	ANSWERABLY	AREOPAGITE
ALTOGETHER	ANSWERLESS	ARGUMENTAL
ALTRUISTIC	ANTAGONISM	ARISTOCRAT
ALUM-SCHIST	ANTAGONIST	ARITHMETIC
AMALGAMATE	ANTECEDENT	ARMIPOTENT
AMANUENSIS	ANTE-CHAPEL	ARRESTMENT
AMATEURISH	ANTEPENULT	ARROGANTLY
AMAZEDNESS	ANTERIORLY	ARROGATION
AMBASSADOR	ANTHRACENE	ARTFULNESS
AMBIDEXTER	ANTHROPOID	ARTHROPODA
AMBULACRUM	ANTICHRIST	ARTICULATE
AMBULATION	ANTICIPATE	ARTIFICIAL
AMBULATORY	ANTI-CLIMAX	ASCENDABLE
AMBUSHMENT	ANTICLINAL	ASCENDANCY
AMELIORATE	ANTIEMETIC	ASCETICISM
AMENDATORY	ANTILITHIC	ASCRIBABLE
AMERCEABLE	ANTIMONIAL	ASCRIPTION
AMERCEMENT	ANTINOMIAN	ASPHYXIATE
AMIABILITY	ANTIPHONAL	ASPIRATION
AMMUNITION	ANTIQUATED	ASPIRINGLY
AMPHIBIOUS	ANTISEPTIC	ASSAILABLE
AMPHIBRACH	ANTITHESIS	ASSEMBLAGE
AMPHIMACER	ANTITHETIC	ASSENTIENT
AMPUTATION	APHAERESIS	ASSESSABLE
AMYGDALATE	APHORISTIC	ASSESSMENT
AMYGDALINE	APICULTURE	ASSEVERATE
AMYGDALOID	APLACENTAL	ASSIBILATE
AMYLACEOUS	APOCALYPSE	ASSIGNABLE
ANABAPTISM	APOCARPOUS	ASSIGNMENT
ANABAPTIST	APOCRYPHAL	ASSIMILATE
ANACAMPTIC	APODEICTIC	ASSISTANCE
ANACLASTIC	APOLOGETIC	ASSOCIABLE
ANADROMOUS	APOLOGIZER	ASSORTMENT
ANAGOGICAL	APOPHTHEGM	ASSUMPTION
ANALOGICAL	APOPLECTIC	ASSUMPTIVE
ANALYSABLE	APOSTATIZE	ASTEROIDAL
ANAMNIOTIC	APOSTOLATE	ASTOMATOUS
ANAPLASTIC	APOSTROPHE	ASTONISHED
ANARTHROUS	APOTHECARY	ASTOUNDING
ANASTOMOSE	APOTHECIUM	ASTRINGENT
ANATOMICAL	APOTHEOSIS	ASTROLATRY
ANCESTRESS	APPARENTLY	ASTROLOGER
ANCHORETIC	APPARITION	ASTROMETER
ANCHOR-HOLD	APPEALABLE	ASTRONOMER
ANDROECIUM	APPEARANCE	ASTRONOMIC
ANDROGYNAL	APPEASABLE	ASTUTENESS
ANDROPHAGI	APPETITIVE	ATHANASIAN
ANECDOTIST	APPLAUSIVE	ATMOSPHERE
ANELECTRIC	APPLICABLE	ATRABILIAR
ANEMOGRAPH	APPLICANCY	ATRAMENTAL
ANEMOMETER	APPOSITELY	ATTACHABLE
ANEMOMETRY	APPOSITION	ATTACHMENT
ANEMOSCOPE	APPOSITIVE	ATTACKABLE
ANEURISMAL	APPRECIATE	ATTAINABLE
ANGIOSPERM	APPRENTICE	ATTAINMENT

ATTENDANCE
ATTRACTION
ATTRACTIVE
AUCTIONEER
AUDIBILITY
AUDIOMETER
AUDITORIUM
AUGUSTNESS
AURICULATE
AURIFEROUS
AURIGATION
AUSPICIOUS
AUSTRALIAN
AUTHORSHIP
AUTOCHTHON
AUTOCRATIC
AUTOGENOUS
AUTOGRAPHY
AUTOMOBILE
AUTONOMOUS
AUTOPTICAL
AVANT-GUARD
AVANTURINE
AVARICIOUS
AVENTURINE
AVERSENESS
AVICULTURE
AVOUCHMENT
AWAKENMENT

B

BABBLEMENT
BABIROUSSA
BABY-FARMER
BABYLONIAN
BACKGAMMON
BACKGROUND
BACKSLIDER
BACKWARDLY
BAFFLINGLY
BALDERDASH
BALNEOLOGY
BALUSTRADE
BANISHMENT
BANKRUPTCY
BAPTISTERY
BARCAROLLE
BAREBACKED
BAREHEADED
BARGE-BOARD
BARKENTINE
BARLEY-CORN
BAROMETRIC
BARREL-BULK
BARRENNESS
BASE-MINDED
BASKET-HILT
BASSET-HORN
BASSOONIST
BASS-RELIEF
BASTIONARY
BAT-FOWLING
BATHING-BOX
BATHOMETER
BATHYMETRY
BATRACHIAN
BATTLEDORE

BATTLEMENT
BATTLE-SHIP
BEADLESHIP
BEARD-GRASS
BEAR-GARDEN
BEAUTIFIER
BEAUTY-SPOT
BECHE-DE-MER
BECOMINGLY
BEDCHAMBER
BEER-ENGINE
BEFOREHAND
BEHINDHAND
BELIEVABLE
BELLADONNA
BELL-FLOWER
BELL-HANGER
BELL-RINGER
BELL-TURRET
BELL-WETHER
BENEDICITE
BENEDICTUS
BENEFACTOR
BENEFICENT
BENEFICIAL
BENEVOLENT
BENUMBMENT
BEQUEATHER
BESOTTEDLY
BESPRINKLE
BESTIALITY
BESTIALIZE
BESTIARIAN
BETTERMENT
BETTERMOST
BETTERNESS
BEVEL-WHEEL
BEWITCHERY
BEWITCHING
BIBLICALLY
BIBLIOLOGY
BIBLIOPEGY
BICHROMATE
BICORPORAL
BIENNIALLY
BIJOUTERIE
BILGE-WATER
BILINGUIST
BILL-BROKER
BILLET-DOUX
BIMACULATE
BIMETALLIC
BIOGENESIS
BIOGRAPHER
BIOPLASMIC
BIRD-CHERRY
BIRD-SPIDER
BIROSTRATE
BIRTHNIGHT
BIRTHPLACE
BIRTHRIGHT
BISHOP-WEED
BISSEXTILE
BISULPHATE
BISULPHITE
BITTERNESS
BITUMINIZE
BITUMINOUS
BLACKAMOOR

BLACKBERRY
BLACK-BOARD
BLACK-CHALK
BLACK-FRIAR
BLACKGUARD
BLACK-SHEEP
BLACKSMITH
BLACKTHORN
BLAMEFULLY
BLANC-MANGE
BLANDISHER
BLANKETING
BLANK-VERSE
BLASPHEMER
BLASTODERM
BLAZONMENT
BLISSFULLY
BLITHENESS
BLITHESOME
BLOCK-HOUSE
BLOOD-HORSE
BLOOD-HOUND
BLOODINESS
BLOOD-MONEY
BLOOD-STONE
BLOODY-FLUX
BLOOMINGLY
BLUBBER-LIP
BLUE-BOTTLE
BLUE-JACKET
BLUISHNESS
BLUSHINGLY
BLUSTERING
BLUSTEROUS
BOARD-WAGES
BOASTFULLY
BOASTINGLY
BODY-COLOUR
BOG-TROTTER
BOISTEROUS
BOMBARDIER
BOMB-VESSEL
BOND-HOLDER
BONDS-WOMAN
BONE-SETTER
BONE-SPAVIN
BOOK-HUNTER
BOOK-KEEPER
BOOK-MUSLIN
BOOKSELLER
BOOTLESSLY
BORDER-LAND
BOTTLE-FISH
BOTTLE-NOSE
BOTTLE-TREE
BOTTOMLESS
BOUTS-RIMES
BOWDLERIZE
BOWIE-KNIFE
BOYISHNESS
BRACHIOPOD
BRACHYLOGY
BRACKETING
BRACTEATED
BRAGGINGLY
BRAHMANISM
BRAIN-FEVER
BRANCHIATE
BRANCHLESS

BRANT-GOOSE
BRAWLINGLY
BRAWNINESS
BRAZENNESS
BRAZIL-WOOD
BRAZILETTO
BREADSTUFF
BREAKWATER
BREAST-BONE
BREAST-DEEP
BREAST-KNOT
BREAST-WALL
BREAST-WORK
BREATHABLE
BREATHLESS
BRENT-GOOSE
BRICK-FILLED
BRICKLAYER
BRIDEGROOM
BRIDESMAID
BRIDGE-DECK
BRIDLE-HAND
BRIDLE-PATH
BRIDLE-ROAD
BRIDLE-REIN
BRIGANDAGE
BRIGANDISM
BRIGANTINE
BRIGHTNESS
BRIGHTSOME
BRILLIANCE
BROAD-CLOTH
BROADSWORD
BROKEN-DOWN
BROKENNESS
BROKEN-WIND
BROME-GRASS
BRONCHITIS
BROOMSTICK
BROOMSTAFF
BROWBEATER
BROWN-STUDY
BRUSQUERIE
BUBONOCELE
BUCCINATOR
BUCK-BASKET
BUCK-JUMPER
BUDDHISTIC
BUFFOONERY
BUFFOONISH
BULLIONIST
BUNGLINGLY
BURDENSOME
BUREAUCRAT
BURROW-DUCK
BUSH-HARROW
BUSH-RANGER
BUSH-SHRIKE
BUTLERSHIP
BUTTER-BIRD
BUTTER-BOAT
BUTTERMILK
BUTTER-TREE
BUTTERWORT
BUTTERY-BAR
BUTTON-PUSH
BUTTON-HOLE
BUTTON-HOOK
BUTTON-WOOD

C

CACOGRAPHY
CADAVEROUS
CADDICE-FLY
CAESPITOSE
CALAMITOUS
CALCAREOUS
CALCINABLE
CALC-SINTER
CALCULABLE
CALCULATED
CALCULATOR
CALEDONIAN
CALIGINOUS
CALIGRAPHY
CALUMNIATE
CALUMNIOUS
CALYCIFORM
CALYPTRATE
CAMELOPARD
CAMERONIAN
CAMPAIGNER
CAMPESTRAL
CAMPHORATE
CAMPHOR-OIL
CANARY-WOOD
CANCELLATE
CANCELLOUS
CANDESCENT
CANDIDNESS
CANDLE-COAL
CANDLE-FISH
CANDLEWICK
CANDY-SUGAR
CANEPHORUS
CANKER-WORM
CANNEL-COAL
CANNON-BALL
CANNON-SHOT
CANONICALS
CANONICITY
CANTATRICE
CANTERBURY
CANTILEVER
CANTONMENT
CANVAS-BACK
CAOUTCHOUC
CAPABILITY
CAPACITATE
CAPILLAIRE
CAPITALIZE
CAPITATION
CAPITULATE
CAPNOMANCY
CAPRICIOUS
CAPTIOUSLY
CARABINEER
CARAVANEER
CARBAZOTIC
CARBONATED
CARBUNCLED
CARDIALGIA
CARELESSLY
CARICATURE
CARNALLITE
CARPELLARY
CARTHUSIAN
CARTWRIGHT

CASCARILLA
CASE-BOTTLE
CASE-HARDEN
CASEMENTED
CASSIA-BARK
CASSIA-BUDS
CASSIOPEIA
CASSOLETTE
CASTIGATOR
CASTRATION
CATAFALQUE
CATALECTIC
CATALEPTIC
CATAMENIAL
CATAPHRACT
CATARRHINE
CATCH-PENNY
CATECHETIC
CATECHUMEN
CHUMENICAL
CATENARIAN
CATENATION
CATHOLICON
CATOPTRICS
CATTLE-SHOW
CAULESCENT
CAUSTICITY
CAUTIONARY
CAUTIOUSLY
CAVALIERLY
CELEBRATED
CELEBRATER
CELLULATED
CENOBITISM
CENSORIOUS
CENSORSHIP
CENSURABLE
CENSURABLY
CENTAURIAN
CENTENNIAL
CENTESIMAL
CENTIGRADE
CENTIMETRE
CENTIPEDAL
CENTRALISM
CENTRALITY
CENTRALIZE
CENTRICITY
CENTRIFUGE
CEPHALITIS
CEPHALOPOD
CEREBELLAR
CEREBELLUM
CEREBRITIS
CEREMONIAL
CEREGRAPHY
CERTIORARI
CERUMINOUS
CESSIONARY
CESTIODEAN
CESTRACION
CHAIN-CABLE
CHALCEDONY
CHALKINESS
CHALLENGER
CHALYBEATE
CHAMAELEON
CHAMBER-POT
CHAMBERTIN
CHAMPIGNON

CHANCELLOR
CHANDELIER
CHANGEABLE
CHANGEABLY
CHANGELESS
CHANGELING
CHANNELLED
CHAPEL-CART
CHAPFALLEN
CHAPLAINCY
CHARGEABLE
CHARIOTEER
CHARITABLE
CHARITABLY
CHARMINGLY
CHARTREUSE
CHARTULARY
CHASTENESS
CHATELAINE
CHATTER-BOX
CHAUCERIAN
CHAUVINISM
CHAUVINIST
CHEEK-POUCH
CHEEK-TOOTH
CHEERFULLY
CHEERINESS
CHEERINGLY
CHEESE-CAKE
CHEESINESS
CHEIROPTER
CHEMICALLY
CHEMISETTE
CHEQUE-BOOK
CHERSONESE
CHERUBIMIC
CHESS-BOARD
CHICKEN-POX
CHIFFONIER
CHILDBIRTH
CHILDISHLY
CHILIASTIC
CHILLINESS
CHILLINGLY
CHIMERICAL
CHIMNEY-CAN
CHIMNEY-TOP
CHIMPANZEE
CHINA-ASTER
CHINCHILLA
CHIP-BONNET
CHIROGNOMY
CHIROGRAPH
CHIROMANCY
CHIRURGEON
CHISELLING
CHIVALROUS
CHLORALISM
CHLORIDIZE
CHLORIDATE
CHLORODYNE
CHLOROFORM
CHOICELESS
CHOLAGOGUE
CHOLIAMBUS
CHOP-FALLEN
CHOPSTICKS
CHORIAMBUS
CHRISTHOOD
CHRISTLESS

CHROMATICS
CHRONICLER
CHRONOGRAM
CHRONOLOGY
CHRYSOLITE
CHUBBINESS
CHURCH-GOER
CHURCHLESS
CHURCH-RATE
CHURCHYARD
CHURLISHLY
CICERONIAN
CINCHONISM
CINENCHYMA
CINQUE-FOIL
CINQUE-PACE
CIRCENSIAN
CIRCUITOUS
CIRCULABLE
CIRCULARLY
CIRCULATOR
CIRCUMCISE
CIRCUMFLEX
CIRCUMFUSE
CIRCUMMURE
CIRCUMVENT
CISMONTANE
CISTERCIAN
CITIZENIZE
CLACK-VALVE
CLAMMINESS
CLANGOROUS
CLANNISHLY
CLARENCEUX
CLASP-KNIFE
CLASSICISM
CLASSICIST
CLAVICHORD
CLAVICULAR
CLAW-HAMMER
CLAY-GROUND
CLEANSABLE
CLEAR-STORY
CLERESTORY
CLERGIABLE
CLEVERNESS
CLIENTSHIP
CLINGSTONE
CLINICALLY
CLINK-STONE
CLINOMETER
CLODHOPPER
CLOISTERER
CLOSE-STOOL
CLOUDBERRY
CLOUD-BUILT
CLOUD-BURST
CLOUDINESS
CLOWNISHLY
CLUB-FOOTED
CLUMSINESS
COACH-STAND
COADJUTRIX
COAGULABLE
COAGULATOR
COALESCENT
COAL-HEAVER
COAL-MASTER
COARSENESS
COAST-GUARD

COASTWARDS
COAT-ARMOUR
COCKATRICE
COCKCHAFER
COCKNEYDOM
COCKNEYISH
COCKNEYISM
COEQUALITY
COERCIVELY
COETANEOUS
COETERNITY
COEXECUTOR
COEXISTENT
COFFEE-MILL
COFFEE-ROOM
COGITATION
COGITATIVE
COGNIZABLE
COGNIZABLY
COGNIZANCE
COGNOMINAL
COHERENTLY
COHESIVELY
COINCIDENT
COLD-CHISEL
COLEORHIZA
COLLAR-BEAM
COLLARLESS
COLLATABLE
COLLATERAL
COLLECTION
COLLECTIVE
COLLEGIATE
COLLIMATOR
COLLINGUAL
COLLIQUATE
COLLOCUTOR
COLLOQUIAL
COLLOQUIST
COLLOQUIZE
COLORATION
COLOURABLE
COLOURABLY
COLOURLESS
COLPORTEUR
COMBATABLE
COMBINABLE
COMBINEDLY
COMBUSTION
COMEDIETTA
COMELINESS
COMESTIBLE
COMFORTING
COMICALITY
COMMANDANT
COMMANDEER
COMMENTARY
COMMERCIAL
COMMISSARY
COMMISSION
COMMISSURE
COMMITMENT
COMMIXTURE
COMMODIOUS
COMMONABLE
COMMONALTY
COMMONNESS
COMMONWEAL
COMMUTABLE
COMPARABLE

COMPARABLY
COMPARISON
COMPASSION
COMPASS-SAW
COMPATIBLE
COMPATIBLY
COMPATRIOT
COMPENDIUM
COMPENSATE
COMPETENCE
COMPETITOR
COMPLACENT
COMPLAINER
COMPLEMENT
COMPLETELY
COMPLETION
COMPLETIVE
COMPLETORY
COMPLEXION
COMPLEXITY
COMPLIANCE
COMPLICACY
COMPLICATE
COMPLICITY
COMPLIMENT
COMPOSEDLY
COMPOSITOR
COMPOUNDER
COMPREHEND
COMPRESSED
COMPRESSOR
COMPROMISE
COMPULSION
COMPULSIVE
COMPULSORY
COMPUTABLE
CONCENTRIC
CONCEPTION
CONCEPTUAL
CONCERNING
CONCERTINA
CONCESSION
CONCESSIVE
CONCHOIDAL
CONCHOLOGY
CONCILIATE
CONCINNITY
CONCLAVIST
CONCLUDING
CONCLUSION
CONCLUSIVE
CONCOCTION
CONCORDANT
CONCRETELY
CONCRETION
CONCUBINAL
CONCURRENT
CONCUSSION
CONCUSSIVE
CONDESCEND
CONDOLENCE
CONDUCTION
CONDUCTIVE
CONFECTION
CONFERENCE
CONFERVOID
CONFESSION
CONFIDANTE
CONFIDENCE
CONFINABLE

CONFISCATE
CONFLUENCE
CONFORMIST
CONFORMITY
CONFOUNDED
CONFOUNDER
CONFUSEDLY
CONFUTABLE
CONGENERIC
CONGENITAL
CONGESTION
CONGESTIVE
CONGLOBATE
CONGREGATE
CONGRUENCE
CONIFEROUS
CONJECTURE
CONJOINTLY
CONJUGALLY
CONJUNCTLY
CONNASCENT
CONNATURAL
CONNECTION
CONNECTIVE
CONNIVANCE
CONNIVENCE
CONQUERING
CONSCIENCE
CONSECRATE
CONSENSUAL
CONSEQUENT
CONSISTENT
CONSISTORY
CONSOCIATE
CONSOLABLE
CONSONANCE
CONSPECTUS
CONSPIRACY
CONSTANTLY
CONSTIPATE
CONSTITUTE
CONSTRAINT
CONSTRINGE
CONSUBSIST
CONSUETUDE
CONSULSHIP
CONSULTING
CONSULTIVE
CONSUMABLE
CONSUMEDLY
CONSUMMATE
CONTACTUAL
CONTAGIOUS
CONTAINANT
CONTENTION
CONTESTANT
CONTEXTUAL
CONTEXTURE
CONTIGUITY
CONTIGUOUS
CONTINENCE
CONTINGENT
CONTINUITY
CONTINUOUS
CONTORTION
CONTRABAND
CONTRACTED
CONTRACTOR
CONTRADICT
CONTRARILY

CONTRAVENE
CONTRIBUTE
CONTRITELY
CONTRITION
CONTROLLER
CONTROVERT
CONVALESCE
CONVECTION
CONVECTIVE
CONVENABLE
CONVENANCE
CONVENIENT
CONVENTION
CONVENTUAL
CONVERGENT
CONVERSANT
CONVERSELY
CONVERSION
CONVEXNESS
CONVEYABLE
CONVEYANCE
CONVICTION
CONVINCING
CONVULSION
CONVULSIVE
COOL-HEADED
CO-OPERATOR
CO-ORDINATE
COPARCENER
COPERNICAN
COPPER-HEAD
COPROLITIC
COPULATION
COPULATIVE
COPULATORY
COPYHOLDER
COQUETTISH
CO-RADICATE
CORDIALITY
CORDILLERA
CORDWAINER
CORELATIVE
CORIACEOUS
CORINTHIAN
CORK-CUTTER
CORKING-PIN
CORK-JACKET
CORN-BEETLE
CORN-COCKLE
CORNERWISE
CORN-FACTOR
CORN-FLOWER
CORNUCOPIA
CORONATION
CORONIFORM
CORPORALLY
CORPOREITY
CORPSE-GATE
CORPULENCE
CORRECTION
CORRECTIVE
CORRECTORY
CORRESPOND
CORRIGENDA
CORRIGIBLE
CORRODIBLE
CORRUGATED
CORRUGATOR
CORRUPTION
CORRUPTIVE

CORSELETED
CORYPHAEUS
COSMICALLY
COSMOGONAL
COSMORAMIC
COSTLINESS
COTHURNATE
COTTIERISM
COTTON-SEED
COTTON-TREE
COTTON-WOOD
COTTON-WOOL
COTYLIFORM
COUCH-GRASS
COUNCILLOR
COUNCIL-MAN
COUNSELLOR
COUNTERACT
COUNTRYMAN
COURAGEOUS
COURT-BARON
COURT-DRESS
COURTHOUSE
COURT-SWORD
COUSINHOOD
COUSINSHIP
COVENANTEE
COVENANTER
COVENANTOR
COVERED-WAY
COVETINGLY
COVETOUSLY
COW-BUNTING
COW-CATCHER
COW-CHERVIL
COW-PARSLEY
COWDIE-PINE
COW-PARSNIP
COWRIE-PINE
CRAFTINESS
CRAGGINESS
CRANE'S-BILL
CRANIOLOGY
CRAPULENCE
CRASSAMENT
CRASSITUDE
CRAWLINGLY
CREAM-FACED
CREAMINESS
CREATIONAL
CREDENTIAL
CREDITABLE
CREDITABLY
CRENELLATE
CRESCENTED
CRESCENTIC
CRETACEOUS
CRIBRIFORM
CRIMINALLY
CRINGELING
CRIO-SPHINX
CRISPATION
CROSS-BREED
CRITICALLY
CRITICIZER
CROSS-BONES
CROSS-BREED
CROSS-STAFF
CROSS-STONE
CROSS-TREES

CROTCHETED
CROW-FLOWER
CROWN-GRASS
CROWN-WHEEL
CRUET-STAND
CRUMB-BRUSH
CRUMB-CLOTH
CRUSTACEAN
CRUSTATION
CRUSTINESS
CRYOPHORUS
CRYPTOGAMY
CRYPTOGRAM
CRYPTOLOGY
CTENOPHORA
CUCKOO-SPIT
CUCURBITAL
CUIRASSIER
CULTIVABLE
CULTIVATOR
CULTURABLE
CULVERTAIL
CUMBERLESS
CUMBERSOME
CUMBROUSLY
CUMMER-BUND
CUMULATION
CUMULATIVE
CURABILITY
CURATESHIP
CURMUDGEON
CURRICULUM
CURSEDNESS
CUSTOMABLE
CUTTLE-FISH
CUTTLE-BONE
CYATHIFORM
CYCLOMETER
CYLINDROID
CZAREVITCH

D

DAGGLE-TAIL
DAINTINESS
DAMAGEABLE
DAMASK-PLUM
DAMASK-ROSE
DAPPLE-GREY
DARK-BROWED
DAUGHTERLY
DAUPHINESS
DAY-DREAMER
DAZZLINGLY
DEACONHOOD
DEACONSHIP
DEAD-LETTER
DEADLINESS
DEAD-NETTLE
DEAD-WEIGHT
DEAD-DOUGHT
DEADHMATE
DEATH-AGONY
DEATH'S-DOOR
DEATH'S-HEAD
DEATH-TOKEN
DEATH-WATCH
DEBASEMENT
DEBAUCHERY

DEBENTURED
DEBILITATE
DEBONAIRLY
DEBOUCHURE
DECAGYNIAN
DECAGYNOUS
DECAHEDRAL
DECALOGIST
DECAMPMENT
DECANDRIAN
DECANDROUS
DECANGULAR
DECAPITATE
DECAPODOUS
DECEIVABLE
DECEMBERLY
DECEMVIRAL
DECIGRAMME
DECIMALIZE
DECIMATION
DECIPHERER
DECISIVELY
DECLAIMANT
DECLARABLE
DECLARATOR
DECLAREDLY
DECLENSION
DECLINABLE
DECLINATOR
DECOLORANT
DECOLORATE
DECOLORIZE
DECOMPOUND
DECORATION
DECORATIVE
DECOROUSLY
DECREEABLE
DECRESCENT
DECUMBENCE
DECUMBENCY
DECURRENCY
DEDICATION
DEDICATORY
DEFACEMENT
DEFALCATOR
DEFAMATION
DEFEASANCE
DEFEASIBLE
DEFECATION
DEFENDABLE
DEFENSIBLE
DEFICIENCE
DEFICIENCY
DEFILEMENT
DEFINITELY
DEFINITION
DEFINITIVE
DEFLAGRATE
DEFLECTION
DEFLOWERER
DEFORMEDLY
DEFRAUDMENT
DEGENERACY
DEGENERATE
DEHISCENCE
DEHUMANIZE
DEJECTEDLY
DEL CREDERE
DELECTABLE
DELECTABLY

DELEGATION
DELIBERATE
DELICATELY
DELIGHTFUL
DELINEATOR
DELINQUENT
DELIQUESCE
DELUSIVELY
DEMAGOGISM
DEMANDABLE
DEMI-QUAVER
DEMOBILISE
DEMOCRATIC
DEMOGORGON
DEMOGRAPHY
DEMOISELLE
DEMOLISHER
DEMOLITION
DEMONETIZE
DEMONOLOGY
DEMORALIZE
DEMURENESS
DEMURRABLE
DENDRIFORM
DENDROLITE
DENDROLOGY
DENIZATION
DENOMINATE
DENOTATION
DENOTATIVE
DENOUEMENT
DENSIMETER
DENTIFRICE
DENUDATION
DENUNCIATE
DEOBSTRUCT
DEODORIZER
DEONTOLOGY
DEPARTMENT
DEPENDABLE
DEPENDANCE
DEPENDENCE
DEPENDENCY
DEPILATION
DEPILATORY
DEPLORABLE
DEPLORABLY
DEPLOYMENT
DEPOLARIZE
DEPOPULATE
DEPORTMENT
DEPOSITARY
DEPOSITION
DEPRAVEDLY
DEPRECATOR
DEPRECIATE
DEPREDATOR
DEPRESSION
DEPRESSIVE
DEPURATION
DEPURATORY
DEPUTATION
DERACINATE
DERIDINGLY
DERISIVELY
DERIVATION
DERIVATIVE
DEROGATION
DEROGATORY
DESCENDANT

DESCENDENT
DESCENDING
DESCENSION
DESECRATER
DESERVEDLY
DESHABILLE
DESICCATOR
DESIDERATE
DESIGNATOR
DESIGNEDLY
DESOLATELY
DESOLATION
DESPAIRING
DESPATCHER
DESPICABLE
DESPICABLY
DESPISABLE
DESPITEFUL
DESPONDENT
DESQUAMATE
DESUDATION
DETACHMENT
DETAINMENT
DETECTABLE
DETERGENCE
DETERGENCY
DETERMINED
DETESTABLE
DETESTABLY
DETONATING
DETONATION
DETRACTION
DETRACTIVE
DETRACTORY
DETRUNCATE
DEUTOPLASM
DEVASTATOR
DEVILISHLY
DEVIL'S-DUST
DEVITALIZE
DEVOLUTION
DEVOTEMENT
DEVOTIONAL
DEVOURABLE
DIABETICAL
DIABOLICAL
DIACAUSTIC
DIACOUSTIC
DIAGLYPHIC
DIAGNOSTIC
DIAGONALLY
DIALECTICS
DIALOGICAL
DIAPEDESIS
DIAPHANOUS
DIAPHONICS
DIASKEUAST
DIATHERMAL
DIATHERMIC
DIATRIBIST
DICTATRESS
DICTIONARY
DIDACTICAL
DIDELPHIAN
DIDUNCULUS
DIDYNAMOUS
DIELECTRIC
DIE-SINKING
DIETETICAL
DIFFERENCE

DIFFICULTY
DIFFIDENCE
DIFFORMITY
DIFFUSIBLE
DIGESTIBLE
DIGITATELY
DIGITATION
DIGITIFORM
DIGITORIUM
DIGRESSION
DIGRESSIVE
DEJUDICATE
DILACERATE
DILAPIDATE
DILATATION
DILATORILY
DILETTANTE
DILIGENTLY
DILLY-DALLY
DILUCIDATE
DIMINISHER
DIMINUENDO
DIMINUTION
DIMINUTIVE
DIMORPHISM
DIMORPHOUS
DINING-ROOM
DINNER-HOUR
DINNERLESS
DINNER-TIME
DIOPTRICAL
DIPETALOUS
DIPHTHERIA
DIPHYLLOUS
DIPHYODONT
DIPLOMATIC
DIPROTODON
DIPSOMANIA
DIRECTNESS
DIRECTRESS
DISABILITY
DISANIMATE
DISAPPAREL
DISAPPOINT
DISAPPROVE
DISARRANGE
DISASTROUS
DISBELIEVE
DISBURTHEN
DISCERNING
DISCHARGER
DISCIPLINE
DISCLAIMER
DISCLOSURE
DISCOMFORT
DISCOMMEND
DISCOMPOSE
DISCONCERT
DISCONNECT
DISCONTENT
DISCOPHORA
DISCORDANT
DISCOUNTER
DISCOURAGE
DISCOURSER
DISCOVERER
DISCREETLY
DISCREPANT
DISCRETION
DISCRETIVE

DISCURSIVE
DISCUSSION
DISCUSSIVE
DISCUTIENT
DISDAINFUL
DISEMBOGUE
DISEMBOSOM
DISEMBOWEL
DISEMBROIL
DISENCHANT
DISENGAGED
DISENNOBLE
DISENSLAVE
DISENTITLE
DISFEATURE
DISFIGURER
DISFURNISH
DISGUSTFUL
DISGUSTING
DISHABILLE
DISHEARTEN
DISHONESTY
DISINCLINE
DISINHERIT
DISJOINTED
DISLOYALLY
DISLOYALTY
DISMALNESS
DISMISSION
DISMISSORY
DISOMATOUS
DISORDERED
DISORDERLY
DISOWNMENT
DISPARAGER
DISPASSION
DISPENSARY
DISPENSING
DISPEOPLER
DISPERMOUS
DISPERSION
DISPERSIVE
DISPIRITED
DISPLEASED
DISPLEASER
DISPOSABLE
DISPOSSESS
DISPUTABLE
DISQUALIFY
DISRESPECT
DISRUPTION
DISSATISFY
DISSECTING
DISSECTION
DISSEMBLER
DISSENSION
DISSENTING
DISSERVICE
DISSIDENCE
DISSILIENT
DISSIMILAR
DISSIPATED
DISSOLUBLE
DISSOLVENT
DISSONANCE
DISSUASION
DISSUASIVE
DISSYMETRY
DISTENSIVE

DISTENTION
DISTICHOUS
DISTILLATE
DISTINCTLY
DISTORTION
DISTORTIVE
DISTRACTED
DISTRAINER
DISTRAINOR
DISTRAUGHT
DISTRESSED
DISTRIBUTE
DITHEISTIC
DIVAGATION
DIVARICATE
DIVERGENCE
DIVERGENCY
DIVINATION
DIVINENESS
DIVING-BELL
DIVISIONAL
DOCIMASTIC
DOCTORSHIP
DOCUMENTAL
DOGGEDNESS
DOGMATIZER
DOG-PARSLEY
DOLOROUSLY
DOMINATION
DOOR-KEEPER
DOUBLE-BASS
DOUBLE-DYED
DOUBLE-LOCK
DOUBLENESS
DOUBLE-STAR
DOUBTFULLY
DOWNLOOKED
DOWN-STAIRS
DRAGON-TREE
DRAMATICAL
DRAMATURGY
DRAUGHT-BAR
DRAWBRIDGE
DRAWLINGLY
DREADFULLY
DREAMINESS
DREARINESS
DRESSMAKER
DROOPINGLY
DROP-HAMMER
DROSOMETER
DROSSINESS
DROWSINESS
DRUDGINGLY
DRUPACEOUS
DRYSALTERY
DUBITATION
DUCK-BILLED
DULL-WITTED
DUMB-WAITER
DUNIWASSAL
DUODECIMAL
DURABILITY
DUUMVIRATE
DWARFISHLY
DYNAMITARD
DYSENTERIC

E

EARTH-BOUND
EARTHINESS
EARTH-PLATE
EARTHQUAKE
EARTH-SHINE
EAR-TRUMPET
EAR-WITNESS
EASTERLING
EASTERTIDE
EBOULEMENT
EBRACTEATE
EBULLIENCE
EBULLIENCY
EBULLITION
ECCHYMOSIS
ECCLESIAST
ECCOPROTIC
ECHINODERM
ECONOMICAL
ECTHLIPSIS
ECZEMATOUS
EDACIOUSLY
EDENTULOUS
EDIBLENESS
EDIFYINGLY
EDITORSHIP
EDULCORATE
EFFACEABLE
EFFACEMENT
EFFECTIBLE
EFFECTLESS
EFFECTUATE
EFFEMINACY
EFFEMINATE
EFFERVESCE
EFFICIENCY
EFFLORESCE
EFFORTLESS
EFFRONTERY
EFFULGENCE
EFFUSIVELY
EGYPTOLOGY
EIGHTEENMO
EIGHTEENTH
EISTEDDFOD
ELABORATOR
ELASTICITY
ELBOW-CHAIR
ELDER-BERRY
ELECAMPANE
ELECTORATE
ELECTRICAL
ELEMENTARY
ELENCHICAL
ELEUSINIAN
ELIMINABLE
ELIQUATION
ELLIPTICAL
ELONGATION
ELOQUENTLY
ELUCIDATOR
EMACIATION
EMANCIPATE
EMARGINATE
EMASCULATE
EMBANKMENT
EMBASSADOR

EMBER-GOOSE
EMBLAZONER
EMBLEMATIC
EMBODIMENT
EMBOLISMAL
EMBOLISMIC
EMBONPOINT
EMBOSSMENT
EMBOUCHURE
EMBROIDERY
EMBRYOGENY
EMBRYOLOGY
EMBRYONARY
EMBRYOTOMY
EMENDATION
EMENDATORY
EMERGENTLY
EMETICALLY
EMIGRATION
EMMETROPIA
EMPHATICAL
EMPIRICISM
EMPLOYABLE
EMPLOYMENT
ENAMELLIST
ENANTIOSIS
ENCAMPMENT
ENCEPHALIC
ENCEPHALON
ENCHANTING
ENCLITICAL
ENCOURAGER
ENCRINITAL
ENCRINITIC
ENCROACHER
ENCYCLICAL
ENCYSTMENT
ENDEARMENT
ENDEMICITY
ENDERMATIC
ENDOGAMOUS
ENDOGENOUS
ENDOPLEURA
ENDORHIZAL
ENDORSABLE
ENDOSMOSIS
ENDOSMOTIC
ENDOSTITIS
ENDURINGLY
ENERVATION
ENFORCIBLE
ENGAGEMENT
ENGAGINGLY
ENGLISHMAN
ENHARMONIC
ENIGMATIST
ENJOINMENT
ENLACEMENT
ENLISTMENT
ENORMOUSLY
ENRICHMENT
ENROCKMENT
ENSANGUINE
ENSIGNSHIP
ENTAILMENT
ENTERALGIA
ENTEROCELE
ENTEROLITE
ENTEROLITH
ENTEROTOMY

ENTERPRISE
ENTHRONIZE
ENTHUSIASM
ENTHUSIAST
ENTICEABLE
ENTICEMENT
ENTICINGLY
ENTIRENESS
ENTOMBMENT
ENTOMOLOGY
ENTOPHYTIC
ENTROCHITE
ENTRY-MONEY
ENUMERATOR
ENUNCIABLE
ENUNCIATOR
EPAULEMENT
EPAULETTED
EPENTHESIS
EPENTHETIC
EPEXEGESIS
EPHEMERIST
EPICYCLOID
EPIDEICTIC
EPIDEMICAL
EPIGASTRIC
EPIGENESIS
EPIGENETIC
EPIGLOTTIC
EPIGLOTTIS
EPIGRAPHIC
EPILEPTOID
EPILOGICAL
EPILOGUIZE
EPIPHLOEUM
EPIRHIZOUS
EPISCOPACY
EPISCOPATE
EPISODICAL
EPISPASTIC
EPISTOLIST
EPISTOLIZE
EPITAPHIAN
EPITAPHIST
EPITHELIAL
EPITHELIUM
EPITOMIZER
EPITOMATOR
EPROUVETTE
EQUABILITY
EQUANIMITY
EQUANIMOUS
EQUATORIAL
EQUESTRIAN
EQUITATION
EQUIVALENT
EQUIVOCATE
ERADICABLE
ERADICATOR
ERECTILITY
EREMITICAL
ERETHISTIC
ERICACEOUS
EROTOMANIA
ERPETOLOGY
ERUBESCENT
ERUCTATION
ERUPTIONAL
ERYSIPELAS
ESCAPEMENT

ESCARPMENT
ESCHAROTIC
ESCRITOIRE
ESCULAPIAN
ESCUTCHEON
ESOPHAGOUS
ESPECIALLY
ESSAYISTIC
ESTEEMABLE
ESTIMATION
ESTIVATION
ESURIENTLY
ETERNALIST
ETERNALIZE
ETHEREALLY
ETHERIFORM
ETHNICALLY
ETHNOLOGIC
ETIOLATION
ETYMOLOGIC
EUCALYPTOL
EUCALYPTUS
EUDEMONISM
EUDEMONIST
EUDIOMETER
EUDIOMETRY
EUHEMERISM
EULOGISTIC
EUPHONIOUS
EUPHORBIUM
EUPHUISTIC
EUSTACHIAN
EUTHANASIA
EVACUATION
EVALUATION
EVANESCENT
EVANGELIST
EVANGELIZE
EVAPORABLE
EVEN-HANDED
EVENTUALLY
EVERLIVING
EVERYWHERE
EVIDENTIAL
EVISCERATE
EVOLVEMENT
EXACERBATE
EXACTITUDE
EXAGGERATE
EXALTATION
EXAMINABLE
EXAMINATOR
EXASPERATE
EX-CATHEDRA
EXCAVATION
EXCELLENCE
EXCELLENCY
EXCERPTION
EXCITATION
EXCITATIVE
EXCITATORY
EXCITEMENT
EXCOGITATE
EXCRESCENT
EXCRUCIATE
EXCUSATORY
EXCUSELESS
EXECRATION
EXECRATIVE
EXECRATORY

EXECUTABLE
EXEGITICAL
EXHALATION
EXHALEMENT
EXHAUSTING
EXHAUSTION
EXHAUSTIVE
EXHIBITION
EXHIBITIVE
EXHIBITORY
EXHILARANT
EXHILARATE
EXHUMATION
EXORBITANT
EXOTERICAL
EXPANSIBLE
EXPATIATOR
EXPATRIATE
EXPECTANCE
EXPECTANCY
EXPEDIENCY
EXPEDITION
EXPELLABLE
EXPERIENCE
EXPERIMENT
EXPERTNESS
EXPIRATORY
EXPLICABLE
EXPLOITAGE
EXPLICITLY
EXPLORABLE
EXPORTABLE
EXPOSITION
EXPOSITIVE
EXPOSITORY
EXPRESSION
EXPRESSIVE
EXPURGATOR
EXSICCATOR
EXTENDIBLE
EXTENSIBLE
EXTENUATOR
EXTERIORLY
EXTERNALLY
EXTINCTEUR
EXTINCTION
EXTINGUISH
EXTIRPABLE
EXTIRPATOR
EXTRACTION
EXTRACTIVE
EXTRAMURAL
EXTRANEOUS
EXTRICABLE
EXUBERANCE
EXUBERANCY
EXULCERATE
EXULTATION
EXUVIATION
EYELET-HOLE
EYE-SERVANT
EYE-SERVICE
■■■ ■■■■■■■■

F

FABRICATOR
FABULOUSLY
FABULOSITY

FACILENESS
FACILITATE
FACTIONARY
FACTIONIST
FACTIOUSLY
FACTITIOUS
FACTORSHIP
FAGOT-VOTER
FAHRENHEIT
FAIR-MINDED
FAIR-SPOKEN
FAITHFULLY
FALLACIOUS
FALLOW-CHAT
FALLOW-DEER
FAMILIARLY
FAMISHMENT
FANATICISM
FANATICIZE
FANCIFULLY
FANTOCCINI
FAN-TRACERY
FARCICALLY
FAR-FETCHED
FARMERSHIP
FAR-SIGHTED
FASCIATION
FASCICULAR
FASCICULUS
FASTIDIOUS
FASTIGIATE
FAT-BRAINED
FATALISTIC
FATHERHOOD
FATHERLAND
FATHERLESS
FATHERSHIP
FATHOMABLE
FATHOMLESS
FAULTINESS
FAVOURABLE
FAVOURABLY
FEARLESSLY
FEATHERING
FEBRIFUGAL
FEDERALISM
FEDERALIST
FEDERALIZE
FEDERATION
FEDERATIVE
FEEBLENESS
FELICITATE
FELICITOUS
FELLMONGER
FELLOW-HEIR
FELLOWSHIP
FELSPATHIC
FEME-COVERT
FEMININELY
FEMININITY
FENESTRATE
FER-DE-LANCE
■■■■■■■■■
■■■■■■■■■
FETTERLESS
FETTERLOCK
FEUILLETON
FEVERISHLY
FIBRILLOUS
FICTIONIST

FICTITIOUS
FIDDLE-WOOD
FIELD-GLASS
FIELD-MOUSE
FIELD-SPORT
FIELD-TRAIN
FIERCENESS
FIGURATION
FIGURATIVE
FIGURE-HEAD
FILE-CUTTER
FILIBUSTER
FILTHINESS
FILTRATION
FIMBRIATED
FINE-SPOKEN
FINGER-POST
FINICALITY
FINITENESS
FIRE-BUCKET
FIRE-ENGINE
FIRE-SCREEN
FIRST-FRUIT
FIRST-WATER
FISH-CARVER
FISHING-ROD
FISHMONGER
FISTICUFFS
FITFULNESS
FLABBINESS
FLABELLATE
FLACCIDITY
FLAGELLANT
FLAGELLATE
FLAGGINESS
FLAGITIOUS
FLAGRANTLY
FLAMBOYANT
FLATTERING
FLATULENCE
FLATULENCY
FLAVESCENT
FLAVOUROUS
FLEABITTEN
FLECTIONAL
FLEDGELING
FLESHINESS
FLINTINESS
FLIPPANTLY
FLIRTATION
FLOATATION
FLOCCULENT
FLORENTINE
FLORIDNESS
FLOSCULOUS
FLUNKEYISM
FLUVIATILE
FLUXIONARY
FOLIACEOUS
FOOTBRIDGE
FOOTLIGHTS
FORAMINULE
■■■■■■■■■
■■■■■■■■■
FORBEARING
FORBIDDING
FORCEFULLY
FORCIPATED
FORCLOSURE
FORECASTLE

FORECHOSEN
FOREFATHER
FOREGROUND
FOREHANDED
FOREORDAIN
FORERUNNER
FORESHADOW
FORETELLER
FORFEITURE
FORGIVABLE
FORMIDABLE
FORMIDABLY
FORNICATOR
FORTHGOING
FORTUITOUS
FOSTERLING
FOUNDATION
FOURCHETTE
FOURSQUARE
FOURTEENTH
FRACTIONAL
FRAGMENTAL
FRAGRANTLY
FRAMBOESIA
FRANCISCAN
FRATERNISE
FRATRICIDE
FRAUDFULLY
FRAUDULENT
FREAKISHLY
FREEBOOTER
FREEHANDED
FREEHOLDER
FREEMARTIN
FREIGHTAGE
FRENETICAL
FRENZIEDLY
FREQUENTER
FRICANDEAU
FRICTIONAL
FRIENDLESS
FRIENDSHIP
FRIGORIFIC
FRISKINESS
FRITILLARY
FROLICSOME
FROSTINESS
FROTHINESS
FROWNINGLY
FRUITERESS
FRUITFULLY
FRUSTRABLE
FRUTESCENT
FUCIVOROUS
FUGITIVELY
FULFILMENT
FUMIGATION
FUNCTIONAL
FUNEREALLY
FUNGACEOUS
FURBELOWED

G

GABIONNADE
GALIMATIAS
GALLOWGLAS
GALVANIZER
GAMEKEEPER

GANGLIONIC
GANGRENOUS
GARISHNESS
GARNISHING
GASTEROPOD
GASTRALGIA
GASTRONOME
GASTRONOMY
GELATINATE
GELATINIZE
GELATINOID
GELATINOUS
GEMINATION
GEMMACEOUS
GENERALITY
GENERALIZE
GENERATION
GENERATIVE
GENERATRIX
GENEROSITY
GENEROUSLY
GENETHLIAC
GENIALNESS
GENICULATE
GENTLEFOLK
GENTLENESS
GEOCENTRIC
GEOGNOSTIC
GEOGRAPHER
GEOLOGICAL
GEOPHAGISM
GEOPONICAL
GEOSELENIC
GEOTROPISM
GINGERBEER
GLACIALIST
GLACIATION
GLANCINGLY
GLANDIFORM
GLANDULOUS
GLASSINESS
GLIMMERING
GLOBULARLY
GLORIOUSLY
GLOSSARIAL
GLOSSARIST
GLOSSINESS
GLOSSOLOGY
GLOTTOLOGY
GLUCOSURIA
GLUMACEOUS
GLUTTONIZE
GNOSTICISM
GONIOMETER
GOODLINESS
GOOSEBERRY
GORGEOUSLY
GORGONEION
GORGONZOLA
GORMANDIZE
GRACEFULLY
GRACIOUSLY
GRAMOPHONE
GRANADILLA
GRANDCHILD
GRANDNIECE
GRANDUNCLE
GRANGERISM
GRAPHOLOGY
GRAPHOTYPE

GRAPTOLITE
GRASSINESS
GRATEFULLY
GRATIFYING
GRATUITOUS
GRAVEOLENT
GRAVIGRADE
GRAVIMETER
GREASINESS
GREGARIOUS
GRESSORIAL
GRIEVOUSLY
GRITTINESS
GROGGINESS
GROUNDLESS
GROUNDSILL
GROUNDWORK
GROVELLING
GRUDGINGLY
GUILLOTINE
GUILTINESS
GUTTURALLY
GYMNASIUMS
GYMNASTICS
GYMNOSPERM
GYNANDROUS
GYRATIONAL

H

HABILIMENT
HABILITATE
HABITUALLY
HACKMATACK
HAEMATOSIS
HAEMATOZOA
HAEMATURIA
HAGIOCRACY
HALBERDIER
HALLELUIAH
HANDICRAFT
HANDMAIDEN
HARASSMENT
HARBOURAGE
HARMLESSLY
HARMONIOUS
HARQUEBUSE
HAUSTELLUM
HEADSTRONG
HEARTINESS
HEAVENWARD
HEBDOMADAL
HECTICALLY
HEEDLESSLY
HELICOIDAL
HELIOGRAPH
HELIOTROPE
HELMINTHIC
HEMIPTERAN
HEMIHEDRAL
HEMIHEDRON
HEMORRHAGE
HENCEFORTH
HENOTHEISM
HENTACHORD
HEPTAGONAL
HEPTARCHIC
HEPTATEUCH
HERBESCENT

HEREABOUTS
HEREDITARY
HERESIARCH
HERMETICAL
HERPETICAL
HESITATION
HETERODOXY
HETEROTOPY
HEXAGYNIAN
HEXAHEDRAL
HEXAHEDRON
HEXAMETRIC
HEXANDRIAN
HIDDENNESS
HIERARCHAL
HIEROPHANT
HIGHWAYMAN
HINDERANCE
HINDUSTANI
HIPPOGRYPH
HIPPOPHILE
HIPPOPHAGY
HITHERMOST
HITHERWARD
HOARSENESS
HOLLOWNESS
HOLOPHOTAL
HOMELINESS
HOMEOPATHY
HOMILETICS
HOMOTONOUS
HONORARIUM
HONOURABLE
HOPELESSLY
HORIZONTAL
HOROGRAPHY
HOROLOGIST
HOROSCOPIC
HOSPITABLE
HOSPITABLY
HOUSEWIVES
HULLABALOO
HUMBLENESS
HUMORALISM
HUMORALIST
HUMORISTIC
HUMOROUSLY
HUMOURSOME
HUMPBACKED
HUSBANDMAN
HYDRAULICS
HYDROMANCY
HYDROMANIA
HYDROPATHY
HYDROPHANE
HYDROPHYTE
HYGROMETER
HYLOTHEISM
HYMENOPTER
HYMENOTOMY
HYPAETHRAL
HYPERBOLIC
HYPERMETER
HYPNOTIZER
HYPODERMAL
HYPOGYNOUS
HYPOTENUSE
HYPSOMETER
HYPSOMETRY

HYSTERICAL

I

ICONOCLASM
ICONOCLAST
ICONOLATRY
IDEOGRAPHY
IDEOLOGIST
IDIOPATHIC
IDOLATROUS
IDOLOCLAST
IGNIPOTENT
IGNORANTLY
ILLATIVELY
ILLEGALITY
ILLITERACY
ILLITERATE
ILLUMINANT
ILLUMINATE
ILLUMINATI
ILLUSTRATE
IMAGINABLE
IMAGINABLY
IMMACULATE
IMMANATION
IMMATERIAL
IMMATURELY
IMMATURITY
IMMEMORIAL
IMMERSIBLE
IMMOBILITY
IMMODERATE
IMMODESTLY
IMMOLATION
IMMORALITY
IMMORTALITY
IMMORTELLE
IMPALPABLY
IMPANATION
IMPASSABLE
IMPASSIBLE
IMPATIENCE
IMPECCABLE
IMPEDIMENT
IMPENITENT
IMPERATIVE
IMPERIALLY
IMPERSONAL
IMPLACABLE
IMPLACABLY
IMPLICITLY
IMPORTABLE
IMPORTANCE
IMPOSINGLY
IMPOSITION
IMPOSSIBLE
IMPOSSIBLY
IMPOSTHUME
IMPOTENTLY
IMPOUNDAGE
IMPREGNATE
IMPRESARIO
IMPRESSION
IMPRIMULAR
IMPROBABLE
IMPROBABLY
IMPROPERLY

IMPRUDENCE
IMPUDENTLY
IMPUGNABLE
IMPUTATION
IMPUTATIVE
INACCURACY
INACCURATE
INACTIVELY
INACTIVITY
INADEQUATE
INAPTITUDE
INAUGURATE
INCAPACITY
INCASEMENT
INCENDIARY
INCESTUOUS
INCHOATELY
INCHOATIVE
INCIDENTAL
INCINERATE
INCLINABLE
INCLUDIBLE
INCOMPLETE
INCONSTANT
INCREDIBLE
INCREDIBLY
INCRESCENT
INCUBATION
INCUBATIVE
INCUMBENCY
INDAGATION
INDECENTLY
INDECISIVE
INDECOROUS
INDEFINITE
INDELICATE
INDICATION
INDICATIVE
INDICTABLE
INDICTMENT
INDIGENOUS
INDIRECTLY
INDISCREET
INDISTINCT
INDITEMENT
INDIVIDUAL
INDOCILITY
INDUCEMENT
INDULGENCE
INDURATION
INDUSTRIAL
INELEGANCE
INELIGIBLE
INELOQUENT
INEQUALITY
INEVITABLE
INEXPIABLE
INFALLIBLE
INFALLIBLY
INFAMOUSLY
INFATUATED
INFECTIOUS
INFELICITY
INFERIORLY
INFERRIBLE
INFIDELITY
INFILTRATE
INFINITELY
INFINITIVE

INFINITUDE
INFLECTION
INFLECTIVE
INFLEXIBLE
INFLICTION
INFLICTIVE
INFORMALLY
INFRACTION
INFREQUENT
INFUSORIAL
INFUSORIAN
INGLORIOUS
INGREDIENT
INGULFMENT
INHABITANT
INHALATION
INHERENTLY
INHERITRIX
INHIBITION
INHIBITORY
INHUMANITY
INHUMATION
INIMICALLY
INIMITABLE
INIQUITOUS
INITIATION
INITIATIVE
INITIATORY
INJUDICIAL
INNATENESS
INNOCENTLY
INNOMINATE
INNOVATION
INNUENDOES
INOCULABLE
INOCULATOR
INOFFICIAL
INOSCULATE
INQUIETUDE
INQUISITOR
INSALUTARY
INSANENESS
INSATIABLE
INSECURELY
INSECURITY
INSENSIBLE
INSENSIBLY
INSINUATOR
INSIPIDITY
INSOBRIETY
INSOLATION
INSOLENTLY
INSOLVABLE
INSOLVENCY
INSOUCIANT
INSPECTION
INSPIRABLE
INSPISSATE
INSTALMENT
INSTIGATOR
INSTILMENT
INSTITUTOR
INSTRUCTOR
INSTRUMENT
INSULARITY
INSULATION
INTANGIBLE
INTANGIBLY
INTEGUMENT
INTENDANCY

INTERBREED
INTERCROSS
INTERESTED
INTERLOPER
INTERLUNAR
INTERMARRY
INTERMEZZO
INTERMURAL
INTERNALLY
INTERSPACE
INTERWEAVE
INTESTABLE
INTESTINAL
INTIMATELY
INTIMATION
INTIMIDATE
INTONATION
INTOXICATE
INTRAMURAL
INTREPIDLY
INTRODUCER
INTROSPECT
INUNDATION
INVAGINATE
INVALIDATE
INVALUABLE
INVARIABLE
INVARIABLY
INVENTIBLE
INVENTRESS
INVESTMENT
INVETERATE
INVIGORATE
INVIOLABLE
INVITATION
INVITATORY
INVITINGLY
INVOCATION
INVOCATORY
INVOLUCRAL
INVOLUCRUM
INVOLUTION
INWARDNESS
IRIDESCENT
IRIDOSMIUM
IRONMONGER
IRRADIANCE
IRRADIANCY
IRRATIONAL
IRRELEVANT
IRRELIGION
IRREMEABLE
IRRESOLUTE
IRREVERENT
IRRIGATION
IRRITATING
IRRITATION
ISAGOGICAL
ISHMAELITE
ISOCHRONAL
ISODYNAMIC
ISOMERICAL
ISRAELITIC

J

JACKANAPES
JAGGEDNESS
JANIZARIES

JARDINIERE
JARGONELLE
JEOPARDIZE
JEOPARDOUS
JESUITICAL
JINRIKISHA
JOCULARITY
JOLTERHEAD
JOURNEYMAN
JOVIALNESS
JOYFULNESS
JOYOUSNESS
JUBILATION
JUDAICALLY
JUDICIALLY
JUGGERNAUT
JUNCACEOUS
JUVENILITY
JUXTAPOSIT

K

KERCHIEFED
KERSEYMERE
KHITMUTGAR
KINDLINESS
KILOGRAMME
KINEMATICS
KINGFISHER
KINGLINESS
KNIGHTHOOD
KNOBKERRIE
KNOTTINESS
KRIEGSPIEL

L

LABORATORY
LACERATION
LACHRYMOSE
LACKADAISY
LACONICISM
LACTOMETER
LACTOSCOPE
LACUSTRINE
LAMBDACISM
LAMBDOIDAL
LAMENTABLE
LAMENTABLY
LAMINATION
LANCEOLATE
LANDHOLDER
LANDLOCKED
LANDLUBBER
LANDSPRING
LANGUOROUS
LANIFEROUS
LANIGEROUS
LANSQUENET
LARDACEOUS
LARYNGITIS
LASCIVIOUS
LAUGHINGLY
LAUREATION
LAWFULNESS
LEADERETTE
LEADERSHIP
LEGATESHIP

LEGISLATOR
LEGITIMACY
LEGITIMATE
LEGITIMIZE
LEGUMINOUS
LENTICULAR
LETHARGIZE
LEUCOPATHY
LEVIGATION
LEVITATION
LEVOGYRATE
LEXICOLOGY
LIBERALISM
LIBERALITY
LIBERALIZE
LIBERATION
LIBERATORY
LIBIDINIST
LIBRETTIST
LICENTIATE
LICENTIOUS
LIEUTENANT
LIFELESSLY
LIGAMENTAL
LIGHTHOUSE
LIKELIHOOD
LIKELINESS
LIMBERNESS
LIMITATION
LINGUIFORM
LINGUISTIC
LIQUESCENT
LITERALISM
LITERALIST
LITERALITY
LITERALIZE
LITERATURE
LITHOGRAPH
LITHOLOGIC
LITHOPHYTE
LITHOTRITY
LITIGATION
LITTLENESS
LITURGICAL
LIVELIHOOD
LIVELINESS
LOCOMOTION
LOCOMOTIVE
LOCULAMENT
LOGGERHEAD
LOGISTICAL
LOGOGRAPHY
LOLLARDISM
LONELINESS
LONESOMELY
LONGHEADED
LOQUACIOUS
LORDLINESS
LORICATION
LOVELINESS
LOWERINGLY
LOXODROMIC
LUBRICATOR
LUCKLESSLY
LUCULENTLY
LUGUBRIOUS
LUMINOSITY
LUMINOUSLY
LUMPSUCKER

LUSCIOUSLY
LUSTRATION
LUSTRELESS
LUXURIANCE
LUTESTRING

M

MACADAMIZE
MACERATION
MACHINATOR
MACULATION
MAGISTRACY
MAGISTRATE
MAGNETIZER
MAGNIFICAL
MAIDENHAIR
MAIDENHEAD
MAIDENHOOD
MAINTAINER
MALACOLOGY
MALAPROPOS
MALCONTENT
MALEFACTOR
MALEVOLENT
MALIGNANCE
MALINGERER
MALODOROUS
MALPIGHIAN
MALVACEOUS
MAMMILLATE
MANAGEABLE
MANAGEMENT
MANCHINEEL
MANDIBULAR
MANFULNESS
MANGOSTEEN
MANIACALLY
MANIFESTLY
MANIFOLDLY
MANIPULATE
MANOEUVRER
MANUSCRIPT
MARASCHINO
MARCESCENT
MARGINALLY
MARGRAVINE
MARIOLATRY
MARIONETTE
MARKETABLE
MARLACEOUS
MARMORATED
MARQUISATE
MARROWLESS
MARSHALLER
MARSHINESS
MARTINGALE
MARVELLOUS
MASQUERADE
MASSASAUGA
MASTERLESS
MASTICABLE
MASTICATOR
MASTODYNIA
MATCHMAKER
MATERIALLY
MATERNALLY
MATHEMATIC

MATRIARCHY
MATRONHOOD
MATURATION
MATURATIVE
MATURENESS
MAXILLIPED
MAYONNAISE
MEAGRENESS
MEASURABLE
MEASURABLY
MECHANICAL
MEDALLURGY
MEDDLESOME
MEDICAMENT
MEDICATION
MEDIOCRITY
MEDITATION
MEDITATIVE
MEERSCHAUM
MEGALITHIC
MEGALOSAUR
MEGAPODIUS
MELANAEMIA
MELANCHOLY
MEMBERSHIP
MEMBRANOUS
MEMORANDUM
MENACINGLY
MENDACIOUS
MENDICANCY
MENSTRUATE
MENSTRUUMS
MENSURABLE
MEPHITICAL
MERCANTILE
MERCHANTRY
MERCIFULLY
MESENTERIC
MESMERIZER
MESOTHORAX
METABOLISM
METACARPUS
METACARPAL
METACENTRE
METAPHORIC
METAPHRASE
METAPHRAST
METAPHYSIC
METASTASIS
METATARSUS
METATARSAL
METATHESIS
METATHORAX
METHODICAL
METHYLATED
METICULOUS
METRICALLY
METROGRAPH
METRONYMIC
METROPOLIS
METTLESOME
MICHAELMAS
MICROMETER
MICROMETRY
MICROPHONE
MICROPHYTE
MICROSCOPE
MICROSCOPY
MICROSEISM

MIDSHIPMAN
MIGHTINESS
MIGNONETTE
MILITARISM
MILITARIST
MILITIAMAN
MILLENNIAL
MILLENNIUM
MILLESIMAL
MINERALIZE
MINERALOGY
MINISTRANT
MINORITIES
MINSTRELSY
MINUTENESS
MIRACULOUS
MIRTHFULLY
MISADVISED
MISARRANGE
MISBELIEVE
MISCELLANY
MISCONDUCT
MISFORTUNE
MISMEASURE
MISOGAMIST
MISOGYNIST
MISPRISION
MISSIONARY
MISTAKABLE
MISTAKENLY
MNEMONICAL
MODERATION
MODERATELY
MODERATISM
MODERNIZER
MODERNNESS
MODIFIABLE
MODISHNESS
MODULATION
MOHAMMEDAN
MOLYBDENUM
MONARCHISM
MONARCHIST
MONASTICON
MONILIFORM
MONITORIAL
MONOCHROME
MONOCHROMY
MONOCULOUS
MONOECIOUS
MONOGAMIST
MONOGAMOUS
MONOLITHIC
MONOLOGIST
MONOMANIAC
MONOPOLIZE
MONOTHEISM
MONOTHEIST
MONOTONOUS
MONSIGNORE
MONUMENTAL
MOPISHNESS
MORATORIUM
MORBIDNESS
MORDACIOUS
MORGANATIC
MOROSENESS
MORPHOLOGY
MORTIFYING
MOSAICALLY

MOTHERHOOD
MOTHERLESS
MOTIONLESS
MOULDINESS
MOUNTEBANK
MOURNFULLY
MOVABILITY
MUCEDINOUS
MUCOUSNESS
MULATTRESS
MULISHNESS
MULTIPLIER
MULTIVALVE
MUMBLINGLY
MUSSULMANS
MUTABILITY
MUTILATION
MUTINOUSLY
MYCOLOGIST
MYSTAGOGUE
MYSTERIOUS
MYTHICALLY
MYTHOLOGIC

N

NAMELESSLY
NAPHTHALIC
NATATORIAL
NATIVENESS
NATTERJACK
NATURALISM
NATURALIST
NATURALIZE
NAUTICALLY
NAVIGATION
NEBULOSITY
NECROLATRY
NECROMANCY
NECROPOLIS
NEGATIVELY
NEGLECTFUL
NEGLIGIBLE
NEGOTIABLE
NEGOTIATOR
NEOLOGICAL
NEOTERICAL
NEPHROTOMY
NETHERMOST
NEUROPATHY
NEUROTONIC
NEUTRALITY
NEUTRALIZE
NEWSMONGER
NIDAMENTAL
NIDIFICATE
NIGHTSHADE
NIGRESCENT
NIHILISTIC
NIMBLENESS
NINCOMPOOP
NINETEENTH
NOBLEWOMAN
NOMINALISM
NOMINATELY
NOMINATION
NOMINATIVE
NONCHALANT
NORTHERNER

NORTHWARDS
NOSOLOGIST
NOTABILITY
NOTARIALLY
NOTEWORTHY
NOTICEABLE
NOTICEABLY
NOURISHING
NOVICESHIP
NUBIFEROUS
NUCIFEROUS
NUMERATION
NUMEROUSLY
NUMISMATIC
NURSERYMAN
NUTRITIOUS
NYCTALOPIA
NYMPHOLEPT

O

OBDURATELY
OBEDIENTLY
OBJECTLESS
OBJURATION
OBLATENESS
OBLIGATION
OBLIGATORY
OBLIGEMENT
OBLIGINGLY
OBLITERATE
OBSEQUIOUS
OBSERVABLE
OBSERVABLY
OBSERVANCE
OBSIDIONAL
OBSOLETELY
OBSTRETRICS
OBSTRUCTOR
OBTAINABLE
OBTAINMENT
OBTURATION
OBTUSENESS
OCCULTNESS
OCCUPATION
OCHLOCRACY
OCHRACEOUS
OCTAHEDRAL
OCTAHEDRON
OCTANDRIAN
OCTANGULAR
OCTOGENARY
OCTOHEDRON
ODIOUSNESS
ODONTALGIC
ODONTOLOGY
OESOPHAGUS
OFFICIALLY
OFFICIATOR
OFTENTIMES
OLEAGINOUS
OLERACEOUS
OLIGARCHIC
OLIGOCLASE
OLIVACEOUS
OMNIFEROUS
OMNIGENOUS
OMNIPOTENT
OMNISCIENT

OMNIVOROUS
ONEIROLOGY
ONTOLOGIST
OPALESCENT
OPERAMETER
OPHTHALMIA
OPHTHALMIC
OPPOSITELY
OPPOSITION
OPPRESSION
OPPRESSIVE
OPPROBRIUM
OPPUGNANCY
OPSIOMETER
OPTATIVELY
OPTIMISTIC
OPTIONALLY
ORACULARLY
ORATORICAL
ORCHESTRAL
ORCHIDEOUS
ORDAINABLE
ORDAINMENT
ORDINATION
OREOGRAPHY
ORGANOGENY
ORGANOLOGY
ORIGINALLY
ORIGINATED
ORIGINATOR
ORNAMENTAL
ORNAMENTER
OROLOGICAL
ORPHANHOOD
ORTHOCERAS
ORTHOCLASE
ORTHODOXLY
ORTHOEPIST
ORTHOPRAXY
OSCILLANCY
OSCULATION
OSCULATORY
OSSIFEROUS
OSSIVOROUS
OSTENSIBLE
OSTEOBLAST
OSTEOCOLIA
OSTEOLOGIC
OTHERWHERE
OUTLANDISH
OUTRAGEOUS
OUTSTRETCH
OVARIOTOMY
OVERBRIDGE
OVERBURDEN
OVERCANOPY
OVERCHARGE
OVERGROWTH
OVERMASTED
OVERSTRAIN
OVERTURNER
OVERWISELY
OXIDIZABLE
OZONOSCOPE

P

PACHYMETER

PACIFIABLE
PAGINATION
PAIDEUTICS
PAINSTAKER
PALAEOZOIC
PALATALIZE
PALATINATE
PALIMPSEST
PALINDROME
PALINODIST
PALLIATION
PALLIATIVE
PALLIDNESS
PALMACEOUS
PALPITATED
PALTRINESS
PALUDINOUS
PANCRATIUM
PANCREATIC
PANEGYRIST
PANEGYRIZE
PANGENESIS
PANICULATE
PANSLAVISM
PAPISTICAL
PARALLELLY
PARALOGISM
PARAPHRASE
PARAPLEGIA
PARAPODIUM
PARASELENE
PARASITISM
PARDONABLE
PARDONABLY
PARENCHYMA
PARENTLESS
PARISIENNE
PARLIAMENT
PARNASSIAN
PARONOMASY
PARONYMOUS
PAROXYSMAL
PAROXYSMIC
PAROXYTONE
PARTIALITY
PARTICIPLE
PARTICULAR
PARTURIENT
PASIGRAPHY
PASQUINADE
PASSIONARY
PASSIONATE
PASTEBOARD
PATENTABLE
PATRIARCHY
PATRICIATE
PATRIOTISM
PATRISTICS
PATRONIZER
PATRONYMIC
PAWNBROKER
PEACEFULLY
PECCADILLO
PECULATION
PECULIARLY
PEDANTICAL
PEDESTRIAN
PEDUNCULAR
PEERLESSLY
PEIRAMETER

PEJORATIVE
PELLICULAR
PENANNULAR
PENDENTIVE
PENETRABLE
PENETRALIA
PENETRATOR
PENGUINERY
PENNYROYAL
PENNYWORTH
PENSIONARY
PENTACHORD
PENTAGONAL
PENTAMETER
PENTASTYLE
PENTATEUCH
PEPPERMINT
PERCENTAGE
PERCEPTIVE
PERCHLORIC
PERCIPIENT
PERCOLATOR
PERCURRENT
PERCUSSION
PERCUSSIVE
PERCUTIENT
PERDURABLE
PERDURABLY
PERFIDIOUS
PERFORATOR
PERFORMING
PERIHELION
PERILOUSLY
PERIODICAL
PERIOSTEAL
PERIOSTEUM
PERIPHRASE
PERIPTERAL
PERISHABLE
PERITONEAL
PERITONEUM
PERIWINKLE
PERLACEOUS
PERMANENCE
PERMEATION
PERMISSION
PERMISSIVE
PERNICIOUS
PERPETRATE
PERPETUATE
PERPETUITY
PERPLEXING
PERPLEXITY
PERQUISITE
PERRUQUIER
PERSIFLAGE
PERSISTENT
PERSISTIVE
PERSONABLE
PERSONALLY
PERSONALTY
PERSONATOR
PERSTRINGE
PERSUASION
PERSUASIVE
PERTINENCE
PERVERSION
PERVERSITY
PERVERSIVE
PESTILENCE

PETITIONER
PETTICHAPS
PETTYCHAPS
PETULANTLY
PHAGEDAENA
PHALANGEAL
PHANEROGAM
PHANTASMAL
PHARISAISM
PHARYNGEAL
PHEASANTRY
PHENOMENAL
PHILOSOPHE
PHILOSOPHY
PHLEBOTOMY
PHLEGMASIA
PHLEGMATIC
PHLOGISTIC
PHLOGISTON
PHLYCTAENA
PHOENICIAN
PHONETICAL
PHONOMETER
PHOSPHORIC
PHOSPHORUS
PHOTOGRAPH
PHOTOMETER
PHOTOMETRY
PHOTOPHONE
PHRENOLOGY
PHYLLOXERA
PHYSICALLY
PHYTOPHAGY
PICKANINNY
PICKPOCKET
PIERCEABLE
PIERCINGLY
PIEZOMETER
PILGRIMAGE
PILIFEROUS
PINNATIFID
PISTILLARY
PISTILLATE
PITCHINESS
PITILESSLY
PITYRIASIS
PLAGIARISM
PLAGIARIST
PLAGIARIZE
PLANIMETER
PLANIMETRY
PLANOMETER
PLASTERING
PLACTICITY
PLATELAYER
PLATYRHINE
PLAUDITORY
PLAYGROUND
PLAYWRIGHT
PLEADINGLY
PLEASANTLY
PLEBISCITE
PLEONASTIC
PLEXIMETER
PLEXOMETER
PLODDINGLY
PLOUGHABLE
PLUMASSIER
PLUPERFECT
PNEUMATICS

POACHINESS
POCULIFORM
POEPHAGOUS
POETICALLY
POIGNANTLY
POLITENESS
POLITICIAN
POLLUTEDLY
POLYANTHUS
POLYCARPIC
POLYCHROME
POLYCHROMY
POLYGAMIST
POLYGAMOUS
POLYGENOUS
POLYGRAPHY
POLYHEDRAL
POLYHEDRON
POLYMERISM
POLYNOMIAL
POLYPOROUS
POLYTHEISM
POLYTHEIST
POMIFEROUS
POMOLOGIST
PONDERABLE
PONTIFICAL
POPULARITY
POPULARIZE
POPULATION
POPULOUSLY
POROUSNESS
PORPHYRITE
PORRACEOUS
PORTCULLIS
PORTENTOUS
PORTLINESS
PORTUGUESE
POSITIVELY
POSITIVISM
POSITIVIST
POSSESSION
POSSESSIVE
POSSESSORY
POSTMASTER
POSTCRIPT
POURPARLER
POWERFULLY
PRACTISING
PRAEMUNIRE
PRAETORIUM
PRAYERLESS
PREADAMITE
PREBENDARY
PRECARIOUS
PRECAUTION
PRECEDENCE
PRECEDENCY
PRECESSION
PRECIOUSLY
PRECLUSION
PRECLUSIVE
PRECOCIOUS
PRECONCERT
PRECURSORY
PREDACEOUS
PREDECEASE
PREDESTINE
PREDICABLE
PREDICTION

PREDICTIVE
PREFECTURE
PREFERABLE
PREFERABLY
PREFERENCE
PREFERMENT
PREHENSILE
PRELATICAL
PREMONITOR
PREPAYMENT
PRESBYOBIA
PRESBYTERY
PRESCIENCE
PRESENTIVE
PRESIDENCY
PRESIGNIFY
PRESSINGLY
PRESUMABLE
PRESUMABLY
PRESUPPOSE
PRETENSION
PREVAILING
PREVALENCE
PRIESTHOOD
PRIESTLIKE
PRIMEVALLY
PRIMORDIAL
PRINCIPLED
PROCEEDING
PROCLIVITY
PROCLIVOUS
PROCOELIAN
PROCREATOR
PROCTORIAL
PROCUMBENT
PROCURABLE
PROCURATOR
PRODUCIBLE
PRODUCTILE
PRODUCTION
PRODUCTIVE
PROFESSION
PROFITABLE
PROFITABLY
PROFLIGACY
PROFLIGATE
PROGENITOR
PROGNATHIC
PROJECTILE
PROJECTION
PROLOCUTOR
PROMINENCE
PROMISSORY
PROMONTORY
PROMPTNESS
PROMULGATE
PRONOMINAL
PROPAGANDA
PROPAGATOR
PROPERNESS
PROPERTIED
PROPITIOUS
PROPORTION
PROPULSION
PROPULSIVE
PROSCENIUM
PROSCRIBER
PROSECUTOR
PROSPECTUS
PROSPERITY

PROSPEROUS
PROSTITUTE
PROTECTION
PROTECTIVE
PROTECTRIX
PROTESTANT
PROTHALLUS
PROTOPHYTE
PROTOPLASM
PROTOPLAST
PROTRACTOR
PROTRUSIVE
PROTRUSION
PROVENANCE
PROVERBIAL
PROVIDENCE
PROVINCIAL
PRUDENTIAL
PSALMODIST
PSALMODIZE
PSITTACINE
PUBESCENCE
PUBLICNESS
PUGILISTIC
PUGNACIOUS
PUISSANTLY
PULSOMETER
PULVERIZER
PUNCTUALLY
PUPILARITY
PUPIPAROUS
PUPIVOROUS
PURBLINDLY
PURITANISM
PURULENTLY
PUTRESCENT
PUZZLEMENT
PYRAMIDION
PYROMETRIC
PYROTECHNY
PYRRHONISM
PYRRHONIST
PYTHOGENIC

Q

QUADRANTAL
QUADRATURE
QUADRICORN
QUADRIVIAL
QUADRUMANA
QUANDARIES
QUARANTINE
QUARRIABLE
QUARTERING
QUATERFOIL
QUATERNARY
QUATERNION
QUEASINESS
QUENCHABLE
QUENCHLESS
QUESTIONER
QUIESCENCE

R

RABBINICAL

RABBLEMENT
RADICALISM
RADIOMETER
RAGAMUFFIN
RAMBLINGLY
RANCIDNESS
RANGERSHIP
RANSOMABLE
RANSOMLESS
RATABILITY
RATTLEWORT
RAVENOUSLY
RAVISHMENT
REACTIVELY
READERSHIP
REAFFOREST
REALIZABLE
REAPPROACH
REASSEMBLE
REBELLIOUS
REBUKINGLY
RECALLABLE
RECEIVABLE
RECENTNESS
RECEPTACLE
RECIPIENCY
RECIPROCAL
RECITATION
RECKLESSLY
RECOMMENCE
RECOMPENSE
RECONCILER
RECONQUEST
RECONSIDER
RECOUPMENT
RECREANTLY
RECREATION
RECREATIVE
RECRUDESCE
RECTORSHIP
RECUMBENCY
RECUPERATE
RECURRENCE
REDEEMABLE
REDELIVERY
REDISCOVER
REDRESSIVE
REDUNDANCY
REDUNDANCE
REFERRIBLE
REFINEMENT
REFLECTING
REFLECTION
REFLECTIVE
REFLEXIBLE
REFORMABLE
REFRACTION
REFRACTING
REFRACTIVE
REFRAGABLE
REFRESHING
REFRINGENT
REFULGENCE
REFUTATION
REFUTATORY
REGALEMENT
REGARDLESS
REGELATION
REGENERATE

REGENERACY
REGENTSHIP
REGIMENTAL
REGISTERED
REGRESSION
REGRESSIVE
REGULATION
REGULATIVE
REJUVENATE
RELATIONAL
RELATIVELY
RELAXATION
RELAXATIVE
RELEASABLE
RELEGATION
RELENTLESS
RELIEVABLE
RELINQUISH
RELISHABLE
RELUCTANCE
RELUCTANCY
REMARKABLE
REMARKABLY
REMARRIAGE
REMEDIALLY
REMEDILESS
REMEMBERER
REMISSIBLE
REMISSNESS
REMITTANCE
REMONETIZE
REMORSEFUL
REMOTENESS
REMUNERATE
RENASCENCE
RENASCENCY
RENCOUNTER
RENDERABLE
RENDEZVOUS
RENOWNEDLY
REPAIRABLE
REPARATION
REPARATIVE
REPATRIATE
REPEALABLE
REPEATABLE
REPEATEDLY
REPELLENCE
REPELLENCY
REPENTANCE
REPERTOIRE
REPETITION
REPETITIVE
REPININGLY
REPLEVISOR
REPORTABLE
REPOSITION
REPOSITORY
REPRESSION
REPRESSIVE
REPROACHER
REPROBATER
REPROVABLE
REPROVABLY
REPUBLICAN
REPUDIATOR
REPUGNANCE
REPURCHASE
REPUTATION

REQUITABLE
RESCISSION
RESEARCHER
RESENTMENT
RESERVEDLY
RESHIPMENT
RESIDENTER
RESILIENCE
RESILIENCY
RESISTANCE
RESONANTLY
RESPECTFUL
RESPECTING
RESPIRABLE
RESPONDENT
RESPONSIVE
RESPONSORY
RESTAURANT
RESTHARROW
RESTLESSLY
RESTORABLE
RESTRAINER
RESULTLESS
RESUMPTION
RESUMPTIVE
RETAINABLE
RETARDMENT
RETICULATE
RETRACTILE
RETRACTION
RETRACTIVE
RETROCHOIR
RETROGRADE
RETROSPECT
RETURNABLE
REVEALABLE
REVELATION
REVENGEFUL
REVERENCER
REVERSIBLE
REVERTIBLE
REVIEWABLE
REVIVALISM
REVOCATION
REVOLUTION
REWARDABLE
RHABDOIDAL
RHAPSODIST
RHAPSODIZE
RHAPSODIST
RHETORICAL
RHEUMATISM
RHINOCEROS
RHINOSCOPE
RHOMBOIDAL
RIDICULOUS
RIGHTFULLY
RIGOROUSLY
RINDERPEST
RINGLEADER
RISIBILITY
ROBUSTNESS
ROMANESQUE
ROOTEDNESS
ROQUELAURE
ROSANILINE
ROTATIONAL
ROTTENNESS
ROUNDABOUT
RUBIGINOUS

RUBBISHING
RUBRICATOR
RUDIMENTAL
RUEFULNESS
RUFFIANISH
RUFFIANISM
RUGGEDNESS
RUMINATION
RUNOLOGIST
RUTHLESSLY

S

SACCHARIFY
SACCHARINE
SACERDOTAL
SACREDNESS
SACRIFICER
SALAMANDER
SALINENESS
SALIVATION
SALLOWNESS
SALMAGUNDI
SALMAGUNDY
SALUBRIOUS
SALUTARILY
SALUTATION
SALUTATORY
SANATORIUM
SANCTIFIED
SANCTIFIER
SANCTIMONY
SANDERLING
SANGUINARY
SANGUINELY
SANITARIAN
SANITATION
SAPPHIRINE
SARCOLEMMA
SARCOPHAGI
SARCOPHILE
SATURATION
SATISFYING
SATURNALIA
SATYRIASIS
SAUROPSIDA
SAVAGENESS
SAVOURLESS
SAXICAVOUS
SAXICOLOUS
SCABBINESS
SCANDALIZE
SCANDALOUS
SCANTINESS
SCARAMOUCH
SCARCENESS
SCARLATINA
SCATHELESS
SCEPTICISM
SCEPTICIZE
SCHEMATIZE
SCHEMINGLY
SCHISMATIC
SCHOLASTIC
SCIAGRAPHY
SCIENTIFIC
SCIOGRAPHY
SCIOLISTIC
SCIRROSITY

SCIRRHOSIS
SCOFFINGLY
SCORNFULLY
SCORZONERA
SCOTOGRAPH
SCOTTICISM
SCOWLINGLY
SCRAMBLING
SCREENINGS
SCRIMPNESS
SCRIPTURAL
SCROFULOUS
SCRUPULOUS
SCRUTINEER
SCRUTINIZE
SCRUTINOUS
SCULLIONLY
SCULPTURAL
SCULPTURED
SCURRILITY
SCURRILOUS
SCURVINESS
SEARCHABLE
SEARCHLESS
SEAREDNESS
SEASONABLE
SEASONABLY
SEASONLESS
SEBIFEROUS
SECRETNESS
SECULARIST
SECULARIZE
SECURENESS
SEDATENESS
SEDUCEMENT
SEDULOUSLY
SEEMLINESS
SEGUIDILLA
SELECTNESS
SEMEIOLOGY
SEMEIOTICS
SEMICIRCLE
SEMPSTRESS
SENATORIAL
SENSUALIST
SENSUALIZE
SEPARATELY
SEPARATION
SEPARATISM
SEPARATIST
SEPTENNIAL
SEPTICIDAL
SEPTILLION
SEQUACIOUS
SERENENESS
SEVENTIETH
SEXAGENARY
SEXTILLION
SHADOWLESS
SHAGGINESS
SHAMEFACED
SHAMPOOING
SHANDYGAFF
SHIBBOLETH
SHIELDLESS
SHIPWRIGHT
SHOCKINGLY
SHOEMAKING
SHOPKEEPER
SHREWDNESS

SHREWISHLY
SHRIEVALTY
SHRILLNESS
SHUDDERING
SIALAGOGUE
SIALOGOGUE
SIBILATORY
SICKLINESS
SIDEROSTAT
SIGILLARIA
SILENTNESS
SILHOUETTE
SIMILARITY
SIMILITUDE
SIMONIACAL
SIMPLICITY
SIMULACRUM
SIMULATION
SIMULATORY
SINECURIST
SINFULNESS
SINGULARLY
SINISTERLY
SINISTROUS
SINOLOGIST
SISTERHOOD
SISTERLESS
SKITTISHLY
SKULKINGLY
SLANDEROUS
SLANTINGLY
SLEETINESS
SLEEVELESS
SLIGHTNESS
SLIPPERILY
SLOPPINESS
SLOTHFULLY
SLUGGISHLY
SLUMBEROUS
SLUTTISHLY
SMATTERING
SMUTTINESS
SNAPPISHLY
SNEAKINGLY
SNEERINGLY
SNIVELLING
SNOBBISHLY
SOCIOLOGIC
SOCRATICAL
SOLACEMENT
SOLDIERING
SOLECISTIC
SOLEMNIZER
SOLICITANT
SOLICITOUS
SOLICITUDE
SOLIDARITY
SOLITARILY
SOLSTITIAL
SOLUBILITY
SOMATOLOGY
SOMBRENESS
SOMERSAULT
SOMNOLENCE
SONOROUSLY
SOOTHINGLY
SOOTHSAYER
SORDIDNESS
SORORICIDE
SOUTHERNER

SPACIOUSLY
SPADICEOUS
SPARSENESS
SPECIALISM
SPECIALITY
SPECIALIZE
SPECIOUSLY
SPECTACLED
SPECTRALLY
SPECULATOR
SPEECHLESS
SPERMACETI
SPHENOGRAM
SPHENOIDAL
SPHERICITY
SPHEROIDAL
SPHRIGOSIS
SPINESCENT
SPIRITEDLY
SPIRITLESS
SPIRITUOUS
SPIROMETER
SPISSITUDE
SPLANCHNIC
SPLEENWORT
SPLENDIDLY
SPLENOLOGY
SPOLIATION
SPONDAICAL
SPONGINESS
SPONSORIAL
SPOTLESSLY
SPRINKLING
SPRUCENESS
SPUMESCENT
SPURIOUSLY
SQUADRONED
SQUALIDITY
SQUARENESS
SQUEEZABLE
SQUIREHOOD
SQUIRESHIP
STABLENESS
STAGNANTLY
STAGNATION
STALACTITE
STALAGMITE
STAMINATED
STAMINEOUS
STAMMERING
STANCHLESS
STANCHNESS
STAPHYLOMA
STARRINESS
STARVATION
STARVELING
STATICALLY
STATIONARY
STATIONERY
STATISTICS
STATUESQUE
STATUTABLE
STATUTORY
STAUROLITE
STEADINESS
STEALTHILY
STEAMINESS
STELLIFORM
STENCILLER
STENOGRAPH

STENTORIAN
STEPFATHER
STEPMOTHER
STERCORATE
STEREOTYPE
STERILIZER
STERTOROUS
STEWARDESS
STICKINESS
STIFFENING
STIGMATIST
STIGMATIZE
STIPULATOR
STOLIDNESS
STOMATITIS
STOOPINGLY
STOREHOUSE
STRABISMUS
STRABOTOMY
STRAIGHTEN
STRAMONIUM
STRATEGIST
STRATHSPEY
STRATIFORM
STRENGTHEN
STRICTNESS
STRIDULOUS
STRINGENCY
STRONGHOLD
STRUCTURAL
STRUCTURED
STRYCHNINE
STUBBORNLY
STUDIOUSLY
STUFFINESS
STULTIFIER
STUPENDOUS
STUPIDNESS
STURDINESS
SUBAQUATIC
SUBAQUEOUS
SUBCLAVIAN
SUBDUCTION
SUBJECTION
SUBJECTIVE
SUBJOINDER
SUBJUGATOR
SUBKINGDOM
SUBLIMABLE
SUBLINGUAL
SUBMERSION
SUBMISSION
SUBMISSIVE
SUBPREFECT
SUBSCRIBER
SUBSECTION
SUBSEQUENT
SUBSIDENCE
SUBSIDIARY
SUBSISTENT
SUBSPECIES
SUBSTITUTE
SUBSTRATUM
SUBTANGENT
SUBTERFUGE
SUBTLENESS
SUBTLETIES
SUBTRACTER
SUBTRAHEND
SUBVENTION

SUBVERSION
SUBVERSIVE
SUCCEDANEA
SUCCEEDING
SUCCESSFUL
SUCCESSION
SUCCESSIVE
SUCCINCTLY
SUCCULENCE
SUCCULENCY
SUCCUSSION
SUCCUSSIVE
SUDATORIUM
SUDDENNESS
SUFFERABLE
SUFFERANCE
SUFFERABLY
SUFFICIENT
SUFFRAGIST
SUGARINESS
SUGGESTION
SUGGESTIVE
SUICIDALLY
SULLENNESS
SULPHURATE
SULTANSHIP
SULTRINESS
SUNSETTING
SUPERCARGO
SUPERHUMAN
SUPERLUNAR
SUPERTONIC
SUPERVISAL
SUPERVISOR
SUPINATION
SUPPERLESS
SUPPLANTER
SUPPLEMENT
SUPPLENESS
SUPPLETORY
SUPPLIANCE
SUPPLICATE
SUPPOSABLE
SUPPRESSOR
SUPRARENAL
SURETYSHIP
SURFACEMAN
SURGICALLY
SURPASSING
SURPLUSAGE
SURPRISING
SUSCEPTIVE
SUSCIPIENT
SUSPENSION
SUSPENSIVE
SUSPENSORY
SUSPICIOUS
SUSTENANCE
SUZERAINTY
SWAGGERING
SWEATINESS
SWEEPINGLY
SWEEPSTAKE
SWEETBREAD
SWEETENING
SWEETHEART
SWIMMINGLY
SYBARITISM
SYCOPHANCY
SYLLABICAL

SYMBOLICAL
SYMMETRIZE
SYNCARPOUS
SYNCHRONAL
SYNCRETISM
SYNECDOCHE
SYNGENETIC
SYNONYMIST
SYPHILITIC
SYSTEMATIC
SYSTEMLESS

T

TABERNACLE
TABULARIZE
TABULATION
TACHOMETER
TACITURNLY
TACTICALLY
TALISMANIC
TALMUDICAL
TAMBOURINE
TANGENTIAL
TANTAMOUNT
TARDIGRADE
TARPAULING
TARTAREOUS
TASTEFULLY
TAUNTINGLY
TAUTOLOGIC
TAWDRINESS
TAXABILITY
TAXIDERMIC
TETCHINESS
TECHNOLOGY
TEETOTALER
TELEGRAPHY
TELEOSTEAN
TELEPATHIC
TELESCOPIC
TELLERSHIP
TELPHERAGE
TEMPERABLE
TEMPERANCE
TEMPORIZER
TEMPTATION
TEMPTINGLY
TENABILITY
TENANTABLE
TENANTLESS
TENDERNESS
TENDRILLED
TENEBRIFIC
TENEMENTAL
TENTACULAR
TERATOLOGY
TESSELLATE
TESTICULAR
TETRACHORD
TETRAGONAL
TETRAMETER
TETRASTICH
TETRASTYLE
TEXTUALIST
THANKFULLY
THEATRICAL
THEMSELVES

THEODICEAN
THEODOLITE
THEOGONIST
THEOLOGIAN
THEOLOGIZE
THEOPHANIC
THEORETICS
THEOSOPHIC
THEOSOPHER
THEREABOUT
THEREAFTER
THEREUNDER
THERIOTOMY
THERMOSTAT
THERMOTICS
THICKENING
THIEVISHLY
THIMBLEFUL
THINKINGLY
THIRTEENTH
THOROUGHLY
THOUGHTFUL
THOUSANDTH
THREADBARE
THREATENER
THREEPENCE
THREEPENNY
THREESCORE
THRIFTLESS
THRIVINGLY
THROMBOSIS
THRONELESS
THROUGHOUT
THUNDERING
TICKLISHLY
TIMELINESS
TIMOROUSLY
TINCTORIAL
TIRESOMELY
TITULARITY
TOILSOMELY
TOLERANTLY
TOLERATION
TOMFOOLERY
TONGUELESS
TOPAZOLITE
TOPOGRAPHY
TORMENTING
TORPIDNESS
TORRENTIAL
TORRENTINE
TORRIDNESS
TORTUOUSLY
TORTURABLE
TOUCHINESS
TOUCHINGLY
TOUCHSTONE
TOURMALINE
TOURNAMENT
TOURNIQUET
TOXICOLOGY
TRABECULAR
TRACHEITIS
TRACTARIAN
TRADESFOLK
TRAFFICKER
TRAGACANTH
TRAGICALLY
TRAITOROUS
TRAJECTORY

TRAMMELLED
TRAMMELLER
TRAMONTANE
TRANQUILLY
TRANSACTOR
TRANSCRIBE
TRANSFEREE
TRANSGRESS
TRANSIENCE
TRANSIENCY
TRANSITION
TRANSITIVE
TRANSITORY
TRANSLATOR
TRANSLUCID
TRANSLUNAR
TRANSPIRES
TRANSPLANT
TRANSPOSAL
TRANSPOSER
TRANSVERSE
TRASHINESS
TRAUMATISM
TRAVAILING
TRAVELLING
TREADWHEEL
TREASURIES
TREMENDOUS
TREPANNING
TRESPASSER
TRIANGULAR
TRICENNIAL
TRICHOTOMY
TRICKINESS
TRICLINIUM
TRICOSTATE
TRIDENTATE
TRIDENTINE
TRIFARIOUS
TRIFLINGLY
TRIFOLIATE
TRIFURCATE
TRIGEMINAL
TRILATERAL
TRILINGUAL
TRILITERAL
TRILOCULAR
TRIMEMBRAL
TRIMESTRAL
TRIMMINGLY
TRIMORPHIC
TRINERVATE
TRINOCTIAL
TRIPARTITE
TRIPHTHONG
TRIPINNATE
TRIPLICATE
TRIPPINGLY
TRIRADIATE
TRISECTION
TRISULCATE
TRITERNATE
TRIUMPHANT
TRIVIALITY
TROCHANTER
TROGLODYTE
TROPAEOLUM
TROPICALLY
TROUBADOUR

TROUSERING
TRUCULENCE
TRUCULENCY
TRUNNIONED
TRUSTFULLY
TRUSTINESS
TRUSTINGLY
TRUTHFULLY
TUBERCULAR
TUBEROSITY
TUBULIFORM
TUITIONARY
TUMBLERFUL
TUMULTANCY
TUMULTUOUS
TUNGSTENIC
TURBULENCE
TURBULENCY
TURBIDNESS
TURGESCENT
TURGIDNESS
TURPENTINE
TWITTERING
TWITTINGLY
TYMPANITIC
TYMPANITIS
TYPOGRAPHY
TYRANNICAL

U

UBIQUITOUS
ULCERATION
ULTIMATELY
ULTRONEOUS
UMBELLIFER
UMBRAGEOUS
UNAFFECTED
UNASPIRING
UNASSISTED
UNATTACHED
UNATTENDED
UNATTESTED
UNAVAILING
UNBALANCED
UNBEARABLE
UNBLUSHING
UNCHANGING
UNCHASTITY
UNCLERICAL
UNCOLOURED
UNCOMMONLY
UNCONFINED
UNCRITICAL
UNCTUOSITY
UNDECAYING
UNDEFENDED
UNDENIABLY
UNDERBRACE
UNDERBRUSH
UNDERDRAIN
UNDERSTATE
UNDERTAKER
UNDERVALUE
UNDERWORLD
UNDERWRITE
UNDETERRED
UNDISMAYED

UNDISPOSED
UNDISPUTED
UNDULATING
UNDULATION
UNDULATORY
UNEASINESS
UNEDIFYING
UNEDUCATED
UNEMPLOYED
UNENVIABLE
UNERRINGLY
UNEVENNESS
UNEXAMINED
UNEXECUTED
UNEXPECTED
UNEXPLORED
UNFAIRNESS
UNFAITHFUL
UNFAMILIAR
UNFATHERED
UNFATHERLY
UNFEMININE
UNFETTERED
UNFINISHED
UNFLAGGING
UNFORESEEN
UNFORGIVEN
UNGENEROUS
UNGOVERNED
UNGRACEFUL
UNGRACIOUS
UNGRATEFUL
UNGROUNDED
UNGRUDGING
UNHALLOWED
UNHAMPERED
UNHANDSOME
UNHISTORIC
UNHOLINESS
UNHONOURED
UNICOSTATE
UNIFLOROUS
UNIFORMITY
UNILATERAL
UNILOCULAR
UNIMAGINED
UNIMPAIRED
UNIMPOSING
UNIMPROVED
UNINCLOSED
UNINSPIRED
UNINVITING
UNISONANCE
UNIVERSITY
UNIVOCALLY
UNKINDNESS
UNLAMENTED
UNLEAVENED
UNLETTERED
UNLICENSED
UNMANNERLY
UNMEASURED
UNMOLESTED
UNMOTHERLY
UNNAMEABLE
UNNUMBERED
UNOBSERVED
UNOFFICIAL
UNPLEASANT

UNPLEASING
UNPOETICAL
UNPOLISHED
UNPOLLUTED
UNPREPARED
UNPROVIDED
UNPROVOKED
UNPUNCTUAL
UNPUNISHED
UNREADABLE
UNRECORDED
UNREDEEMED
UNREFORMED
UNREGARDED
UNRELIABLE
UNRELIEVED
UNREPEALED
UNREPENTED
UNREQUITED
UNRESERVED
UNRESISTED
UNRESOLVED
UNRESTORED
UNREVENGED
UNREWARDED
UNRIVALLED
UNROMANTIC
UNRULINESS
UNSALEABLE
UNSCHOOLED
UNSEASONED
UNSECONDED
UNSISTERLY
UNSMIRCHED
UNSOCIABLE
UNSOCIABLY
UNSTEADILY
UNSTRAINED
UNSUITABLE
UNSUITABLY
UNSWERVING
UNTAMEABLE
UNTEMPERED
UNTENANTED
UNTHANKFUL
UNTHINKING
UNTIDINESS
UNTILLABLE
UNTOWARDLY
UNTROUBLED
UNTRUTHFUL
UNWARINESS
UNWAVERING
UNWEARABLE
UNWEIGHING
UNWIELDILY
UNWONTEDLY
UNWORTHILY
UNYIELDING
UPBRAIDING
UPBRINGING
UPHOLSTERY
UPPISHNESS
UPROARIOUS
URINOSCOPY
URTICATION
USEFULNESS
USURPATION
UTRICULATE
UXORIOUSLY

V

VALOROUSLY
VANQUISHED
VANQUISHER
VARICOSITY
VARIEGATED
VARIOLITIC
VATICANISM
VATICINATE
VAUDEVILLE
VAUNTINGLY
VEGETALITY
VEGETARIAN
VEGETATION
VEGETATIVE
VEHEMENTLY
VEHICULARY
VELOCIPEDE
VELOCITIES
VELUTINOUS
VENERATION
VENGEFULLY
VENIALNESS
VENOMOUSLY
VENTILATOR
VENTRICOUS
VENTRICOSE
VERIFIABLE
VERMICELLI
VERMICULAR
VERNACULAR
VERTEBRAT .
VERTEBRATE
VERTICALLY
VESICATION
VESICATORY
VESICULATE
VESICULOSE
VESICULOUS
VESPERTINE
VESTIBULAR
VETERINARY
VIBRACULUM
VICEREGENT
VICTORIOUS
VICTUALLER
VIGILANTLY
VIGOROUSLY
VILLAINOUS
VILLEINAGE
VINAIGROUS
VINDICATOR
VINDICTIVE
VIOLACEOUS
VIRTUELESS
VIRTUOUSLY
VIRULENTLY
VISITATION
VITRESCENT
VITRIOLATE
VITRIOLIZE
VITUPERATE
VIVANDIERE
VIVIPARITY
VIVISECTOR
VOCABULARY
VOCATIONAL
VOCIFERATE

VOCIFEROUS
VOLATILITY
VOLATILIZE
VOLITIONAL
VOLTAMETER
VOLUBILITY
VOLUMETRIC
VOLUMINOUS
VOLUPTUARY
VOLUPTUOUS
VOMITORIES
VORTIGINAL
VOYAGEABLE
VULNERABLE

W

WAPINSCHAW
WARDENSHIP
WASTEFULLY
WATCHFULLY
WATERINESS
WATERPROOF
WAVERINGLY
WEATHERING
WELLINGTON
WESTWARDLY
WHARFINGER
WHATSOEVER
WHENSOEVER
WHEREABOUT
WHIMPERING
WHISPERING
WHITSUNDAY
WHIZZINGLY
WICKEDNESS
WILDEREDLY
WILDERNESS
WILDERMENT
WILFULNESS
WITCHCRAFT
WITHDRAWAL
WITHHOLDER
WOEFULNESS
WOMANISHLY
WONDERMENT
WONDROUSLY
WOODPECKER
WORRYINGLY
WORSHIPFUL
WORSHIPPER
WORTHINESS
WRATHFULLY
WRETCHEDLY
WRITERSHIP
WRONGFULLY

X

XYLOGRAPHY

Y

YEARNINGLY
YEASTINESS
YESTEREVEN

YESTERMORN
YOURSELVES
YOUTHFULLY

Z

ZINCOGRAPH

ZOOMORPHIC
ZOOPHAGOUS
ZOOTOMICAL

ELEVEN-LETTER WORDS

A

AARON'S-BEARD
ABANDONMENT
ABBREVIATOR
ABECEDARIAN
ABHORRENTLY
ABIOGENESIS
ABLACTATION
ABNORMALITY
ABOLISHABLE
ABOMINATION
ABOVE-GROUND
ABRACADABRA
ABRANCHIATE
ABSENTATION
ABSENTEEISM
ABSOLVATORY
ABSTINENTLY
ABSTRACTION
ABSTRACTIVE
ABUSIVENESS
ACADEMICIAN
ACATALECTIC
ACCELERATOR
ACCEPTATION
ACCESSIONAL
ACCESSORIAL
ACCESSORILY
ACCIPITRINE
ACCLAMATION
ACCLAMATORY
ACCLIMATIZE
ACCOMMODATE
ACCOMPANIER
ACCOMPANIST
ACCORDANTLY
ACCORDINGLY
ACCOUCHEUSE
ACCOUNTABLE
ACCOUNTABLY
ACCUMULATOR
ACHIEVEMENT
ACIDIFIABLE
ACINACIFORM
ACKNOWLEDGE
ACOUSTICIAN
ACQUIESCENT
ACQUIREMENT
ACQUISITION
ACQUISITIVE
ACQUITTANCE
ACRIMONIOUS
ACTINOMETER
ACUMINATION
ACUPRESSURE
ACUPUNCTURE
ADAM'S-NEEDLE
ADDLE-HEADED
ADIAPHOROUS
ADIATHERMIC
ADJECTIVELY
ADJOURNMENT
ADJUDICATOR

ADMINICULAR
ADMIRALSHIP
ADOLESCENCE
ADOLESCENCY
ADSTRICTION
ADUMBRATION
ADUMBRATIVE
ADVANCEMENT
ADVENTURESS
ADVENTUROUS
ADVERBIALLY
ADVERSATIVE
ADVERSENESS
ADVERTISING
ADVISEDNESS
AEROLOGICAL
AERONAUTICS
AEROSTATICS
AEROSTATION
AESCULAPIAN
AESTIVATION
AFFECTATION
AFFECTINGLY
AFFECTIONED
AFFILIATION
AFFIRMATION
AFFIRMATIVE
AFFRANCHISE
AFTER-GROWTH
AGATIFEROUS
AGGLOMERATE
AGGLUTINANT
AGGLUTINATE
AGGRANDIZER
AGGRAVATING
AGGRAVATION
AGGREGATELY
AGGREGATION
AGNOSTICISM
AGNUS-CASTUS
AGONIZINGLY
AGRARIANISM
AGRICULTURE
AGUARDIENTE
AIMLESSNESS
ALBUMINURIA
ALCHEMISTIC
ALEXANDRIAN
ALEXANDRINE
ALKALESCENT
ALKALIMETER
ALKALIMETRY
ALLEVIATION
ALLEVIATE
ALL-FOOLS' DAY
ALLOPHYLIAN
ALL-SOULS' DAY
ALTERCATION
ALTERNATELY
ALTERNATION
ALTERNATIVE
ALTO-RILIEVO
AMALGAMATOR
AMARANTHINE
AMATIVENESS

AMBIGUOUSLY
AMBITIOUSLY
AMBROSIALLY
AMELANCHIER
AMELIORATOR
AMENORRHOEA
AMENTACEOUS
AMERICANISM
AMERICANIZE
AMETHYSTINE
AMIABLENESS
AMOENOMANIA
AMONTILLADO
AMOROUSNESS
AMPHIBIOLOGY
AMPHISBAENA
AMPLEXICAUL
ANACANTHOUS
ANACHRONISM
ANACOLUTHON
ANACREONTIC
ANAESTHESIA
ANAESTHETIC
ANALLANTOIC
ANALOGOUSLY
ANAPLEROTIC
ANASTOMOSIS
ANASTOMOTIC
ANCHORITESS
ANCHOVY-PEAR
ANCIENTNESS
ANDROSPHINX
ANECDOTICAL
ANFRACTUOUS
ANGELICALLY
ANGELOLATRY
ANGELOPHANY
ANGLICANISM
ANGLO-INDIAN
ANGLOPHOBIA
ANIMALCULAR
ANIMATINGLY
ANNIHILABLE
ANNIHILATOR
ANNIVERSARY
ANNUNCIATOR
ANOMALISTIC
ANONYMOUSLY
ANTECEDENCE
ANTE-CHAMBER
ANTEMUNDANE
ANTENUPTIAL
ANTEPASCHAL
ANTEPENDIUM
ANTERIORITY
ANTHRACITIC
ANTIBILIOUS
ANTICARDIUM
ANTICYCLONE
ANTIFEBRILE
ANTIFEDERAL
ANTIPHRASIS
ANTIPYRETIC
ANTIQUARIAN
ANTIQUENESS

ANTIRRHINUM
ANTISPASTIC
ANTISTROPHE
ANTITYPICAL
ANTONOMASIA
ANXIOUSNESS
APHRODISIAC
APOCALYPTIC
APOLOGETICS
APONEUROSIS
APOPETALOUS
APOSIOPESIS
APOSTERIORI
APOSTLESHIP
APOSTROPHIC
APPALLINGLY
APPELLATION
APPELLATIVE
APPLE-BLIGHT
APPLICATION
APPLICATIVE
APPLICATORY
APPOINTMENT
APPORTIONER
APPRECIABLE
APPRECIABLY
APPREHENDER
APPROBATION
APPROPRIATE
APPROVINGLY
APPROXIMATE
APPURTENANT
ARBITRAMENT
ARBITRARILY
ARBITRATION
ARBITRAMENT
ARBORESCENT
ARCHAEOLOGY
ARCHANGELIC
ARCHDUCHESS
ARCHEGONIUM
ARCHIMEDEAN
ARCHIPELAGO
ARDUOUSNESS
ARISTOCRACY
ARMINIANISM
ARMOUR-PLATE
ARQUEBUSIER
ARRAIGNMENT
ARRANGEMENT
ARROW-HEADED
ARTERIALIZE
ARTERIOTOMY
ARTILLERIST
ARTLESSNESS
ASCENSIONAL
ASCERTAINER
ASCITITIOUS
ASPORTATION
ASSAFOETIDA
ASSASSINATE
ASSESTATION
ASSENTINGLY
ASSESTIVELY
ASSESSIONAL
ASSIDUOUSLY
ASSIGNATION
ASSOCIATION
ASSOCIATIVE
ASSUAGEMENT

ASSUREDNESS
ASSYRIOLOGY
ASTIGMATISM
ASTONISHING
ASTRINGENCY
ATHERMANOUS
ATHLETICISM
ATMIDOMETER
ATMOSPHERIC
ATOMIZATION
ATRABILIOUS
ATROCIOUSLY
ATTEMPTABLE
ATTENTIVELY
ATTENUATION
ATTESTATION
ATTITUDINAL
ATTRACTABLE
ATTRIBUTION
ATTRIBUTIVE
AUDACIOUSLY
AUDIBLENESS
AUDITORSHIP
AURICULARLY
AUSCULTATOR
AUSTERENESS
AUTOGRAPHIC
AVOIRDUPOIS
AWKWARDNESS

B

BACCHANALIA
BACCIFEROUS
BACCIVOROUS
BACILLICIDE
BALEFULNESS
BANDY-LEGGED
BARBAROUSLY
BAREFACEDLY
BARLEY-SUGAR
BARLEY-WATER
BARN-SWALLOW
BARQUENTINE
BARREL-ORGAN
BARYCENTRIC
BASHFULNESS
BASTARD-WING
BEAM-COMPASS
BEAR-BAITING
BEARING-REIN
BEAR'S-GREASE
BEASTLINESS
BEAUTEOUSLY
BEAUTIFULLY
BEDIZENMENT
BEGUILEMENT
BELIEVINGLY
BELL-FOUNDER
BELLIGERENT
BELLOWS-FISH
BENEDICTINE
BENEDICTION
BENEFACTION
BENEFICENCE
BENEFICIARY
BENEVOLENCE
BENGAL-LIGHT

BENIGNANTLY
BEREAVEMENT
BESEEMINGLY
BEWITCHMENT
BIBLIOLATER
BIBLIOLATRY
BIBLIOMANCY
BIBLIOMANIA
BIBLIOPHILE
BIBLIOTHECA
BICARBONATE
BICENTENARY
BIFURCATION
BILIOUSNESS
BILL-STICKER
BILOPHODONT
BIMETALLISM
BIMETALLIST
BIODYNAMICS
BIOGENESIST
BIPARTITION
BIQUADRATIC
BITTER-SWEET
BITUMINATED
BLACK-BEETLE
BLACK-LETTER
BLACK-MONDAY
BLADDER-FERN
BLADDERWORT
BLAMELESSLY
BLAMEWORTHY
BLASPHEMOUS
BLEACHFIELD
BLEPHARITIS
BLESSEDNESS
BLOCK-SYSTEM
BLOOD-BOUGHT
BLOOD-GUILTY
BLOODLESSLY
BLOOD-SUCKER
BLOOD-VESSEL
BLUE-COAT-BOY
BLUNDERBUSS
BOARD-SCHOOL
BODY-SERVANT
BOHEMIANISM
BOLTING-MILL
BOLT-UPRIGHT
BOMBARDMENT
BONAPARTIST
BONNET-ROUGE
BOOKBINDING
BOOKISHNESS
BOOK-KEEPING
BOOK-LEARNED
BOOK-SELLING
BOORISHNESS
BORBORYGMUS
BOTANICALLY
BOTHERATION
BOTTLE-CHART
BOTTLE-GLASS
BOTTLE-GREEN
BOTTLE-NOSED
BOULDER-CLAY
BOUNDLESSLY
BOUNTEOUSLY
BOUNTIFULLY
BOURGEOISIE
BOXING-GLOVE

BOXING-MATCH
BRABBLEMENT
BRACHIOPODA
BRAGGADOCIO
BRANCHIOPOD
BRAZEN-FACED
BREADTHWAYS
BREAD-WINNER
BREAST-PLATE
BREAST-WHEEL
BREECH-BLOCK
BRICKLAYING
BRILLIANTLY
BRINE-SHRIMP
BRISTLINESS
BRITTLENESS
BRONCHOCELE
BRONCHOTOMY
BRONZE-STEEL
BROTHERHOOD
BROTHERLESS
BRUSH-TURKEY
BRUSQUENESS
BRUTISHNESS
BUCKET-WHEEL
BUFFALO-ROBE
BULL-BAITING
BULLET-MOULD
BULLET-PROOF
BULL-FIGHTER
BULL-TERRIER
BUNCH-BACKED
BUREAUCRACY
BURGESS-SHIP
BURGLARIOUS
BURGOMASTER
BURNT-SIENNA
BUSYBODYISM
BUTCHER-BIRD
BUTTER-KNIFE
BUTTER-MOULD
BUTTER-PRINT
BUTYRACEOUS
BYSSIFEROUS

C

CABBAGE-MOTH
CABBAGE-PALM
CABBAGE-TREE
CABBAGE-ROSE
CABBAGE-WORM
CABBALISTIC
CACOGASTRIC
CACOPHONOUS
CALCEOLARIA
CALCIFEROUS
CALCINATION
CALCOGRAPHY
CALCULATING
CALCULATION
CALCULATIVE
CALEFACIENT
CALEFACTION
CALEFACTORY
CALIBRATION
CALLIGRAPHY
CALLING-CRAB
CALLOUSNESS

CALORIMETER
CALORIMETRY
CALUMNIATOR
CALVINISTIC
CAMARADERIE
CAMEL'S-THORN
CAMPANOLOGY
CAMPANULATE
CAMPHOR-TREE
CAMP-MEETING
CANARY-GRASS
CANCERATION
CANDELABRUM
CANDESCENCE
CANDIDATURE
CANDLE-BERRY
CANDLELIGHT
CANDLE-POWER
CANDLESTICK
CANNIBALISM
CANONICALLY
CANTHARIDES
CAPACIOUSLY
CAPILLAMENT
CAPILLARITY
CAPILLIFORM
CAPITULATOR
CAPTAINSHIP
CAPTIVATING
CARAVANSARY
CARBON-POINT
CARBUNCULAR
CARBURETTED
CARCINOLOGY
CARDINALATE
CARDIOGRAPH
CARD-SHARPER
CAREFULNESS
CARESSINGLY
CARMINATIVE
CARNATIONED
CARNIVOROUS
CAROLINGIAN
CARRIAGE-WAY
CARRION-CROW
CARTOGRAPHY
CARUNCULATE
CARVEL-BUILT
CASSITERITE
CASTELLATED
CASTIGATION
CASTIGATORY
CASTILE-SOAP
CASTING-VOTE
CATACAUSTIC
CATACHRESIS
CATACLYSMAL
CATACLYSMIC
CATAPHONICS
CATASTROPHE
CATECHETICS
CATEGORICAL
CATER-COUSIN
CATERPILLAR
CATHEDRATIC
CATHOLICISM
CATHOLICITY
CATHOLICIZE
CAULIFLOWER
CAUSATIVELY

CAUSATIVITY
CAUSELESSLY
CAUSTICALLY
CAVE-DWELLER
CAVERNULOUS
CAVO-RILIEVO
CEASELESSLY
CELEBRATION
CELESTIALLY
CELLIFEROUS
CEMENTATION
CENTENARIAN
CENTRE-BOARD
CENTRE-PIECE
CENTRICALLY
CENTRIFUGAL
CENTRIPETAL
CENTROBARIC
CEPHALALGIC
CEPHALASPIS
CEPHALOTOMY
CEREBRALISM
CEREBRATION
CEREBRIFORM
CEREMONIOUS
CEROPLASTIC
CERTAINNESS
CERTIFICATE
CESAREWITCH
CHAFING-DISH
CHAIN-BRIDGE
CHAIN-STITCH
CHALCEDONIC
CHALCEDONYX
CHALK-STONES
CHAMBERLAIN
CHAMBER-MAID
CHAMPIONESS
CHANGEFULLY
CHANTERELLE
CHANTICLEER
CHAOTICALLY
CHAPERONAGE
CHARLATANIC
CHARLATANRY
CHARTACEOUS
CHASTISABLE
CHECK-STRING
CHEERLESSLY
CHEESE-PRESS
CHEF-D'OEUVRE
CHEQUER-WORK
CHERRY-STONE
CHESS-PLAYER
CHEVAL-GLASS
CHIAROSCURO
CHIEFTAINCY
CHIEFTAINRY
CHILOGNATHA
CHIROGRAPHY
CHIROMANCER
CHIROMANTIC
CHIROPODIST
CHIRURGICAL
CHISEL-TOOTH
CHITTERLING
CHLOROMETER
CHLOROPHYLL
CHOIR-SCREEN
CHONDROLOGY

CHOROGRAPHY
CHRISMATORY
CHRISTENDOM
CHRISTENING
CHRISTOLOGY
CHROMATROPE
CHRONOGRAPH
CHRONOLOGER
CHRONOLOGIC
CHRONOMETER
CHRONOMETRY
CHRONOSCOPE
CHRYSOBERYL
CHRYSOCOLLA
CHRYSOPHYLL
CHRYSOPRASE
CHURCH-COURT
CHURCH-GOING
CHURCHWOMAN
CICATRICULE
CINERACEOUS
CINERITIOUS
CINNABARINE
CINQUE-PORTS
CIRCULARITY
CIRCULATING
CIRCULATION
CIRCULATIVE
CIRCULATORY
CIRCUMPOLAR
CIRCUMSPECT
CIRCUMVOLVE
CITIZENSHIP
CLAIRVOYANT
CLAMOROUSLY
CLANDESTINE
CLASS-FELLOW
CLASSICALLY
CLEAN-HANDED
CLEAN-LIMBED
CLEANLINESS
CLEAR-HEADED
CLEARING-NUT
CLEAR-STARCH
CLEFT-PALATE
CLEPTOMANIA
CLERICALISM
CLIMACTERIC
CLIMATOLOGY
CLINOMETRIC
CLOG-ALMANAC
CLOSE-FISTED
CLOSE-HANDED
CLOSE-HAULED
CLOTHES-MOTH
CLOUD-CAPPED
CLOVER-GRASS
COACH-OFFICE
COAGULATION
COAGULATIVE
COALESCENCE
COAL-TRIMMER
COAL-WHIPPER
■■■■■■ ■ ■ ■■■
COCHIN-CHINA
COCK-AND-BULL
CODICILLARY
COD-LIVER-OIL
COEFFICIENT
COESSENTIAL

COETERNALLY
COEXISTENCE
COEXTENSIVE
COFFEE-BERRY
COFFEE-HOUSE
COGNOSCIBLE
COINCIDENCE
COLD-BLOODED
COLD-HEARTED
COLLABORATE
COLLAPSIBLE
COLLECTANEA
COLLECTEDLY
COLLIMATION
COLLOCATION
COLLUSIVELY
COLONIALISM
COLORIMETER
COLUMBARIUM
COLUMNARITY
COMBINATION
COMBUSTIBLE
COMET-FINDER
COMFORTABLE
COMFORTABLY
COMFORTLESS
COMMANDMENT
COMMEMORATE
COMMENDABLE
COMMENDABLY
COMMENDATOR
COMMENTATOR
COMMINATION
COMMINATORY
COMMINUTION
COMMISERATE
COMMISSURAL
COMMONPLACE
COMMUNALISM
COMMUNALIST
COMMUNICANT
COMMUNICATE
COMMUNISTIC
COMMUTATION
COMMUTATIVE
COMPACTNESS
COMPARATIVE
COMPARTMENT
COMPASSABLE
COMPASS-CARD
COMPELLABLE
COMPENDIOUS
COMPENSATOR
COMPETENTLY
COMPETITION
COMPETITIVE
COMPILATION
COMPLACENCE
COMPLACENCY
COMPLAINANT
COMPLAISANT
COMPLIANTLY
COMPLICATED
COMPORTMENT
COMPOSITELY
COMPOSITION
COMPOSSIBLE
COMPRESSION
COMPRESSIVE
COMPRESSURE

COMPROMISER
COMPTROLLER
COMPUNCTION
COMPURGATOR
COMPUTATION
COMRADESHIP
CONCATENATE
CONCEALABLE
CONCEALMENT
CONCEITEDLY
CONCEIVABLE
CONCEIVABLY
CONCENTRATE
CONCEPTACLE
CONCERNMENT
CONCILIABLE
CONCILIATOR
CONCISENESS
CONCOMITANT
CONCORDANCE
CONCUBINAGE
CONCUBINARY
CONCURRENCE
CONDEMNABLE
CONDENSABLE
CONDITIONAL
CONDITIONED
CONDOLATORY
CONDOLEMENT
CONDONATION
CONDUCTIBLE
CONDUCTRESS
CONFABULATE
CONFEDERACY
CONFEDERATE
CONFERRABLE
CONFESSEDLY
CONFIDENTLY
CONFIDINGLY
CONFINEMENT
CONFIRMABLE
CONFISCABLE
CONFISCATOR
CONFLAGRATE
CONFLICTING
CONFLICTION
CONFORMABLE
CONFORMABLY
CONFUTATION
CONGEALABLE
CONGELATION
CONGRUOUSLY
CONIROSTRAL
CONJECTURAL
CONJUGALITY
CONJUGATION
CONJUNCTION
CONJUNCTIVE
CONJUNCTURE
CONJURATION
CONNECTEDLY
CONNOISSEUR
CONNOTATION
CONNUBIALLY
CONQUERABLE
CONSCIOUSLY
CONSECRATOR
CONSECUTION
CONSECUTIVE

CONSENTIENT
CONSEQUENCE
CONSERVABLE
CONSERVANCY
CONSERVATOR
CONSIDERATE
CONSIDERING
CONSIGNMENT
CONSILIENCE
CONSISTENCE
CONSOLATION
CONSOLATORY
CONSOLIDANT
CONSOLIDATE
CONSONANTAL
CONSORTSHIP
CONSPICUOUS
CONSPIRATOR
CONSTELLATE
CONSTERNATE
CONSTITUENT
CONSTITUTER
CONSTRAINED
CONSTRAINER
CONSTRICTOR
CONSTRUCTER
CONSTRUCTOR
CONSUMPTION
CONSUMPTIVE
CONTAINABLE
CONTAMINATE
CONTEMPLATE
CONTENTEDLY
CONTENTIOUS
CONTESTABLE
CONTINENTAL
CONTINENTLY
CONTINGENCE
CONTINGENCY
CONTINUABLE
CONTINUALLY
CONTINUANCE
CONTINUATOR
CONTINUEDLY
CONTRABASSO
CONTRACTILE
CONTRACTION
CONTRAJERVA
CONTRARIANT
CONTRARIETY
CONTRARIOUS
CONTRA-TENOR
CONTRAVENER
CONTRAYERVA
CONTRE-TEMPS
CONTRIBUTOR
CONTRIVABLE
CONTRIVANCE
CONTROLMENT
CONTROVERSY
CONVENIENCE
CONVENIENCY
CONVENTICLE
CONVERGENCE
CONVERSABLE
CONVERSABLY
CONVERTIBLE
CONVERTIBLY
CONVEYANCER
CONVINCIBLE

CONVIVIALLY
CONVOCATION
CONVOLUTION
CONVOLVULUS
CONVULSIBLE
COOL-TANKARD
CO-OPERATION
CO-OPERATIVE
COPARCENARY
COPIOUSNESS
COPPERPLATE
COPPERSMITH
COQUILLA-NUT
CORALLIFORM
CORBEL-TABLE
CORNER-STONE
CORNICULATE
CORNIGEROUS
CORPORALITY
CORPORATELY
CORPORATION
CORPOREALLY
CORPULENTLY
CORPUSCULAR
CORRECTABLE
CORRECTNESS
CORRELATION
CORRELATIVE
CORROBORANT
CORROBORATE
CORROSIVELY
CORRUGATION
CORRUPTIBLE
CORRUPTIBLY
CORRUPTLESS
CORRUPTNESS
CORUSCATION
CO-SIGNATORY
COSMOGONIST
COSMOGRAPHY
COSMOLOGIST
COSTIVENESS
COTERMINOUS
COTTON-GRASS
COTTON-PLANT
COTTON-PRESS
COTYLEDONAL
COUNTENANCE
COUNTERFEIT
COUNTERFOIL
COUNTERFORT
COUNTERMAND
COUNTERMARK
COUNTERMINE
COUNTER-MOVE
COUNTERPANE
COUNTERPART
COUNTERPLOT
COUNTERSEAL
COUNTERSIGN
COUNTERSINK
COUNTERVAIL
COUNTERWORK
COUNTRIFIED
COUNTRY-SIDE
COURTEOUSLY
COURTLINESS
COXCOMBICAL
CRABBEDNESS
CRACOVIENNE

CRANIOMETER
CRANIOMETRY
CRANIOSCOPY
CRATERIFORM
CREAM-CHEESE
CREATORSHIP
CREDIBILITY
CREDULOUSLY
CREMATORIUM
CREOPHAGOUS
CREPITATION
CREPUSCULAR
CRESTFALLEN
CRIMINALIST
CRIMINALITY
CRIMINATION
CRIMINATIVE
CRITICASTER
CROCIDOLITE
CROCODILIAN
CROOK-BACKED
CROOKEDNESS
CROSS-ACTION
CROSS-LEGGED
CROTCHETEER
CROWN-PRINCE
CRUCIFEROUS
CRUCIFIXION
CRUCIGEROUS
CRUSTACEOUS
CRYPTOGAMIC
CRYPTOGRAPH
CRYSTALLINE
CRYSTALLIZE
CRYSTALLOID
CUBICALNESS
CUIR-BOUILLI
CULMIFEROUS
CULMINATION
CULPABILITY
CULTIVATION
CUPELLATION
CUPRIFEROUS
CURATORSHIP
CURLY-HEADED
CURRANT-WINE
CURRY-POWDER
CURSORINESS
CURTAILMENT
CURVILINEAR
CURVILINEAL
CUSTOMARILY
CUSTOM-HOUSE
CYCADACEOUS
CYCLOPAEDIA
CYCLOPAEDIC
CYNOPHILIST
CYPERACEOUS
CYTOGENESIS

D

DACTYLOLOGY
DAMPISHNESS
DANCING-GIRL
DANGEROUSLY
DAUNTLESSLY
DAY-LABOURER
DEATH-RATTLE

DEATH-STROKE
DEBARKATION
DEBAUCHMENT
DECARBONIZE
DECEITFULLY
DECEMVIRATE
DECEPTIVELY
DECLAMATION
DECLAMATORY
DECLARATION
DECLARATIVE
DECLARATORY
DECLINATION
DECLINATORY
DECLINATURE
DECOLLATION
DECOMPOSITE
DECORTICATE
DECREPITATE
DECREPITUDE
DECRESCENDO
DECUMBENTLY
DECURRENTLY
DECUSSATELY
DECUSSATION
DEDUCTIVELY
DEEP-MOUTHED
DEER-STALKER
DEFALCATION
DEFECTIVELY
DEFENCELESS
DEFENSIVELY
DEFERENTIAL
DEFIANTNESS
DEFIBRINIZE
DEFIBRINATE
DEFICIENTLY
DEFLAGRATOR
DEFLORATION
DEFOLIATION
DEFORCEMENT
DEFORMATION
DEGLUTITION
DEGLUTITORY
DEGRADATION
DEGRADINGLY
DEHORTATION
DEHORTATIVE
DEHORTATORY
DEHYDRATION
DEICTICALLY
DEIFICATION
DEISTICALLY
DELECTATION
DELETERIOUS
DELICIOUSLY
DELIGHTEDLY
DELIGHTLESS
DELIGHTSOME
DELINEATION
DELINQUENCY
DELIRIOUSLY
DELITESCENT
DELIVERANCE
DEMAGNETIZE
DEMARCATION
DEMESMERIZE
DEMI-BASTION
DEMI-CADENCE

DEMOCRATIZE
DEMOGRAPHIC
DEMONIACISM
DEMONOLATRY
DEMONOLOGIC
DEMONSTRATE
DENIZENSHIP
DENOMINABLE
DENOMINATOR
DENTICULATE
DENTIGEROUS
DENUNCIATOR
DEOBSTRUENT
DEOXIDATION
DEPAUPERATE
DEPAUPERIZE
DEPENDENTLY
DEPHLEGMATE
DEPOPULATOR
DEPORTATION
DEPRAVATION
DEPRECATION
DEPRECATORY
DEPRECATIVE
DEPREDATION
DEPREDATORY
DEPRIVATION
DEPRIVEMENT
DERANGEMENT
DERELICTION
DERMATOLOGY
DESCENDABLE
DESCENDIBLE
DESCRIBABLE
DESCRIPTION
DESCRIPTIVE
DESECRATION
DESERVINGLY
DESICCATION
DESIDERATUM
DESIGNATION
DESIGNATIVE
DESPERATELY
DESPERATION
DESPISINGLY
DESPONDENCE
DESPONDENCY
DESTINATION
DESTITUTION
DESTROYABLE
DESTRUCTION
DESTRUCTIVE
DESULTORILY
DETERIORATE
DETERMINANT
DETERMINATE
DETERMINISM
DETERMINIST
DETESTATION
DETRIMENTAL
DEUTEROGAMY
DEUTERONOMY
DEVASTATION
DEVELOPMENT
DEVIOUSNESS
DEVOLVEMENT
DEVOTEDNESS
DEXTEROUSLY
DIACRITICAL

DIAGNOSTICS
DIALECTICAL
DIALOGISTIC
DIAMAGNETIC
DIAMETRICAL
DIAPHANCITY
DIAPHORESIS
DIAPHORETIC
DIARTHROSIS
DIATHERMOUS
DICEPHALOUS
DICHOGAMOUS
DICHOTOMOUS
DICHROMATIC
DICHROSCOPE
DICOTYLEDON
DICTATORIAL
DIDACTYLOUS
DIFFERENTIA
DIFFERENTLY
DIFFICULTLY
DIFFIDENTLY
DIFFRACTION
DIFFRACTIVE
DIFFUSENESS
DIFFUSIVELY
DIGITIGRADE
DILAPIDATED
DILAPIDATOR
DILUVIALIST
DIMENSIONAL
DIMENSIONED
DINNER-TABLE
DINOSAURIAN
DINOTHERIUM
DIPHTHONGAL
DIPHYCERCAL
DIPLOMATICS
DIPLOMATIST
DIPLOMATIZE
DIPRISMATIC
DIPSOMANIAC
DIRECTORATE
DIRECTORIAL
DIREFULNESS
DISACCUSTOM
DISAFFECTED
DISAFFOREST
DISAPPROVAL
DISARMAMENT
DISBANDMENT
DISBELIEVER
DISCERNIBLE
DISCERNIBLY
DISCERNMENT
DISCONTINUE
DISCORDANCE
DISCORDANCY
DISCOURAGER
DISCOURTESY
DISCREPANCE
DISCREPANCY
DISCUSSABLE
DISENCUMBER
DISENTANGLE
DISENTHRALL
DISENTHRONE
DISENTRANCE
DISGRACEFUL

DISGUISEDLY
DISHONESTLY
DISINTHRALL
DISJUNCTION
DISJUNCTIVE
DISLOCATION
DISMASTMENT
DISOBEDIENT
DISOBLIGING
DISORGANIZE
DISPENSABLE
DISPERSEDLY
DISPIRITING
DISPLEASING
DISPLEASURE
DISPOSITION
DISPUTATION
DISPUTATIVE
DISQUIETING
DISQUIETUDE
DISSECTIBLE
DISSENTIENT
DISSEPIMENT
DISSERTATOR
DISSILIENCE
DISSIMULATE
DISSIPATION
DISSOLUTELY
DISSOLUTION
DISSOLVABLE
DISSYLLABIC
DISSYLLABLE
DISTASTEFUL
DISTEMPERED.
DISTENSIBLE
DISTILLABLE
DISTINCTION
DISTINCTIVE
DISTINGUISH
DISTRACTING
DISTRACTION
DISTRESSFUL
DISTRESSING
DISTRIBUTOR
DISTRUSTFUL
DISTURBANCE
DITHYRAMBIC
DITHYRAMBUS
DIVERSIFIED
DIVERTINGLY
DIVING-DRESS
DIVINING-ROD
DIVORCEABLE
DIVORCEMENT
DOCK-WARRANT
DOCTRINAIRE
DOCTRINALLY
DOCUMENTARY
DOLABRIFORM
DOLEFULNESS
DOMESTICATE
DOMESTICITY
DOMICILIARY
DOMICILIATE
DOMINEERING
DOUBLE-EDGED
DOUBLE-ENTRY
DOUBLE-FACED
DOUBLE-FIRST
DOUBLE-QUICK

DOUBTLESSLY
DOUGHTINESS
DOWNTRODDEN
DOXOLOGICAL
DRAMATURGIC
DRAUGHTSMAN
DREADNOUGHT
DREAMLESSLY
DRUNKENNESS
DUBIOUSNESS
DUCTILENESS
DUPLICATION
DUPLICATIVE
DUPLICATURE
DUTIFULNESS
DYNAMICALLY
DYSLOGISTIC

E

EARNESTNESS
EARTHENWARE
EARTHLINESS
ECCENTRICAL
ECLECTICISM
EDIFICATION
EDITOR'ALLY
EDUCATIONAL
EFFECTIVELY
EFFICACIOUS
EFFICIENTLY
EFFOLIATION
EFFULGENTLY
EGLANDULOSE
EGLANDULOUS
EGREGIOUSLY
EIDOLOCLAST
EJACULATION
ELABORATELY
ELABORATIVE
ELABORATION
ELASTICALLY
ELECTIONEER
ELECTORSHIP
ELECTRICIAN
ELECTROCUTE
ELECTROGILD
ELECTROLYSE
ELECTROLYTE
ELECTROTYPE
ELEMENTALLY
ELEPHANTINE
ELEPHANTOID
ELIGIBILITY
ELIZABETHAN
ELLIPSOIDAL
ELLIPTICITY
ELUCIDATION
ELUCIDATIVE
ELUSORINESS
ELUTRIATION
EMANCIPATOR
EMBARKATION
EMBARRASSED
EMBLEMATIST
EMBLEMATIZE
EMBOWELMENT
EMBRACEMENT
EMBROCATION

EMBROILMENT
EMBRYOLOGIC
EMMENAGOGUE
EMMENAGOGIC
EMPIRICALLY
EMULATIVELY
EMULSIONIZE
ENARTHROSIS
ENCEPHALOID
ENCEPHALOUS
ENCHAINMENT
ENCHANTMENT
ENCHANTRESS
ENCOMIASTIC
ENCOURAGING
ENCUMBRANCE
ENCYSTATION
ENDOCARDIAC
ENDEMICALLY
ENDLESSNESS
ENDOCARDIUM
ENDORHIZOUS
ENDORSEMENT
ENDOSMOSMIC
ENDOSPERMIC
ENERGETICAL
ENFEOFFMENT
ENFORCEABLE
ENFORCEMENT
ENFRANCHISE
ENGINEERING
ENGORGEMENT
ENGRAILMENT
ENGROSSMENT
ENHANCEMENT
ENIGMATICAL
ENLARGEMENT
ENLIGHTENED
ENLIVENMENT
ENNEAGYNOUS
ENNEAHEDRAL
ENNEAHEDRON
ENNOBLEMENT
ENOUNCEMENT
ENSLAVEMENT
ENTABLATURE
ENTEROPATHY
ENTERTAINER
ENTHRALMENT
ENTOMOLOGIC
ENTOZOOLOGY
ENTREATABLE
ENTWINEMENT
ENUCLEATION
ENUMERATION
ENUNCIATION
ENUNCIATIVE
ENUNCIATORY
ENVELOPMENT
ENVIRONMENT
EPIDICTACAL
EPIGASTRIUM
EPIGRAPHICS
EPILOGISTIC
EPIPETALOUS
EPIPHYLLOUS
EPIPHYTICAL
EPISCOPALLY
EPISTOLICAL
EPITHALAMIC

EPITHELIOMA
EPITHETICAL
EQUABLENESS
EQUIANGULAR
EQUIDISTANT
EQUILATERAL
EQUILIBRATE
EQUILIBRIST
EQUILIBRIUM
EQUINOCTIAL
EQUIPOLLENT
EQUIVALENCE
EQUIVALENCY
EQUIVOCALLY
EQUIVOCATOR
ERADICATION
ERADICATIVE
ERASTIANISM
EREMACAUSIS
ERRATICALLY
ERRONEOUSLY
ERUBESCENCE
ERYTHEMATIC
ESCHATOLOGY
ESCHEATABLE
ESOTERICISM
ESSENTIALLY
ESTABLISHED
ESTABLISHER
ETHEREALITY
ETHEREALIZE
ETHNOGRAPHY
ETHNOLOGIST
ETYMOLOGIST
ETYMOLOGIZE
EUCHARISTIC
EUDAEMONISM
EUDAEMONIST
EUPHEMISTIC
EUROPEANIZE
EVANESCENCE
EVANGELICAL
EVAPORATION
EVAPORATIVE
EVENTUALITY
EVENTUATION
EVERLASTING
EVOLUTIONAL
EXAGGERATOR
EXAMINATION
EXCEEDINGLY
EXCELLENTLY
EXCEPTIONAL
EXCESSIVELY
EXCLAMATION
EXCLAMATORY
EXCLUSIVELY
EXCLUSIVISM
EXCORIATION
EXCORTICATE
EXCRESCENCE
EXCULPATION
EXCULPATORY
EXCURSIVELY
EXECUTIONER
EXECUTORIAL
EXEMPLARILY
EXEMPLIFIER
EXFOLIATION
EXHAUSTIBLE

EXHAUSTLESS
EXHORTATION
EXHORTATIVE
EXHORTATORY
EXISTENTIAL
EXONERATION
EXONERATIVE
EXORBITANCE
EXORBITANCY
EXOSKELETON
EXOSKELETAL
EXOTERICISM
EXPANSIVELY
EXPATIATION
EXPATIATORY
EXPECTATION
EXPECTATIVE
EXPECTORANT
EXPECTORATE
EXPEDIENTLY
EXPEDITIOUS
EXPENDITURE
EXPENSIVELY
EXPERIENCED
EXPISCATION
EXPLANATION
EXPLANATORY
EXPLICATION
EXPLICATIVE
EXPLICATORY
EXPLOITABLE
EXPLORATION
EXPLORATORY
EXPLOSIVELY
EXPONENTIAL
EXPORTATION
EXPOSEDNESS
EXPOSTULATE
EXPRESSIBLE
EXPROPRIATE
EXPURGATION
EXPURGATORY
EXQUISITELY
EXTEMPORARY
EXTEMPORIZE
EXTENSIVELY
EXTENUATION
EXTENUATORY
EXTERIORITY
EXTERMINATE
EXTERNALISM
EXTERNALITY
EXTERNALIZE
EXTIRPATION
EXTIRPATORY
EXTORTIONER
EXTRACTIBLE
EXTRADITION
EXTRAVAGANT
EXTRAVASATE
EXTRICATION
EXTRINSICAL
EXUBERANTLY

F

FABRICATION
FACETIOUSLY

FACSIMILIST
FACULTATIVE
FADDISHNESS
FAITHLESSLY
FALLIBILITY
FALTERINGLY
FAMILIARITY
FAMILIARIZE
FANATICALLY
FANFARONADE
FANTASTICAL
FARTHERMORE
FARTHERMOST
FARTHINGALE
FASCINATING
FASCINATION
FASHIONABLE
FASTIGIATED
FAULTLESSLY
FAUSSEBRAYE
FAVOURITISM
FEARFULNESS
FEASIBILITY
FEATHERLESS
FEATURELESS
FEBRICULOSE
FEBRIFEROUS
FECUNDATION
FELONIOUSLY
FELSPATHOSE
FERMENTABLE
FEROCIOUSLY
FERRIFEROUS
FERRUGINOUS
FERULACEOUS
FIDGETINESS
FILAMENTARY
FILAMENTOSE
FILAMENTOUS
FILAMENTOID
FILLIBUSTER
FIMETARIOUS
FINANCIALLY
FINICALNESS
FIRMAMENTAL
FISSIPAROUS
FLABBERGAST
FLACCIDNESS
FLATULENTLY
FLAVOURLESS
FLESHINESS
FLEXIBILITY
FLIGHTINESS
FLOCCULENCE
FLORESCENCE
FLORILEGIUM
FLOURISHING
FLOWERINESS
FLUCTUATING
FLUCTUATION
FLUORESCENT
FOMENTATION
FOOLISHNESS
FORAMINATED
FORAMINIFER
FORBEARANCE
FORCIPATION
FORECLOSURE
FOREIGNNESS

FOREPAYMENT
FORESHORTEN
FORESTALLER
FORETHOUGHT
FORFEITABLE
FORGIVENESS
FORMICATION
FORMULARIZE
FORMULATION
FORNICATION
FORTHCOMING
FORTIFIABLE
FORTNIGHTLY
FORTUNATELY
FORWARDNESS
FRACTIONIZE
FRACTIONATE
FRACTIOUSLY
FRAGILENESS
FRAGMENTARY
FRANGIPANNI
FRANTICALLY
FRATERNALLY
FRATRICIDAL
FRAUDLESSLY
FRAUDULENCE
FREEBOOTING
FREEMASONRY
FRETFULNESS
FRIGHTFULLY
FRIVOLOUSLY
FROWARDNESS
FRUGIFEROUS
FRUGIVOROUS
FRUITLESSLY
FRUSTRATION
FULGURATION
FULMINATING
FULMINATION
FULSOMENESS
FUNAMBULIST
FUNCTIONATE
FUNCTIONARY
FUNDAMENTAL
FUNGIVOROUS
FURIOUSNESS
FURTHERANCE
FURTHERMORE
FURTHERMOST

G

GAINFULNESS
GALLIMAUFRY
GALLOWGLASS
GAMOGENESIS
GARNISHMENT
GARRULOUSLY
GASTRONOMER
GEMMIPAROUS
GENDARMERIE
GENEALOGIST
GENERALSHIP
GENERICALLY
GENETICALLY
GENICULATED
GENTEELNESS
GENTLEMANLY
GENTLEWOMAN

GENTLEWOMEN
GENUFLEXION
GENUINENESS
GEOMETRICAL
GERMINATION
GERMINATIVE
GERRYMANDER
GESTICULATE
GHASTLINESS
GHOSTLINESS
GIGANTESQUE
GILLYFLOWER
GINGERBREAD
GIRLISHNESS
GLAUCESCENT
GLOBIGERINA
GLOBULARITY
GLOMERATION
GLUMIFEROUS
GLYPTOTHECA
GOATISHNESS
GODDAUGHTER
GODLESSNESS
GONFALONIER
GORMANDIZER
GOURMANDIZE
GRACELESSLY
GRADATIONAL
GRAMMATICAL
GRANDFATHER
GRANDIOSITY
GRANDMOTHER
GRANDNEPHEW
GRANIFEROUS
GRANITIFORM
GRANIVOROUS
GRANULATION
GRAPHICALLY
GRATULATION
GRATULATORY
GRAVIMETRIC
GRAVITATION
GRAVITATIVE
GREENGROCER
GRISTLINESS
GROTESQUELY
GROTESQUERY
GUANIFEROUS
GUARDEDNESS
GUILELESSLY
GUILTLESSLY
GULLIBILITY
GUMMIFEROUS
GUTTIFEROUS
GUTTURALIZE
GYNECOCRACY
GYNAECOLOGY
GYNAEOLATRY

H

HABERDASHER
HABITUATION
HAEMOGLOBIN
HAEMOPHILIA
HAEMOPTYSIS
HAEMORRHAGE
HAGIOGRAPHY
HAGIOLOGIST

HANDBREADTH
HANDICAPPER
HANDWRITING
HARBOURLESS
HARMFULNESS
HARPSICHORD
HATEFULNESS
HAUGHTINESS
HAUSTELLATE
HAZARDOUSLY
HEALTHFULLY
HEALTHINESS
HEARTHSTONE
HEARTLESSLY
HEAVENWARDS
HEBDOMADARY
HEEDFULNESS
HEINOUSNESS
HELIOCHROMY
HELIOGRAPHY
HELLENISTIC
HELLISHNESS
HELMINTHOID
HELPFULNESS
HEMATOXYLIN
HEMERALOPIA
HEMIHEDRISM
HEMIPTEROUS
HEMISPHERIC
HEMITROPOUS
HEMORRHAGIC
HEMORRHOIDS
HEPTAGYNOUS
HEPTAGYNIAN
HEPTAHEDRON
HEPTAHEDRAL
HEPTAMEROUS
HEPTANDROUS
HEPTANGULAR
HERBIVOROUS
HEREDITABLE
HEREINAFTER
HERESIOLOGY
HERETICALLY
HERMENEUTIC
HERPETOLOGY
HESPERORNIS
HETEROCLITE
HETEROPHEMY
HEXAGONALLY
HIBERNATION
HIBERNICISM
HIDEOUSNESS
HIERARCHISM
HIPPOCAMPUS
HISTORIETTE
HISTRIONISM
HOBBLEDEHOY
HOLOGRAPHIC
HOLOTHURIAN
HOMILETICAL
HOMOEOPATHY
HOMOGENEITY
HOMOGENEOUS
HOMOGENESIS
HOMOGENETTE
HOMOIOUSIAN
HOMOMORPHIC
HOMOPLASTIC
HONEYSUCKLE

HONOURABLES
HOPEFULNESS
HOROLOGICAL
HOROSCOPIST
HOSPITALITY
HOSPITALLER
HOUSEHOLDER
HOUSEKEEPER
HOUSEWIFELY
HOUSEWIFERY
HUCKLEBERRY
HUCKSTERAGE
HUMECTATION
HUMILIATING
HUMILIATION
HUMORSOMELY
HUNCHBACKED
HURTFULNESS
HYACINTHINE
HYALOGRAPHY
HYDROCARBON
HYDROCYANIC
HYDROGENOUS
HYDROGRAPHY
HYDROMETRIC
HYDROPATHIC
HYDROPHOBIA
HYDROPHOBIC
HYDROSTATIC
HYDROTHORAX
HYETOGRAPHY
HYGROMETRIC
HYGROSCOPIC
HYMNOGRAPHY
HYMNOLOGIST
HYPERBOLISM
HYPERBOLIZE
HYPERBOREAN
HYPERCRITIC
HYPERSTHENE
HYPERTROPHY
HYPOGASTRIC
HYPOGLOSSAL
HYPOSTATIZE
HYPOSTASIZE
HYPOTHECATE
HYPOTHENUSE
HYPOTHESIZE
HYSTEROTOMY

I

ICHTHYOLITE
ICHTHYOLOGY
ICHTHYORNIS
ICONOGRAPHY
ICOSAHEDRAL
IDENTICALLY
IDEOGRAPHIC
IDIOMATICAL
IDIOMORPHIC
IDIOTICALLY
IGNOMINIOUS
IGNORAMUSES
ILLIBERALLY
ILLIMITABLE
ILLOGICALLY
ILLUMINATOR

ILLUSIONIST
ILLUSTRATOR
ILLUSTRIOUS
IMAGINATION
IMAGINATIVE
IMBRICATION
IMITABILITY
IMITATIVELY
IMMEDIATELY
IMMENSENESS
IMMIGRATION
IMMORTALITY
IMMORTALIZE
IMPANELMENT
IMPARTATION
IMPARTIALLY
IMPASSIONED
IMPASSIVELY
IMPATIENTLY
IMPEACHABLE
IMPEACHMENT
IMPECUNIOUS
IMPENITENCE
IMPERFECTLY
IMPERFORATE
IMPERIALISM
IMPERIALIST
IMPERIALIZE
IMPERIOUSLY
IMPERMEABLE
IMPERMEABLY
IMPERSONATE
IMPERTINENT
IMPETUOSITY
IMPETUOUSLY
IMPIOUSNESS
IMPLACENTAL
IMPLEMENTAL
IMPLICATION
IMPLICATIVE
IMPLORATION
IMPLORATORY
IMPORTANTLY
IMPORTATION
IMPORTUNATE
IMPORTUNITY
IMPRECATION
IMPRECATORY
IMPREGNABLE
IMPREGNABLY
IMPRESSIBLE
IMPRESSIBLY
IMPRESSMENT
IMPROPRIATE
IMPROPRIETY
IMPROVEMENT
IMPRUDENTLY
IMPULSIVELY
INADVERTENT
INALIENABLE
INALIENABLY
INALTERABLE
INATTENTION
INATTENTIVE
INAUGURATOR
INCANTATION
INCANTATORY
INCARCERATE
INCARNADINE

INCARNATION
INCEPTIVELY
INCERTITUDE
INCESSANTLY
INCLEMENTLY
INCLINATION
INCLUSIVELY
INCOGITABLE
INCOHERENCE
INCOHERENCY
INCOMPETENT
INCONGRUENT
INCONGRUOUS
INCONSONANT
INCONSTANCY
INCONTINENT
INCORPORATE
INCORPOREAL
INCORRECTLY
INCREASABLE
INCREDULITY
INCREDULOUS
INCREMATION
INCRIMINATE
INCULCATION
INCULPATION
INCULPATORY
INCUMBRANCE
INCURIOUSLY
INCURVATION
INCURVATURE
INDECIDUATE
INDEFINABLE
INDENTATION
INDEPENDENT
INDEXTERITY
INDIFFERENT
INDIGESTION
INDIGNANTLY
INDIGNATION
INDIVIDUATE
INDIVISIBLE
INDIVISIBLY
INDOMITABLE
INDOMITABLY
INDORSEMENT
INDUBITABLE
INDUBITABLY
INDUCTIONAL
INDUCTIVELY
INDULGENTLY
INDUPLICATE
INDUSTRIOUS
INEBRIATION
INEFFECTIVE
INEFFECTUAL
INEFFICIENT
INELEGANTLY
INEQUITABLE
INESCAPABLE
INESSENTIAL
INESTIMABLE
INEXCUSABLE
INEXCUSABLY
INEXPEDIENT
INEXPENSIVE
INEXPLOSIVE
INFANTICIDE
INFATUATION

INFECUNDITY
INFERENTIAL
INFERIORITY
INFERTILELY
INFERTILITY
INFESTATION
INFEUDATION
INFINITIVAL
INFLAMMABLE
INFLAMMABLY
INFLUENTIAL
INFORMALITY
INFORMATION
INFRACOSTAL
INFRANGIBLE
INFREQUENCY
INGATHERING
INGENIOUSLY
INGENUOUSLY
INGRATITUDE
INGURGITATE
INHABITABLE
INHERITABLE
INHERITABLY
INHERITANCE
INJUDICIOUS
INJURIOUSLY
INNAVIGABLE
INNERVATION
INNOCUOUSLY
INNOXIOUSLY
INNUMERABLE
INNUMERABLY
INNUTRITION
INOBSERVANT
INOBTRUSIVE
INOCULATION
INOFFENSIVE
INOPERATIVE
INOPPORTUNE
INORGANIZED
INQUISITION
INQUISITIVE
INSALUBRITY
INSATIATELY
INSCRIPTION
INSCRIPTIVE
INSCRUTABLE
INSCRUTABLY
INSECTICIDE
INSECTIVORE
INSENSITIVE
INSEPARABLE
INSEPARABLY
INSESSORIAL
INSIDIOUSLY
INSINCERELY
INSINCERITY
INSINUATING
INSINUATION
INSINUATIVE
INSOUCIANCE
INSPIRATION
INSPIRATORY
INSTABILITY
INSTIGATION
INSTINCTIVE
INSTITUTION
INSTRUCTION
INSTITUTIVE

INSTRUCTIVE
INSULTINGLY
INSUPERABLY
INTEGRATION
INTELLIGENT
INTEMPERANT
INTEMPERATE
INTENSENESS
INTENSIVELY
INTENTIONAL
INTENTIONED
INTERACTION
INTERCALARY
INTERCALATE
INTERCESSOR
INTERCHANGE
INTERCOSTAL
INTERCOURSE
INTERESTING
INTERFLUENT
INTERFUSION
INTERIORITY
INTERJACENT
INTERLINEAR
INTERLINEAL
INTERMEDDLE
INTERMEDIAL
INTERMEDIUM
INTERMINATE
INTERMINGLE
INTERNALITY
INTERNECINE
INTERNUNCIO
INTEROCULAR
INTERPOLATE
INTERPRETER
INTERREGNUM
INTERROGATE
INTERRUPTED
INTERSPERSE
INTERVIEWER
INTOLERABLE
INTOLERABLY
INTOLERANCE
INTRACTABLE
INTRACTABLY
INTREPIDITY
INTRICATELY
INTRINSICAL
INTRUSIVELY
INTUITIONAL
INTUITIVELY
INTUMESCENT
INVECTIVELY
INVENTIVELY
INVENTORIAL
INVESTIGATE
INVESTITURE
INVIDIOUSLY
INVIOLATELY
INVOLUNTARY
INVOLVEMENT
IPECACUANHA
IRIDESCENCE
IRKSOMENESS
IRONMONGERY
IRRADIATION
IRREDUCIBLE
IRREDUCIBLY
IRREFUTABLE

IRREFUTABLY
IRREGULARLY
IRRELEVANCE
IRRELEVANCY
IRRELIGIOUS
IRREMOVABLE
IRREMOVABLY
IRREPARABLE
IRREPARABLY
IRREVERENCE
IRREVOCABLE
IRREVOCABLY
ISOCHRONOUS
ISOCHRONISM
ISOMETRICAL
ISOMORPHISM
ISOMORPHOUS
ISRAELITISH
ITHYPHALLIC

J

JACOBITICAL
JACTITATION
JOYLESSNESS
JUDICIOUSLY
JURIDICALLY
JUSTICESHIP
JUSTIFIABLY
JUVENESCENT

K

KAMPTULICON
KINEMATICAL
KLEPTOMANIA
KNAVISHNESS

L

LABEFACTION
LABORIOUSLY
LABRADORITE
LACONICALLY
LACRYMATORY
LACTESCENCE
LACTIFEROUS
LAMELLICORN
LAMELLIFORM
LAMENTATION
LAMMERGEIER
LANCEOLATED
LANCINATING
LANCINATION
LANGUIDNESS
LANGUISHING
LAPIDESCENT
LARVIPAROUS
LARYNGOTOMY
LATIFOLIATE
LATIFOLIOUS
LATITUDINAL
LAURUSTINUS
LAWLESSNESS
LEASEHOLDER
LECHEROUSLY

LECTURESHIP
LEGERDEMAIN
LEGISLATION
LEGISLATIVE
LEGISLATURE
LENGTHINESS
LENTIGINOUS
LEPIDOSIREN
LETHARGICAL
LEUCORRHOEA
LIBELLOUSLY
LIBERTARIAN
LIBERTICIDE
LIBERTINISM
LICHENOLOGY
LICKERISHLY
LICKSPITTLE
LIEUTENANCY
LIGAMENTOUS
LIGHTKEEPER
LILLIPUTIAN
LINGERINGLY
LINGUISTICS
LIQUEFIABLE
LIQUESCENCY
LIQUIDAMBAR
LIQUIDATION
LISSOMENESS
LITERALNESS
LITHOGRAPHY
LITHOTOMIST
LITHOTRIPSY
LITHOTRITOR
LITIGIOUSLY
LITTERATEUR
LOATHLINESS
LOATHSOMELY
LOGARITHMIC
LOGICALNESS
LOGOMACHIST
LUBRICATION
LUDICROUSLY
LUMPISHNESS
LUSTFULNESS
LUTHERANISM
LUXURIANTLY
LUXURIOUSLY
LYCANTHROPE
LYCANTHROPY

M

MACHINATION
MACROBIOTIC
MAGISTERIAL
MAGISTRATIC
MAGNANIMITY
MAGNETICIAN
MAGNIFIABLE
MAGNIFICENT
MAGNIFICOES
MAINTENANCE
MALEDICTION
MALEFICENCE
MALEVOLENCE
MALFEASANCE
MALICIOUSLY
MALIGNANTLY
MALPOSITION

MALPRACTICE
MAMMIFEROUS
MANDARINATE
MANDIBULATE
MANDUCATION
MANDUCATORY
MANGANESIAN
MANIPULATOR
MANUFACTORY
MANUFACTURE
MANUMISSION
MARCHIONESS
MARMORATION
MARSHALLING
MARSHALSHIP
MARTYROLOGY
MASCULINITY
MASQUERADER
MASTICATION
MASTICATORY
MATCHLESSLY
MATERIALISM
MATERIALIST
MATERIALIZE
MATHEMATICS
MATRIARCHAL
MATRICULATE
MATRIMONIAL
MAWKISHNESS
MEANINGLESS
MEASURELESS
MEASUREMENT
MECHANICIAN
MECHANOLOGY
MEDIASTINUM
MEDIATENESS
MEDIATORIAL
MEDICINALLY
MEDIEVALISM
MEDIEVALIST
MEGALOMANIA
MEGATHERIUM
MELANCHOLIA
MELIORATION
MELLIFEROUS
MELLIFLUENT
MELLIFLUOUS
MELLIVOROUS
MELODIOUSLY
MEMORABILIA
MEMORANDUMS
MEMORIALIST
MEMORIALIZE
MENORRHAGIA
MENSURATION
MENTIONABLE
MERCENARILY
MERCHANDISE
MERCHANTMAN
MERCILESSLY
MERCURIALLY
MERITORIOUS
MESALLIANCE
MESOPHLOEUM
MESSIAHSHIP
METAGENESIS
METAMORPHIC
METAPHYSICS
METEOROLITE
METEOROLOGY

METHODISTIC
METHODOLOGY
METONYMICAL
MICROCOCCUS
MICROGRAPHY
MICROLITHIC
MICROMETRIC
MICROSCOPIC
MICTURITION
MILLENARIAN
MILLIGRAMME
MILLIONAIRE
MINDFULNESS
MINERALIZER
MINERALOGIC
MINIATURIST
MINISTERIAL
MINISTERING
MINNESINGER
MISALLIANCE
MISANTHROPE
MISANTHROPY
MISBECOMING
MISBEGOTTEN
MISBELIEVER
MISCARRIAGE
MISCHIEVOUS
MISCONCEIVE
MISCONSTRUE
MISFEASANCE
MISSPELLING
MISTRUSTFUL
MITIGATIONS
MIXTILINEAL
MIXTILINEAR
MOLESTATION
MOMENTARILY
MOMENTOUSLY
MONARCHICAL
MONASTICISM
MONODELPHIA
MONOGENESIS
MONOGRAPHER
MONOGRAPHIC
MONOMORPHIC
MONOPHTHONG
MONOPHYSITE
MONOPOLIZER
MONOTREMATA
MONSTROSITY
MONSTROUSLY
MOONLIGHTER
MORAVIANISM
MORPHOLOGIC
MOUNTAINEER
MOUNTAINOUS
MOVABLENESS
MULTANGULAR
MULTANIMOUS
MULTILINEAL
MULTIPOTENT
MULTISERIAL
MULTISONOUS
MULTITUDINESS
MUNIFICENCE
MURDEROUSLY
MURMURINGLY
MUSCULARITY
MUTABLENESS
MYCOLOGICAL

MYTHOLOGIST
MYTHOLOGIAN
MYTHOLOGIZE
MYTHOPOETIC

N

NARRATIVELY
NATIONALISE
NATIONALISM
NATIONALIST
NATIONALITY
NATURALNESS
NAUGHTINESS
NECESSARILY
NECESSITATE
NECESSITOUS
NECKERCHIEF
NECROBIOSIS
NECROLOGIST
NECROMANCER
NECROMANTIC
NEEDFULNESS
NEFARIOUSLY
NEGLIGENTLY
NEGOTIATION
NEGOTIATORY
NEIGHBOURLY
NEOTROPICAL
NEPHRITICAL
NEUTRALIZER
NICTITATION
NIGHTINGALE
NIMBIFEROUS
NITROGENIZE
NITROGENOUS
NOCTILUCOUS
NOCTIVAGANT
NOCTURNALLY
NOISELESSLY
NOISOMENESS
NOMENCLATOR
NOMINATIVAL
NONCHALANCE
NONDESCRIPT
NONSENSICAL
NORTHWARDLY
NOSOLOGICAL
NOTABLENESS
NOTHINGNESS
NOTORIOUSLY
NOURISHABLE
NOURISHMENT
NOXIOUSNESS
NUMERICALLY
NUMISMATICS
NUMISMATIST
NUNCUPATIVE
NUNCUPATORY
NUTRIMENTAL
NUTRITIVELY
NYCTITROPIC
NYMPHOLEPSY
NYMPHOMANIA

O

OBEDIENTIAL

OBFUSCATION
OBJECTIVELY
OBJECTIVITY
OBJURGATION
OBJURGATORY
OBLIQUENESS
OBLIVIOUSLY
OBNOXIOUSLY
OBSCENENESS
OBSCURATION
OBSCUREMENT
OBSCURENESS
OBSECRATION
OBSECRATORY
OBSERVANTLY
OBSERVATION
OBSERVATIVE
OBSERVATORY
OBSOLESCENT
OBSTETRICAL
OBSTINATELY
OBSTIPATION
OBSTRUCTION
OBSTRUCTIVE
OBTESTATION
OBTRUSIVELY
OBVIOUSNESS
OCCULTATION
OCHLOCRATIC
ODONTOPHORE
ODORIFEROUS
OENOPHILIST
OESOPHAGEAL
OFFENSIVELY
OFFICIALISM
OFFICIOUSLY
OFFSCOURING
OMINOUSNESS
OMNIFARIOUS
OMNIPOTENCE
OMNIPRESENT
OMNISCIENCE
OMNISCIENCY
OMPHALOTOMY
ONEIROMANCY
ONIROCRITIC
ONOMASTICON
ONOMATOLOGY
ONTOGENESIS
ONTOLOGICAL
OPALESCENCE
OPEIDOSCOPE
OPERATIVELY
OPEROSENESS
OPINIONABLE
OPINIONATED
OPPORTUNELY
OPPORTUNISM
OPPORTUNIST
OPPORTUNITY
OPPROBRIOUS
ORBICULARLY
ORBICULATED
ORCHESTRION
ORCHIDOLOGY
ORDERLINESS
ORGANICALLY
ORGANIZABLE
ORIENTALISM
ORIENTALIST

ORIENTALIZE
ORIGINALITY
ORIGINATION
ORIGINATIVE
ORNAMENTIST
ORNITHOLITE
ORNITHOLOGY
ORTHOGRAPHY
ORTHOPAEDIA
ORTHOPAEDIC
ORTHOPEDIST
ORTHOTROPAL
OSCILLATING
OSCILLATION
OSCILLATORY
OSTENTATION
OSTEOGRAPHY
OSTEOLOGIST
OSTEOPLASTY
OSTREACEOUS
OUTDISTANCE
OUTSTANDING
OVERBALANCE
OVERBEARING
OVERFLOWING
OVERWEENING
OVERWROUGHT
OXYGENATION
OXYHYDROGEN

P

PACIFICALLY
PACIFICATOR
PAEDAGOGICS
PAINFULNESS
PAINSTAKING
PALAEARCTIC
PALEOGRAPHY
PALMIFEROUS
PALPABILITY
PALPITATION
PALPIGEROUS
PALSGRAVINE
PAMPHLETEER
PAMPINIFORM
PANDEMONIUM
PANDURIFORM
PANEGYRICAL
PANHELLENIC
PANTHEISTIC
PAPYRACEOUS
PAPYROGRAPH
PARABOLICAL
PARACENTRIC
PARADOXICAL
PARAGOGICAL
PARAGRAPHIC
PARALLACTIC
PARALLELISM
PARASITICAL
PARCHEDNESS
PARENTHESIS
PARENTHESES
PARENTHETIC
PARENTICIDE
PARIPINNATE
PARISHIONER
PAROCHIALLY

PARONOMASIA
PARTIBILITY
PARTICIPATE
PARTICIPIAL
PARTICULATE
PARTITIVELY
PARTNERSHIP
PARTURITION
PARVANIMITY
PASSIBILITY
PASSIONLESS
PASSIVENESS
PASTURELESS
PATERNOSTER
PATHOLOGIST
PATRIARCHIC
PATRIMONIAL
PATRONIZING
PEARLACEOUS
PECCABILITY
PECTINATION
PECULIARITY
PECUNIARILY
PEDAGOGICAL
PEDICELLATE
PEDOBAPTISM
PEDOBAPTIST
PEDUNCULATE
PEEVISHNESS
PELAGIANISM
PELARGONIUM
PELLUCIDITY
PENETRATING
PENETRATION
PENETRATIVE
PENINSULATE
PENITENTIAL
PENNONCELLE
PENNYWEIGHT
PENSIVENESS
PENTAGYNIAN
PENTAGYNOUS
PENTAHEDRAL
PENTAHEDRON
PENTANDROUS
PENTANGULAR
PENTECOSTAL
PENULTIMATE
PENURIOUSLY
PERAMBULATE
PERCEIVABLE
PERCEIVABLY
PERCEPTIBLE
PERCEPTIBLY
PERCIPIENCE
PERCIPIENCY
PERCOLATION
PEREGRINATE
PERENNIALLY
PERFECTIBLE
PERFECTNESS
PERFORATION
PERFORATIVE
PERFORMABLE
PERFORMANCE
PERFUMATORY
PERFUNCTORY
PERICARDIAL
PERICARDIAC
PERICARDIUM

PERICARPIAL
PERICRANIUM
PERIGASTRIC
PERIODICITY
PERIOSTEOUS
PERIPATETIC
PERIPHRASIS
PERIPHRASES
PERISTALTIC
PERITONAEAL
PERITONAEUM
PERITONITIS
PERMANENTLY
PERMISSIBLE
PERMISSIBLY
PERMUTATION
PERPETRATOR
PERPETUABLE
PERPETUALLY
PERSECUTION
PERSECUTRIX
PERSEVERING
PERSISTENCE
PERSISTENCY
PERSONALISM
PERSONALITY
PERSONALIZE
PERSONATION
PERSPECTIVE
PERSPICUITY
PERSPICUOUS
PERSPIRABLE
PERSUADABLE
PERSUASIBLE
PERTINACITY
PERTINENTLY
PERTURBABLE
PERTURBANCE
PERVERTIBLE
PESSIMISTIC
PESTIFEROUS
PESTILENTLY
PETITIONARY
PETRIFIABLE
PETROGRAPHY
PETROLOGIST
PETTIFOGGER
PHAGEDAENIC
PHANTOMATIC
PHARISAICAL
PHARYNGITIS
PHENOMENISM
PHENOMENIST
PHILATELIST
PHILHELLENE
PHILOLOGIST
PHILOLOGIAN
PHILOMATHIC
PHILOSOPHER
PHILOSOPHIC
PHOSPHORATE
PHOSPHORIZE
PHOSPHOROUS
PHOTOCHROMY
PHOTOGLYPHY
PHOTOGRAPHY
PHOTOMETRIC
PHOTOSPHERE
PHRASEOLOGY
PHTHIRIASIS

PHYLACTERIC
PHYLLOTAXIS
PHYSIOGNOMY
PHYSIOLATRY
PHYSIOLOGIC
PHYTOGRAPHY
PHYTOLOGIST
PICROTOXINE
PICTORIALLY
PICTURESQUE
PIETISTICAL
PINNATISECT
PIPERACEOUS
PIPISTRELLE
PIRATICALLY
PISCATORIAL
PISCIVOROUS
PITEOUSNESS
PITIFULNESS
PLACABILITY
PLAGIOSTOME
PLAINTIVELY
PLANETARIUM
PLANETOIDAL
PLANISPHERE
PLANTIGRADE
PLATINOTYPE
PLAYFULNESS
PLEASURABLE
PLEASURABLY
PLEBEIANISM
PLEBEIANIZE
PLEISTOCENE
PLENARINESS
PLENIPOTENT
PLENTEOUSLY
PLENTIFULLY
PLETHORICAL
PLEURITICAL
PLIABLENESS
PLOUGHSHARE
PLURIPAROUS
PLUTOCRATIC
PLUVIOMETER
PNEUMOMETER
PNEUMONITIS
POCOCURANTE
PODOPHYLLIN
POINTEDNESS
POISONOUSLY
POLARIMETER
POLARISCOPE
POLARIZABLE
POLEMICALLY
POLITICALLY
POLTROONERY
POLYCARPOUS
POLYCHROMIC
POLYGASTRIC
POLYGENESIS
POLYMORPHIC
POLYONYMOUS
POLYPHONISM
POLYPHONIST
POLYPLASTIC
POLYRHIZOUS
POLYSPOROUS
POLYTECHNIC
POMEGRANATE
POMPELMOOSE

POMPOUSNESS
PONDEROSITY
PONDEROUSLY
PONTIFICATE
PORNOGRAPHY
PORPHYRITIC
PORTABILITY
PORTMANTEAU
PORTRAITURE
POSSIBILITY
POSTERIORLY
POSTULATORY
POTENTIALLY
POWERLESSLY
PRACTICABLE
PRACTICABLY
PRACTICALLY
PRAGMATICAL
PRAYERFULLY
PREAUDIENCE
PRECEPTRESS
PRECIPITANT
PRECIPITATE
PRECIPITOUS
PRECISENESS
PRECOGNOSCE
PRECONCEIVE
PRECONTRACT
PREDECESSOR
PREDICAMENT
PREDICATION
PREDICATIVE
PREDICATORY
PREDOMINANT
PREDOMINATE
PREHENSILE
PREHISTORIC
PREJUDGMENT
PREJUDICATE
PREJUDICIAL
PRELATESHIP
PRELIBATION
PRELIMINARY
PREMATURELY
PREMATURITY
PREMEDITATE
PREMIERSHIP
PREMONITION
PREMONITORY
PREOCCUPIED
PREPARATION
PREPARATIVE
PREPARATORY
PREPOSITION
PREPOSITIVE
PREROGATIVE
PRESAGEMENT
PRESENTABLE
PRESENTNESS
PRESERVABLE
PRESUMPTION
PRESUMPTIVE
PRETENDEDLY
PRETENTIOUS
PRETERITION
PRETERITIVE
PREVALENTLY
PREVENTABLE
PRICKLINESS
PRIESTCRAFT

PRIMATESHIP
PRIMIGENIAL
PRIMITIVELY
PRINCIPALLY
PRISMATICAL
PRIVATIVELY
PROBABILITY
PROBATIONER
PROBLEMATIC
PROBOSCIDES
PROCONSULAR
PROCREATION
PROCTORSHIP
PROCURATION
PROCUREMENT
PRODIGALITY
PROFANATION
PROFANENESS
PROFICIENCY
PROFUSENESS
PROGNATHISM
PROGNATHOUS
PROGRESSION
PROGRESSIVE
PROHIBITION
PROHIBITIVE
PROHIBITORY
PROLEGOMENA
PROLEPTICAL
PROLETARIAN
PROMINENTLY
PROMISCUOUS
PROMISINGLY
PROMPTITUDE
PROMULGATOR
PRONOUNCING
PROPAGATION
PROPAGATIVE
PROPHETICAL
PROPINQUITY
PROPITIABLE
PROPITIATOR
PROPOSITION
PROPRIETARY
PROPRIETRIX
PROPRIETIES
PROROGATION
PROSAICALLY
PROSECUTION
PROSECUTRIX
PROSELYTISM
PROSELYTIZE
PROSENCHYMA
PROSOPOPEIA
PROSPECTION
PROSPECTIVE
PROSTITUTOR
PROSTRATION
PROTECTORAL
PROTECTRESS
PROTOMARTYR
PROTONOTARY
PROTRACTILE
PROTRACTION
PROTRACTIVE
PROTRUSIBLE
PROTUBERANT
PROTUBERATE
PROVIDENTLY
PROVOCATION

PROVOCATIVE
PROVOKINGLY
PROVOSTSHIP
PROXIMATELY
PRUDISHNESS
PRURIGINOUS
PSALMODICAL
PSEUDOPODIA
PSITTACEOUS
PSYCHOLOGIC
PTERIDOLOGY
PTERODACTYL
PUBLICATION
PUBLISHABLE
PUERILITIES
PULVERULENT
PULVINIFORM
PUNCTILIOUS
PUNCTUALITY
PUNCTUATION
PURCHASABLE
PURGATIVELY
PURGATORIAL
PURGATORIAN
PURITANICAL
PURPOSELESS
PUTRIDINOUS
PUTRIFIABLE
PUTRESCENCE
PUTRESCIBLE
PYRAMIDACLE
PYRAMIDALLY
PYROTECHNIC
PYTHAGORIAN
PYTHAGORISM

Q

QUACKSALVER
QUADRENNIAL
QUADRILLION
QUALITATIVE
QUARRELSOME
QUERULOUSLY
QUESTIONARY
QUIBBLINGLY
QUICKSILVER
QUIESCENTLY
QUINCUNCIAL
QUINTILLION
QUIVERINGLY

R

RALLENTANDO
RAPACIOUSLY
RAPSCALLION
RAPTUROUSLY
RAREFACTION
RATIOCINATE
RATIONALISM
RATIONALIST
RATIONALITY
RAVISHINGLY
REACTIONARY
REACTIONIST
READABILITY
READMISSION

REALIZATION
REANIMATION
REASSERTION
REASSURANCE
RECANTATION
RECELEBRATE
RECEPTIVITY
RECIPROCATE
RECIPROCITY
RECLAIMABLE
RECLAMATION
RECLINATION
RECOMMENDER
RECONNOITRE
RECONSTRUCT
RECOVERABLE
RECREMENTAL
RECRIMINATE
RECRUITMENT
RECTANGULAR
RECTIFIABLE
RECTILINEAL
RECTILINEAR
RECTISERIAL
RECUMBENTLY
REDDISHNESS
REDISCOVERY
REDOUBTABLE
REDRESSIBLE
REDUPLICATE
REDUNDANTLY
REFERENTIAL
REFLECTIBLE
REFLEXIVELY
REFORMATION
REFORMATIVE
REFORMATORY
REFRACTABLE
REFRAINMENT
REFRANGIBLE
REFRESHMENT
REFRIGERANT
REFRIGERATE
REFULGENTLY
REGARDFULLY
REGIMENTALS
REGRETFULLY
REGRETTABLE
REGURGITATE
REINSERTION
REINTRODUCE
REITERATION
REITERATIVE
RELIABILITY
RELIGIONISM
RELIGIONIST
RELIGIOUSLY
RELUCTANTLY
REMEMBRANCE
REMIGRATION
REMINISCENT
REMONSTRANT
REMONSTRATE
RETTORSELESS
REMUNERABLE
RENAISSANCE
REPENTANTLY
REPLACEMENT
REPLENISHER
REPLEVIABLE

REPLICATION
REPORTORIAL
REPREHENDER
REPRESENTER
REPRESSIBLE
REPRESSIBLY
REPROACHFUL
REPROBATION
REPROVINGLY
REPUDIATION
REPUGNANTLY
REPULSIVELY
REQUIREMENT
REQUISITION
RESCINDMENT
RESEMBLANCE
RESENTFULLY
RESERVATION
RESIDENTIAL
RESIGNATION
RESPECTABLE
RESPECTABLY
RESPIRATION
RESPIRATORY
RESPLENDENT
RESPONDENCE
RESPONDENCY
RESPONSIBLE
RESPONSIBLY
RESPONSIONS
RESTITUTION
RESTIVENESS
RESTORATION
RESTORATIVE
RESTRICTION
RESTRICTIVE
RESUSCITATE
RETALIATION
RETALIATIVE
RETALIATORY
RETARDATION
RETARDATIVE
RETENTIVELY
RETICULARLY
RETICULATED
RETIREDNESS
RETRACTABLE
RETRANSLATE
RETRIBUTION
RETRIBUTIVE
RETRIBUTORY
RETRIEVABLE
RETRIEVABLY
RETROACTIVE
REVERBERANT
REVERBERATE
REVERENTIAL
REVERSELESS
REVERSIONER
REVOLTINGLY
RHABDOMANCY
RHAPSODICAL
RHETORICIAN
RHINOCLERIAL
RIFACIMENTO
RIGHTEOUSLY
RIOTOUSNESS
RISIBLENESS
RITUALISTIC
RODOMONTADE

ROMANTICISM
ROMANTICIST
ROMPISHNESS
ROSICRUCIAN
RUBEFACIENT
RUDIMENTARY
RURIDECANAL
RUSTICATION

S

SABBATARIAN
SACRAMENTAL
SACRIFICIAL
SADDUCEEISM
SAGACIOUSLY
SALINOMETER
SALVABILITY
SANSKRITIST
SAPONACEOUS
SARACENICAL
SARCASTICAL
SARCOMATOUS
SARCOPHAGUS
SATIRICALLY
SATURNALIAN
SAVOURINESS
SAXIFRAGOUS
SCAFFOLDING
SCALPRIFORM
SCANDINAVIA
SCAPULARIES
SCENOGRAPHY
SCEPTICALLY
SCHOLARSHIP
SCHOLIASTIC
SCHOTTISCHE
SCIATICALLY
SCINTILLANT
SCINTILLATE
SCIRRHOSITY
SCLEROBASIC
SCLEROMETER
SCLEROTITIS
SCOLOPENDRA
SCOPIFEROUS
SCOUNDRELLY
SCRAGGINESS
SCRUTINIZER
SEARCHINGLY
SECONDARILY
SECONDARIES
SECRETARIAL
SECTIONALLY
SECULARNESS
SEDENTARILY
SEDIMENTARY
SEDITIONARY
SEDITIOUSLY
SEDUCTIVELY
SEGREGATION
SEIGNIORAGE
SEIGNIORIAL
SEISMOGRAPH
SEISMOMETER
SIESMOSCOPE
SIESMOMETRY
SELFISHNESS
SEMIOGRAPHY

SEMPITERNAL	SOPHISTICAL	SUBCONTRACT
SENSATIONAL	SORROWFULLY	SUBCONTRARY
SENSELESSLY	SOTERIOLOGY	SUBDEACONRY
SENSIBILITY	SOTTISHNESS	SUBDIVISION
SENSIFEROUS	SOVEREIGNTY	SUBDOMINANT
SENSITIVELY	SPARKLINGLY	SUBGLOBULAR
SENSITIVITY	SPATHACEOUS	SUBJUGATION
SENTENTIOUS	SPECTACULAR	SUBJUNCTIVE
SENTIMENTAL	SPECTATRESS	SUBLIMATION
SENTINELLED	SPECTROLOGY	SUBLIMATORY
SEPTICAEMIA	SPECULATION	SUBLIMENESS
SEPTIFEROUS	SPECULATIVE	SUBMERGENCE
SEQUESTERED	SPENDTHRIFT	SUBMETALLIC
SEQUESTRATE	SPHERICALLY	SUBMULTIPLE
SERICULTURE	SPHEROMETER	SUBORDINACY
SERIOUSNESS	SPICIFEROUS	SUBORDINATE
SERVICEABLE	SPINIFEROUS	SUBORNATION
SERVICEABLY	SPONSORSHIP	SUBSCAPULAR
SESQUIPEDAL	SPONTANEITY	SUBSENSIBLE
SEVENTEENTH	SPONTANEOUS	SUBSEQUENCE
SEXAGESIMAL	SPRINGINESS	SUBSERVIENT
SEXENNIALLY	SPUMIFEROUS	SUBSISTENCE
SHADOWINESS	SQUALIDNESS	SUBSTANTIAL
SHALLOWNESS	SQUEAMISHLY	SUBSTANTIVE
SHAMELESSLY	SQUIREARCHY	SUBTILENESS
SHAPELINESS	STALACTICAL	SUBTRACTION
SHAREHOLDER	STALACTITIC	SUBTROPICAL
SHELTERLESS	STAPHYLOSIS	SUCCEDANEUM
SHEPHERDESS	STARCHINESS	SUCCOURLESS
SHERIFFALTY	STATELINESS	SUFFICIENCY
SHERIFFSHIP	STATISTICAL	SUFFOCATING
SHIFTLESSLY	STEADFASTLY	SUFFOCATION
SHIVERINGLY	STEEPLEJACK	SUFFOCATIVE
SHOPKEEPING	STENOGRAPHY	SUFFRAGETTE
SHORTCOMING	STEPBROTHER	SUFFUMIGATE
SHOWERINESS	STEREOSCOPE	SUGGESTIBLE
SHRINKINGLY	STEREOTROPE	SUITABILITY
SHRUBBINESS	STEREOTYPED	SULPHURATOR
SHUFFLINGLY	STEREOTYPER	SULPHUREOUS
SIDEROSCOPE	STEREOTYPIC	SUMMERSAULT
SIGHTLINESS	STETHOMETER	SUMPTUOUSLY
SIGNIFICANT	STETHOSCOPE	SUPERABOUND
SILVERSMITH	STETHOSCOPY	SUPERFETATE
SIMPERINGLY	STEWARDSHIP	SUPERFICIAL
SINGULARITY	STICHOMANCY	SUPERFICIES
SINISTRALLY	STICHOMETRY	SUPERFLUITY
SINISTRORSE	STICKLEBACK	SUPERFLUOUS
SINLESSNESS	STIGMATICAL	SUPERIMPOSE
SKETCHINESS	STIMULATING	SUPERINDUCE
SKILFULNESS	STIMULATION	SUPERINTEND
SLAUGHTERER	STIMULATIVE	SUPERIORESS
SLEEPLESSLY	STINTEDNESS	SUPERIORITY
SLENDERNESS	STIPENDIARY	SUPERJACENT
SLIGHTINGLY	STIPULATION	SUPERLATIVE
SLUMBERLESS	STOCKBROKER	SUPERLUNARY
SOCIABILITY	STOCKHOLDER	SUPERNATANT
SOCINIANISM	STRAIGHTWAY	SUPERSCRIBE
SOJOURNMENT	STRAMINEOUS	SUPERSUBTLE
SOLANACEOUS	STRANGENESS	SUPERVISION
SOLDATESQUE	STRANGULATE	SUPERVISORY
SOLDIERSHIP	STRATEGETIC	SUPPLIANTLY
SOLEMNITIES	STRATEGICAL	SUPPORTABLE
SOLILOQUIES	STRENUOUSLY	SUPPORTABLY
SOLILOQUIZE	STRINGENTLY	SUPPOSITION
SOLMIZATION	STRINGINESS	SUPPRESSION
SOLUBLENESS	STUDENTSHIP	SUPPRESSIVE
SOLVABILITY	STUNTEDNESS	SUPPURATION
SOMEWHITHER	STYLISHNESS	SUPPURATIVE
SOMNAMBULIC	STYLOGRAPHY	SUPRACOSTAL
SOOTHSAYING	SUBAXILLARY	SUPRAORBITS

SUPRASPINAL
SURGEONSHIP
SURREBUTTER
SURROUNDING
SUSCEPTIBLE
SUSCEPTIBLY
SWARTHINESS
SWEEPSTAKES
SWINISHNESS
SYCOPHANTIC
SYLLABARIUM
SYLLABICATE
SYLLOGISTIC
SYMMETRICAL
SYMPATHETIC
SYMPATHIZER
SYMPHONIOUS
SYMPOSIARCH
SYMPTOMATIC
SYNCHRONISM
SYNCHRONIZE
SYNCHRONOUS
SYNCOPATION
SYNODICALLY
SYNTACTICAL
SYSTEMATIZE

T

TABEFACTION
TACHYGRAPHY
TACITURNITY
TALKATIVELY
TANGIBILITY
TASTELESSLY
TAUTOLOGIST
TAUTOLOGIZE
TAXABLENESS
TEARFULNESS
TEDIOUSNESS
TEETOTALLER
TEETOTALISM
TEGUMENTARY
TELEGRAMMIC
TELEGRAPHIC
TELESCOPIST
TEMERARIOUS
TEMPERATELY
TEMPERATURE
TEMPESTUOUS
TEMPORALITY
TEMPORARILY
TEMPORIZING
TENABLENESS
TENEBROSITY
TENEMENTARY
TENTATIVELY
TEPEFACTION
TEREBRATULA
TERMINATION
TERMINATIVE
TERMINOLOGY
TERRAQUEOUS
TERRESTRIAL
TERRICOLOUS
TERRIGENOUS
TERRITORIAL
TESSELLATED
TESTAMENTAL

TESTICULATE
TETRAGYNOUS
TETRAHEDRAL
TETRAHEDRON
TETRAMEROUS
TETRANDROUS
THALLOPHYTE
THANATOLOGY
THANKLESSLY
THANKSGIVER
THAUMATROPE
THAUMATURGE
THAUMATURGY
THEATRICALS
THENCEFORTH
THEODOLITIC
THEOLOGIZER
THEOPNEUSTY
THEOREMATIC
THEORETICAL
THEOSOPHIST
THEOTECHNIC
THEREABOUTS
THEREWITHAL
THERMOMETER
THERMOSCOPE
THITHERWARD
THOUGHTLESS
THRASONICAL
THREADINESS
THREATENING
THRIFTINESS
THRILLINGLY
THUNDERBOLT
TITILLATION
TITILLATIVE
TOBACCONIST
TONSILLITIS
TOPOGRAPHER
TOPOGRAPHIC
TORMENTILLA
TORPESCENCE
TORTURINGLY
TOTIPALMATE
TOTTERINGLY
TOXOPHILITE
TRACHEOTOME
TRACHEOTOMY
TRACKLESSLY
TRADITIONAL
TRADUCEMENT
TRAFFICLESS
TRAGEDIENNE
TRANSACTION
TRANSALPINE
TRANSCRIBER
TRANSFERRER
TRANSFIXION
TRANSFLUENT
TRANSFUSION
TRANSFUSIVE
TRANSIENTLY
TRANSLATION
TRANSLATORY
TRANSLUCENT
TRANSMARINE
TRANSMITTAL
TRANSMITTER
TRANSPARENT
TRANSPORTED

TRANSPORTER
TRANSVERSAL
TRAPEZIFORM
TRAPEZOIDAL
TREACHEROUS
TREASONABLE
TREASONABLY
TREMBLINGLY
TREMULOUSLY
TREPIDATION
TRIANGULATE
TRIBULATION
TRIBUNICIAN
TRIBUNITIAL
TRIBUTARILY
TRIBUTARIES
TRICAPSULAR
TRICKSINESS
TRICOLOURED
TRICUSPIDAL
TRIENNIALLY
TRIFOLIATED
TRIGEMINOUS
TRIMESTRIAL
TRINITARIAN
TRIPERSONAL
TRIPETALOUS
TRIPHYLLOUS
TRIQUETROUS
TRISEPALOUS
TRISTICHOUS
TRISYLLABLE
TRITURATION
TRITURATURE
TRIUMVIRATE
TRIVIALNESS
TROCHOIDALS
TROGLODYTIC
TROUBLESOME
TRUCULENTLY
TRUEHEARTED
TRUNCHEONED
TRUNCHEONER
TRUSTEESHIP
TRUSTWORTHY
TUBERCULATE
TUBERCULINE
TUBERCULIZE
TUBERCULOSE
TUBERCULOUS
TUMEFACTION
TUNABLENESS
TURBULENTLY
TURGESCENCE
TYPOGRAPHER
TYPOGRAPHIC
TYRANNICIDE
TYRANNOUSLY

U

ULTRAMARINE
UNABOLISHED
UNADVISABLE
UNADVISABLY
UNADVISEDLY
UNALTERABLE
UNAMBIGUOUS
UNAMBITIOUS

UNAPOSTOLIC
UNASPIRATED
UNBEFITTING
UNBLEMISHED
UNCANONICAL
UNCEASINGLY
UNCERTAINTY
UNCHRISTIAN
UNCIVILIZED
UNCOMMITTED
UNCONCEALED
UNCONCERNED
UNCONDEMNED
UNCONFIRMED
UNCONNECTED
UNCONSCIOUS
UNCONTESTED
UNCONVERTED
UNCORRECTED
UNCOURTEOUS
UNCOUTHNESS
UNDAUNTEDLY
UNDEFINABLY
UNDERCHARGE
UNDERGROUND
UNDERGROWTH
UNDERSTROKE
UNDERTAKING
UNDESERVING
UNDESIRABLE
UNDEVIATING
UNDIGNIFIED
UNDISGUISED
UNDISTURBED
UNDOUBTEDLY
UNDUTIFULLY
UNEMOTIONAL
UNENDURABLE
UNENLIVENED
UNESSENTIAL
UNEXERCISED
UNEXHAUSTED
UNFAILINGLY
UNFALTERING
UNFEELINGLY
UNFEIGNEDLY
UNFERMENTED
UNFLINCHING
UNFORGIVING
UNFORGOTTEN
UNFORTUNATE
UNFULFILLED
UNFURNISHED
UNGALLANTLY
UNGENTEELLY
UNGODLINESS
UNGUARDEDLY
UNGUICULATE
UNHARBOURED
UNHEALTHFUL
UNHEALTHILY
UNHEEDFULLY
UNHUMANISED
UNICELLULAR
UNIFICATION
UNIFORMNESS
UNIMPORTANT
UNINHABITED
UNIPERSONAL
UNIPETALOUS

UNIVALVULAR
UNIVERSALLY
UNKNOWINGLY
UNLUCKINESS
UNMANLINESS
UNMEANINGLY
UNMELODIOUS
UNMINDFULLY
UNMITIGABLE
UNMITIGATED
UNMURMURING
UNMUTILATED
UNNATURALLY
UNNECESSARY
UNOBSERVANT
UNOBSERVING
UNOBTRUSIVE
UNOFFENDING
UNORGANISED
UNPALATABLE
UNPARAGONED
UNPATRIOTIC
UNPERFORMED
UNPERVERTED
UNPOPULARLY
UNPRACTICAL
UNPRACTISED
UNPRESUMING
UMPROMISING
UNPROTECTED
UNPUBLISHED
UNQUALIFIED
UNREADINESS
UNREASONING
UNRECLAIMED
UNREDRESSED
UNRELENTING
UNREMITTING
UNREPENTANT
UNRESISTING
UNRIGHTEOUS
UNSATISFIED
UNSEAWORTHY
UNSECTARIAN
UNSENTENCED
UNSHRINKING
UNSMIRCHING
UNSOLICITED
UNSOUNDNESS
UNSPEAKABLE
UNSPEAKABLY
UNSPECIFIED
UNSPIRITUAL
UNSUPPORTED
UNSURPASSED
UNSUSPECTED
UNTARNISHED
UNTEACHABLE
UNTHINKABLE
UNTHRIFTILY
UNTINCTURED
UNTRACTABLE
UNTRAVELLED
UNUTTERABLE
UNUTTERABLY
UNVARNISHED
UNVERACIOUS
UNWARRANTED
UNWEDGEABLE
UNWHOLESOME

UNWILLINGLY
UNWITNESSED
UNWITTINGLY
UPHOLSTERER
URANOGRAPHY
URTICACEOUS
USELESSNESS
UTILITARIAN

V

VACCINATION
VACILLATING
VACILLATION
VAGABONDAGE
VAGABONDISM
VALEDICTION
VALEDICTORY
VARIABILITY
VARIEGATION
VARSOVIENNE
VASCULARITY
VATICINATOR
VELLICATION
VENDIBILITY
VENESECTION
VENTILATION
VENTRICULAR
VENTRILOQUY
VENTURESOME
VENTUROUSLY
VERACIOUSLY
VERBOSENESS
VERISIMILAR
VERMICULATE
VERMICULOUS
VERMIVOROUS
VERSATILELY
VERSATILITY
VERSICOLOUR
VERTEBRATED
VERTIGINOUS
VEXATIOUSLY
VICARIOUSLY
VICEREGENCY
VICEROYALTY
VICEROYSHIP
VICIOUSNESS
VICISSITUDE
VINAIGRETTE
VINCIBILITY
VINDICATION
VINDICATIVE
VINDICATORY
VINEGARETTE
VIOLONCELLO
VISCOUNTESS
VISIBLENESS
VISIONARIES
VITICULTURE
VITRESCENCE
VITRIFIABLE
VITUPERABLE
VITUPERATOR
VIVACIOUSLY
VIVISECTION
VOLCANICITY
VOLUBLENESS
VOLUNTARILY

VOLUNTARIES
VORACIOUSLY
VULCANICITY

W

WAGGISHNESS
WAKEFULNESS
WANDERINGLY
WARRANTABLY
WASHERWOMAN
WASPISHNESS
WAYWARDNESS
WEALTHINESS
WEARISOMELY
WEATHERMOST
WEIGHTINESS
WESLEYANISM
WESTERNMOST
WHEREABOUTS
WHERESOEVER
WHEREWITHAL
WHICHSOEVER
WHIMSICALLY

WHISKEYFIED
WHITSUNTIDE
WHOLESOMELY
WHOREMONGER
WILLINGNESS
WINDLESTRAW
WINSOMENESS
WISHFULNESS
WITENAGEMOT
WITHERINGLY
WITHSTANDER
WITLESSNESS
WOMANLINESS
WONDERFULLY
WONDERINGLY
WORKMANLIKE
WORKMANSHIP
WORLDLINESS
WORTHLESSLY

X

XANTHOPHYLL
XYLOGRAPHER

XYLOGRAPHIC
XYLOPHAGOUS
XYLOPHYLOUS

Y

YESTERNIGHT

Z

ZEALOUSNESS
ZINCIFEROUS
ZINCOGRAPHY
ZOANTHARIAN
ZOOMORPHISM
ZOROASTRIAN
ZYGODACTYLE
ZYMOTICALLY

TWELVE-LETTER WORDS

A

ABBREVIATION
ABBREVIATORY
ABOLITIONIST
ABORTIVENESS
ABSOLUTENESS
ABSORPTIVITY
ABSTEMIOUSLY
ABSTRACTEDLY
ABSTRACTEDNESS
ABSTRUSENESS
ACADEMICALLY
ACANTHACEOUS
ACCELERATION
ACCELERATIVE
ACCELERATORY
ACCENTUATION
ACCIDENTALLY
ACCOMMODATOR
ACCOMPLISHER
ACCOUCHEMENT
ACCUMULATION
ACCUMULATIVE
ACCURATENESS
ACHLAMYDEOUS
ACKNOWLEDGER
ACOUSTICALLY
ACQUAINTANCE
ACQUIESCENCE
ACROCEPHALIC
ACROSTICALLY
ADAPTABILITY
ADDER'S-TONGUE
ADDICTEDNESS
ADDITIONALLY
ADHESIVENESS
ADJUDICATION
ADJUNCTIVELY
ADMONITORIAL
ADORABLENESS
ADSCITITIOUS
ADULTERATION
ADULTEROUSLY
ADVANTAGEOUS
ADVENTITIOUS
ADVENTUREFUL
ADVOCATESHIP
AERODYNAMICS
AEROSIDERITE
AESTHETICISM
AETIOLOGICAL
AFFECTEDNESS
AFFECTIONATE
AFFLICTINGLY
AFTER-THOUGHT
AGALMATOLITE
AGAMOGENESIS
AGRICULTURAL
ALCOHOLMETER
ALEXIPHARMIC
ALIENABILITY
ALIMENTATION
ALKALESCENCE

ALLITERATION
ALLITERATIVE
ALLOMORPHISM
ALL-SAINTS' DAY
ALLUSIVENESS
ALMIGHTINESS
ALTERABILITY
AMALGAMATION
AMBASSADRESS
AMBIDEXTROUS
AMELIORATION
AMELIORATIVE
AMENABLENESS
AMICABLENESS
AMMONIAPHONE
AMORTIZATION
AMORTIZEMENT
AMPHICOELOUS
AMPHISTOMOUS
AMPHITHEATRE
AMYGDALOIDAL
ANABAPTISTIC
ANAESTHETIZE
ANALOGICALLY
ANALYTICALLY
ANAMORPHOSIS
ANAPODEICTIC
ANARTHROPODA
ANATHEMATIZE
ANATOMICALLY
ANEMOPHILOUS
ANGIOCARPOUS
ANGUILLIFORM
ANIMALCULINE
ANITROGENOUS
ANNIHILATION
ANNOMINATION
ANNOUNCEMENT
ANNUNCIATION
ANNUNCIATORY
ANOTHER-GUESS
ANTAGONISTIC
ANTARTHRITIC
ANTASTHMATIC
ANTEBRACHIAL
ANTECEDENTLY
ANTEDILUVIAN
ANTEMERIDIAN
ANTEPILEPTIC
ANTEPRANDIAL
ANTHELMINTIC
ANTHOCARPOUS
ANTHOLOGICAL
ANTHROPOGENY
ANTHROPOLOGY
ANTHROPOTOMY
ANTICIPATION
ANTICIPATIVE
ANTICIPATORY
ANTIDEMOCRAT
ANTIFRICTION
ANTIHYPNOTIC
ANTILEGOMENA
ANTI-MACASSAR
ANTIMONIATED

ANTIPATHETIC
ANTIPHRASTIC
ANTISTROPHIC
ANTITHEISTIC
ANTIVENEREAL
APHORISMATIC
APOSTROPHIZE
APPARITIONAL
APPENDICITIS
APPENDICULAR
APPERCEPTION
APPOGGIATURA
APPOSITIONAL
APPRAISEMENT
APPRECIATION
APPRECIATORY
APPREHENSION
APPREHENSIVE
APPROACHABLE
APPROPRIABLE
APPROPRIATOR
APPURTENANCE
ARBORESCENCE
ARBORIZATION
ARCHDEACONRY
ARCHIPELAGIC
ARCHITECTURE
ARGILLACEOUS
ARISTOCRATIC
ARISTOTELIAN
ARITHMETICAL
ARITHMOMETER
ARMOUR-BEARER
ARMOUR-PLATED
ARTICULATELY
ARTICULATION
ARTIFICIALLY
ARTIODACTYLE
ARTISTICALLY
ASH-WEDNESDAY
ASPHYXIATION
ASSASSINATOR
ASSEVERATION
ASSIMILATION
ASSIMILATIVE
ASTONISHMENT
ASTRINGENTLY
ASTROLOGICAL
ASYMMETRICAL
ASYMPTOTICAL
ATHEROMATOUS
ATTITUDINIZE
ATTORNEYSHIP
ATTRACTIVELY
ATTRIBUTABLE
AUGMENTATION
AUGMENTATIVE
AUSCULTATION
AUSPICIOUSLY
AUSTRALASIAN
AUTHENTICATE
AUTHENTICITY
AVANT-COURIER
AVARICIOUSLY
AVERRUNCATOR

B

BACCHANALIAN
BACHELORHOOD
BACHELORSHIP
BACKWARDNESS
BACTERIOLOGY
BALANCE-SHEET
BALANCE-WHEEL
BALLAD-MONGER
BARBETTE-SHIP
BATTERING-RAM
BATTLEMENTED
BEATIFICALLY
BEETLE-BROWED
BENEFACTRESS
BENEFICENTLY
BENEFICIALLY
BENEVOLENTLY
BEQUEATHABLE
BEQUEATHMENT
BESEECHINGLY
BESOTTEDNESS
BEWILDERMENT
BEWITCHINGLY
BIARTICULATE
BIBLIOGRAPHY
BIBLIOMANIAC
BIBLIOPOLIST
BICENTENNIAL
BILLINGSGATE
BIOGRAPHICAL
BLACK-CURRANT
BLACK-DRAUGHT
BLACKGUARDLY
BLACK-HEARTED
BLACK-MOUTHED
BLACK-PUDDING
BLAMABLENESS
BLANDISHMENT
BLAST-FURNACE
BLENNORRHOEA
BLISSFULNESS
BLISTER-STEEL
BLOOD-LETTING
BLOODSHEDDER
BLOOD-STAINED
BLOODTHIRSTY
BLUE-STOCKING
BOARDING-PIKE
BODY-SNATCHER
BOISTEROUSLY
BOLTING-CLOTH
BOOK-LEARNING
BOOK-SCORPION
BOOTLESSNESS
BOTTLE-HOLDER
BOW-COMPASSES
BOWLING-ALLEY
BOWLING-GREEN
BRACHYGRAPHY
BRACKISHNESS
BRANCHIOPODA
BRASS-FOUNDER
BREAST-PLOUGH
BREATHLESSLY
BREECH-LOADED
BREVIPENNATE
BRIDE-CHAMBER

BRIGADE-MAJOR
BRISTOL-BOARD
BRISTOL-BRICK
BRISTOL-PAPER
BROTHER-IN-LAW
BUCCANEERING
BUFFALO-CHIPS
BUFFLE-HEADED
BURDENSOMELY
BUREAUCRATIC
BURNING-GLASS
BURROWING-OWL
BUTTER-SCOTCH
BUTTERY-HATCH
BUZZARD-CLOCK

C

CABINET-MAKER
CACHINNATION
CADAVEROUSLY
CALABASH-TREE
CALAMITOUSLY
CALISTHENICS
CALLIGRAPHER
CALLIGRAPHIC
CALLISTHENIC
CALORESCENCE
CALUMNIATION
CALUMNIATORY
CALUMNIOUSLY
CALYCIFLORAL
CAMP-BEDSTEAD
CAMP-FOLLOWER
CANALICULATE
CANCELLARIAN
CANCELLATION
CANDLE-HOLDER
CANONIZATION
CANTABRIGIAN
CANTANKEROUS
CANTHARIDINE
CAPERCAILZIE
CAPITULATION
CAPPAGH-BROWN
CAPRICIOUSLY
CAPTIOUSNESS
CARBONACEOUS
CARDINAL-BIRD
CARELESSNESS
CARICATURIST
CARLOVINGIAN
CARPENTER-BEE
CARPET-BAGGER
CARPET-KNIGHT
CARRIAGEABLE
CARTE-BLANCHE
CARTHAGINIAN
CARTRIDGE-BOX
CASE-HARDENED
CATACHRESTIC
CATACOUSTICS
CATADIOPTRIC
CATALLACTICS
CATASTROPHIC
CATELECTRODE
CATTLE-PLAGUE
CAUSATIONISM
CAUTIOUSNESS

CEMENTITIOUS
CENSORIOUSLY
CENTENNIALLY
CENTIFOLIOUS
CENTUPLICATE
CEREMONIALLY
CEROPLASTICS
CHAIRMANSHIP
CHALCOGRAPHY
CHAMPIONSHIP
CHANCE-MEDLEY
CHAPLAINSHIP
CHAPTER-HOUSE
CHARACTERIZE
CHARLES'S-WAIN
CHARNEL-HOUSE
CHARTER-PARTY
CHARTOGRAPHY
CHASTISEMENT
CHAUVINISTIC
CHECKER-BOARD
CHEERFULNESS
CHEESEMONGER
CHEESE-PARING
CHEIROPODIST
CHEQUER-BOARD
CHERRY-BRANDY
CHERRY-LAUREL
CHERRY-PEPPER
CHIEF-JUSTICE
CHIEFTAINESS
CHILD-BEARING
CHILD-GROWING
CHILDISHNESS
CHIMERICALLY
CHIMNEY-PIECE
CHIMNEY-SHAFT
CHIMNEY-STACK
CHIMNEY-STALK
CHIMNEY-SWEEP
CHIROGRAPHER
CHIROGRAPHIC
CHIVALROUSLY
CHOLESTERINE
CHRESTOMATHY
CHRISTIANITY
CHRISTIANIZE
CHRISTMAS-BOX
CHRISTMAS-DAY
CHRISTMAS-EVE
CHRIST'S-THORN
CHROMATOLOGY
CHROMOSPHERE
CHRONOGRAPHY
CHRONOLOGIST
CHRONOMETRIC
CHRYSOPHANIC
CHURCHWARDEN
CHURLISHNESS
CHYLIFACTIVE
CIRCUITOUSLY
CIRCUMCISION
CIRCUMFLUENT
CIRCUMFUSION
CIRCUMGYRATE
CIRCUMJACENT
CIRCUMNUTATE
CIRCUMSCRIBE
CIRCUMSTANCE
CIVILIZATION

CLAIRVOYANCE
CLAIRVOYANTE
CLANNISHNESS
CLASSICALISM
CLASSIFIABLE
CLEAR-SIGHTED
CLEISTOGAMIC
CLIMATICALLY
CLINKER-BUILT
CLOTHES-HORSE
CLOUD-KISSING
CLOVEN-FOOTED
CLOVEN-HOOFED
CLOWNISHNESS
COACHMANSHIP
COALITIONIST
COAL-MEASURES
CODIFICATION
COELENTERATE
COENESTHESIS
COHABITATION
COHESIVENESS
COINCIDENTLY
COLEOPTEROUS
COLLABORATOR
COLLATERALLY
COLLECTIVELY
COLLECTIVISM
COLLECTIVIST
COLLECTORATE
COLLIGUATIVE
COLLOQUIALLY
COLOGNE-EARTH
COLONIZATION
COLOQUINTIDA
COMMEMORABLE
COMMEMORATOR
COMMENCEMENT
COMMENDATION
COMMENDATORY
COMMENSALISM
COMMENSURATE
COMMENTATION
COMMENTATIVE
COMMERCIALLY
COMMISERATOR
COMMISSARIAL
COMMISSARIAT
COMMISSIONED
COMMISSIONER
COMMODIOUSLY
COMMONWEALTH
COMMUNICABLE
COMMUNICABLY
COMMUNICATOR
COMPELLATION
COMPENSATION
COMPENSATIVE
COMPENSATORY
COMPLACENTLY
COMPLAISANCE
COMPLEMENTAL
COMPLETENESS
COMPLEXIONAL
COMPLEXIONED
COMPLICATION
COMPLICATIVE
COMPLIMENTER
COMPOSEDNESS
COMPREHENDER

COMPRESSIBLE
COMPULSIVELY
COMPUNCTIOUS
COMPURGATION
CONCENTRATED
CONCHIFEROUS
CONCHOLOGIST
CONCILIATION
CONCILIATORY
CONCLAMATION
CONCLUSIVELY
CONCOMITANCE
CONCOMITANCY
CONCORDANTLY
CONCREMATION
CONCRESCENCE
CONCRETENESS
CONCUPISCENT
CONCURRENTLY
CONDEMNATION
CONDEMNATORY
CONDENSATION
CONFABULATOR
CONFECTIONER
CONFERENTIAL
CONFESSIONAL
CONFIDENTIAL
CONFIRMATION
CONFIRMATIVE
CONFIRMATORY
CONFISCATION
CONFISCATORY
CONFORMATION
CONFOUNDEDLY
CONFUCIANISM
CONGENIALITY
CONGLOBATION
CONGLOMERATE
CONGLUTINATE
CONGRATULANT
CONGRATULATE
CONGREGATION
CONNUBIALITY
CONSCIONABLE
CONSCRIPTION
CONSECRATION
CONSENTIENCE
CONSEQUENTLY
CONSERVATION
CONSERVATISM
CONSERVATIVE
CONSERVATORY
CONSIDERABLE
CONSIDERABLY
CONSIGNATION
CONSISTENTLY
CONSISTORIAL
CONSOCIATION
CONSOLE-TABLE
CONSOLIDATOR
CONSTABULARY
CONSTIPATION
CONSTITUENCY
CONSTITUTION
CONSTITUTIVE
CONSTRICTION
CONSTRICTIVE
CONSTRINGENT
CONSTRUCTION
CONSTRUCTIVE

CONSULTATION
CONSULTATIVE
CONSUMMATELY
CONSUMMATION
CONSUMMATIVE
CONTABESCENT
CONTAGIOUSLY
CONTAMINABLE
CONTEMPLATOR
CONTEMPORARY
CONTEMPTIBLE
CONTEMPTIBLY
CONTEMPTUOUS
CONTERMINOUS
CONTESTATION
CONTIGUOUSLY
CONTINGENTLY
CONTINUATION
CONTINUOUSLY
CONTRACTEDLY
CONTRACTIBLE
CONTRADICTER
CONTRAPUNTAL
CONTRARINESS
CONTRARIWISE
CONTRIBUTION
CONTRIBUTIVE
CONTRIBUTORY
CONTRITENESS
CONTROLLABLE
CONTROVERTER
CONTUMACIOUS
CONTUMELIOUS
CONVALESCENT
CONVECTIVELY
CONVENIENTLY
CONVENTICLER
CONVENTIONAL
CONVERSANTLY
CONVERSATION
CONVEXO-PLANE
CONVEYANCING
CONVINCINGLY
CONVIVIALIST
CONVIVIALITY
CONVULSIONAL
CONVULSIVELY
CO-ORDINATELY
CO-ORDINATION
CO-ORDINATIVE
COPROPHAGOUS
COPULATIVELY
COPYING-PRESS
COQUETTISHLY
CORALLACEOUS
CO-RESPONDENT
CORN-EXCHANGE
CORN-MARIGOLD
COROLLACEOUS
CORPORALSHIP
CORPOREALISM
CORPOREALIST
CORPOREALITY
CORPSE-CANDLE
CORRADIATION
CORRECTIONAL
CORRELATABLE
CORROBORATOR
COSMOGRAPHER
COSMOGRAPHIC

COSMOLOGICAL
COSMOPLASTIC
COSMOPOLITAN
COSTERMONGER
COTYLEDONARY
COTYLEDONOUS
COUNCIL-BOARD
COUNSELLABLE
COUNTENANCER
COUNTER-AGENT
COUNTERCHARM
COUNTERCHECK
COUNTER-FORCE
COUNTER-MARCH
COUNTERPOINT
COUNTERPOISE
COUNTER-PROOF
COUNTERSCARP
COUNTER-TENOR
COUNTERWEIGH
COUNTRY-DANCE
COUNTRYWOMAN
COURAGEOUSLY
COURT-MARTIAL
COURT-PLASTER
COUSIN-GERMAN
COVETOUSNESS
COWARDLINESS
COXCOMICALLY
CRACK-BRAINED
CRANIOLOGIST
CREDIBLENESS
CREMATIONIST
CRENELLATION
CRITICIZABLE
CROSS-EXAMINE
CROSS-GRAINED
CROSS-PURPOSE
CRYPTOGAMOUS
CRYPTOGRAPHY
CUCKING-STOOL
CULPABLENESS
CUPPING-GLASS
CUPULIFEROUS
CURLING-IRONS
CURLING-TONGS
CURLING-STONE
CURRANT-JELLY
CURVIROSTRAL
CUSTARD-APPLE
CYCLOSTOMOUS
CYLINDRIFORM

D

DACTYLIOLOGY
DACTYLORHIZA
DAMNABLENESS
DANGER-SIGNAL
DEAMBULATORY
DEATH-WARRANT
DEBILITATING
DEBILITATION
DECAPITATION
DECASYLLABIC
DECENTRALIZE
DECIPHERABLE
DECIPHERMENT
DECISIVENESS

DECLINOMETER
DECOLORATION
DECOMPOSABLE
DECONSECRATE
DECREASINGLY
DECREPITNESS
DECRUSTATION
DEDICATORIAL
DEDUCIBILITY
DEER-STALKING
DEFAMATORILY
DEFINITENESS
DEFINITIONAL
DEFINITIVELY
DEFLAGRATION
DEFORCIATION
DEFORMEDNESS
DEFRAUDATION
DEGENERATELY
DEGENERATION
DEJECTEDNESS
DELIBERATELY
DELIBERATION
DELIBERATIVE
DELICATENESS
DELIGHTFULLY
DELIMITATION
DELIQUESCENT
DELITESCENCE
DELITESCENCY
DELUSIVENESS
DEMONIACALLY
DEMONOLOGIST
DEMONSTRABLE
DEMONSTRABLY
DEMONSTRATOR
DEMORALIZING
DENATURALIZE
DENDROLOGIST
DENOMINATION
DENOMINATIVE
DENOUNCEMENT
DENTICULATED
DENTIROSTRAL
DENUNCIATION
DENUNCIATORY
DENUNCIATIVE
DEONTOLOGIST
DEPARTMENTAL
DEPOPULATION
DEPRAVEDNESS
DEPRECIATION
DEPRECIATIVE
DEPRECIATORY
DEPRESSINGLY
DERIVATIONAL
DERIVATIVELY
DERMATOPHYTE
DESCENSIONAL
DESIDERATIVE
DESIRABILITY
DESOLATENESS
DESPAIRINGLY
DESPITEFULLY
DESPOLIATION
DESPONDENTLY
DESPOTICALLY
DESQUAMATION
DESQUAMATIVE
DESQUAMATORY

DESSERT-SPOON
DESTRUCTIBLE
DESULPHURIZE
DESULPHURATE
DESYNONYMIZE
DETERMINABLE
DETERMINATOR
DETERMINEDLY
DETHRONEMNET
DETONIZATION
DETRUNCATION
DEUTEROPATHY
DEUTEROSCOPY
DEVILISHNESS
DEVIL-MAY-CARE
DEVOTIONALLY
DEXTRO-GYRATE
DIABOLICALLY
DIAGRAMMATIC
DIALECTICIAN
DIALECTOLOGY
DIALOGICALLY
DIAMAGNETISM
DIAMOND-DRILL
DIAPHANOUSLY
DIATOMACEOUS
DIATONICALLY
DIBRANCHIATE
DICHROSCOPIC
DICTATORSHIP
DIDACTICALLY
DIETETICALLY
DIFFERENTIAL
DIGRESSIONAL
DIGRESSIVELY
DIJUDICATION
DILACERATION
DILAPIDATION
DILATABILITY
DILATORINESS
DILETTANTISM
DIMINISHABLE
DIMINUTIVELY
DIPHTHERITIC
DIPHTHONGIZE
DIPLOMATICAL
DIRECTORSHIP
DISADVANTAGE
DISAFFECTION
DISAGGREGATE
DISAGREEABLE
DISAGREEABLY
DISAGREEMENT
DISALLOWABLE
DISALLOWANCE
DISANNULMENT
DISAPPOINTED
DISASSOCIATE
DISASTROUSLY
DISBURSEMENT
DISCERNINGLY
DISCIPLESHIP
DISCIPLINARY
DISCOMFITURE
DISCOMMODITY
DISCOMPOSURE
DISCONSOLATE
DISCONTENTED
DISCORDANTLY
DISCOUNTABLE

DISCOURAGING
DISCOURTEOUS
DISCOVERABLE
DISCREETNESS
DISCRETIONAL
DISCRETIVELY
DISCRIMINATE
DISCURSIVELY
DISDAINFULLY
DISEASEDNESS
DISEMBARRASS
DISEMBELLISH
DISENCHANTER
DISENDOWMENT
DISESTABLISH
DISFRANCHISE
DISGORGEMENT
DISGUISEMENT
DISGUSTINGLY
DISINFECTANT
DISINFECTION
DISINGENUOUS
DISINTEGRATE
DISINTERMENT
DISLODGEMENT
DISOBEDIENCE
DISORGANIZER
DISPAUPERIZE
DISPENSATION
DISPENSATORY
DISPIRITEDLY
DISPLACEABLE
DISPLACEMENT
DISPLEASEDLY
DISPUTATIOUS
DISQUISITION
DISQUISITORY
DISREGARDFUL
DISREPUTABLE
DISREPUTABLY
DISSATISFIED
DISSEMINATOR
DISSENTERISM
DISSERTATION
DISSEVERANCE
DISSIMILARLY
DISSIMULATOR
DISSOCIATION
DISSUASIVELY
DISSYLLABISM
DISTILLATION
DISTILLATORY
DISTINCTNESS
DISTRACTEDLY
DISTRAINABLE
DISTRIBUTION
DISTRIBUTIVE
DITHEISTICAL
DIVARICATION
DIVISIBILITY
DOCTRINARIAN
DODECAHEDRAL
DODECAHEDRON
DODECANDROUS
DOGMATICALLY
DOMESTICALLY
DONKEY-ENGINE
DOUBLE-ACTING
DOUBLE-DEALER
DOUBLE-MINDED

DOUBTFULNESS
DRAGON'S-BLOOD
DRAMATICALLY
DRAUGHT-BOARD
DRAWING-BOARD
DRAWING-PAPER
DREADFULNESS
DRESSING-CASE
DRESSING-GOWN
DRESSING-ROOM
DRIVING-SHAFT
DRIVING-WHEEL
DROUGHTINESS
DUCKING-STOOL
DWARFISHNESS

E

EARNEST-MONEY
EAU DE COLOGNE
EAVESDROPPER
ECCENTRICITY
ECCLESIASTES
ECCLESIASTIC
ECCLESIOLOGY
ECLECTICALLY
ECONOMICALLY
ECSTATICALLY
ECTOPARASITE
EDUCATIONIST
EDUCTION-PIPE
EDULCORATION
EDULCORATIVE
EFFECTUATION
EFFEMINATELY
EFFERVESCENT
EFFLORESCENT
EFFUSIVENESS
EGOISTICALLY
EGYPTOLOGIST
ELECTRICALLY
ELECTROLYSIS
ELECTROLYTIC
ELECTROMETER
ELECTROMETRY
ELECTROMOTOR
ELECTROPLATE
ELECTROSCOPE
ELECTROTYPIC
ELEEMOSYNARY
ELEMENTARITY
ELLIPTICALLY
ELOCUTIONIST
EMANCIPATION
EMARGINATION
EMASCULATION
EMASCULATORY
EMBEZZLEMENT
EMBITTERMENT
EMBLAZONMENT
EMIGRATIONAL
EMOLLESCENCE
EMOTIONALISM
EMPHATICALLY
EMPRESSEMENT
EMPYREUMATIC
ENCEPHALITIS
ENCHANTINGLY
ENCLITICALLY

ENCROACHMENT
ENCUMBRANCER
ENCYCLOPEDIA
ENDOCARDITIS
ENDOPARASITE
ENDOPHYLLOUS
ENDOSMOMETER
ENDOSKELETON
ENFEEBLEMENT
ENHARMONICAL
ENTANGLEMENT
ENTERPRISING
ENTERTAINING
ENTHRONEMENT
ENTHUSIASTIC
ENTOMOLOGIST
ENTOMOSTRACA
ENTRANCEMENT
ENTREATINGLY
ENVISAGEMENT
EPENCEPHALON
EPEXEGETICAL
EPHEMERALITY
EPHEMERIDIAN
EPICUREANISM
EPICYCLOIDAL
EPIDEICTICAL
EPIDERMICALLY
EPIDEMIOLOGY
EPIGRAMMATIC
EPISCOPALIAN
EPISODICALLY
EPISTEMOLOGY
EPITHALAMIUM
EQUALIZATION
EQUANIMOUSLY
EQUATORIALLY
EQUESTRIENNE
EQUIMULTIPLE
EQUIPOLLENCE
EQUIPOLLENCY
EQUIVALENTLY
EQUIVOCATORY
ERYTHEMATOUS
ESCHATOLOGIC
ESCUTCHEONED
ESOTERICALLY
ESSENTIALITY
ESTRANGEMENT
ETHERIZATION
ETHNOGRAPHER
ETHNOLOGICAL
ETYMOLOGICAL
EUPHONIOUSLY
EVANESCENTLY
EVANGELICISM
EVIDENTIALLY
EVISCERATION
EVOLUTIONARY
EVOLUTIONIST
EXACERBATION
EXAGGERATION
EXAGGERATIVE
EXAGGERATORY
EXALBUMINOUS
EXANTHEMATIC
EXASPERATION
EXASPERATING
EXCHANGEABLE
EXCITABILITY

EXCLUSIONIST
EXCOGITATION
EXCRUCIATING
EXCURSIONIST
EXECUTORSHIP
EXERCITATION
EXHAUSTIVELY
EXHIBITIONER
EXHILARATION
EXORBITANTLY
EXOTERICALLY
EXPATRIATION
EXPERIENTIAL
EXPERIMENTAL
EXPERIMENTER
EXPLICITNESS
EXPLOITATION
EXPOSTULATOR
EXPRESSIONAL
EXSANGUINOUS
EXTEMPORIZER
EXTERMINATOR
EXTERMINABLE
EXTINGUISHER
EXTORTIONARY
EXTRAMUNDANE
EXTRANEOUSLY
EXTRAVAGANCE
EXTRAVAGANCY
EXTRAVAGANZA

F

FACTIOUSNESS
FACTITIOUSLY
FAITHFULNESS
FALLACIOUSLY
FANCIFULNESS
FARADIZATION
FARCICALNESS
FASCICULARLY
FASCICULATED
FASTIDIOUSLY
FATHERLASHER
FEARLESSNESS
FEBRIFACIENT
FELICITATION
FELICITOUSLY
FEMININENESS
FENESTRATION
FERMENTATION
FERMENTATIVE
FEVERISHNESS
FICTITIOUSLY
FISSILINGUAL
FISSIROSTRAL
FLAGELLATION
FLAGITIOUSLY
FLATTERINGY
FLEXIBLENESS
FLITTERMOUSE
FLORICULTURE
FLUORESCENCE
FORAMINIFERA
FORBIDDINGLY
FORCIBLENESS
FORDABLENESS
FOREBODEMENT
FOREKNOWABLE

FORNICATRESS
FORTUITOUSLY
FOUNDATIONER
FRANKINCENSE
FRAUDULENTLY
FREQUENTNESS
FROLICSOMELY
FRONDESCENCE
FRONDIFEROUS
FRONTISPIECE
FRUCTESCENCE
FUGITIVENESS
FUNCTIONALLY
FURFURACEOUS
FUTILITARIAN

G

GALACTAGOGUE
GALACTOMETER
GALLIGASKINS
GALLINACEOUS
GALVANOMETRY
GALVANOSCOPE
GAMOPETALOUS
GASIFICATION
GELATINATION
GENEALOGICAL
GENICULATION
GENTILITIOUS
GENUFLECTION
GEOGRAPHICAL
GEOLOGICALLY
GEOMETRICIAN
GERONTOCRACY
GESTICULATOR
GLADIATORIAL
GLANDIFEROUS
GLAUCOMATOUS
GLOSSOGRAPHY
GLOSSOLOGIST
GLOTTOLOGIST
GLUTTONOUSLY
GLYPHOGRAPHY
GOVERNMENTAL
GOVERNORSHIP
GRACEFULNESS
GRACIOUSNESS
GRADUATESHIP
GRALLATORIAL
GRAMMATICIZE
GRATEFULNESS
GRATUITOUSLY
GREENISHNESS
GREGARIOUSLY
GRIEVOUSNESS
GROUNDLESSLY
GYMNOCARPOUS
GYMNOSOPHIST

H

HABERDASHERY
HAGIOGRAPHER
HAGIOGRAPHIC
HANDKERCHIEF
HARMONIOUSLY
HEADQUARTERS

HELIOCENTRIC
HELIOTROPISM
HENCEFORWARD
HERMENEUTICS
HERMETICALLY
HERPETOLOGIC
HESITATINGLY
HETEROGAMOUS
HETEROLOGOUS
HIBERNACULUM
HIBERNIANISM
HIEROGLYPHIC
HINDOOSTANEE
HIPPOCENTAUR
HIPPOPHAGIST
HIPPOPOTAMUS
HISTORICALLY
HISTRIONICAL
HOMOEOPATHIC
HOMOLOGATION
HOMOMORPHISM
HORIZONTALLY
HORTICULTURE
HOUSEKEEPING
HUMOROUSNESS
HYDROFLUORIC
HYDROGRAPHER
HYDROPATHIST
HYDROSTATICS
HYDROTHERMAL
HYGIENICALLY
HYMNOGRAPHER
HYPERBOLICAL
HYPNOTIZABLE
HYPOCHONDRIA
HYPOCRITICAL
HYPOSTATICAL
HYPOTHECATOR
HYPOTHETICAL
HYSTERICALLY

I

IAMBOGRAPHER
ICHTHYOLATRY
ICHTHYOPSIDA
IDENTIFIABLE
IDIOELECTRIC
IDIOSYNCRASY
IDOLATROUSLY
ILLEGIBILITY
ILLEGITIMACY
ILLEGITIMATE
ILLIBERALITY
ILLUMINATION
IMMACULATELY
IMMATURENESS
IMMEASURABLE
IMMEASURABLY
IMMEMORIALLY
IMMENSURABLE
IMMERSIONIST
IMMETHODICAL
IMMODERATELY
IMMUTABILITY
IMPARTIALITY
IMPENETRABLE
IMPENETRABLY
IMPENITENTLY

IMPERATORIAL
IMPERATIVELY
IMPERFECTION
IMPERFORABLE
IMPERISHABLE
IMPERISHABLY
IMPERSONALLY
IMPERSONATOR
IMPERTINENCE
IMPERVIOUSLY
IMPETIGINOUS
IMPONDERABLE
IMPOSTHUMATE
IMPRESSIVELY
IMPRISONMENT
IMPROPRIATOR
IMPROVIDENCE
INACCURATELY
INADEQUATELY
INADMISSIBLE
INADVERTENCE
INADVERTENCY
INAPPLICABLE
INAPPLICABLY
INAPPOSITELY
INARTICULATE
INARTIFICIAL
INAUSPICIOUS
INCALCULABLE
INCANDESCENT
INCAPACITATE
INCAUTIOUSLY
INCENDIARISM
INCIDENTALLY
INCINERATION
INCOMMODIOUS
INCOMPARABLE
INCOMPARABLY
INCOMPATIBLE
INCOMPATIBLY
INCOMPETENCE
INCOMPETENCY
INCOMPLETELY
INCONCLUSIVE
INCONSEQUENT
INCONSISTENT
INCONSOLABLE
INCONSOLABLY
INCONSTANTLY
INCORPOREITY
INCORRODIBLE
INCORRUPTION
INCREASINGLY
INCURABILITY
INDEBTEDNESS
INDECISIVELY
INDECLINABLE
INDECOROUSLY
INDEFEASIBLE
INDEFENSIBLE
INDEFINITELY
INDELIBILITY
INDEPENDENCE
INDICATIVELY
INDIFFERENCE
INDIGESTIBLE
INDIRECTNESS
INDISCREETLY
INDISCRETION
INDISPUTABLE

INDISSOLUBLE
INDOCTRINATE
INEFFACEABLE
INEFFICIENCY
INELASTICITY
INERADICABLE
INERADICABLY
INEXPEDIENCE
INEXPEDIENCY
INEXPERIENCE
INEXPERTNESS
INEXPLICABLE
INEXTRICABLE
INFECTIOUSLY
INFELICITOUS
INFILTRATION
INFINITIVELY
INFLECTIONAL
INFREQUENTLY
INFRINGEMENT
INFUNDIBULAR
INFUSIBILITY
INHABITATION
INHOSPITABLE
INNUTRITIOUS
INOSCULATION
INSALUBRIOUS
INSECURENESS
INSOLUBILITY
INSPECTORATE
INSPISSATION
INSTALLATION
INSTRUCTRESS
INSTRUMENTAL
INSUFFERABLE
INSUFFERABLY
INSUFFLATION
INSURRECTION
INTEGUMENTAL
INTELLECTION
INTELLECTIVE
INTELLECTUAL
INTELLIGENCE
INTEMPERANCE
INTERCESSION
INTERCONNECT
INTERCURRENT
INTERDICTION
INTERDICTORY
INTERDIGITAL
INTERFERENCE
INTERFEMORAL
INTERGLACIAL
INTERJECTION
INTERLINEARY
INTERLOCUTOR
INTERMEDDLER
INTERMEDIACY
INTERMEDIARY
INTERMEDIATE
INTERMINABLE
INTERMINABLY
INTERMISSION
INTERMITTENT
INTERMIXTURE
INTERMUNDANE
INTERNUNCIAL
INTEROCEANIC
INTERORBITAL
INTERPELLATE

INTERPLEADER
INTERRUPTION
INTERRUPTIVE
INTERSTITIAL
INTERTEXTURE
INTERVENTION
INTERVOCALIC
INTIMIDATION
INTOLERANTLY
INTOXICATION
INTOXICATING
INTRANSIGENT
INTRANSITIVE
INTRENCHMENT
INTRODUCTION
INTRODUCTIVE
INTROMISSION
INTUSSUSCEPT
INVALIDATION
INVEIGLEMENT
INVERTEBRATE
INVESTIGABLE
INVISIBILITY
INVOLUCELLUM
INVULNERABLE
IRASCIBILITY
IRONICALNESS
IRRATIONALLY
IRREDEEMABLE
IRREDEEMABLY
IRREFLECTIVE
IRREFRAGABLE
IRREGULARITY
IRREMEDIABLE
IRREMEDIABLY
IRREMISSIBLE
IRREPEALABLE
IRREPROVABLE
IRRESISTENCE
IRRESISTIBLE
IRRESISTIBLY
IRRESOLUTION
IRRESOLVABLE
IRRESPECTIVE
IRRESPIRABLE
IRRESPONSIVE
IRREVERENTLY
IRREVERSIBLE
IRREVERSIBLY
IRRITABILITY

J

JOHANNISBERG
JOURNALISTIC
JURISCONSULT
JURISPRUDENT
JUVENESCENCE

K

KALEIDOSCOPE
KINDERGARTEN
KLEPTOMANIAC

L

LACHRYMATORY
LAEMMERGEIER
LAEMMERGEYER
LANGUISHMENT
LARYNGOSCOPE
LASCIVIOUSLY
LATICIFEROUS
LAUDABLENESS
LAUREATESHIP
LEGITIMATELY
LEGITIMATION
LEIOTRICHOUS
LENTICULARLY
LEPTOCARDIAN
LEXICOGRAPHY
LEXICOLOGIST
LIBIDINOUSLY
LIBIDINOSITY
LICENTIOUSLY
LIFELESSNESS
LIGNIPERDOUS
LIKEABLENESS
LIQUEFACIENT
LIQUEFACTION
LISTLESSNESS
LITHOGRAPHER
LITHOGRAPHIC
LITHOLOGICAL
LITHOPHAGOUS
LITURGIOLOGY
LOCALIZATION
LOMENTACEOUS
LONESOMENESS
LONGITUDINAL
LOQUACIOUSLY
LUGUBRIOUSLY
LUKEWARMNESS
LUMINIFEROUS
LUMINOUSNESS

M

MACHICOLATED
MACROPTEROUS
MADEMOISELLE
MAGNETICALLY
MAGNETIZABLE
MAGNIFICENCE
MAGNILOQUENT
MAIDENLINESS
MAINTAINABLE
MAJESTICALLY
MALEVOLENTLY
MALFORMATION
MALLEABILITY
MALTREATMENT
MALVERSATION
MANIFESTABLE
MANIFESTIBLE
MANIPULATION
MANIPULATIVE
MANIPULATORY
MANSLAUGHTER
MANUFACTURER
MARLINESPIKE

MARRIAGEABLE
MARVELLOUSLY
MATERIALNESS
MATHEMATICAL
MECHANICALLY
MEDIATORSHIP
MEDITATIVELY
MEGALOSAURUS
MELODRAMATIC
MENSTRUATION
MERCHANTABLE
MERCIFULNESS
MERCURIALIZE
MERETRICIOUS
MERIDIONALLY
METEMPIRICAL
METEOROGRAPH
METHODICALLY
METROPOLITAN
MEZZORILIEVO
MICROBIOLOGY
MICROGEOLOGY
MICROPHONOUS
MICROSCOPIST
MINISTRATION
MINISTRATIVE
MIRACULOUSLY
MIRTHFULNESS
MISAPPREHEND
MISBELIEVING
MISCALCULATE
MISDEMEANANT
MISDEMEANOUR
MISDIRECTION
MISINTERPRET
MISPLACEMENT
MISPRONOUNCE
MISREPRESENT
MISSTATEMENT
MISTRANSLATE
MITRAILLEUSE
MOBILIZATION
MODIFICATION
MODIFICATORY
MOIREANTIQUE
MONASTICALLY
MONETIZATION
MONODELPHIAN
MONOGRAPHIST
MONOMANIACAL
MONOMETALLIC
MONOMORPHOUS
MONOPETALOUS
MONOPHYLLOUS
MONSEIGNEURS
MONUMENTALLY
MORPHOLOGIST
MOURNFULNESS
MUCILAGINOUS
MUCOPURULENT
MULLIGATAWNY
MULTICOSTATE
MULTIFARIOUS
MULTIFORMITY
MULTILATERAL
MULTIPLIABLE
MULTIPLICAND
MULTIPLICITY
MULTITUBULAR
MUNICIPALIZE

MYSTERIOUSLY
MYTHOGRAPHER

N

NAMELESSNESS
NARCOTICALLY
NATURALISTIC
NAVIGABILITY
NECTOCALYCES
NEEDLESSNESS
NEGLECTFULLY
NEOLOGICALLY
NEVERTHELESS
NIDIFICATION
NOCTAMBULIST
NOMENCLATURE
NOMINATIVELY
NONAGENARIAN
NONCHALANTLY
NORTHERNMOST
NOTIFICATION
NUTRITIOUSLY

O

OBDURATENESS
OBLIGATORILY
OBLIGINGNESS
OBLITERATION
OBLITERATIVE
OBSCURANTIST
OBSEQUIOUSLY
OBSOLESCENCE
OBSOLETENESS
OBSTREPEROUS
OCCIDENTALLY
OCEANOGRAPHY
OCTOGENARIAN
OCTOPETALOUS
OLEOMARGARIN
OMNIPOTENTLY
OMNIPRESENCE
OMNISCIENTLY
ONOMATOPOEIA
ONOMATOPOEIC
OPHIOPHAGOUS
OPINIONATIVE
OPPRESSIVELY
ORATORICALLY
ORGANIZATION
ORGANOGRAPHY
ORNAMENTALLY
ORNITHOMANCY
ORNITHOSCOPY
OROGRAPHICAL
ORTHOGNATHIC
ORTHOGRAPHER
ORTHOGRAPHIC
OSSIFICATION
OSTENTATIOUS
OSTEODENTINE
OSTEOGRAPHER
OSTEOMALACIA
OUTMANOEUVRE
OUTRAGEOUSLY
OVERESTIMATE

P

PAEDOBAPTIST
PALAEOBOTANY
PALAEOGRAPHY
PALAEOLITHIC
PALINGENESIS
PALPABLENESS
PANHELLENISM
PANTISOCRACY
PAPISTICALLY
PARACENTESIS
PARADISIACAL
PARAGRAPHIST
PARALIPOMENA
PARASITICIDE
PARENCHYMOUS
PARIDIGITATE
PARISYLLABLE
PAROCHIALISM
PAROCHIALIZE
PARONOMASTIC
PARSIMONIOUS
PARTICIPATOR
PARTISANSHIP
PARTIZANSHIP
PATHETICALLY
PATHOLOGICAL
PATRIARCHATE
PATRIARCHISM
PEACEFULNESS
PELLUCIDNESS
PENTAGONALLY
PERAMBULATOR
PERCEPTIVITY
PEREGRINATOR
PEREMPTORILY
PERFIDIOUSLY
PERGAMENEOUS
PERICARDITIS
PERIOSTEITIS
PERIPHERICAL
PERIVISCERAL
PERMEABILITY
PERPETRATION
PERPLEXINGLY
PERQUISITION
PERSEVERANCE
PERSISTENTLY
PERSPICACITY
PERSPIRATION
PERSPIRATORY
PERSUASIVELY
PERTINACEOUS
PERTURBATION
PERVICACIOUS
PESTILENTIAL
PETRIFACTION
PETRIFACTIVE
PETROGRAPHER
PETTIFOGGERY
PHAENOGAMOUS
PHARMACOLOGY
PHARYNGOTOMY
PHILANTHROPY
PHILHARMONIC
PHILHELLENIC
PHILISTINISM
PHILOSOPHISM

PHILOSOPHIZE
PHLEBOTOMIST
PHONETICALLY
PHOSPHORESCE
PHOTOGRAVURE
PHRASEOLOGIC
PHRENOLOGIST
PHYLOGENESIS
PHYLOGENETIC
PHYSIOCRATIC
PHYSIOGRAPHY
PHYTOGENESIS
PHYTOPHAGOUS
PISCICULTURE
PITIABLENESS
PITILESSNESS
PLACABLENESS
PLANISPHERIC
PLEASANTRIES
PLEBISCITARY
PLENIPOTENCE
PLENIPOTENCY
PLURILITERAL
PLURILOCULAR
PNEUMATOLOGY
POLLUTEDNESS
POLYANTHUSES
POLYMORPHISM
POLYPHYLLOUS
POLYSPERMOUS
POLYSYLLABLE
POLYSYNDETON
POLYTECHNICS
POPULOUSNESS
PORCELLANEOUS
PORTABLENESS
PORTENTOUSLY
POSITIVENESS
POSSESSIVELY
POWERFULNESS
PRACTICALITY
PRACTITIONER
PRECEPTORIAL
PRECIOUSNESS
PRECIPITABLE
PRECISIANISM
PRECOCIOUSLY
PRECOGNITION
PREDESTINATE
PREFERENTIAL
PRELATICALLY
PREMAXILLARY
PREOCCUPANCY
PREPONDERATE
PRESBYTERIAL
PRESBYTERIAN
PREREQUISITE
PRESCRIPTION
PRESCRIPTIVE
PRESENTATION
PRESIDENTIAL
PRESUMPTUOUS
PREVAILINGLY
PRUDEFULNESS
PRIESTLINESS
PRIMIGENIOUS
PRIMOGENITOR
PRINCIPALITY
PROBATIONARY
PROCLAMATION

PRODIGIOUSLY
PROFESSORATE
PROFOUNDNESS
PROLEGOMENON
PROLETARIATE
PROLIFICNESS
PROLONGATION
PROMULGATION
PROPAGANDISM
PROPENSENESS
PROPITIATION
PROPITIOUSLY
PROPORTIONAL
PROSCRIPTION
PROSCRIPTIVE
PROSELYTIZER
PROSOPOPOEIA
PROSPEROUSLY
PROSTITUTION
PROTESTATION
PROTHONOTARY
PROTOPLASMIC
PROTRACTEDLY
PROTUBERANCE
PROVERBIALLY
PROVIDENTIAL
PRUDENTIALLY
PSEUDONYMOUS
PSYCHOLOGIST
PSYCHROMETER
PTERODACTYLE
PUGNACIOUSLY
PULVERACEOUS
PULVERIZABLE
PURBLINDNESS
PURIFICATION
PUTREFACTION
PYROMETRICAL
PYROTECHNIST

Q

QUADRAGESMIA
QUADRANGULAR
QUADRINOMIAL
QUADRUMANOUS
QUALMISHNESS
QUANTITATIVE
QUAQUAVERSAL
QUERIMONIOUS
QUESTIONABLE
QUESTIONABLY
QUINQUENNIUM

R

RAMIFICATION
RATIFICATION
READJUSTMENT
READMITTANCE
REANNEXATION
REAPPEARANCE
REASSUMPTION
REBELLIOUSLY
RECALCITRANT
RECAPITULATE
RECENSIONIST
RECEPTACULAR

RECIPROCALLY
RECKLESSNESS
RECOMMITMENT
RECONCILABLE
RECONVEYANCE
RECORDERSHIP
RECRUDESCENT
RECUPERATION
RECUPERATIVE
RECUPERATORY
REDINTEGRATE
REDISTRIBUTE
REFLECTIVELY
REFRACTORILY
REFRESHINGLY
REFUTABILITY
REGARDLESSLY
REGENERATION
REGENERATIVE
REGENERATORY
REGISTRATION
REHABILITATE
REILLUMINATE
REIMPOSITION
REINSPECTION
REINSTALMENT
REINVESTMENT
REINVIGORATE
REJUVENATION
RELATIONSHIP
RELATIVENESS
RELENTLESSLY
RELIABLENESS
RELIGIONLESS
RELINQUISHER
REMEMBRANCER
REMINISCENCE
REMONSTRANCE
REMORSEFULLY
REMOVABILITY
REMUNERATION
REMUNERATIVE
RENEWABILITY
RENOUNCEMENT
RENUNCIATION
REPARABILITY
REPERCUSSION
REPERCUSSIVE
REPREHENSION
REPRESSIVELY
REPROACHABLE
REPROACHABLY
REPRODUCTION
REPRODUCTIVE
REPUBLICATES
REQUIESCENCE
RESIDENTIARY
RESINIFEROUS
RESISTLESSLY
RESOLUTENESS
RESOLUTIONER
RESOLVEDNESS
RESOURCELESS
RESPECTFULLY
RESPECTIVELY
RESPLENDENCE
RESPLENDENCY
RESPONDENTIA
RESPONSIVELY
RESTAURATEUR

RESTRAINABLE
RESTRAINABLY
RESURRECTION
RESUSCITABLE
RESUSCITATOR
RETICULATION
RETRACTATION
RETRENCHMENT
RETRIEVEMENT
RETROCESSION
REVENGEFULLY
REVERBERATOR
RHINOPLASTIC
RHIZOPHAGOUS
RHODODENDRON
RHODOMONTADE
RHOMBOHEDRAL
RHOMBOHEDRON
RHYTHMICALLY
RIDICULOUSLY
ROMANTICALLY
RUTHLESSNESS

S

SACERDOTALLY
SACRAMENTARY
SACRILEGIOUS
SACROSANCTLY
SALEABLENESS
SALUBRIOUSLY
SALUTARINESS
SALVATIONIST
SANGUIFEROUS
SANGUINENESS
SANGUINOLENT
SAPONIFIABLE
SAPROPHAGOUS
SARCOPHAGOUS
SARSAPARILLA
SATISFACTION
SATISFACTORY
SCANDALOUSLY
SCANDINAVIAN
SCARIFICATOR
SCARLATINOUS
SCENOGRAPHIC
SCHOOLMASTER
SCHORLACEOUS
SCLERODERMIC
SCORNFULNESS
SCOUNDRELISM
SCRIPTURALLY
SCROFULOUSLY
SCROPHULARIA
SCRUPULOSITY
SCRUPULOUSLY
SCULPTURALLY
SCURRILOUSLY
SCUTELLIFORM
SECESSIONISM
SECESSIONIST
SECRETARIATE
SECTARIANISM
SECTARIANIZE
SEDULOUSNESS
SEGMENTATION
SEIGNIORALTY
SEISMOLOGIST

SELENOGRAPHY
SEMEIOGRAPHY
SEMINIFEROUS
SEMPERVIRENT
SENATORIALLY
SENSIBLENESS
SENSIFACIENT
SEPARABILITY
SEPARATENESS
SEPTENNIALLY
SEPTUAGENARY
SEPTUAGESIMA
SEQUESTRATOR
SERAPHICALLY
SERPENTIFORM
SHAKSPEARIAN
SHAMEFACEDLY
SHAMEFULNESS
SHEEPISHNESS
SHREWISHNESS
SHUDDERINGLY
SIDEROGRAPHY
SIGNIFICATOR
SIMONIACALLY
SIMULTANEITY
SIMULTANEOUS
SLANDEROUSLY
SLAUGHTEROUS
SLIPPERINESS
SLOVENLINESS
SLUGGISHNESS
SLUTTISHNESS
SNAPPISHNESS
SNOBBISHNESS
SOCRATICALLY
SOLICITATION
SOLICITOUSLY
SOLIDIFIABLE
SOLISEQUIOUS
SOLITARINESS
SOMNAMBULATE
SOMNAMBULISM
SOMNAMBULIST
SONOROUSNESS
SOPHISTICATE
SOPORIFEROUS
SOUTHERNMOST
SPACIOUSNESS
SPECIALITIES
SPECIFICALLY
SPECTROMETER
SPECTROSCOPE
SPECTROSCOPY
SPERMATOZOON
SPHENOGRAPHY
SPHRAGISTICS
SPHYGMOGRAPH
SPIRITEDNESS
SPIRITLESSLY
SPIRITUALISM
SPIRITUALIST
SPIRITUALITY
SPIRITUALIZE
SPITEFULNESS
SPORADICALLY
SPOTLESSNESS
SPURIOUSNESS
STALWARTNESS
STANNIFEROUS
STATISTICIAN

STEATOPYGOUS
STENOGRAPHIC
STEPDAUGHTER
STEREOGRAPHY
STEREOPTICON
STEREOTYPIST
STERNUTATION
STERNUTATIVE
STERNUTATORY
STOCKBROKING
STRAIGHTNESS
STRAWBERRIES
STRENGTHENER
STRIDULATION
STUBBORNNESS
STUDIOUSNESS
STUPEFACIENT
STUPEFACTIVE
STUPEFACTION
STUPENDOUSLY
STYLOGRAPHIC
SUBCOMMITTEE
SUBCUTANEOUS
SUBDIVISIBLE
SUBEPIDERMAL
SUBFEUDATORY
SUBJECTIVELY
SUBJECTIVITY
SUBLINEATION
SUBMAXILLARY
SUBMISSIVELY
SUBOCCIPITAL
SUBSCRIPTION
SUBSEQUENTLY
SUBSERVIENCE
SUBSERVIENCY
SUBSTANTIATE
SUBSTANTIVAL
SUBSTITUTION
SUBSTRUCTION
SUBSTRUCTURE
SUBTERRANEAN
SUCCEDANEOUS
SUCCESSFULLY
SUCCESSIONAL
SUCCESSIVELY
SUCCINCTNESS
SUDORIFEROUS
SUFFICIENTLY
SUFFRUTICOSE
SUGGESTIVELY
SUITABLENESS
SULPHURATION
SULPHURETTED
SUPERANNUATE
SUPERCILIARY
SUPERCILIOUS
SUPEREMINENT
SUPERMUNDANE
SUPERNACULAR
SUPERNACULUM
SUPPLICATORY
SUPPRESSIBLE
SUPRAMUNDANE
SUPRAORBITAL
SURMOUNTABLE
SURPRISINGLY
SURREJOINDER
SURVEILLANCE
SURVEYORSHIP

SURVIVORSHIP
SUSCEPTIVITY
SUSPICIOUSLY
SUSTENTATION
SYCOPHANTISH
SYCOPHANTISM
SYLLABICALLY
SYMBOLICALLY
SYNANTHEROUS
SYNARTHROSIS
SYNONYMOUSLY
SYNOPTICALLY
SYSTEMATICAL

T

TABERNACULAR
TACHYGRAPHIC
TALISMANICAL
TAMELESSNESS
TANGENTIALLY
TANGIBLENESS
TASTEFULNESS
TECHNOLOGIST
TELAUTOGRAPH
TELEGRAPHIST
TELEOLOGICAL
TEMPERAMENTS
TEMPORALNESS
TENUIROSTRAL
TERCENTENARY
TEREBINTHINE
TERGIVERSATE
TERRIBLENESS
TERRIFICALLY
TETRAPTEROUS
THALLOGENOUS
THANKFULNESS
THANKSGIVING
THEATRICALLY
THEOCRATICAL
THEOREMATIST
THEOSOPHICAL
THERAPEUTICS
THERAPEUTIST
THICKSKINNED
THIEVISHNESS
THITHERWARDS
THOUGHTFULLY
THRIFTLESSLY
TICKLISHNESS
TITANIFEROUS
TOPOGRAPHIST
TORREFACTION
TORRICELLIAN
TORTUOUSNESS
TOXICOLOGIST
TRADITIONIST
TRADUCIANISM
TRAITOROUSLY
TRANQUILLIZE
TRANQUILLITY
TRANSFERABLE
TRANSFERENCE
TRANSFUSIBLE
TRANSGRESSOR
TRANSHIPMENT
TRANSITIONAL
TRANSITIVELY

TRANSITORILY
TRANSLATABLE
TRANSLUCENCY
TRANSMIGRATE
TRANSMISSION
TRANSMUTABLE
TRANSMUTABLY
TRANSPARENCE
TRANSPARENCY
TRANSPICUOUS
TRANSPLANTER
TRANSPONTINE
TRANSPORTING
TRANSPOSABLE
TRANSUDATION
TRANSUDATORY
TRANSUMPTIVE
TRANSVERSELY
TRIADELPHOUS
TRIANGULARLY
TRICENTENARY
TRICHINIASIS
TRICHOMATOSE
TRICUSPIDATE
TRIDACTYLOUS
TRIGRAMMATIC
TRIPARTITELY
TRIPHTHONGAL
TRIUMPHANTLY
TROPOLOGICAL
TRUNCHEONEER
TRUTHFULNESS
TUBERCULATED
TUBERCULOSIS
TUMULTUOUSLY
TYRANNICALLY

U

UBIQUITOUSLY
ULTRAMONTANE
UMBRAGEOUSLY
UNACCEPTABLE
UNACCUSTOMED
UNACQUAINTED
UNADULTERATE
UNANSWERABLE
UNANSWERABLY
UNAPPEALABLE
UNAPPEASABLE
UNASPIRINGLY
UNASSAILABLE
UNBECOMINGLY
UNBREATHABLE
UNCHALLENGED
UNCHANGEABLE
UNCHARITABLE
UNCHARITABLY
UNCOMMERCIAL
UNCOVENANTED
UNCTUOUSNESS
UNCULTIVATED
UNDECEIVABLE
UNDECLINABLE
UNDERCLOTHES
UNDERCURRENT
UNDERSTRATUM
UNDERWRITING
UNDESERVEDLY

UNDETERMINED
UNDISCERNING
UNDISCHARGED
UNEXPECTEDLY
UNFAITHFULLY
UNFATHOMABLY
UNFAVOURABLE
UNFAVOURABLY
UNFRANCHISED
UNFREQUENTED
UNFRUITFULLY
UNGENEROUSLY
UNGOVERNABLE
UNGOVERNABLY
UNGRACEFULLY
UNGRACIOUSLY
UNGRATEFULLY
UNHANDSOMELY
UNHESITATING
UNHISTORICAL
UNIMPORTANCE
UNIMPUGNABLE
UNINSTRUCTED
UNINTERESTED
UNITARIANISM
UNIVERSALISM
UNIVERSALIST
UNIVERSITIES
UNIVERSOLOGY
UNKINDLINESS
UNLAWFULNESS
UNLIKELIHOOD
UNLIKELINESS
UNMANAGEABLE
UNMARKETABLE
UNMERCIFULLY
UNMISTAKABLE
UNOBSERVEDLY
UNOBSTRUCTED
UNPARALLELED
UNPATRONIZED
UNPLEASANTLY
UNPLEASINGLY
UNPOETICALLY
UNPOPULARITY
UNPREJUDICED
UNPREPAREDLY
UNPRETENDING
UNPRINCIPLED
UNPRIVILEGED
UNPRODUCTIVE
UNPROFITABLE
UNPROPITIOUS
UNPROSPEROUS

UNQUENCHABLE
UNQUENCHABLY
UNQUESTIONED
UNREASONABLE
UNREASONABLY
UNRECONCILED
UNREGENERACY
UNREGISTERED
UNRESERVEDLY
UNRESTRAINED
UNRESTRICTED
UNSANCTIFIED
UNSATISFYING
UNSCRIPTURAL
UNSCRUPULOUS
UNSEARCHABLE
UNSEEMLINESS
UNSTABLENESS
UNSTEADINESS
UNSTRATIFIED
UNSUCCESSFUL
UNSUPPRESSED
UNSUSPECTING
UNSUSPICIOUS
UNSYSTEMATIC
UNTENANTABLE
UNTHINKINGLY
UNTOWARDNESS
UNTRAMMELLED
UNTRUTHFULLY
UNWIELDINESS
UNWONTEDNESS
UNWORTHINESS
UPROARIOUSLY

V

VAINGLORIOUS
VALETUDINARY
VALUABLENESS
VANQUISHABLE
VAPORIZATION
VARIABLENESS
VATICINATION
VELOCIPEDIST
VENDIBLENESS
VERIFICATION
VERNACULARLY
VERSIFICATOR
VERTICILLATE
VICTORIOUSLY
VIGOROUSNESS
VILIFICATION

VILLAINOUSLY
VINDICTIVELY
VISCOUNTSHIP
VISITATORIAL
VITALIZATION
VITREOUSNESS
VITRIFACTION
VITRIFACTURE
VITRIOLATION
VITUPERATION
VITUPERATIVE
VIVIPAROUSLY
VOCABULARIES
VOCALIZATION
VOCIFERATION
VOCIFEROUSLY
VOLUMINOUSLY
VOLUPTUARIES
VOLUPTUOUSLY

W

WAREHOUSEMAN
WATCHFULNESS
WELLINGTONIA
WHENCESOEVER
WHERETHROUGH
WHIMSICALITY
WHISPERINGLY
WHORTLEBERRY
WOMANISHNESS
WORSHIPFULLY
WRANGLERSHIP
WRATHFULNESS
WRETCHEDNESS

X

XYLOBALSAMUM

Y

YOUTHFULNESS

Z

ZINCOGRAPHIC
ZOOCHEMISTRY
ZOOPHYTOLOGY

THIRTEEN-LETTER WORDS

A

ABSORBABILITY
ACCESSIBILITY
ACCIDENTALISM
ACCIDENTALLY
ACCLIMATATION
ACCOMMODATING
ACCOMMODATION
ACCOMMODATIVE
ACCOMPANIMENT
ACCOUTREMENTS
ACETABULIFORM
ACETIFICATION
ACIDIFICATION
ACOTYLEDONOUS
ACQUISITIVELY
ACRIMONIOUSLY
ADMEASUREMENT
ADMINISTRATOR
ADMIRABLENESS
ADMISSIBILITY
ADUMBRATIVELY
ADVENTUROUSLY
ADVERTISEMENT
ADVISABLENESS
AESTHESIOLOGY
AESTHETICALLY
AFFIRMATIVELY
AFFORESTATION
AGGLOMERATION
AGGLUTINATION
AGGLUTINATIVE
AGGRAVATINGLY
AGREEABLENESS
AGRICULTURIST
ALCOHOLOMETER
ALGEBRAICALLY
ALLEGORICALLY
ALLOWABLENESS
ALTERNATIVELY
ALUMINIFEROUS
AMBASSADORIAL
AMBIDEXTERITY
AMPLIFICATION
AMPLIFICATIVE
AMPLIFICATORY
ANACHRONISTIC
ANAGRAMMATIST
ANAPHRODISIAC
ANDROPETALOUS
ANGIOSPERMOUS
ANGLO-AMERICAN
ANGLO-CATHOLIC
ANIMADVERSION
ANIMALIZATION
ANNEXATIONIST
ANTAPHRODITIC
ANTHROPOLATRY
ANTHROPOLOGIC
ANTHROPOMETRY
ANTHROPOPATHY
ANHROPOPHAGI
ANTHROPOPHAGY

ANTIARTHRITIC
ANTIASTHMATIC
ANTICHRISTIAN
ANTICORROSIVE
ANTIEPHIALTIC
ANTIEPISCOPAL
ANTILOGARITHM
ANTIMONARCHIC
ANTIMONIANISM
ANTINEPHRITIC
ANTISCORBUTIC
ANTISPASMODIC
ANTITYPICALLY
APHANIPTEROUS
APOGEOTROPISM
APOSTOLICALLY
APPELLATIVELY
APPENDICULATE
APPLICABILITY
APPORTIONMENT
APPREHENSIBLE
APPROPRIATELY
APPROPRIATION
APPROXIMATELY
APPROXIMATION
APPROXIMATIVE
ARBITRARINESS
ARBORICULTURE
ARCHAEOLOGIST
ARCHAEOPTERYX
ARCHBISHOPRIC
ARCHIDIACONAL
ARCHIMANDRITE
ARCHITECTURAL
ARGENTIFEROUS
ARGUMENTATION
ARGUMENTATIVE
ARITHMETICIAN
ARUNDINACEOUS
ASCERTAINABLE
ASCERTAINMENT
ASCRIPTITIOUS
ASSASSINATION
ASSIDUOUSNESS
ASSOCIATESHIP
ASSYRIOLOGIST
ASTHMATICALLY
ASTONISHINGLY
ATHEISTICALLY
ATROCIOUSNESS
ATTAINABILITY
ATTENTIVENESS
ATTRIBUTIVELY
AUDACIOUSNESS
AUTHENTICALLY
AUTHORITATIVE
AUTOBIOGRAPHY
AUTOCHTHONOUS
AVAILABLENESS
AXIOMATICALLY

B

BACCALAUREATE

BACKWARDATION
BALLAST-HEAVER
BALL-CARTRIDGE
BALSAMIFEROUS
BAREFACEDNESS
BEATIFICATION
BEAUTIFULNESS
BEGINNINGLESS
BELIEVABILITY
BELLES-LETTRES
BESSEMER-STEEL
BIBLIOGRAPHER
BIBLIOLOGICAL
BIBLIOTHECARY
BLACKGUARDISM
BLAMELESSNESS
BLASPHEMOUSLY
BLINDMAN'S-BUFF
BLISTER-BEETLE
BLOCK-PRINTING
BLOOD-RELATION
BLOODSHEDDING
BLOOD-SPILLING
BLOTTING-PAPER
BOARDING-HOUSE
BOMBASTICALLY
BOOKING-OFFICE
BOROGLYCERIDE
BOUNDLESSNESS
BOUNTIFULNESS
BREECH-LOADING
BREVILOQUENCE
BREVIROSTRATE
BROKEN-HEARTED
BROTHERLINESS
BUMPTIOUSNESS
BURGLARIOUSLY
BURNING-MIRROR
BURNT-OFFERING
BUTCHER'S-BROOM

C

CALCIFICATION
CALICO-PRINTER
CALLISTHENICS
CALORIFACIENT
CAMPANOLOGIST
CAMPEACHY-WOOD
CAMPHORACEOUS
CANDIDATESHIP
CAPACIOUSNESS
CARBONIFEROUS
CARBONIZATION
CARNIFICATION
CARPET-BEDDING
CARRIER-PIGEON
CARTE-DE-VISITE
CARTILAGINOUS
CASTLE-BUILDER
CATASTROPHISM
CATECHISTICAL
CATEGOREMATIC
CATEGORICALLY

CAT-O'-NINE TAILS
CAUSELESSNESS
CAUTERIZATION
CEPHALO-THORAX
CEREBRO-SPINAL
CEREMONIOUSLY
CERTIFICATION
CHALCOGRAPHER
CHALLENGEABLE
CHANCEL-SCREEN
CHANGEABILITY
CHANGEFULNESS
CHARACTERLESS
CHARTOGRAPHIC
CHEERLESSNESS
CHEIROPTEROUS
CHEVAL-DE-FRISE
CHIMNEY-CORNER
CHOPPING-KNIFE
CHOREPISCOPAL
CHREMATISTICS
CHRISTMAS-ROSE
CHRISTMAS-TREE
CHROMATOPHORE
CHRONOGRAPHER
CHRYSANTHEMUM
CHUCK-FARTHING
CHURCHMANSHIP
CHURCH-SERVICE
CHYLIFICATION
CHYMIFICATION
CICATRIZATION
CINCHONACEOUS
CINEMATOGRAPH
CINNAMON-STONE
CIRCUMAMBIENT
CIRCUMDUCTION
CIRCUMFERENCE
CIRCUMFLUENCE
CIRCUMJACENCE
CIRCUMJACENCY
CIRCUMSPECTLY
CIRCUMVALLATE
CIRCUMVENTION
CIRCUMVENTIVE
CLAMOROUSNESS
CLANDESTINELY
CLARIFICATION
CLEARING-HOUSE
CLEISTOGAMOUS
CLIMATOGRAPHY
CLINCHER-BUILT
CLOISTER-GARTH
COADJUTORSHIP
COARSE-GRAINED
CO-BELLIGERENT
COCHLEARIFORM
COESSENTIALLY
COEXTENSIVELY
COLLABORATION
COLLABORATEUR
COLLECTEDNESS
COLLOQUIALISM
COLLOQUIALIST
COMBATIVENESS
COMMANDERSHIP
COMMEMORATIVE
COMMENSURABLE
COMMENSURABLY
COMMISERATION

COMMISERATIVE
COMMUNICATIVE
COMMUTABILITY
COMMUTATIVELY
COMMUNICATION
COMPANIONABLE
COMPANIONABLY
COMPANIONLESS
COMPANIONSHIP
COMPARATIVELY
COMPASSIONATE
COMPATIBILITY
COMPENDIOUSLY
COMPLAININGLY
COMPLAISANTLY
COMPLEMENTARY
COMPLIMENTARY
COMPREHENSION
COMPREHENSIVE
CONCATENATION
CONCAVO-CONVEX
CONCEITEDNESS
CONCENTRATION
CONCENTRATIVE
CONCEPTUALISM
CONCEPTUALIST
CONCOMITANTLY
CONCRETIONARY
CONCUPISCENCE
CONDESCENDING
CONDESCENSION
CONDITIONALLY
CONDUCIVENESS
CONFABULATION
CONFABULATORY
CONFECTIONARY
CONFECTIONERY
CONFEDERATION
CONFEDERATIVE
CONFESSIONARY
CONFESSORSHIP
CONFIDINGNESS
CONFIGURATION
CONFLAGRATION
CONFRATERNITY
CONFRONTATION
CONGRATULATOR
CONJECTURABLE
CONJECTURALLY
CONJUGATIONAL
CONJUNCTIONAL
CONJUNCTIVELY
CONSANGUINITY
CONSCIENTIOUS
CONSCIOUSNESS
CONSECUTIVELY
CONSENTANEOUS
CONSEQUENTIAL
CONSERVATOIRE
CONSIDERATELY
CONSIDERATION
CONSOLIDATION
CONSPICUOUSLY
CONSPIRATRESS
CONSTABLESHIP
CONSTELLATION
CONSTERNATION
CONSTRAINABLE
CONSTRAINEDLY
CONSUMPTIVELY

CONTABESCENCE
CONTAMINATION
CONTAMINATIVE
CONTEMPLATION
CONTEMPLATIVE
CONTENTEDNESS
CONTENTIOUSLY
CONTORTIONIST
CONTRABANDISM
CONTRABANDIST
CONTRACTILITY
CONTRADICTION
CONTRADICTIVE
CONTRADICTORY
CONTRAPUNTIST
CONTRATE-WHEEL
CONTRAVENTION
CONTRIBUTABLE
CONTROVERSIAL
CONTROVERTIST
CONVALESCENCE
CONVALESCENCY
CONVENTIONARY
CONVENTIONIST
CONVERSAZIONE
CONVEXO-CONVEX
CONVOCATIONAL
CONVULSIONARY
COPARTNERSHIP
CORALLIFEROUS
COROLLIFLORAL
CORRELATIVELY
CORRESPONDENT
CORRESPONDING
CORRESPONSIVE
CORROBORATION
CORROBORATIVE
CORROBORATORY
CORRODIBILITY
CORROSIVENESS
CORRUPTIONIST
CORYMBIFEROUS
COSMOPOLITISM
COTTON-SPINNER
COTTON-THISTLE
COUNTERACTION
COUNTERACTIVE
COUNTERCHANGE
COUNTERCHARGE
COUNTERFEITER
COUNTER-MOTION
COUNTER-POISON
COUNTER-SIGNAL
COUNTER-STROKE
COUNTERWEIGHT
COURTEOUSNESS
COXCOMBICALLY
CRAFTSMANSHIP
CRANIOSCOPIST
CREDITABILITY
CREDULOUSNESS
CROSS-BREEDING
CROSS-GARTERED
CROSS-HATCHING
CROSS-QUESTION
CROTCHETINESS
CRUSTACEOLOGY
CRYPTOGRAPHER
CRYPTOGRAPHIC
CUSTOMARINESS

CYLINDRICALLY

D

DACTYLIOGLYPH
DADDY-LONG-LEGS
DAGUERREOTYPE
DANCING-MASTER
DANGEROUSNESS
DASTARDLINESS
DAUGHTER-IN-LAW
DAUNTLESSNESS
DEAD-RECKONING
DEATH-STRUGGLE
DECEITFULNESS
DECEPTIVENESS
DECOMPOSITION
DECONCENTRATE
DECORTICATION
DECREPITATION
DEFECTIVENESS
DEFENCELESSLY
DEFENSIBILITY
DEFERENTIALLY
DEFERVESCENCE
DEFERVESCENCY
DEFIBRINATION
DELICIOUSNESS
DELIQUESCENCE
DELIRIFACIENT
DELIRIOUSNESS
DEMONSTRATION
DEMONSTRATIVE
DENATIONALIZE
DENTICULATELY
DENTICULATION
DEODORIZATION
DEONTOLOGICAL
DEPHOSPHORIZE
DEPRECATINGLY
DERMATOLOGIST
DERMO-SKELETON
DESCRIPTIVELY
DESIRABLENESS
DESTRUCTIVELY
DESULTORINESS
DETERIORATION
DETERMINATELY
DETERMINATION
DETERMINATIVE
DETRIMENTALLY
DEUTEROGAMIST
DEVELOPMENTAL
DEXTEROUSNESS
DIALECTICALLY
DIALOGISTICAL
DIAMESOGAMOUS
DIAMETRICALLY
DIAPHRAGMATIC
DIATHERMANOUS
DICHLAMYDEOUS
DICHOTOMOUSLY
DICTATORIALLY
DIFFERENTIATE
DIFFUSIBILITY
DIFFUSIVENESS
DIGESTIBILITY
DIPHTHONGALLY
DIPSOMANIACAL

DISAPPEARANCE
DISCIPLINABLE
DISCOLORATION
DISCONNECTION
DISCONTINUITY
DISCONTINUOUS
DISCREDITABLE
DISCREDITABLY
DISCRETIONARY
DISCRIMINATOR
DISEMBARKMENT
DISENGAGEMENT
DISESTIMATION
DISFIGURATION
DISFIGUREMENT
DISGRACEFULLY
DISHONOURABLE
DISHONOURABLY
DISINTEGRABLE
DISINTERESTED
DISJUNCTIVELY
DISMEMBERMENT
DISNATURALIZE
DISOBEDIENTLY
DISOBLIGEMENT
DISOBLIGINGLY
DISPARAGINGLY
DISPARAGEMENT
DISPASSIONATE
DISPLANTATION
DISPOSSESSION
DISPROPORTION
DISRESPECTFUL
DISSEMINATION
DISSIMILARITY
DISSIMILATION
DISSIMILITUDE
DISSIMULATION
DISSOLUBILITY
DISSOLUTENESS
DISTASTEFULLY
DISTINCTIVELY
DISTINGUISHED
DISTRESSFULLY
DISTRESSINGLY
DISTRIBUTABLE
DISTRUSTFULLY
DIVERSIFIABLE
DOMESTICATION
DOMICILIATION
DOUBLE-DEALING
DOUBLE-HEARTED
DOUBLE-TONGUED
DRAGGLE-TAILED
DRAWING-MASTER
DRESSING-TABLE
DRILL-SERGEANT
DRINK-OFFERING
DWELLING-HOUSE
DYNAMO-MACHINE
DYSMENORRHOEA

E

EARTHLY-MINDED
ECCENTRICALLY
ECHINODERMATA
ECONOMIZATION
EDUCATIONALLY

EFFECTIVENESS
EFFERVESCENCE
EFFERVESCIBLE
EFFICACIOUSLY
EFFLORESCENCE
EGOTISTICALLY
EGPYTOLOGICAL
ELABORATENESS
ELECTRIFIABLE
ELECTROCUTION
ELECTRO-MAGNET
ELECTROMETRIC
ELECTROMOTIVE
ELECTROPHORUS
ELEPHANTIASIS
EMBARRASSMENT
EMBELLISHMENT
EMBRYOLOGICAL
EMIGRATIONIST
ENCOMIASTICAL
ENCOMPASSMENT
ENCOURAGEMENT
ENCOURAGINGLY
ENCYCLOPAEDIA
ENCYCLOPAEDIC
ENCYCLOPEDISM
ENCYCLOPEDIST
ENDURABLENESS
ENERGETICALLY
ENIGMATICALLY
ENLIGHTENMENT
ENTERTAINMENT
ENTOMOLOGICAL
ENTOMOPHAGOUS
ENTOMOPHILOUS
ENTOZOOLOGIST
EPIGRAMMATIST
EPIGRAMMATIZE
EPIPERIPHERAL
EQUESTRIANISM
EQUIDIFFERENT
EQUIDISTANTLY
EQUILIBRATION
EQUIPONDERANT
EQUIPONDERATE
EQUISETACEOUS
EQUITABLENESS
EQUIVOCALNESS
ERYSIPELATOUS
ESTABLISHMENT
ESTIMABLENESS
EUCHARISTICAL
EVANGELICALLY
EVERLASTINGLY
EXANTHEMATOUS
EXCEPTIONABLE
EXCEPTIONALLY
EXCITABLENESS
EXCLUSIVENESS
EXCOMMUNICATE
EXCORTICATION
EXCUSABLENESS
EXPANSIBILITY
EXPANSIVENESS
EXPECTORATION
EXPECTORATIVE
EXPEDITIONARY
EXPEDITIOUSLY
EXPENSIVENESS
EXPERIMENTIST

EXPOSTULATION
EXPOSTULATORY
EXPROPRIATION
EXQUISITENESS
EXSANGUINEOUS
EXTEMPORARILY
EXTENSIBILITY
EXTENSIVENESS
EXTERMINATION
EXTERMINATORY
EXTERRITORIAL
EXTRAJUDICIAL
EXTRAOFFICIAL
EXTRAORDINARY
EXTRATROPICAL
EXTRAVAGANTLY
EXTRAVASATION
EXTRINSICALLY

F

FACETIOUSNESS
FALSIFICATION
FANTASTICALLY
FARINACEOUSLY
FAULTLESSNESS
FEATHERWEIGHT
FEROCIOUSNESS
FERTILIZATION
FILIBUSTERISM
FLASHINGPOINT
FLESHCOLOURED
FLOCCILLATION
FLORICULTURAL
FOOLHARDINESS
FORAMINIFERAL
FOREKNOWLEDGE
FOREMENTIONED
FORGETFULNESS
FORMULIZATION
FORTIFICATION
FOSSILIFEROUS
FOSSILIZATION
FRACTIOUSNESS
FREQUENTATIVE
FRIGHTFULNESS
FRIVOLOUSNESS
FRUMENTACEOUS
FUNAMBULATION
FUNDAMENTALLY

G

GALVANIZATION
GALVANOPLASTY
GASTEROPODOUS
GASTROCNEMIUS
GENERALISSIMO
GENTLEMANLIKE
GEOMETRICALLY
GESTICULATION
GLORIFICATION
GLOSSOGRAPHER
GLOSSOLOGICAL
GOODNATUREDLY
GRACELESSNESS
GRAMINIVOROUS

GRAMMATICALLY
GRANDILOQUENT
GRANDMOTHERLY
GRAPPLINGIRON
GRATICULATION
GRATIFICATION
GROSSULACEOUS
GROTESQUENESS
GUBERNATORIAL
GUILTLESSNESS
GYMNASTICALLY
GYMNOSPERMOUS

H

HAEMAGLOBULIN
HAIRSPLITTING
HALLUCINATION
HALLUCINATORY
HARBOURMASTER
HARMONIZATION
HEALTHFULNESS
HEARTBREAKING
HEARTLESSNESS
HELMINTHOLOGY
HEMIMETABOLIC
HEMISPHERICAL
HERMAPHRODISM
HERMAPHRODITE
HERMENEUTICAL
HERPETOLOGIST
HETEROCARPOUS
HETERODACTYLE
HETEROGENEITY
HETEROGENEOUS
HETEROGENESIS
HETEROMORPHIC
HETEROPLASTIC
HETEROPTEROUS
HIEROGLYPHIST
HOLOMETABOLIC
HOMOEOPATHIST
HORIZONTALITY
HORRIPILATION
HORTICULTURAL
HOUSEBREAKING
HUNDREDWEIGHT
HYDROCEPHALUS
HYDRODYNAMICS
HYDROKINETICS
HYDROMETRICAL
HYMENOPTEROUS
HYPERCRITICAL
HYPERMETROPIA
HYPOCHONDRIAC
HYPOCONDRIUM
HYPOPHOSPHITE
HYPOTHECATION
HYSTERANTHOUS

I

IATROCHEMICAL
ICHTHYOLOGIST
IDEOGRAPHICAL
IDIOMATICALLY
IDIOSYNCRATIC
IGNOMINIOUSLY

ILLEGIBLENESS
ILLUSTRIOUSLY
IMMATERIALISM
IMMATERIALISTS
IMMATERIALITSY
IMMOVABLENES
IMMUTABLENES
IMPARIPINNATE
IMPARTIBILITY
IMPASSIBILITY
IMPASSIONABLE
IMPASSIVENESS
IMPECCABILITY
IMPECUNIOSITY
IMPERFECTNESS
IMPERIOUSNESS
IMPERSONALITY
IMPERSONATION
IMPERTINENTLY
IMPERTURBABLE
IMPETUOUSNESS
IMPLACABILITY
IMPORTUNATELY
IMPOSSIBILITY
IMPRACTICABLE
IMPRACTICABLY
IMPRESSIONIST
IMPRESSIONISM
IMPROBABILITY
IMPROPRIATION
IMPROVABILITY
IMPROVIDENTLY
IMPROVISATION
IMPROVISATORY
INADVERTENTLY
INAPPRECIABLE
INAPPROPRIATE
INATTENTIVELY
INCANDESCENCE
INCARCERATION
INCOGNOSCIBLE
INCOMBUSTIBLE
INCOMPETENTLY
INCONCEIVABLE
INCONCEIVABLY
INCONDENSABLE
INCONGRUOUSLY
INCONSEQUENCE
INCONSIDERATE
INCONSISTENCE
INCONSISTENCY
INCONSPICUOUS
INCONTESTABLE
INCONTESTABLY
INCONTINENTLY
INCONVENIENCE
INCONVERTIBLE
INCONVINCIBLE
INCORPORATION
INCORPOREALLY
INCORRECTNESS
INCORRUPTIBLE
INCREDIBILITY
INCREDULOUSLY
INCURABLENESS
INDEFATIGABLE
INDEFATIGABLY
INDEPENDENTLY
INDESCRIBABLE

INDETERMINATE
INDIFFERENTLY
INDISPENSABLE
INDISPENSABLY
INDISPOSITION
INDISSOCIABLE
INDISSOLVABLE
INDIVIDUALISM
INDIVIDUALITY
INDIVIDUALIZE
INDIVIDUATION
INDUSTRIALISM
INDUSTRIOUSLY
INEFFECTIVELY
INEFFECTUALLY
INEFFICACIOUS
INEFFICIENTLY
INELIGIBILITY
INEXHAUSTIBLE
INEXHAUSTIBLY
INEXPEDIENTLY
INEXPENSIVELY
INEXPERIENCED
INEXPRESSIBLE
INEXPRESSIBLY
INFALLIBILISM
INFALLIBILIST
INFERENTIALLY
INFINITESIMAL
INFLEXIBILITY
INFLORESCENCE
INFLUENTIALLY
INFUNDIBULATE
INGENIOUSNESS
INHOSPITALITY
INJUDICIOUSLY
INOBSERVANTLY
INOFFENSIVELY
INOPPORTUNELY
INQUISITIONAL
INQUISITIVELY
INQUISITORIAL
INSATIABILITY
INSECTIVOROUS
INSENSIBILITY
INSIDIOUSNESS
INSIGNIFICANT
INSINUATINGLY
INSPECTORSHIP
INSTANTANEOUS
INSTINCTIVELY
INSTITUTIONAL
INSTRUCTIVELY
INSUBORDINATE
INSUFFICIENCY
INSUPPORTABLE
INSUPPORTABLY
INSUSCEPTIBLE
INTANGIBILITY
INTEGUMENTARY
INTELLIGENCER
INTELLIGENTLY
INTEMPERATELY
INTENSIVENESS
INTENTIONALLY
INTERCALATION
INTERCELLULAR
INTERCOLONIAL
INTERDIGITATE
INTERESTINGLY

INTERLACEMENT
INTERLINEARLY
INTERLOCUTION
INTERLOCUTORY
INTERMARRIAGE
INTERMEDIATOR
INTERMITTANCE
INTERMUSCULAR
INTERNATIONAL
INTEROSCULATE
INTERPETIOLAR
INTERPOLATION
INTERPOSITION
INTERPRETABLE
INTERRELATION
INTERROGATION
INTERROGATIVE
INTERROGATORY
INTERRUPTEDLY
INTERSIDEREAL
INTERSPERSION
INTERSTELLARY
INTERSTRATIFY
INTERTROPICAL
INTRAPARIETAL
INTRATROPICAL
INTRINSICALLY
INTROSPECTION
INTROSPECTIVE
INTRUSIVENESS
INVENTORIALLY
INVESTIGATION
INVESTIGATIVE
INVIDIOUSNESS
INVINCIBILITY
INVIOLABILITY
INVISIBLENESS
INVOLUNTARILY
IRASCIBLENESS
IRRATIONALITY
IRRECLAIMABLE
IRRECOVERABLE
IRRECOVERABLY
IRRELIGIOUSLY
IRREPRESSIBLE
IRREPRESSIBLY
IRRESPONSIBLE
IRRESPONSIBLY
IRRETRIEVABLE
IRRETRIEVABLY

J

JOLLIFICATION
JUDICIOUSNESS
JURISPRUDENCE
JUSTIFICATION
JUSTIFICATIVE
JUSTIFICATORY

K

KALEIDOSCOPIC

L

LABYRINTHODOM

LACKADAISICAL
LANGUISHINGLY
LARYNGOSCOPIC
LAUGHABLENESS
LECHEROUSNESS
LEPIDODENDRON
LEPIDOPTEROUS
LETHARGICALLY
LEUCOCYTHEMIA
LEXICOGRAPHER
LEXICOGRAPHIC
LIBRARIANSHIP
LICHENOGRAPHY
LICKERISHNESS
LIGHTSOMENESS
LIGNIFICATION
LIPOGRAMMATIC
LITHOFRACTEUR
LITHOGLYPHICS
LITIGIOUSNESS
LOATHSOMENESS
LOGARITHMICAL
LUDICROUSNESS
LUXURIOUSNESS
LYENCEPHALOUS

M

MACHICOLATION
MAGISTERIALLY
MAGNANIMOUSLY
MAGNETIZATION
MAGNIFICENTLY
MAGNILOQUENCE
MALACOSTRACAN
MALICIOUSNESS
MALLEABLENESS
MANIFESTATION
MANUFACTURING
MARSIPOBRANCH
MARTYROLOGIST
MASCULINENESS
MATERFAMILIAS
MATERIALISTIC
MATHEMATICIAN
MATRICULATION
MATRIMONIALLY
MEDIATORIALLY
MEDITERRANEAN
MEGACEPHALOUS
MELLIFLUENTLY
MELLIFLUOUSLY
MELODIOUSNESS
MELODRAMATIST
MEMBRANACEOUS
MENSURABILITY
MERCENARINESS
MERCILESSNESS
MERITORIOUSLY
MESENCEPHALON
MESOCEPHALOUS
METALLIFEROUS
METAMORPHOSIS
METAPHYSICIAN
METEMPIRICISM
METEOROLOGIST
METHODISTICAL
METONYMICALLY
MICROMETRICAL

MICROSCOPICAL
MINERALOGICAL
MINISTERIALLY
MISADVERTENCE
MISCEGENATION
MISCELLANEOUS
MISCHIEVOUSLY
MISCONCEPTION
MISERABLENESS
MISGOVERNMENT
MISMANAGEMENT
MISUNDERSTAND
MODERATORSHIP
MOHAMMEDANISM
MOHAMMEDANIZE
MOLLIFICATION
MOMENTARINESS
MOMENTOUSNESS
MONARCHICALLY
MONOCHROMATIC
MONOCOTYLEDON
MONOGRAMMATIC
MONOGRAPHICAL
MONOMETALLISM
MONOMETALLIST
MONOTHALAMOUS
MONOTREMATOUS
MONSTROUSNESS
MORPHINOMANIA
MORTIFICATION
MOUNTAINOUSLY
MULTANGULARLY
MULTICAPSULAR
MULTIPLICATOR
MULTIPRESENCE
MULTISYLLABLE
MULTITUDINOUS
MUMMIFICATION
MYSTIFICATION

N

NECESSITARIAN
NECESSITOUSLY
NEGOTIABILITY
NEIGHBOURHOOD
NICKELIFEROUS
NIGGARDLINESS
NOISELESSNESS
NONCONFORMING
NONCONFORMIST
NONCONFORMITY
NONSENSICALLY
NOTORIOUSNESS
NULLIFICATION

O

OBJECTIONABLE
OBJECTIONABLY
OBJECTIVENESS
OBLIVIOUSNESS
OBNOXIOUSNESS
OBSERVATIONAL
OBSTINATENESS
OBSTRUCTIVELY
OCCIDENTALIZE

ODONTOGLOSSUM
ODORIFEROUSLY
OFFENSIVENESS
OFFICIOUSNESS
OPERASBOUFFES
OPHIOMORPHOUS
OPHTHALMOLOGY
OPHTHALMOTOMY
OPPORTUNENESS
OPPOSITIONIST
OPPROBRIOUSLY
ORCHESTRATION
ORGANOGENESIS
ORGANOLOGICAL
ORNAMENTATION
ORNITHICHNITE
ORNITHOLOGIST
ORTHOEPICALLY
ORTHOGNATHOUS
OSTENSIBILITY
OSTREACULTURE
OUTSETTLEMENT
OVERFLOWINGLY
OVERSTATEMENT
OVERVALUATION
OVOVIVIPAROUS

P

PALAEOCRYSTIC
PALAEOGRAPHIC
PALAEONTOLOGY
PALAEOTHERIUM
PALAEOZOOLOGY
PALATABLENESS
PANDICULATION
PANEGYRICALLY
PANSPERMATISM
PANTHEISTICAL
PAPAVERACEOUS
PARABOLICALLY
PARADOXICALLY
PARAGRAPHICAL
PARALLELOGRAM
PARAPHERNALIA
PARASITICALLY
PARENTHETICAL
PARLIAMENTARY
PARTICIPATION
PARTICIPIALLY
PARTICOLOURED
PARTICULARISM
PARTICULARIST
PARTICULARITY
PARTICULARIZE
PATERFAMILIAS
PATHOGNOMONIC
PATRIMONIALLY
PATRIOTICALLY
PATRONIZINGLY
PEACEABLENESS
PEDESTRIANISM
PENDULOUSNESS
PENETRABILITY
PENETRATINGLY
PENITENTIALLY
PENNILESSNESS
PENTADELPHOUS
PENTAPETALOUS

PENTAPHYLLOUS
PENTASTICHOUS
PENURIOUSNESS
PERAMBULATION
PEREGRINATION
PERFECTIONISM
PERFECTIONIST
PERFUNCTORILY
PERICHONDRIUM
PERIPATETICAL
PERISHABILITY
PERPENDICULAR
PERSCRUTATION
PERSEVERINGLY
PERSONALITIES
PERSPECTIVELY
PERSPICACIOUS
PERSPICUOUSLY
PESTIFEROUSLY
PHANEROGAMOUS
PHARISAICALLY
PHARMACEUTICS
PHARMACEUTIST
PHARMACOPOEIA
PHENOMENALISM
PHILANTHROPIC
PHILHELLENISM
PHILOMATHICAL
PHILOSOPHICAL
PHILOSOPHIZER
PHONAUTOGRAPH
PHONOGRAPHIST
PHOSPHURETTED
PHOTOMETRICAL
PHRASEOLOGIST
PHRENOLOGICAL
PHYLACTERICAL
PHYLACTERICAL
PHYLLOPHAGOUS
PHYSIOGNOMIST
PHYSIOLOGICAL
PICTURESQUELY
PISCICULTURAL
PLAINTIVENESS
PLATITUDINOUS
PLATYCEPHALIC
PLAUSIBLENESS
PLECTOGNATHIC
PLENTEOUSNESS
PLETHORICALLY
PLURALIZATION
PNEUMATICALLY
PNEUMATOMETER
PNEUMOGASTRIC
POCOCURANTISM
POISONOUSNESS
POLLINIFEROUS
POLYCHROMATIC
POLYCOTYLEDON
POLYDACTYLISM
POLYSYNTHETIC
POLYTHALAMOUS
PONDERABILITY
PONDEROUSNESS
PORCELLANEOUS
PORPHYRACEOUS
POSSESSIONARY
POWERLESSNESS
PRACTICALNESS
PRAGMATICALLY

PRAYERFULNESS
PRECAUTIONARY
PRECENTORSHIP
PRECIPITANTLY
PRECIPITATELY
PRECIPITATION
PRECIPITOUSLY
PRECONCEPTION
PREDESTINATOR
PREDICABILITY
PREDICAMENTAL
PREDICATIVELY
PREDOMINANTLY
PREFIGURATION
PREFIGUREMENT
PREJUDICATION
PREJUDICIALLY
PRELIMINARILY
PREMATURENESS
PREMEDITATION
PREOCCUPATION
PREORDINATION
PREPARATIVELY
PREPONDERANCE
PREPOSITIONAL
PREPOSSESSING
PREPOSSESSION
PRESBYTERSHIP
PRESCIENTIFIC
PRESCRIPTIBLE
PRESIDENTSHIP
PRESSIROSTRAL
PRESUMPTIVELY
PRETENTIOUSLY
PRETERMISSION
PRETERNATURAL
PRETERPERFECT
PREVARICATION
PRIMITIVENESS
PRIMOGENITURE
PRISMATICALLY
PRIVATEERSMAN
PROBABILITIES
PROBLEMATICAL
PROCONSULSHIP
PROCRASTINATE
PROFESSORIATE
PROGNOSTICATE
PROGRESSIONAL
PROGRESSIVELY
PROLEPTICALLY
PROMISCUOUSLY
PRONOUNCEABLE
PRONOUNCEMENT
PRONUNCIATION
PROPAEDEUTICS
PROPHETICALLY
PROPORTIONATE
PROPOSITIONAL
PROPRIETORIAL
PROSPECTIVELY
PROTECTIONISM
PROTECTIONIST
PROTECTORSHIP
PROTERANDROUS
PROTEROGYNOUS
PROTESTANTISM
PROTESTANTIZE
PROVERBIALIST
PROVINCIALISM

PROVISIONALLY
PSYCHOLOGICAL
PULMONIFEROUS
PULVERIZATION
PUNCTILIOUSLY
PURITANICALLY
PUSILLANIMITY
PUSILLANIMOUS
PYRHELIOMETER
PYROTECHNICAL

Q

QUADRAGESIMAL
QUADRIFOLIATE
QUADRILATERAL
QUADRILITERAL
QUADRILOCULAR
QUADRIPARTITE
QUADRUPLICATE
QUALIFICATION
QUALIFICATIVE
QUALITATIVELY
QUERULOUSNESS
QUINCENTENARY
QUINQUAGESIMA
QUINQUANGULAR

R

RAPACIOUSNESS
RATIOCINATION
RATIOCINATIVE
RATIOCINATORY
RATIONALISTIC
READJOURNMENT
REALISTICALLY
REAPPOINTMENT
REARRANGEMENT
RECEIVABILITY
RECIPROCATION
RECOMMENDABLE
RECONCILEMENT
RECRIMINATION
RECRIMINATIVE
RECRIMINATORY
RECRUDESCENCE
RECRUDESCENCY
RECTANGULARLY
RECTIFICATION
RECTILINEALLY
REDUPLICATION
REFLEXIBILITY
REFRIGERATION
REFRIGERATIVE
REFRIGERATORY
REGISTRARSHIP
REGURGITATION
REIMBURSEMENT
REIMPORTATION
REINFORCEMENT
REINSTATEMENT
REINTERROGATE
REINVESTIGATE
REJUVENESCENT
RELIGIOUSNESS
REMISSIBILITY
REMONSTRATIVE

REMONSTRATORY
REMORSELESSLY
REPLENISHMENT
REPREHENSIBLE
REPREHENSIBLY
REPRESENTABLE
REPROACHFULLY
REPROBATENESS
REPUBLICATION
REPULSIVENESS
RESISTIBILITY
RESOLVABILITY
RESPIRABILITY
RESPIRATIONAL
RESPLENDENTLY
RESTRICTIVELY
RESUSCITATION
RETENTIVENESS
RETROGRESSION
RETROGRESSIVE
RETROSPECTION
RETROSPECTIVE
REVERBERATION
REVERBERATORY
REVERENTIALLY
REVERSIBILITY
REVOLUTIONARY
REVOLUTIONISM
REVOLUTIONIST
REVOLUTIONIZE
RHAPSODICALLY
RHIZOMORPHOUS
RHOPALOCEROUS
RIGHTEOUSNESS
RUSSOPHOBISTS

S

SACCHAROMETER
SACCHARIMETER
SACERDOTALISM
SACRAMENTALLY
SACROSANCTIFY
SAGACIOUSNESS
SALACIOUSNESS
SANCTIMONIOUS
SARCASTICALLY
SCARIFICATION
SCEPTICALNESS
SCHIZOMYCETES
SCHOLASTICISM
SCINTILLATION
SCRIPTURALISM
SCRIPTURALIST
SCULPTURESQUE
SECONDARINESS
SECRETARYSHIP
SECRETIVENESS
SEDENTARINESS
SEDIMENTATION
SEDITIOUSNESS
SEISMOGRAPHIC
SENESCHALSHIP
SENSELESSNESS
SENSITIVENESS
SENTENTIOUSLY
SENTIMENTALLY
SEPARABLENESS
SEPTISYLLABLE

SEPTUAGESIMAL
SEQUESTRATION
SESQUILATERAL
SHAMELESSNESS
SHAPELESSNESS
SIGHTLESSNESS
SIGILLOGRAPHY
SIGNIFICANTLY
SIGNIFICATION
SIGNIFICATIVE
SIGNIFICATORY
SINGULARITIES
SOLEMNIZATION
SOLICITORSHIP
SOLIDUNGULATE
SOMNAMBULATOR
SOMNILOQUENCE
SOPHISTICALLY
SOPHISTICATOR
SORROWFULNESS
SPASMODICALLY
SPECIFICATION
SPECTROSCOPIC
SPECULATIVELY
SPERMATORRHEA
SPLANCHNOLOGY
SPLENETICALLY
SPONTANEOUSLY
SPORTSMANSHIP
SPRIGHTLINESS
SQUEAMISHNESS
SQUEEZABILITY
STALACTITICAL
STALAGMITICAL
STALWORTHNESS
STAMINIFEROUS
STAPHYLORAPHY
STATESMANLIKE
STATESMANSHIP
STATISTICALLY
STEADFASTNESS
STEGANOGRAPHY
STENOGRAPHIST
STERCORACEOUS
STEREOGRAPHIC
STETHOSCOPIST
STOLONIFEROUS
STRANGULATION
STRATEGETICAL
STRATEGICALLY
STRATIGRAPHIC
STRENGTHENING
STRUCTURELESS
SUBDEACONSHIP
SUBORDINATELY
SUBORDINATION
SUBORDINATIVE
SUBPERITONEAL
SUBSTANTIALLY
SUBSTANTIVELY
SUBTILIZATION
SUCCESSIONIST
SUFFRAGANSHIP
SUFFUMIGATION
SULPHUREOUSLY
SUPERABUNDANT
SUPERADDITION
SUPERANNUATED
SUPERDOMINANT
SUPEREMINENCE

SUPERFETATION
SUPERFICIALLY
SUPERFLUITIES
SUPERFLUOUSLY
SUPERFORTRESS
SUPERLATIVELY
SUPERPOSITION
SUPERSATURATE
SUPERSENSIBLE
SUPERSTITIOUS
SUPPLANTATION
SUPPLEMENTARY
SUPPOSITIONAL
SUPRASCAPULAR
SURREPTITIOUS
SYLLOGISTICAL
SYMMETRICALLY
SYMPATHETICAL
SYMPIESOMETER
SYMPTOMATICAL
SYNCHRONOUSLY
SYNECDOCHICAL
SYNECPHONESIS
SYNTACTICALLY
SYNTHETICALLY
SYPHILIZATION

T

TALKATIVENESS
TANTALIZATION
TASTELESSNESS
TEACHABLENESS
TELEGRAPHICAL
TEMPERATENESS
TEMPESTUOUSLY
TEMPORALITIES
TEMPORIZATION
TENACIOUSNESS
TERGIVERSATOR
TERMINATIONAL
TERPSICHOREAN
TERRESTRIALLY
TERRITORIALLY
TETRASYLLABLE
THALAMIFLORAL
THANKFULNESS
THAUMATURGIST
THAUMATURGICS
THEANTHROPISM
THEATRICALITY
THEOLOGICALLY
THEORETICALLY
THERIOMORPHIC
THOUGHTLESSLY
THREATENINGLY
TINTINNABULAR
TOLERABLENESS
TOPOGRAPHICAL
TOXICOLOGICAL
TRACKLESSNESS
TRADITIONALLY
TRANQUILLIZER
TRANSATLANTIC
TRANSCENDENCE
TRANSCENDENCY
TRANSCRIPTION
TRANSCRIPTIVE
TRANSGRESSION

TRANSIENTNESS
TRANSITIONARY
TRANSLUCENTLY
TRANSMIGRATOR
TRANSMISSIBLE
TRANSMITTABLE
TRANSMITTANCE
TRANSMUTATION
TRANSPARENTLY
TRANSPIRATION
TRANSPORTABLE
TRANSPOSITION
TRANSPOSITIVE
TRANSVERSALLY
TREMULOUSNESS
TRIANGULARITY
TRIANGULATION
TRIPINNATIFID
TROUBLESOMELY
TYPOGRAPHICAL

U

UMBELLIFEROUS
UMBRACULIFORM
UNACCOMPANIED
UNACCOUNTABLE
UNAPOSTOLICAL
UNAPPRECIATED
UNASSIMILATED
UNCERTAINTIES
UNCOMFORTABLE
UNCOMFORTABLY
UNCOMPLAINING
UNCONDITIONAL
UNCONDITIONED
UNCONFORMABLE
UNCONFORMABLY
UNCONQUERABLE
UNCONQUERABLY
UNDERCLOTHING
UNDERGRADUATE
UNDERESTIMATE
UNDERSTANDING
UNDERSTRAPPER
UNDISCERNIBLE
UNDISCIPLINED
UNDISSOLVABLE
UNDISTURBEDLY
UNDIVERSIFIED
UNEMBARRASSED
UNENLIGHTENED
UNFAMILIARITY
UNFASHIONABLE
UNFASHIONABLY
UNFORTUNATELY
UNGRAMMATICAL
UNGUARDEDNESS
UNIMPASSIONED
UNIMPEACHABLE
UNIMPRESSIBLE
UNINHABITABLE
UNINSTRUCTIVE
UNINTERESTING
UNINTERMITTED
UNINTERRUPTED
UNJUSTIFIABLE
UNJUSTIFIABLY
UNMENTIONABLE

UNMINDFULNESS
UNNECESSARILY
UNNEIGHBOURLY
UNOBTRUSIVELY
UNPERCEIVABLE
UNPHILOSOPHIC
UNPRECEDENTED
UNPRESENTABLE
UNRECOMPENSED
UNREPRESENTED
UNRIGHTEOUSLY
UNSAVOURINESS
UNSERVICEABLE
UNSIGHTLINESS
UNSKILFULNESS
UNSUBSTANTIAL
UNSURPASSABLE
UNSUSCEPTIBLE
UNSYMMETRICAL
UNTHRIFTINESS
UNTRUSTWORTHY
UNWARRANTABLE
UNWARRANTABLY
UNWILLINGNESS
UNWORKMANLIKE
UNWORLDLINESS

V

VEGETARIANISM
VENERABLENESS
VENTRILOQUIAL
VENTRILOQUISM
VENTRILOQUIST
VENTRILOQUIZE
VENTRILOQUOUS
VERMICULATION
VERNACULARISM
VERSICOLOURED
VERSIFICATION
VEXATIOUSNESS
VIOLONCELLIST
VISIONARINESS
VITRIFICATION
VIVACIOUSNESS
VOLATILIZABLE
VOLUMENOMETER
VOLUNTARINESS
VORACIOUSNESS
VULCANIZATION
VULNERABILITY

W

WEARISOMENESS
WHITHERSOEVER
WHOLESOMENESS
WONDERFULNESS
WORTHLESSNESS

X

XEROPHTHALMIA
XYLOGRAPHICAL

Y

YACHTSMANSHIP
YELLOWISHNESS

Z

ZYGODACTYLOUS

FOURTEEN-LETTER WORDS

A

ABOMINABLENESS
ABSTEMIOUSNESS
ABSTRACTEDNESS
ACCEPTABLENESS
ACCOMPLISHABLE
ACCOMPLISHMENT
ACCOUNTABILITY
ACCOUNTANTSHIP
ACKNOWLEDGMENT
ADMINISTRATION
ADMINISTRATIVE
ADSCITITIOUSLY
ADVANTAGEOUSLY
ADVENTITIOUSLY
AFFECTIONATELY
AFOREMENTIONED
AGGRANDIZEMENT
AGGRESSIVENESS
ALPHABETICALLY
AMPHIBOLOGICAL
ANAGRAMMATICAL
ANTAPHRODISIAC
ANTHROPOGRAPHY
ANTIPHLOGISTIC
ANTIQUARIANISM
ANTISCRIPTURAL
ANTISYPHILITIC
ANTITHETICALLY
APHELIOTROPISM
APHORISTICALLY
APOLOGETICALLY
APOPHTHEGMATIC
APPREHENSIVELY
APPRENTICESHIP
ARBORICULTURAL
ARCHAEOLOGICAL
ARCHDEACONSHIP
ARCHIEPISCOPAL
ARITHMETICALLY
ASTROLOGICALLY
ASTRONOMICALLY
ATTAINABLENESS
ATTRACTIVENESS
AUGMENTATIVELY
AURORA BOREALIS
AUSPICIOUSNESS
AUTHENTICATION
AUTOBIOGRAPHER
AUTOBIOGRAPHIC

B

BACTERIOLOGIST
BAROMETRICALLY
BATHING-MACHINE
BEAUTIFICATION
BELIEVABLENESS
BILLIARD-MARKER
BIOGRAPHICALLY
BIRD-OF-PARADISE
BITUMINIFEROUS

BLANK-CARTRIDGE
BLITHESOMENESS
BOA-CONSTRICTOR
BOARDING-SCHOOL
BOISTEROUSNESS
BOROUGH-ENGLISH
BOULEVERSEMENT
BRACHYCEPHALIC
BRANCHIOSTEGAL
BREADFRUIT-TREE
BREATHLESSNESS
BRIGHT'S-DISEASE
BRISTOL-DIAMOND
BRITANNIA-METAL
BROBDINGNAGIAN
BRUSSELS-CARPET

C

CABINET-COUNCIL
CALAMANDER-WOOD
CALCOGRAPHICAL
CALICO-PRINTING
CAPITALIZATION
CAPRICIOUSNESS
CAPTAIN-GENERAL
CARDINAL-FLOWER
CARLINE-THISTLE
CARTRIDGE-PAPER
CASTLE-BUILDING
CASTRAMETATION
CATADIOPTRICAL
CATECHETICALLY
CATHERINE-WHEEL
CENSORIOUSNESS
CENSURABLENESS
CENTRALIZATION
CHALCOGRAPHIST
CHAMBER-COUNSEL
CHANCELLORSHIP
CHANGEABLENESS
CHARACTERISTIC
CHARGEABLENESS
CHARITABLENESS
CHICKEN-HEARTED
CHIMNEY-SWALLOW
CHOROGRAPHICAL
CIRCUITOUSNESS
CIRCUMAMBIENCY
CIRCUMAMBU LATE
CIRCUMFERENTOR
CIRCUMGYRATION
CIRCUMLITTORAL
CIRCUMLOCUTION
CIRCUMLOCUTORY
CIRCUMNAVIGATE
CIRCUMNUTATION
CIRCUMSPECTION
CIRCUMSTANTIAL
CIRCUMVOLUTION
CLASSIFICATION
COESSENTIALITY
COGNOSCIBILITY
COLORADO BEETLE

COLOURABLENESS
COLOUR-SERGEANT
COMMENSURATELY
COMMENSURATION
COMMENTATORIAL
COMMISSARYSHIP
COMMODIOUSNESS
COMPOSING-STICK
COMPREHENSIBLE
COMPREHENSIBLY
CONCAVO-CONCAVE
CONCEIVABILITY
CONCENTRICALLY
CONCESSIONAIRE
CONCLUSIVENESS
CONDENSABILITY
CONDITIONALITY
CONFIDENTIALLY
CONGLOMERATION
CONGLUTINATION
CONGLUTINATIVE
CONGRATULATION
CONGRATULATORY
CONGREGATIONAL
CONSANGUINEOUS
CONSCRIPTIONAL
CONSTITUTIONAL
CONSTITUTIVELY
CONSTRUCTIONAL
CONSTRUCTIVELY
CONSUBSTANTIAL
CONSUETUDINARY
CONTAGIOUSNESS
CONTEMPTUOUSLY
CONTIGUOUSNESS
CONTINENTALIST
CONTINENTALISM
CONTINUOUSNESS
CONTRACTEDNESS
CONTRADICTABLE
CONTRADICTIOUS
CONTRAINDICATE
CONTRAPOSITION
CONTROLLERSHIP
CONTROVERTIBLE
CONTROVERTIBLY
CONTUMACIOUSLY
CONTUMELIOUSLY
CONVALESCENTLY
CONVENTIONALLY
CONVERSATIONAL
CONVERTIBILITY
CONVEXO-CONCAVE
CO-ORDINATENESS
COPPER-BOTTOMED
COPPER-FASTENED
CORNET-A-PISTONS
COROLLIFLOROUS
CORRESPONDENCE
CORRESPONDENCY
CORRUPTIBILITY
COSMOPOLITICAL
COTEMPORANEOUS
COUNSELLORSHIP
COUNTERBALANCE

COURAGEOUSNESS
CREDITABLENESS
CROSSREFERENCE
CRYSTALLIZABLE
CRYSTALLOMANCY
CUCURBITACEOUS
CURTAINLECTURE

D

DACTYLIOGLYPHY
DECEIVABLENESS
DECHRISTIANIZE
DECOLORIZATION
DECONSECRATION
DECORATIVENESS
DEFINITIVENESS
DEGENERATENESS
DELIBERATENESS
DELIGHTFULNESS
DEMOBILISATION
DEMOCRATICALLY
DEMONETIZATION
DEMORALIZATION
DENOMINATIONAL
DENOMINATIVELY
DEPLORABLENESS
DEPOLARIZATION
DEROGATORINESS
DESCENDIBILITY
DESPICABLENESS
DESPITEFULNESS
DESTRUCTIONIST
DETESTABLENESS
DIABOLICALNESS
DIAHELIOTROPIC
DICOTYLEDONOUS
DIFFUSIBLENESS
DIGESTIBLENESS
DIMINUTIVENESS
DIPHTHONGATION
DIPLOMATICALLY
DISAGGREGATION
DISAPPOINTEDLY
DISAPPOINTMENT
DISAPPROPRIATE
DISAPPROVINGLY
DISARRANGEMENT
DISCIPLINARIAN
DISCONSOLATELY
DISCONTENTEDLY
DISCONTENTMENT
DISCONTINUANCE
DISCOUNTENANCE
DISCOURAGEMENT
DISCOURAGINGLY
DISCOURTEOUSLY
DISCRETIONALLY
DISCRIMINATELY
DISCRIMINATING
DISCRIMINATION
DISCRIMINATIVE
DISCURSIVENESS
DISDAINFULNESS
DISEMBARKATION
DISEMBOGUEMENT
DISEMBOWELMENT
DISENCHANTMENT
DISENCHANTRESS

DISENCUMBRANCE
DISENGAGEDNESS
DISENTHRALMENT
DISGUSTFULNESS
DISILLUSIONIZE
DISINCLINATION
DISINCORPORATE
DISINGENUOUSLY
DISINHERITANCE
DISINTEGRATION
DISINVESTITURE
DISJOINTEDNESS
DISORDERLINESS
DISQUISITIONAL
DISRESPECTABLE
DISSERTATIONAL
DISTEMPERATURE
DISTENSIBILITY
DISTINGUISHING
DISTRACTEDNESS
DISTRIBUTIVELY
DIVERTISSEMENT
DODECASYLLABLE
DOUBLEBREASTED

E

ECCLESIASTICAL
ECCLESIOLOGIST
EDUCATIONALIST
EFFEMINATENESS
ELECTIONEERING
ELECTROBIOLOGY
ELECTRODYNAMIC
ELECTROKINETIC
ELECTROLYTICAL
ELEMENTARINESS
ELEUTHEROMANIA
EMBLEMATICALLY
EMPYREUMATICAL
ENCYCLOPAEDIST
ENHARMONICALLY
ENTERPRISINGLY
ENTHRONIZATION
ENTHUSIASTICAL
ENTOPERIPHERAL
EPIGRAMMATICAL
EQUIPONDERANCE
ETHNOGRAPHICAL
ETYMOLOGICALLY
EULOGISTICALLY
EVANGELICALISM
EVANGELIZATION
EXCOMMUNICABLE
EXCREMENTITIAL
EXCRUCIATINGLY
EXPERIMENTALLY
EXPRESSIONLESS
EXPRESSIVENESS
EXTEMPORANEOUS
EXTINGUISHABLE
EXTINGUISHMENT
EXTORTIONATELY
EXTRAPAROCHIAL
EXTRINSICALITY

F

FAINTHEARTEDLY
FALLACIOUSNESS
FANTASTICALITY
FARSIGHTEDNESS
FASTIDIOUSNESS
FAVOURABLENESS
FELLOWCOMMONER
FELLOWCREATURE
FIBROCARTILAGE
FIGURATIVENESS
FLAGITIOUSNESS
FLORICULTURIST
FORAMINIFEROUS
FOREORDINATION
FORISFAMILIATE
FORMIDABLENESS
FORTUITOUSNESS
FRATERNIZATION
FREESPOKENNESS
FRIENDLESSNESS
FRINGILLACEOUS
FROLICSOMENESS
FRUCTIFICATION

G

GASTROVASCULAR
GENEALOGICALLY
GENERALIZATION
GEOCENTRICALLY
GEOGRAPHICALLY
GOODHUMOUREDLY
GRANDILOQUENCE
GREGARIOUSNESS
GROUNDLESSNESS
GUILLOTINEMENT
GYRENCEPHALATE

H

HANDICRAFTSMEN
HARMONIOUSNESS
HELMINTHAGOGUE
HEMISPHEROIDAL
HERESIOGRAPHER
HERMAPHRODITIC
HETEROCLITICAL
HETEROMORPHOUS
HETEROPHYLLOUS
HIEROGLYPHICAL
HIPPOPOTAMUSES
HISTRIONICALLY
HONOURABLENESS
HORTICULTURIST
HYDROGRAPHICAL
HYPERAESTHESIA
HYPERBOLICALLY
HYPERCRITICISM
HYPOCRITICALLY
HYPOSTATICALLY
HYPOTHETICALLY

I

ICHNOLITHOLOGY
ICHTHYOLOGICAL
ICHTHYOPHAGOUS
ICHTHYOPHAGIST
IDENTIFICATION
IDIOPATHICALLY
ILLEGITIMATELY
ILLUSTRATIVELY
IMPARIDIGITATE
IMPASSABLENESS
IMPERVIOUSNESS
IMPLACABLENESS
IMPOVERISHMENT
IMPRESSIBILITY
IMPRESSIONABLE
IMPRESSIVENESS
IMPROVABLENESS
IMPROVISATRICE
INALIENABILITY
INAPPREHENSION
INAPPROACHABLE
INARTICULATELY
INARTIFICIALLY
INAUSPICIOUSLY
INCAPACITATION
INCAUTIOUSNESS
INCOMMENSURATE
INCOMMUNICABLE
INCOMPRESSIBLE
INCONCLUSIVELY
INCONSIDERABLE
INCONSIDERABLY
INCONSISTENTLY
INCONVENIENTLY
INCORPOREALITY
INDECIPHERABLE
INDECOMPOSABLE
INDECOROUSNESS
INDEFINITENESS
INDESTRUCTIBLE
INDESTRUCTIBLY
INDETERMINABLE
INDIFFERENTISM
INDISCREETNESS
INDISCRIMINATE
INDISPOSEDNESS
INDISTINCTNESS
INDIVISIBILITY
INDOCTRINATION
INEXPRESSIBLES
INFECTIOUSNESS
INFLEXIBLENESS
INHARMONIOUSLY
INORDINATENESS
INQUISITIONARY
INSATIABLENESS
INSEPARABILITY
INSIGNIFICANCE
INSTITUTIONARY
INSTRUMENTALLY
INSUFFICIENTLY
INSUPERABILITY
INSUPPRESSIBLE
INSURMOUNTABLE
INSURRECTIONAL
INTANGIBLENESS

INTELLECTUALLY
INTERCESSIONAL
INTERCOMMUNION
INTERCOMMUNITY
INTERDEPENDENT
INTERJECTIONAL
INTERLINEATION
INTERMAXILLARY
INTERMEDIATELY
INTERMEDIATION
INTERMIGRATION
INTERPELLATION
INTERPENETRATE
INTERPLANETARY
INTERPRETATION
INTERPRETATIVE
INTRACTABILITY
INTRANSITIVELY
INTRANSMUTABLE
INVARIABLENESS
INVINCIBLENESS
INVIOLABLENESS
IRRATIONALNESS
IRRECOGNIZABLE
IRRECONCILABLE
IRRECONCILABLY
IRREMOVABILITY
IRREPARABILITY
IRREPROACHABLE
IRREPROACHABLY
IRRESOLUTENESS
IRRESPECTIVELY

J

JURISDICTIONAL

K

KNICKERBOCKERS

L

LAMELLIROSTRAL
LAPIDIFICATION
LATITUDINARIAN
LEUCOCYTHAEMIA
LIBERTARIANISM
LIBIDINOUSNESS
LICENTIOUSNESS
LIEUTENANTSHIP
LONGITUDINALLY

M

MACADAMIZATION
MACROCEPHALOUS
MAGNILOQUENTLY
MATHEMATICALLY
MENSURABLENESS
MERETRICIOUSLY
METAPHORICALLY
METAPHYSICALLY
METEMPSYCHOSIS
METENSOMATOSIS
METEOROLOGICAL

METROPOLITICAL
METTLESOMENESS
MICROCEPHALOUS
MINERALIZATION
MINISTERIALIST
MIRACULOUSNESS
MISANTHROPICAL
MISAPPLICATION
MISCALCULATION
MISINFORMATION
MISMEASUREMENT
MULTIFARIOUSLY
MULTIPLICATION
MULTIPLACATIVE
MYSTERIOUSNESS
MYTHOLOGICALLY

N

NATURALIZATION
NEUROHYPNOTISM
NEUROHYPNOLOGY
NEUROPATHOLOGY
NEUTRALIZATION

O

OBLIGATORINESS
OBSEQUIOUSNESS
OBSTREPEROUSLY
OBSTRUCTIONIST
OPHTHALMODYNIA
OPHTHALMOSCOPE
OPHTHALMOSCOPY
OPINIONATIVELY
OPISTHOCOELOUS
OPISTHOGRAPHIC
OPPRESSIVENESS
ORNITHODELPHIA
ORNITHODELPHIC
ORNITHOLOGICAL
ORTHOGRAPHICAL
OSTENTATIOUSLY
OUTRAGEOUSNESS
OVERPOWERINGLY

P

PACHYDACTYLOUS
PACHYDERMATOUS
PALAEOGRAPHIST
PAPILIONACEOUS
PARAGRAMMATIST
PARALLELEPIPED
PARALLELOPIPED
PARAPHRASTICAL
PARENCHYMATOUS
PARSIMONIOUSLY
PASSIONATENESS
PATHOLOGICALLY
PENTADACTYLOUS
PERCEPTIBILITY
PERFECTIBILITY
PERFIDIOUSNESS
PERIPATETICISM
PERIPHRASTICAL
PERISHABLENESS

PERISSODACTYLE
PERMISSIBILITY
PERNICIOUSNESS
PERSPIRABILITY
PERSUASIVENESS
PERTINACIOUSLY
PESTILENTIALLY
PHANTASMAGORIC
PHANTASMAGORIA
PHARMACEUTICAL
PHARMACOLOGIST
PHARMACOPOLIST
PHELLOPLASTICS
PHILANTHROPIST
PHONOGRAPHICAL
PHRASEOLOGICAL
PHYSIOGNOMICAL
PHYTOGEOGRAPHY
PHYTOPATHOLOGY
PISCICULTURIST
PLECTOGNATHOUS
PLEONASTICALLY
PLEURAPOPHYSIS
PNEUMATOLOGIST
POLYSYLLABICAL
POLYTHEISTICAL
POPULARIZATION
PRACTICABILITY
PREBENDARYSHIP
PRECARIOUSNESS
PRECOCIOUSNESS
PRECONCERTEDLY
PREDESTINARIAN
PREDESTINATION
PREDETERMINATE
PREFERENTIALLY
PREPONDERATION
PREPOSTEROUSLY
PRESUMPTUOUSLY
PROCRASTINATOR
PROCURATORSHIP
PRODUCTIVENESS
PROFESSIONALLY
PROGNOSTICATOR
PROHIBITIONIST
PROLETARIANISM
PROPAEDEUTICAL
PROPITIATORILY
PROPITIOUSNESS
PROPORTIONABLE
PROPORTIONABLY
PROPRIETORSHIP
PROCENCEPHALON
PROSPEROUSNESS
PROVIDENTIALLY

Q

QUADRAGENARIAN
QUADRIDIGITATE
QUADRIGEMINOUS
QUADRISYLLABLE
QUANTIFICATION
QUANTITATIVELY
QUERIMONIOUSLY
QUINQUEPARTITE

R

RANUNCULACEOUS
REASONABLENESS
RECALCITRATION
RECAPITULATION
RECAPITULATORY
RECEIVABLENESS
RECOMMENDATION
RECOMMENDATORY
RECONCILIATION
RECONNAISSANCE
RECONSTRUCTION
RECTILINEARITY
RECURVIROSTRAL
REDINTEGRATION
REDISTRIBUTION
REFLECTIVENESS
REFRACTORINESS
REGARDLESSNESS
REGENERATENESS
REHABILITATION
REIMPRISONMENT
REINTRODUCTION
REJUVENESCENCE
RELENTLESSNESS
RELINQUISHMENT
REMINISCENTIAL
REMONETIZATION
REMORSEFULNESS
REMUNERABILITY
REORGANISATION
REPREHENSIVELY
REQUISITIONIST
RESISTIBLENESS
RESOLVABLENESS
RESPECTABILITY
RESPIRABLENESS
RESPONSIBILITY
RESPONSIVENESS
RETROGRADATION
REVENGEFULNESS
REVIVIFICATION
ROSICRUCIANISM

S

SABBATARIANISM
SACCHARIFEROUS
SACRAMENTARIAN
SACRILEGIOUSLY
SANCTIFICATION
SANGUINIVOROUS
SATISFACTORILY
SCANDALOUSNESS
SCHOLASTICALLY
SCIENTIFICALLY
SCRUPULOUSNESS
SCURRILOUSNESS
SEASONABLENESS
SECULARIZATION
SENSATIONALISM
SENSATIONALIST
SENTIMENTALISM
SENTIMENTALIST
SENTIMENTALITY
SENTIMENTALIZE
SESQUIPEDALIAN

SESQUIALTERATE
SIMPLIFICATION
SIMULTANEOUSLY
SLATTERNLINESS
SOLIDIFICATION
SOMNAMBULATION
SOMNAMBULISTIC
SOPHISTICATION
SPECIALIZATION
SPECTROSCOPIST
SPEECHLESSNESS
SPHAERISTERIUM
STATIONARINESS
STENOGRAPHICAL
STIGMATIZATION
STRATIFICATION
STUPENDOUSNESS
SUBARBORESCENT
SUBCONSCIOUSLY
SUBINFEUDATION
SUBMISSIVENESS
SUBSTANTIALITY
SUBSTANTIALIZE
SUBSTANTIATION
SUFFERABLENESS
SUPERABUNDANCE
SUPERANNUATION
SUPERCELESTIAL
SUPERCILIOUSLY
SUPEREMINENTLY
SUPEREROGATORY
SUPERFICIALITY
SUPERINCUMBENT
SUPERINTENDENT
SUPERNATURALLY
SUPERSCRIPTION
SUPERSENSITIVE
SUPERPHOSPHATE
SUPERSTRUCTURE
SUPPOSITITIOUS
SUPRAMAXILLARY
SUSCEPTIBILITY
SUSPICIOUSNESS
SYNCHRONICALLY
SYSTEMATICALLY

T

TABULARIZATION
TATTERDEMALION
TAUTOLOGICALLY
TELEOLOGICALLY
TELESCOPICALLY
TERMINOLOGICAL
TETRADACTYLOUS
THOUGHTFULNESS
THRIFTLESSNESS
TINTINNABULARY
TRADITIONALISM
TRANSCENDENTAL
TRANSITORINESS
TRANSMIGRATORY
TRANSVERBERATE
TRIDIMENSIONAL
TRIPERSONALIST
TUMULTUOUSNESS

U

ULTRAMONTANISM
ULTRAMONTANIST
UNACKNOWLEDGED
UNAPPROPRIATED
UNCONSCIONABLE
UNCONSCIONABLY
UNCONTROLLABLE
UNCONTROLLABLY
UNDECOMPOSABLE
UNDERSTATEMENT
UNDISCOVERABLE
UNFAITHFULNESS
UNFRUITFULNESS
UNGRACEFULNESS
UNGRATEFULNESS
UNINCORPORATED
UNINTELLIGIBLE
UNINTELLIGIBLY
UNINTERMITTING
UNIPERSONALIST

UNMERCIFULNESS
UNOSTENTATIOUS
UMPREMEDITATED
UNPREPOSSESSED
UNPRESUMPTUOUS
UNPROSPEROUSLY
UNQUESTIONABLE
UNQUESTIONABLY
UNRECOGNIZABLE
UNRELIABLENESS
UNRESTRAINEDLY
UNSATISFACTORY
UNSCRIPTURALLY
UNSCRUPULOUSLY
UNSOCIABLENESS
UNSUCCESSFULLY
UNSUITABLENESS
UNTRANSLATABLE

V

VALETUDINARIAN

VILLAINOUSNESS
VINDICTIVENESS
VITUPERATIVELY
VIVIPAROUSNESS
VOLATILIZATION
VULNERABLENESS

W

WONDERSTRICKEN

Z

ZINCOGRAPHICAL
ZINGIBERACEOUS
ZINZIBERACEOUS
ZOROASTRIANISM

FIFTEEN-LETTER WORDS

A

ACCLIMATIZATION
ACCOUNTABLENESS
ACQUISITIVENESS
ADDISON'S-DISEASE
ADVENTUROUSNESS
AFFRANCHISEMENT
AMPHITHEATRICAL
ANNIHILATIONIST
ANTEPENULTIMATE
ANTERO-POSTERIOR
ANTHROPOLOGICAL
ANTHROPOMORPHIC
ANTHROPOPHAGOUS
ANTI-EVANGELICAL
ANTIMONARCHICAL
ANTISABBATARIAN
ANTITRINITARIAN
APPROPRIATENESS
ARBORICULTURIST
ARCHIEPISCOPACY
ARGUMENTATIVELY
AUTHORITATIVELY

B

BIBLIOGRAPHICAL
BLEACHING-POWDER
BLOOD-GUILTINESS
BRACHYCEPHALOUS
BRANCHIOSTEGOUS
BRUSSELS-SPROUTS

C

CAMPYLOSPERMOUS
CATECHISTICALLY
CEREMONIOUSNESS
CHAMBERLAINSHIP
CHAMBER-PRACTICE
CHARGE D'AFFAIRES
CHEMICO-ELECTRIC
CHRISTADELPHIAN
CHRONOGRAMMATIC
CHRONOLOGICALLY
CIRCUMFORANEOUS
CIRCUMNAVIGABLE
CIRCUMNAVIGATOR
CIRCUMSCRIBABLE
CIRCUMSCRIPTION
CIRCUMSCRIPTIVE
CIRCUMSPECTNESS
CIRCUMSTANTIATE
CIRCUMVALLATION
COLOUR-BLINDNESS
COMBUSTIBLENESS
COMMONPLACE-BOOK
COMMUNICABILITY
COMMUNICATIVELY
COMPASSIONATELY
COMPREHENSIVELY

COMPRESSIBILITY
COMPTROLLERSHIP
CONCEIVABLENESS
CONDESCENDINGLY
CONFESSIONALIST
CONJUNCTIONALLY
CONNOISSEURSHIP
CONSCIENTIOUSLY
CONSENTANEOUSLY
CONSEQUENTIALLY
CONSIDERATENESS
CONSPICUOUSNESS
CONSUBSTANTIATE
CONTEMPLATIVELY
CONTEMPORANEITY
CONTEMPORANEOUS
CONTEMPTIBILITY
CONTENTIOUSNESS
CONTRACTIBILITY
CONTRADICTORILY
CONTRAVALLATION
CONTROVERSIALLY
CONVENTIONALISM
CONVENTIONALIST
CONVENTIONALITY
CONVENTIONALIZE
CONVERSABLENESS
CONVOLVULACEOUS
CORRELATIVENESS
CORRESPONDENTLY
CORRESPONDINGLY
CORRUPTIBLENESS
COSMOPOLITANISM
COUNTER-APPROACH
COUNTER-EVIDENCE
COUNTER-IRRITANT
COUNTER-MOVEMENT
COUNTER-PRESSURE
CROOK-SHOULDERED
CRYPTOGRAPHICAL
CRYSTALLIZATION
CRYSTALLOGRAPHY

D

DECALCIFICATION
DECARBONIZATION
DECARBURIZATION
DEFENCELESSNESS
DELIGHTSOMENESS
DEMAGNETIZATION
DEMONSTRABILITY
DEMONSTRATIVELY
DEPHLOGISTICATE
DESCRIPTIVENESS
DESTRUCTIBILITY
DESTRUCTIVENESS
DETERMINABILITY
DETERMINATENESS
DEVITRIFICATION
DIAHELIOTROPISM
DIALOGISTICALLY
DIAPHORETICALLY
DIAPHRAGMATITIS

DIFFERENTIATION
DISADVANTAGEOUS
DISCONTINUATION
DISCOUNTENANCER
DISCRETIONARILY
DISENTANGLEMENT
DISGRACEFULNESS
DISINTERESTEDLY
DISINTHRALLMENT
DISORGANIZATION
DISPASSIONATELY
DISPROPORTIONAL
DISRESPECTFULLY
DISSATISFACTION
DISSATISFACTORY
DISTASTEFULNESS
DISTINGUISHABLE
DISTINGUISHABLY
DISTRUSTFULNESS
DIVERSIFICATION
DOLICHOCEPHALIC
DOUBLE-BARRELLED
DRAUGHTSMANSHIP
DREDGING-MACHINE

E

ECCLESIASTICISM
ECHINODERMATOUS
ECLAIRCISSEMENT
EFFICACIOUSNESS
ELDER-FLOWER-WINE
ELECTRIFICATION
ELECTRO-DYNAMICS
ELECTRO-KINETICS
ELECTRO-MAGNETIC
ELECTRO-NEGATIVE
ELECTRO-POSITIVE
ELEUTHEROMANIAC
EMANCIPATIONIST
ENCOMIASTICALLY
ENFRANCHISEMENT
ENTENTE CORDIALE
ENTOMOLOGICALLY
EPIDEMIOLOGICAL
EPISCOPALIANISM
ETHEREALIZATION
EXCHANGEABILITY
EXCOMMUNICATION
EXCREMENTITIOUS
EXEMPLIFICATION
EXPERIENTIALISM
EXPERIENTIALIST
EXPERIMENTALIST
EXPERIMENTALIZE
EXPERIMENTATION
EXTERNALIZATION
EXTRAJUDICIALLY
EXTRAORDINARILY

F

FALLING-SICKNESS
FANTASTICALNESS
FORMULARIZATION
FOUNDATION-STONE
FRAGMENTARINESS

G

GENTLEMANLINESS
GOVERNOR-GENERAL

H

HENDECASYLLABLE
HERMENEUTICALLY
HETERODACTYLOUS
HISTORIOGRAPHER
HISTORIOGRAPHIC
HOMOGENEOUSNESS
HUMANITARIANISM
HYDROSTATICALLY
HYPERCRITICALLY
HYPOCHONDRIACAL

I

IDEOGRAPHICALLY
IMPRESCRIPTIBLE
IMPENETRABILITY
INACCESSIBILITY
INALIENABLENESS
INAPPLICABILITY
INAPPROPRIATELY
INATTENTIVENESS
INAUTHORITATIVE
INCOMMENSURABLE
INCOMMUNICATIVE
INCOMPATIBILITY
INCOMPREHENSIVE
INCONSIDERATELY
INCONSPICUOUSLY
INCORRIGIBILITY
INDEMNIFICATION
INDETERMINATELY
INDETERMINATION
INDIVIDUALISTIC
INDOMITABLENESS
INEFFICACIOUSLY
INEXCUSABLENESS
INEXPLICABILITY
INFLAMMABLENESS
INFUNDIBULIFORM
INJUDICIOUSNESS
INOFFENSIVENESS
INQUISITIVENESS
INQUISITORIALLY
INSCRUTABLENESS
INSEPARABLENESS
INSIGNIFICANTLY
INSTRUMENTALIST
INSTRUMENTALITY
INSTRUMENTATION
INSUBORDINATION
INSURRECTIONARY
INSURRECTIONIST
INTELLECTUALIST
INTELLECTUALITY
INTELLECTUALIZE
INTELLIGIBILITY
INTEMPERATENESS
INTERCHANGEABLE

INTERCHANGEABLY
INTERCOLONIALLY
INTERCOMPARISON
INTERCONNECTION
INTERDIGITATION
INTERFOLIACEOUS
INTERJECTIONARY
INTERNATIONALLY
INTERROGATIVELY
INTOLERABLENESS
INTRACTABLENESS
INTRANSMISSIBLE
INTROSUSCEPTION
INVULNERABILITY
IRRELIGIOUSNESS
IRREPREHENSIBLE
IRRESISTIBILITY
ISOPERIMETRICAL

PHENAKISTOSCOPE
PHOSPHORESCENCE
PHRENOLOGICALLY
PHYSIOGRAPHICAL
PHYSIOLOGICALLY
PICTURESQUENESS
PLEURO-PNEUMONIA
PRACTICABLENESS
PREPOSITIONALLY
PRESTIDIGITATOR
PRETENTIOUSNESS
PRIVY-COUNCILLOR
PROCRASTINATION
PROGNOSTICATION
PROMISCUOUSNESS
PROPORTIONATELY
PROTEMPORANEOUS
PULMOBRANCHIATE

J

JURISPRUDENTIAL

K

KALEIDOSCOPICAL

L

LEXICOGRAPHICAL
LOPOBRANCHIATE

M

METROPOLITANATE
MICROSCOPICALLY
MISCHIEVOUSNESS
MISCONSTRUCTION
MONOCHLAMYDEOUS
MORPHOLOGICALLY

N

NATIONALIZATION
NOTWITHSTANDING

O

OPHTHALMOPLEGIA
ORNITHORHYNCHUS

P

PALAEOGRAPHICAL
PALAEONTOLOGIST
PALAEOPHYTOLOGY
PARTHENOGENESIS
PARTHENOGENETIC
PERGAMENTACEOUS
PERPENDICULARLY
PERSONIFICATION
PERSPICACIOUSLY
PERSPICUOUSNESS

Q

QUATERCENTENARY

R

REPROACHFULNESS
RETROGRESSIVELY

S

SABBATH-BREAKING
SELF-EXAMINATION
SELF-EXPLANATORY
SENTENTIOUSNESS
SHOOTING-GALLERY
SPEAKING-TRUMPET
STRAIGHTFORWARD
STRAIT-WAISTCOAT
STRATEGETICALLY
STRATIGRAPHICAL
SUPEREXCELLENCE
SUPERFICIALNESS
SUPERNATURALISM
SUPERNATURALIST
SUPERNUMERARIES
SYMPATHETICALLY
SYMPTOMATICALLY

T

TETRASYLLABICAL
TONOGRAPHICALLY
TRANSFIGURATION
TRANSLITERATION
TRANSMUTABILITY
TRANSPARENTNESS
TRANSPLANTATION
TRANSPOSITIONAL
TREACHEROUSNESS
TREASONABLENESS
TRIGONOMETRICAL
TROUBLESOMENESS
TRUSTWORTHINESS

U

UNCEREMONIOUSLY
UNCOMMUNICATIVE
UNCONDITIONALLY
UNCONSCIOUSNESS
UNCONSTRAINEDLY
UNDEMONSTRATIVE
UNEXCEPTIONABLE
UNGENTLEMANLIKE
UNGRAMMATICALLY
UNPARLIAMENTARY
UNPHILOSOPHICAL
UNPRONOUNCEABLE
UNRIGHTEOUSNESS
UNSOPHISTICATED

V

VICISSITUDINARY
VICISSITUDINOUS

W

WHEEL-ANIMALCULE
WOODY-NIGHTSHADE
WRITING-CHAMBERS

X

—

Y

—

Z

—

SIXTEEN-LETTER WORDS

A

ACANTHOPTERYGIAN
ACQUAINTANCESHIP
ADVANTAGEOUSNESS
ANAGRAMMATICALLY
ANGLO-CATHOLICISM
ANTHROPOMORPHISM
ANTHROPOMORPHOUS
ANTIPHRASTICALLY
APPREHENSIVENESS
ARCHAEOLOGICALLY
ARISTOCRATICALLY
AUTOBIOGRAPHICAL

B
—

C

CADUCIBRANCHIATE
CARYOPHYLLACEOUS
CHONDROPTERYGIAN
CHROMO-LITHOGRAPH
CHRONOGRAMMATIST
CHRYSELEPHANTINE
CIRCUMAMBULATION
CIRCUMNAVIGATION
CIRCUMSTANTIALLY
CLEAR-SIGHTEDNESS
CLIMATOGRAPHICAL
COMMANDER-IN-CHIEF
COMMENSURABILITY
COMMISSIONERSHIP
CONSTRUCTIVENESS
CONSUBSTANTIALLY
CONTEMPORARINESS
CONTEMPTIBLENESS
CONTEMPTUOUSNESS
CONTRADICTIOUSLY
CONTRAINDICATION
CONTUMACIOUSNESS
COSMOGRAPHICALLY
COUNTER-SIGNATURE
CROSS-EXAMINATION
CRYPTOBRANCHIATE
CRYSTALLOGRAPHER
CRYSTALLOGRAPHIC

D

DECENTRALISATION
DEMONSTRABLENESS
DENOMINATIONALLY
DIAGRAMMATICALLY
DIPHTHONGISATION
DISAGREEABLENESS
DISCONTENTEDNESS
DISCRIMINATIVELY
DISESTABLISHMENT

DISFRANCHISEMENT
DISINGENUOUSNESS
DISPROPORTIONATE
DISQUALIFICATION
DISTINGUISHINGLY
DOLICHOCEPHALISM
DOLICHOCEPHALOUS
DRINKING-FOUNTAIN

E

ECCLESIASTICALLY
ELASMOBRANCHIATE
ELECTRO-BALLISTIC
ELECTRO-BIOLOGIST
ENTHUSIASTICALLY
EPIGRAMMATICALLY
EXTEMPORANEOUSLY
EXTERRITORIALITY
EXTRAPAROCHIALLY

F

FAINTHEARTEDNESS
FALSE-HEARTEDNESS
FELLOW-COUNTRYMAN
FORISFAMILIATION

G
—

H

HERMAPHRODITICAL
HIEROGLYPHICALLY
HIGGLEDY-PIGGLEDY
HOMOEOPATHICALLY
HYDROGRAPHICALLY

I

IMMEASURABLENESS
IMPERCEPTIBILITY
IMPERISHABLENESS
IMPERTURBABILITY
IMPRACTICABILITY
INACCESSIBLENESS
INCOMBUSTIBILITY
INCOMPARABLENESS
INCOMPREHENSIBLE
INCOMPREHENSIBLY
INCONCLUSIVENESS
INCONTROVERTIBLE
INCONTROVERTIBLY
INCONVERTIBILITY
INCORRIGIBLENESS
INCORRUPTIBILITY
INDISCRIMINATELY
INEXHAUSTIBILITY

INEXPRESSIVENESS
INEXTINGUISHABLE
INEXTINGUISHABLY
INSUSCEPTIBILITY
INTELLIGIBLENESS
INTERCOMMUNICATE
INTERCONTINENTAL
INTERJECTIONALLY
INTERPENETRATION
IRRESPONSIBILITY

J
—

K
—

L
—

M

MALACOPTERYGIOUS
MALAGUETTA-PEPPER
MELODRAMATICALLY
MICROCHRONOMETER
MICROPHOTOGRAPHY
MISANTHROPICALLY
MISAPPROPRIATION
MISPRONUNCIATION
MISUNDERSTANDING
MONOCOTYLEDONOUS
MUSCULOCUTANEOUS

N

NECESSITARIANISM

O

OBSTREPEROUSNESS
ORTHOGRAPHICALLY

P

PALAEONTOLOGICAL
PARADIGMATICALLY
PARALLELEPIPEDON
PARAPHRASTICALLY
PERIPHRASTICALLY
PERISSODACTYLOUS
PERPENDICULARITY
PHARMACEUTICALLY
PHONOGRAPHICALLY
PHOTOGRAPHICALLY
PHOTO-MICROGRAPHY
POLYCOTYLEDONOUS
PRAISEWORTHINESS
PREDETERMINATION
PRE-ESTABLISHMENT

PRESTIDIGITATION
PRESUMPTUOUSNESS
PRETERPLUPERFECT

Q

QUERIMONIOUSNESS
QUESTIONABLENESS

R

REPRESENTATIONAL
REPRESENTATIVELY
RETRANSFORMATION
RETURNING-OFFICER

S

SCENOGRAPHICALLY
SELF-PRESERVATION
SHORT-SIGHTEDNESS
SIMPLE-MINDEDNESS
SIMULTANEOUSNESS
SOPHONOSTOMATOUS
SPHYGMOMANOMETER
SPIRITUALIZATION
STEREOSCOPICALLY
STEREOTYPOGRAPHY
STETHOSCOPICALLY
SUPERCILIOUSNESS
SUPPOSITITIOUSL
SUSCEPTIBILITIES

T

TELESPECTROSCOPE
THEOPHILANTHROPY
THERMOMETROGRAPH
THERMOMETRICALLY
TINTINNABULATION
TRANSCENDENTALLY
TRANSFERRIBILITY
TRANSMISSIBILITY
TRANSMUTABLENESS
TRANSMUTATIONIST
TRANSPORTABILITY
TRANSUBSTANTIATE
TRESPASS-OFFERING

U

UNCHARITABLENESS
UNCONSTITUTIONAL
UNDENOMINATIONAL
UNDISCRIMINATING
UNGOVERNABLENESS
UNPRODUCTIVENESS
UNPROFITABLENESS
UNREASONABLENESS
UNSUBSTANTIALITY

W

WELL-PROPORTIONED

SEVENTEEN-LETTER WORDS

A
ADMINISTRATORSHIP
ANTIHYPOCHONDRIAC
AUTHORITATIVENESS

B
BEGGAR-MY-NEIGHBOUR

C
CHROMO-LITHOGRAPHY
CHRONOGRAMMATICAL
CIRCUMSTANTIALITY
COMMUNICATIVENESS
COMPREHENSIBILITY
COMPREHENSIVENESS
CONCENTRATIVENESS
CONGREGATIONALISM
CONGREGATIONALIST
CONSCIENTIOUSNESS
CONSEQUENTIALNESS
CONSTITUTIONALISM
CONSTITUTIONALIST
CONSTITUTIONALITY
CONSUBSTANTIALITY
CONSUBSTANTIATION
CONTEMPLATIVENESS
CONTEMPORANEOUSLY
CONTRADICTORINESS
CONTRADISTINCTION
CONTRADISTINCTIVE
CONVERSATIONALIST
COUNTER-ATTRACTION
COUNTER-ATTRACTIVE
COUNTER-IRRITATION
COUNTER-REVOLUTION

D
DEMONSTRATIVENESS
DENATIONALISATION
DENOMINATIONALISM
DISADVANTAGEOUSLY
DISHONOURABLENESS
DISINTERESTEDNESS
DISPROPORTIONABLE
DISPROPORTIONALLY

E
EARTHLY-MINDEDNESS
ELECTRO-METALLURGY
ELECTRO-PHYSIOLOGY
EXTRAORDINARINESS

F — G
—

H
HETEROGENEOUSNESS

I
IMPERCEPTIBLENESS
IMPRACTICABLENESS
INCOMMUNICABILITY
INCOMPRESSIBILITY
INCONCEIVABLENESS
INCONSEQUENTIALLY
INCONSIDERATENESS
INDISTINGUISHABLE
INEFFICACIOUSNESS
INSUPPORTABLENESS
INTERCOLUMNIATION
INTERCOMMUNICABLE
IRRECONCILABILITY

J
—

K
—

L
LAMELLIBRANCHIATE
LATITUDINARIANISM
LIEUTENANT-COLONEL
LIEUTENANT-GENERAL

M
MALADMINISTRATION
MARSIPOBRANCHIATE
MISINTERPRETATION
MISREPRESENTATION

N
—

O
OPISTHOBRANCHIATE

P
PALAEOICHTHYOLOGY
PARTICULARIZATION
PERENNIBRANCHIATE
PHILANTHROPICALLY

PREDESTINARIANISM

Q
—

R
REPREHENSIBLENESS

S
SELF-CONSCIOUSNESS
SELF-CONTRADICTION
SELF-CONTRADICTORY
SELF-FERTILIZATION
SELF-RIGHTEOUSNESS
SPECTROSCOPICALLY
SPLANCHNO-SKELETON
STEREOGRAPHICALLY
STEREOTYPOGRAPHER
STRAIGHTFORWARDLY

T
THEOPHILANTHROPIC
THERMO-ELECTRICITY
TRANSCENDENTALISM
TRANSCENDENTALIST
TRANSUBSTANTIATOR
TRIGONOMETRICALLY

U
UNFASHIONABLENESS
UNGENTLEMANLINESS

V
VALETUDINARIANISM

W — X
—

Y — Z

EIGHTEEN-LETTER WORDS

A

ANTI-CONSTITUTIONAL

C

CHARACTERISTICALLY
CHROMO-LITHOGRAPHER
COMPREHENSIBLENESS
CROSS-FERTILIZATION
CRYSTALLOGRAPHICAL

D

DISPROPORTIONATELY

E

ESTABLISHMENTARIAN

I

INCOMMENSURABILITY

INCOMMUNICABLENESS
INTERCOMMUNICATION
IRRECONCILABLENESS

L

LIGHTNING-CONDUCTOR

P

PARALLELOGRAMMATIC
POCKET-HANDKERCHIEF
PUBLIC-SPIRITEDNESS

T

THEOPHILANTHROPIST
TRANSUBSTANTIATION
TRAVERSING-PLATFORM

U

UNCONSTITUTIONALLY

NINETEEN-LETTER WORDS

C

CONTEMPORANEOUSNESS

D

DISADVANTAGEOUSNESS

I

INCONTROVERTIBILITY
INCOMPREHENSIBILITY
INTERSTRATIFICATION

S

STRAIGHTFORWARDNESS

TWENTY-LETTER WORD

P

PHILOPROGENITIVENESS